T0137000

Lecture Notes in Computer Science   14027

The series Lecture Notes in Computer Science (LNCS), including its subseries Lecture Notes in Artificial Intelligence (LNAI) and Lecture Notes in Bioinformatics (LNBI), has established itself as a medium for the publication of new developments in computer science and information technology research, teaching, and education.

LNCS enjoys close cooperation with the computer science R & D community, the series counts many renowned academics among its volume editors and paper authors, and collaborates with prestigious societies. Its mission is to serve this international community by providing an invaluable service, mainly focused on the publication of conference and workshop proceedings and postproceedings. LNCS commenced publication in 1973.

Jessie Y. C. Chen · Gino Fragomeni
Editors

Virtual, Augmented and Mixed Reality

15th International Conference, VAMR 2023
Held as Part of the 25th HCI International Conference, HCII 2023
Copenhagen, Denmark, July 23–28, 2023
Proceedings

 Springer

Editors
Jessie Y. C. Chen
U.S. Army Research Laboratory
Aberdeen Proving Ground, MD, USA

Gino Fragomeni
U.S. Army Combat Capabilities
Development Command Soldier Center
Orlando, FL, USA

ISSN 0302-9743 ISSN 1611-3349 (electronic)
Lecture Notes in Computer Science
ISBN 978-3-031-35633-9 ISBN 978-3-031-35634-6 (eBook)
https://doi.org/10.1007/978-3-031-35634-6

This Springer imprint is published by the registered company Springer Nature Switzerland AG
The registered company address is: Gewerbestrasse 11, 6330 Cham, Switzerland

Foreword

Human-computer interaction (HCI) is acquiring an ever-increasing scientific and industrial importance, as well as having more impact on people's everyday lives, as an ever-growing number of human activities are progressively moving from the physical to the digital world. This process, which has been ongoing for some time now, was further accelerated during the acute period of the COVID-19 pandemic. The HCI International (HCII) conference series, held annually, aims to respond to the compelling need to advance the exchange of knowledge and research and development efforts on the human aspects of design and use of computing systems.

The 25th International Conference on Human-Computer Interaction, HCI International 2023 (HCII 2023), was held in the emerging post-pandemic era as a 'hybrid' event at the AC Bella Sky Hotel and Bella Center, Copenhagen, Denmark, during July 23–28, 2023. It incorporated the 21 thematic areas and affiliated conferences listed below.

A total of 7472 individuals from academia, research institutes, industry, and government agencies from 85 countries submitted contributions, and 1578 papers and 396 posters were included in the volumes of the proceedings that were published just before the start of the conference, these are listed below. The contributions thoroughly cover the entire field of human-computer interaction, addressing major advances in knowledge and effective use of computers in a variety of application areas. These papers provide academics, researchers, engineers, scientists, practitioners and students with state-of-the-art information on the most recent advances in HCI.

The HCI International (HCII) conference also offers the option of presenting 'Late Breaking Work', and this applies both for papers and posters, with corresponding volumes of proceedings that will be published after the conference. Full papers will be included in the 'HCII 2023 - Late Breaking Work - Papers' volumes of the proceedings to be published in the Springer LNCS series, while 'Poster Extended Abstracts' will be included as short research papers in the 'HCII 2023 - Late Breaking Work - Posters' volumes to be published in the Springer CCIS series.

I would like to thank the Program Board Chairs and the members of the Program Boards of all thematic areas and affiliated conferences for their contribution towards the high scientific quality and overall success of the HCI International 2023 conference. Their manifold support in terms of paper reviewing (single-blind review process, with a minimum of two reviews per submission), session organization and their willingness to act as goodwill ambassadors for the conference is most highly appreciated.

This conference would not have been possible without the continuous and unwavering support and advice of Gavriel Salvendy, founder, General Chair Emeritus, and Scientific Advisor. For his outstanding efforts, I would like to express my sincere appreciation to Abbas Moallem, Communications Chair and Editor of HCI International News.

July 2023   Constantine Stephanidis

HCI International 2023 Thematic Areas and Affiliated Conferences

Thematic Areas

- HCI: Human-Computer Interaction
- HIMI: Human Interface and the Management of Information

Affiliated Conferences

- EPCE: 20th International Conference on Engineering Psychology and Cognitive Ergonomics
- AC: 17th International Conference on Augmented Cognition
- UAHCI: 17th International Conference on Universal Access in Human-Computer Interaction
- CCD: 15th International Conference on Cross-Cultural Design
- SCSM: 15th International Conference on Social Computing and Social Media
- VAMR: 15th International Conference on Virtual, Augmented and Mixed Reality
- DHM: 14th International Conference on Digital Human Modeling and Applications in Health, Safety, Ergonomics and Risk Management
- DUXU: 12th International Conference on Design, User Experience and Usability
- C&C: 11th International Conference on Culture and Computing
- DAPI: 11th International Conference on Distributed, Ambient and Pervasive Interactions
- HCIBGO: 10th International Conference on HCI in Business, Government and Organizations
- LCT: 10th International Conference on Learning and Collaboration Technologies
- ITAP: 9th International Conference on Human Aspects of IT for the Aged Population
- AIS: 5th International Conference on Adaptive Instructional Systems
- HCI-CPT: 5th International Conference on HCI for Cybersecurity, Privacy and Trust
- HCI-Games: 5th International Conference on HCI in Games
- MobiTAS: 5th International Conference on HCI in Mobility, Transport and Automotive Systems
- AI-HCI: 4th International Conference on Artificial Intelligence in HCI
- MOBILE: 4th International Conference on Design, Operation and Evaluation of Mobile Communications

List of Conference Proceedings Volumes Appearing Before the Conference

1. LNCS 14011, Human-Computer Interaction: Part I, edited by Masaaki Kurosu and Ayako Hashizume
2. LNCS 14012, Human-Computer Interaction: Part II, edited by Masaaki Kurosu and Ayako Hashizume
3. LNCS 14013, Human-Computer Interaction: Part III, edited by Masaaki Kurosu and Ayako Hashizume
4. LNCS 14014, Human-Computer Interaction: Part IV, edited by Masaaki Kurosu and Ayako Hashizume
5. LNCS 14015, Human Interface and the Management of Information: Part I, edited by Hirohiko Mori and Yumi Asahi
6. LNCS 14016, Human Interface and the Management of Information: Part II, edited by Hirohiko Mori and Yumi Asahi
7. LNAI 14017, Engineering Psychology and Cognitive Ergonomics: Part I, edited by Don Harris and Wen-Chin Li
8. LNAI 14018, Engineering Psychology and Cognitive Ergonomics: Part II, edited by Don Harris and Wen-Chin Li
9. LNAI 14019, Augmented Cognition, edited by Dylan D. Schmorrow and Cali M. Fidopiastis
10. LNCS 14020, Universal Access in Human-Computer Interaction: Part I, edited by Margherita Antona and Constantine Stephanidis
11. LNCS 14021, Universal Access in Human-Computer Interaction: Part II, edited by Margherita Antona and Constantine Stephanidis
12. LNCS 14022, Cross-Cultural Design: Part I, edited by Pei-Luen Patrick Rau
13. LNCS 14023, Cross-Cultural Design: Part II, edited by Pei-Luen Patrick Rau
14. LNCS 14024, Cross-Cultural Design: Part III, edited by Pei-Luen Patrick Rau
15. LNCS 14025, Social Computing and Social Media: Part I, edited by Adela Coman and Simona Vasilache
16. LNCS 14026, Social Computing and Social Media: Part II, edited by Adela Coman and Simona Vasilache
17. LNCS 14027, Virtual, Augmented and Mixed Reality, edited by Jessie Y. C. Chen and Gino Fragomeni
18. LNCS 14028, Digital Human Modeling and Applications in Health, Safety, Ergonomics and Risk Management: Part I, edited by Vincent G. Duffy
19. LNCS 14029, Digital Human Modeling and Applications in Health, Safety, Ergonomics and Risk Management: Part II, edited by Vincent G. Duffy
20. LNCS 14030, Design, User Experience, and Usability: Part I, edited by Aaron Marcus, Elizabeth Rosenzweig and Marcelo Soares
21. LNCS 14031, Design, User Experience, and Usability: Part II, edited by Aaron Marcus, Elizabeth Rosenzweig and Marcelo Soares

47. CCIS 1836, HCI International 2023 Posters - Part V, edited by Constantine Stephanidis, Margherita Antona, Stavroula Ntoa and Gavriel Salvendy

https://2023.hci.international/proceedings

Preface

With the recent emergence of a new generation of displays, smart devices, and wearables, the field of virtual, augmented, and mixed reality (VAMR) is rapidly expanding, transforming, and moving towards the mainstream market. At the same time, VAMR applications in a variety of domains are also reaching maturity and practical usage. From the point of view of the user experience, VAMR promises possibilities to reduce interaction efforts and cognitive load, while also offering contextualized information, by combining different sources and reducing attention shifts, and opening the 3D space. Such scenarios offer exciting challenges associated with underlying and supporting technologies, interaction and navigation in virtual and augmented environments, and design and development. VAMR themes encompass a wide range of areas such as education, aviation, social, emotional, psychological, and persuasive applications.

The 15th International Conference on Virtual, Augmented and Mixed Reality (VAMR 2023), an affiliated conference of the HCI International conference, provided a forum for researchers and practitioners to disseminate and exchange scientific and technical information on VAMR-related topics in various applications. The presentations covered a wide range of topics, centered on themes related to the design of VAMR applications and environments, as well as multimodal interaction in VAMR. With recent advances in robotics, topics of interest have expanded to include VAMR-based techniques for human-robot interaction. Applications of VAMR this year focus on medicine and health as well as aviation. Finally, several papers address various aspects of the user experience with and acceptance of VAMR technologies.

One volume of the HCII 2023 proceedings is dedicated to this year's edition of the VAMR conference. It focuses on topics related to designing VAMR applications and environments, visualization, image rendering and 3D in VAMR, multimodal interaction in VAMR, robots and avatars in Virtual and Augmented Reality, VAMR in medicine and health, VAMR in aviation, and user experience in VAMR. Papers of this volume are included for publication after a minimum of two single-blind reviews from the members of the VAMR Program Board or, in some cases, from members of the Program Boards of other affiliated conferences. We would like to thank all of them for their invaluable contribution, support, and efforts.

July 2023

Jessie Y. C. Chen
Gino Fragomeni

15th International Conference on Virtual, Augmented and Mixed Reality (VAMR 2023)

Program Board Chair(s): **Jessie Y. C. Chen**, *U.S. Army Research Laboratory, USA* and **Gino Fragomeni**, *U.S. Army Combat Capabilities Development Command Soldier Center, USA*

Program Board:

- Shih-Yi Chien, *National Chengchi University, Taiwan*
- Avinash Gupta, *University of Illinois Urbana-Champaign, USA*
- Sue Kase, *U.S. Army Research Laboratory, USA*
- Daniela Kratchounova, *Federal Aviation Administration (FAA), USA*
- Fotis Liarokapis, *CYENS, Cyprus*
- Chao Peng, *Rochester Institute of Technology, USA*
- Jose San Martin, *Universidad Rey Juan Carlos, Spain*
- Andreas Schreiber, *German Aerospace Center (DLR), Germany*
- Sharad Sharma, *University of North Texas, USA*
- Simon Su, *National Institute of Standards and Technology (NIST), USA*
- Denny Yu, *Purdue University, USA*

The full list with the Program Board Chairs and the members of the Program Boards of all thematic areas and affiliated conferences of HCII2023 is available online at:

http://www.hci.international/board-members-2023.php

HCI International 2024 Conference

The 26th International Conference on Human-Computer Interaction, HCI International 2024, will be held jointly with the affiliated conferences at the Washington Hilton Hotel, Washington, DC, USA, June 29 – July 4, 2024. It will cover a broad spectrum of themes related to Human-Computer Interaction, including theoretical issues, methods, tools, processes, and case studies in HCI design, as well as novel interaction techniques, interfaces, and applications. The proceedings will be published by Springer. More information will be made available on the conference website: http://2024.hci.international/.

General Chair
Prof. Constantine Stephanidis
University of Crete and ICS-FORTH
Heraklion, Crete, Greece
Email: general_chair@hcii2024.org

https://2024.hci.international/

Contents

Visualization, Image Rendering and 3D in VAMR

Multimodal Interaction in VAMR

VAMR in Aviation

User Experience in VAMR

Designing VAMR Applications and Environments

UI Design Recommendations for Multimodal XR Interfaces Using a Collaborative System

Sarah Garcia[✉] and Marvin Andujar

University of South Florida, Tampa, FL 33620, USA
{sarahgarcia,andujar1}@usf.edu

Abstract. Over the past years, various design guidelines such as Nielsen's heuristics have been proposed in order to guide researchers and developers in creating usable and consistent user interfaces (UIs) [12]. However, within the field of Extended Reality (XR), existing relevant design guidelines are still limited due to the newness of spatial technologies such as head-mounted displays (HMDs) now entering the consumer market. As applications continue to emerge that span multiple modalities and realities, guidance for researchers and developers in initial design stages is needed. This paper presents results of 1-on-1 interview sessions with UX experts in industry, using an existing collaborative multimodal system as a use case. After a brief introduction to the use case, researchers were asked questions regarding application-specific considerations, as well as broader scalability implications. Thematic analysis was conducted using interview audio transcripts to determine the most prominent themes. Results include a set of general recommendations that can be used to guide researchers in early design stages of creating multimodal user interfaces for XR applications, such as evaluation of form-factor capabilities and determination of the context of use.

Keywords: Extended Reality · User Interface Design · Guidelines · Design Recommendations

1 Introduction

Over the past few decades, growth in augmented reality (AR), virtual reality (VR) and mixed reality (MR) has led to expansion of novel research fields. The use of Extended Reality (XR), often used as an umbrella term to encompass these realities [11,13], has experienced significant growth and popularity with advances in mobile and head-mounted display (HMD) technology. Recent releases with improved hardware and software capabilities have entered the market, such as the HoloLens 2[TM] [2] and HTC VIVE Pro 2[TM] [1]. This is only expected to increase, as markets for XR technology are anticipated to reach upwards of $2 billion by 2027 [14].

© The Author(s), under exclusive license to Springer Nature Switzerland AG 2023
J. Y. C. Chen and G. Fragomeni (Eds.): HCII 2023, LNCS 14027, pp. 3–14, 2023.
https://doi.org/10.1007/978-3-031-35634-6_1

Demand for XR technology has also allowed systems to become increasingly more accessible, as more affordable options have entered the consumer market. As a result, development of applications in industry and academia have increased, and can be seen in education and training across various fields [16]. However, development of XR applications, particularly those that function across more than one modality, is still in its early stages. Additionally, as a whole, development of user interface design standards, conventions, and best practices in XR are still considered to require additional research [8,9].

In this paper, we contribute to the discussion of creating UI design recommendations for multimodal applications in XR by presenting results from interviews with experts using an existing collaborative military system as a use case. To explore key interface requirements, 1-on-1 interview sessions with subject-matter experts in the field of UX design and Human-Computer Interfaces were conducted. The goal of this study was to gain various expert opinions on the creation of UI designs that span across interaction modalities (virtual reality, augmented reality), as well as to explore concepts that contribute to design guidelines in the XR field.

2   Related Works

2.1   Existing Design Guidance and Heuristics

Work has been done regarding creation of principles for design of user interfaces, such as the well-known ten usability heuristics developed by Nielsen [12]. However, these existing heuristics are limited, as they were not created with the intention of being used for XR interfaces and technology. XR interfaces, such as HMDs, differ from existing non-spatial interfaces in how users view and interact with information. For example, they provide the user with additional interactivity due to motion and direction tracking, 360° viewing of information, and more. Moreover, the implementation of haptic capabilities, spatial audio, and additional sensors continue to be explored in combination with XR platforms. Therefore, work regarding design guidelines across various subsets of XR design contributes to the research community in expanding current well-known design principles. Additionally, recommendations or design guidelines for XR can be used to highlight what not to do when designing UIs. This would help mitigate some of the known issues and considerations to be taken into account that arise in various XR systems.

Some research has been conducted for AR-specific development guidance. Endsley et al. created a set of guidelines targeted towards AR practitioners, to better address the challenges in designing that Nielsen's heuristics do not cover [7]. Their heuristics were developed through use of affinity diagramming using existing guidelines and heuristics in the AR space at the time.

Vi et al. builds on this by developing a set of eleven design guidelines for head-mounted display hardware [15]. Work by Vi et al was derived from existing research as well as from online documentation sources for major HMD developers as well as other developers, examining more than 60 different resources.

This work pulls insights from additional communities to combine with academic published work, for a set of eleven guidelines.

However, researchers have found existing work limited in its ability to be practically applied. In work by Krauss et. Al. design recommendations for MR were analyzed from various scientific papers and industry practitioners [8]. They found that existing design recommendations often do not "state their intended use, goals, and target group". To address this, our research provides recommendations that can be applied specifically during initial design stages for scaling interface designs across XR modalities. Additionally, it describes the intended goals and target group, to better assist future researchers in determining if design recommendations suit their needs.

2.2   Scalability in XR

Minimal research has been done regarding scalability of XR systems. However, in work by Memmesheimer and Ebert, they introduce the concept of scalable extended reality (XR^s) [10]. The authors define it as the concept of scaling between both displays and degrees of virtuality, with a goal of increasing memorability that allows users to switch more easily between differing degrees of XR. They believe that lack of scalability limits the adoption of XR technology, which offers potential in areas such as training and working environments. They conclude that there are multiple topics of future research that are needed to support scalable XR systems. For instance, "interaction techniques ... that remain intuitive to users even when they switch between devices or degrees of virtuality". The authors propose combining existing independent research fields in order to create and study scalable XR systems.

While some work exists in working towards guidelines in XR, little to no work has been done in providing recommendations for designing interfaces that work successfully across XR. Current interfaces for multimodal systems are often based on hardware and software limitations, convenience or speed of development, and have low importance placed on interfaces as a whole. As the number of applications that make use of more than one type of reality continue to grow, there is additional research needed regarding the interfaces developed for these systems.

3   Methodology

3.1   Participants

The study consisted of five participants, three male and two female, ages 24–44. As shown in Table 1, workplaces and experiences of participants include Honda, Adobe, Intel and New Relic. Their length of years of experience varied; however four out of five participants held a PhD in UX related fields, with the fifth holding a Master's. In the context of this work, a participant was determined an expert by having advanced degrees or work experience in the area.

Table 1. Table with UX subject-matter expert data, where Years is the amount of years experience each participant had with UI/UX Design.

ID	Degree	Years	Field	Title	Employer
1	Doctoral	14	Innovation/Product	UX Architect	Intel
2	Doctoral	15	User Experience	Experience Architect	Intel
3	Masters	3	AR/VR Software Eng	Software Engineer	Adobe
4	Doctoral	12	UX Research	UX Research Lead	Honda
5	Doctoral	15	User Experience	Sr. Manager of UX Research	New Relic

3.2   Study Design

This research was conducted using the Battlespace Visualization and Interaction (BVI) software as the proposed use case, an active US Army Science and Technology project that supports research and development for complex military scenario mission planning and control [3]. It allows for visualization and annotation of military information to facilitate a variety of soldier needs. Motivation for conducting this study was to collect exploratory data before creating initial mockup designs for UI changes to the BVI software. This software provides a real-world use case to explore key interface requirements for scaling user interfaces across interaction modalities (AR, VR, etc.).

To do this, 1-on-1 interview sessions with subject-matter experts in the field of UX design and Human-Computer Interfaces were conducted to collect qualitative data. The goal of this study was to gain various expert opinions on the creation of UI designs that span across interaction modalities (virtual reality, augmented reality), as well as to explore concepts that contribute to design guidelines in the XR field. During each session, participants were given background information and asked to view the current system interface, as well as answer a set of interview questions. Audio and video data were captured during each session for later review using thematic analysis, discussed in further detail in the following sections. This research study was approved by the University of South Florida's Institutional Review Board (IRB) for data collection with human subjects under IRB Study #003637.

3.3   Procedure

To begin, known researchers in the field were reached out to via email request. Those that responded to the invitation scheduled a time with the PI to meet virtually via Microsoft Teams™. Meetings were held virtually in part due to COVID-19-related restrictions of meeting in person, as well as due to specialized UX researchers being spread geographically/non-local.

Study sessions were semi-structured interviews, approximately one hour each in duration. After reiterating the study procedures that they were about to participate in, verbal consent to participate was obtained. Participants then completed a short pre-interview survey using Qualtrics survey software, shared via Microsoft Teams^{TM}, to gather basic demographic information as well as information regarding experience in the field. Next, permission was requested from participants to record audio and screen data during the interview session. All participants approved, with only one participant electing to disable their front-facing camera. Audio recording allowed for transcribing of the interviews during post-processing of the data. Additionally, screen-recorded information was used to review any instances were participants referenced slides that were shown.

Semi-structured interviews consisted of a PowerPoint^{TM} presentation given by the PI with background information. This information included: key terms, the current problem space, and overview information regarding an existing collaborative XR system (BVI) as a real-world use case. After the presentation, participants were asked a set of interview questions as a guide for the conversation. Questions were centered around participant experience, application-specific design considerations, as well as broader scalability implications. The list of questions in order can be found in Table 2.

Table 2. Interview questions asked to participants during the session, organized in chronological order and by intended purpose.

Purpose	Interview Question
Researcher Experience	What types of roles have you had related to UI/UX design? What is your experience with XR (VR, MR, AR, etc.)?
Application Specific	Which features of the user interface do you consider to be the most important? Most important to be consistent across modalities? Why? Which features of the user interface do you consider to be the least important? Least important to be consistent across modalities? Why?
Broader Scalability	What are the major challenges you foresee in the creation of a universal UI framework? How would you envision a scalable UI across multiple systems? Where do you see UX going? What are the trends you anticipate moving forward?

Following this, participants were shown draft mockups of a potential user interface and provided their feedback on the initial designs. These mockups were first iterations of designs later implemented in this work.

3.4   Thematic Analysis Methodology

To begin, participant transcripts were anonymized using participant identifiers rather than names. Audio transcriptions were done using Dovetail software, an online assistive research tool that allows for transcription of audio [6]. It provides methods for researchers to rapidly highlight and organize information, allowing for analysis of large amounts of interview data. Interviews were uploaded and transcribed verbatim using this software and then verified manually by the principal investigator for any errors in automated transcriptions.

Following this, thematic analysis was conducted. Prior work from Braun and Clarke was used as a guide for research steps to successfully analyze data into meaningful themes and results [4,5]. The six-step procedure detailed in their work is as follows: 1) Familiarization of data, 2) generating initial codes, 3) search for themes, 4) reviewing themes, 5) defining and naming themes, and finally 6) producing the report. To familiarize with the data, the author read the interview transcripts multiple times. Initial codes were then added manually to the transcripts, such as "following form factor expectations", "understanding context", and more. These can be seen, along with their frequencies, in Fig. 1. Codes were added to the data using Dovetail software, allowing for color-coding of different ideas and concepts. Areas of the transcript where the PI was speaking were not taken into account. Next, these initial codes were reviewed then grouped into themes and sub-themes, as seen in Fig. 2. Themes were scored by importance using the frequency in which they were encountered.

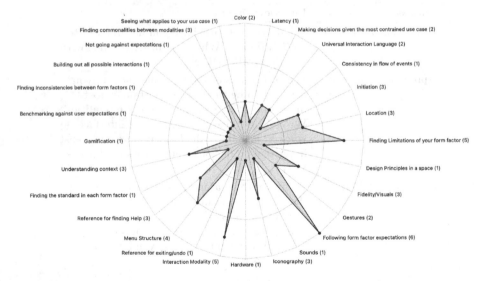

Fig. 1. Radar plot depicting thematic analysis codes in user interview transcripts and their frequencies.

4   Results

The thematic analysis of qualitative interviews revealed five primary themes: visual consistency, evaluating form-factor capabilities, establishing consistent

Codes	Themes
• Color • Iconography • Fidelity • Location of features	Creating visual consistency
• Making decisions given the most constrained case • Finding Commonalities between modalities • Finding Limitations of the form factor • Finding inconsistencies between form factors • Building out all possible interactions initially	Evaluating form-factor capabilities
• User Flow of Events • Initiation • Menu Structure • Reference for finding help • Reference for exiting	Establishing consistent user flow of events
• Following expectations of each form factor • Finding the standard in each form factor • Benchmarking against user expectations • Not going against user expectations • Researching design principles in a space • Consistent Interaction Modality	Working with form-factor norms and expectations
• Seeing what applies to your use case • Understanding the context	Determining the context of use

Fig. 2. Chart of generated thematic analysis codes grouped to associated themes.

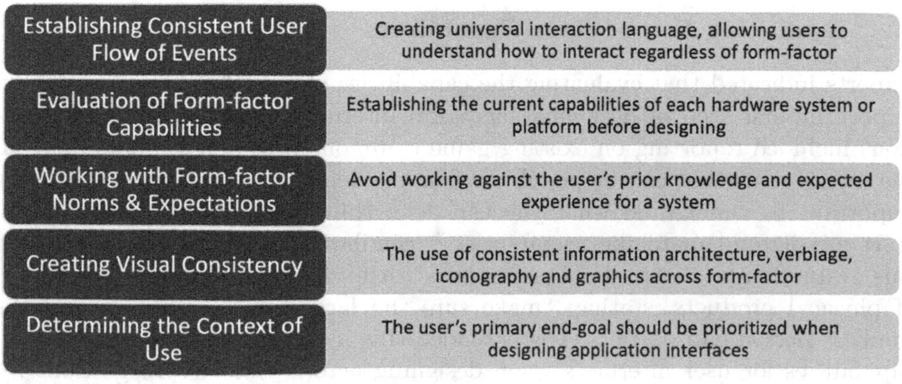

Establishing Consistent User Flow of Events	Creating universal interaction language, allowing users to understand how to interact regardless of form-factor
Evaluation of Form-factor Capabilities	Establishing the current capabilities of each hardware system or platform before designing
Working with Form-factor Norms & Expectations	Avoid working against the user's prior knowledge and expected experience for a system
Creating Visual Consistency	The use of consistent information architecture, verbiage, iconography and graphics across form-factor
Determining the Context of Use	The user's primary end-goal should be prioritized when designing application interfaces

Fig. 3. Five primary themes identified by the thematic analysis process, with a short summarization of each.

user flow of events, working with form-factor norms and expectations, and determining context of use. These themes and their short summaries can be seen in Fig. 3. These themes are discussed in further detail in the following sections.

4.1   Creating Visual Consistency

Participant feedback regarding visual consistency is in line with current guidelines for user interface design. Experts commented that the use of simple iconography that can be transitioned across all experiences is ideal, as well as the use of a clear coloring visual to guide users. Three participants indicated that visuals and their fidelity were of relatively high importance, and should be replicated across realities. Therefore if graphics, animations or interactions are of high quality in one, they should be in all.

Consistency of the location of tool placement within 3D space, however, had mixed feedback. One expert advocated for consistency, commenting that wherever interactable items are located in one experience should remain consistent for all other experiences or modalities. They continued, "I don't want to have to figure out and learn, 'oh where are the tools located in this new experience', right?". On the other hand, another subject matter expert opposed this thought. They describe tool location consistency as less important than identifiability of each item, due to the idea that in "AR and VR, you instinctively know you have an entire world to discover". As users in AR and VR may be more comfortable with the idea that they need to discover the area around them, placement of tools may allow for more variability. Although these responses seem opposing at initial glance, they align in that both place importance on making it so that the user understands the iconography or symbology easily. In this way, reducing learning curves when switching modalities and general barrier of entry on first use are considered of high importance when designing UIs successful across modalities.

4.2   Evaluating Form-Factor Capabilities

Experts indicated that evaluating the capabilities of each XR modality was an important first step of designing successful interfaces across realities. Suggestions included reporting on existing game commonalities and "building out all the interactions that can be possible". One participant noted that it was "very important to understand what you can do within an environment before you start mixing and matching [capabilities]". Similarly, another expert compared this evaluation to the study of ergonomics within human factors for the design of physical products, stating: "make sure the largest person can fit and the smallest person can reach". They extended this idea to the selection of feature capabilities for user interfaces when designing across systems. Suggestions for starting this process were to begin with one to two form-factors to begin, in order to understand them as comprehensively as possible, before building out further.

Additionally, finding limitations of each form factor was discussed by 4 out of 5 participants as a method for making design choices, as some decisions may be dictated by the most constrained use case. Experts posed questions such as: "If you were to look at or develop some principles, well in which case or which scenario would that not be? What is the edge case? What is the corner case?". One example of this brought up by an expert during the interviews, is choosing iconography when faced with design considerations of an augmented reality headset, as not all colors in UIs will work effectively in AR for viewing. This can be especially important to consider for applications that are intended to be used both indoors and outdoors, or in particularly harsh lighting conditions.

Moreover, understanding additional tools that the user is expected to use or has access to when interacting with the system such as a stylus pen with a tablet, controllers, etc., was suggested. Having an understanding of what hardware or interactions that can and cannot be supported per each form-factor may be useful. Overall, through the evaluation of each form-factors capabilities, commonalities, inconsistencies and limitations, researchers and designers could better inform their design choices.

4.3   Establishing Consistent User Flow of Events

Factors that determine the flow events such as menu structure and information architecture should have minimal variations across form-factor. Regardless of some changes being present due to each form-factor, the data hierarchy should maintain as consistent as reasonably allowed, said participants. This is similar to the creation of visual consistency as described in prior subsections. One participant says, "Are the menus labeled the same? Do they have the same verbiage? Are the same features stored under the same menu topics?". Similarly, options within menus or feature sets should be similar as users will "have an expectation of what's going to be there".

Initial engagement with the information architecture should also be similar. A user should be able to launch and pull up tools in the same manner across systems, as well as close them. Additionally, there should be consistent reference points for key locations that users will access, such as methods for finding help, fixing mistakes using undo commands, or going back. "Whether that means cancel, back, escape, whatever, however you're labeling it... trying to make that selection similar", says one participant. In this way, no matter the form-factor they know where their necessary options and controls should be located.

4.4   Working with Form-Factor Norms and Expectations

Experts recommended that designers "immerse [themselves] in other similar experiences" in order to become more familiar with the design principles in that space. Understanding the experience in each space or form-factor is key to knowing what feels natural, normal, and comfortable. They posed questions such as "What experiences are you comparing or basing that off of?" and "How do they move something from point A to point B?". For example in a tablet, expectations are that the menu is located at the top of the page or sometimes towards the left. While in virtual reality, this may differ. Finding where menus are typically found in each system and adhering to that. At the bare minimum, noted one participant, you shouldn't be actively going against these norms.

One participant asked, "what do people normally do?", explaining that while existing applications should not necessarily dictate the 'standard' for that space, they may be the only thing that user has interacted with prior in VR/AR. Finding existing norms between existing software's or games in that space, and deciding if they work well for your application may help with transferability of knowledge from prior experiences. Similarly, another participant noted that there are "preconceived expectations for each modality" and that "people expect to be able to do certain things in each modality that you may not be able to do in the others". Suggestions for becoming more informed included playing existing games, documenting notes about other experiences, and existing research publications.

4.5   Determining the Context of Use

While there can be several sets of heuristic design choices or guidelines that one should follow when designing across form-factors, taking that information in to account while still maintaining consideration for the specific context of use is important. Principles to follow should be focused on a particular interaction with it's context of use, "opposed to a broad set of principles that may not be applicable here" as mentioned by one expert.

When posed with considering a specific use case, in this case the BVI software, one participant suggested finding out what users are "used to using, what they currently use, and what interactions are they used to" when completing their desired task. The BVI software's primary use case was interpreted as annotation for mission planning. In this case, one would investigate how they are currently achieving those goals as there are "different tools for different contexts of use".

5   Discussion

The resulting themes determined by thematic analysis present general recommendations for researchers and developers seeking information on creation of UI designs in the XR space. While limited existing research exists for novel HMD interface design, as seen in MR-specific or VR-specific guidelines discussed, these guidelines provide an initial starting point for researchers designing for multiple modalities.

Some resulting themes are aligned with prior heuristics such as Nielsen's usability heuristics for interface design. However, Nielsen's heuristics are intended as a broad rule of thumb, and not intended to refer to XR or multimodal systems. Establishing consistent user flow of events is similar to Nielsen's "Consistency and Standards" heuristic, in that they both refer to the end user's expectation that words and actions such as menu item structure mean the same thing. In contrast, the recommendations presented are further specialized to multimodal XR systems, and as a result, include heavy consideration for form-factor capabilities and expectations in each system modality.

Endsley et al. presented design heuristics that are intended to be specific to AR [7]. While those heuristics include "Accounting for hardware capabilities", multimodal design practices were explicitly excluded from consideration. The recommendation presented in this paper to evaluate form-factor capabilities is intended to guide the system designer towards understanding of the most-constrained modality, and to consider the commonalities and limitations of each modality.

Results of this study primarily consist of feedback centered around a collaborative system, with the main use case being annotation of military information and symbology. While participants were also asked to generalize their feedback, as seen in research questions that are not use-case specific, this is a current limitation to the scope of this study. Researchers should keep this in mind when deciding to apply this research to their own work, as additional themes may emerge due to expansion to other use cases that are significantly different, such as tele-communication Additionally, the participant sample size interviewed was relatively small, with a total of five expert participants. As a result, findings are considered exploratory and can be used as a starting point for conversation surrounding scalability of UIs across XR modalities.

Through establishing themes that may improve designing for applications that span multiple realities, there is opportunity for validation of the concepts conveyed through evaluation of design prototypes created in the next stages of development. Vi et. al discusses that through their literature search, few examples of developed XR software exist to convey concepts [15]. Continuation of this research by development of prototype interfaces and their evaluation contributes to existing research by applying principles within actual applications.

6   Conclusion and Future Work

This work presents a set of five initial recommendations determined through thematic analysis of subject-matter experts in the UX field. Results may provide guidance to researchers and developers in the field during the initial design stages of XR interface design, and may increasing the limited existing information available for development in such an emerging field. Results from this research will be applied to creating initial redesigned user interfaces for an existing collaborative military system. Future experiments on prototype UI designs, such as usability studies with subject-matter experts, will be used to test applicability of principles in practice.

References

1. HTC Vive Pro 2 Virtual Reality Headset. vive.com (2022). https://myshop-us.vive.com/
2. Microsoft HoloLens 2. microsoft.com (2022). https://www.microsoft.com/en-us/d/hololens-2/
3. Amburn, C., Vey, N., Boyce, M., Mize, J.: The augmented reality sandtable (ARES)(No. ARL-SR-0340). Army Res. Lab. (2015)
4. Braun, V., Clarke, V.: Using thematic analysis in psychology. Qual. Res. Psychol. **3**(2), 77–101 (2006)
5. Clarke, V., Braun, V., Hayfield, N.: Thematic analysis. Qual. Psychol.: Pract. Guide Res. Methods **3**, 222–248 (2015)
6. Dovetail. https://dovetailapp.com/
7. Endsley, T.C., Sprehn, K.A., Brill, R.M., Ryan, K.J., Vincent, E.C., Martin, J.M.: Augmented reality design heuristics: designing for dynamic interactions. In: Proceedings of the Human Factors and Ergonomics Society Annual Meeting, vol. 61, pp. 2100–2104. Sage Publications Sage CA, Los Angeles, CA (2017)
8. Krauß, V., Jasche, F., Saßmannshausen, S.M., Ludwig, T., Boden, A.: Research and practice recommendations for mixed reality design-different perspectives from the community. In: Proceedings of the 27th ACM Symposium on Virtual Reality Software and Technology, pp. 1–13 (2021)
9. Krauß, V., Nebeling, M., Jasche, F., Boden, A.: Elements of XR prototyping: characterizing the role and use of prototypes in augmented and virtual reality design. In: Proceedings of the 2022 CHI Conference on Human Factors in Computing Systems, pp. 1–18 (2022)
10. Memmesheimer, V.M., Ebert, A.: Scalable extended reality: a future research agenda. Big Data Cogn. Comput. **6**(1), 12 (2022)
11. Milgram, P., Kishino, F.: A taxonomy of mixed reality visual displays. IEICE Trans. Inf. Syst. **77**(12), 1321–1329 (1994)
12. Nielsen, J.: Enhancing the explanatory power of usability heuristics. In: Proceedings of the SIGCHI Conference on Human Factors in Computing Systems, pp. 152–158 (1994)
13. Parveau, M., Adda, M.: Toward a user-centric classification scheme for extended reality paradigms. J. Ambient. Intell. Humaniz. Comput. **11**(6), 2237–2249 (2020)
14. Vardomatski, S.: Council post: augmented and virtual reality after COVID-19, November 2022. https://www.forbes.com/sites/forbestechcouncil/2021/09/14/augmented-and-virtual-reality-after-covid-19/?sh=57711d092d97
15. Vi, S., da Silva, T.S., Maurer, F.: User experience guidelines for designing HMD extended reality applications. In: Lamas, D., Loizides, F., Nacke, L., Petrie, H., Winckler, M., Zaphiris, P. (eds.) INTERACT 2019. LNCS, vol. 11749, pp. 319–341. Springer, Cham (2019). https://doi.org/10.1007/978-3-030-29390-1_18
16. Xing, Y., Liang, Z., Shell, J., Fahy, C., Guan, K., Liu, B.: Historical data trend analysis in extended reality education field. In: 2021 IEEE 7th International Conference on Virtual Reality (ICVR), pp. 434–440. IEEE (2021)

Modular 3D Interface Design for Accessible VR Applications

Corrie Green[✉] [iD], Yang Jiang, and John Isaacs

Robert Gordon University, Aberdeen AB10 7AQ, Scotland
`c.green1@rgu.ac.uk`

Abstract. Designed with an accessible first design approach, the presented paper describes how exploiting humans' proprioception ability in 3D space can result in a more natural interaction experience when using a 3D graphical user interface in a virtual environment. The modularity of the designed interface empowers the user to decide where they want to place interface elements in 3D space allowing for a highly customizable experience, both in the context of the player and the virtual space. Drawing inspiration from today's tangible interfaces used, such as those in aircraft cockpits, a modular interface is presented taking advantage of our natural understanding of interacting with 3D objects and exploiting capabilities that otherwise have not been used in 2D interaction. Additionally, the designed interface supports multimodal input mechanisms which also demonstrates the opportunity for the design to cross over to augmented reality applications. A focus group study was completed to better understand the usability and constraints of the designed 3D GUI.

Keywords: Virtual Reality · Interaction · Accessibility · 3D GUI

1 Introduction

The progression of the graphical user interface (GUI) has reached a level of ubiquitous understanding, allowing users who are accustomed to desktop or mobile device interfaces to interact through familiar interface elements such as windows, icons, menus, and pointers (WIMP).

However, with the adoption of virtual reality, these design decisions have for the most part been directly translated to work in a 360° experience supporting, 6 degrees of freedom (DOF). Resulting in the same 2D elements being used in virtual reality (VR) with user selection primarily being a ray cast in the form of a laser. This allows designers to use existing design concepts by placing elements in a similar fashion to a traditional desktop environment would use.

If we depend just on conventional interface design choices, we are not necessarily taking advantage of the extra dimension made available. Existing interaction techniques for VR have resulted in a novel and diverse set of designs that have primarily been developed for the VR games market [1].

J. Y. C. Chen and G. Fragomeni (Eds.): HCII 2023, LNCS 14027, pp. 15–32, 2023.
https://doi.org/10.1007/978-3-031-35634-6_2

3D interfaces provide the opportunity to utilize our sense of proprioception as we physically surround ourselves with static interfaces in the form of 3D objects akin to that of the real world. Proprioception can also be referred to as kinesthesia and is the ability to know where your body is in space and has been referred to as our "six sense" [2]. It gives the user an idea of where their body parts are in relation to their environment and how they may be able to interact with it. Drawing closer to incorporating the human body fully can increase our understanding of the 3D digital environment presented, by using our natural understanding of the world [3].

As VR has the potential to provide more presence than a traditional interface, the idea requires more interface design evolution to become more flexible and human-oriented. An example study simulated wind; the breeze enhanced presence among users [4]. Showing that somewhat unconventional methods can enhance presence, to which, natural interaction for the user may furthermore provide fewer constraints leading to increased presence. The developed interface outlined in this paper provides a multimodal approach to interaction design and fully supports existing ray-based input controls. Thereby reducing the adoption effort required by users who may have accessibility constraints, requiring them to use ray-based interaction. Using a new medium of fully 3D panels over traditional 2D windows or forms, the system in addition to supporting novel 3D interaction also allows for the migration of ray-based interaction techniques typical for existing VR applications. Gesture-based interaction approaches have been used for input, allowing the users' hands to be tracked with or without a controller during selection and navigation. The system is modular allowing users to move the location of all UI components in 3D space to suit their preference, with the addition of contextual-based UI being explored where UI elements appear only when relevant to the task being completed.

Predicting what an interactive element will achieve is largely responsible for its placement, context, and iconography. A skeuomorph is a design concept that is used to represent objects with their real-world counterparts, primarily used in user interface design - such as associating a floppy disk with a save icon. In Ivan Sutherlands' famous essay "The Ultimate Display" he opens with "We sense an involvement with this physical world which gives us the ability to predict its properties well. For example, we can predict where objects will fall, how well-known shapes look from other angles, and how much force is required to push objects against friction." Using the real world as a guide for the GUI we can cross over our ability for pattern recognition in context using inductive thinking, with the potential to enhance memory by association with their real-world counterparts. An important aspect to consider before exploring the opportunities made available by a 3D GUI was the vehicle in which to showcase the interface itself. Usability discussions were completed in focus groups which allowed participants to share their experience using the developed interface alongside peers and provide insight into the satisfying and frustrating aspects of the interaction. Establishing a familiar metaphor was important for this reason, as recruitment targeted users' previous exposure to VR applications, where novice to intermediate users was selected to participate. The selected demographic was used, as the study's focus was to understand the usability of the designed interface and highlight issues and struggles with a 3D modular GUI without significant context to current design philosophies.

A conceptual model was therefore established to understand the problem space for a new medium of interaction. To present the interface in an application that a 3D GUI may be applicable to, the development of a 3D visualization platform for geospatial positions was developed. Allowing for visualization of various forms of 3D spatial data including point cloud scans, video playback, and geospatial data which was represented by electric vehicle (EV) chargers' latitude and longitude positions. Querying of EV charger locations was completed based on their charging type and availability. This allowed for a selection of chargers to be scanned and linked to their real-world position visualized by their point cloud scan using the Microsoft Azure Kinect. The map was selected as the primary visualization tool as a homage to the map being the "graphic representation of the milieu" [5] but primarily due to it being a familiar visualization medium for many people.

2 Modular Interface Concepts

The definition of modular by the Oxford dictionary states, "employing or involving a module or modules as the basis of design or construction." In programming design practices, modular code is to divide the functionality of the system into separate modules that are independent of one another. The concept also stretches into UI design where interface elements are created for a variety of environments. An example of this is during website development, where interface elements are isolated with their own set of constraints, allowing them to be independent and dynamically adjust based on the user's device. This approach to a responsive layout allows for support across various platforms; mobile, desktop, tablet, and even VR. In contrast, defining constraints for 3D UI in immersive environments have been explored [3] but have also yet to be fully integrated into real-world applications. UI Elements without any constraint are problematic as the increased design space leaves many design choices at the discretion of the developer. The key areas in the presented 3D interface include the following and will be discussed further.

- Free-floating allows for adjustment in 6-DOF for users with specific viewing angle requirements and allows for anchored placement in 3D space.
- Contextual, allowing elements to only be displayed when relevant to the location in the environment resulting in;
- Predictable task-focused interactions, using skeuomorphs and colors around 3D interface trims in designated context zones

Key to the naming conventions definition, it aims to provide the "basis of design or construction." The presented 3D interface allows users to move the UI to a location in 3D space, that isn't dictated by the application being presented. Rather than employing rigorous design methodologies to focus on the layout of interactable element positions such as the location of buttons and sliders, we can instead empower the user to place interactive elements best suited to their needs.

By interacting with VR interface elements repeatedly, the user can learn the spatial location of objects and understand the interaction mechanism employed by them [6]. As a user completes their desired task, they can adjust the placement of immediate controls in location to suit their preference. This allows users who may have accessibility constraints to adjust the UI to a location that is suitable for their interaction (Fig. 1).

Fig. 1. Render of the developed 3D interface panels, allowing for manipulation of the 3D map visualization by querying a geospatial dataset

The concept of consistently visible UI controls stems from traditional fixed UI elements. An example is the toolbar on most WIMP interfaces where the close, expand, and minimize buttons are always available to the user. The developed interface has included this fixed UI concept through an iterative development process ensuring users can show and hide 3D panels in a single action.

Panels containing UI elements such as buttons can be moved in 3D space with no gravity influencing them, resulting in panels being *free-floating*. The user interacting to move the placement of panels uses natural gestures such as grabbing and releasing. These panels can be fixed to the user's virtual body for movement around the environment but also when not fixed to the user's movement (controlled via button press) they are instead anchored in place in relation to the desired task being carried out in the environment. A paper exploring new directions and perspectives of 3D GUI [6] notes that "standard 3D UI techniques can and should be based on object attachment" when regarding interfaces floating in space. In addition, the author describes this as an exception, not a rule when relating real-world interaction to virtual interaction. The designed interface presented in this paper includes panels that are free floating based on the user's exposure to existing interfaces in the real world that may have free-floating connotations. Primarily being, the computer tablet. Although the paper's release was in 2008, many users would not have been familiar with the concept of the digital tablet as the original iPad was released in 2010, two years after the initial paper's release.

The panel is a key component to the design of the modular interface, allowing for relocation in free-floating space and anchored to user movement or left static in a location desired by the user. This is consistent across all panel and UI elements, keeping interaction between elements predictable. Using panel color and shape to direct the user to these interfaces with predictable interaction areas. This was created by adding trim around all panels in a color that can be selected by the user. In Fig. 2 the trim is white around the grey panel, with various transparency properties on the back panel to provide contrast to the surrounding environment.

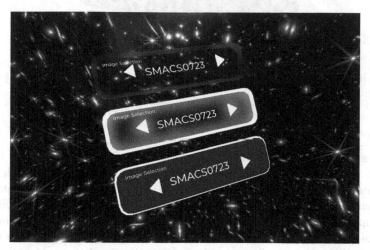

Fig. 2. 3D UI Panels allowing for side navigation using buttons, demonstrating three different contrast approaches in a noisy background environment

The key to natural interaction is the use of gestures and physical movement to move panels, to support accessibility, it is intended that the interface can be customized via a configuration file that has values of key elements pre-placed in the environment allowing them to interact with the interface. For example, if a user is unable to stand and lie down, they may not be able to reach for the interface components at first, instead, another user or a configuration file can be used to allow the user to interact with the elements from their position. Further exploration into the availability of interaction techniques is discussed in Sect. 4.

The redesign of the traditional 2D slider into its 3D counterpart was centered around ensuring it doesn't require a complex interaction, being a variation of small and large movements in a single action. Instead, the slider allows for scrolling via small movements at a fixed distance, not requiring movement across the entirety of the slider. Prioritizing shoulder and elbow movement over wrist movement. Due to the spring physics associated with the anchor point in the center, the slider's anchor always returns to the center position upon release. Scroll speed scales as it is moved further from the origin. This design is like that of the middle mouse click auto-scroll on existing 2D scroll-bar elements (Fig. 3).

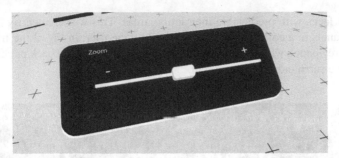

Fig. 3. Reimagined 3D slider using physic spring joints to return anchor to the center point after an interaction

2.1 Required Constraints

With the addition of the third dimension being added to interface design, there becomes more opportunity for additional confusion in establishing a mental model of the system for end users, due to the context space in which the interface may be presented. With more freedom of space, there becomes an increased availability for the placement of GUI components. Existing 3D applications such as CAD software on 2D interfaces are designed for professionals and as such, provide a plethora of options in tabs and sub-menus. With the extra dimensionality of visualization VR provides, there is an opportunity for an excess of choice, consequently, an intelligent reduction of choice needs to be integrated into its design. It is therefore important to consider constraining the system to allow interface elements to display only when necessary.

The panels developed are a key area to which add constraints to. The button and slider elements that are traditionally found in forms or menu systems can be located via panels in the designed interface. These panels act as grabbable containers allowing the interface elements to be arranged inside an area that can be moved in 3D space to suit the user's preference. The borders of these panels are consistent in color and style to highlight their interactivity, a consistent interaction color theme was established to convey to the user that elements in this color can be interacted with. Such as a white button, white panel border, and white slider anchor.

2.2 Contextual Interface

Contextual UI location allows for interactable features to only appear when in proximity to the task at hand. Much like the real world, computer users can physically walk to a monitor to select its controls. If the monitor is fixed into world space in a virtual world, the question must be asked, is it appropriate for the monitor to be fixed? The two contexts described below, show how local user space and world space can be used effectively to provide UI context to the task being carried out.

Player Context. Consistent user interface elements are concepts that can be found in the WIMP design structure. A common feature of window controls allows for minimize, maximize, and float controls of windows or form containers. These are always available to the user and are persistent throughout the navigation of an application. In a virtual reality environment, the player's space can also be divided into fixed player UI and environment UI. The developed system shown in Fig. 4 shows specific UI elements that can be locked to the player's position while navigating each zone. Controls available to them may be consistent throughout environment contexts, such as loading a settings menu, resetting player position, or closing the application. The specifics of what events the UI elements complete are at the discretion of the developer, however the separation between environment-specific controls and player controls is the context in which they are displayed.

For example, closing the application would likely be best suited as *player context* UI as it is always linked to the player regardless of *environmental context*. Entering an environment focused on video playback in Fig. 4 annotated as "zone 2", can allow for a play button to be locked and added to the player's context while navigating in this zone, but not necessarily. The player may choose to keep UI in a fixed location in world space close to the interface's *environment context*, which is the virtual screen in this example.

Environment Context. Based on the player's location in the virtual environment, it may be appropriate to hide all UI and only display relevant UI elements based on the task in the environment. For example, if the user is interacting with the 3D map in Fig. 4 "zone 1", then the controls for this map should be located near the map itself, as the user would be unable to see details of the map if controlling at a distance. The context here is the environment which is map control. In the other example described above, video playback, the screen is the environment context and the UI elements that are in the proximity of this will be displayed.

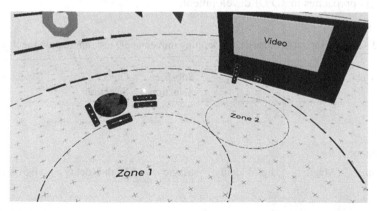

Fig. 4. Environment context UI zones, demonstrating UI elements only visible to the task

2.3 Natural Interaction Matrix

This section explores the requirements for a VR application, and how planning inter-action mechanisms can support engagement with the task being completed. Evolving technologies and newer interaction techniques will likely result in the matrix chang-ing for the requirements of an application over time however it serves as a baseline to understand the input techniques made available to complete an action.

In questioning naturalism in 3D interfaces [7], two high-level mechanisms for 3D interaction design are discussed. A design technique with *interaction fidelity* and another with a focus on enhancing usability and performance by using *"magic techniques."* The two techniques contrast in strategy, where interaction fidelity focuses on how natural the interaction is in relation to a real-world environment, and "magic techniques" focuses on task completion in an unnatural environment.

Such as using the teleporting locomotion strategy due to lack of physical play space which would otherwise be a high-fidelity interaction. Each actionable task in virtual space will need to be broken down to fully understand the potential options made available and select the best-suited technique for the interaction. The paper [7] notes 3 universal UI tasks that can be viewed as high-level requirements for a 3D application, travel, selection, and manipulation.

Travel is movement in the virtual space, where both high interaction fidelity - physically walking in a tracked environment - and "magic" mechanisms - such as teleporting are options available to the user. In visualizing big data challenges [8], a set of requirements were provided that describe features a VR visualization platform should achieve in the context of 3D visualization of multidimensional datasets. This was used as a guide for the development of the conceptual model for an application with a 3D GUI focus presented in this paper. The matrix shown in Table 1 categorizes these requirements into three interaction tasks, travel, selection, and manipulation. These are categorized further by a potential choice for their interaction mechanism, high fidelity, or a "magic technique". Based on the requirement type, developers decided what category of interaction it falls under. The matrix is to encourage the exploration of High-fidelity and Magic interaction approaches in 3D UI development.

Table 1. Natural interaction matrix for defining universal 3D task interaction mechanisms

Requirement	Scaling	Navigation	Subspace Selection	Object Selection	Object Move
Travel		x			
Selection			x	x	
Manipulation	x				x
Mechanism	Magic	High-Fidelity	Magic	High-Fidelity	High-Fidelity

3   Multimodal Input

In the following sections, multimodal input and selection approaches are discussed. Providing a multimodal approach to user input has been shown to allow more users to interact with the system more effectively [9]. The availability of various input mediums is an important accessibility design consideration and is a critical component of the modular system.

Input modality is discussed in the web accessibility guidelines for "pointers" [10] where timed and complex gestures may be inaccessible for some users. Although not to be avoided in its entirety, the functional recommendation is to offer alternative methods of inputs to enable users with motor impairments to interact with the interface still. The input control mechanism for the discussed 3D modular interface is supported by ray-based interaction. In addition to this popular method of input, by using gestures recorded with hand tracking - with or without controllers - we can support the user in deciding their preferred input medium.

As the user can freely move in 6 DOF, they are away from surfaces that can support fine motor skills for accurate selection of objects at range. Mouse and keyboard interaction approaches limit natural interaction grasp because of this and why for natural interaction approaches, hand tracking is a lucrative opportunity for improved immersion and intuition.

In comparison to 2D input approaches which are traditionally 4-DOF, 6-DOF interaction approaches have the caveat of requiring more physical movement which can be restrictive to some users. 2D input mediums have been shown to be two orders of magnitude more precise and have less latency [11, 12]. Although attempts have been made to alleviate this, more study is required to see what other algorithmic approaches can be used.

It is for this reason that supporting numerous input mediums should be considered when developing a 3D GUI. Every panel in the designed interface has elements of buttons and or sliders.

3.1 Hand Tracking with Controllers

Ray-based UI interaction systems can support controller input with the use of a laser pointer. In augmented reality, the same concept of laser pointers is used as a metaphor for interacting with an augmented environment [13]. For 3D interfaces that can rely on gestures followed by the selection of interface elements, there is an opportunity for the support of controller and hand-tracking input. Supporting both allow for user preference to be exploited and the potential to use the same interface system as new input mediums are supported. At Meta reality labs, research into using electromyography (EMG) where electrical motor nerve signals are translated into actionable input for a virtual interface [14]. With new different input mediums, the interfaces currently developed in VR based on the WIMP concept may have to be redefined to support such an input. Whereas the opportunity with a modular 3D GUI, a multimodal input mechanism can be established from the start, including an accessible first design philosophy.

Not all VR headsets require controllers as they have inside-out hand tracking capability which at a minimum allows for navigation around the headsets OS via gestures – such as pointing. Specifically, in 2022 the Meta Quest 2 headset allows for navigation on the browser and loading of applications without the use of a controller. This has its advantages such as user convenience for a more passive experience such as video playback, however not all VR applications support hand tracking. By doing so developers are limiting those with hand-tracking headsets to experiencing their product. As the future could contain more and more hand-tracking supported headsets, it was therefore deemed important to develop support for hand-tracking and controller-based input.

The Valve Index controllers can be seen in the Fig. 5 with input mappings highlighted. These controllers use infrared on the index fingers to track the user's finger at a distance without touching any of the controller itself. The grip around the controller support tracking other fingers with the thumb having more infrared sensors available on each button at the top of the controller. This provides finger-tracking capability while also being able to support feedback via haptics.

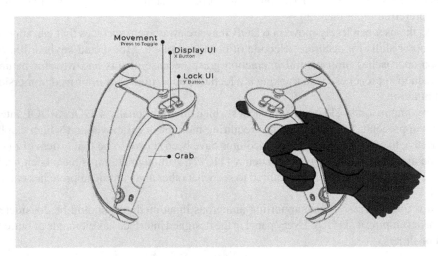

Fig. 5. Exclusive finger tracking approach supported with Valve Index controllers, allowing for locomotion using the joystick and two buttons for displaying and hiding the 3D UI

The environment is manipulated exclusively with hand tracking for this reason but selection/input with ray-based mechanisms can be used via toggle. The buttons on the controller do however provide additional functionality such as virtual space movement. Room-scale tracking is enabled by default; however, it is not always convenient, and designing for every room layout is not feasible. The joysticks are therefore used for locomotion techniques supporting teleporting and standing movement by clicking down the joystick. This keeps both mediums of movement selected by one control mechanism. In addition, this supports the same controls for each hand, allowing users to navigate using their preferred hand and further supporting temporary accessibility issues, such as users having a broken dominant hand.

The UI displayed around the user at any given time can be hidden and redisplayed at their own preference via a toggle on the controller's button. The UI can also be locked to the user's position as they navigate around the map. In Sect. 2.2, contextual UI is discussed where this feature opens a lot of opportunities for hidden control mechanisms in the virtual space.

3.2 Eye Tracking

With the adoption of variable rate shading and foveated rendering based on eye tracking, there presents an even larger opportunity than physical interaction design, to intelligently introduce a new input medium into virtual reality interfaces. Rather than selecting a UI component using physical hand tracking, the gaze-based selection is an alternative ray-based interaction technique, that can be used as an additional input mechanism [15] demonstrated in Fig. 6. Where the user can select a UI element for interaction and confirm their selection with a button press or with a countdown while gazing at a specific element for a specified duration based on a ray directed by the user's eye gaze. By designing an interface that supports both gesture and ray-based interaction we can exploit eye tracking as it becomes more available in VR headsets, such as the Quest Pro and HTC Vive Pro.

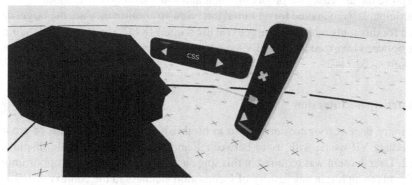

Fig. 6. Ray casting approach of selection can also be used with the 3D UI by using visual cues to show where the virtual "cursor" is being displayed

3.3 Voice Input

Buttons on panels can be selected using voice input using the Azure Voice SDK. Each button has a required value to be said such as "left charger status." Each panel is named appropriately allowing any user who can view the panel to know its primary identifier. Every button that can be interacted with via voice commands requires a primary key to be said to activate the correct event. Alternatively, a hierarchy can be established if a button is the only one displayed on a panel. For example, the panel tag title followed by the button. Due to the significant amount of UI displayed, this was only implemented on a set few buttons for experimentation. An example of the keyword followed by a command is as follows broken down into the primary key and command associated with a button. "Charger panel, next."

Beyond the selection of buttons, such a mechanism can be used to expand menus into further groups without alternative interaction. Such a mechanism can enhance the usability and performance of the task being completed by the user by being presented with only relevant information to the task being carried out. This allows preparation for the next task while still immersed in one.

Emerging user interaction design principles could also have a place in a virtual environment. Sonic interaction design (SID) can play a key role in supporting the quality of an interactive experience. Paper [16] describes how multimodal listening approaches such as "listening in, up, out, through and around" a play space can help form shape perception.

Although not directly implemented in this conceptual model, it does provide a notion for further expansion by exploiting audio cues for 3D objects beyond selection feedback.

4 Research Design and Methodology

The preliminary focus group study provided qualitative data about how 6 users reacted to a 3D GUI, allowing the ability to query a database and update visual cues on a 3D topographical map. The aim of the study is to identify potential accessibility constraints and explore the use cases for producing high and low usability satisfaction.

Participants were invited for an initial interview to confirm they are the target demographic for this study which was targeted at users aged 18 to 55 and classified their experience between intermediate use of virtual reality and inexperienced. The participating users were aged 24–29.

4.1 Participant Interview

Preliminary interviews were carried out to establish a baseline user base of novice to intermediate VR users, with users between 1 and 3 on the Likert scale displayed in Table 2. User consent was required at this stage and was followed by an opportunity for participants to highlight any history of locomotion sickness in the context of VR.

Table 2. Initial interview questions to target users VR exposure

Initial Interview Questions
Do you have experience with motion sickness from VR or other?
Are you at present comfortable to proceed?
Scale from 1 to 5, where would you place your VR experience?

1	2	3	4	5
Once or Never	Rarely	Occasionally	Frequently	Very Frequently

4.2 Process

The in-person study was completed where participants were in the same room around a screen which allowed the current user's VR headset perspective to be displayed, this was to encourage discussion about experienced interactions with the system. Firstly, a tutorial demonstration was provided by the chair to the entire group, allowing them to view the external screen and ask questions about what they are seeing. This provided an overview of the interface to give some context and expectations on interactions.

Once an overview of the experience was presented by the chair of the focus group, the first user was placed into VR, this was selected based on their experience in VR.

Those who are novices with little to no experience – Likert scale 1 – were asked to go first and users were then selected incrementing in VR exposure until everyone had completed the task.

The study demographic only had novice to intermediate experience with VR. Requiring headset adjustment and fine control over the IPD for each user which took 2–5 min per user. Participants only started the experience once their headset was comfortable and they could see text in the environment clearly. Users were asked the following.

1. Walk around the space and select a locomotion technique of their choice (if the default joystick wasn't comfortable, they could opt for teleport)
2. Interact with the 3D UI Panels that interface with the map and move the map to latitude–longitude locations queried.
3. Interact with the point cloud playback and view the cloud alongside the video counterpart.

During the interaction, the user in the experience was asked to share their unfiltered thoughts about their interactions. Other members of the focus group could spectate from the perspective of the VR user and participate in the conversation as well due to displaying on an external screen. After 10 min or so the next user would be placed into the same experience. Once half of the users have completed their experience further questions were added to the group discussed in Sect. 4.3.

4.3 Assessment Criteria

Notes were carried out during each participant interaction in the focus group session. Questions were asked to support in identifying areas of interaction satisfaction partnered with the observation notes taken. **Thematic analysis** was used and will be outlined in the following section which allows for themes and patterns to be identified that can be further explored with further questioning. Key questions for discussion were asked throughout and open to anyone to respond, not just the user in the experience at the time. Two key research questions are focused on and are supported by three follow-up questions.

Research Objective 1: What aspects did you see as high usability satisfaction?
Research Objective 2: What aspects did you see as low usability satisfaction?
Question 1: How was the experience overall?
Question 2: Where do you see the application of such an experience?
Question 3: What do you think of using a 3D Interface?

4.4 Results

A total of 6 adults participated with initial interviews indicating their exposure to VR was 1–3 on a Likert scale of VR experience, with 4 users being inexperienced at 1 on the scale, and 2 being at scale 3. This defined a baseline demographic of novice VR users. No candidates were disqualified at the initial stage due to experience with motion sickness. One participant reported they do get travel sick, but due to their exposure to

VR in the past were comfortable to proceed as previous VR motion sickness exposure was due to a sharp drop in HMD framerate.

Users who stated 1 on in the initial stage said they have only used VR for demonstrations at short intervals at shopping centers or at a friend's house. Users who put their experience as a 3 on the Likert scale shared that they have previously owned headsets, however, it has been "a few years since using it." Key themes were consistently brought up by all users, these included, controls haptic feedback, multimodal input, task-specific usability, and UI functionality.

Haptics. One of the points of discussion was how users know that they have interacted with a game world object. Responses here ranged from desiring more vibration feedback to having unique sound prompts for every type of action completed. A frequent comment was that users didn't know when their finger had entered the actionable UI element such as a button. They suggested visual effects that could be added to let the user know that the button was ready to be interacted with. Due to the 3D depth requirement to trigger a button, this comment came up more than once. One comment discussed how haptic feedback wasn't fully recognized due to the sound that was played back, they said they heard the button press, and that indicated selection to them without vibrational haptics, which went unnoticed upon reflection.

Multimodal Input. Users had the capability to select their desired locomotion technique, either teleporting or using the joystick for a more natural walking experience. Two users brought up that they instead felt comfortable physically walking in the place space and found that using the joystick to navigate was to move larger distances to interact with the floating interactable around the environment. Another user did mention that a larger play space would have been preferred but also commented that if they were familiar with their physical surroundings, they would feel more comfortable. Ideas discussed regarding this included demonstrating the pass-through VR mode that allows the VR headsets camera to be displayed to allow the user time to become more familiar with the physical environment. The joysticks however were not favored by one user who hasn't spent much time in VR apart from one previous demonstration, this made them "feel sick" and preferred to use the teleportation mode.

Two users once entered the environment instinctively looked for a laser pointer to interact with the UI, even after watching other participants interact. They shared that this was something they are used to in VR and haven't interacted with UI in this way before. One user stated they preferred to use their finger to interact with the slider using physics colliders rather than grabbing the slider's anchor handle.

Virtual Environment. One user shared that they are never in a cockpit-like environment with so many controls floating around them so learning how the elements interact with their hands was a learning curve. In addition, it wasn't always clear what elements are interactable with their virtual hands, once informed that everything in the environment is interactable participants ventured away from the menu to explore the floating 3D models in the distance. Visualization of the point cloud scan of the geospatial location selected proved to be an exciting point of discussion. One user mentioned that they haven't experienced anything like this before and had ideas for virtual meeting rooms to be presented like this, allowing for a fully collaborative 3D experience. Further to this discussion comments on collaborating in this environment were discussed as a benefit for sharing 3D data, with use cases being discussed in the tourism sector for viewing hotels and in the real estate sector for viewing the property.

Video playback was also a discussion once a geospatial location was selected, a user mentioned it felt unnatural to look at the video and said it was something they would have to get used to seeing a video "floating" in space. Furthermore, one user adjusted their headset and went back into the experience, and instinctively tried to grab the interface without the controllers being placed on them.

UI Functionality. The users were tasked to interact with the menus and panels surrounding the 3D map which allowed for zooming and navigating around the world. One user shared a creative comment, that moving the UI system between locked and unlocked positions "felt like a Star Wars cockpit more than a menu" another user praised its interaction as feeling more "natural" than a conventional UI. Users unanimously enjoyed being able to hide and show the UI based on what they were doing in the environment, allowing them to walk without the intrusion of the objects being displayed in the environment, allowing for less distraction when completing tasks. However, one user mentioned that there could be an annoyance if the UI panels are obfuscating a task being carried out at the time. In such a scenario the UI panels would be required to be displayed while also interacting with the 3D map movement.

Pertaining to extending functionality, some users felt there was a lot of freedom to move and place the UI in different locations but would have additionally liked to scale the UI elements presented allowing for complete customization of the interface elements. In addition, two users stated that they always customize the UI for applications they have and saw the benefit of real-time manipulation of the UI's location, allowing for specific UI priorities to be "kept close" to the user at relevant tasks.

High Usability Satisfaction Highlights. One user who was rated 1 on the scale admitted to not using their less dominant hand – left – for anything other than movement. They preferred to use their dominant hand for interacting with UI elements and having the freedom to select the hand they use for movement as both controllers supported movement was a benefit.

Another high usability feature that was discussed was how close the UI was to them after the initial setup, they found it helpful to have the controls move around with them as they explored the environment with the addition of the locking and unlocking feature. One of the more experienced users shared that they wanted to move the UI as soon as they were placed into the environment to locations that they prefer, and further discussion exposed that having UI not relevant to the current task at hand would be cumbersome.

Users thought highly of the UI being displayed only at relevant locations where tasks were completed showing a clear indication of what task the UI elements were associated with. The contextual UI in this scenario allowed users to explore without requiring them to manually disable the UI based on where they were in the world "the map UI disappears when I can't see the map which makes sense."

Low Usability Satisfaction Highlights. One user stated while using the joystick locomotion technique that looking at their feet made them feel "wobbly" this was discussed where a virtual set of legs may benefit them. Novice users shared that they were concerned with how long it took them to set up their IPD and adjust the headset which was large, and one comment suggested wireless headsets may provide less of a cumbersome experience. They shared that they were confused as to why distant objects were blurry.

Some users were concerned with the haptics vibrational frequency being set too low. It wasn't consciously noticed that it was being used, although it was admitted that they could hear the sound which may have distracted them from the vibration.

Although UI elements could be moved, one user desired to scale and snap the elements to ensure they are always straight. The current implementation allows full rotational freedom resulting in some UI panels not being "straight or parallel."

One user with a 3 on the experience scale shared they prefer to have the traditional first-person joystick rotation movement over snapping rotation to 45°. This was described as a "smoother" transition for turning on the spot.

4.5 Discussion

The focus group study targeted users with little to intermediate exposure to VR applications, with the goal of supporting an unbiased view from existing VR interface design aiming to encourage discussion on novel ideas the interface presents. It provided insight into usability concerns when interacting with an exclusive 3D interface environment. Findings concluded high usability satisfaction when interacting using natural interaction approaches, such as the manipulation of the interface in 3D space via hand gestures. Low usability satisfaction was primarily focused on the haptic feedback of the interface, where depth perception using hand tracking was a concern for multiple users as they were unsure if the UI element had been interacted with.

User safety is of the highest concern when working with any population Initially users were asked if they had experienced motion sickness from travel or VR in the past [17]. The study was designed to focus on users' movement being minimal in the real world and virtual world as motion sickness is primarily experienced by those who passively travel [18] ensuring they are as comfortable as possible while interacting with the presented interface. All users felt comfortable proceeding with the focus group as the one user who has experienced motion sickness in the past had intermediate exposure to virtual reality experiences. Users were also offered to sit down if it would make them more comfortable as the experience is also possible to do this way, but users wanted to physically walk between interfaces which drove discussion around how UI is presented in different areas of the environment. Topics such as object occlusion between interaction areas were raised because of this.

Participants expressed that they enjoyed being in the environment and interacting with the various objects and interface it presented. Users were encouraged to discuss between them in an informal manner what they enjoyed and what made them uncomfortable to interact with, this generated a significant amount of relevant conversation exposing ideas on how the presented interface could be used in various applications along with their usability considerations. The 3D map of the world provided an element of familiarity to users, standing as a metaphor that all participants reported being exposed to in the past in a more traditional way via smartphone and desktop applications.

Interacting with the map in a fully 3D immersive environment was reported to be an enjoyable and memorable experience due to the familiarity and comparison users could provide.

The study format was focused on the user discussion with the headset being rotated between each user leaving time for discussion while one user was interacting with the various panels containing buttons and sliders. This allowed for the formulation of thematic discussion, leading from one idea area to the next and exploring the usability considerations in various contexts.

4.6 Conclusion

This qualitative study explored the use of a modular 3D interface presented in an inter-active VR setting. An important aspect to consider before exploring the opportunities made available by a 3D GUI was the vehicle in which to showcase the interface itself to participants with appropriate feedback. The developed application provided a concep-tual model using a 3D topographical map, linked to geospatial locations allowing for navigation and view selected locations through a point cloud scan. The modular panels provided a novel interaction mechanism that leverages the strengths humans use in their day-to-day interactions and empowers the user to adjust real-time interface elements to suit their exact needs and preferences.

Overall, the focus group discussion provided key areas of future work, where notably low usability satisfaction was perceived with appropriate haptic feedback being a primary concern. The participant's sentiment overall however was positive during the experience, with many ideas being generated for how such an interface could be used in a practical application.

Limitations of the study included time allocation per user, where some users took longer to adjust to the virtual environment than others. Some users naturally immersed themselves in the VR environment and were comfortable interacting with the various elements it provided with minimal direction. Whereas other users needed more guid-ance through the applications flow, and to understand that the entire environment is interactable with their virtual hands.

With the rapid adoption of VR headsets and their sensor capabilities - such as eye-tracking, this growing area of study appears to lack a multimodal development approach beyond using typical ray-based interaction. It is therefore important to iterate 3D GUI design concepts with users to expose usability constraints with various input mediums. The implications of the presented study will provide a framework for future VR focus groups, allowing for developed 3D GUI components allowing for faster iteration of high and low usability satisfaction.

References

1. Steed, A., Takala, T.M., Archer, D., Lages, W., Lindeman, R.W.: Directions for 3D user interface research from consumer VR games. IEEE Trans. Vis. Comput. Graph **27**, 4171–4182 (2021). https://doi.org/10.48550/arxiv.2106.12633

2. Zakharov, A.V., Kolsanov, A.V., Khivintseva, E.V., Pyatin, V.F., Yashkov, A.V.: Proprioception in immersive virtual reality. Proprioception (2021). https://doi.org/10.5772/INTECHOPEN. 96316
3. Stuerzlinger, W., Wingrave, C.A.: The value of constraints for 3d user interfaces. Virtual Realities: Dagstuhl Seminar **2008**, 203–223 (2011). https://doi.org/10.1007/978-3-211-99178-7_11/COVER
4. Noël, S., Dumoulin, S., Whalen, T., Ward, M., Stewart, J.A., Lee, E.: A breeze enhances presence in a virtual environment. In: Proceedings - 3rd IEEE International Workshop on Haptic, Audio and Visual Environments and their Applications - HAVE 2004, pp. 63–68 (2004). https://doi.org/10.1109/HAVE.2004.1391883
5. Robinson, A.H.: The Nature of Maps, 1st edn. University of Chicago Press, Chicago (1976)
6. Atta, M.T., Romli, A., Majid, M.A.: The impact of AR/VR on spatial memory performance of learners: a review. In: Proceedings - 2021 International Conference on Software Engineering and Computer Systems and 4th International Conference on Computational Science and Information Management, ICSECS-ICOCSIM 2021, pp. 75–79 (2021). https://doi.org/10.1109/ICSECS52883.2021.00021
7. Bowman, D.A., McMahan, R.P., Ragan, E.D.: Questioning naturalism in 3D user interfaces. Commun. ACM **55**, 78–88 (2012). https://doi.org/10.1145/2330667.2330687
8. Olshannikova, E., Ometov, A., Koucheryavy, Y., Olsson, T.: Visualizing big data with augmented and virtual reality: challenges and research agenda. J. Big Data **2**, 1–27 (2015). https://doi.org/10.1186/S40537-015-0031-2/FIGURES/14
9. (PDF) The efficiency of various multimodal input interfaces evaluated in two empirical studies. https://www.researchgate.net/publication/49392564_The_Efficiency_of_Various_Multimodal_Input_Interfaces_Evaluated_in_Two_Empirical_Studies. Accessed 10 Feb 2023
10. Understanding Guideline 2.5: Input Modalities | WAI | W3C. https://www.w3.org/WAI/WCAG21/Understanding/input-modalities. Accessed 6 Jan 2023
11. Teather, R.J., Pavlovych, A., Stuerzlinger, W., MacKenzie, I.S.: Effects of tracking technology, latency, and spatial jitter on object movement. In: 3DUI - IEEE Symposium on 3D User Interfaces 2009 – Proceedings, pp. 43–50 (2009). https://doi.org/10.1109/3DUI.2009.4811204
12. Teather, R.J., Stuerzlinger, W.: Assessing the effects of orientation and device on (constrained) 3D movement techniques. In: 3DUI - IEEE Symposium on 3D User Interfaces 2008, pp. 43–50 (2008). https://doi.org/10.1109/3DUI.2008.4476590
13. Ro, H., Byun, J.-H., Park, Y.J.: AR pointer: advanced ray-casting interface using laser pointer metaphor for object manipulation in 3D augmented reality environment (2019)
14. Inside Facebook Reality Labs: Wrist-based interaction for the next computing platform. https://tech.fb.com/ar-vr/2021/03/inside-facebook-reality-labs-wrist-based-interaction-for-the-next-computing-platform/. Accessed 6 Sept 2022
15. Piotrowski, P., Nowosielski, A.: Gaze-based interaction for VR environments. In: Choraś, M., Choraś, R.S. (eds.) IP&C 2019. AISC, vol. 1062, pp. 41–48. Springer, Cham (2020). https://doi.org/10.1007/978-3-030-31254-1_6
16. Summers, C., Lympouridis, V., Erkut, C.: Sonic interaction design for virtual and augmented reality environments. In: 2015 IEEE 2nd VR Workshop on Sonic Interactions for Virtual Environments (SIVE), pp 1–6. IEEE (2015)
17. Brown, J.A.: An exploration of virtual reality use and application among older adult populations. Gerontol. Geriatr. Med. **5**, 233372141988528 (2019). https://doi.org/10.1177/2333721419885287
18. Recenti, M., et al.: Toward predicting motion sickness using virtual reality and a moving platform assessing brain, muscles, and heart signals. Front. Bioeng. Biotechnol. **9**, 132 (2021). https://doi.org/10.3389/FBIOE.2021.635661/BIBTEX

Development and Discussion of an Authentic Game to Develop Cleaning Skills

Takayuki Kosaka(✉) ⓘ and Mari Kosaka

Tokai University, Hiratsuka, Kanagawa, Japan
kosaka@kosaka-lab.com

Abstract. Recently, there has been an increase in the number of children who do not help clean their homes. This is claimed to be due to children's negative perception of cleaning as "tedious" and "boring." We focused on vacuuming as a part of the cleaning process and developed a serious game using real-world vacuuming as a game content to encourage children to enjoy cleaning. Although studies on entertainment have been conducted using vacuum cleaners, these studies focused on vacuuming virtual garbage projected by projectors, not on vacuuming garbage in the real world. The Monster Cleaners that we have developed take advantage of vacuum cleaners' original function, which is to vacuum up trash in the real world, but with the setting that virtual monsters are hidden among the trash. Monster Cleaners is a vacuum cleaner that can collect virtual monstrosities based on the amount of garbage that it sucks up in the real world. The winner is the one who sucks up more monstrosities while competing with two other people. It is recommended to use the vacuum cleaner slowly, and by setting the vacuum cleaner so that it cannot suck up any monstrosities if it is used too fast, the player can learn how to use the vacuum cleaner correctly. In this study, we implemented and demonstrated a game system. Although the proposed game system can be enhanced, we suggest that the system can be used to learn how to use a vacuum cleaner correctly.

Keywords: Serious game · Gamification · Cleaning game · cleaning skills

1 Introduction

Nowadays, the number of children who do not help with housework such as sweeping, washing, and dish cleaning is increasing. Although many children like playing video games, few like housework. This is because they have a negative feeling toward housework, such as "it is unpleasant" or "it is not fun." Housework tends to be tedious, boring, and stressful, but it is crucial for our daily life. It is necessary to develop technologies that will eliminate the negative image of housework and encourage children to help with housework of their motivations. To achieve this, this study focuses on sweeping and proposes a system called the "Monster Cleaners." The system not only encourages children to clean their room in a fun manner but also teaches them how to use a vacuum cleaner.

© The Author(s), under exclusive license to Springer Nature Switzerland AG 2023
J. Y. C. Chen and G. Fragomeni (Eds.): HCII 2023, LNCS 14027, pp. 33–42, 2023.
https://doi.org/10.1007/978-3-031-35634-6_3

2 Related Works

Many studies have been conducted to make cleaning and housework entertaining.

Ogasawara et al. [1] proposed an interactive vacuum cleaner that uses a projector to project a virtual object. The system sucks the virtual object with a vacuum cleaner-like device, and the user enjoys cleaning as a result of the game-like interaction. The "VACUUU (· ∀ ·) UUUM" system developed by Tada et al. [2] extends the sucking feeling of a vacuum cleaner. This system projects a large object on the floor that a real vacuum cleaner cannot suck. A vacuum cleaner-like device sucks the projected virtual dust. In accordance with the size of the virtual dust sucked, the system gives the user a sucking-like feeling by changing the shape of the device's hose, providing vibration feedback, and deforming the projected object.

These systems try to make cleaning enjoyable using a special vacuum cleaner. However, they use mechanisms for sucking virtual objects and dust, projected using a projector, leaving real dust scattered on the floor. The room does not become clean even if a virtual dust pile is collected. This is also a matter of instilling good habits. For instance, even if trash is left on the floor, children can ignore it and only suck virtual garbage projected by the projector. The function of a vacuum cleaner is to collect "real dust." Therefore, it is crucial to make cleaning enjoyable without impairing its primary function.

Oono et al. proposed a small robot that can be attached to an arbitrary appliance [3]. The robot can express the state of the appliances in motion. Their research aimed to make monotonous housework enjoyable. Furthermore, studies on display robots [4] have been conducted to describe the function of home appliances by anthropomorphizing them by attaching pseudoeyes and pseudoarms to them. These attempts claim that providing enjoyment and information should be conducted without impairing the functions of conventional vacuum cleaners and home appliances.

We have been investigating the use of people's behavior in the real world as a game content to guide their action in the real world by stimulating their intention and interest.

For example, we proposed a serious game for dietary education that intends to improve children's nutrition [5–7]. The player's actions such as "eating," "chewing," and "smiling" are used as conditions in the game. To beat monsters that appear on the game screen, the player must eat his/her least favorite foods, such as green peppers, tomatoes, and carrot cookies. By acting on nutritional advice during the game such as "It seems better to drink tomato juice to beat Dracula," many players eat their least favorite foods. This behavior surprises the players' parents because their children eat nutritious food without being forced. Because children are motivated to advance to higher levels in the game and beat it, they overcome their dislike toward food. As this example demonstrates, it is possible to use serious games for training people to change their daily behavior.

With this background, this study proposes a serious game that uses cleaning in the real world as a game content while maintaining the vacuum cleaner's original purpose of motivating children to clean their rooms in the real world.

3 Design Principle

This study proposes a serious game in which children collect virtual monsters by sucking dust with a vacuum cleaner-like device. The system aims to change children's behavior so that they enjoy cleaning. The game objective is to suck dust in the real world using a vacuum cleaner-like device. Depending on the type and place of the dust collected in the real world, different events occur in the game. The system was developed with the following guidelines.

The System Should Clean in the Real World. In a game with "cleaning" as the theme, instead of collecting virtual trash, the vacuum cleaner should collect dust in the real world. Therefore, it is crucial to develop games that make use of the vacuum cleaner's original functions.

The Base Cleaner Should not be Modified. The proposed system uses a commercially available vacuum cleaner for ease of manufacture. If a special modification is performed on the vacuum cleaner, its warranty is voided. Therefore, it is crucial not to conduct any special modification on the cleaner. In this system, all devices, including the sensor and display, are connected as commonly used attachments, which are developed using a 3D printer. Thus, the system can be attached to any general vacuum cleaner that you already have.

The System Should make the Player Learn to Use the Cleaner. This system is a serious game that makes players learn how to use a vacuum cleaner. In general, vacuum cleaners should be moved slowly. The approach of performance measurement for home electric cleaners given by Japan Industrial Standards regulates the moving speed of a cleaner's head to a maximum of 50 cm/s [8]. Therefore, the system is designed such that it cannot suck monsters if the speed exceeds 50 cm/s. This teaches the players to keep the speed below 50 cm/s.

Additionally, when cleaning a Japanese tatami mat, it is important to vacuum along the grain of the mat. To teach children how to clean a tatami mat, the Monster Cleaners system can be set such that no monsters are sucked unless the vacuum is pushed along the grain of the mat. In this way, children can learn to use a vacuum cleaner properly by playing a game.

4 Monster Cleaners

The game's primary objective is to clean a room by collecting dust in the real world using a vacuum cleaner. Two people competitively participate in the game. The player starts the vacuum by depressing the cleaner's trigger. Players cannot advance in the game unless they suck dust in the real world. The more dust a player sucks, the more monsters the player collects. Points are added according to the amount of dust collected, area cleaned, and cleaner's head speed. The player with the highest score wins the game.

The monsters sucked are collected using a hosepipe in a backpack carried on the player's back. Using full-color light-emitting diodes (LEDs) and vibration motors, an impression is presented that the monsters are resisting being vacuumed.

Apart from ordinary monsters, the game includes hidden boss monsters to guide the player to the intended place. The player performs cleaning while looking for a boss by monitoring a boss sensor mounted on the tip of the Monster Cleaners. The boss sensor indicates the distance and direction to the nearest boss monster. During the game's configuration, the boss monsters can be placed at an arbitrary position. For example, if the number of boss monsters in the living room is higher, the player is expected to clean the living room extensively while searching for a boss monster.

4.1   System Configuration

Figure 1 shows the system configuration of Monster Cleaners. The system consists of a vacuum cleaner device that actually cleans, a Dust Sensor Device that detects the sucked dust, a Tube device that shows how it is being sucked, a backpack device that controls them, a Position Sensor Device that measures the position, It consists of game devices.

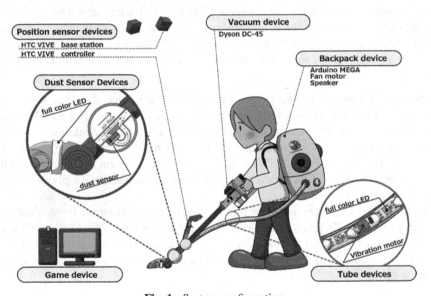

Fig. 1. System configuration.

4.2   Vacuum Device

The vacuum cleaner device is a vacuum cleaner that sucks up real-world debris. A stick-type cordless vacuum cleaner (Dyson Digital Slim DC-45) was used in this system to encourage free action by the experiencer. The DC-45 introduced a trigger-button power switch and suctioned only while the trigger button was pulled. It weighs 2.3 kg. It is connected to the dust sensor device by a joint.

4.3 Dust Sensor Device

The vacuum cleaner is activated by pulling the trigger button on the vacuum device, and dust is sucked from the suction head through the pipe. A dust sensor is mounted in the pipe to measure the dust concentration during suction and determine if dust has been sucked (Fig. 1). The dust sensor device is equipped with a dust sensor (SHARP GP2Y1010AU) to detect the amount of dust inhaled, and the GP2Y1010AU is capable of detecting the concentration of fine dust particles (PM0.8 or greater) based on an optical detector. In this system, when the dust concentration exceeds the threshold value, it was determined that dust was aspirated. The dust sensor device is also equipped with a full-color LED that indicates the distance from the floor monster. The LED changes to blue when the player is far away from the floor monster and red when the player is close to the floor monster. Players can rely on the LEDs to locate the floor monster.

4.4 Tube Device

The tube device is a device that presents the aspirated monster being sent to the back-pack device. A tube extending from the dust sensor device to the backpack device is installed, and 60 full-color LEDs (NeoPixel) and 8 vibration motors (TAMIYA FA-130 with weights attached) are mounted inside the tube (Fig. 3). When judging trash suction, the LEDs and vibration motors are operated at different times to reproduce the monster being sent to the backpack device through the tube. The color of the LED and the intensity of the vibration are changed according to the type of monster suctioned (Fig. 6). If the suction head was moving at a speed of 50 cm/s or faster, the LED was set to turn off and no vibration was presented. This is expected to encourage the experiencer to move at an appropriate speed (Fig. 2).

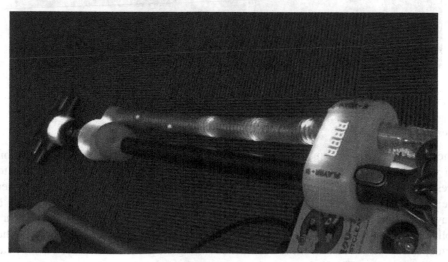

Fig. 2. Tube device.

4.5 Backpack Device

A backpack that the user carries on his/her back houses all equipment to control the system. The backpack comprises an Arduino Mega microcontroller board for system control, a speaker for expressing the monsters' scream, and a large fan motor to give an impression that the monster is resisting being vacuumed. Furthermore, the backpack contains a Bluetooth module for wireless communication with the game device (Fig. 3). The backpack device weighs approximately 3 kg. The power supply (100 V) is wired.

Fig. 3. Display device.

4.6 Game Device

The game device is a computer that controls the system's status, including information on whether devices are connected and the game level configuration. It is also used to present instructions for playing the game, the current game situation, and results. After the game ends, the game device displays the activation ratio (the areas cleaned by a player), distance covered, average speed, maximum speed, and the number of monsters collected along with the total score (Fig. 4). The player with the highest score wins the game. The location and amount of dust sucked during the game are displayed using heat map visualization (Fig. 5).

In general, cleaning efficiency is enhanced by intensively cleaning areas that collect dust easily instead of cleaning from corner to corner every day. However, it is difficult to determine where the room is dirty. Because heat map visualization contributes to locating dirty areas, the users can clean their room more efficiently.

Fig. 4. Game Screen.

4.7 Pseudo-dust

In this system, it is possible to use dust particles such as dust and dirt collected from households in advance. However, dust and dirt are generally considered to be a mixture of sand, mud, fragments of human skin, dandruff, and hair, dead insects such as mites, mold spores, cloth, and cotton dust. It is a hygienic problem to scatter them on the floor at the experience. Therefore, sodium bicarbonate (sodium bicarbonate), which is said to have no effect on the environment or human body, was used as a pseudo-dust. The particle size of sodium bicarbonate is estimated to average 75–1300 μm, which can be measured by the dust sensor mounted on the dust sensor device. The pseudo-dust was spread on the floor by the exhibitor as needed prior to the start of the experience.

Fig. 5. Heat map visualization.

5 Exhibition

We conducted an exhibition to investigate whether using sweeping as a game content influenced children's behavior.

In the exhibition, we observed children who actively vacuumed to collect more monsters than their opponents did. Many parents said, "I wish they could do vacuuming so diligently at home." Fig. 6 shows a scene from the exhibition.

Soon after the game started, we observed that a player moved the cleaner head rapidly. As the system detected the speed was over the limit, a warning expressing "move slowly" was presented and the LEDs were turned off, indicating that the player could no longer suck monsters. He soon realized this and slowly moved the cleaner head. This scenario demonstrates that players can learn how to use the vacuum cleaner properly through playing the game.

Two possible factors may have caused the experiencer to move the cleaner head at a high speed immediately after the start. The first is that they do not recognize that the vacuum cleaner must be moved at a low speed to get the suction effect probably because they move the vacuum cleaner at a high speed on a daily basis. The second factor is that this game system is designed for two players to compete against each other, and it is assumed that the players moved the game quickly and energetically to beat their opponents. Therefore, it is necessary to change the game system so that the players can cooperate to fight off the monsters instead of competing with each other.

To guide the player to an arbitrary position, we placed a boss monster on the floor and observed the players' reactions. We observed that players slowly moved the cleaner's head to look for the boss monster. Parents and the audience around the players also

Fig. 6. Demonstration of Monster Cleaners (Japan).

whooped, for example, "That is it there!" and "I found the monster there!" indicating that the audience was involved in the game.

However, by the middle of the day, many of the children were so engrossed in collecting the boss monster that they did not inhale the visible lumps of baking powder. Therefore, it is necessary to develop a system of boss monsters that react to the amount of garbage that they inhale, rather than their position on the floor. Furthermore, some participants seemed to be only focused on the game screen on the display in front of them and made contact with their opponents. In the future, we need to improve the system by removing the front display or attaching a display to the vacuum cleaner.

6 Conclusion

This study proposed a serious game system called Monster Cleaners that aims to motivate children to clean their rooms. This system, which adds a gaming aspect to cleaning, allows children to not only clean while having fun but also learn how to use a vacuum cleaner. Although there were some elements of improvement in the proposed system, it was suggested that this system could be used to learn how to use a vacuum cleaner properly.

In the future, we will focus on training players in specific uses of vacuum cleaners. For example, we will implement a system to train players how to clean Japanese tatami mats.

Furthermore, most vacuum cleaners today are motorhead vacuum cleaners that assist in cleaning. It runs by itself with just a light touch on the vacuum cleaner's handle. The self-propelled speed of the motorhead can be changed by controlling its self-propelled motor. By stopping the motor when it sucks up trash, it can be expected to stop more in place and suck up more trash.

There are two types of interest: direct interest and indirect interest. The former is an interest in an object and/or an activity itself, whereas the latter is an interest that emerges from a liking toward a previously considered uninteresting object and/or action by undertaking some activities. It is suggested that the indirect interest can be changed to a direct interest by analyzing the activities [9]. Our research is oriented toward an indirect-interest-based approach, and the result presented in the study suggests its usefulness. Matsumura pointed out that it is crucial to consider both physical aspects (e.g., system and equipment) and psychological aspects (e.g., curiosity and self-esteem) to develop such efforts [10]. We intend to incorporate these enforcements and extend the research targets to include other housework apart from cleaning.

References

1. Ogasawara, R., Yamaki, T., Tsukada, K., Watanabe, K., Siio, I.: Interactive cleaner. In: Proceedings of the Entertainment Computing 2007, Osaka, Japan, 1–3 October 2007, pp. 71–74 (2007)
2. Tada, K., Yamaji, D., Kanno, K., Kawabata, Y.: VACUUUUUUM. In: Proceedings of the Virtual Reality society of Japan Annual Conference, Osaka, Japan, 18–20 September 2013, p. 19 (2014)
3. Oono, K., Tsukada, K., Siio, I.: Kadebo: a small robot attached on home appliances for joyful household chores. In: Proceedings of the Entertainment Computing 2013, Kagawa, Japan, 4–6 October 2013, pp. 288–291 (2013)
4. Osawa, H., Imai, M.: Evaluation of direct function explanation using agentized object. In: Proceedings of the Interaction 2008, Tokyo, Japan, 3–4 March 2008, pp. 167–168 (2008)
5. Iwamoto, T., Sasayama, Y., Motoki, M., Kosaka, T.: Back to the mouth. In: Proceedings of the ACM SIGGRAPH 2009 Emerging Technologies. SIGGRAPH '09, New Orleans, Louisiana, 3–7 August 2009. ACM New York (2009). https://doi.org/10.1145/1597956.1597960
6. Kosaka, T., Iwamoto, T.: Serious dietary education system for changing food preferences "food practice shooter". In: Proceedings of the Virtual Reality International Conference, VRIC '13. Laval, France, 20–22 March 2013. ACM New York (2013). https://doi.org/10.1145/2466816.2466841
7. Bannai, Y., Kosaka, T., Aiba, N.: Food practice shooter: a serious game with a real-world interface for nutrition and dietary education. In: Yamamoto, S. (ed.) HCI 2014. LNCS, vol. 8521, pp. 139–147. Springer, Cham (2014). https://doi.org/10.1007/978-3-319-07731-4_14
8. Japanese Industrial Standards: Methods of measurement of performance of vacuum cleaners for household and similar use. JISC9802 (1999)
9. Silvia, P.J.: Exploring the Psychology of Interest. Oxford University Press, Oxford (2006)
10. Matsumura, N., Fruchter, R., Leifer, L.: Shikakeology: designing triggers for behavior change. AI & Soc. 30(4), 419–429 (2014). https://doi.org/10.1007/s00146-014-0556-5

Gender Stereotypes in Interaction Design. Render Me – Augmented Reality Masks to Inhabit the Metaverse

Inês Matos Tuna[1], Sónia Rafael[2]([✉]) [iD], Victor M. Almeida[3] [iD], and Ana O. Henriques[3] [iD]

[1] Faculty of Fine-Arts, University of Lisbon, Largo da Academia Nacional de Belas Artes, 1249-058 Lisboa, Portugal

[2] Faculty of Fine-Arts, ITI/LARSyS, University of Lisbon, Largo da Academia Nacional e Belas Artes, 1249-058 Lisboa, Portugal
srafael@campus.ul.pt

[3] CIEBA – Artistic Studies Research Center, Faculty of Fine-Arts, University of Lisbon, Largo da Academia Nacional e Belas Artes, 1249-058 Lisboa, Portugal
{victoralmeida,ana.gfo.henriques}@campus.ul.pt

Abstract. The purpose of this article is to understand how digital systems interact, reproduce societal power structures, and mimic the male canon in digital systems. Thus, it is necessary to understand how the algorithms of biometric technologies and Artificial Intelligence systems used in the categorization of images contribute to the inception of biases and stereotypes. In response to this question, the *Render Me* project was developed, which simulates how biometric technologies and design choices can marginalize individuals.

Through a Feminist Speculative Design methodology, a fictional brand was developed that sells digital skins (augmented reality filters in Spark AR Studio) that protect the physical identity of its users against data capture and against surveillance of their real faces. This is meant as a satirical approach, as the female subject is placed as the main figure, abandoning the ideal of the man at the centre of the world that served its humanist desires. This female subject, however, is crossed by all the stereotypes attributed to her in the physical world. A skin is assigned to the user through the choice of keywords derived from the Myers-Brigg Type Indicator (MBTI) model. Additionally, only female masks can be purchased to navigate the entire metaverse, which vary their visual configuration according to female stereotypes. There are six skins in its current iteration, but it is intended that others can be developed in the future, representing other axes of identity such as race, class, and gender. In this way, the project aims to be an awareness tool for the perpetuation and amplification of gender stereotypes in digital systems. In short, by centering the female subject as the main figure, the Render Me project hopes to stimulate critical thinking about how technological objects reproduce ingrained prejudices and preestablished ideas and paradigms which might actually be causing harm.

Keywords: interaction design · gender stereotypes · biometric systems · augmented reality

J. Y. C. Chen and G. Fragomeni (Eds.): HCII 2023, LNCS 14027, pp. 43–57, 2023.
https://doi.org/10.1007/978-3-031-35634-6_4

1 Introduction

The male model prevails – the classic ideal of Man formulated by Protagoras, as "the measure of all things" [1] and the woman emerges as a deviant being, as different, as "other", although the condition of contemporary woman is generally more favorable.

To speak of women as the main subject is, therefore, to question the male pattern that has been used to describe all of humanity. As Criado Perez exposes in *Invisible Women*, masculinity and whiteness are assumed precisely because they do not need to be expressed. They are implied. They are unquestionable. They are the default. And that reality is inevitable for those whose identity needs to be mentioned, for those whose needs and perspectives are repeatedly forgotten [2].

According to the 2019 European Commission's *Report on equality between women and men in the EU* [3], gender disparity is present in various social behaviours, which translates into the reinforcement of stereotypes, gender violence, lack of economic independence and disproportionate participation in various diverse areas. Women continue, in our cultural context, to play stereotyped and insulting roles, which devalue their status as specialists, whether in technical or scientific areas. In the political context, leadership positions are still mostly held by men, even with the implementation of quotas, Incidentally, according to data from the European Commission, men still outnumber women by at least 4 to 1 (i.e., <20% of women) [3] in technical or scientific fields.

Gender violence, moreover, is one of the greatest forms of oppression. Indeed, in the European Union, around half of all women say they have been victims of sexual harassment and one in three over the age of 15 have experienced physical and/or sexual violence. Further, in countries like Mexico, the number of femicides is not tracked in any tangible way [4]. In addition to femicide and sexual harassment, violence against women can also take the form of cyber harassment, honour-related violence, dating/domestic violence, and the practice of female genital mutilation [4].

The European Commission report [3] also points to the devaluation of mostly female occupations, such as positions related to assistance and education. When women occupy positions linked to the Scientific-Humanistic areas instead of Technological areas such as engineering, for instance, they often suffer a salary penalty for this. The European Commission's report also points to a strong division, in the digital areas, related to "insensitive" working conditions, and proposes greater support and funding directed towards digital media, to achieve gender parity.

2 The Role of Design

If an intersectional perspective on the feminist movement allows us to explore the plurality of experiences—not only of gender, but also of other social and cultural aspects of individuals who do not see themselves in the dominant group—design practices must also recognize these ingrained power structures. In other words, it is necessary to promote a design practice that is cognizant of communities and individuals who are systematically socially and politically othered.

The author Luiza Prado [5] promotes an intersectional feminist perspective in design that offers a deep analysis about the impact of design objects in society. For Prado, it is pertinent to analyse how power structures and discrimination in the relationship between human beings and technology have been ignored. In this sense, her work proposes a design practice close to Critical and Speculative Design, developed by Anthony Dunne and Fiona Raby [6], but which, based on the observation of daily interactions with technology, allows for the role of these objects to be revealed within the complex systems of oppression of a capitalist, heteronormative, sexist, and racist society.

That is, design, by simultaneously addressing issues of race, class, or gender, and by challenging assumptions and preconceptions made about the role of various objects in everyday life, can produce a critical stance that encourages small changes toward a more equitable future.

3   The Absence of Female Representation in the Digital World

Statistically, the digital world is dominated by men, as women occupy only 21.5% of all jobs available in the digital context, according to the 2018 European Commission report entitled *Women in the Digital Age* [3]. However, the first digital computer, the ENIAC, was programmed by women in 1946, and for most of the 20th century, women were the dominant gender in programming [2].

According to a study published by the consulting company Accenture [7], only 68% of female university students chose to take coding and computing classes in 2017, in contrast to 83% of male students, which shows a strong discrepancy between the sexes. This disparity can be explained by the persistence of an unconscious bias related to the ability that each gender has, as well as the working conditions in the workplace.

These biases range from feeling a lack of freedom to present ideas in the same way as male colleagues, as well as the devaluation of programming and computer skills in relation to men's skills—which discourages women from following a career in this sector. At the same time, the report [3] identified that the lack of diversity and representativeness, in a technological context increasingly marked by Big Data and algorithms, will imply that digital systems reflect only the values, information and ideas of their developers, who are, as a rule, male, middle class, privileged and predominantly white.

Although, currently, the recommendations of international agencies point toward the inclusion of more women in the digital sphere and the creation of an algorithm verification system, in addition to the devolpment of Artificial Intelligence systems to guarantee their neutrality, authors such as Schlesinger [8], Shaowen Bardzell [9] and Sasha Costanza-Chock [10] point to the difficulty of the field of Information and Communication Technologies in incorporating marginalized groups in its design process. In fact, it is possible to find situations of discrimination based on gender that could be avoided if more women (of different contexts) were part of the design team [2, 7].

Nowadays there is a plausible trend of trans people (specifically trans-feminine individuals) entering the fields of computer science. Research by Skye Kychenthal [34] may help address the social issues of gender difference in computer science with a broader and more detailed perspective, considering that gender difference issues exist across the gender spectrum.

4   Bias in Biometric Systems

Since the field of Artificial Intelligence is in such rapid development, it is essential to question what kind of information is provided to machine learning algorithms which help perpetuate and amplify stereotypes, based either on gender, race, age, and others. That is, how do Artificial Intelligence systems reproduce discrimination and cultural prejudices based on available data.

It is possible to conclude that "the machines are not just reflecting our prejudices. Sometimes they significantly amplify them" [2] because they learn from the information provided to them and thus directly reflect the values of those who program them. For example, identifying faces is a simple task for humans [11], but for Artificial Intelligence it requires understanding the geometric structure (3D) and confronting it with external factors such as light and the position of the face.

Biometric systems work through two main processes: verification (or authentication) and recognition. The verification process determines whether a face exists, and the recognition system determines the identity of the image from a database. When facial recognition technology companies claim to have an identification rate above 95% [12], their verification is limited to their database sample.

Organizations and institutions have every interest in collecting information about the largest number of individuals, including an intention to supervise, control and punish the bodies of people and groups that hold less power in society, especially as these are seen as a "commodity" [13]. It is in this context that it is plausible to determine that the development of biometric technologies, which allow for the coding of certain physical aspects, can be an obstacle for marginalized communities, since they algorithmically define physical traits with which users might not identify, such as race or gender, or even the assumption of a person's character, just by algorithmic observation of their characteristics.

4.1   The Case of Aspire Mirror

Joy Buolamwini, in 2016, realized that the facial recognition software she used in the university project "Aspire Mirror" could not recognize her face. The code, written in JavaScript, could not detect Buolamwini's face, only that of her lighter-skinned colleagues. She noticed, when examining the database of the facial analysis technology at her disposal, that it was composed of 77.5% of male faces and 83.5% of white faces.

As such, the truth is that this supposed representative sample, from which the algorithm had to learned to verify and recognize different faces, was reduced to a small percentage of the world's population: men and Caucasian people. This is further highlighted by the fact that the misrecognition rate of fair-skinned men is only 0.8%. [14].

In addition, through an intersectional analysis of Microsoft, IBM, and Face++ systems, the researcher, together with Timnit Gebru, observed that "darker-skinned women were up to forty-four times more likely to be misclassified than lighter-skinned males" [13]. It is possible, therefore, to confirm that social inequalities are also reflected in digital systems through the excessive representation of a very specific part of the population. Indeed, according to Buolamwini, these systems could only identify 10% of the world's population.

Looking at biometric systems from an intersectional perspective and demanding transparency is exceedingly important to make these technologies less harmful to marginalized communities.

Thus, data scientists, programmers, and designers should be concerned both with developing bias-preventive mechanisms and with the effectiveness of the artifacts they develop, so that users are not directly or indirectly affected by an unfair status quo [13].

5   The Render Me Project

The project at the core of this paper, entitled *Render Me* deals with a satirical approach to the deterministic effects of biometric systems that reinforce gender stereotypes. It considers a speculative future where "skins" define the social construction of identity and only through these skins can the metaverse be explored.

The methodology applied to the project follows the research process developed by Anthony Dunne and Fiona Raby [6]—Critical and Speculative Design. This design methodology aims to reveal the values and ideologies absorbed in digital systems and how they transform the relationship with human beings. This is especially relevant as Dunne and Raby specifically intend to take advantage of design as a tool for raising awareness of less recognized issues, allowing for the emancipation of human beings as consumers: "design can help to expand awareness about the consequences of our actions as citizens and consumers" [6]. As James Auger states, "speculative design proposals are essentially questioning tools" [15] and not proposals for new technological products.

5.1   Scenario

This project is intended to discuss gender from an intersectional perspective within a constructed society, postulated to have become completely conquered by technology and in which control and surveillance are no longer framed by a democratic system.

The digital economy has taken over all interactions and avatars are necessary for us to relate to the world (parasocial relationships). The idea of human ceases to be that of "Man" espoused by Protagoras [1], to become that of the avatar. Offline identity has little impact and interactions are mostly conducted online.

Thus, a scenario is built where 3D masks ("augmented reality filters") are needed for the avatars through which interaction in the metaverse is possible. These masks are digital skins that protect the physical identity of their users, both against data extraction and against surveillance and the capture of their real faces. The name of the brand, *Render Me* intends to exalt the connection between the concept of "render"—which, according to the Cambridge Dictionary [16], means "to translate words into another language," or according to the Oxford dictionary, Lexicon [17], "to represent or portray artistically"—and the pronoun "Me".

5.2   Digital Skins and the MBTI Model

For the development of these digital skins, a concept of persona was used, which comprises the notion of identity "for several individuals to inhabit" [18], based on a study of Carl Jung [19].

According to Jung's psychology [20] the conception of persona is the version of the individual that is presented to the world, but in the context of the digital economy this idea has been characterized by the "sum of available data about an individual"—which results in their digital persona.

However, for the investigation of this project, the model developed by Isabel Myres and Katharine Briggs, "Myres-Briggs Type Indicator" (MBTI) [21], was chosen based on that of Carl Jung, as it is currently the most popular and widely used personality mapping method [22] in the context of appropriating behavioural surplus.

According to the MBTI, it is possible to analyse the behaviour and social identity of users based on four dichotomies: extroversion vs. introversion; sensing vs. intuition; thinking vs. feeling; judging vs. perceiving [23], which results in 16 different combinations/types. Each of these four dimensions concerns how the individual interacts, processes information, makes decisions and decides to live life, respectively.

We present a graphic with the MBTI and with the developed skins (marked with colours). It is our goal to continue this investigation and develop skins for the other personalities and genders (Fig. 1).

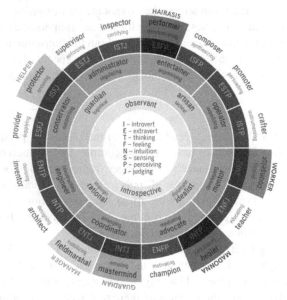

Fig. 1. Carl Jung Psychological Types, Myers-Briggs Indicator (MBTI), David Keirsey Temperament Sorter [30] as well as the masks.

It is based on these studies that we intend to develop the "look and feel," that is, an aesthetic of the digital skins for six of the personalities identified in the MBTI model. These skins would then function as a digital presence of the gender stereotypes associated with women and, at the same time, as "performance," in the sense that they are controlled by the user.

The digital skins were developed through the Spark AR Studio platform, as it allows their circulation through the most frequently used social networks, Instagram in particular. For this reason, a moodboard was designed for each of the personas, which served as inspiration for the development of Augmented Reality filters.

The Helper Skin

The Helper focuses on highlighting the woman's role as protector and caretaker of the physical and emotional well-being of men.

About the construction of this identity as an archetype, it is possible to trace, alongside the MBTI model, a more introverted and sensorial projection of the world and a more sentimental and perceptive way of making decisions (ISFJ)—that is, the type and personality of "Protector" [23]. As such, The Helper's main qualities are sensitivity, cooperation, kindness, and empathy.

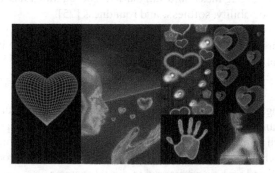

Fig. 2. Inspiration moodboard (images taken from Pinterest) and a screenshot from the Helper skin.

On a visual level, an effort was made to evoke both virtual assistants and the idea of a "cyborg" by resorting to imagery projected in the Microsoft program Cortana. In particular, the filter shares the visual language of the videogame character Cortana, from *Halo*. Cortana is a hyperfeminine "cyborg", represented by a "networked circuit full of currents of vibrating light" [24]. This is an idea also conveyed in The Helper's skin through its representation in a hologram with "glitches" (errors). Additionally, pink was chosen because it is associated, in Western cultures, with feminine attributes, preserving the delicacy and sweetness linked to the figure of the woman (Fig. 2).

The Guardian Skin

The Guardian skin presents male stereotypes, such as qualities that enhance introversion and intuition, the predominance of rational thinking, a "Mastermind-type" personality, and preference for a style where the characteristic of judgment predominates (INTJ) [23]. Specifically, The Guardian presents a more assertive, cold, and competitive type of behaviour.

As far as visual choices are concerned, The Guardian offers an association of geometric figures. There is a correlation between abstract figures and qualities associated

Fig. 3. Inspiration moodboard (images taken from Pinterest) and a screenshot from the Guardian skin.

with men, namely independence, roughness, and angularity. The qualities associated with women are, for example, sociability, softness, and roundness [25].

Given that The Guardian persona expresses a typically masculine archetype, the decision was made to represent the outline of the face in a bulk and superimpose it with angular geometric figures, typically associated with the male gender (Fig. 3).

The Madonna Skin

This skin is based on the imagery of the Virgin Mary and her adoration, as pure and virginal. It explores the binary and antagonistic understanding of female gender representation in digital systems, which reinforces the patriarchal system and restricts women's autonomy. Freud's Madonna-whore complex [24] consists of reductive visions produced by the male perspective, which end up being mirrored in digital systems.

A persona analogous to the artistic representation of Mary and the "Healer" personality-type of the MBTI model [23] was developed, with traits such as purity, affection, altruism, and warmth, and which assumes an introverted and intuitive functioning style—a more feeling and perceptive interpretation of the world (INFP).

On a visual level, the skin appropriates the artistic representation of the figure of the Virgin Mary by the Renaissance painter Rafael Sanzio (1483–1520), Madonna with Child (1505). Likewise, it was decided to place a halo, in gold leaf, and to imprison its image in a frame in order to enhance the idea of admiration and worship (Fig. 4).

The Hairesis Skin

Hairesis intends to represent the biblical figure of Eve and, at the same time, women in heretical communities of the Feudal period [26]. This personification of Eve presents herself as an antagonistic character to Maria. In this sense, it symbolizes the role of a seductive, confident, and vile woman, who is often represented in literature and cinema.

This persona has a "Performer" personality type (ESFP), that is, they are extroverted and confident in their sensory experiences [23], as they apprehend reality through their perception and emotional nature.

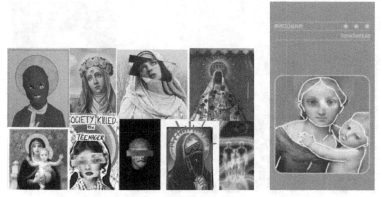

Fig. 4. Inspiration moodboard (images taken from Pinterest) and a screenshot from the Madonna skin.

Fig. 5. Inspiration moodboard (images taken from Pinterest) and a screenshot from the Hairesis skin.

On a visual level, red was used to represent the idea of seduction and conflict associated with the "femme fatale," presented as an irresistible and dangerous figure with pronounced feminine traits (Fig. 5).

The Worker Skin

The Worker intends to emphasize the multiplicity of women's tasks (professional, domestic, conciliatory, etc.). It is a persona with traits usually associated with women, such as a sense of responsibility, and a human, polite and cooperative side. Therefore, the construction of the archetype, based on the MBTI model of the "Counselor" personality (INFJ) highlights this introversion and the intuitive way one apprehends the world, as well as a cooperative and organized mode of operation [23].

Regarding the visual plan, The Worker features a small, coloured animation on a black and white background, covering the face, with the title of professional careers typically linked to the female gender, such as "caregiver", "au pair", "assistant", "housework" and "nursing", to recall its importance in the current cultural panorama (Fig. 6).

Fig. 6. Inspiration moodboard (images taken from Pinterest) and a screenshot from the Worker skin.

Since, according to the World Economic Forum, women take on extra work supporting the well-being, diversity, equity, and inclusion of their peers. But it's 'invisible' work—because companies aren't recognizing and rewarding [27].

The Manager Skin

The Manager intends to evoke a masculine archetype, as a way of appropriating the "sexist and misogynistic culture of the Silicon Valley tech community" [28]. That is, one that represents the desired qualities in men: competitiveness, leadership, and independence. This persona, in the context of this work, represents the annihilation of the intelligent and feminine woman.

The construction of this archetype, according to the MBTI Model, presents a "Field Marshall" personality type, that is, ENTJ, which translates into an extroverted way of interacting, an intuitive way of analysing the world, which values logic and judgment in the way of living [23].

The visual representation of this persona translates to the complete erasure of the female subject, through the construction of a figure represented by a contour line, hiding all the physical characteristics of the user and, thus, neutralizing their definition of social identity.

The decision to completely abdicate any visual symbol, in addition to the use of genderless tones: yellow and green, refers to the feminist perspective that "all human beings are equal" [29]. Choosing, therefore, to place this persona in a more neutral plane as possible (Fig. 7).

5.3   The Instagram Account and the Filters with the Skins

The Instagram account, which hosts the augmented reality filters, is part of the narrative and interactive logic and, therefore, a publication plan was developed to better clarify the concept of each of the six digital "skins" developed. These publications are in line with the graphic language developed for each of the filters, present the name of the "skin"

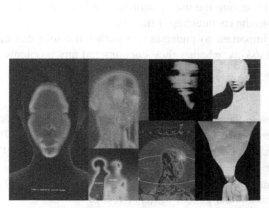
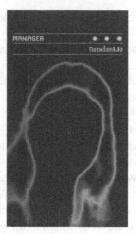

Fig. 7. Inspiration moodboard (images taken from Pinterest) and a screenshot from the Manager skin.

and contain a small description (Fig. 8). The Instagram page can be visited through this link: https://www.instagram.com/rndr.me.

Fig. 8. Preview of the Instagram account feed of the "Render Me" platform.

5.4 User Testing

To carry out the User Test, the "Single Ease Question" (SEQ) method was used, which allows determining the difficulty of performing one or more tasks using a 7-point scale [31]. This tool enables a metric analysis of the user experience and a greater correlation with a qualitative analysis, as it works for a variety of questions during the usability evaluation.

The SEQ makes it possible to measure the platform's usability even from a distance—that is, without directly observing the user's actions—and leaves room for an understanding of what exactly was the encountered difficulty.

During the User Test, it is important to understand whether the user can easily interact with the Instagram filters/skins, whether they encountered any problems, and their reaction/experience.

Participants

The evaluation and perception test of the users in relation to the filters/skins was carried out based on a questionnaire given to 12 people between the ages of 21 and 45. 41.7% of these were in the 21 to 24 age group ($N = 5$); 41.7% between 25 and 30 ($N = 5$); 8.3% between 36 and 40 years old ($N = 1$); and 8.3% between 41 and 45 years old ($N = 1$). 41.7% of the sampled respondents identified as being female ($N = 5$), another 41.7% as being male ($N = 5$), and 16.7% as another gender (other) ($N = 2$).

It is also acknowledged that 58.3% of the sample has a degree ($N = 7$); 33.3% completed a Master's degree ($N = 4$); and 8.3% claim to have completed secondary education ($N = 1$). Most respondents ($N = 5$) work as a designer or similar (41.7%) but it was also possible to poll a consultant in telecommunications, a student, a researcher, two project managers, a receptionist, and a shopkeeper in this survey sample.

The test was carried out through an online questionnaire where the following scenario was presented: "You are at home and decide to open the social network Instagram. You start watching Stories and one of your friends shares a video of himself wearing an augmented reality mask. You get curious and decide to click on the profile of the author of the mask. At that moment, you notice the link in the description and access the Rndr.me account." The following tasks were requested: a) access https://www.instagram.com/rndr.me; b) read the descriptions of the skins in the Posts; c) select the AR Filters tab (⚜); d) choose an augmented reality filter; e) select "try it on" and explore.

Results and Discussion

Regarding the analysis and interpretation of the Likert Scale responses, it is considered necessary to calculate the mean and standard deviation. To complete the test with this type of scale, each potential user marked their response in a spectrum of 7 degrees of agreement, from 1 (strongly disagree) to 7 (strongly agree), on the Likert Scale.

The following table presents the mean and standard deviation (STDEV) results of the responses obtained (Table 1).

Given these results, according to the "Single Ease Question" method, most markers have a mean greater than 5.5, representing a score within the average on the SEQ scale [32]. This analysis shows that participants were able to easily interact with the skins and had a generally positive experience. The standard deviation (STDEV), in general, demonstrates that most of the values that represent the responses in the Likert Scale of the test are not very homogeneous, since they are greater than 1.0.

Table 1. Mean and Standard Deviation (STDEV) results of the responses (Likert Scale).

	Q1 It was easy to read the description of the skins	Q2 I understand the objectives of the skins	Q3 The experience of using the skins was positive	Q4 I would use the Augmented Reality skins	Q5 I don't need technical support to use the skins	Q6 The graphical language used is adequate
FEM	5,8	5,2	6	6	6,2	6,4
MASC	5,6	4,6	5,8	5	6,8	6
OTHER	6	6,5	5	6	6	6
MEAN	**5,75**	**5,16**	**5,75**	**5,58**	**6,41**	**6,16**
STDEV	**1,22**	**2,08**	**1,48**	**1,78**	**1**	**1,19**

6 Conclusion

From the analysis of the cultural meaning of gender, the analysis of biometric systems of facial recognition and the investigation of different perspectives on design practice, it was possible to develop a speculative artifact that communicates and questions the dominant culture, exposing established gender stereotypes.

It was based on this idea that a fictional brand was developed, under the name *Render Me*, which develops digital skins (augmented reality filters in Spark AR) that protect the physical identity of its users against data extraction. However, this is a satirical approach, as it explores how stereotypes associated with gender, race, ethnicity, and sexuality cross the physical world into digital systems. In this sense, an aesthetic was constructed for six different augmented reality filters, based on the gender stereotypes identified throughout this research article. This was also done in accordance with the MBTI model, which provides a behavioural dimension with cultural meaning imposed by the conception of gender roles.

The project proposed here intends to be an awareness tool regarding the perpetuation and amplification of gender stereotypes in digital systems, specifically in biometric systems.

In short, the *Render Me* project seeks to place the female subject as the main figure, abandoning the harmful notion of the man at the centre that served humanist desires, and inciting critical thinking about how technological objects reproduce long-formulated prejudices and ideals. Designers must remain agents of change, increasingly aware of these issues.

References

1. Braidotti, R.: The Posthuman. Polity Press, Berlin (2013)
2. Criado-Perez, C.: Invisible Women. Exposing Data Bias in a World Designed for Men. Abrams Press, New York (2019)

3. European Commission: 2019 Report on equality between women and men in the EU. Office for Official Publications of the European Communities, Luxembourg (2019)
4. Miller, M.: Finding the Blank Spots in Big Data. AIGA Eye on Design, New York (2020). https://eyeondesign.aiga.org/finding-the-blank-spots-in-big-data. Accessed 12 Mar 2021
5. Martins, L.: Privilege and oppression: towards a feminist speculative design. In: Lim, Y., Niedderer, K., Redström, J., Stolterman, E., Valtonen, A. (eds.) Design's Big Debates - DRS International Conference 2014, 16–19 June, Umeå, Sweden (2014). https://dl.designresear chsociety.org/drs-conference-papers/drs2014/researchpapers/75. Accessed 10 Apr 2022
6. Dunne, A., Raby, F.: Speculative Everything Design, Fiction, and Social Dreaming. MIT Press, Cambridge (2013)
7. European Commission: Women in the Digital Age. Office for Official Publications of the European Communities, Luxembourg (2018)
8. Schlesinger, A., Edwards W.K., Grinter, R.E.: Intersectional HCI: engaging identity through gender, race, and class. In: Proceedings of the 2017 CHI Conference on Human Factors in Computing Systems (CHI '17), pp. 5412–5427. Association for Computing Machinery, New York (2017). https://doi.org/10.1145/3025453.3025766
9. Bardzell, S.: Feminist HCI: taking stock and outlining an agenda for design. In: Proceedings of the SIGCHI Conference on Human Factors in Computing Systems (CHI '10), pp. 1301–1310. Association for Computing Machinery, New York (2010). https://doi.org/10.1145/175 3326.1753521
10. Costanza-Chock, S.: Introduction: #TravelingWhileTrans, design justice, and escape from the matrix of domination. In: Design Justice. 1st ed. (2020). https://designjustice.mitpress. mit.edu/pub/ap8rgw5e. Accessed 12 Apr 2022
11. Zhou, S.K., Chellappa, R., Zhao, W.: Unconstrained Face Recognition. Springer, New York (2006). https://doi.org/10.1007/978-0-387-29486-5
12. Garvie, C., Frankle, J.: Facial-Recognition Software Might Have a Racial Bias Problem. The Atlantic. Washington (2016). https://www.theatlantic.com/technology/archive/2016/04/the-underlying-bias-of-facial-recognition-systems/476991. Accessed 26 Feb 2022
13. D'Ignazio, C., Klein, L.: 1. The Power Chapter. In: Data Feminism (2020). https://data-fem inism.mitpress.mit.edu/pub/vi8obxh7. Accessed 17 Feb 2022
14. Buolamwini, J., Gebru, T.: Gender shades: intersectional accuracy disparities in commercial gender classification, PMLR (81), 77–91 (2018). http://proceedings.mlr.press/v81/buolam wini18a/buolamwini18a.pdf. Accessed 03 Jan 2022
15. Mitrović, I., Auger, J., Hanna, J., & Helgason, I.: Beyond speculative design: Past – Present – Future. Arts Academy, University of Split, Split (2021)
16. Cambridge Dictionary, https://dictionary.cambridge.org/pt/dicionario/ingles/render, last accessed 2022/01/03
17. Misak, C.: The Oxford Handbook of American Philosophy (2008; online edn, Oxford Academic, 2 Sept. 2009), https://doi.org/10.1093/oxfordhb/9780199219315.001.0001. Accessed 23 Mar 2022
18. Giles, D.C.: A typology of persona as suggested by jungian theory and the evolving persona studies literature. Persona Stud. 6(1), 15–29 (2020). https://doi.org/10.21153/psj2020vol6n o1art99
19. Jung, C.G.: Collected works of C.G. Jung, Volume 6: In: Adler, G., Hull, R.F.C. (eds.) Psychological Types (6). Princeton University Press, New Jersey (1971) http://www.jstor.org/sta ble/j.ctt5hhqtj. Accessed 24 Mar 2022
20. Clarke, R.: The digital persona and its application to data surveillance. Inf. Soc. 10(2), 77–92 (1994)
21. Briggs-Myers, I., Briggs, K.C.: Myers-Briggs Type Indicator (MBTI). Consulting Psychologists Press, Palo Alto (1985)

22. Escobido, M., Stevens, G.: Can personality type be predicted by social media network structures? In: The Asian Conference on Psychology & the Behavioral Sciences, pp. 159–173. IAFOR, Osaka (2013)
23. Amirhosseini, M.H., Kazemian, H.: Machine learning approach to personality type prediction based on the Myers-Briggs Type Indicator®. Multimodal Technol. Interact. **4**(1), 9 (2020)
24. Bergen, H.: 'I'd blush if I could': digital assistants, disembodied cyborgs and the problem of gender. Word Text J. Liter. Stud. Linguist. **6**(01), 95–113 (2016)
25. Martin, A.E., Slepian, M.L.: Dehumanizing gender: the debiasing effects of gendering human-abstracted entities. Pers. Soc. Psychol. Bull. **44**(12), 1681–1696 (2018)
26. Federici, S.: Caliban and the Witch: Women, the Body and Primitive Accumulation. Autonomedia, Brooklyn (2014)
27. Masterson, V.: Women are burning out doing invisible 'office housework'. World Economic Forum (2021). https://www.weforum.org/agenda/2021/11/women-workplace-2021-invisible-labour. Accessed 11 Apr 2022
28. Donald, S.: Societal Implications of Gendering AI. Arizona State University, Arizona (2019)
29. Effiong, A., Inyang, S.: A brief history and classification of feminism. In: Patu, S.A. (eds.) A Brief History of Feminism. MIT Press, Cambridge (2017)
30. Keirsey, D.: Please Understand Me II: Temperament, Character, Intelligence. Prometheus Nemesis Book Company, California (1998)
31. Likert, R.: A technique for the measurement of attitudes. Arch. Psychol. **22**(140), 1–55 (1932)
32. Sauro, J.: 10 Things to Know About the Single Ease Question (SEQ). Measuring U (2012). https://measuringu.com/seq10. Accessed 29 Dec 2020
33. Scherer, K.R.: What are emotions? And how can they be measured? Soc. Sci. Inf. **44**(4), 695–729 (2005)
34. Kychenthal, S.: Why the trans programmer? IEEE (2022). https://arxiv.org/pdf/2205.01553.pdf. Accessed 6 Mar 2022

A Metaverse Interactive Experience Space Based on Oriental Prayer Culture

Jiawei Ou, Jing Luo[✉], Yiyong Zeng, Jiajun Huang, Jun Zou, and Pei Cheng

College of Art and Design, Shenzhen University, Shenzhen, Guangdong, China
luojng@szu.edu.cn

Abstract. With the development and maturity of the new generation of information technology, the concept of the metaverse is becoming more and more popular. Major technology companies are investing a lot of money to create the metaverse [1], and governments around the world have also introduced policies to support the development of the metaverse industry [2]. As a product of the integration and development of various cutting-edge technologies [3], the metaverse can inject strong impetus into the development of economic and cultural industries. This research aims to combine the oriental prayer culture with the metaverse concept, to design an interactive space with an immersive experience, to provide people with a place for spiritual sustenance, and to explore a new direction for the development of the prayer culture industry, and to provide other cultures industry development inspiration. This study sorts out the development history of the metaverse and the current development status of virtual technology, analyzes the new characteristics of prayer culture in Chinese youth groups, understands user needs through questionnaires, collects user feedback, and verifies the interactive experience through scene simulation Interesting. The study concludes that the interactive experience space of the Oriental Prayer Culture Metaverse can be used in shopping malls, theme parks, and other public places to provide interesting and immersive interactive experiences for young groups mainly aged 18–35, which has great commercial value and is achievable.

Keywords: Metaverse · Oriental Prayer Culture · Interactive Experience Space

1 Introduction

As one of China's traditional cultures, "prayer culture" has experienced thousands of years of ups and downs, and has taken root in the hearts of the Chinese people. Based on the pursuit of "prayer culture", consumers will have prayer consumption behavior [4]. Nowadays, China is in a period of profound transformation, social contradictions are prominent, people's life pressure is increasing, and members of society, especially young people, generally have emotions such as anxiety and loss [5]. In addition, the economic difficulties and life troubles brought about by the epidemic have significantly reduced people's expectations for future life [6]. Epidemic disasters and secondary disasters will have a great negative impact on people's mental health [7]. When individuals cannot

J. Y. C. Chen and G. Fragomeni (Eds.): HCII 2023, LNCS 14027, pp. 58–71, 2023.
https://doi.org/10.1007/978-3-031-35634-6_5

control their living environment, people often resort to praying to gods to regain a sense of control [8]. Under such a social background, people's demand for prayer culture is increasing.

At the same time, with the development and maturity of the new generation of digital technology, the concept of the metaverse is becoming more and more popular. The major technology companies are investing significant sums of money in the creation of the metaverse whose main feature will be the fusion between the virtual world and the physical one [1]. The term "metaverse" emerged to further facilitate the digital transformation of all aspects of our physical lives [9]. Metaverse, as an integrated innovation and integrated application integrating Internet, big data, cloud computing, AI, blockchain, VR, AR and other technologies, has attracted the attention of all countries in the world [2], and the Chinese government has also issued corresponding The policy supports the development of metaverse industry, and hopes to inject strong development momentum into the real economy industry through virtual technology [10].

This study explores the phenomenon of new forms of Chinese contemporary prayer culture and hopes that the interactive experience space designed by combining the oriental prayer culture with the concept of metaverse can be applied to shopping malls, theme parks, and other public places, through installation art, laser projection, AR, VR, AI, and other technologies provide people with interesting and shocking sensory interaction experience. The target users of this project are mainly the "M generation" group, that is, young people aged 18–35.

2   The Development of the Metaverse and Related Technologies

The concept of "metaverse" first appeared in the novel Snow Crash by American science fiction writer Neal Stephenson in 1992. What he described was a virtual world corresponding to the real world, in which people could have a unique Digital avatar [11]; the game "second life" released in 2003 is considered to be the first metaverse game [12]. Users can socialize with others through a movable virtual avatar in the game, which provides high-level Social networking services; "Ready Player One" written by Ernest Cline in 2011 is another novel depicting the virtual world of the Metaverse [13], which was later adapted into a 2018 movie, which vividly shows the infinite possibilities of the metaverse world; in 2014, Sony, Samsung, and Google released VR headsets [3]; VR devices can greatly enhance people's sensory experience; in 2017, Microsoft acquired the VR company Altspace VR [14], allowing virtual reality technology and avatars to be used in the office field; in 2021, Facebook, the world's largest social platform, officially changed its name to Meta, emphasizing its important role in the development of the Metaverse [3], and was called Metaverse No. One share of Roblox is also officially listed on the New York Stock Exchange, so 2021 is called the first year of the Metaverse. As for the review of the development process of the metaverse, we can find that although the concept of the metaverse appeared very early, in recent years, as the technologies related to the metaverse began to mature, the metaverse began to enter the public's field of vision, becoming Get hot. Today, the research on the metaverse is still in its early stages, and different scholars have different definitions of the metaverse [3]. Therefore, the metaverse space described in this article is not only the virtual world but also includes the interactive space of the real world.

This article also briefly sorts out the technologies related to the Metaverse, which can also be applied in the real interactive experience space to provide people with a more realistic and shocking experience. The advancement of these technologies will provide a basis for the realization of the interactive experience space. Today, the technologies related to the metaverse mainly include blockchain, AR, VR, 3D reconstruction, AI, IoT, edge computing [3], etc. Blockchain technology is mainly used in fields such as cryptocurrency, financial services, risk management, and the IoT [15]. It can guarantee the ownership of NFTs in the Metaverse, which will benefit the development of cultural and creative digital collections. Create huge commercial value while inheriting. AR and VR technology can provide users with immersive sensory experience and a variety of interactive possibilities, increasing the fun of users in the prayer process, especially in the real experience space, AR Technology is a supplement to reality, not a complete replacement [16]. Each user can see different content in the same space. 3D reconstruction technology has been widely used in real estate, virtual museums, and many other fields. Users don't have to come to the scene to see a real physical scene. AI can quickly analyze existing data and learn from it, and quickly generate brand new 2D pictures or even 3D scenes. AI can also answer people's questions and provide unique insight. The IoT can connect all devices in the scene to operate more efficiently. Its core is sensors. These sensors can collect information about people and the environment. The collection of different information can make the elements in the metaverse scene ever-changing. These technologies are combined and used in real scenes or virtual environments to create infinite possibilities. For example, AI can generate unique digital collections according to people's wishes. In addition to the technologies mentioned above, installation art, laser projection, etc. may also be used in the experience space studied in this project. The combination of various advanced technologies will bring unique experiences to users.

3 Oriental Prayer Culture

Considering that it will take some time for the wide application of the metaverse, and the groups interested in the metaverse are mainly young people, the oriental prayer culture described in this study is not a traditional Chinese cultural activity of praying for blessings, but a cultural activity among young people in China in recent years. A new form of online praying for blessings phenomenon prevailing in China. In 2013, koi became synonymous with luck and became popular on the Internet in China. Major media and businesses continued to use the image of koi to create new topics, and many people reposted pictures of koi on the Internet to pray for blessings [17]. Like many buzzwords on the Internet, after being widely used by netizens, its meaning will be weakened, and koi will soon be replaced by other things in this trend of blessing. Later, images that were only novel and unique without auspicious cultural meanings could also become the objects of blessings reposted by netizens, such as cute cats and even leaves with unique shapes.The sacred features of the blessing content reposted by netizens are gradually weakening and becoming abstract, the interestingness and innovation of content are more important than effectiveness in repost behavior. These phenomena show that young people's prayer behavior does not require the participation of gods in the traditional sense, and the needs of young people for spiritual comfort can be met through the reposting of blessing pictures.

With the iterative update of the virus version, the end of the epidemic is nowhere in sight, and people's daily life and the social economy have been greatly affected. The rat race social status has exacerbated the youth group's confusion about the future [17]. Studies have shown that when individuals cannot control their living environment, people often resort to praying to gods to regain a sense of control [8]. People often use these superstitious behaviors to relieve their anxiety, nervousness, and fear when they are threatened or uncertain [18]. In modern society, people face more pressure and uncertainty in life and are often in a state of anxiety, which makes people expect to solve problems at low cost and seek spiritual comfort [5]. Recreational online prayer behavior is a positive social strategy for young people to relieve the pressure of life [17]. People don't need to pay "faith costs", but they can still have expectations for the future. In such a situation, it is easy for people to make "Pascal's bet" (it is better to believe in something than not in nothing).

In addition, with the popularization of online payment, the development of technology and the enhancement of people's awareness of environmental protection, many temples have also begun to innovate the traditional way of praying. Here are two cases, a temple in Quanzhou, Fujian introduced an electronic prayer device. By scanning the QR code on the screen of the device to pay, people can make donations on the device to accumulate merit, and they can also make wishes on the device, user's wishes will be preserved in the temple. Another temple in Shanghai has established an online prayer platform, where people can perform various prayer activities. These forms of online and offline blessings existed before the popularity of the metaverse concept, and metaverse technology, as an important development direction of the next generation Internet, will surely give offline prayer activities better opportunities for development. Therefore, on this basis, the prayer interactive experience space explored in this study is also an innovation of offline blessing methods.

Compared with the objects of traditional praying behaviors, the objects of prayer behaviors designed in the "Prayer Metaverse Experience Space" are actually "not emphasizing god". Although we refer to the design of East Asian native religious culture in terms of visual style, we do not use specific gods as the basis for users to pray, but from the space design style, the characteristics of the behavior itself, and the feedback after prayer behavior, users can get a positive psychological feeling. The online prayer phenomenon that has become popular among young people in recent years is also different from traditional prayer behaviors. It has evolved from the initial rise to almost no "sacred features". As a youth subculture, it conveys the participants' yearning for a better life. The phenomenon of online blessings inspires us that the blessings that young people need in the future can no longer be limited to concrete gods, but also abstract symbols. At the same time, we should also pay attention to the entertainment of the blessing process. The "Prayer Metaverse Experience Space" provides people with a more interesting form of prayer in a more abstract way. While expressing their expectations for a better life, people can also obtain a unique experience that is different from the traditional way of prayer.

4   Questionnaire

This study also designed a questionnaire and filled it out on the network platform to determine the target users through the questionnaire, to understand the user's real thoughts, psychological state, and psychological expectations for the experience space. In the end, a total of 90 valid questionnaires were obtained, including 26 male samples (28.89%) and 64 female samples (71.11%). This data is similar to the distribution of online prayer user data [17], and the majority are female. Through data analysis, it is found that the people who are interested in the concept of prayer metaverse are mainly concentrated in the age group of 18–35, mainly in the "M generation", which is consistent with the age distribution in the "2017 Weibo User Development Report" [20]. Through data analysis, it is found that the higher the frequency of participation in traditional prayer activities, the higher the degree of education, and the younger people are, the more inclined they are to participate in new forms of prayer activities, and the new forms of prayer activities have the same psychological comfort as traditional prayer activities. More than 84% of users have participated in offline or online prayer activities, more than 62% of users participated in prayer activities because of seeking spiritual comfort, and more than 78% of users have the willingness to continue praying. More than 80% of the users have a relatively high acceptance of the metaverse prayer activity and are willing to try it. In addition, the results of the questionnaire also show that the main motivations of users to participate in prayer activities are an academic success (70%), physical health (68.89%), the blessing of safety (55.56%), career success (42.22%) and changes in fortune (31.11%), etc., as shown in Fig. 1. In the experience space, users hope to get the feeling of audio-visual interaction.

Question: What is your motivation for participating in online prayer activities?[multiple choice]

options	sub-total	Proportion	
academically successful	63		70%
In good health	62		68.89%
Bless peace	50		55.56%
career successful	38		42.22%
change of fortune	28		31.11%

Fig. 1. Motivation of users to participate in online prayer activities

5   Concept Design and Interaction Process

Based on the analysis of technologies related to the metaverse concept, the analysis of the new form of prayer culture, and the results of the questionnaire, we designed a prayer culture metaverse interactive experience space and named it "Prayer Metaverse", and its conceptual design is shown in Fig. 2. The experience space includes three interactive scenes: the wishing pool, the wall of answers, and the wishing lamp. Corresponding to the offline experience space, there is also an online mini-program, which serves as a bridge connecting users and the space. Users can share their wishes, wishing experience, and purchase wish-related peripherals in this mini-program, which is convenient for users While knowing the interactive process of the experience space, it can also realize commercial realization.

The prayer meataverse mainly provides people with a unique prayer experience through space design, music, lighting effects, augmented reality and other information technologies. When people enter the space, scan the QR code of the space to open the "Prayer Metaverse" online mini-program, and come to the wishing stone, people can choose different types of wishes through the mini-program, such as praying for wealth, safety, fame, love, then enter the specific wish on the mobile phone, and then use NFC technology, when the user brings the mobile phone close to the wishing stone, the type of wish and the specific wish selected by the user on the mobile phone will be uploaded to the cloud of the "Prayer Metaverse" space, and the user wears the wishing stone in the space. With the AR glasses inside, user can see the brilliant light effects on the wishing stone, these light effects will guide the user to slide the virtual wishing coin on the wishing stone platform to the central wishing tree, and the user can see the light effect track of virtual wishing coin which flying from the wishing stone to the wishing tree. The wishing tree will also shine after receiving the wishing coin, as the "god" to the user's feedback, in addition, the user can also see a shimmering Buddha's hand virtual image floating in the wishing pool through AR glasses to interact with the user, according to the different types of wishes, the forms of Buddha's hand are also different, as shown in Fig. 3. The Buddha's hand that the user sees through the AR glasses will interact with the user in specific actions, which can leave a unique visual, auditory and emotional experience for the user. The wishing stones and wishing trees in the space are not only artistic installations that can interact with users, but also symbols of gods. These symbols give users interactive feedback and can bring positive psychological hints to users. The forms of interaction are mainly visual and auditory.

Fig. 2. The wishing scene of the prayer metaverse space

In addition, after completing the blessing, users can purchase products related to the prayer activity and digital collections unique to the user in the experience space or online mini-program. Digital collections are 2D images or 3D models generated by AI according to the user's wishes. Users can also share their experiences in the user community through the mini-program. User sharing is conducive to attracting more audiences to experience

Fig. 3. Different gestures symbolize different types of wishes and interactions

and building a user ecosystem. We can set up a reward mechanism to encourage users to share. The experience process of the wishing scene in the "Prayer Metaverse" experience space is shown in Fig. 4, and the system framework and prototype of the online mini-program are shown in Fig. 5.

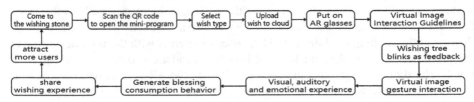

Fig. 4. The experience process of the wishing scene in the space

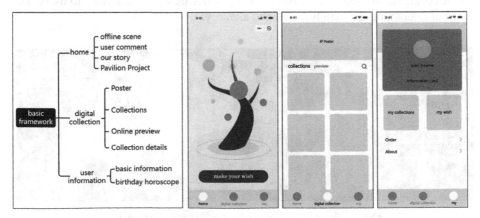

Fig. 5. The mini-program system framework and its prototype

6 Feasibility Analysis

We used the PEST analysis model and SWOT analysis method to analyze the feasibility of this project. The business model of "Prayer Metaverse" belongs to the category of creative industries, and creative industries, as the "old partner" of Metaverse commercial applications, are the most suitable industries for the development of Metaverse-related commercial applications [21]. The "Prayer Metaverse" experience space is mainly used in large shopping malls, and it can also be specially built in theme parks. These places are crowded with people, which is conducive to the widespread and promotion of the metaverse prayer culture.

6.1 PEST Analysis

For the analysis of the external environment of the "Prayer Metaverse" project, this study constructed a PEST analysis model, and proposed the feasibility of "Prayer Metaverse" in it based on the analysis of the environment. The model is shown in Fig. 6.

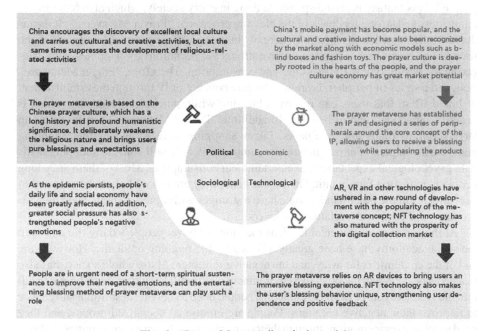

Fig. 6. "Prayer Metaverse" analysis model

At the level of the political environment, China is accelerating the construction of a socialist cultural power, encouraging the inheritance and development of local excellent traditional culture, and vigorously carrying out various cultural and creative activities. "Prayer Metaverse" relies on China's traditional prayer culture and has a long-term historical accumulation and profound humanistic significance, combined with the international cutting-edge technology and the concept of the metaverse, can be said to inject the spirit of the times into traditional culture and has great potential for cultural dissemination. However, it should also be noted that the country is constantly reducing the cultural spread of religious beliefs, so the "Prayer Metaverse" culture, as a new type of "Non-religious" prayer activity, can also effectively avoid such political environmental influences.

In terms of the economic environment, Chinese mobile payment technology has been popularized, and the cultural and creative industry has also begun to flourish as economic models such as blind boxes and trendy toys have been recognized by the market. The motivations of blessing consumption behavior can be divided into the following seven types: habitual, communicative, contractual, occasional, reminiscent, cognitive, and functional [4]. Among them, the communicative type, the contractual type, and the occasional type are closely related to the consumption pattern of "Prayer Metaverse". Communicative motivation means that consumers are aware that the "prayer culture" has taken root in the hearts of the Chinese people, so using products as a means of communication is easy to understand, low in communication costs, and can well convey wishes to gift recipients; contractual motivation means that consumers will Consumption behavior is regarded as an expectation in exchange for "the right time, place and people". This fantasy is an indispensable thing in every society, which also requires the uniqueness and strong feedback of the blessing process of "Prayer Metaverse"; It means that in festivals with a strong atmosphere of "blessing", the reunion of family members, friends, and lovers makes consumers have stronger expectations for happiness, thus triggering the desire to pray for blessings and consumption. Therefore, "Prayer Metaverse" designed a series of peripherals around the core concept of IP through the establishment of brand IP, so that users can receive a blessing while purchasing products, which is beautiful, practical, and gift-giving. In addition, "Prayer Metaverse" can be set up in large shopping malls or theme parks. Taking shopping malls as an example, shopping malls are a complex of entertainment consumption. People will come to shopping malls with psychological expectations of entertainment consumption. Most of them are young people in pairs or a family unit. On the one hand, they are more likely to be attracted to new things. On the other hand, people have a stronger willingness to pray when they are accompanied by friends, relatives, or lovers.

At the social environmental level, as mentioned above, people's daily life and even the social economy have been greatly affected by the ongoing epidemic. However, the end of the epidemic is far away, and the negative sentiment of the whole society has also reached a peak. When the objective environment is difficult to change, in order not to fall into the vicious cycle of negative emotions, people need a short-term spiritual sustenance to improve their negative emotions. People are emotional socialized groups, and they need to release their emotions through their own actions. Taking prayer activities as short-term spiritual sustenance can effectively make up for their own feelings of powerlessness, panic, guilt, etc. [22].

At the level of technical environment, virtual reality technologies have been developed for a long time, and the technology is becoming more mature, and the popularity of the Metaverse concept in 2021 has broadened the application scenarios and demands of virtual reality technology. The technology brings a new round of development. In addition, the metaverse is accompanied by the development of NFT digital collection technology and market, although there is still some chaos in the NFT market, which needs to be regulated by the introduction of relevant policies. "Prayer Metaverse" brings a brand-new immersive prayer experience to users relying on AR glasses equipment. NFT technology also makes it unique for users to participate in blessing, which further strengthens user viscosity and positive feedback received by users.

6.2 SWOT Analysis

To promote the development of "Prayer Metaverse" new prayer activities, this study uses the SWOT analysis method to analyze the internal advantages and disadvantages of "Prayer Metaverse" as well as external opportunities and threats and establishes a table to propose corresponding strategies, as shown in Fig. 7.

internal factors ＼ external factors	Opportunities 1.Prayer culture is rooted in the hearts of the people 2.Metaverse is hot, related technology development 3.The social environment makes people urgently need spiritual sustenance 4.Cultural and creative economy has a large market	Threats 1.The Impact of Traditional Blessing Culture
Strengths 1.Novel and unique user experience 2.Good visual style 3.Positive implication of content of prayer activities 4.Combination of mini-program and physical space	SO Strategy 1.Establish brand IP and related peripheral design 2.Realize emotional design in the design of scenes, interactions, surroundings, etc 3.Using cutting-edge technology to enhance the sense of immersion experience	ST Strategy 1.Improve the function of mini-program 2.Weaken the religious nature, focus on aesthetic immersion experience and promote prayer culture
Weaknesses 1.The technical and site requirements of the real space are high 2.The concept of prayer metaverse is complex 3.With novel experience as the main selling point, business sustainability is poor	WO Strategy 1.The space is set in the shopping mall to meet the requirements of the flow of people, consumption scenes and installation space 2.Cooperate with other brands to use traditional holiday promotion	WT Strategy 1.Enhance the visual style design, and the space can be used as public art during non-event hours for viewing 2.Expand user groups,plan activities for target users

Fig. 7. "Prayer Metaverse" SWOT analysis

In terms of internal factors, the main advantage of "Prayer Metaverse" is that it combines physical devices with virtual imaging, offline venues and online platforms, bringing users an unprecedented immersive experience and positive feedback. At the same time, the visual style of the space's architecture, interaction, and surroundings has also been in-depth designed concerning the oriental Zen style, which has a strong sense of unity and high level. However, the "dual combination" model of physical installations and virtual imaging, offline venue, and online platform also mean that this project has relatively high requirements for venue space and technology, and also has a high threshold for users. Another disadvantage of "Prayer Metaverse" is that it combines the concept of the metaverse to form the Oriental metaverse. The related concept settings are relatively complicated, and it is difficult to sum them up in one word. Finally, because the "Prayer Metaverse" prayer activity is "not emphasizing god" compared with traditional prayer activities, a big selling point has become a novel and unique prayer experience, so it is difficult to have a high user viscosity and sustainable in business aspect.

In terms of external factors, "Prayer Metaverse" has great opportunities for development, but at the same time faces certain threats. First of all, China's prayer culture is rooted in the hearts of the people, so the form of activities can easily be recognized by users; secondly, the popularity and spread of the metaverse concept can attract a large number of people who are interested in the metaverse concept as a publicity point for the concept Users; thirdly, with the deepening of the risk society and the uncertain situation of the epidemic situation, the overall sentiment of the society is negative, and there is a high demand for new prayer activities with healing and spiritual sustenance; the last is the promotion of the country and the improvement of the quality of the people under the current circumstances, the cultural and creative payment economy has a better market prospect and great commercial potential. The threat that "Prayer Metaverse" is facing is that the rationality of praying is questioned because of the lack of specific gods.

SO strategy refers to the strategy of realizing development by using the advantages obtained from the analysis. This analysis mainly includes three points. The first is to take advantage of the cultural and creative economy through the advantages of visual style and positive implication, establish a brand IP and carry out a series of related peripheral designs around IP; the second is to realize emotional design in the design of scenes, interactions, and peripherals so that users who hope to obtain spiritual sustenance in the prayer activities can obtain corresponding positive feedback; the third is to make good use of the technological content of technology and devices, and adopt cutting-edge technologies to enhance and optimize the user experience.

ST strategy refers to the strategy of preventing possible threats through advantages, and this analysis mainly includes two points. The first is to build a good online platform design, and improve the functions of online simple blessing, wish fulfillment, and digital collection transactions so that users can better understand, be familiar with, and remember this project through online interaction. The second is to weaken the "sacred features" in prayer activities, and use the aesthetic and immersive prayer experience combined with cutting-edge technology and the new prayer culture as the highlight of publicity, so as to distinguish it from the traditional blessing that emphasizes the belief in gods.

WO strategy refers to the strategy of using external opportunities to minimize internal weaknesses. This analysis mainly includes three points. The first is to set the experience space in the shopping mall, which can achieve the following benefits at the same time: (1)The offline installation of "Prayer Metaverse" requires a large space and financial support, and the business district can meet this condition; (2) "Prayer Metaverse" activities can be used as an innovative cultural activity to attract traffic to the business district, and the business district, as a place with dense traffic, can also create the greatest economic benefits and cultural influence for the project; (3) The target group of "Prayer Metaverse" is mainly those who are interested in metaverse technology Interested groups, groups who are willing to participate in online prayer activities, groups that pursue visual styles, etc. These groups are concentrated in the age group of 18–35 years old, and they are also the main users of the business district and the main force of consumption. (4) During traditional Chinese holidays, family members, friends, and couples often come to the business district together. At this time, the "Prayer Metaverse" experience space will strengthen the interest of these users because of the meaning of "beautiful" and "blessing". Experience and consumption intention will bring stronger positive feedback to it. The second strategy is similar to the above-mentioned benefits. It is necessary to grasp the cultural meanings of traditional festivals and different brands, and cooperate with them to improve the commercial sustainability of the brand; the last point is to use the concept of the metaverse and new technologies to carry out sufficient preliminary

Announcement, let users understand and be familiar with the concept setting of "Prayer Metaverse" in advance.

WT strategy refers to the strategy of minimizing potential danger, and this analysis mainly includes two points. First of all, it is necessary to strengthen the design of the visual style, so that the venues can be used as public art in non-event hours with enough ornamental value, and can get the support of shopping malls and the public; then, it is necessary to clarify its user group and make event planning for this group, to To achieve the greatest economic benefits and cultural influence.

7 Scenario Simulation and User Feedback

We held a small exhibition on campus to attract users to simulate the wishing scene, observe users' behavior during the wishing process, and collect user feedback. We made a wishing tree with some simple materials, and invited users to choose different wishing types, then write their wishes on the back of the wishing card of the corresponding wishing type, and hang the wishing card on the wishing tree. We also used 3D printing technology to manufacture different types of wishing coins and invited users to play a game of throwing wishing coins. Our exhibition is welcomed by many people. Since the exhibition is held on campus, the participants are mainly college students. They have a higher degree of awareness of the metaverse and a higher acceptance of entertainment-based blessings. We have classified the wish types and wishes of users, and most of the wish types they choose are wealth and fame, which is consistent with our previous research results. In addition, we have also received feedback from users, for example, the content of the project is not perfect, the continuous innovation experience needs to be strengthened, the reproducible implementation is difficult, the uniqueness is not reflected enough, the prayer metaverse without god may not be sustainable, the connection between virtual image interactive gestures and the wishing tree is not rigorous enough. Due to the big difference between the scene simulation and our concept design of the interactive experience space, the participants cannot experience the cutting-edge technology mentioned above, but the scene simulation proves that the young people have a strong interest in the metaverse and the new form of prayer interest.

8 Conclusion

By reviewing the metaverse and related technologies, this study demonstrates that the metaverse is characterized by the combination of fiction and reality, and the existence and progress of related technologies can also prove the technical feasibility of this interactive experience space. This article expounds on the concept of Eastern prayer culture, and also analyzes the phenomenon of online prayer culture in China, and demonstrates the feasibility and rationality of the new form of prayer culture, through questionnaires to determine user groups and user needs, through PEST analysis model and SWOT analysis the commercial feasibility of the design is analyzed, and finally, the acceptance of the target user to the prayer metaverse is verified through scene simulation.

The metaverse interactive experience space based on oriental prayer culture is an innovative design that combines the current fiery metaverse concept and emerging technologies with traditional prayer culture. It creates a new form of prayer experience space based on the needs of modern young people to seek new forms of spiritual sustenance in the face of life pressure and the innovative development needs of the traditional prayer industry, providing entertainment for young people mainly "M generation" unique and immersive prayer interactive experience. "Prayer Metaverse" combines virtual technology with physical scenes, online platforms and offline space creates a "god" carrier that is more in line with the spiritual entertainment consumption needs of young people, and creates a business model that can operate effectively. Metaverse empowers the real economy and revitalizes traditional industries, has high commercial value and good market prospects, and also provides ideas for the innovative development of other cultural industries.

References

1. Riva, G., Wiederhold, B.K.: What the Metaverse is (really) and why we need to know about it (2022)
2. 3D virtual worlds and the metaverse: current status and future possibilities
3. A review of metaverse's definitions, architecture, applications, challenges, issues, solutions, and future trends
4. Fengna, S.: A preliminary study on the motivation of Chinese blessing consumption behavior. Mod. Econ. Inf. **19**, 3–4 (2015)
5. Huang, Y., Yang, Y.: Research on influencing factors of Chinese social network mascots reposting blessings: taking koi-related Weibo as an example. Inf. Sci. **37**(04), 86–91+121 (2019). https://doi.org/10.13833/j.issn.1007-7634.2019.04.013
6. Wang, J. (ed.): Research report on chinese social mentality (2020), Beijing: Social Sciences Literature Press, pp. 1–11 (2021), Junxiu, W. (ed.) Research Report on Chinese Social Mentality (2021), Beijing: Social Science Press, pp. 4–9 (2021)
7. Wang, J., Zhang, Y.: Risk perception, social emotions and future expectations: changes in social mentality at different stages of the epidemic. Soc. Sci. Front **10**, 220–237 (2022)
8. Chen, Y., Zhang, J., Liu, J.: Review of superstitious psychology research. Adv. Psychol. Sci. **17**(1), 218–226 (2009)
9. Lee, L.H., Braud, T., Zhou, P., et al.: All one needs to know about metaverse: a complete survey on technological singularity, virtual ecosystem, and research agenda. arXiv preprint arXiv:2110.05352 (2021)
10. Wang, W.: Policies released in many places, metaverses scrambling to implement. China Electronics News, 2022-10-14 (007). https://doi.org/10.28065/n.cnki.ncdzb.2022.001225
11. Stephenson, N.: Snow crash: A novel: Spectra (2003)
12. Tidy, J.: Zuckerberg's metaverse: lessons from second life. BBC News. Archived from the original on November 13, 2021. Retrieved November 17 (2021)
13. Cline, E.: Ready Player One: A Novel. Broadway Books (2012)
14. Langston, J.: 'You can actually feel like you're in the same place': microsoft mesh powers shared experiences in mixed reality. Innovation Stories. Archived from the original on 3 November 2021. Accessed 3 Nov 2021
15. Zheng, Z., Xie, S., Dai, H.N., et al.: Blockchain challenges and opportunities: a survey. Int. J. Web Grid Serv. **14**(4), 352–375 (2018)

16. Azuma, R.T.: A survey of augmented reality. Presence: Teleoper. Vir. Environ. **6**(4), 355–385 (1997)
17. Fu, L.: Red and grey: perspective on the duality of contemporary youth's daily life from the custom of "Blessing of Koi Carp." Cult. Herit. **05**, 116–125 (2021)
18. Luo, H.: Analysis on the learning mechanism of superstition—from the perspective of learning psychology to see the formation of superstition. J. Gansu Normal Univ. **6**(4), 85–89 (2001)
19. Lai, S.: Research on factors affecting users' microblog information forwarding. Libr. Work Res. **08**, 31–37 (2015). https://doi.org/10.16384/j.cnki.lwas.2015.08.008
20. Sina Weibo Data Center: Weibo User Development Report [EB/OL] (2017). http://www.useit.com.cn/thread-17562-1-1.html. Accessed 17 Feb 2018
21. Xu, X., Chen, W.: The commercial application of metaverse. Zhang Jiang Sci. Technol. Rev. **03**, 10–13 (2022)
22. Qin, M.: A psychological analysis of social media users' "prayer" behavior—Taking the phenomenon of "lighting candles" after major emergencies as an example. Journal. Res. Guide **8**(11), 56+96 (2017)

Physiological Data Placement Recommendations for VR Sport Applications

Dirk Queck[1]([✉])[iD], Iannis Albert[1,2][iD], Georg Volkmar[2][iD], Rainer Malaka[2][iD],
and Marc Herrlich[1][iD]

[1] University of Kaiserslautern-Landau (RPTU), 67653 Kaiserslautern, Germany
queck@eit.uni-kl.de
[2] University of Bremen, 28359 Bremen, Germany

Abstract. VR sports applications and exergames offer opportunities to improve users' health playfully. Evidence from various investigations on the combinations of physiological data and VR show that visualized biofeedback supports physical training in many dimensions. Display physiological data can help improve virtual exercises' effectiveness by observing, maintaining, and regulating physical stress areas. While guidelines for graphical user interfaces in VR have been derived from research, especially for information placement and notifications, it does not offer recommendations for the design of displaying live physiological data. To investigate physiological data placement for VR sports applications, we conducted a user study with 29 participants. We compared different types of placements with a head-up display (*HUD*), a virtual fitness tracker (*Watch*), and a static world space placement (*In-Situ*) in a VR squash-based game. We found a significant effect on game performance between *In-Situ* and *HUD*. We analyzed subjective user feedback concerning the topic and found that most users preferred the *In-Situ* placement. Based on the findings we derived recommendations for physiological data placement in VR sports applications.

Keywords: 3D-User Interfaces · Recommendations · Wearables · Virtual Reality · Physiological Data

1 Introduction

Researchers investigated the positive effects of physical VR exercises [8] and proved that VR training has positive effects on physical and psychological health [23]. Investigations from sports science show that displaying and monitoring physiological data during exercise are effective means to improve training effects [2, 16]. This beneficial training concept has been successfully transferred

---

Supported by organization x.

to VR applications [14]. To support VR exercises for users by displaying physiological data, it is essential to know where and how this data should be placed in virtual space.

General user interface (UI) concepts from the desktop domain are not easily transferable to VR. Fast-paced applications with a lot of head movements, often seen in many commercial applications (e.g. BeatSaber), are particularly difficult to design without affecting users in gameplay or evoking cognitive overload. While there is research for example on VR menu design [6,9], text placement in HMDs [7,28], and notifications in VR [27], displaying physiological data in VR evokes new interaction challenges. A suitable visualization is needed that allows users easy access to their physiological parameters.

To gain initial insights into the design of physiological data displays in VR, we conducted a user study with 29 participants. We began with a fundamental investigation of display type and placement and developed a VR sports game similar to Squash, in which we implemented and compared three techniques to present the physiological data in the virtual environment. The displays were used to allow the users to monitor their physiological parameters (heart rate and calories) during gameplay. For this purpose, we implemented an open-source sensor platform for evaluating physiological data and sending this data directly to the application. We defined a heart rate range, based on sports science training concepts, that the users were supposed to maintain during the game. The study aimed to find out:

(RQ 1) What effects (if any) do placement and presentation of physiological data have on the user experience and usability of VR exergames and sports applications?

(RQ 2) How does the placement and presentation of physiological data affect game performance in particular?

We investigated three types of placements: (A) (*In-Situ*) data placement static in the virtual environment, (B) VR head-up display (*HUD*), known from many first-person games, and (C) a virtual watch (*Watch*) on the wrist as a representative of the on-body placement. In this contribution, we provide recommendations for the placement of physiological data displays. Further, we suggest design parameters for physical data displays in VR sports and exercise applications.

2   Related Work

In the following section, we discuss relevant factors for the design of physiological data displays and general conditions for the VR exergame context.

2.1   Influencing Factors for Physiological Data Display Design

Rzayev et al. studied the placement of notifications in VR while playing, learning, and solving problems [27]. They compared this to a head-up display, on-body, floating, and in-situ representations in open, semi-open, and closed VR environments.

The purpose of notification differs from physiological data monitoring but we will use their range of placement variants for our investigation. For each placement design, we consider evaluated guidelines of GUIs for virtual reality games [3].

HUD Background Information. In a placement investigation for HMDs, Rzayev et al. found that text displayed in smart glasses in the center and bottom center positions compared to the top right leads to higher comprehension [28]. They further showed that text in the top right position increased subjective workload and decreased comprehension [28]. In another investigation focused on notification placement in VR, Rzayev et al. found that displaying notifications in a head-up display decreased reaction time and the number of missed notifications [27]. Chua et al. did a further notification placement study for monocular HMDs [7]. They investigated nine physical display positions for showing notifications. They found that top and peripheral positions were more comfortable and unobtrusive and that the notifications that were in the middle, bottom-middle, and lower positions were the most noticeable [7]. These results motivate our preferred position of the physiological data display in the HMD-location in VR. We assume that the upper and peripheral positions are more inconspicuous and better suited for our use case.

In-Situ Background Information. The study from Rzayev et al. on notification placement in VR gained some knowledge about in-situ placement. They found that displaying notifications in the in-situ position increases the response time [27]. They further recommended that this placement can be used to visualize "non-essential" information because it can deliver data without interrupting VR experiences [27], which is quite useful in our use case.

Watch Background Information. In Rzayev et al.'s investigation "hovering" and "near-body" were the preferred variants for displaying notifications in VR [27]. The near-body placement is similar to our watch placement idea but the VR Sports application context seems to change the specific requirements. Li et al. in their work *Armstrong* evaluated the performance and limitations of 3D UIs for non-dominant arms in VR environments. They show that targets placed closer to the skin, around the wrist, or on the medial side of the forearm can be selected faster than targets placed farther from the skin (around the elbow or on the lateral side of the forearm) [18].

2.2   General Conditions for VR Exergames

Virtual reality exergames (VRE) have a positive influence on health through physical activity and support cognitively stimulating training that goes with interaction in the virtual environment [8]. An important factor in the virtual environment is the user's Field of View (FOV). Ragan et al. have shown that a higher FOV leads to better target detection during a scanning task. In addition, a larger FOV allowed users to identify targets in the periphery and change the visual scanning pattern to detect them [25]. They additionally mentioned that higher visual complexity resulted in poorer target detection during a scanning task [25]. The size of the FOV can also have a negative impact on the cognitive load of the user [4], reducing their task performance if the FOV is too small. Users often have less FOV available than the theoretical maximum FOV due to headset fit and individual face geometries [15] which might have an impact.

This leads to the consideration that a higher complexity in the game (e.g., a larger number of game objects, complicated geometries, complex environments, difficult game modalities or detailed textures) leads to the need of a more minimalistic and strongly contrasted design approach for the physiological data display in a VR sports application context.

3   Data Placement and Design Strategy

We implemented three placement strategies for physiological data displays in VR: the In-Situ placement on a wall (Fig. 1, top), the HUD (Fig. 1, bottom right), and the On-Body placement in form of a digital watch (Fig. 1, bottom left). We chose the same UI design concept for all three variations with small adjustments for their individual UI requirements to ensure comparability as much as possible: the heart rate is shown in a color-coded range visualization (*slider*) as well as a numerical representation of the current heart rate below the visualization.

In-Situ. *In-Situ* physiological data is placed on a wall in the vicinity of the target area. We consider FOV influences [5, 25] and placed the UI in the peripheral FOV, as well as close as possible to the principal direction of play.

HUD. The *HUD* resembles the interface design as seen in HMDs [7, 26, 28], cars [1], or traditional video games [27]. Rzayev et al. placed the notifications 0.25 m from the front of the VR headset at an angle of 25°. We used this as an orientation and iteratively refined the design based on user tests. We consider the effects mentioned in Sect. 2 and place the physiological data in the center near the bottom of the FOV.

Watch. The *Watch* condition is similar to the on-body placement for notification by Rzayev et al. and inspired by VR smartwatch UI [11]. The UI is placed on the non-dominant hand, since the player holds a game device (racket) in the dominant hand. Care is taken to attach the display as close as possible to the lower arm. We determine the display size and angle iteratively with subjects of different heights. Compared to the In-Situ UI design, only the lower dashboard with the numerical representation is reduced in size and fit to a round box to represent a virtual watch.

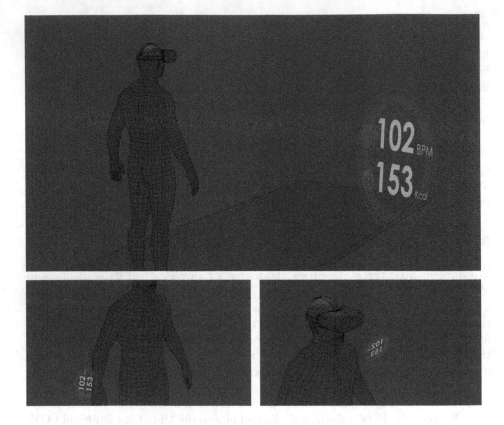

Fig. 1. Placement Strategies

4 Game Concept and Evaluation System

In the following section, we describe the heart rate measurement mechanism and our game concept. Further, we present the evaluation system and the design of the physiological data placements strategies.

4.1 Game Concept

Wearables provide acceptable accuracy in measuring physiological data [20], though they are not always without controversy [22]. However, as an exercise monitoring instrument [10] and basis for reflection [12] to motivate behavior change, wearables are already being used successfully. This motivates us to integrate wearable technology in our game mechanic. We developed a VR sports game inspired by squash using the 3D engine *Unity*[1]. A virtual target is placed in front of the user (see Fig. 2). The users have a racket in their hand and a virtual watch on their wrist. Behind the participant is a spawning button to

---

[1] Unity Game Engine (Unity), https://unity.com/, visited 06.09.2022.

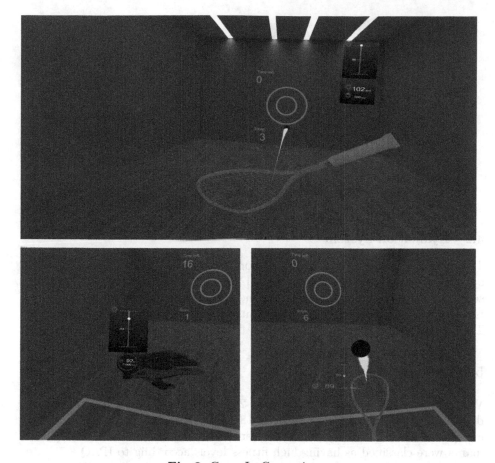

Fig. 2. Cases In-Game views

respawn the ball when the ball is not inside of the gaming area. The goal of the game is to hit the ball with the bat inside of the target and score as many points as possible. For each hit with the ball on the target, the player gets one point. This type of game is well suited because it includes movements with the arms, bending the knees, ducking, and lateral movements, but also requires precise movements. During gameplay, users are provided with a display with physiological parameters (heart rate and calories) and an exercise intensity visualization based on their heart rate. To display the respective exercise intensity, we use classical interval displays. For the exercise intensity measurement (heart rate range), we calculated ±15 beats per minute (BPM) to the average exercise heart rate. We determined this number on the basis of moderate training recommendations and pre-tests.

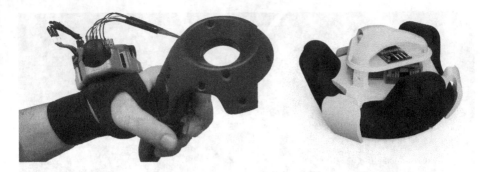

Fig. 3. Evaluation System

4.2 Evaluation System

The evaluation system (Fig. 3) is a custom VR-enabled wearable based on our open-source sensor platform framework [24]. The modules are a core hardware sensor platform, a software framework, and a 3D-printed housing. The heart rate is measured via a pulse oxymeter sensor attached to the handle of the controller. The system uses a Bluetooth connection to communicate with a PC.

5   User Study

We conducted a laboratory study with 29 participants and a within-subjects design. Six participants were between 18–25 years and 23 participants in the group of 25–35. 17 of the participants were female and 12 were male. 17 participants were classified as having high fitness levels according to IPAQ [17] categorization, nine participants had a moderate and three a low level. The participant's highest IPAQ MET was $max = 118320.0$ and the lowest was $min = 396.0$. The average IPAQ MET was $m = 7556.81$. The experiment lasted approximately 35 min per participant. The goal of the study was to find out what effects (if any) placement and presentation of physiological data have on the user experience and usability of VR exergames and sports applications (RQ1), and how the placement and presentation of physiological data affects game performance in particular (RQ2). Further, we investigated whether some placements might lead to e.g. motion sickness, presence reduction, or game impairment. During the experiment, users wore the evaluation system, as described in the section before. We have one nominal independent variable (display placement type). In this context we investigated three different experimental conditions: *In-situ* (Fig. 2, top)-, *HUD* (Fig. 2, bottom left)- and *Watch* (Fig. 2, bottom right)-placement.

5.1 Apparatus

An HTC Vive VR system was used for this study. This included the HMD, a Vive Tracker (2018) and two base stations. To attach the tracker to the wrist, we used a hand strap for HTC Vive trackers. We used the evaluation system as mentioned before and clamped them onto the Vive tracker. The evaluation system was attached to a strap worn around the user's non-dominant hand. The HR sensor was taped to the VR Controller on the handle in an ergonomic way around the shaft.

5.2 Procedure

At the beginning of each session, participants were informed about the general procedure and gave their informed consent to participate. Each user received a brief introduction to the virtual wearable and visualization of the heart rate range. The experiment began with a warm-up session to the VR game. Depending on their skill level, the participants needed 5–15 min of warm-up with the game before they felt comfortable. Then we started to calculate the average heart rate during gaming by using the evaluation system (Sect. 4.2). The range was set at plus and minus 15 bpm (Sect. 4.1) buffer zone from the calculated average heart rate. We introduce the participants to stay within the visualized range throughout the game. For this, they had to monitor their physical data via the different display types. Each condition lasted three minutes of gameplay after which the participants were asked to fill out the NASA-TLX questionnaire to assess their task load during the condition [21]. We did the NASA-TLX scoring directly after each condition so that the user could give their feedback directly. The order of conditions was counter-balanced across participants using the latin square method [13]. After the VR session, we asked the participants in a qualitative interview to provide feedback on different aspects on each display type and experience.

6 Results

We investigated the effects of different placement strategies for physiological data in VR. For this purpose, we performed quantitative analysis and qualitative feedback. The average heart rate in all experiments was $m = 102.35$ BPM (beats per minute). For the *In-Situ* the average BPM was 103.49, for *HUD* $m = 101.12$ BPM, and the *Watch* $m = 102.44$ BPM. The participant with the highest average heart rate had $max = 132.35$ BPM and the one with the lowest average was 78.50 BPM.

6.1 Game Performance

With the quantitative analysis we investigated two game performance aspects. First, the *score* (in-game points) during the game. Second, the seconds out of heart rate range (*SOOR*). Both aspects were checked seperately for each placement. Further, we employed the *NASA-TLX* [21] questionnaire to measure perceived workload for the user. For the three conditions, we used a repeated-measures analysis of variance (ANOVA) for each variable (*score, SOOR, NASA TLX*). For this, we used paired samples t-tests with Bonferroni correction as post-hoc test.

Score. The overall mean *score* during VR training in all three conditions combined was $m = 11.67$ and $\sigma = 5.48$. The maximum *score* in a condition was $max = 32$ and was achieved with the watch placement. The lowest *score* was $min = 2$ (two times), both achieved during the *HUD* placement. The average *score* for the *In-Situ* was $m = 13.31$ and $\sigma = 5.48$. The minimum for this placement was $min = 3$ and the maximum $max = 24$. The average *score* for the HUD was $m = 10.24$ and $\sigma = 4.53$ and the average *score* for the *Watch* was $m = 11.45$ and $\sigma = 6.56$. The minimum *score* during the *HUD* placement was $min = 2$ and the maximum $max = 20$. For the *Watch* was $min = 4$ and the maximum was $max = 32$. We checked the sample distribution using Q-Q Plots and did tests for normality. For the ANOVA we checked for sphericity and the preconditions. There is a statistically significant difference between *In-Situ* and *HUD* scores. The other comparisons showed no statistically significant results (Table 1).

Table 1. Post Hoc Comparisons - RM Factor Score

RM Factor Score	RM Factor Score	Mean Difference	SE	df	t	p_{Turkey}	$p_{Bonferroni}$
In-Situ	- HUD	3.07	1.17	28.0	2.620	0.036	0.042
	- Watch	1.86	1.21	28.0	1.540	0.288	0.405
HUD	- Watch	−1.21	1.31	28.0	−0.921	0.632	1.000

Seconds Out of Range. The mean *SOOR* over all three conditions was $m = 18.73$ and $\sigma = 33.69$. The average *SOOR* for the *In-Situ* was $m = 12.29$ and $\sigma = 24.60$ with $max = 99.48$ and $min = 0$. The average for *SOOR* of the *HUD* placement was $m = 23.049$ and $\sigma = 31.19$ with $max = 113.03$ and $min = 0$. The average *SOOR* for the *Watch* was $m = 20.86$ and $\sigma = 42.91$ with $max = 174.46$ and $min = 0$. Post-hoc test showed no statistically significant results.

Perceived Workload. The overall *NASA-TLX* average score in all three conditions combined was $m = 7.25$. The mean overall attributes for *In-Situ* was $m = 7.09$, for *HUD* was $m = 7.086$ and for the *Watch* $m = 7.39$. There was no statistically significant result between the placements. We also compared all individual dimensions of the perceived workload. For these attributes, no significant results were found.

6.2   Qualitative Feedback

The results showed that 14 of 29 participants preferred the *In-Situ* placement for heart rate range monitoring during VR sport exercise. Ten participants preferred the *HUD* placement for staying inside of the range and five people mentioned that the *Watch* performed best. For the qualitative feedback analysis, the inductive category formation after Mayring [19] was used. Figure 4 shows the subjects' responses to all three conditions summarized by reduction to the essentials.

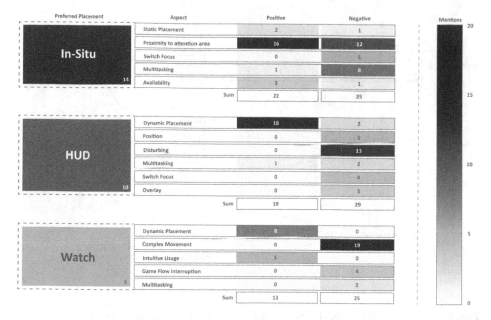

Fig. 4. The color-coding shows the number of mentions. The answers were classified in similar information categories which led to aspect groups. (Color figure online)

7   Suggested Recommendations

We identified specific relationships between response categories. Some responses describe implicit design decisions and influence mentioned problems. Figure 5 shows that the design decision affects aspects that influence the user experience positively or negatively.

In-Situ Design Decisions
Proximity to the Primary Area of Attention. The proximity to the principal game direction (target) was a prominent aspect (28 mentions). This design parameter is closely related to the "Switch Focus" and "Multitasking" problems and influences the degree of "Availability". The negatively perceived aspects could be avoided with suitable positioning of the display (or dynamical positioning) and a prominent design.

Permanent Static Placement. This is similar to the "proximity to the primary area of attention". The game context is particularly relevant. For applications where the principal game direction does not change, the In-Situ placement is suitable.

HUD Design Decisions
Permanent and Dynamic Placement. The dynamic placement of the HUD is the main advantage. It was also seen as disturbing by the participants. The placement of the data in the HUD is nevertheless customizable by the designer.

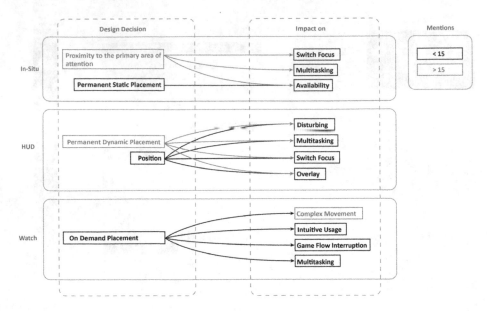

Fig. 5. The model shows which design decisions caused several issues or were important aspects for the user (positive and negative) and thus require higher attention during the design process, or which design decision emerged as a prominent feature from the user survey.

Position. The position of the data in the HUD variant plays an important role in the usability of the display. It can be guided by related work [7,28], but it depends on the context if the game takes place in the middle or lower field of view (FOV) (like in our game) or rather in the upper area.

Watch Design Decision
On Demand. The Watch placement is intuitive to use, but the complex movement made information retrieval a time-consuming burden for users. In some cases, this also led to users being interrupted in their game flow.

8   Discussion and Limitations

The results show that the type of placement does not influence the intensity of the exercise.

We can answer RQ1 ("What effects (if any) do placement and presentation of physiological data have on the user experience and usability of VR exergames and sports applications?") due to the qualitative feedback for our application example. Almost half of the users prefer *In-Situ* placement. *In-Situ* placement is a functional solution to prevent occlusion problems between physiological data display and game objects (for example with *HUD* placement) or elaborate movements to monitor current physical data (for example with *Watch* placement).

Nevertheless, some users criticized the long distance from the data display to the center of the FOV. If the distance of *In-Situ* placement to the center of the FOV can be reduced without disturbing gameplay, users can be supported in their focus-switching task. These aspects can only be determined from our example. For other application contexts, more research needs to be done. In addition, advanced features for the different placements could be implemented, e.g. *In-Situ* display only appears during looking at the display (e.g. by eye-tracking). This would minimize the negative aspect of distraction. Also, the support of placement strategies by additional signal modalities (e.g. sound, vibration) is conceivable.

We can not answer RQ2 ("How does the placement and presentation of physiological data affect game performance in particular?") by the quantitative data we measured. There was a statistically significant difference in the *score* between *In-Situ* and *HUD*. But the other comparisons regarding performance (*score* and *SOOR*) or perceived workload showed no statistically significant differences. We assume that the relatively low speed of the game for the majority of participants (recognizable by the low average heart rate) reduced exercise stress of users. Another indicator for that is the measured low perceived workload. The participants probably had enough time to make use of the display effectively in each condition. Furthermore, the qualitative feedback showed that the *In-Situ* placement was not placed sufficiently close to the center of the FOV. Our design decision could lead to non-optimal use of *In-Situ* placement.

The study design imposes some limitations. The measurements of the evaluation system had a high, but no continuous measurement confidence. Due to the movements of the participants during the VR training, the measuring process could be impaired, so the sensor could not measure any heart rate during these periods. This led to small adjustment issues in the range visualization. The design of the conditions, especially the *In-Situ*, has not been ideally placed. Some users noted that the data is placed too far from the target (center FOV) which is shown in Fig. 4. This may have influenced the evaluation and subjective perception of the users as well as the quantitative results. In addition, the sample of 29 subjects is not yet sufficient to make general statements about the placement of physiological data.

9   Conclusion

In this work, we provide recommendations for the placement of physiological data displays in VR sports applications. Almost half of the users prefer In-Situ placement. We found a statistically significant difference between In-Situ and HUD scores. For other game performance parameters, comparisons showed no statistically significant results. We give recommendations of which placement is appropriate in terms of monitoring performance and maintaining heart rate zones to improve physical training in VR.

Acknowledgements. This work is supported by the DFG within the SPP 2199.

References

1. Ablaßmeier, M., Poitschke, T., Wallhoff, F., Bengler, K., Rigoll, G.: Eye gaze studies comparing head-up and head-down displays in vehicles. In: 2007 IEEE International Conference on Multimedia and Expo, pp. 2250–2252. IEEE (2007)
2. Achten, J., Jeukendrup, A.E.: Heart rate monitoring: applications and limitations. Sports Med. **33**(7), 517–538 (2003)
3. Alves, S., Callado, A., Jucá, P.. Evaluation of graphical user interfaces guidelines for virtual reality games. In: 2020 19th Brazilian Symposium on Computer Games and Digital Entertainment (SBGames), pp. 71–79 (2020). https://doi.org/10.1109/SBGames51465.2020.00020
4. Baumeister, J., et al.: Cognitive cost of using augmented reality displays. IEEE Trans. Visual Comput. Graphics **23**(11), 2378–2388 (2017)
5. Bowman, D.A., Kruijff, E., LaViola, J.J., Poupyrev, I.: 3D User Interfaces: Theory and Practice. Addison Wesley Longman Publishing Co. Inc., USA (2004)
6. Bowman, D.A., Wingrave, C.A.: Design and evaluation of menu systems for immersive virtual environments. In: Proceedings IEEE Virtual Reality 2001, pp. 149–156. IEEE (2001)
7. Chua, S.H., Perrault, S.T., Matthies, D.J.C., Zhao, S.: Positioning glass: investigating display positions of monocular optical see-through head-mounted display. In: Proceedings of the Fourth International Symposium on Chinese CHI (ChineseCHI2016). Association for Computing Machinery, New York, NY, USA (2016). https://doi.org/10.1145/2948708.2948713
8. Costa, M.T.S., et al.: Virtual reality-based exercise with exergames as medicine in different contexts: a short review. Clin. Pract. Epidemiol. Ment. Health **15**, 15 (2019)
9. Davis, M.M., Gabbard, J.L., Bowman, D.A., Gracanin, D.: Depth-based 3D gesture multi-level radial menu for virtual object manipulation. In: 2016 IEEE Virtual Reality (VR), pp. 169–170. IEEE (2016)
10. Düking, P., Hotho, A., Holmberg, H.C., Fuss, F.K., Sperlich, B.: Comparison of non-invasive individual monitoring of the training and health of athletes with commercially available wearable technologies. Front. Physiol. **7**, 71 (2016)
11. Fit, Y.: Yur fit (2022). https://yur.fit/. Accessed 14 Feb 2022
12. Gal, R., May, A.M., van Overmeeren, E.J., Simons, M., Monninkhof, E.M.: The effect of physical activity interventions comprising wearables and smartphone applications on physical activity: a systematic review and meta-analysis. Sports Med.-Open **4**(1), 1–15 (2018)
13. Grant, D.A.: The Latin square principle in the design and analysis of psychological experiments. Psychol. Bull. **45**(5), 427 (1948)
14. Houzangbe, S., Christmann, O., Gorisse, G., Richir, S.: Integrability and reliability of smart wearables in virtual reality experiences: a subjective review. In: Proceedings of the Virtual Reality International Conference - Laval Virtual (VRIC 2018). Association for Computing Machinery, New York, NY, USA (2018). https://doi.org/10.1145/3234253.3234305
15. Index, V.: Field of view (fov) (2008). https://www.valvesoftware.com/en/index/deep-dive/fov. Accessed 8 Feb 2022
16. Jeukendrup, A., Diemen, A.V.: Heart rate monitoring during training and competition in cyclists. J. Sports Sci. **16**(sup1), 91–99 (1998)
17. Lee, P.H., Macfarlane, D.J., Lam, T., Stewart, S.M.: Validity of the international physical activity questionnaire short form (IPAQ-SF): a systematic review. Int. J.

Behav. Nutr. Phys. Act. **8**(1), 115 (2011). https://doi.org/10.1186/1479-5868-8-115

18. Li, Z., Chan, J., Walton, J., Benko, H., Wigdor, D., Glueck, M.: Armstrong: an empirical examination of pointing at non-dominant arm-anchored uis in virtual reality. In: Proceedings of the 2021 CHI Conference on Human Factors in Computing Systems (CHI 2021). Association for Computing Machinery, New York, NY, USA (2021). https://doi.org/10.1145/3411764.3445064

19. Mayring, P.: Qualitative Inhaltsanalyse, vol. 14. UVK Univ.-Verl, Konstanz (1994)

20. Nelson, B.W., Allen, N.B.: Accuracy of consumer wearable heart rate measurement during an ecologically valid 24-hour period: intraindividual validation study. JMIR Mhealth Uhealth **7**(3), e10828 (2019)

21. Pfendler, C.: Zur messung der mentalen beanspruchung mit dem nasa-task load index. Zeitschrift für Arbeitswissenschaft **44**(3), 158–163 (1990)

22. Piwek, L., Ellis, D.A., Andrews, S., Joinson, A.: The rise of consumer health wearables: promises and barriers. PLoS Med. **13**(2), e1001953 (2016)

23. Qian, J., McDonough, D.J., Gao, Z.: The effectiveness of virtual reality exercise on individual's physiological, psychological and rehabilitative outcomes: a systematic review. Int. J. Environ. Res. Public Health **17**(11), 4133 (2020)

24. Queck, D., et al.: SpiderClip: towards an open source system for wearable device simulation in virtual reality. In: Extended Abstracts of the 2022 CHI Conference on Human Factors in Computing Systems (CHI EA 2022). Association for Computing Machinery, New York, NY, USA (2022). https://doi.org/10.1145/3491101.3519758

25. Ragan, E.D., Bowman, D.A., Kopper, R., Stinson, C., Scerbo, S., McMahan, R.P.: Effects of field of view and visual complexity on virtual reality training effectiveness for a visual scanning task. IEEE Trans. Visual Comput. Graphics **21**(7), 794–807 (2015). https://doi.org/10.1109/TVCG.2015.2403312

26. Rothe, S., Tran, K., Hußmann, H.: Dynamic subtitles in cinematic virtual reality. In: Proceedings of the 2018 ACM International Conference on Interactive Experiences for TV and Online Video (TVX 2018), pp. 209–214. Association for Computing Machinery, New York, NY, USA (2018). https://doi.org/10.1145/3210825.3213556

27. Rzayev, R., Mayer, S., Krauter, C., Henze, N.: Notification in VR: the effect of notification placement, task and environment. In: Proceedings of the Annual Symposium on Computer-Human Interaction in Play (CHI PLAY 2019), pp. 199–211. Association for Computing Machinery, New York, NY, USA (2019). https://doi.org/10.1145/3311350.3347190

28. Rzayev, R., Woźniak, P.W., Dingler, T., Henze, N.: Reading on smart glasses: the effect of text position, presentation type and walking, pp. 1–9. Association for Computing Machinery, New York, NY, USA (2018). https://doi.org/10.1145/3173574.3173619

Iterative Design of an Immersive Analytics Environment Based on Frame of Reference

Disha Sardana[1]([⊠])[iD], Nikitha Donekal Chandrashekhar[1][iD], Denis Gračanin[1][iD], Krešimir Matković[2][iD], and Gregory Earle[1][iD]

[1] Virginia Tech, Blacksburg, VA, USA
{dishas9,nikitha,gracanin,earle}@vt.edu
[2] VRVis Research Center, Vienna, Austria
matkovic@vrvis.at

Abstract. Immersive analytics is an active research area that explores human-centric approaches to data exploration and analysis based on spatial arrangement and visualization of data elements in immersive 3D environments. The proliferation of extended reality (XR) technologies amplifies the need for design guidelines to help create coherent user experiences in XR environments. One of the important challenges is the accurate placement and identification of various visual elements. We explore the iterative design of the placement of visual elements and interaction with them in an immersive analytics environment based on frames of reference. The choice of a frame of reference can impact usability, ease of interaction, degree of immersion, and task performance, among other things. Our first design iteration explores the impact of visualization scale for two frames of reference: egocentric and exocentric. In response to the findings from the first study and based on performance measures such as degree of immersion, rank order, and subjective user feedback, tethered frame of reference is added to the second iteration. The second design iteration uses the collected user feedback to explore and compare the advantages and limitations of these three frames of reference. The findings are used to inform design guidelines.

Keywords: Immersive Analytics · Mixed Reality · Embodied Interaction · Coordinated Multiple Views

1 Introduction

The growing interest in extended reality (XR) motivates researchers to study the design of immersive virtual environments (IVE). The goal is to clearly understand the advantages and disadvantages based on the types of IVE, tasks, modalities, and interaction techniques. One of the essential concepts related to human spatial cognition and navigation in these environments is a frame of reference (FOR). FOR is a way of representing how we place various entities in space [9].

It characterizes the relations between the objects and the user in space and is often dependent on the viewpoint, which may or may not be controlled by the user. FOR may impact the extent of immersion, which could affect the usability, learnability, and interaction capabilities of users in various contexts. The effects of FOR have been explored previously in research areas such as flight navigation [23], architectural design [11], scientific visualization [13], immersive analytics [21,24,25], collaborative virtual environments [3,18], memorability studies [7] and auditory research [14,19]. Although various studies have explored the impact of FOR in many different contexts, very few studies have focused on the *design* of IVEs based on FOR.

A user's physical surroundings can vary widely, and this may create practical limits on IVEs. It is challenging to determine where to place visual elements in an IVE. Depending on the scale of visualization, the optimal placement of visual elements may vary. Furthermore, a wide range of techniques can be used to allow a user to interact with the elements. Depending on the type of FOR, it is vital to determine which techniques work efficiently. For example, in terms of interaction techniques, in an FOR where a user is outside of the IVE, raycasting is often used as a selection technique for interactions with distant objects. In contrast, users tend to prefer touch interactions when selecting nearby objects [8]. Researchers investigating the impact of mixed modes that allow seamless switching between touching and pointing have found that users prefer the mixed mode for specific analytical tasks [20].

We focus on some specific visual and interaction elements relevant to the design of an immersive analytics environment. Immersive analytics is an advancing field that lies at the intersection of visual analytics and human-computer interaction, supporting data science, analytical reasoning, and decision-making in immersive 3D environments. A few serious challenges in the field are concerned with the accurate placement of visualizations in space and interaction capabilities with the developed immersive analytics systems [4]. Our primary goal is to evaluate the impact of the visualization scale and, therefore, FOR on the placement of visual elements and disparate interaction techniques in an immersive analytics environment. Our approach utilizes a coordinated multiple views (CMV) paradigm in a mixed reality (MR) environment. A unique aspect of our work is that we focus on interaction with different visual elements in the environment rather than performing analytical tasks, such as finding extrema, counting, sorting, etc. This allows us to isolate the user experience of interacting with the visual elements at various scales. A related goal of the study is to analyze which FOR is preferred by users for some typical interactive tasks in an immersive analytics environment.

2 Related Work

Previous studies have defined broadly two FORs to convey spatial representations: an egocentric FOR and an exocentric FOR (sometimes also called allocentric or geocentric FOR). In general, an egocentric FOR is where the spatial locations are referenced with respect to the point of view of the user. An exocentric FOR is where the locations of entities in space are referenced with respect to a framework external to a user, independent of their location [9].

The definitions of these FORs change somewhat depending on the context and the environment. For example, FORs defined for a *desktop virtual environment (DVE)* by McCormick et al. [13] and Schafer et al. [18] are, egocentric FOR: an immersed perspective of a user's viewpoint inside the virtual environment; exocentric FOR: a bird's-eye perspective allowing a user to view a large portion of the virtual environment; tethered FOR: incorporating the essence of both the egocentric and exocentric FORs, i.e., allowing an immersed but a broader viewpoint than the egocentric FOR, but not as wide as the exocentric FOR; and 'fly' mode: where the users can move in and out of the VE, allowing them to cross the boundaries between egocentric and exocentric FORs.

In Chellali et al.'s [3] work for a *collaborative DVE*, an egocentric FOR is associated with an individualistic profile, and personal pronouns (I, you) are used to specify the locations of objects in the environment relative to the user's own body; for example, "in front of me". In contrast, an exocentric FOR is associated with a teamwork profile, where impersonal pronouns (we, one) are used, and team members refer to elements within their shared environment with respect to the spatial description of the room.

Recently, with advances in head-mounted displays, Wagner et al. [21] studied the effect of FORs based on the scales of data visualization in a fully *virtual reality (VR) environment*. The egocentric FOR is developed at a room-sized scale, designed for walking. Their exocentric FOR is a tabletop-sized environment that occupies 60% of the volume of the room. They introduced a third FOR named 'Huge', which is possible in a fully virtual environment. It allows users to access the data at all heights in their developed space-time cube implementation. Yang et al. [26] explored various ways to visualize geographical maps and globes in a *VR environment*. In their work, an exocentric globe is defined when a user is outside the globe, and an egocentric globe is defined when a user is inside the globe. They also explored two additional viewpoints: a worldwide flat map rendered to a plane in the VR environment and a worldwide curved map projected onto a section of a sphere surrounding the user.

Markov et al. [12] investigated the effect of FOR on visual attention and mental workload using head-mounted *augmented reality displays*. They defined an egocentric FOR where the cues are presented with respect to the user's field of view. In contrast, an exocentric FOR presents cues relative to objects in the surrounding IVE. Bukvic et al., in their studies [2,16] of the human perception of sound in an *immersive auditory environment*, defined an egocentric FOR as body-stabilized, where a user is not allowed to move in the immersive auditory space, but can only move their head or rotate their body while standing at a fixed location. In contrast, an exocentric FOR is defined as world-stabilized, where a user is free to walk in the surrounding space to facilitate the localization of a sound source.

Previous work has shown that egocentric FORs are better suited for focusing on local details, and exocentric FORs work better when learning global concepts [15] and/or grasping the overall structure of the environment [5]. This difference motivates researchers to think about how the technology and interfaces should be designed. Egocentric room-scale exploration in an IVE may significantly reduce mental workload [21]. Egocentric room-scale FOR has also been found to be the fastest in counting tasks [24]. Tasks involving the fine detailing and precise movements of objects work better when a user is in an egocentric FOR [18].

Exocentric FORs, on the other hand, are significantly better in terms of accuracy in an information-seeking task in a VR environment [21]. An exocentric FOR has been found to work better when users search for patterns in datasets [13]. Research has suggested that an exocentric FOR supports global judgments better than the egocentric FOR [22]. Manipulating large objects is also found to be easier and faster in an exocentric FOR [18].

A tethered FOR blends the egocentric and exocentric capabilities to provide users with multiple views of the same problem. It can provide an overview of a problem while allowing users to zoom in for details when required.

The studies described here suggest that no particular FOR performs significantly better in all types of visualization tasks. These findings motivate our research to study the impact of FOR on various visual analytics tasks. We focus our study on how the placement of visual elements within different frames of reference and interaction with them affects the user's experience in an immersive analytics environment.

In the remainder of this paper, our use of the terms egocentric and exocentric FORs most closely follow the definitions of Wagner et al. [21]. Our egocentric FOR is a room-sized environment where users are encouraged to move into the data for exploration and analysis. The exocentric FOR is described as a table-top environment that allows users to look at the data from outside the visualization. In the latter scenario, users are encouraged to move around the visualization instead of walking into it.

3   Problem Definition and Approach

One of the challenges when studying the FOR effects is to choose the appropriate scales for the various FORs. Most studies use the same placement of visual elements for various FORs while conducting experiments [21]. However, this approach may lead to an unfair comparison among various analytical tasks in different FORs. For example, an analytical task asking users to find the minimum value in a histogram plot may depend on the location of the histogram view. The scale of the data visualization is usually large enough in an egocentric FOR, and data may be clearly visible. However, since an exocentric FOR is compact, there may be some occlusions that affect the visibility of some features. Ideally, the location of the histogram view should be optimized to offer the same visibility to users in both views, so the performance of the analytical task can be fairly assessed.

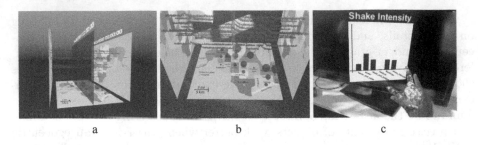

a   b   c

Fig. 1. User study tasks. **a)** Interaction with the slicing plane. **b)** Brushing the data spheres. **c)** Reading labels in the histogram view.

Similarly, the interaction techniques required to perform the analytical task and record the responses of the users need to be optimized for each FOR, so they do not cause any bias while recording user performances of various analytical tasks in experiments studying the impact of FOR. Therefore, there is a need to explore different design approaches in each FOR to have grounds for future experiments studying the efficiency and performance of data analytical tasks in an immersive analytics environment.

We explore various visual and interactive elements in an immersive analytics environment through an iterative design process. Our approach to iteratively improve analysis in an FOR is to design, implement, evaluate, and analyze [6].

3.1   Dataset

For our experiment, we choose the IEEE VAST challenge 2019 dataset [1], which relates to the aftermath of an earthquake. The data contain the time-stamped reports sent from earthquake victims to an emergency response team using custom software (an app). The reports include damage to various utilities such as power, medical facilities, water, and sewer lines, in addition to reports of the shake intensity. Our implementation is motivated by the goal of finding when and where the maximum damage happens. The implementation of this heterogeneous spatial and temporal dataset and key choices for our design are explained in detail in our previous work [17]. The following subsections explain some of the key implementation choices briefly.

3.2   Prototype Design

In the prototype, the map of the affected region is shown on the floor and on the left-hand side and the right-hand side planes (Fig. 1). The left-hand side and the right-hand side planes are placed in parallel to each other to link the geographical information for each region with time-series line plots (Fig. 1a). These time-series line plots show an aggregate of damage reports and, therefore, allow a user to examine the time of maximum damage. A slicing plane is used to navigate along the time axis, which is made semi-transparent to allow users to look at the data despite its presence. The start and end timestamps are placed on top of the left-hand and right-hand side planes. The current timestamp is placed above the slicing plane (Fig. 1a).

One dimension of the data is shown on the floor map as a scatter plot (Fig. 1b), i.e., Power damage. This view allows a user to focus on the power damage reports for all the regions shown on the map at a particular timestamp. Users can interactively select these data spheres over the floor map. This is called brushing, and once a user brushes a data sphere, its color toggles from blue to pink. The technique allows users to focus on the details of the region where the maximum power damage has happened.

One of the coordinated views, a 2D histogram view, is kept in front of the users, as shown in Fig. 1c. The histogram view shows data for the brushed region at the timestamp corresponding to the location of the slicing plane. This view gives details of all other damages happening in the brushed region and at the particular time-stamp selected via the slicing plane. If there is no brushed region, the histogram view may not show anything.

4   Iterative Design

We first explore only two FORs: egocentric and exocentric, since these are the most common FORs used in literature across various domains. The experiment was conducted in a quiet, closed room with dimensions 8.92 m × 9.25 m. The room was well-lit, and the space was unobstructed to allow users to move around freely. The participants wore the Microsoft HoloLens 2 device with a horizontal field of view of 43° and a vertical field of view of 29°. Once users wore the device, they ran an eye-calibration test with a built-in calibration scheme.

In our experiment, the egocentric FOR covered the room floor, allowing users to walk over the virtual floor map. The three egocentric FORs presented to the users are termed Ego-S, Ego-M, and Ego-L, for egocentric FOR at small, medium, and large scales, respectively. The three scales chosen for the egocentric FOR utilized a floor map area of 2 m × 2 m, 3 m × 3 m, and 4 m × 4 m, respectively. These scales were chosen after considerable testing and were large enough to allow users to walk in the space for exploring data. Since the same geographical map was placed vertically on the left-hand side and the right-hand side, the vertical scale of the side planes matched those of the floor map.

The size of the exocentric FOR corresponded to a typical tabletop. The three exocentric FORs are termed Exo-S, Exo-M, and Exo-L, which designate exocentric FORs at small, medium, and large scales, respectively. The three scales chosen for the exocentric FOR utilized a floor map area of 0.4 m × 0.4 m, 0.6 m × 0.6 m, and 0.8 m × 0.8 m, respectively. The center of the exocentric environment was set up at the eye level of the users. This choice kept the prototype at the same relative height despite differences in users' heights.

To interact with the elements in the developed prototype, participants used an air-tap gesture with their dominant hand, i.e., bringing the index finger and thumb closer to each other. This gesture was intuitive, and most participants learned it quickly.

In the pilot studies, feedback from users was gathered to assess the difficulty of the various interaction tasks. In the first pilot study, three different visualization scales for each egocentric and exocentric FOR were investigated, leading to a total of six scenarios. The three scenarios within each FOR were presented to the users in random order, and the order of FOR was also randomized. Switching from one scenario to another was controlled by voice commands such as 'Show Scene 1'. Users were allowed to move in each of the scenes. They were given three tasks in a specified order within each scene as follows:

1. The first task involved interaction with the slicing plane, which is a movable plane used for navigating through the time-series data (Fig. 1a). Users were asked to move the slicing plane to one of six specific dates and times.
2. The second task required the user to brush data spheres of their choice in the floor view (Fig. 1b).
3. The third task asked users to read the nth label from the 2D histogram view (Fig. 1c). We used a 2D view in our study to test the strength of MR environments for exploring both 2D and 3D views simultaneously.

The user study tasks focused on interaction with different visual elements in the environment rather than performing analytical tasks, such as finding extrema, counting, sorting, etc. This approach helped us isolate how users felt about interacting with the visual elements at various scales. After completing the three tasks in the first pilot study, users were encouraged to freely explore the scene. Data relevant to user performance, degree of immersion, and rank order were collected using a survey, which users answered orally while in the data environment. We also recorded participants' level of self-reported immersion for each FOR by using a single question about subjectively perceived immersion [10], i.e., "How immersed did you feel in this data environment?". Additional subjective feedback regarding their responses and experience was collected at the end of the questionnaire.

4.1   User Feedback from the First Design Iteration

The first pilot study includes data from five male and one female participant. Five participants had previously experienced the prototype about 9 months prior to the study, and one was familiar with our work through a presentation. Below we present the qualitative user feedback from this group, where the responses are broken down by their relevance to specific views and tasks.

Within-Egocentric FORs. Overall, users felt that the advantage of Ego-S was that they could get into it and out of it easily and quickly. Ego-L, on the other hand, covered most of the room and was more suitable for an immersive walk-through experience. Users reported feeling more immersed in Ego-L and they noted that the Ego-L experience felt closer to VR. Moving on the map in Ego-L made sense to the users since it led to a more immersive view of everything, which might have helped with data exploration and improved spatial memory.

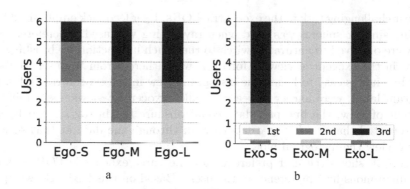

Fig. 2. User rankings for the first design iteration. **a)** Within-egocentric. **b)** Within-exocentric.

On the other hand, we also deduced from the user feedback that the slicing plane was too large in the Ego-L case. Users found it more difficult to interact with because it required both walking and the use of their hands. In the Ego-M and Ego-L scenarios, users reported that the timestamps were too high overhead, making it uncomfortable for them to move the slicing plane while reading the timestamps. In the smaller-scale views, users reported that some of the data spheres were too small to be easily selected using the ray-casting approach. In contrast, the larger views allowed users to walk close to the data spheres, which facilitated easier selection. Hence, brushing the spheres was easiest for users at the Ego-L scale. In relation to the third task, users reported that the labels and the data shown in the histogram view were easy to read in the egocentric views because of the scale of the environment, especially in Ego-M and Ego-L. An observed drawback of the Ego-L scenario was that users must walk to the histogram view to read the labels and view the data, and this added physical effort and took more time to complete the task.

Figure 2a shows user preferences within the three egocentric FORs. Three users prefer Ego-S, and two prefer Ego-L. Based on the rank order and the subjective feedback provided by the users, we opt to investigate these two scales in our second design iteration.

Within-Exocentric FORs. The users reported that exocentric FORs were fine for an overview because all the data were in front of the users, making it easy for them to focus on the visualization. Reading the timestamps was also generally easier in the exocentric views. In terms of limitations, users expressed discomfort while interacting with the slicing plane in the exocentric FORs. Small-scale movements, such as moving the slicing plane to a precise timestamp, were harder to perform accurately in the smaller exocentric views. This was because as the visualization scale decreased, the window of the time-axis slide became smaller too. However, this could be a limitation of the visualization design rather than that of FOR. The study data also revealed that users found brushing to be the most challenging task in the exocentric FORs. User feedback emphasized that brushing smaller spheres was hard when raycasting was used. Therefore, some users were observed to naturally switch to the touch interaction for brushing the spheres in the exocentric views. Moreover, we gathered from the user feedback that while it was easy to locate the histogram view in the exocentric FORs, the histogram labels were harder to see in smaller exocentric views. Depending on the point of view, the line plot data could obscure the histogram labels, and users reported that it felt unnatural to walk through the data at that scale in order to view the histogram plot.

Figure 2b shows the user preference for the three exocentric FORs. Exo-M is the unanimous first preference of the users. Based on this feedback, we opted for the Exo-M scale for the exocentric FOR in the subsequent design iteration.

4.2 Second Design Iteration

Based on the user feedback collected in the first pilot study, three FORs seemed to warrant further study: Ego-L, Ego-S, and Exo-M, which we will now denote as egocentric, tethered, and exocentric, respectively (Figs. 3a, b, and c). The second design iteration involved changes related to the initial position of the prototype, the scale and position of the 2D histogram view, the brushing interaction with the data spheres, and the addition of audio feedback for interaction with the environment.

- User feedback from the first pilot study indicated that the scenes opened too close to the users. We changed the initial position of the tethered FOR such that the entire prototype was in the field of view while allowing the users to step into it and walk over the map when they wanted to focus on details. For the exocentric FOR, we shifted the position downward and forward such that it appeared as it would if placed on a standard height (0.9 m) table. We scaled down the vertical dimension of the egocentric FOR such that the prototype was lower than the height of the ceiling while retaining the immersive walk-through experience.
- As a result of user feedback, we increased the histogram scale to make it easier to read the data and labels. We also changed the location of the histogram in the exocentric FOR, moving it up such that the line plot data no longer obstructed the histogram (Figure 3c).
- During the first pilot study, users also mentioned that brushing the smaller data spheres was often hard to do, irrespective of the FOR. To improve the brushing experience, we increased the size of the data spheres in the second iteration while working to ensure that increasing their size did not cause the bigger spheres to overlap. Another design change in the second design iteration was to make the spheres that were brushed semi-transparent, such that it was easier to read the region names on the floor map below them.
- In the domain of sound, we added an aural notification feature. This was a 'tap' sound that augmented the visual feedback when using the brushing technique. This audible change imitated the real-world experience in which

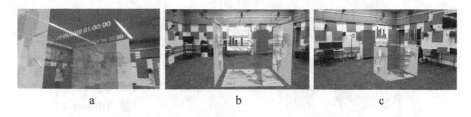

Fig. 3. Three FORs based on various scales of visualization in the second design iteration. a) Egocentric FOR. b) Tethered FOR. c) Exocentric FOR.

tapping on an object generally produces a sound. This feature created a more cognitively coherent experience. An aural notification for FOR switching was also implemented in the second study, in addition to a visual tooltip indicating when users were transported to a new scene.

4.3   User Feedback from the Second Design Iteration

Fourteen users, nine male, and five female, comprised the second pilot study. The user group did not overlap with users from the first pilot study. Five of these users had never experienced AR/VR devices before, four had less than 1 h of previous experience, and two had less than 3 h of prior experience with AR/VR devices. Each of the remaining three had more than 20 h of previous AR/VR experience. Four users had previously experienced our prototype, with three of them only experiencing it once in an hour-long study almost 9 months prior to the second pilot study. Three of the users had previously experienced our work only once in a non-immersive desktop setting (between 9–12 months ago), and one of them had known about our work only through a presentation.

Based on user feedback from the first pilot study, two questions were added to the questionnaire in the second round of the study. They focused specifically on obtaining the experience of users related to reading the timestamps and the histogram labels. Figure 4 shows the data collected for the following user tasks:

- **T1:** Interaction with the slicing plane
- **T2:** Brushing the spheres on the floor
- **T3:** Locating the histogram view
- **T4:** Reading the histogram labels
- **T5:** Reading the timestamps

Figure 4 shows the boxplots of user responses for the task performance in egocentric, tethered & exocentric FORs in the second design iteration. The Kruskal-Wallis test, a non-parametric test, is used to find significant differences in the performance measure for each task in different FORs. Tasks T1, T3, and T4 show no significant differences among the three FORs. In task T5, all the users found it extremely easy to read the timestamps in the exocentric FOR. As the height of the timestamps was increased, it became more difficult for users to

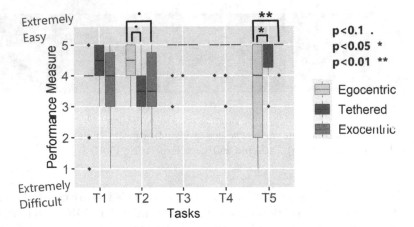

Fig. 4. Performance results for the second design iteration. The Kruskal-Wallis test is used to find significant differences in the performance measure for each task in different FORs.

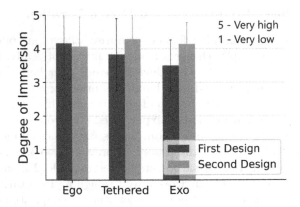

Fig. 5. Mean of the user responses regarding how immersed they felt in Egocentric, Tethered, and Exocentric FORs.

read the timestamps, as evidenced in the statistical analysis (Fig. 4). Brushing the data spheres in the floor view (task T2) was reported to be most comfortable in the egocentric FOR because of the scale. As the visualization scale decreased, brushing the spheres became slightly less easy. Nonetheless, the second design iteration provided significant improvement in brushing the spheres for all FORs, compared to the first design iteration, and showed statistical differences only at an α value of 0.1. The second design iteration also showed improvement in terms of users' self-reported immersion in tethered and exocentric FORs, as indicated in Fig. 5.

Figure 6 shows the rank order among the egocentric, tethered, and exocentric FORs. Nine users ranked the tethered FOR as their first preference. Two of the users preferred the egocentric FOR because they were visually impressed by

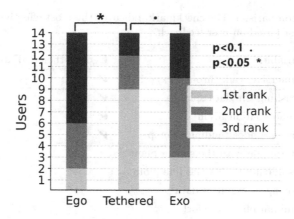

Fig. 6. User rankings for the second design iteration.

the scale of the environment. Three users chose the exocentric FOR to be their preference because of their liking to see everything in one view and thereby get an overview of the data visualization. We used the Kruskal-Wallis test to find significant differences in the user rankings in the three FORs. We infer that the tethered FOR is preferred by users over the Egocentric FOR significantly by an α level of 0.05.

5   Discussion

Table 1 shows the user feedback and the most effective FOR for each variable of interest. The general observations, design limitations, and possible solutions based on the user feedback for interaction and visualization aspects in the three FORs include:

- **Orientation of the time-stamps:** When users moved the slicing plane to a location that was very close to the left-hand side map, the slicing plane's timestamp became occluded by the timestamp over the left-hand side map. An adaptive approach for the orientation of the time stamps dependent on the user's point of view could be developed to resolve this issue. Moreover, when data are placed at an unfamiliar location or at a higher viewing angle, the task should be designed such that the users do not have to use that data often but only gaze at it occasionally.
- **Brushing the data spheres:** In the first design iteration, users report that it is harder to brush the small-sized spheres irrespective of the visualization scale. This led us to increase the size of the spheres in the second design iteration. Despite this change, users experience some minor difficulty in brushing the smaller spheres in the exocentric FOR. Future studies should explore scaling the data values or switching the data variable shown in the floor view. In the context of our data visualization, the values show considerable variation, and that variation needs to be seen to make sense of the data. If there is a

Table 1. FORs comparison. The checkmark indicates the most effective FOR for each variable of interest based on user feedback.

Variables	Ego	Tethered	Exo
Immersive walk-through experience	✔		
Brushing the data spheres	✔		
Sound spatialization	✔		
Spatial understanding of map	✔		
Interaction with the slicing plane		✔	
Visualizing time-series line-plots		✔	
Moving in & out of data		✔	
Minimal physical effort			✔
Overview of data			✔
Finding data correlations			✔
Reading the time-stamps			✔

situation where smaller data values are of higher importance and the brushing technique is significant, then changing the interaction style may help. For example, instead of the '*point and pinch*' technique, '*point*' and using voice command '*Select*'.

- **Time-series line plots:** A large number of line plots made the visualization appear noisy. In the egocentric FOR, once the users were inside the visualization, the time-series line plots became the dominant visual element. One possible approach to mitigate this is to have a disable feature if the tasks do not require that information. For example, if users want to focus on the data in the histogram view solely, a 'turn-off' feature to hide the time-series line plots could be implemented. Another approach is depicting only a single trend line or taking a moving average of the time-series data, which may help users objectively identify meaningful peaks and valleys. An approach like this might reduce the noisy/spiky elements of the data and help eliminate the feeling of visual clutter in the line plots.

- **Adaptive font color:** A constraint relevant to improving the location of the histogram was the overlap between the timestamps and the light-colored background of the histogram. A white font was used for the timestamps since the physical environment may vary, and the background colors may distract the users from reading the text correctly. The white color is preferred for text in an MR environment since it has high contrast with dark backgrounds and is less likely to appear muted in real physical environments. An adaptive system could be developed that assesses the background and uses white font color against dark backgrounds and black against light backgrounds. If not easily implementable, the location of the light-colored elements should be modified such that they do not affect the readability of the white-colored fonts.

6   Conclusion

Our studies examine the design of a multi-modal immersive analytics environment based on various FORs. We examine the strengths and limitations of our data visualization design in each FOR based on the placement of various 2D and 3D views and the interaction techniques. The first pilot study identifies comfortable scales for egocentric and exocentric FORs. A third scale emerged from this study – a tethered FOR. It provides the affordances of both FORs, an overview of the data visualization, and an immersive walk-through experience. The second pilot study incorporated improvements in the user experience in terms of the performance of interactive tasks and the degree of immersion in the three FORs.

This iterative design process allowed us to evaluate and improve the visual and interaction design by laying out the design guidelines for each FOR. It helped us to identify and mitigate biases in terms of visual placement and interaction of various elements for performing fair assessments in the future in different FORs. Based on these pilot studies, we will use informed design guidelines to study the impact of FOR on data analytics tasks in an immersive analytics context. Moreover, studies focusing on sitting, standing, and walking scenarios, and sound versus no sound scenarios will be explored to evaluate the physical and mental demands in various FORs.

References

1. Bukvic, I.I., Earle, G., Sardana, D., Joo, W.: IEEE VIS 2019 conference: VAST challenge (2022). https://vast-challenge.github.io/2019/. Accessed 17 June 2022
2. Bukvic, I.I., Earle, G., Sardana, D., Joo, W.: Studies in spatial aural perception: establishing foundations for immersive sonification. In: International Conference on Auditory Display (2019)
3. Chellali, A., Milleville-Pennel, I., Dumas, C.: Elaboration of a common frame of reference in collaborative virtual environments. In: Proceedings of the 15th European Conference on Cognitive Eergonomics: The Ergonomics of Cool Interaction, pp. 1–8 (2008)
4. Ens, B., et al.: Grand challenges in immersive analytics. In: Proceedings of the 2021 CHI Conference on Human Factors in Computing Systems, pp. 1–17 (2021)
5. Ferland, F., Pomerleau, F., Le Dinh, C.T., Michaud, F.: Egocentric and exocentric teleoperation interface using real-time, 3D video projection. In: Proceedings of the 4th ACM/IEEE international Conference on Human Robot Interaction, pp. 37–44 (2009)
6. Hartson, R., Pyla, P.S.: The UX Book: Agile UX Design for a Quality User Experience, second ed. Morgan Kaufmann, Cambridge, MA (2019)
7. Jund, T., Capobianco, A., Larue, F.: Impact of frame of reference on memorization in virtual environments. In: 2016 IEEE 16th International Conference on Advanced Learning Technologies (ICALT), pp. 533–537. IEEE (2016)
8. Kim, W., Xiong, S.: ViewfinderVR: configurable viewfinder for selection of distant objects in VR. arXiv preprint arXiv:2110.02514 (2021)
9. Klatzky, R.L.: Allocentric and egocentric spatial representations: definitions, distinctions, and interconnections. In: Freksa, C., Habel, C., Wender, K.F. (eds.) Spatial Cognition. LNCS (LNAI), vol. 1404, pp. 1–17. Springer, Heidelberg (1998). https://doi.org/10.1007/3-540-69342-4_1

10. Kraus, M., Weiler, N., Oelke, D., Kehrer, J., Keim, D.A., Fuchs, J.: The impact of immersion on cluster identification tasks. IEEE Trans. Vis. Comput. Graph. **26**(1), 525–535 (2019)

11. Leigh, J., Johnson, A.E., Vasilakis, C.A., DeFanti, T.A.: Multi-perspective collaborative design in persistent networked virtual environments. In: Proceedings of the IEEE 1996 Virtual Reality Annual International Symposium, pp. 253–260. IEEE (1996)

12. Markov-Vetter, D., Luboschik, M., Islam, A.T., Gaugor, P., Staadt, O.: The effect of spatial reference on visual attention and workload during viewpoint guidance in augmented reality. In: Symposium on Spatial User Interaction, pp. 1–10 (2020)

13. McCormick, E.P., Wickens, C.D., Banks, R., Yeh, M.: Frame of reference effects on scientific visualization subtasks. Hum. Factors **40**(3), 443–451 (1998)

14. Navolio, N., Lemaitre, G., Forget, A., Heller, L.M.: The egocentric nature of action-sound associations. Front. Psychol. **7**, 231 (2016)

15. Salzman, M.C., Dede, C., Loftin, R.B.: VR's frames of reference: a visualization technique for mastering abstract multidimensional information. In: Proceedings of the SIGCHI conference on Human Factors in Computing Systems, pp. 489–495 (1999)

16. Sardana, D., Joo, W., Bukvic, I.I., Earle, G.: Perception of spatial data properties in an immersive multi-layered auditory environment. In: Proceedings of the 15th International Conference on Audio Mostly, pp. 30–37 (2020)

17. Sardana, D., Kahu, S.Y., Gračanin, D., Matković, K.: Multi-modal data exploration in a mixed reality environment using coordinated multiple views. In: Yamamoto, S., Mori, H. (eds.) HCII 2021. LNCS, vol. 12765, pp. 337–356. Springer, Cham (2021). https://doi.org/10.1007/978-3-030-78321-1_26

18. Schafer, W.A., Bowman, D.A.: Evaluating the effects of frame of reference on spatial collaboration using desktop collaborative virtual environments. Virtual Real. **7**(3), 164–174 (2004)

19. Voss, P.: Auditory spatial perception without vision. Front. Psychol. **7**, 1960 (2016)

20. Wagner, J., Stuerzlinger, W., Nedel, L.: Comparing and combining virtual hand and virtual ray pointer interactions for data manipulation in immersive analytics. IEEE Trans. Vis. Comput. Graph. **27**(5), 2513–2523 (2021)

21. Wagner, J., Stuerzlinger, W., Nedel, L.: The effect of exploration mode and frame of reference in immersive analytics. IEEE Trans. Vis. Comput. Graph. (2021)

22. Wickens, C.D., Liang, C.C., Prevett, T., Olmos, O.: Electronic maps for terminal area navigation: effects of frame of reference and dimensionality. Int. J. Aviat. Psychol. **6**(3), 241–271 (1996)

23. Wickens, C.D., Prevett, T.T.: Exploring the dimensions of egocentricity in aircraft navigation displays. J. Exp. Psychol. Appl. **1**(2), 110 (1995)

24. Yang, Y., Cordeil, M., Beyer, J., Dwyer, T., Marriott, K., Pfister, H.: Embodied navigation in immersive abstract data visualization: Is overview+detail or zooming better for 3D scatterplots? IEEE Trans. Vis. Comput. Graph. **27**(2), 1214–1224 (2021)

25. Yang, Y., Dwyer, T., Jenny, B., Marriott, K., Cordeil, M., Chen, H.: Origin-destination flow maps in immersive environments. IEEE Trans. Vis. Comput. Graph. **25**(1), 693–703 (2018)

26. Yang, Y., Jenny, B., Dwyer, T., Marriott, K., Chen, H., Cordeil, M.: Maps and globes in virtual reality. Comput. Graph. Forum **37**(3), 427–438 (2018)

A VR Office Applying Modern Search and Filter Concepts for Knowledge Workers

Fanny Weidner[1]([⊠]), Laurenz Bischoff[1], Johannes Bätz[1], Robin Schöppach[1], Peter Meineke[1], Kevin Kambach[1], Jannick Mitsch[1], Andreas Motuzov[1], Martin Mieth[1], Andreas Schulz[2], Melissa Weidlich-Rau[1], Christian Roschke[1], Matthias Vodel[1], Alexander Kühn[1], Tobias Czauderna[1][ID], Daniel Müssig[2], Manuel Heinzig[1], Jörg Lässig[2][ID], and Marc Ritter[1]

[1] Faculty of Applied Computer Sciences and Biosciences, University of Applied Sciences Mittweida, Technikumplatz 17, 09648 Mittweida, Germany
{fanny.weidner,laurenz.bischoff,johannes.baetz,robin.schoeppach, peteralexander.meineke,kevin.kambach,jannick.mitsch,andreas.motuzov, martin.mieth,melissa.rau,christian.roschke,matthias.vodel, alexander.thomas.kuehn.1,tobias.czauderna,manuel.heinzig, marc.ritter}@hs-mittweida.de
[2] Department of Computer Science, University of Applied Sciences Zittau/Görlitz, Theodor-Körner-Allee 16, 02763 Zittau, Germany
{a.schulz,daniel.muessig,j.laessig}@hszg.de

Abstract. Virtual, Augmented and Mixed Reality (VAMR) fields of applications are met with the demand for innovation within the field to build the bridge between the theory of its use and our daily life. However, much of the innovation stops at conceptualising the opportunities that virtual environments offer and instead drifts back to our familiar 2D screens.

This work presents the design of interactive 3D tools for a VR-simulated office space to support tasks related to the workflow of a knowledge worker with the focus on one part of a knowledge worker's workflow: the collection of knowledge. We propose two tools for a VR-Office environment primarily targeting the facilitation of manually acquiring and sorting research publications related to specific topics of interest.

In the process of our work, we created a unique virtual office environment offering two prototype research tools *Synonym Finder* and *Pyramid*, which aim to support a knowledge worker's tasks. Throughout our project, we conducted a qualitative user evaluation with seven participants. Overall, we achieved excellent results with the VR prototype and received insightful feedback to improve our application.

Keywords: Training education and tutoring · Virtual environments · VR tools · Knowledge worker

1 Introduction

Over the last few years, the interest and willingness to invest time and money in Virtual, Augmented and Mixed Reality (VAMR) have steadily increased. More

---

F. Weidner and L. Bischoff—Contributed equally.

© The Author(s), under exclusive license to Springer Nature Switzerland AG 2023
J. Y. C. Chen and G. Fragomeni (Eds.): HCII 2023, LNCS 14027, pp. 101–113, 2023.
https://doi.org/10.1007/978-3-031-35634-6_8

and more VR head-mounted displays (HMDs) get purchased, and Meta did a big push with their investment into the VR space [2].

VAMR fields of applications are met with the demand for innovation within the field to build the bridge between the theory of its use and our daily life. When it comes to VR applications, many drift back to the familiar and everyday use of conventional 2D screens. The possibilities offered by the VR space are not used to their full potential, and the work within them feels less intuitive than it helps. An example of this is the latest Metaverse trailer by Meta[1].

VR is not seen as a completely new universe, with new ways of working on problems and finding novel solutions, but merely as an alternative. This is especially the case when looking at Meta's most recent product, the Meta Quest Pro[2]. The trailer for the Meta Quest Pro demonstrates various methods of incorporating 2D screens into the typical workday and quickly accessing more screens within VR. At the same time, it shows little use of VR, and the creative expression appears minimal. With Meta mainly focusing on solutions for VR and stagnating in creative terms, a considerable number of users are still left wondering if daily work in VR is a viable alternative and if it can be preferential to working with conventional 2D screens.

This contribution describes the conceptualisation and implementation of the two tools *Synonym Finder* and *Pyramid* in a VR prototype aiming to support a knowledge worker's tasks, and evaluates how the VR prototype fares against its 2D counterpart. The working environment and the didactic concept in which our group worked on this project were described by Ritter et al. [12].

With this study, we want to compare whether working in a VR environment can be part of the work process of knowledge workers and highlight possible challenges commonly faced when working in a VR space. We start by highlighting similar and helpful studies on the topic in Sect. 2 followed by a description of our development process in Sects. 3 and 4. Afterwards, in Sect. 5, we present the findings of a qualitative user evaluation that we conducted to measure and compare the performance of a knowledge worker working with 2D tools and with our 3D tools in a VR environment. We finish with a conclusion and an outlook to future work in Sect. 6.

2   Related Work

The four main tasks of a knowledge worker are creating (publications), connecting (with other researchers), finding/gathering and sharing knowledge. In our project, we primarily focused on the aspect of collecting knowledge on the example of the research process. Therefore, our task demanded that we find a solution where the knowledge worker could benefit from interactive 3D tools within a simulated VR office space. At the same time, we need to consider potential health issues to assess them and incorporate them into the general concept of the workflow [1]. If narrowed down to the topic of applying VAMR technology to

---

[1] https://youtu.be/Uvufun6xer8.
[2] https://www.meta.com/de/en/quest/quest-pro/.

improve the workflow of knowledge workers, the amount of scientific work that still needs to be done is immense. Studies on the topic are not always limited to using VAMR in an office environment. Biener [4] proposes using Mixed Reality to help knowledge workers work in other environments and more mobile settings. Exploring the usage of a three-dimensional display in combination with several other tools lays a solid foundation for the concept of a 3D VR environment for knowledge workers.

Another critical factor for us was to improve the productivity in the office. But delivering fast and quality work comes not only from an office that is perfectly designed to do the job but also from how comfortable it is to use, as Haynes [8] suggests. The study describes four components as most important: comfort, office layout, interaction, and negative distractions. Depending on these factors, we have set ourselves the task of designing a VR office that considers all of these aspects. VR is also an excellent way to encourage interaction but quickly leads to distractions. Handling and turning those distractions into a fun VR activity can help ease work stress. The office layout was a key aspect we also took care of by developing different environments as well as dedicated rooms for the tools.

A few studies specifically focus on the comparative productivity of applying VR to knowledge work. Aufegger et al. [3] focus on this problem in a study highlighting various factors that contribute or even hinder productivity in a VR context. In this, we tried to apply concepts to improve the productivity of knowledge workers such as reflecting office spaces and different surroundings.

However, the current state-of-the-art VR technology still has hardware and technical issues that can affect working with VR. These problems include cybersickness, motion sickness, and the weight and warmth of the glasses can hamper navigation in the 3D environment. Although some of these problems, such as moving around in VR, can be solved by technical workarounds, the physical issues that wearing VR goggles create cause users discomfort that cannot be solved with current developments and research [5,6].

A topic that is notably underrepresented in the aforementioned discussions of VR in a knowledge work context is the usage of other forms of representation and interaction that stray away from the usage of 2D screens in a 3D VR environment. VR offers a more creative approach to user experience design and using the potential to apply more innovative concepts is a key aspect of this paper.

3   Concept of the VR Prototype

The concept of our VR prototype as a simplified office portrays the capabilities of a fully 3D interactable environment. It strives to use as little as possible 2D screens to interact with the user. The concept of the prototype is to support every major working field of a knowledge worker, which includes *Research*, *Writing Publications*, and *Presentation of Knowledge*. Collecting and sorting publications can be challenging. The first challenge is to find valuable related topics for the research. Our concept's second challenge is collecting and sorting qualified publications for research.

The *Synonym Finder* and the *Pyramid* are the tools built to contribute to these use cases. Both tools should be objects that are not static within the office space but can be arranged according to the user's requirements. In addition, the two tools require cloud services to store and access respective data.

3.1 Synonym Finder

One aspect that research faces is the collection of documents using general search engines. The knowledge worker researches by using related topics to find useful resources. The *Synonym Finder* therefore acquires possible related topics. It offers the possibility to utilise each search result in the 3D space as a spherical bubble. The result is presented as text in the middle of the bubble. Bubbles serve as UI for the user to interact with. They can start a new search starting with a result or create a mind map out of the results. The development of the tool is inspired by the synonym library of the University of Leipzig [11].

3.2 Collecting and Storing Data

Sorting and reviewing publications for the own research can be time-consuming. A knowledge worker can subscribe to notifications from ResearchGate or Google Scholar. Our concept plans to automate the analysis of this notifications by extracting attached publications and information about them called publication data. Publication data is exemplified through topics, release date, author(s), and title. This data is further stored and can be accessed by the *Pyramid* tool.

3.3 Pyramid

Finding a fitting publication in a vast collection takes time. Therefore, the *Pyramid* can be used by a knowledge worker to sort the collection of publications according to their requirements. We decided that a user should be able to differentiate the resources by their gathered publication data. This way, the documents can be easily accessed, and there should be a coherent overview. It is called *Pyramid* because, in the initial concept, the user should work from bottom to top starting at the bottom with all publications available and working towards the top with the filtered publications. However, based on feedback from the qualitative user evaluation (see Sect. 5), the *Pyramid* was turned upside down to make it feel more natural by working from top to bottom.

3.4 Tutorial

Considering users are not familiar with our tools or not even with working in VR itself, we created a tutorial covering both cases. Delivering the training for both cases an assistant was developed. It presents an overview of tasks (task

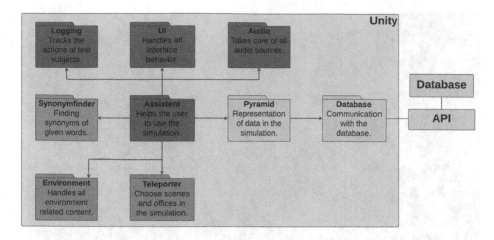

Fig. 1. The system architecture of the VR prototype.

board), teaching users how to interact with VR and our tools. For both cases, different training tasks were developed. These tasks include simple moving in the environment, pointing with the controllers (of the according HMD), grabbing objects like a task board, and interacting with the UI. Every tool and the general interactions have an individual task board. After completing the tutorials, the virtual assistant supporting the user during the tutorial is still available to the user to, e.g., look up the controls.

4   Implementation

This section elaborates on our approaches to developing prototypes based on the concepts and how our Unity application is structured.

The prototype uses Unity Version 2020.3.19f1 with the VR Interaction Framework (VRIF) plugin[3] to enable fast prototyping and SteamVR[4] for compatibility. For further use cases, the PDF Reader Plugin[5] and the Open Thesaurus [10] are used in our prototype. Additionally, we developed a connection between Unity and a database that provides necessary publication data and a Google Drive to access the stored publications. The code is written in C#, additionally we used PHP for a custom API for the database input. Figure 1 shows an overview of the system architecture. Testing took place using the Vive Eye Pro and Valve Index HMDs.

---

[3] https://assetstore.unity.com/packages/templates/systems/vr-interaction-framework-161066.

[4] https://store.steampowered.com/app/250820/SteamVR/.

[5] https://assetstore.unity.com/packages/tools/gui/pdf-renderer-32815.

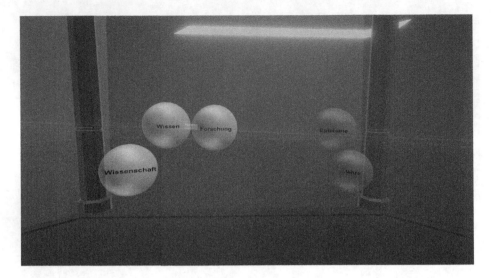

Fig. 2. The *Synonym Finder* with five synonym bubbles which have been arranged by the user. Additionally, the three synonym bubbles "Wissenschaft", "Wissen", "Forschung" on the left have been marked to continue working with them. The bubbles "Wissen" and "Forschung" have been connected to each other.

4.1   VR Environment

The 3D-modelled VR environment comprises different Unity scenes based on our tools. The Main Menu environment offers an introductory options menu to choose starting with or without a tutorial, and instructions for the VR setup. After starting, our developed Tutorial scene helps with a preface to VR interactions and the environment. Afterwards, the user enters the Central Office environment from which they can choose to go to the *Synonym Finder* Room or the *Pyramid* Room.

4.2   Synonym Finder

Our *Synonym Finder* is a tool implemented in our office environment that grants access to "OpenThesaurus" [10], a free online synonym database. The user can enter a word into a search bar which is sent to the Open Thesaurus API. Synonyms received from Open Thesaurus and related topics that match the synonyms are converted into bubbles in the VR environment (see Fig. 2). The VRIF plugin allows double-handed interaction with the bubbles, such as moving, discarding (moving into a bin), and highlighting them (grab them and use a trigger button on the controller of the HMD) to mark them for future searches. The user can also grab two bubbles and press a trigger button to connect these bubbles by a link as part of a mind map.

Fig. 3. The *Pyramid* with filters in the second layer. The first layer (top layer) has been removed by the user and can be seen to the right; the third and fourth layer are still in place below the second layer. The PDF Reader (right) and the login screen for the database (left) can be seen in the background.

4.3   Database and Google Drive

The database and Google Drive serve as the central repositories for all publication data that can be filtered in the *Pyramid*. The *Pyramid* tool requires the user to set up and log into a MySQL database and Google Drive account before use. Google Drive stores all PDF resources the *Pyramid* can access, while the MySQL database holds the publication data which is used for the filter system.

A custom PHP API was developed that enables the communication between the Unity VR application and the database via JSON sent by HTTP requests. The JSON is interpreted by the API which executes the queries and sends the answers back to the application.

4.4   Pyramid

The *Pyramid* is horizontally divided into four layers based on criteria of the publication data and looks like an upside-down pyramid (see Fig. 3). The top three layers are filter layers, including "topic", "publication", "date and author" as filter options. The last layer (bottom layer) is the result layer that offers the user the option to download a publication. Every new layer adds a filter to the search. Each option is represented by objects looking like folders, the folders for each layer have a unique colour. The filters are applied by interacting first with the folder objects followed by the pyramid layer. Based on the choice of the previous layer(s), the next one only shows filtered results. If the user reaches the last layer (the bottom layer), they can download the fitting resources to their computer.

The user can then read the publication with the PDF Reader Plugin in VR or use a PDF reader of their choice outside the VR application.

4.5 Tutorial

The virtual assistant plays a central role in the tutorial. It manages the task board and the tutorial progress. Depending on the current application, the user can refer to the assistant as a guide to monitor all tasks and tips. These are displayed and updated on the task board.

The tutorial and the tasks are structured into sections: VR Tutorial, *Synonym Finder*, and *Pyramid*. Each section has a unique set of tasks supported by voice lines from the virtual assistant to facilitate understanding and make the tasks more accessible.

5 Evaluation

We conducted a qualitative user evaluation to gather feedback on our VR prototype and to compare its applicability with a conventional method and a 2D tool.

5.1 Participants

A total of seven participants took part in our evaluation, all of whom were male and aged between 20 and 33 years. Three stated no prior experience with VR, while the rest split evenly between 1–3 interactions and 5–20 interactions.

The participants were divided into two groups of 3 and 4. One group conducted the 2D part of the evaluation first, followed by the VR part, while the second group started with the VR part. The groups conducted the evaluation in opposite orders to observe and balance out possible effects the first part could have on the second.

5.2 Software and Hardware

We have used an implementation of our VR prototype based on the initial concept for the *Pyramid* (see Sect. 3). To evaluate the usability of this VR prototype, a 2D desktop wireframe prototype (see Fig. 4) was created in addition as a reference point. It followed a similar structure to the *Pyramid* feature of the VR prototype. By testing both prototypes and the conventional method of sorting and searching through an e-mail inbox, one can derive statements about the relative effectiveness of both prototypes.

For the evaluation, we used four head-mounted displays: two Oculus Rift, one Oculus Quest 2 and one HTC Vive Pro. These were connected to four gaming computers capable of running the application smoothly.

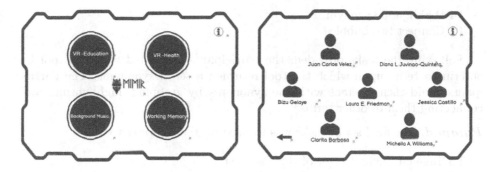

Fig. 4. Wireframe prototype showing research topic selection (left) and author selection (right).

5.3 2D Part

Comparison to Standard E-Mail Processing. Before the participants could evaluate the wireframe prototype, they first had to evaluate how easy it was to get a specific publication via the conventional method of manual e-mail processing. The participants were given an instruction sheet explaining how the e-mail inbox with Google Scholar notifications and the wireframe prototype work. Four inboxes were prepared with 50–100 notification e-mails about newly published publications on various topics. Each participant was given a task sheet describing which publications to search for. Additionally, the participants were tasked to create categories ("work", "education", "tech", and "VR") and to categorise the publications.

Wireframe Prototype. To adequately evaluate the wireframe prototype, all participants were given a set of tasks to complete. They were asked to navigate through the *Pyramid* structure and find specific publications. On average, the time for both 2D parts was 10–15 minutes each.

5.4 Virtual Reality

Tutorial and Guiding. Before evaluating the VR prototype, the participants had to complete the integrated tutorial. During this process, a participant could get helpful information from the virtual assistant to complete several training tasks designed to help them navigating the VR environment and learn actions like grabbing and moving objects.

Synonym Finder. After finishing the tutorial, the participants were guided to another virtual room to evaluate the *Synonym Finder* tool. Here the participants were instructed to complete the following tasks:

- T1 Enter a search term into the search bar.
- T2 Grab and move the *Synonym Finder*.
- T3 Move synonyms in the *Synonym Finder*.

- T4 Highlight a synonym.
- T5 Connect two bubbles.

Following the tasks provided, the participants interacted with the tool by entering a term, upon which the tool returned a set of synonyms. The participants could then interact with the synonyms by grabbing, highlighting, and connecting them to other terms.

Pyramid. The final set of tasks was focused on the *Pyramid* tool:

- T6 Take off the first layer of the *Pyramid.*
- T7 Choose a folder and grab it.
- T8 Take off the next layer.
- T9 Work through the next layers until you reach the bottom.
- T10 Take a PDF out of the final layer and open it in the PDF reader.

The participants tested working through the layers of the *Pyramid* by choosing the respective folder to get to the next layer. Upon reaching the final layer, they chose a publication to read on the integrated PDF reader.

Including the tutorial, the VR section of the evaluation lasted anywhere between 25 to 40 min per participant.

5.5   Data

In order to gauge the usability of the prototype, each participant filled out a questionnaire ahead of the evaluation and two surveys after finishing the two parts of the evaluation. The questionnaire was used to collect demographic information and the level of experience with VR. The first survey was conducted through Google Forms and participants were asked to rate their agreement with the following statements from 1 to 5 on a Likert scale [9]:

- S1 I found the e-mail distribution pleasant to use.
- S2 The e-mails were arranged clearly in the mailbox.
- S3 The wireframe prototype was pleasant to use.
- S4 I understood the categorising system.
- S5 I understood the basics of VR thanks to the tutorial.
- S6 The tutorial helped me to complete tasks in VR later.
- S7 I completely understood how the *Synonym Finder* works.
- S8 I had no problems grabbing bubbles, moving them, or making connections between them.
- S9 I had no problems grabbing the *Pyramid*, taking off layers or grabbing folders.
- S10 I completely understood how the *Pyramid* works.
- S11 I had no problems reading the PDFs in VR.
- S12 Wearing the VR Headset for an extended time was strenuous.
- S13 The checklist helped me to navigate the VR environment.
- S14 The assistant was irritating.

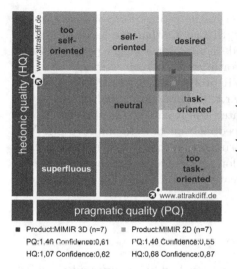

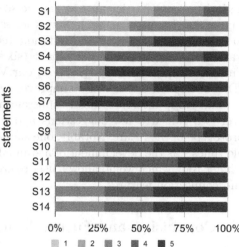

Fig. 5. AttrakDiff survey results (blue – VR prototype, orange – 2D wireframe prototype). (Color figure online)

Fig. 6. Survey results for statements S1 to S14 rated on a Likert scale (1 – strongly disagree, 5 – strongly agree).

For the second survey AttrakDiff was used [7] (see Fig. 5). It utilises semantic differentials to assess the practical viability (pragmatic quality, PQ) and more emotional aspects (hedonic quality, HQ). Lastly, we held a group interview to allow the participants to give feedback beyond the surveys provided.

5.6   Results

There are a few observations one can derive from this qualitative evaluation. First, the VR prototype we built outperformed the 2D wireframe prototype in terms of hedonic quality and was evenly rated concerning the pragmatic quality. Thus, our VR prototype ostensibly provided the participants with more enjoyment. This can be explained by a more stimulating environment and the participants' predominantly inexperience in the field of virtual reality. Furthermore, due to the significantly high AttrakDiff scores for both prototypes, one could assume that both surpass the conventional method. This is corroborated by the results of the other survey (see Fig. 6), which rated this method notably lower than the wireframe prototype and the VR prototype. Only one of the seven participants found that the conventional method was pleasant to use. At the same time the response to statements S3 and S4 show the wireframe prototype and its categorisation system were easy to work with. In general, all participants rated the statements S5 to S11 and S13 about the VR prototype from "neutral" to "strongly agree". However, the *Pyramid* tool of the VR prototype seem to have caused some issues for a few participants as shown by the ratings for S9 (one rating "strongly disagree" and one rating "disagree") and S10 (one rating "disagree"). Surprisingly, the virtual assistant was evidently irritating to the majority of our participants as can be seen in the ratings for S14 (five ratings "agree" or "strongly agree"). Nevertheless, S12 shows that the hardware needs to be refined as the usage of head-mounted displays for a longer period of time was exhausting for most participant (six ratings "agree" or "strongly agree"). Finally, while the hedonic quality of our VR prototype outdoes the result of its 2D counterpart, it can still be improved w.r.t. the pragmatic quality.

The group interview mostly substantiated the results of the surveys. Moreover, we gained a few suggestions and feedback on how to improve our VR prototype in the future. Notably, one such suggestion that was mentioned multiple times was the development of a standalone system analogue to the *Synonym Finder* tool, which would allow a user to create a 3D mind map using the bubbles and connection features.

6 Conclusion and Future Work

The results of the qualitative user evaluation were highly positive and provided valuable feedback to improve our VR application. VR knowledge work, as it is now, is still in its early stages. Commercial products are just getting around to incorporating the initial features beyond a conventional 2D screen. Perhaps, an essential aspect of working within VAMR and making it more accessible to the public with such applications would be to view head-mounted displays as we tried to: as a tool. They can ease aspects of an otherwise dull and drawn-out workflow, a tool that enriches our work and turns it into a vivid experience. The entirety of our project shows only a small portion of what is possible. All of this is the result of a student project, and if more research is conducted in the field, the future of knowledge work in virtual worlds will look bright.

We were able to change vital parts of the *Pyramid* and *Synonym Finder* tool interaction in retrospect of the user evaluation, and more development and progress can and should be made. To align the *Pyramid* concept to the feedback from the evaluation, the bottom layer of the *Pyramid* became the top layer, flipping the 3D model of the *Pyramid* upside down. In addition to that, more mind map uses for the *Synonym Finder* as mentioned before are being introduced and tested out. While working on the prototype, we also created a concept for how it could be envisioned. More tools, rooms, and environments should be added to improve the way of working in the VR space. A healthy approach to the work in VR is a big part that is important to us but still needs to be implemented in our VR prototype. Scheduling and reminders to take off the HMD or to take breaks with exercises are only small features that could ensure a healthy approach since working with the (still) heavy and bulky head-mounted displays might pose yet unknown health risks. In the same way, one should feel comfortable while working. For this, we will create more virtual environments which will be even more adaptable so that each user can adjust them to their own requirements and comfort.

References

1. Aaltonen, I., et al.: State-of-the-Art Report on Knowledge Work - New Ways of Working. Technical report, VTT Technical Research Centre of Finland (2012). https://cris.vtt.fi/en/publications/state-of-the-art-report-on-knowledge-work-new-ways-of-working. Accessed 10 Feb 2023
2. Alsop, T.: Virtual reality (VR) headset unit sales worldwide from 2019 to 2024 (2021). https://www.statista.com/statistics/677096/vr-headsets-worldwide/. Accessed 10 Feb 2023
3. Aufegger, L., Elliott-Deflo, N.: Virtual reality and productivity in knowledge workers. Front. Virtual Real. 3 (2022). https://doi.org/10.3389/frvir.2022.890700
4. Biener, V.: [DC] Mixed reality interaction for mobile knowledge work. In: 2022 IEEE Conference on Virtual Reality and 3D User Interfaces Abstracts and Workshops (VRW), pp. 928–929 (2022). https://doi.org/10.1109/VRW55335.2022.00315
5. Chattha, U.A., Janjua, U.I., Anwar, F., Madni, T.M., Cheema, M.F., Janjua, S.I.: Motion sickness in virtual reality: an empirical evaluation. IEEE Access 8, 130486–130499 (2020). https://doi.org/10.1109/ACCESS.2020.3007076
6. Dörner, R., Steinicke, F.: Wahrnehmungsaspekte von VR, pp. 43–78. Springer, Berlin, Heidelberg (2019). https://doi.org/10.1007/978-3-662-58861-1_2
7. Hassenzahl, M., Burmester, M., Koller, F.: AttrakDiff: Ein Fragebogen zur Messung wahrgenommener hedonischer und pragmatischer Qualität. In: Szwillus, G., Ziegler, J. (eds.) Mensch & Computer, pp. 187–196 (2003). https://doi.org/10.1007/978-3-322-80058-9_19
8. Haynes, B.P.: Office productivity: a theoretical framework. J. Corp. Real Estate 9(2), 97–110 (2007). https://doi.org/10.1108/14630010710828108
9. Likert, R.: A technique for the measurement of attitudes. Arch. Psychol. 22(140), 1–55 (1932)
10. Naber, D.: OpenThesaurus: ein offenes deutsches Wortnetz. In: Sprachtechnologie, mobile Kommunikation und linguistische Ressourcen: Beiträge zur GLDV-Tagung 2005 in Bonn, pp. 422–433 (2005)
11. Quasthoff, U.: Projekt "Der Deutsche Wortschatz". In: Heyer, G., Wolff, C. (eds.) Linguistik und neue Medien [10. Jahrestagung der GLDV]. Deutscher Universitätsverlag (1998)
12. Ritter, M., Roschke, C., Tolkmitt, V.: Finanzmars im Kosmos von Blended Learning. In: CARF Luzern 2019: Controlling. Accounting. Risiko. Finanzen, pp. 327–344 (2019)

A Bibliometric-Based Study of Virtual Reality User Interface Design

Yang Xu and Honghai Zhang[✉]

Beijing Institute of Technology, No. 5 Zhongguancun South Street, Haidian District, Beijing, China
1500266716@qq.com

Abstract. To systematically understand the global characteristics of virtual reality user interface design research in the international context, grasp the current research hotspots and theoretical foundations of virtual reality user interface design, and explore new trends in future development based on current research hotspots. Using the literature related to virtual reality user interface design collected by Web of Science as the data source, we use VOSviewer and CiteSpace to map the scientific knowledge in terms of year output distribution, country, research institution, author, reference co-citation and keyword clustering, and conduct visual analysis to sort out the research. The results show that the overall number of literature in the search area is on the rise, and China and the United States are in the leading position in research. The research hotspots are mainly focused on "user interface design", "hci", "system", "virtual environment", "visualization", etc., and the research status is relatively mature. Human-centered computing, mixed reality, augmented reality, education, experience, immersive virtual reality, interaction paradigm, and 3D modeling become the new trend of future development. The lack of close collaboration between research institutions and authors and the small number of high-production authors are the main limitations of this stage of research.

Keywords: Virtual Reality · User Interface · Design · Bibliometrics · VOSviewer

1 Introduction

Virtual Reality (VR) technology is a new practical technology that has emerged in recent years with the development of information technology. The basic principle is to use computers to simulate virtual scenes to give users an immersive sensory experience, and users can interact with the virtual scenes to immerse themselves in the virtual world for recreation, work, learning, and other operations [1]. User interface (UI) is the medium through which users interact with computer information systems, and it is also the functional carrier and main feature of information products [2]. As a tool for exchanging information between users and devices and their applications, user interface design aims to enable users to easily and efficiently operate devices and their applications

J. Y. C. Chen and G. Fragomeni (Eds.): HCII 2023, LNCS 14027, pp. 114–129, 2023.
https://doi.org/10.1007/978-3-031-35634-6_9

to achieve human-computer interaction and thus achieve the goals that users want to accomplish with the help of such devices and applications. With the development of virtual reality applications, new changes and features have emerged in the user interface design of virtual reality-based interactive systems to meet the product positioning and usage requirements of virtual reality interactive systems.

In recent years, virtual reality has been more and more widely used in various fields of human society. At the same time, user interface design, to guide and assist users in software applications by means of human-computer interaction, plays a very important role in innovating the way of using applications and improving the quality of user experience. The user interface design based on virtual reality interactive systems has many new changes and features compared with computer and mobile electronic device applications, so the research on user interface design based on virtual reality interactive systems has attracted a lot of attention from scholars. At the same time, with the extensive attention of the academic community, the field has produced many literature results, and the knowledge structure is diverse and complex, involving different fields of subject knowledge. It is difficult to objectively analyze the current situation of research in this field and the changes in research hotspots. It is even more difficult to accurately grasp the basic theories and research paradigms of user interface design in virtual reality by relying only on the stage review and summary. Therefore, to comprehensively explore the current situation, research hotspots, and development trends of user interface design in virtual reality, we use knowledge mapping to visualize and analyze the literature related to user interface design in virtual reality based on a scientific bibliography.

2   Study Design

2.1   Data Sources

Since high-quality scientific literature is subject to strict peer review and rigorous scrutiny by published journals, its research results are more representative of the discipline [3]. In this study, the Web of Science database was used as the data source, and the search strategy was set as TS = ((vr OR virtual reality) AND (user interface design)) to ensure the accuracy of the results, and the four commonly used citation indexes in the WOS database, SCI-Expanded, SSCI, CPCI-S and The four major citation indexes, SCI-Expanded, SSCI, CPCI-S and CPCI-SSH, were selected as the search sources. To ensure the comprehensiveness of the test data, the search scope was the full year of journal literature included in the database (i.e., July 1993 to October 16, 2022). To avoid the loss of interdisciplinary literature, the literature sources were not streamlined. The retrieved literature was exported as txt files in the format of "full records and cited references", and articles that deviated from the research topic, missing field information (such as time, keywords, authors, and other key information), and duplicate data were excluded. A total of 820 articles were obtained for further quantitative analysis.

2.2 Research Methodology

In this paper, we use scientific bibliometrics to generate a visual knowledge map by combining CiteSpace and VOSviewer software to analyze the literature output, keyword clustering, and highly cited literature of this research topic and then combine them with relevant parameters for comprehensive analysis. Bibliometrics, which refers to the quantitative analysis of various types of literature to discover potential patterns and information in a large amount of literature data, was first proposed by Pritchard in 1969. Vos viewer, developed by van Eck and Waltman at the Center for Scientific and Technological Research, Leiden University, The Netherlands, in 2009, has a powerful user graphical interface and mapping visualization [4]. CiteSpace is a citation visualization and analysis software developed by Prof. Chaomei Chen's team at Drexel University, USA, and has been widely used for bibliometric analysis in recent years [5]. In the paper, keyword co-occurrence clustering is used to analyze the overall research overview and research perspective of VR user interface research; time-keyword clustering mapping and Burst high-density emergence are used to obtain the research evolution path and future hot trends of virtual reality user interface design from the time dimension; classical highly cited literature is used to analyze the research paradigm of VR user interface research from the micro level; reference co-occurrence is used to explore the underlying theoretical model of VR user interface design research.

3 Results and Analysis of Virtual Reality User Interface Design Literature Measurements

3.1 Basic Characteristics of Virtual Reality User Interface Design Research

The pattern of change in the output of academic literature developed over time is an important method to measure the development trend of research topics and can effectively assess the research dynamics of the discipline [6]. After cleaning and de-weighting, the retrieved data for field extraction, the distribution of annual publications in virtual reality user interface design literature is shown in Fig. 1. as seen from the publications of WOS, the number of annual articles published has generally shown an upward trend since 1993–2022, with the total number of annual publications peaking at 80 in 2019, reflecting some extent that the field has 2019 reached the maturity of the research phase. The development history of international research on virtual reality user interface design has roughly gone through three stages: the initial stage, the development stage, and the maturity stage, in which the first literature was published in 1993, and 1993–2000 was the initial stage of international academic research, with an average annual number of about 4 articles and a slow growth rate; 2001–2015 was the growth period of research, with fast growth of literature output, reaching an average annual The period of 2001–2015 is the growth period of research, and the literature output grows rapidly, reaching an average of about 24 articles per year; 2016–2022 is the maturity period of research, with an average annual output of 61 articles, but the overall fluctuation of the literature output in this period is large and tends to fall back.

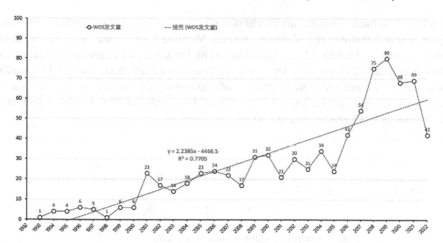

Fig. 1. Annual publication volume distribution of virtual reality user interface design literature

3.2 Distribution of Literature by Country and Research Institution

The number of publications and the number of citations by country/region in the dataset describes the high-producing countries in the research field and their impact. In terms of country/region output, a total of 63 countries/regions worldwide contribute to this research area. Among them, the top 10 countries account for more than 73% of the total number of publications and are important sources of output for virtual reality user interface design research worldwide. The United States is the most productive country in virtual reality user interface design research, with 183 publications (20% of total publications), ranking first in total publications, followed by China (146 publications, 11.4% of total publications), followed by Germany (64 publications), Korea (63 publications), Italy (52 publications), Japan (46 publications), the United Kingdom (42 publications), Canada (35 publications), and Australia (35 publications). In terms of the number of publications, the US and Canada accounted for 11.4% of the total number of publications. In terms of the number of articles published, the US and China both have more than 100 articles, while other countries have much fewer. In addition, the U.S., Australia, and the U.K. have the highest number of citations, with more than 1000 citations. In the research cooperation network, the US, China, Japan, Germany, UK, Korea, and Australia maintain cooperation relations, but they are not close enough and are mostly scattered.

823 research institutions worldwide have conducted research related to "Virtual Reality User Interface Design" from 1993–2022. The number of nodes is 211 and the number of collaborative relationships is 113, see Fig. 2. From the distribution of cooperation strength (number of times of cooperation) within each sub-network, the international cooperation in virtual reality user interface design research is not close and shows strong geographical characteristics, mainly cooperation between institutions in their own countries and regions. The institutional cooperation is regionally concentrated but overall scattered, with "Virginia Polytechnic Institute and State University", "University of Canterbury", "University of the United States", "University of Canterbury" and "Korea

Advanced Institute of Science and Technology" forming three large subgroups of high-impact research institutions. Within the search, Virginia Polytechnic Institute and State University ranked 1st with 14 articles, followed by University of Canterbury (9 articles), Korea Advanced Institute of Science and Technology (9 articles), and the University of Canterbury (9 articles). The University of Canterbury (9 articles), Korea Advanced Institute of Science and Technology (9 articles), University of Illinois (9 articles), and Korea University (8 articles) were next in line.

Fig. 2. Cooperative institutions co-occurrence network

3.3 Most Influential Journals and Author Collaboration Networks

The top 10 most prolific journals in terms of the number of articles published from 1993–2022 and their respective 5-year IFs (impact factors), which account for about 23% of the total number of articles published, are listed in Table 1. The No. 1 publisher is Virtual Reality, with 19 articles, 244 citations, and an impact factor of 4.697; the No. 2 publisher is Applied Scienced-Basel, with 12 articles, 37 citations, and an impact factor of 2.838; the No. 3 publisher is Ieee Transactions on Visualization and Computer Graphics, with 8 articles, 186 citations, and an impact factor of 5.838. Among them, Virtual Reality is the first in terms of output and citations per article (244), reflecting its significant influence in the field of virtual reality user interface design and its core position in this field.

Authors are the smallest unit of literature output and direct contributors to virtual reality user interface design research. By examining author co-citations, it is possible to identify the more active scholars in this field worldwide. Through preliminary analysis of authors' names and disambiguation of authors for co-citation analysis, the largest sub-network of authors' output and collaboration for virtual reality user interface design research was extracted from 2654 authors and 301 pairs of collaborations. The statistics reveal that there are not many authors with high output, among which Mark Billinghurst from the University of South Australia has the most publications with an H-index of 86 and is ranked No. 1 with 11 publications within the search area, followed by Jinmo Kim (Hansung University), Mingyu Kim (Catholic University of Pusan), Ernst Kruijff (Bonn-Rhein-Sieg University of Applied Sciences), Joseph L. Gabbard (Virginia Polytechnic Institute and State University), Bernstein University (University of Pusan), and the University of California. Institute and State University), and Bernhard E. Riecke (Simon Fraser University). In addition, the collaborative research among scholars is not close and mostly sporadic between institutions, which is the status of virtual reality user interface design research.

Table 1. Virtual Reality User Interface Design High Yield Journal Distribution

Ranking	Journals	Country	Number Of Articles Published	Number Of Citations	Average Citations	Five-Year Impact Factor
Virtual Reality	England	19	244	12.8421	5.471	England
Applied Sciences-Basel	Switzerland	12	37	3.0833	2.921	Switzerland
Ieee Transactions On Visualization And Computer Graphics	USA	8	186	23.25	5.37	USA
Presence-Virtual And Augmented Reality	USA	8	88	11	1.835	USA
Computers & Graphics-Uk	England	7	132	18.8571	1.952	England
International Journal Of Human-Computer Studies	England	7	109	15.5714	4.435	England
Multimedia Tools And Applications	Netherlands	7	52	7.4286	2.395	Netherlands
Symmetry-Basel	Switzerland	7	35	5	2.834	Switzerland
International Journal Of Advanced Manufacturing Technology	England	6	36	6	3.471	England
Electronics	Switzerland	5	8	1.6	2.657	Switzerland

3.4 Analysis of Hot Topics and Frontier Trends in Virtual Reality User Interface Design Research

The keywords of literature are a high distillation of the authors' research results, and the keyword frequency can measure the importance of their related topics in a specific field, thus allowing quantitative analysis and comparison of scientists' creative activities. Cooccurrence analysis, as an important element in bibliometric methods, can be used to express the research theme of a discipline or the research direction of a field, and usually contains research objects, research perspectives, research methods, etc. The high frequency cooccurrence keywords reflect the long-term research hotspots of virtual reality user interface design [7]. In this study, 820 documents containing a total of 2339 keywords within the search scope were selected for subsequent analysis.

It is worth noting that not all the keywords provided by the authors were normalized. Therefore, the extracted keywords were normalized using affinity propagation according to the method mentioned by Frey and Dueck (2007) [8]. The algorithm takes as input the similarity matrix of the dataset. In the initial stage of the algorithm, all samples are considered as potential clustering centroids. Also, each sample point is considered a node in the network. The keywords were normalized to ensure that the singular and plural forms of the words were treated consistently, the synonyms were uniform, and the homonyms were clear. For example, "systems" is replaced by "system" and "head mounted display" is replaced by "head-mounted display". Head-mounted display" was replaced by "head-mounted display", and "human-computer interaction" was replaced by "hci". Removed search terms and generic terms such as "VR", "AR", and "MR". Table 2 shows the top 20 keywords, each of which can be considered as a focus of the field to a different degree. Based on the word frequency and co-word frequency, the overall attributes of the keyword or topic can be made clearer.

Table 2 lists the top 20 keywords for virtual reality user interface design. It can be seen that "user interface design", "hci", "system", " virtual environment" and "visualization" are the top 5 high-frequency keywords. Terms such as usability, environment, reality, human-centered computing, and simulation are also considered high-frequency keywords. These keywords provide an overall perception of the research in the field of virtual reality user interface design.

Table 2. Top 20 keywords of virtual reality user interface design

NO	Keyword	Fre	NO	Keyword	Fre
1	User interface design	85	11	user experience	19
2	Hci	50	12	immersion	18
3	System	38	13	interaction	18
4	Virtual environment	34	14	model	15
5	Visualization	28	15	natural user interface	14
6	Usability	27	16	performance	14
7	Environment	25	17	education	13
8	Reality	25	18	experience	13
9	Human-centered computing	24	19	rehabilitation	13
10	Simulation	20	20	interaction design	12

Co-word analysis is based on counting and analyzing the co-occurrence of words in different parts of domain-specific articles [9]. It is generally a method of extracting words from articles in the corresponding subject area and calculating the co-occurrence frequency of each word pair to obtain the correlation between words, for example, using various indexes and mapping subdomains. After frequency analysis, we selected keywords with a frequency of 3 or more, and ran Vosviewer to set the keyword co-occurrence frequency to 3. The keyword co-occurrence clustering formed by 196 keywords after screening and merging synonyms is shown in Fig. 3.

The size of the nodes indicates the frequency of the subject words, and the high-frequency words of the subject words reflect the hot spots of the long-term research on virtual reality user interface design. From Fig. 3, we can see that "vr", "ar", "user interface design", "design" and "hci" are the most frequently co-occurring keywords, indicating that they are most directly related to other keywords and act as a bridge in the research system. The keywords cover a wide range of topics, such as "environment", "surgical training", "mental health ", "eeg", "animation", "architecture", etc., indicating that virtual reality user interface design research is highly comprehensive, with a wide range of research objects and multiple research perspectives. The keyword co-occurrence clustering network also shows that virtual reality user interface design research has strong interdisciplinary characteristics, involving knowledge from different disciplines, such as psychology, human factors, visualization, medical health, emotional computing, eye-tracking, education, etc., reflecting that virtual reality application areas are very broad, empowering various disciplinary fields and opening new paradigms for scientific research.

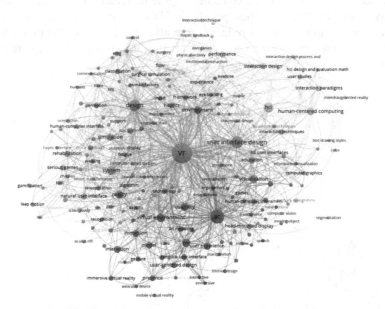

Fig. 3. Keywords co-occurrence clustering network

To further study the frontier themes and development trends of virtual reality user interface design, the average occurrence time of keywords was statistically analyzed separately to obtain Fig. 4 (keyword co-occurrence time zone map), which visually reflects the evolution of the themes of virtual reality user interface design and the development trends of keywords in each time period within the search scope [10]. From Fig. 4, we can find that the keywords that appear on average later than 2018 in the WOS data are mainly mr, game, midi controller, 3d modeling, hci, vr, positional interaction, ar, user-defined interface, creativity, and human-center computing. Creativity, and human-center computing. Figure 5 lists the top 30 keywords in terms of emergence intensity, where the darker part characterizes the years with relatively prominent keyword citation frequency in the literature, reflecting the changing trend of the study. Time zone map (Fig. 4) and Burst keyword high-density emergence (Fig. 5) are both indicators for the analysis of keyword introduction of the time dimension, and they can be cross-referenced to obtain more objective and accurate results [11].

As shown in Fig. 5, the Top 30 emergent keywords are sorted by time, which shows that the WOS research hotspots are divided into 3 distinct intervals. From the keyword evolution of the three intervals, the early research on virtual reality user interface design mainly focuses on virtual environment, construction, hci, vrml, interaction technique, conceptual design, framework, tangible interaction, and so on. Since 2013, with the advancement of technology, the research perspective and focus have gradually shifted to immersion, ar, simulation, serious game, Leap motion, user study, and presence. A comprehensive analysis of the time zone map and the high-density emergent words shows that the future research content of the international academic community is focused on human-centered computing, mixed reality, augmented reality, education, experience, immersive virtual reality, interaction paradigm, 3D modeling, etc. The research trend shows that the research content is refined, more attention is paid to the user's psychological feelings and personalized needs, and a better user experience is created by the immersive interface operation feeling.

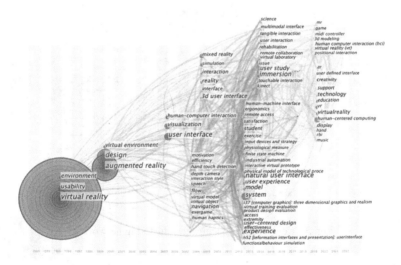

Fig. 4. Keywords Timezone View of WOS

Top 30 Keywords with the Strongest Citation Bursts

Keywords	Year	Strength	Begin	End	1993 - 2022
cad	1993	1.9563	1996	2001	
virtual environment	1993	4.1376	1999	2010	
construction	1993	1.9488	2003	2005	
human-computer interaction	1993	2.9568	2004	2009	
vrml	1993	2.5833	2005	2006	
interaction technique	1993	2.0073	2005	2010	
conceptual design	1993	1.9634	2006	2012	
framework	1993	2.073	2006	2010	
tangible interaction	1993	2.1996	2009	2015	
reality	1993	2.6695	2011	2012	
and virtual reality	1993	2.1749	2013	2017	
immersion	1993	1.9931	2013	2018	
augmented	1993	2.6215	2013	2017	
simulation	1993	2.4043	2014	2019	
serious game	1993	3.0614	2014	2018	
leap motion	1993	2.1307	2015	2018	
user study	1993	1.9334	2017	2020	
presence	1993	1.9195	2017	2020	
system	1993	5.4525	2018	2019	
display	1993	2.2197	2018	2022	
technology	1993	2.3	2018	2020	
human computer interaction (hci)	1993	3.7431	2019	2022	
experience	1993	2.382	2019	2022	
education	1993	3.4761	2019	2022	
immersive virtual reality	1993	2.9452	2019	2020	
vr	1993	2.7297	2019	2022	
human-centered computing	1993	6.5404	2019	2022	
model	1993	2.1381	2019	2022	
interactionparadigm	1993	2.3413	2020	2022	
mixed/augmented reality	1993	1.8953	2020	2022	

Fig. 5. Keywords Burst Term

3.5 Theoretical Foundations of Virtual Reality User Interface Design Research

According to the statistics, the 820 documents in the search area cited 16,971 valid references from 12,650 scholars. As some references are cited in pairs, co-citation relationships are formed, and the entire reference collection forms a co-citation network. The co-citation network shows the evolution of virtual reality user interface design research at the basic knowledge level. The co-citation network was constructed by extracting references with a citation frequency of no less than 4 from 1993 to 2022, and the co-citation clusters consisting of 261 references and 3885 co-citation relationships were generated by the LLR text mining algorithm, as shown in Fig. 6. The top 15 citations ranked classical literature are shown in Table 3.

Among this highly cited literature, number 1 is Ronald T. Azuma's review of augmented reality and its application scope, which summarizes the problems in building effective augmented reality systems and discusses the directions and areas for further research in augmented reality in the future [12]. Number 2 literature reviews the results of a multi-year research project to obtain subjective ratings of 10 workload-related factors from 16 different experiments and proposes a multidimensional rating scale to derive reliable predictions of workload by combining information on the magnitude and source of six workload-related factors [13]. No. 3 investigates visual displays for mixed reality, identifies six categories of mixed reality display environments, and proposes a three-dimensional classification including world perception, reproduction fidelity, and presence level metaphor [14]. No. 4 proposes that 3D UI researchers should develop new research approaches around the concepts of specificity, flavor, implementation, and emerging technologies by looking at the history of 3D UI and the latest technologies of the time and illustrating and discussing the new directions involved in using a real-world case study completed by his team [15]. Number 5 reviewed some of the main confounding factors identified or hypothesized to lead to the presence in virtual environments and developed a long-term tendency questionnaire (ITQ) to investigate relevant factors that may indicate the tendency of individuals to be present in artificial social environments. The Presence Questionnaire (PQ) addresses different factors or features specific to an artificial environment that may influence the experience of the presence or the ability to immerse oneself in that environment [16]. No. 6 addresses a wide range of generic metrics and provides a systematic, reliable, and low-cost usability scale that can be used for the global assessment of system usability [17]. Number 7 describes the development of a simulator sickness Questionnaire (SQ) that is derived from the MSQ using a series of factor analyses and illustrates its use in monitoring simulator performance using computerized SSQ survey data from 3691 simulator hops. The database used for development included more than 1100 MSQs representing data from 10 Navy simulators. SQ provided direct computer or manual scoring, enhanced the ability to identify "problem" simulators, and improved diagnostic capabilities [18]. No. 8 provides a comprehensive review of the current state of development of augmented reality technology and provides a detailed description of the latest developments in augmented reality technology from different aspects such as the definition of the concept, development history, and application directions [19]. Number 9 provides a broad overview of 3-D interaction and user interfaces, discusses the impact of common VE hardware devices on user interaction, as well as interaction techniques for general 3-D tasks and the use of traditional 2-D interaction styles in 3-D environments, with a focus on not only presenting available techniques but also practical guidelines and widely circulated myths for 3-D interaction design, and concludes with a discussion of 3-D interaction design and some example applications with complex 3-D interaction requirements, and provides an annotated online bibliography as a reference for the article [20]. No. 10 presents a knowledge-based design testbed for generating maintenance and repair instructions using head-mounted see-through displays implemented through graphics technology, and based on this study looks at how graphics can be combined with speech and non-speech audio and localized in 3D using spatial sound processors to tell users where to look and what to look for and concludes by suggesting that advances in display technology will soon make wearable see-through displays possible, which will be smaller and lighter, but with higher resolution and a wider field of view [21]. Number 11 describes three forms of body-related interaction: a direct manipulation approach that uses body sensations to help control actions, a physical memory approach that stores and recalls body-related information, and a gestural approach that uses body-related actions to execute commands. The results of informal user trials and formal user studies investigating the usability of body-related interaction techniques are also reported [22]. Number 12 proposes that as a form of communication, real walking is significantly superior to virtual walking and flying (simple, straightforward, and natural), with the greatest differences in subjective presence between flyers and the two types of walkers. In addition, real walkers had higher subjective perceptions than virtual walkers, but this difference was only statistically significant in some models. Virtual walking was found to be significantly improved by detecting footsteps using a head accelerometer, and subjective presence was significantly correlated with the degree to which subjects associated with their virtual bodies (avatars) [23]. Number 13 introduces the authors' vision of human-computer interaction (HCI): 'Tangible Bits'. Tangible Bits allow users to "master and manipulate" Bits at the user's center of attention by coupling them to everyday physical objects and architectural surfaces. Tangible Bits also enable users to use environmental display media (e.g., light, sound, airflow, and water movement in augmented space) to Perceive the background Bits around human perception [24]. No. 14 implements a new highly interactive 3D modeling system, currently called JDCAD, in which the user is equipped with six degrees of freedom input devices. They allow the user to directly manipulate objects in 3D space without having to map the task to 1D or 2D space [25]. The naturalness and intuitiveness of this interaction can greatly improve the efficiency of geometric design, thus making it possible to sketch using a computer. Number 15 describes usability checking methods [26].

The literature above links up most of the fundamentals of virtual reality user interface design, which are of great significance and impetus to the development and improvement of research methods in this field and bring many insights to the subsequent research.

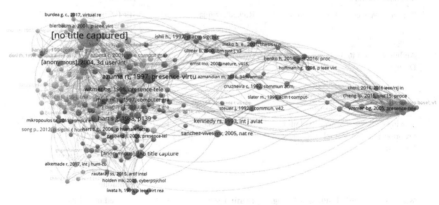

Fig. 6. Reference co-citation clustering network

Table 3. WOS Highly Cited Scholastic Citations

Rank	Title	Author	Year	Source	Number of citations
1	A Survey of Augmented Reality	Ronald T. Azuma	1997	Presence: Teleoperators & Virtual Environments	37
2	Development Of NASA-TLX (Task Load Index): Results of Empirical and Theoretical Research	Sandra G.Hart	1988	Advances in Psychology	21
3	A Taxonomy of Mixed Reality Visual Displays	Paul Milgram	1994	IEICE Transactions on Information and Systems	20
4	New Directions In 3D User Interfaces	DougA.Bowman	2006	The International Journal of Virtual Reality	19
5	Measuring Presence in Virtual Environments: A Presence Questionnaire	Bob G. Witmer	1994	Teleoperators and Virtual Environments	18
6	SUS – A Quick and Dirty Usability Scale	John Brooke	1996	Usability evaluation in industry	14
7	Simulator Sickness Questionnaire: An Enhanced Method for Quantifying Simulator Sickness	Kennedy R S	1993	The international journal of aviation psychology	14
8	Recent Advances in Augmented Reality	Ronald Azuma	2001	IEEE Computer Graphic and Applications	13
9	An Introduction to 3-D User Interface Design	Doug A. Bowman	2001	Teleoperators and Virtual Environments	12
10	Knowledge-Based Augmented Reality	Steven Feiner	1993	Communications of the ACM	12
11	Moving Objects in Space: Exploiting Proprioception In Virtual-Environment Interaction	Mark R. Mine	1997	Proceedings of the 24th annual conference on Computer graphics and interactive techniques	12
12	Walking > Walking-In-Place > Flying, In Virtual Environments	Martin Usoh	1999	Proceedings of the 26th annual conference on Computer graphics and interactive techniques	12
13	Tangible Bits: Towards Seamless Interfaces Between People, Bits and Atoms	Hiroshi Ishii	1997	Proceedings of the ACM SIGCHI Conference on Human factors in computing systems	11

(continued)

Table 3. (*continued*)

Rank	Title	Author	Year	Source	Number of citations
14	Jdcad – A Highly Interactive 3d Modeling System	LIANG, JD	1994	Computers & graphics	11
15	Usability Inspection Methods	Jakob Nielse	1994	Conference companion on Human factors in computing systems	11

4 Conclusion and Discussion

Virtual reality user interface design research has generally shown an upward trend in literature output, with the total number of annual publications peaking in 2019, the overall fluctuation of literature output in the past five years, and a tendency to fall back. "Virginia Polytechnic Institute and State University" "University of Canterbury" and "Korea Advanced Institute of Science and Technology" is the main application institutions in the field of international virtual reality user interface design research. Australia), Jinmo Kim (Hansung University), Mingyu Kim (Catholic University of Pusan), Ernst Kruijff (Bonn-Rhein-Sieg University of Applied Sciences), Joseph L. Gabbard (Virginia Polytechnic Institute and State University), Bernhard E. Riecke (Simon Fraser University), and other authors' teams are the main application teams for virtual reality user interface The main application team of the virtual reality user interface design research.

The keyword clustering shows that the research content of virtual reality user interface design is comprehensive and diversified, "user interface design", "hci", "system ", "virtual environment", and "visualization" are the top 5 high-frequency keywords. Terms such as usability, environment, reality, human-centered computing, and simulation are also hot topics in this field, and these keywords provide an overall perception of the research in the field of virtual reality user interface design. The research hotspots indicate that virtual reality user interface design research is comprehensive, has strong interdisciplinary characteristics, and is at the forefront of the research field. Combining Burst high-density emergence, time-keyword clustering overlay, and the trend of high-frequency keyword distribution in the time zone diagram can predict that future research will focus on human-centered computing, mixed reality, augmented reality, education, experience, immersive virtual reality, interaction paradigm, 3d modeling and so on.

In the field of virtual reality user interface design research, several influential and highly cited pieces of literature have been generated. This literature links up most of the basic knowledge in the field and plays an important role in promoting the development of subsequent research on virtual reality user interface design.

References

1. Zhu, R.: Research and Application of Pen-based Interactive Interface Supported by Handpad. Shandong Normal University, Jinan (2009)
2. Li, R.: Research and application of user interface design for virtual reality interactive system. Sci. Technol. Wind **25**, 65–68 (2022)
3. Chalcraft, A.: Encyclopedia of library and information science (2nd edition). Ref. Rev. **18**(7), 8–9 (2004)
4. Vaneck, N.J., Waltman, L.: Software survey: VOS-viewer, a computer program for bibliometric mapping. Scientometrics **84**(2), 523–538 (2010)
5. Chen, C.: CiteSpace II: detecting and visualizing emerging trends and transient patterns in scientific literature. J. Am. Soc. Inform. Sci. Technol. **57**(3), 359–377 (2006)
6. Chen, Y.K., Jiang, Y., He, R., Wu, X.: Analysis of research progress, hot spots and trends of emotional design based on bibliometrics. Packag. Eng. **43**(06), 32–40 (2022)
7. Callon, M., Courtial, J.P., Turner, W.A.: From translations to problematic networks: an introduction to co-word analysis. Soc. Sci. Inf. **22**(2), 191–235 (1983)
8. Frey, B.J., Dueck, D.: Clustering by passing messages between data points. Science **315**(5814), 972–976 (2007)
9. Callon, M., Courtial, J.P., Laville, F.: Co-word analysis as a tool for describing the network of interactions between basic and technological research: the case of polymer chemistry. Scientometrics **22**(1), 155–205 (1991)
10. Chen, C., Dubin, R., Kim, M.C.: Emerging trends and new developments in regenerative medicine: a scientometric update (2000–2014). Expert Opin. Biol. Ther. **14**(9), 1295–1317 (2014)
11. Kleinberg, J.: Bursty and hierarchical structure in streams. Data Min. Knowl. Disc. **7**(4), 373–397 (2003)
12. Azuma, R.T.: A survey of augmented reality. Presence: Teleoperators and Virtual Env. **6**(4), 355–385 (1997)
13. Hart, S.G., Staveland, L.E.: Development of NASA-TLX (Task Load Index): results of empirical and theoretical research. Adv. Psychol. **52**, 139–183 (1988)
14. Milgram, P., Kishino, F.: A taxonomy of mixed reality visual displays. IEICE Trans. Inf. Syst. **77**(12), 1321–1329 (1994)
15. Bowman, D.A., Chen, J., Wingrave, C.A.: New directions in 3d user interfaces. Int. J. Virtual Reality **5**(2), 3–14 (2006)
16. Witmer, B.G., Singer, M.J.: Measuring presence in virtual environments: a presence questionnaire. Presence **7**(3), 225–240 (1998)
17. Brooke, J.: SUS-A quick and dirty usability scale. Usability Eval. Ind. **189**(194), 4–7 (1996)
18. Kennedy, R.S., Lane, N.E., Berbaum, K.S.: Simulator sickness questionnaire: an enhanced method for quantifying simulator sickness. Int. J. Aviat. Psychol. **3**(3), 203–220 (1993)
19. Azuma, R., Baillot, Y., Behringer, R.: Recent advances in augmented reality. IEEE Comput. Graphics Appl. **21**(6), 34–47 (2001)
20. Bowman, D.A., Kruijff, E., LaViola, J.J.: An introduction to 3-D user interface design. Presence **10**(1), 96–108 (2001)
21. Feiner, S., MacIntyre, B., Seligmann, D.: Knowledge-based augmented reality. Commun. ACM **36**(7), 53–62 (1993)
22. Mine, M.R., Brooks, Jr., F.P., Sequin, C.H.: Moving objects in space: exploiting proprioception in virtual-environment interaction. In: Proceedings of the 24th Annual Conference on Computer Graphics and Interactive Techniques, pp. 19–26. ACM Press, New York (1997)
23. Usoh, M., Arthur, K., Whitton, M.C.: Walking > walking-in-place > flying, in virtual environments. In: Proceedings of the 26th Annual Conference on Computer Graphics and Interactive Techniques, pp. 359–364. ACM Press, New York (1999)

24. Ishii, H., Ullmer, B.: Tangible bits: towards seamless interfaces between people, bits, and atoms. In: Proceedings of the ACM SIGCHI Conference on Human Factors in Computing Systems, pp. 234–241. Association for Computing Machinery Press, New York (1997)
25. Liang, J., Green, M.: JDCAD: a highly interactive 3D modeling system. Comput. Graph. **18**(4), 499–506 (1994)
26. Nielsen, J.: Usability inspection methods. In: Conference Companion on Human Factors in Computing Systems, pp. 413–414. Association for Computing Machinery press, New York (1994)

Teamwork in Software Development and What Personality Has to Do with It - An Overview

Philipp M. Zähl[1]([⊠])(iD), Sabine Theis[2](iD), Martin R. Wolf[1],
and Klemens Köhler[1](iD)

[1] Institute for Digitization, FH Aachen University of Applied Sciences,
Aachen, Germany
{zaehl,m.wolf,k.koehler}@fh-aachen.de
[2] Institute of Software Engineering, German Aerospace Center (DLR),
Cologne, Germany
sabine.theis@dlr.de

Abstract. Due to the increasing complexity of software projects, software development is becoming more and more dependent on teams. The quality of this teamwork can vary depending on the team composition, as teams are always a combination of different skills and personality types. This paper aims to answer the question of how to describe a software development team and what influence the personality of the team members has on the team dynamics. For this purpose, a systematic literature review ($n = 48$) and a literature search with the AI research assistant Elicit ($n = 20$) were conducted. Result: A person's personality significantly shapes his or her thinking and actions, which in turn influences his or her behavior in software development teams. It has been shown that team performance and satisfaction can be strongly influenced by personality. The quality of communication and the likelihood of conflict can also be attributed to personality.

Keywords: teamwork · software · personality · performance · elicit

1 Introduction

Nowadays, software development is mainly done in teams [11,47,86], in order to cope with the growing complexity of IT projects [19]. Teams represent a combination of different people (here: software developers) who have not only professional but also human differences [14,63]. In addition, extra-personal factors such as the characteristics of the leader or the organizational structures of the company also have an effect on teams [17]. Despite this, the software industry has focused primarily on enterprise and development processes [10]. There is now a large body of evidence in the literature that the human characteristics of team members have a significant impact on team performance [55]. Personality traits are particularly important because they shape our actions and thus our

J. Y. C. Chen and G. Fragomeni (Eds.): HCII 2023, LNCS 14027, pp. 130–153, 2023.
https://doi.org/10.1007/978-3-031-35634-6_10

behavior within the team. [49] For example, communication, conflict management, or team climate can be influenced by certain personality traits [75,81,91].
Team performance as a whole can be deliberately improved by taking personality
into account. Thus, when considering team performance, not only professional
but also said human factors of the team should be considered [15]. The purpose
of this paper is to provide an overview of teamwork in software development. To
this end, we will examine how software teams are formed and in what kind of
embedded structures. In addition, we consider the factors that have been associated with high team performance and try to identify which measurable variables
have a high impact. Finally, we look separately at the influence of the developer's
personality on teamwork in software development. To this end, we answer the
following research questions:

- RQ1: How are software development teams defined in the literature and what
  attributes are used to define them?
- RQ2: What impact do team members' personalities have on the team dynamics?

In contrast to other publications on this topic (e.g., [40,56,74]), our focus will
not lie exclusively on the individual developer. Indeed, it has often been studied
how the characteristics of a developer influence other developers or activities of
the team. We want to look at the issue at the team level. Thus, we also deal with
impacts on individuals discovered in the publications, but beyond that, we will
identify additional variables that affect the team or arise from within the team.

The article's structure will be as follows: after having shown the relevance and
our motivation, as well as deriving research questions in Sect. 1, we will introduce
the research method in the Sect. 2. Section 3 contains the results, which will be
evaluated in Sect. 4. Finally, Sect. 5 provides a summary and a description of
future work.

2   Review Methodology

2.1   Search Strategy

This paper follows the search strategy proposed by [22], which consists of three
stages (see Fig. 1): manual and automated searches are performed in the first
stage, followed by a manual reference search in the second stage. Duplicates are
removed in both phases. The third and final stage involves further deduplica-
tion, after which the search is completed. If additional literature is necessary for
contextualizing specific research items, it can be added at this point in the process. The automated search was limited to the databases ACM Digital Library,
Clarivate WebOfScience, Elsevier ScienceDirect and IEEE Xplore.

We excluded papers that meet at least one of the following criteria: (1) being
written in a language other than English, (2) not being accessible on the Web,
and (3) being incomplete documents, drafts, slides of presentations, or extended
abstracts.

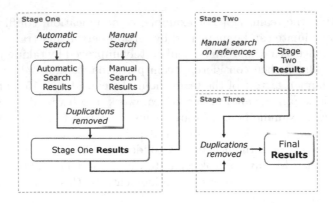

Fig. 1. Stages of search strategy according [22]

2.2 Search String Construction

A search string is created for the automatic search. Relevant keywords were selected for this based on the research questions. These are also extended by some synonyms or family terms for a higher sensitivity [22].

1. Primary search terms: software development, team
2. Secondary search terms: description model, information model, characteristics, formation, personality
3. Synonyms and familiar terms
   (a) software development: software engineering
   (b) personality: character trait

The primary search terms are linked by "And" and should always appear in the results. The secondary search terms, on the other hand, are linked as a whole by "And", but among themselves only by "Or". Thus, at least one of the secondary search terms is used in each result. Synonyms and similar terms complement the corresponding words and are trivially linked to them by "Or". This results in the following search string:

```
("software development" OR "software engineering") AND team
    AND ("description model" OR "information model" OR
    characteristics OR personality OR formation OR "character
    trait")
```

The search string may vary slightly depending on the syntax of the respective database, but the specified keywords should be indicated at least in the title of the reviewed publication.

Figure 2 summarizes the search process performed.

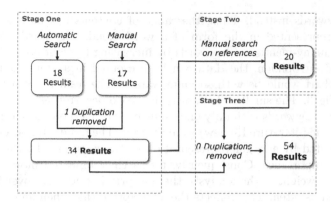

Fig. 2. Search strategy results

2.3   Literature Analysis

After the articles were checked again for suitability and quality, a narrative review was conducted [90]. The data extraction is done using the following scheme: Each article was reviewed section by section, extracting key statements and text passages relevant to our research questions. These were then summarized or at least shortened so that, if possible, the most important statements could be extracted for citation or aggregation. In this phase, another six papers were removed from the analysis due to insufficient data/literature base or because they had no relevance to our research questions despite the above selection criteria. The removed papers are from Stage 1A, where literature was searched exclusively by an automatic search string. Since the selected search procedure does not include a quality or content check, the actually usable literature can only be determined here during the analysis.

Fig. 3. Word cloud representing the keywords of the analyzed papers

In addition, the keywords of all reviewed papers were collected. If no keywords were available for a paper, key terms from the title or abstract were used to fill in keywords instead. Thus, the range of contents of this research could be visually represented in the form of a word cloud. The word cloud allows highlighting many-mentioned keywords by increasing the font size [29,38]. Furthermore, in our opinion, the data can be presented in a more compact form than a bar chart would be with so many values. The resulting word cloud can be seen in Fig. 3. The smallest keywords have two occurrences, and the largest more than 10. Keywords with only one occurrence or methodological procedures (e.g. Systematic Literature Review) were ignored. The more often a term is mentioned (indicated by a larger representation in the word cloud), the higher we valuated its importance. Consequently, terms that appeared more often were given a higher weight in the analysis, thereby prioritizing them over items that were not used as often. This reflects the assumption that phenomena that were mentioned more often are also better studies and understood. Consequently, the word cloud not only shows the abundance of each term, but it also gives an impression of the priorities assigned by us to contents of this paper.

2.4 Extension of the Literature Sample with AI

We decided to conduct another more novel literature review in addition to the conventional approach of a literature review just presented. For this purpose, we instructed the AI research assistant Elicit (https://elicit.org/) to expand our literature sample with suitable literature. The Elicit results were limited to publication years from 2015. In addition, the number of results was extended three times, by using the "Show more results" button in order to reduce the number of less applicable publications. We then supplemented this dataset with information on whether and which personality model was used, and whether the study results indicated a direct impact of personality traits on team dynamics (see RQ2). Table entries no meeting these criteria were excluded.

Not only do we expect to gain more knowledge regarding our research questions, but we used this opportunity to explore the viability of this method for future literature studies. To ensure the possibility to compare both methods, we seperated the results. Thus, Elicit results are listed separately throughout the paper.

3 Results

3.1 Software-Engineering

This paper focuses on teams in software development, which involves the systematic and disciplined approach to the development, operation, and maintenance of software, commonly known as software engineering (SE) [12,54]. Software development requires technical and analytical skills as well as continuous learning to produce high quality results [4,21,31]. Due to the increasing complexity of software projects [19], a division of labor by teamwork has become essential, requiring a range of skills and roles [4] and involving negotiation and communication [26,31]. Effective teamwork is crucial for the success of software projects, and has been associated with communication, coordination, balance of contributions, mutual support, effort, and team cohesion being key factors [28,47,79]. In addition, successful software development requires high organizational and interpersonal skills to manage interactions with customers and identify their needs [10,14]. Meeting budget, time, and quality requirements is critical for software project success, as exceeding the budget is a major reason for project failure [21].

Figure 4 shows the 44 factors and 170 subfactors [18,19] have found to influence the software development process. They created a model consisting of the eight factor classes: organization, business, application, management, requirements, technology, personnel and operation. These classes are assigned altogether 44 factors with again altogether 170 Sub factors.

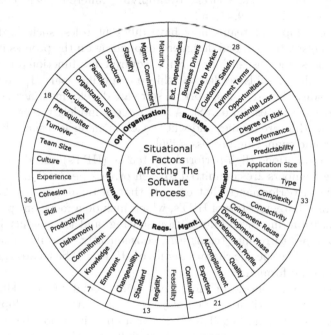

Fig. 4. Situational Factors Affecting the Software Process according to [18,19]

3.2 Teams

Following [6,41,67], we define a team as a group of two or more individuals working together to achieve one or more common goals directed toward a productive outcome. Teamwork is a complex and dynamic system that evolves and adapts based on the interaction of its members and situational requirements [11]. The activities of team members can be divided into task-related and teamwork-related behaviors [77]. It is important to note that teams can operate both inside and outside organizations, as well as over an organizations boundaries. Their defining characteristic is not being part of the same organization but working towards a common goal. Teams are essential for accomplishing complex and difficult tasks, allowing *ordinary* people to achieve *extraordinary* results through a collaborative process [47,76]. Teamwork makes it possible to absorb differences in competence among group members and leads to higher commitment, fidelity and quality of work [28]. As already mentioned, it is not only more effective to work in teams, but also a necessity, due to the increasing complexity and size of software projects [26,43]. Moreover, due to the increasing requirements for knowledge, skills, and abilities, individual employees cannot achieve results independently. Thus the survival and success of software developing enterprises is determined by their ability to form and facilitate teams [28,52]. They can influence the organizational context by applying different team compositions and working methods [11,19,41,85].

Software development teams may have different roles, such as developers, architects, analysts, testers, and designers, depending on the process model used [67]. Some process models, such as Scrum, require cross-functional teams whose members have all the skills needed to achieve a specific goal [21]. New types of teams, such as distributed teams, work on software development across locations, cultures, and time zones [26,65,88]. Agile process models typically have self-managed teams that are smaller and where each member is responsible for both implementing and managing processes [26].

One source mentions High-performance teams (HPTs) and defines them as groups whose members are committed to each other's personal growth and success, resulting in performance that exceeds that of regular teams [28]. Table 1 summarizes the characteristics of HPTs, which include a focus on specific tasks, better organization, improved information sharing, and less conflict [28]. These findings also apply to regular teams [67], consequently, we will not distinguish between the two. The specific characteristics of HPTs will be treated as generally improving team performance.

The effective assignment of employees is a crucial process [4]. Different approaches exist to distribute the employees to the software development roles or to different teams (e.g. [32,71,89]). For example, it is possible to map the software development roles to recommended skills. People who have these skills can then be deployed more appropriately according to the roles. It was shown that this skill-based role assignment has motivated developers [1]. A number of other methods exist for allocating employees to teams or roles. Since this was not within the scope of our research questions, we will not introduce them here.

When putting together teams, the focus should not only be on the technical aspects [21]. Homogeneous teams may be more appropriate than diverse teams in some software development phases (e.g., requirements elicitation) [34]. In principle, however, many studies share the opinion that diverse teams are more advantageous overall: Diversity among team members has been shown to have a positive impact on team performance. This includes diversity in characteristics and perspectives, as well as in knowledge and experience [14,15,43,52,57,61].

Table 1. Characteristics of HPTs for Software Development regarding [28]

Organizational Characteristics	Contextual Characteristics				Technical Characteristics	
Team Diversity	Team Work	Communication	Motivation	Intelligence	Coordination	Managerial Involvement
Team size	Team Leadership	Team Cohesion	Unexpected Challenges	Analytic	Professional Orientation	Restriction of External Influence
Team's autonomy	Personality	Improvisation	Attitude	Less tendency to conflicts	Teamwork Orientation	Performance Evaluation
Work less hours	Organization	Respect	Passion to Teach	Socialization	Focus on Specific Tasks	Competencies of Management
Organizational Commitment	Coprehension	Empathy	Better sharing Information	Confidence	Experience in Propagation	Usage of Resources
Life quality at work	Accountability	Emotional Intelligence	Believe on own abilities	Awareness	Knowledge	Work Tasks Division
Low Turnover	Flexibility	Cognitive Work / Abilities	Tasks Participation		Less Decision Made	Goals Fixing

By having a wider range of perspectives, teams are more likely to come up with innovative solutions to problems. In addition, having a variety of skills and personalities among team members can help distribute work more efficiently and prevent conflict [50]. Depending on the country, the diversity-performance ratio may vary [36]. At the same time, care should be taken to ensure that not only highly qualified specialists are in a team, as this can lead to unproductive conflicts [35].

In conclusion, creating an appropriate team composition is challenging due to the increasing complexity with a growing number of candidates. This problem is classified as NP-hard, making it difficult to test all possibilities. While new research on this topic is emerging, it remains difficult to validate the approaches presented [21].

3.3   Team-Success

In our understanding, a team is successful when it is successful on a project level and on a personal level. We are guided by Hoegl's team effectiveness model [41], which is based on the variables of teamwork quality, team performance and personal success (see Fig. 5). According to this understanding, a successful team achieves quantitative and qualitative goals, provides its team members with satisfaction and learning opportunities, and is based on good professional teamwork.

Teamwork quality is essential to team performance and the personal success of team members. It includes open communication, goal coordination, cooperation, contribution, shared responsibility, and a sense of belonging to the group. [41,43] Soft factors play an important role in maintaining good teamwork quality. Even a mediocre or chaotic team can have good teamwork quality if its members feel they belong and contribute. Some studies define team effectiveness differently (e.g. [47]), such as combining quality and quantity of output with attitudes

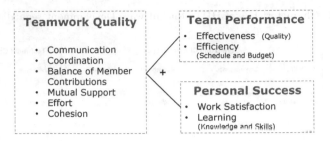

Fig. 5. Team success according to [41]

such as commitment. We do not see any contradiction in terms of content here, just a different perspective on known variables.

Team performance refers to the effectiveness and efficiency of a team in achieving its goals, including adherence to time, budget, and requirements, as well as communication among team members. Soft factors such as team climate, innovation, member competencies, top management support, and leader behavior strongly influence team performance. The performance of individual members also affects this metric. Project management metrics can objectively capture team performance, but if they are not available, subjective feedback from team members can provide a good impression of the project. [17, 24, 39, 41, 67, 70] Further influencing factors are shown in Fig. 6.

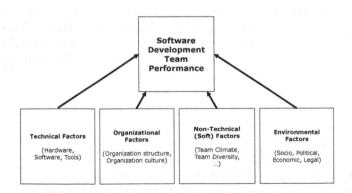

Fig. 6. Factors affecting the software development team performance according to [67]

The personal success factor refers to the success of individual team members, which can be achieved by maintaining satisfaction and providing learning opportunities. Satisfaction is a good measure because it takes into account all personal and subjective factors in the professional and corporate environment. Learning, on the other hand, is a challenging process that allows individuals to feel they are making progress, which requires motivation generated by the learning content or some aspects at the project or organizational level. According to the definition provided for HPTs, inclusion of personal success is their distinguishing feature in contrast to ordinary teams [5, 33, 42].

3.4   Organization and Leadership

A team's success is influenced by the organization and its leaders, who can foster social relationships to enhance team quality. Effective time management is also critical to success, requiring a balance of formal direction, external control, and internal flexibility. In addition, leadership plays a critical role in team success, and it is important to involve team members in the decision making process to maintain the quality of teamwork and prevent sole reliance on the leader. [35, 43, 47].

3.5   Communication

Communication in particular has been cited in many studies as a success factor for teamwork [41, 43, 64]. This does not always have to take place in large quantities if the quality of the exchange is sufficient. Thus, even short, spontaneous, informal conversations can have an extremely positive influence on the team [41]. However, communication within the team becomes more difficult the larger the team [64]. Lastly, by facilitating exchange of information communication enables the formation of shared mental models - which again can be classified as a decisive success factor [41, 72].

3.6   Conflicts

A variety of conflicts can arise during teamwork, including relationship conflicts, which involve personal differences between members, and task conflicts, which involve disagreements about the work. Relationship conflicts have a negative effect on productivity and satisfaction [11, 36, 65], while small task conflicts can have a positive effect [11]. However, higher levels of conflict can lead to better decisions, higher levels of understanding and acceptance, and more employee engagement [20, 27]. When conflicts escalate, the positive effect on team performance disappears [27] and lack of conflict resolution due to time constraints or lack of motivation has a negative impact on team success [48]. Conflict is a common occurrence in team settings and is often caused by perceptions of limited resources, creative or multiple demand tasks, and interdependence among team members [11, 67]. Lack of communication, individual differences, behaviors, and social pressures in teams can also contribute to conflict [65, 67]. Virtual, diverse teams face particular challenges due to communication difficulties, which can lead to more unresolved conflicts and higher error rates in produced software [88].

Trust is useful in conflict resolution and is positively correlated with productivity and team satisfaction [11]. Trust can be divided into cognitive trust, which is confidence in the abilities of others, and affective trust, which is belief in the trustworthy intentions of others. During stressful periods, mistakes and performance deficits can reduce cognitive trust, making affective trust more important for effective teamwork [11]. The interaction between the manager and the development team can also be improved by a high level of trust [77]. Conflict management can reduce the negative impact of conflict on team performance [67,75]. Social loafing is a motivation problem that can be avoided by emphasizing the importance of each team member [11]. Other factors that influence a team's potential for conflict include social differences, generational differences, personal priorities, and ideologies [36].

3.7   Developer Motivation

Motivation is an essential factor for team performance as it moderates the relationship between team input and output, resulting in a significant impact on team performance [17]. Motivation can come from various sources, including job satisfaction, professional and organizational commitment, which have a direct relationship with performance [17]. Employees tend to perform better when they believe their work is important, which provides them with a sense of purpose and intrinsic motivation [17]. Personality traits can also have an impact on motivation, as individuals with high levels of conscientiousness and openness to experience are more motivated to perform their tasks [62]. In addition, higher levels of productivity require higher levels of motivation, which can be achieved by setting clear goals and providing appropriate incentives [69].

3.8   Team-Climate

Team climate describes the ability of a team to create a shared mental model and the ability to obtain, process, and share information with each other, as measured by four dimensions: Vision, Participative Safety, Task Orientation, and Support for Innovation. A positive team climate leads to team satisfaction, better software quality, and higher productivity and team success, while learning and reflection are also important for developers to improve. [2,11,43,78]

3.9   Influence of Personality

The intention of this chapter is to examine what influence the personal characteristics, especially the personality, of software developers have on the team and the software development process. The model assumes that characteristics can be examined on two levels: Superficially based on demographic data (e.g. gender, age, education, origin) or deeply cognitive (personality, knowledge, skills, experiences) [47].

The personality is generally viewed as a dynamic organization of psychophysical systems within the person that produce the person's characteristic patterns of behavior, thoughts, and feelings [22,25]. And since software development processes involve people, the human aspects are a clear part of it [31,59]. Studies show that personality influences the results of software development projects more than technologies, processes or tools [23,31,72]. Meanwhile, improvements in project success, code quality, and individual satisfaction have been demonstrated [22,24]. Project managers can take advantage of these insights to increase developer satisfaction and thus improve product quality [2]. In addition, awareness of other team members' personalities can increase team acceptance and understanding [22,55], as well as motivation [91]. Software project failures can also be reduced by taking the human factor into account [31,63].

In the previous chapters the shared mental model (SMM) was mentioned more often. The mental model is an knowledge structure that helps to describe, explain and forecast our environments [47]. At the same time, they enable information to be selected more easily and corresponding actions to be taken. Without SMM, information may exceed individual mental capacity due to its volume or complexity. [72] Such a mental model can arise at the team level if the team members have the same mental model, or at least same expectations, with regard to a context. In order for a shared mental model to develop, some motivation is needed among team members. However, once the mental model has been developed, trust, satisfaction, cohesiveness, group efficacy and commitment increase. [47] SMM thus has a strong influence on the quality of teamwork and thus on team performance [47].

In software development, the composition of the team is an important factor in the success of a project. Several studies have been conducted to investigate the relationship between team members' personalities and team performance. Several personality models have been used as a basis for exploring the impact of their constituent personality traits. One of the most prevalent being the Myers-Briggs Type Indicator (MBTI). Software developers with high scores in its categories of Agreeableness and Extraversion can have a positive impact on team performance. By taking these personality factors into account, software development teams can become more efficient [2,81]. Empirical studies have identified the ISTJ type as the most prominent among software developers. IS professionals are introverted, highly rational and analytical "thinkers" rather than "feelers" [87].

Moderately diverse teams consisting of members with different personalities reduce the risk of software project failure [79] and increase team success [34]. There is a relationship between team personality composition and team performance and climate [23,81]. Teams with different personality types perform better than the homogeneous ones [67]. Team characteristics, team member characteristics, and the level of intra-group conflict account for half of the variance between the best and worst performing teams [67].

Personal characteristics have a significant impact on team performance and attitude [79,81]. Software developers with low scores on the Five-Factor Model (FFM) of neuroticism have a high ability to handle stress. Teams with low variance in neuroticism have better team cooperation. Team members with high levels of Extroversion take on leadership roles and can improve teamwork. Teams with high levels of Openness have high levels of learning effectiveness. Team members who are too agreeable may avoid discussion. Similar values of Conscientiousness can distribute the burden fairly among team members, resulting in a better team [79]. Extroverted software developers are more effective in group decision making [34]. Teams with extroverted developers achieve higher software quality [61].

A lack of openness can lead to a lack of involvement of other team members, resulting in less knowledge and experience being shared [41]. A high level of openness in the team have been shown to lead to higher team performance [67, 81]. Cognitive differences can have a negative impact on teamwork as unconscious biases and beliefs can lead to coordination difficulties. Even subtle differences in perspectives or assumptions can have a negative effect [47]. Larger, more diverse teams in which team members are not subject to a rigid structure (e.g., in agile development) may increase the frequency of personal incompatibilities and thus the potential for conflict [52]. This finding is also supported by [11], as already mentioned in the chapter on conflict.

Finally, the leadership of software teams is also influenced by the personality of the leader. According to the FFM, the personality dimensions of Openness, Agreeableness, Conscientiousness, and Extraversion in leaders lead to higher project success rates [87]. It has been observed that certain personality types get along better with each other and thus achieve better team efficiency [31,52]. Personality influences the way team members communicate and thus the quality of teamwork [52].

3.10 Elicit-Results

As part of our literature search, we used Elicit to identify additional sources, which are listed in the Table 2, which also includes the main results for each article. The use of Elicit identified additional publications not found by either manual or automated searches, and the Elicit results are consistent with the results of the conventional literature search. For example, other significant personality correlates related to teamwork are listed. Job demands or job satisfaction are also related. We did not find any contradictions between the previous statements and the Elicit results.

Table 2. Elicit Results

Index	Main Findings
[13]	Project manager **personality** (MBTI) does not have a statistically significant influence on project effort deviation. Project manager teamwork behavior, assessed by Belbin's BTRSPI, has a statistically significant influence on project effort deviation
[60]	**Personality** and problem difficulty have a significant influence on the efficiency of pairs
[16]	**Personality** types have an influence on software development tasks choices

(*continued*)

Table 2. (*continued*)

Index	Main Findings
[53]	Top Members occupied critical roles in knowledge diffusion and demonstrated more openness to experience than the Others. No specific **personality** predicted members' involvement in knowledge diffusion
[58]	Conscientiousness is an important factor in the performance of student software engineering project teams. Team identification and the team's performance norms have a substantial influence on the team's performance
[32]	The RAMSET methodology had an impact on the **personality** preferences of Malaysian students. Personality preferences can affect the overall success of a software development project. It is important to consider effective **personality** preferences when creating software development team models and methodologies
[9]	Developers with MBTI type "INTJ" presented lower levels of depth of inheritance tree (DIT) and "slightly" smaller methods (LOC)
[30]	Combination of intuitive (N) and feeling (F) traits is not a suitable **personality** choice for programmer role
[7]	Consciousness, Neuroticism and Openness to Experience have a significant relationship with the Cyclomatic Complexity metric. Extroversion, Agreeableness and Neuroticism have significant relation with metric Coupling between Objects. Extroversion and Neuroticism have a significant relationship with metric Depth of Inheritance Tree
[83]	Personality has a significant relationship with task selection. Intuitive (N) and feeling (F) **personality** traits are primarily focused on the time duration of a project
[91]	Effective team structures support teams with higher emotional stability, agreeableness, extroversion, and conscientiousness **personality** traits. Extroversion trait was more predominant than previously suggested in the literature, especially among agile software development teams
[51]	Intuition and Sensing **personality** traits had an effect on programming performance. Intuition type students wrote more efficient code than Sensing type students. There was a significant linear correlation between Intuition and programming performance
[37]	Tester, team lead, and project manager are found to be ENFJs, which is the least common type in software developers. ISFJ is found to be the most preferable type for web developers and software engineers, with an edge over ENFJ
[8]	The Response For a Classe(RFC) and Weighted Methods Per Class (WMC) metric do not have a significant relationship with MBTI types. Depth of Inheritance(DIT) metric have a significant relationship with MBTI types

(*continued*)

Table 2. (*continued*)

Index	Main Findings
[44]	Productive software development teams can be formed by mapping the Big-Five Personality Traits with the software development tasks
[45]	Personality traits of software developers can be used to match their skills with the tasks associated with their job descriptions
[73]	40 discrete emotions have been reported in software engineering studies, with the most frequent being anger, fear, disgust, sadness, joy, love, and happiness
[3]	Higher levels of introversion are observed in isolated teams that have less contact with customers. Agile software development teams tend to have high levels of agreeableness and conscientiousness
[46]	Extraversion and feeling **personality** traits are the most suitable **personality** traits for requirements analysts/engineers who are assigned the task of requirements elicitation
[84]	A set of tools based on Myers-Briggs type indicators can be used to assess a candidate's natural disposition for a software development role. A mathematical coefficient was developed to evaluate the natural disposition of candidates during the allocation process
[80]	Personality type prediction can be applied in Turkish language. Social media posts can be used to predict MBTI **personality** traits
[68]	We proposed an improved version of Team Homogeneity Index called Weighted Team Homogeneity Index. We found that weights assigned to **personality** traits make a difference and Weighted Team Homogeneity Index is more strongly correlated than Team Homogeneity Index for almost all of the teams
[82]	Conscientiousness emerged as the strongest predictor of life satisfaction. Neuroticism and extraversion were found to predict negative affect and positive affect, respectively

4 Discussion

A three-stage search according to [22] was used as the methodological approach for the literature search. This approach facilitated the combination of manual and automated searches. Although the methodology is valid and reproducible, it could have been improved by adhering to the PRISMA procedure [66] to improve the transparency of the process.

The addition of the AI-based literature search has provided a selection of literature that complements this paper well. These findings suggest that purely Elicit-based studies may yield viable results. As our exploration was very promising, we suggest further research. In order to verify our positive conclusion, the completion of a research cycle is necessary. Based on our empirical findings, theoretical assumptions are possible, which in turn would inform experiments to verify these theories.

To answer RQ1, this paper emphasizes that teams as socio-dynamic systems are complex and cannot be fully described with infinite precision. The paper focuses on the level of teams transforming resources into value and presents Fig. 4 and Table 1 as the most relevant models to answer RQ1 based on the current state of research. In addition, we have presented various team metrics (team success, teamwork quality, team performance, personal success, team climate) that can describe or even measure team functioning. However, our literature review did not provide a holistic picture of personality or team characteristics and their specific impact on teams. Therefore, either our study design was not sufficient to find all relevant research, or further research on these phenomena is needed.

Regarding RQ2, personality was found to have a strong impact on individual processes at the team and product level. Our study demonstrates the benefits of considering personality when planning team-based software development processes. Furthermore, it suggests that certain phases of a software development project rely heavily on personality-based (emergent) phenomena, such as communication. This is because communication can be an output of a process (e.g., in the requirements phase) as well as a variable for various processes that have positive or negative effects. This suggests that future research on personality traits and their influence on communication would be particularly rewarding. In conclusion, we can say that regardless of the specific mechanisms, developers' personalities have been shown to have a strong influence on teamwork and team performance.

The following limitations apply to this study: (1) Some analyzed studies, which measured personality traits using national surveys, can only generalize their statements to the general population software developers to a limited extent. Alternatively, they could suggest that there is no general population and some findings will always remain specific to external circumstances. Thus, their conclusions for teamwork in software development must be treated with caution. (2) With more than 40 search results, the literature search carried out reached a high number of sources for non-automated analyzes. At the same time, only the basic chapters of many papers could be used - a number of papers even had to be removed manually. A specific search string or a topic-separated search might have been appropriate here.

Some studies in our sample (e.g., [86]) report skills such as creativity as important for software teams. The method used in these studies were surveys among software engineers. Thus, they represent the subjective perception of software engineers. Consequently, they did not provide information on how these characteristics correlate to team performance.

In contrast to most of our findings, one study suggested that including personality has little potential for optimization: According to [11], research should be focused in the area of processes and tools, since it is easier to achieve results here. This statement is in contrast to many other publications, that identified or mentioned much untapped potential in the field of personality research in IT [22,26,67,79,91]. The main contradiction found between [11] and other publications is based on a different perspective, as [11] consider the opportunity costs of focusing on efforts on personality-based approaches. We consider this a valuable finding.

It is not possible to clearly identify from the studies when a team can be described as diverse or until when a team can be described as homogeneous, precisely because diversity can be defined differently depending on the context. In the context of personality diversity, we see the greatest insight in the conclusion that it is sensible to record the personality of the team members in the first place. This would allow incompatibilities or even strengths to be identified earlier, and make controlled interventions possible.

5 Conclusion and Future Work

In this paper, we answered the question of what constitutes teamwork in software development and what impact the personality traits of developers have on the team. For this purpose, we conducted a three-stage literature search (n=48) according to [22].

Teams today are necessary constructs in which two or more people work together to achieve a common goal. As teams adapt and develop dynamically through interaction and changes of the environment, they meet the definition are a complex social system.

The personality of a person shapes his behavior patterns, thoughts and feelings. Especially in software development, where a high percentage of communication and work has to be done with people, the personality of the developers has a high, but often still unrecognized value. Although some studies have not been able to prove an effect of personality on programming results, personality does have a high influence on the team. For example, studies have measured an improvement in project success or developer satisfaction.

There are different approaches to assemble teams - but generally the goal is to optimize team performance. We have defined team performance as a metric to evaluate the effectiveness and efficiency in terms of results, but also the team's ability to work and communicate. One finding was that conflicts can have both positive and negative impact on team performance. The challenge is to combine teams in a way that enables more productive forms of conflict while reducing the probability of harmful ones. One finding was that an abundant number of small conflicts can increase understanding and acceptance within the team and thus sustainably improve team performance.

We see several opportunities for further research in this area. One possibility would be to examine the relationships between the team metrics presented here and personalities. Another possibility would be to "translate" one personality type into the type of another personality model, making the findings of different studies comparable. Additionally, it would be helpful to be able to determine which personality constellations have which influence on conflicts.

The contrasting views of [11] should motivate research into the efficiency of personality-based approaches to improve team performance, especially with regard to opportunity costs.

Most of the studies reviewed looked for relationships between individual personality traits and performance. In retrospect, our review revealed three perspectives: The influence of individual personality traits on individual function within a team - which most of the reviewed publications examined; the influence of individual personality traits on team parameters such as "communication" - which some studies focused on; and the influence of the abundance of certain personality traits in teams on team performance - which we tried to make accessible. As we found, the first two perspectives and the results of the publications that include them strongly imply correlations with team performance. However, they do not yet support the formulation of general statements. Further research on all three levels is needed. We suggest that future research should coordinate studies on these three levels. The goal would be to produce generalized findings about the influence of specific personality traits of individuals within teams, as expressed in team dynamics, which in turn determine team performance.

Overall, the resulting model linking performance indicators to personality characteristics could be used by practitioners to assemble teams.

References

1. Acuna, S.T., Juristo, N., Moreno, A.M.: Emphasizing human capabilities in software development. IEEE Softw. **23**(2), 94–101 (2006). https://doi.org/10.1109/MS.2006.47
2. Acuña, S.T., Gómez, M.N., Hannay, J.E., Juristo, N., Pfahl, D.: Are team personality and climate related to satisfaction and software quality? Aggregating results from a twice replicated experiment. Inf. Softw. Technol. **57**, 141–156 (2015). https://doi.org/10.1016/j.infsof.2014.09.002
3. Akarsu, Z., Orgun, P., Dinc, H., Gunyel, B., Yilmaz, M.: Assessing personality traits in a large scale software development company: exploratory industrial case study. In: Walker, A., O'Connor, R.V., Messnarz, R. (eds.) EuroSPI 2019. CCIS, vol. 1060, pp. 192–206. Springer, Cham (2019). https://doi.org/10.1007/978-3-030-28005-5_15
4. Assavakamhaenghan, N., Suwanworaboon, P., Tanaphantaruk, W.: Towards team formation in software development: a case study of moodle: Ecti-con 2020 : 24–27 June 2020, virtual conference hosted by college of computing, prince of Songkla University. In: 2020 17th International Conference on Electrical Engineering/Electronics, Computer, Telecommunications and Information Technology (ECTI-CON) (2020). https://doi.org/10.1109/ECTI-CON49241.2020
5. Aziri, B.: Job satisfaction: a literature review. Manag. Res. Pract. **3**(4), 77–86 (2011)
6. Baker, D.P., Horvarth, L., Campion, M., Offermann, L., Salas, E.: The all teamwork framework. Int. Adult Lit. Surv. Meas. Adult Lit. Life Skills New Framew. Assess. **13**, 229–272 (2005)
7. Barroso, A.S., et al.: Relationship between Personality Traits and Software Quality (2017)
8. Barroso, A.S., de J. Prado, K.H., Soares, M.S., do Nascimento, Rogerio P. C.: How personality traits influences quality of software developed by students. In: Proceedings of the XV Brazilian Symposium on Information Systems. ACM, New York, NY, USA (2019). https://doi.org/10.1145/3330204.3330237

9. Barroso, A.S., Madureira, J.S., Melo, F.S., Souza, T.D.S., Soares, M.S., do Nascimento, R.P.C.: An evaluation of influence of human personality in software development: an experience report. In: 2016 8th Euro American Conference on Telematics and Information Systems (EATIS). IEEE (2016). https://doi.org/10.1109/eatis.2016.7520108

10. Beaver, J.M., Schiavone, G.A.: The effects of development team skill on software product quality. ACM SIGSOFT Softw. Eng. Notes **31**(3), 1–5 (2006)

11. Borrego, M., Karlin, J., McNair, L.D., Beddoes, K.: Team effectiveness theory from industrial and organizational psychology applied to engineering student project teams: a research review. J. Eng. Educ. **102**, 472–512 (2013)

12. Bourque, P., Fairley, R.E. (eds.): SWEBOK: guide to the software engineering body of knowledge. IEEE Computer Society, Los Alamitos, CA, 3.0 edn. (2014). http://www.swebok.org/

13. Branco, D.T.M.C., de Oliveira, E.C.C., Galvão, L., Prikladnicki, R., Conte, T.: An empirical study about the influence of project manager personality in software project effort. In: ICEIS (2), pp. 102–113 (2015)

14. Capretz, L.F., Ahmed, F.: Making sense of software development and personality types. IT Prof. **12**(1), 6–13 (2010). https://doi.org/10.1109/MITP.2010.33

15. Capretz, L.F.: Personality types in software engineering. Int. J. Hum.-Comput. Stud. **58**(2), 207–214 (2003)

16. Capretz, L.F., Varona, D., Raza, A.: Influence of personality types in software tasks choices. Comput. Hum. Behav. **52**, 373–378 (2015). https://doi.org/10.1016/j.chb.2015.05.050

17. Chen, P.C., Chern, C.C., Chen, C.Y.: Software project team characteristics and team performance: team motivation as a moderator. In: 2012 19th Asia-Pacific Software Engineering Conference, pp. 565–570. IEEE (2012). https://doi.org/10.1109/APSEC.2012.152

18. Clarke, P., O'Connor, R.V.: The situational factors that affect the software development process: towards a comprehensive reference framework. Inf. Softw. Technol. **54**(5), 433–447 (2012). https://doi.org/10.1016/j.infsof.2011.12.003

19. Clarke, P., O'Connor, R.V., Leavy, B.: A complexity theory viewpoint on the software development process and situational context. In: Perry, D.E., Raffo, D. (eds.) Proceedings of the International Conference on Software and Systems Process, pp. 86–90. ACM, New York, NY, USA (2016). https://doi.org/10.1145/2904354.2904369

20. Cohen, S.G., Bailey, D.E.: What makes teams work: group effectiveness research from the shop floor to the executive suite. J. Manag. **23**(3), 239–290 (1997). https://doi.org/10.1177/014920639702300303

21. Costa, A., et al.: Team formation in software engineering: a systematic mapping study. IEEE Access **8**, 145687–145712 (2020). https://doi.org/10.1109/ACCESS.2020.3015017

22. Cruz, S., Da Silva, F.Q., Capretz, L.F.: Forty years of research on personality in software engineering: a mapping study. Comput. Hum. Behav. **46**, 94–113 (2015). https://doi.org/10.1016/j.chb.2014.12.008

23. Cruz, S., Da Silva, F., Monteiro, C., Santos, C.F., dos Santos, M.T.: Personality in software engineering: preliminary findings from a systematic literature review. In: 15th Annual Conference on Evaluation & Assessment in Software Engineering (EASE 2011), pp. 1–10. IET (2011). https://doi.org/10.1049/ic.2011.0001

24. Da Silva, F.Q., et al.: Team building criteria in software projects: a mix-method replicated study. Inf. Softw. Technol. **55**(7), 1316–1340 (2013). https://doi.org/10.1016/j.infsof.2012.11.006

25. Dafoulas, G.A., Macaulay, L.A.: Facilitating group formation and role allocation in software engineering groups. In: Proceedings ACS/IEEE International Conference on Computer Systems and Applications, pp. 352–359. IEEE Computer Society (2001). https://doi.org/10.1109/AICCSA.2001.934012

26. Dingsoyr, T., Dyba, T.: Team effectiveness in software development: human and cooperative aspects in team effectiveness models and priorities for future studies. In: 2012 5th International Workshop on Co-operative and Human Aspects of Software Engineering (CHASE), pp. 27–29. IEEE (2012). https://doi.org/10.1109/CHASE.2012.6223016

27. de Dreu, C.K.W., Weingart, L.R.: Task versus relationship conflict, team performance, and team member satisfaction: a meta-analysis. J. Appl. Psychol. **88**(4), 741–749 (2003). https://doi.org/10.1037/0021-9010.88.4.741

28. Dutra, A.C.S., Prikladnicki, R., Conte, T.: What are the main characteristics of high performance teams for software development? In: Proceedings of the 17th International Conference on Enterprise Information Systems, pp. 145–152. SCITEPRESS - Science and and Technology Publications (2015). https://doi.org/10.5220/0005375601450152

29. Felix, C., Franconeri, S., Bertini, E.: Taking word clouds apart: an empirical investigation of the design space for keyword summaries. IEEE Trans. Vis. Comput. Graph. **24**(1), 657–666 (2018). https://doi.org/10.1109/TVCG.2017.2746018

30. Gilal, A.R., Jaafar, J., Abro, A., Omar, M., Basri, S., Saleem, M.Q.: Effective personality preferences of software programmer: a systematic review (2017)

31. Gilal, A.R., Jaafar, J., Basri, S., Omar, M., Tunio, M.Z.: Making programmer suitable for team-leader: software team composition based on personality types. In: 2015 International Symposium on Mathematical Sciences and Computing Research (iSMSC), pp. 78–82. IEEE (2015). https://doi.org/10.1109/ISMSC.2015.7594031

32. Gilal, A.R., Jaafar, J., Omar, M., Basri, S., Waqas, A.: A rule-based model for software development team composition: team leader role with personality types and gender classification. Inf. Softw. Technol. **74**, 105–113 (2016). https://doi.org/10.1016/j.infsof.2016.02.007

33. Gopalan, V., Bakar, J.A.A., Zulkifli, A.N., Alwi, A., Mat, R.C.: A review of the motivation theories in learning. In: AIP Conference Proceedings, vol. 1891, p. 020043 (2017)

34. Gorla, N., Lam, Y.W.: Who should work with whom? building effective software project teams. Commun. ACM **47**(6), 79–82 (2004)

35. Gratton, L., Erickson, T.J.: Eight ways to build collaborative teams. Harv. Bus. Rev. (2007)

36. Hartono, B., Dzulfikar, L., Damayanti, R.: Impact of team diversity and conflict on project performance in Indonesian start-ups. J. Ind. Eng. Manag. **13**(1), 155 (2020). https://doi.org/10.3926/jiem.3037

37. Hasan, A., Moin, S., Pasha, M.: Prediction of personality profiles in the Pakistan software industry-a study. Psych **1**(1), 320–330 (2019). https://doi.org/10.3390/psych1010022

38. Heimerl, F., Lohmann, S., Lange, S., Ertl, T.: Word cloud explorer: text analytics based on word clouds. In: 2014 47th Hawaii International Conference on System Sciences, pp. 1833–1842. IEEE (2014). https://doi.org/10.1109/HICSS.2014.231

39. Henderson, J.C., Lee, S.: Managing I/S design teams: a control theories perspective. Manag. Sci. **38**(6), 757–777 (1992). https://doi.org/10.1287/mnsc.38.6.757

40. Hidellaarachchi, D., Grundy, J., Hoda, R., Mueller, I.: Does personality impact requirements engineering activities? arXiv preprint arXiv:2210.07807 (2022)

41. Hoegl, M., Gemuenden, H.G.: Teamwork quality and the success of innovative projects: a theoretical concept and empirical evidence. Organ. Sci. **12**(4), 435–449 (2001). https://doi.org/10.1287/orsc.12.4.435.10635

42. Hofer, B.K.: Personal epistemology research: implications for learning and teaching. Educ. Psychol. Rev. **13**(4), 353–383 (2001)

43. Hogan, J.M., Thomas, R.: Developing the software engineering team. In: Australasian Computing Education Conference 2005 (2005)

44. Iqbal, M.A., Aldaihani, A.R., Shah, A.: Big-five personality traits mapped with software development tasks to find most productive software development teams. Int. J. Innov. Technol. Explor. Eng. **8**(12), 965–971 (2019). https://doi.org/10.35940/ijitee.j9755.1081219

45. Iqbal, M.A., Ammar, F.A., Aldaihani, A.R., Khan, T.K.U., Shah, A.: Predicting most effective software development teams by mapping MBTI personality traits with software lifecycle activities. In: 2019 IEEE 6th International Conference on Engineering Technologies and Applied Sciences (ICETAS). IEEE (2019). https://doi.org/10.1109/icetas48360.2019.9117370

46. Iqbal, M.A., Shah, A. and Khan, T.K.: Predicting most productive requirements elicitation teams using MBTI personality traits model. Int. J. Eng. Adv. Technol. **9**(1), 3809–3814 (2019). https://doi.org/10.35940/ijeat.a9833.109119

47. Kang, H.R., Yang, H.D., Rowley, C.: Factors in team effectiveness: cognitive and demographic similarities of software development team members. Hum. Relat. **59**(12), 1681–1710 (2006). https://doi.org/10.1177/0018726706072891

48. Karn, J.S., Cowling, A.J.: Using ethnographic methods to carry out human factors research in software engineering. Behav. Res. Methods **38**(3), 495–503 (2006). https://doi.org/10.3758/bf03192804

49. Karn, J., Cowling, T.: A follow up study of the effect of personality on the performance of software engineering teams. In: 5th ACM-IEEE International Symposium on Empirical Software Engineering, pp. 232–241 (2006)

50. LeJeune, N.F.: A real-world simulation technique for forming software development teams in a capstone course. J. Comput. Sci. Coll. **50**(1), 247–253 (2008)

51. Li, X., Shih, P.C., Daniel, Y.: Effects of intuition and sensing in programming performance using mbti personality model. In: Proceedings of the 2nd International Conference on Advances in Image Processing. ACM, New York, NY, USA (2018). https://doi.org/10.1145/3239576.3239608

52. Licorish, S., Philpott, A., MacDonell, S.G.: Supporting agile team composition: a prototype tool for identifying personality (in)compatibilities. In: 2009 ICSE Workshop on Cooperative and Human Aspects on Software Engineering, pp. 66–73. IEEE (2009). https://doi.org/10.1109/CHASE.2009.5071413

53. Licorish, S.A., MacDonell, S.G.: Communication and personality profiles of global software developers. Inf. Softw. Technol. **64**, 113–131 (2015). https://doi.org/10.1016/j.infsof.2015.02.004

54. Ludewig, J., Lichter, H.: Software Engineering: Grundlagen, Menschen, Prozesse, Techniken. dpunkt. Verl., Heidelberg, 3, korrigierte aufl. edn. (2013)

55. Matturro, G., Raschetti, F., Fontan, C.: Soft skills in software development teams: a survey of the points of view of team leaders and team members. In: 2015 IEEE/ACM 8th International Workshop on Cooperative and Human Aspects of Software Engineering, pp. 101–104. IEEE (2015). https://doi.org/10.1109/CHASE.2015.30

56. Mendes, F., Mendes, E., Salleh, N., Oivo, M.: Insights on the relationship between decision-making style and personality in software engineering. Inf. Softw. Technol. **136**, 106586 (2021)

57. Menezes, Á., Prikladnicki, R.: Diversity in software engineering. In: Sharp, H., de Souza, C.R.B., Graziotin, D., Levy, M., Socha, D. (eds.) Proceedings of the 11th International Workshop on Cooperative and Human Aspects of Software Engineering, pp. 45–48. ACM, New York, NY, USA (2018). https://doi.org/10.1145/3195836.3195857

58. Monaghan, C., Bizumic, B., Reynolds, K., Smithson, M., Johns-Boast, L., van Rooy, D.: Performance of student software development teams: the influence of personality and identifying as team members. Eur. J. Eng. Educ. **40**(1), 52–67 (2015). https://doi.org/10.1080/03043797.2014.914156

59. Nesterenko, O., Selin, Y.: The teams information model for software engineering management. In: 2021 IEEE 16th International Conference on Computer Sciences and Information Technologies (CSIT), pp. 341–344. IEEE (2021). https://doi.org/10.1109/CSIT52700.2021.9648737

60. Noori, F., Kazemifard, M.: Simulation of pair programming using multi-agent and MBTI personality model. In: 2015 Sixth International Conference of Cognitive Science (ICCS), pp. 29–36 (2015)

61. Omar, M., Syed-Abdullah, S.L.: Identifying effective software engineering (se) team personality types composition using rough set approach. In: 2010 International Symposium on Information Technology, pp. 1499–1503. IEEE (2010). https://doi.org/10.1109/ITSIM.2010.5561479

62. Parks, L., Guay, R.P.: Personality, values, and motivation. Pers. Individ. Differ. **47**(7), 675–684 (2009)

63. Pieterse, V., van Eekelen, M.: How personality diversity influences team performance in student software engineering teams. In: 2018 Conference on Information Communications Technology and Society (ICTAS) (2018)

64. Prashandi, W.A.C., Kirupananda, A.: Automation of team formation in software development projects in an enterprise: what needs to improve? In: 2019 International Conference on Advanced Computing and Applications (ACOMP), pp. 16–22. IEEE (2019). https://doi.org/10.1109/ACOMP.2019.00010

65. Presler-Marshall, K., Heckman, S., Stolee, K.T.: What makes team[s] work? A study of team characteristics in software engineering projects. In: Vahrenhold, J., Fisler, K., Hauswirth, M., Franklin, D. (eds.) Proceedings of the 2022 ACM Conference on International Computing Education Research, vol. 1, pp. 177–188. ACM, New York, NY, USA (2022). https://doi.org/10.1145/3501385.3543980

66. PRISMA: Transparent reporting of systematic reviews and meta-analyses (2023). https://www.prisma-statement.org/

67. Purna Sudhakar, G., Farooq, A., Patnaik, S.: Soft factors affecting the performance of software development teams. Team Perform. Manag. Int. J. **17**(3/4), 187–205 (2011). https://doi.org/10.1108/13527591111143718

68. Qamar, N., Malik, A.A.: Determining the relative importance of personality traits in influencing software quality and team productivity (2020)

69. Rehman, M., Mahmood, A.K., Salleh, R., Amin, A.: Motivation in software engineering & personal characteristics of software engineers. In: 2011 National Postgraduate Conference, vol. 2, pp. 216–226 (2011)

70. Robey, D., Smith, L.A., Vijayasarathy, L.R.: Perceptions of conflict and success in information systems development projects. J. Manag. Inf. Syst. **10**(1), 123–139 (1993)

71. Rutherfoord, R.H.: Using personality inventories to help form teams for software engineering class projects. In: Proceedings of the 6th Annual Conference on Innovation and Technology in Computer Science Education, vol. 33, no. 3, pp. 73–76 (2001). https://doi.org/10.1145/507758.377486

72. Ryan, S., O'Connor, R.V.: Development of a team measure for tacit knowledge in software development teams. J. Syst. Softw. **82**(2), 229–240 (2009). https://doi. org/10.1016/j.jss.2008.05.037
73. Sánchez-Gordón, M., Colomo-Palacios, R.: Taking the emotional pulse of software engineering – a systematic literature review of empirical studies. Inf. Softw. Technol. **115**, 23–43 (2019). https://doi.org/10.1016/j.infsof.2019.08.002
74. Sánchez-Gordón, M., Colomo-Palacios, R.: Taking the emotional pulse of software engineering a systematic literature review of empirical studies. Inf. Softw. Technol. **115**, 23–43 (2019)
75. Sawyer, S.: Effects of intra-group conflict on packaged software development team performance. Inf. Syst. J. **11**(2), 155–178 (2001)
76. Scarnati, J.T.: On becoming a team player. Team Perform. Manag. Int. J. **7**(1/2), 5–10 (2001). https://doi.org/10.1108/13527590110389501
77. Shaikh, M.K.: How to form a software engineering capstone team? Heliyon **7**(4), e06629 (2021). https://doi.org/10.1016/j.heliyon.2021.e06629
78. Shameem, M., Kumar, C., Chandra, B.: A proposed framework for effective software team performance: a mapping study between the team members' personality and team climate. In: 2017 International Conference on Computing, Communication and Automation (ICCCA), pp. 912–917. IEEE (2017). https://doi.org/10. 1109/CCAA.2017.8229936
79. Shuto, M., Washizaki, H., Kakehi, K., Fukazawa, Y.: Relationship between the five factor model personality and learning effectiveness of teams in three information systems education courses. In: 2017 18th IEEE/ACIS International Conference on Software Engineering, Artificial Intelligence, Networking and Parallel/Distributed Computing (SNPD) (2017)
80. Sonmezoz, K., Ugur, O., Diri, B.: MBTI personality prediction with machine learning. In: 2020 28th Signal Processing and Communications Applications Conference (SIU). IEEE (2020). https://doi.org/10.1109/siu49456.2020.9302239
81. Soomro, A.B., Salleh, N., Nordin, A.: How personality traits are interrelated with team climate and team performance in software engineering? A preliminary study. In: 2015 9th Malaysian Software Engineering Conference (MySEC), pp. 259–265. IEEE (2015). https://doi.org/10.1109/MySEC.2015.7475230
82. Tanksale, D.: Big five personality traits: are they really important for the subjective well-being of Indians? Int. J. Psychol. **50**(1), 64–69 (2015). https://doi.org/10. 1002/ijop.12060
83. Tunio, M.Z., et al.: Impact of personality on task selection in crowdsourcing software development: a sorting approach. IEEE Access **5**, 18287–18294 (2017). https://doi.org/10.1109/access.2017.2747660
84. Varona, D., Capretz, L.F.: Assessing a candidate's natural disposition for a software development role using MBTI (2020)
85. Vijayasarathy, L.R., Butler, C.W.: Choice of software development methodologies: do organizational, project, and team characteristics matter? IEEE Softw. **33**(5), 86–94 (2016). https://doi.org/10.1109/MS.2015.26
86. Weilemann, E.: A winning team - what personality has to do with software engineering. In: 2019 IEEE/ACM 41st International Conference on Software Engineering: Companion Proceedings (ICSE-Companion), pp. 252–253. IEEE (2019). https://doi.org/10.1109/ICSE-Companion.2019.00100
87. Wiesche, M., Krcmar, H.: The relationship of personality models and development tasks in software engineering. In: SIGSIM-CPR 2014: Proceedings of the 52nd ACM Conference on Computers and People Research, pp. 149–161 (2014). https://doi. org/10.1145/2599990.2600012

88. Wong, S.S., Burton, R.M.: Virtual teams: what are their characteristics, and impact on team performance? Comput. Math. Organ. Theory **6**, 339–360 (2000)
89. Wu, J., Jiang, Y., Zhu, J.: Human resource allocation combined with team formation. In: 2016 International Conference on Computational Intelligence and Applications (ICCIA), pp. 67–71. IEEE (2016). https://doi.org/10.1109/ICCIA.2016.20
90. Xiao, Y., Watson, M.: Guidance on conducting a systematic literature review. J. Plan. Educ. Res. **39**(1), 93–112 (2019)
91. Yilmaz, M., O'Connor, R.V., Colomo-Palacios, R., Clarke, P.: An examination of personality traits and how they impact on software development teams. Inf. Softw. Technol. **86**, 101–122 (2017). https://doi.org/10.1016/j.infsof.2017.01.005

Visualization, Image Rendering and 3D in VAMR

Enhanced Scene Interpretation and Perception Through 3D Virtual Thermal Imaging

Vlassis Fotis$^{(\boxtimes)}$, Ioannis Romanelis$^{(\boxtimes)}$, Sokratis Zouras, Athina Kokonozi, and Konstantinos Moustakas$^{(\boxtimes)}$

University of Patras, Patras, Achaia, Greece
{vfotis,iroman,zouras,athinakokonozi,moustakas}@ece.upatras.gr
https://www.vvr.ece.upatras.gr/

Abstract. Thermal imaging is a widely used technique in several real-world applications in which a clear view of an object or scene is required, and obstruction thereof cannot be tolerated. By visualizing the received thermal radiation in the infrared spectrum, a clear depiction of the thermal profile of objects is obtained, that is information-rich and invariant to most severe atmospheric conditions. However, using thermal imaging hardware requires training and hands-on experience that is difficult to obtain. In this paper we explore PICTUM, a fully parameterizable thermal imaging simulation software that can be used to train personnel in various scenarios and digitally recreated atmospheric conditions, in order to provide sufficient experience in a controlled environment, before using the actual hardware.

Keywords: Thermal imaging · virtual reality · Simulation

1 Introduction

Thermal infrared imaging of objects in a scene presents their thermal radiation profile in the infrared spectrum. This alternate view of the scene objects contributes to the extraction of additional information like temperature or material and can be effectively used for detection or tracking in video sequences. Measured thermal radiation includes thermal radiation emitted by objects, reflected by their surface, and is also affected by the atmosphere; some is transmitted, some is absorbed, and some is even emitted from the atmosphere itself, while the thermal camera itself emits thermal radiation during operation. Therefore, thermal imaging depends on the properties of the objects in the area and their surroundings and is used in several applications such as building inspection, fire monitoring, industry, medical and marine search and rescue applications. The method is widely used in surveillance applications for the enhancement of vision and for the detection of objects, due to limitations of CCD cameras to operate properly, under conditions of limited or no optical visibility (night, fog, smoke etc.).

© The Author(s), under exclusive license to Springer Nature Switzerland AG 2023
J. Y. C. Chen and G. Fragomeni (Eds.): HCII 2023, LNCS 14027, pp. 157–167, 2023.
https://doi.org/10.1007/978-3-031-35634-6_11

Although, thermal cameras are ideal for surveillance in low visibility situations, it is important to note that handling them properly and being able to detect potential hazards requires training and hands-on experience. More specifically, the user's eye needs to adjust to the thermal visualization framework and familiarity with the appearance of objects and surroundings in general must be established. The variety of the thermal camera's functionalities and visualization modes are also extremely important in detecting a specific target and each functionality might accommodate a scenario better than others. Typically, a trainee gains experience by participating in real-life scenarios and exercises on the thermal headset itself. However, this process involves many caveats, inefficiencies and unnecessary costs. In order to experience various atmospheric conditions using the thermal headset, one has to wait for them to occur naturally, making it nearly impossible to plan specific training sessions ahead of time. Additionally, direct supervision from an expert is constantly required, and mistakes made during an actual rescue could be potentially lethal.

This paper presents activities towards the development of PICTUM, a fully customizable thermal imaging simulation software for the training of personnel to understand and correctly perceive content in the field of view of a thermal camera in applications for the surveillance and guarding of outdoor and indoor spaces, under different environmental and lighting conditions, and through immersion in the virtual environment of the field of view of the thermal camera.

The proposed workflow includes the creation of 3D thermal imaging of the virtual objects which are created based on the thermal coefficients and thermal properties of the static and dynamic objects of interest, the multimodal rendering of surface/volume models as well as the simulation and visualization of data and motion performance in the virtual environment. The aim is to provide a functional prototype which will allow the dynamic interaction of the trainee with the virtual objects and with the content of the training scenarios in real time, while being fully extensible with new script libraries allowing the adaptation to personalized training scenarios in order to address the needs of different trainee and application scenario.

The framework of PICTUM follows an instructor-trainee interface architecture and includes the design and development of GUI components, networking, and the structure of the communication system between them. The functional prototype will be tested in a pilot study for marine area surveillance and for training students at the Hellenic Naval Academy [5], a university-level institution providing naval education. The main contributions of this thermal headset simulation application are:

- The VR thermal headset allows the user to practice using thermal imaging technology in a safe and controlled environment, allowing consequence-free errors and eliminating risks of damage to the thermal imaging equipment.
- The presented framework is fully extensible and atmospheric phenomena can be replicated, diversifying the content into a complete collection of training exercises.
- It provides a cost-effective alternative to buying and using actual thermal imaging equipment.

– The instructor-trainee system architecture allows for live supervision from the experienced instructor who conducts the training session.

2 Related Work

Virtual reality has exploded in popularity over the past decade. While initially it was focused on the gaming and entertainment industry, its obvious merits have attracted interest from other industries and domains. In medicine, virtual reality is still in its early stages but several studies have revealed potential with regards to rehabilitation [2] as well as mediating the effects of various psychological disorders [1,4]. Virtual environments have also been shown to cause a certain level of distraction to the user, which in term has been utilized to attenuate pain in patients [3] undergoing invasive medical procedures. In retail, the effects of virtual reality applications on consumer preferences and behavior in general are extensively studied [10,11] and findings suggest that this consumer-based technology is bound to change the on and off-store experience completely in the next few years. The usage of virtual reality is also being explored in the manufacturing industry [8]. Researchers believe that it can be effectively utilized as a training tool for workers, in order to acquire experience in assembly [9] and improve collaboration between the workers and robots/heavy machinery as well as safety [7].

Virtual reality is extremely popular for simulation tasks and the versatility it provides makes it suitable for our work. However there are several challenges that need to be addressed, since there is no actual thermal camera involved in the simulation software, begging the question of how the thermal representation of the environment will be created. Research works in image analysis use fusion of thermal and visual images [12,14], in an attempt to augment the information that visual images normally provide. Advances in photogrammetry and laser scanning have enabled thermal mapping to be applied directly in the 3D domain, through RGB-D data [15] as well as point clouds in both static [16] and dynamic [17] settings. Nevertheless, the location has to be scanned and processed with appropriate equipment first, and the virtual environment is restricted to places that actually exist. We opt to go for a physics-based approach instead, using triangular meshes and temperature textures to represent our objects and running the resources through the real camera's post-processing pipeline to obtain the same effect.

3 Methodology

The objective of this study is to create a virtual reality simulation of a thermal imaging headset, incorporating the thermal and material properties of objects in a three-dimensional (3D) environment. To achieve this, volumetric and multimodal rendering techniques for surface and volume models have been adapted to operate within the thermal pipeline, instead of conventional rendering methods. The ultimate goal of this project is to produce a functional prototype that enables the user to engage dynamically with the virtual environment and acclimate themselves with the thermal imaging equipment.

In addition to incorporating thermal and material properties, the virtual reality simulation of the thermal imaging headset must operate in real-time to enhance the realism of the user experience. The application must also be adjustable, allowing the trainer to modify parameters such as atmospheric conditions (e.g. day/night, rain/smoke/fog), and the season (e.g. summer/winter). Furthermore, it should be extensible, enabling the addition of new training scenarios to accommodate varying training needs and application contexts.

In the initial stage of the project, two distinct scenarios are developed. The first scenario will focus on familiarization with the VR equipment, where the trainee is placed in a closed room with a Leslie's cube in front, which they can manipulate (translate and rotate) using controllers. A Leslie's cube, a benchmark model in thermal imaging, is a cube whose faces are made of different materials with varying reflective and emmissive properties, which as a result emits different levels of infrared radiation from each face (at the same temperature). Therefore, it serves as an excellent guideline for understanding the basic principles of thermal imaging, especially for inexperienced users. The second scenario will involve a coastal rescue exercise, where the user must locate a drowning target and observe the rescue procedure as the boat approaches. These scenarios aim to provide a realistic and immersive experience for the trainee.

Additionally, the application will feature a trainer's graphical user interface (GUI) that allows the trainer to set the parameters for the training scenario and monitor the progress of all participants in real-time. Multiple participants can be trained simultaneously, and the trainer can view the world as the participants see it and communicate with them through a chat. This comprehensive functionality offers a versatile tool for trainers, giving them the opportunity to provide personalized feedback to each trainee in real time, by advising them based on what they are actually seeing, and in real time.

The virtual reality simulation of the thermal imaging headset will be evaluated in a pilot study for marine area surveillance and for training students at the Hellenic Naval Academy, a university-level institution providing naval education. The functional prototype will be tested to determine its effectiveness in these real-world scenarios.

3.1   Virtual Thermal Imaging

The creation of the thermal imaging component in the virtual reality simulation requires several steps. First, a 3D scene is assembled by gathering objects, represented as 3D meshes, which can be either custom made or obtained from online sources, and optimizing the models for real-time performance by reducing their polygon count. The virtual environment is then built by defining the location of these objects in the scene. The thermal properties of objects, including temperature and emissivity, are assigned to the 3D meshes using two different textures. The first texture assigns each vertex to a material ID and is later sampled from a material database to obtain the emissivity value. A database with

256 different Material IDs is sufficient for this project, so the material texture is a single-channel PNG 8-bit. The second texture holds the temperature value for each fragment, in Kelvin degrees, which is stored in a 32-bit single-channel EXR file. A rescaling module maps the values from 0 to 1, as specified by most image editing software, to actual Kelvin degrees, resulting to a temperature map.

By combining the temperature information and the material properties of each object we can calculate the emitted radiation that is captured by the thermal headset. We render the scene from the camera perspective and store the image (one for each eye) that the thermal headset would capture. This simulates the raw data that the thermal sensors would capture. Then we virtually follow the same post-processing pipeline as the original thermal headset to produce as accurate results as possible. It is worth mentioning that since the application has to run in real-time all post-processing steps are optimized and run directly in the GPU with custom shader programs. These post-processing steps are mostly image processing algorithms that are applied on the captured image frame, a process that is similar to deferred rendering.

The virtual reality thermal imaging simulation offers three viewing modes for the user: white-hot, black-hot, and red-hot. In white-hot mode, the highest temperatures are represented by white and the lowest by black. In black-hot, the colors are reversed with the highest temperatures being represented by black and the lowest by white. The red-hot mode uses a range of colors, starting with black and gradually transitioning to white, then to various shades of red. This allows the user to differentiate between a range of luminance values, with the highest values being represented by the reddest shade (Fig. 1).

Fig. 1. The three thermal representations. Red-Hot, White-Hot, Black-Hot (from left to right) (Color figure online)

3.2   Post-processing Pipeline

An arbitrary object's thermal visualization mainly depends on two factors, the temperature distribution throughout the object's volume, and the material properties that comprise it. Atmospheric conditions, and scattering phenomena influence the emitted radiation that ultimately reaches the lens of the thermal camera producing the final output. We choose to go with a simple approach that allows us to represent the scene with arbitrary accuracy while also allowing easy extensions and modifications. Using the object representation mentioned previously, the temperature and material properties (emmissivity) at each point allow us to calculate the light intensity that reaches the lens. Following that, a series of post processing effects are applied before the output image is reached. Atmospheric phenomena can be modeled as intermediate processing steps at this stage.

The early luminance image is denoised in order to rid the image of non-uniformities caused by faulty sensors in the camera's sensor array. The non-uniformities appear in the image similar to salt and pepper noise and naturally do not occur in the simulation due to the absence of sensors. Their presence is added digitally and can be remedied by a calibration mechanism that is available in the actual headset, as a training exercise. The image is then subjected to contrast enhancement via histogram equalization. This is step is of particular importance, as thermal cameras tend to be used in low visibility situations, where most of the image's color values are concentrated in a narrow dynamic range of colors, obstructing the view of the scene. The histogram equalization spreads the values throughout the entire dynamic range creating a more clear view. The final step is an edge-preserving filtering operation, realized through bilateral filtering. This has a smoothing effect over the image but retains important edge details.

3.3   Graphical User Interface

This section will focus on the trainers and trainees GUI, and the networking technology utilized for communication between them. The trainers and trainees GUI allow for an intuitive and user-friendly interface for training and feedback, with the networking technology ensuring efficient and seamless communication.

Trainee's GUI. The trainee's GUI has a streamlined design, as the user will be immersed in the virtual environment and may have difficulty operating a complex interface. The GUI provides basic features such as adjusting the headset display mode and requesting assistance from the trainer through a predefined set of questions/responses. This is due to the limitations of the virtual environment, which may prevent the user from accessing a keyboard to communicate through chat.

Instructor's GUI. The trainer's GUI is more complex and consists of five main components in order to accommodate all that an instructor might require during a training session.

- The first component allows the trainer to set up the training scenario and conditions by choosing from available scenarios and adjusting options such as time of day, atmospheric conditions such as rain, fog, or smoke, and season. This last option is particularly important as the summer season can result in temperatures above the human body in some areas exposed to the sun.
- Next up is the participant list, where the trainer can view all connected users, monitor their status, and track their progress. The trainer can also select a participant and view their perspective to assist or send a direct message.
- The third component is a designated viewing area that displays and live-streams the perspective of the selected participant.
- The fourth component is the chat, where the trainer can send messages to all or selected participants and view messages and requests from trainees.
- Finally, a mini map helps the trainer track the positions of trainees in the virtual world and monitor their progress.

The UI widgets are designed to maintain their size and position regardless of display size and resolution through the use of percentage-based sizing.

3.4   Communication System

The communication between the trainer and trainees is established through a server-client model. This model was chosen to support asynchronous communication and manage incoming connections and messages efficiently. A Listener is in charge of monitoring incoming communications, while a Dispatcher reads each message's metadata, identifies the sender and the "purpose" of the message, then forwards it to the relevant operator. The Handler component features a set of message processing procedures designed to handle specific types of messages. It stores the data in shared registers that the main program can access. Data processing and networking are handled in the background, with automated processes. The trainer sets up and adjusts the parameters of the training scenario through the input components in the GUI during initialization.

4   Training Scenarios

4.1   Leslie's Cube

The first scenario aims to help the user become familiar with the VR equipment, controls, and thermal imaging. The user will find themselves in a virtual room with a cube in front of them, known as Leslie's cube, consisting of faces made of different materials. In the center of each face, a constant temperature is applied that decreases towards the edges of the cube.

By manipulating the cube with the controls, the user will observe that the different sides of the cube emit different radiation levels based on their material emissivity, despite having the same temperature. However, the limited temperature values in this scenario can cause issues with histogram equalization in the post-processing pipeline, as the scene has very few models. To address this, the temperature on the walls of the room is changed from a uniform temperature to a higher temperature at the corners that decreases towards the center (Fig. 2).

Fig. 2. Leslie's cube scenario in Black-Hot representation

4.2   Human Rescue on a Coastal Area

After the user has familiarized themselves with the VR equipment and thermal imaging, they will progress to a more realistic training scenario, which is a key part of their training. In this scenario, the user will be placed in a watch-house (Fig. 3) located on a cliff, which serves as the local navy post. From this vantage point, they will be able to survey the surrounding scenery, including the coast, various objects such as a changing room, shower, and jetty, as well as a wooden boat and a naval rescue ship. In the sea, there is a buoy and several rocks.

The objective of the user is to locate a drowning target and alert the naval ship to perform the rescue. They must also monitor the rescue process to ensure that it runs smoothly. Throughout the scenario, the user will repeat the task in different seasons and weather conditions, showcasing the importance of thermal imaging equipment in harsh environments and their ability to quickly familiarize themselves with the equipment and reduce response time.

5   Limitations

By faithfully following the actual thermal camera's pipeline we are able to produce an effect that is similar to that of the camera. While this approach has several advantages (as discussed in the previous sections), it is a double-edged sword, in that it needs extremely detailed temperature and material textures to achieve the exact same effect. Detailed temperature textures are hard to come by however, as one needs to perform extensive experiments and simulations using quality equipment, which defeats the purpose of this project. Material textures also require high levels of precision to model each individual object. The latter can be alleviated by choosing simpler object with fewer materials or by skimping on minor material details. Having low levels of detail in the temperature can cause problems for the post-processing pipeline, especially if the values are concentrated in a rather narrow range, due to the histogram equalization (Fig. 4).

Fig. 3. Human rescue on the coastal area scenario. View from the watch-house. Red-Hot representation. The scene provided by MILTECH [6] (PICTUM partner) (Color figure online)

Fig. 4. Human rescue on the coastal area scenario. View from the watch-house. Black-Hot representation.

In order to mitigate the temperature problem we incorporate more objects in the scene in order to increase the luminance variation in the frame and model the temperature as gaussian distributions with higher temperature in the center and decreasing towards the edges. Through this simplified version of the actual thermal image, the simulation is accurate enough to get the point across and help users understand the fundamentals behind this technology.

An interesting approach is to enrich the temperature textures with appropriately mathematically modeled kinds of noise, replicating the level of detail that would normally be found in a physically-accurate temperature texture. This however exceeds the scope of this project so we leave it as future work.

6 Conclusion

The VR thermal headset simulation is an innovative application of VR technology that provides a realistic and cost-effective way to train personnel in the use of thermal imaging technology. We are hoping that this application will serve as an easy, convenient and most of all safe alternative to traditional training methods involving the actual headset.

Acknowledgements. This research project has been co-financed by the European Regional Development Fund of the European Union and Greek national funds through the Operational Program Competitiveness, Entrepreneurship and Innovation, under the call RESEARCH - CREATE - INNOVATE (project code: T2EΔK-03941).

References

1. Gega, L.: The virtues of virtual reality in exposure therapy. Br. J. Psychiatry **210**, 245–246 (2018)
2. Dockx, K., et al.: Virtual reality for rehabilitation in Parkinson's disease. Cochrane Database Syst. Rev. (2016)
3. Gold, J.I., Belmont, K.A., Thomas, D.A.: The neurobiology of virtual reality pain attenuation. Cyberpsychol. Behav. **10**, 536–544 (2007)
4. Beidel, D.C., et al.: Trauma management therapy with virtual-reality augmented exposure therapy for combat-related PTSD: a randomized controlled trial. J. Anxiety Disord. **61**, 64–74 (2019)
5. Hellenic Naval Academy (PICTUM partner). https://www.hna.gr/en/
6. MILTECH Hellas (PICTUM partner). https://www.miltech.gr
7. Malik, A.A., Masood, T., Bilberg, A.: Virtual reality in manufacturing: immersive and collaborative artificial-reality in design of human-robot workspace. Int. J. Comput. Integr. Manuf. **33**, 22–37 (2020)
8. Berg, L.P., Vance, J.M.: Industry use of virtual reality in product design and manufacturing: a survey. Virtual Reality **21**, 1–17 (2017)
9. Abidi, M.H., Al-Ahmari, A., Ahmad, A., Ameen, W., Alkhalefah, H.: Assessment of virtual reality-based manufacturing assembly training system. Int. J. Adv. Manuf. Technol. **105**(9), 3743–3759 (2019). https://doi.org/10.1007/s00170-019-03801-3
10. Bonetti, F., Warnaby, G., Quinn, L.: Augmented reality and virtual reality in physical and online retailing: a review, synthesis and research agenda. Augmented Reality Virtual Reality (2018)
11. Pizzi, G., Scarpi, D., Pichierri, M., Vannucci, V.: Virtual reality, real reactions?: comparing consumers' perceptions and shopping orientation across physical and virtual-reality retail stores. Comput. Hum. Behav. **96**, 1–12 (2019)
12. Bai, X., Zhou, F., Xue, B.: Fusion of infrared and visual images through region extraction by using multi scale center-surround top-hat transform. Opt. Express **19**, 8444–8457 (2011)

13. Borrmann, D., Elseberg, J., Nuchter, A.: Thermal 3D mapping of building facades. In: Lee, S., Cho, H., Yoon, K.J., Lee, J. (eds.) Intelligent Autonomous Systems 12. Advances in Intelligent Systems and Computing, vol. 193, pp. 173–182. Springer, Heidelberg (2012). https://doi.org/10.1007/978-3-642-33926-4_16

14. Chen, S., Leung, H.: An EM-CI based approach to fusion of IR and visual images. In: International Conference on Information Fusion (2009)

15. Vidas, S., Moghadam, P., Bosse, M.: 3D thermal mapping of building interiors using an RGB-D and thermal camera. In: International Conference on Robotics and Automation (2013)

16. De Pazzi, D., Pertile, M., Chiodini, S.: 3D radiometric mapping by means of LiDAR SLAM and thermal camera data fusion. Sensors **22**, 8512 (2022)

17. Weinmann, M., Leitloff, J., Hoegner, L., Jutzi, B., Stilla, U., Hinz, S.: Thermal 3D mapping for object detection in dynamic scenes. Ann. Photogram. Remote Sens. Spat. Inf. Sci. (2014)

Interactive Avatar Creation System from Learned Attributes for Virtual Reality

Tomohiro Hibino$^{(\boxtimes)}$, Haoran Xie , and Kazunori Miyata

Japan Advanced Institute of Science and Technology, Nomi, Ishikawa, Japan
t_hibino@jaist.ac.jp

Abstract. Demands for 3D models are increasing rapidly as metaverse culture rises. Communication in virtual spaces with avatars is supposed to play an important role in the near future. While photo-realistic 3D avatars are already available to be made by many methods, anime-like avatars are seldom considered due to their difficulties in analysis. Existing creation support systems like for character modeling need to operate too many parameters, so a user may lose what they want to make and what to do. Our main goal of this work is to help users to create it interactively with no work stress and low time cost. To solve this issue, we developed Subdivison Shrink method and implemented interactive VR (Virtual Reality) anime-like avatar creation system. In the proposed system, a user can create an anime-like avatar model in VR space and modify it interactively.

Keywords: Virtual Reality · 3D CG · Creation Assistance

1 Introduction

Computer graphics have been developed with online games such as MMORPG (Massively Multiplayer Online RPG) and communication services such as Second Life. In recent years, advances in computing power have enabled users to experience the virtual world as a three-dimensional space using a HMD (Head Mount Display) or smart glasses. The VR worlds where users can do communication and economic activities like real world is called metaverse application. Metaverse services, such as VRChat and Meta Horizons, are expected to become a major means of communication near future [1, 2].

The human 3D model in VR space is called avatar. While photo-realistic ones are mainly used as means of telecommunication. On the other hand, anime-like avatars are mainly used for role-playing in video games or in the situation where user's physical bodies are hidden, such as SNS (Social Networking Servise).

Creating a 3D model involves a wide range of tasks, including image sketching, vertex mesh creation, material creation for surface textures, and rigging to associate joints and mesh. Each process requires specialized skills, so the learning costs for a beginner is too huge.

© The Author(s), under exclusive license to Springer Nature Switzerland AG 2023
J. Y. C. Chen and G. Fragomeni (Eds.): HCII 2023, LNCS 14027, pp. 168–181, 2023.
https://doi.org/10.1007/978-3-031-35634-6_12

For this reason, many 3D video game have a system called "character making", in which the character's face and body shape are determined by manipulating many parameters [3]. Even though, it is a difficult task for beginners to manipulate dozens, or even hundreds, of parameters in order to create the intended character. In adjusting many parameters and checking the created avatar in long time, user may get tired and lose what they want to create.

Our contributions in this reserach are

- To develop a method to extract characteristics as a few attributes from anime-like avatars with fine detail
- To enable users to operate these attributes interactively
- To enable users to see the created avatar realtime in VR space

so that user with no skill of 3DCG can create anime-like avatars easily and fast.

2 Related Works

2.1 Analysis for 3D Models

When 3D models are analyzed in a conventional method, it is more difficult to analyze than 2D data such as images. This is because image data has fixed data structure in the form of pixels and RGB values. Whereas, 3D models have data in the form of vertices, edges, and faces. Different numbers of vertices and the order of connection (topology) lead different dimensions of data, that makes it difficult to analyze data in fixed data structure.

In recent years, deep learning methods have succeeded in generating new images with texture and style almost the same to the training data [4,5], but it is impossible to apply such methods directly to 3D data.

In the case of realistic avatars, the body shape is almost the same and the range of variation is small, and the shape is smooth and continuous. Therefore, a model such as SMPL [6] can generate almost all body shapes and poses. Because of this ease of generation, methods have already been established to automatically generate avatars, including textures, based on image data from cameras and other sources [7,8]. Recently, text-prompt based method using CLIP [9] succeeded to create 3D human models with combining text-to-image method [10].

In contrast, anime-like avatars often have cartoon-like expressions on their faces, deformed body shapes, and wide and irregular variations. Therefore, more parameters and resolutions are required to express fine details compared to photo-realistic avatars. Research on the automatic generation of anime-like avatars is limited to fixing the basic model [11,12], and no methods has yet been developed to extract features from a wide range of details in the various models.

2.2 Deep Learning Based Approaches

We discuss the relationship between 3DCG and deep learning. 3D data rarely has common topology, so a desirable method is needed to analyze them across different topology.

The most naive approach is using voxels (unit cubes) in 3D space. However, voxel-based methods such as [13,14] have a certain limit to the resolution. Because this type of methods needs the memory space growing exponentially in $O(n^3)$ order.

The point cloud-based method [15] is efficient in terms of memory savings and is suitable for rendering backgrounds (e.g., walls and a large number of objects along them at different scales). But its lack of mesh and rig information makes it impossible to apply to avatar generation.

A method to estimate parameters before by inverse rendering from training data images [16,17] is a robust 3D reconstruction technique. Also, to estimate the parameters of the implicit function [18,19] is a powerful method in the generation of morphological data. However, the application of these methods is still limited to the reproduction of simple models such as desks and airplanes.

Since anime-like avatars have unrealistic proportion of body parts, that need a wide range of variations than photo-realistic avatars. In addition, the shape of anime-like avatars are generally simplified but locally have protruding features like emphasized eyebrow that need a high resolution in shape expression. This is why it is difficult to analyze anime-like characters shape, even using machine learning methods. So, robust and high-fidelity methods for anime-like avatars are needed.

3   Proposed Method

In this paper, we propose a method named **Subdivision Shrink** to unify differences in topology between training data. This method learns the details of the training data while keeping the common topology by matching the position of each landmarks to the training data at the low polygon level, and then iterating the process of high-polygonization and approximation.

3.1   Template Matching

First, a process named template matching is performed between the training data and a low-polygon common mesh as a template. 90 landmarks (composed of eyebrow lie, eye line, nose line, mouse line etc.) are set on this template and set close to the corresponding (Fig. 1).

3.2   Subdivison Surface and Shrink Wrap

The template was then performed subdivision surface and shrink wrap. These processes are performed in Blender API. The method of the subdivision surface is simple tessellation, and the method of shrink wrap is above-surface mode. Since the template is set closer to the vertices near the training data, the multiplied vertices by the subdivision surface are set closer to the training data, too. So the detail of the training data can be studied with keeping a common topology.

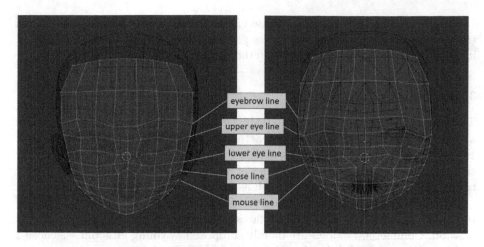

Fig. 1. Template matching among different training data. We approximate 90 of landmarks of the templates to training data. The landmarks are composed of facial key points, eyebrow, eye, nose, mouse.

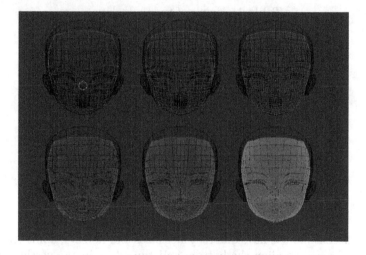

Fig. 2. Proceedings of subdivison shrink. The first template is the top left one and the 5th one is the down right. The template mesh gets high-polygoned learning the details of the training data.

By repeating this operation, data with sufficient precision was obtained in a common topology (Fig. 2).

Since the number of vertices multiplies exponentially with each subdivision, the memory limit is reached after several iterations. In this study, we decided six iterations (number of template vertices $90 \leftarrow 296,001$) is accurate enough to reproduce the detail.

Blender, a 3D CG Software, was used for template matching and iterations of the operations. Template matching was performed manually, and the subsequent iteration process was performed by Python scripts in Blender.

3.3   Dataset and Analysis

The most efficient way to automatically create a wide range of high-quality avatars is to learn from existing character. Conventionally, high-quality models such as those used in video games were not available for customers, but recently there has been a rapid increase in sales of 3D models by individual creators due to demand for metaverse services such as VRChat.

We bought 40 commercial 3D models from BOOTH [20] and then obtained topology-unified mesh data for the faces and bodies using Subdivison Shrink method. Commercial models are mainly composed of young girls but we chose 2 male models and 12 deformed models to include not only feminine elements but also masculine elements and cartoon character elements (Table 1).

Table 1. Sample of trainindg data

Type	Sample	n
female		26
male		2
deformed		12

Since different models have different face sizes and heights, affine transformation was performed to align the bottom and top edges in the vertical direction (min-max normalization), and to align the center of the model in the front-back and horizontal directions to average zero (mean normalization). Variations between these meshes were recorded as shape keys (the shifts of positions of vertices from mean).

With the same topology, We succeeded to interpolate from a model to another model continuously by adjusting corresponding shape keys. The generated meshes keeps the both the global features (overall shape and the positions of landmarks) and the local features (e.g. deformed eye line and deformed mouth shape) (Fig. 3).

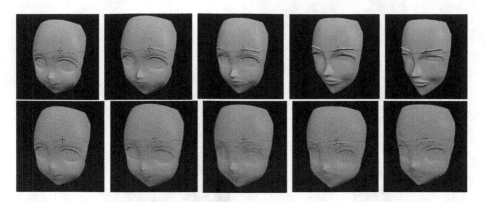

Fig. 3. The samples of interpolation. The upper row shows an interpolation from feminine features to masculine features. The lower row shows an interpolation from tail-falling features to tail-rising features.

We performed principal components were extracted as feature attributes by principal component analysis.

The cumulative explained variance ratios of the top three principal components were 0.76, 0.09, and 0.06 (cumulative 0.91) for the face components, and 0.76, 0.13, and 0.04 (cumulative 0.94) for the body components, respectively (Fig. 4).

4   VR Application

Based on the extracted attributes, we developed an application that user can create avatars in VR space (Fig. 5). Unity, a gaming middleware, was used to create the application. The HTC Vive Pro Eye was used for the HMD, and the Vive Controller was used for the controller. The user can change the avatar located in the center of the VR space by operating the controller (Table 2).

The shape of avatar is changed by operating the controller. The rotation of the left-hand controller was linked to body features. The right-hand controller to facial features. The vertical height of the left-hand controller was linked to the avatar's height. The vertical height of the right-hand controller was linked to the avatar's facial scale (Fig. 6). These changes are only applied while the user is pressing the controller trigger.

For the hair mesh data, we use a fixed mesh in this study because it was difficult to unify the topology.

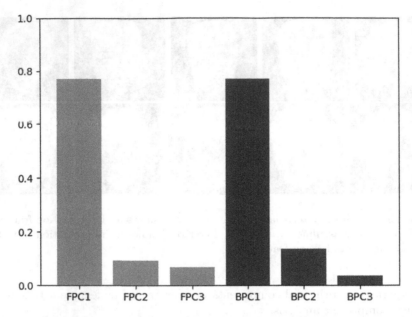

Fig. 4. Cumulative explained variance ratio of PCA. The left 3 are FPC (Face Principal Component), The right 3 are BPC(Body Principal Component)

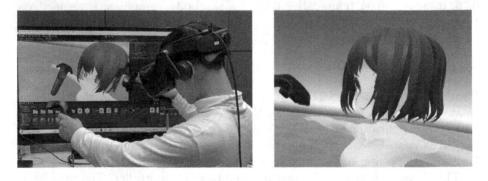

Fig. 5. Left: A user using our system. Right: The image the user sees via HMD display. The user can feel the avatar as if they are in front of the user.

Table 2. The changes of shape based on PC. The upper 3 rows show the changes about face, and the lower 3 rows show the changes about body. We extend the range of PC from ±3 SD to ±6 SD to exaggerate the changes.

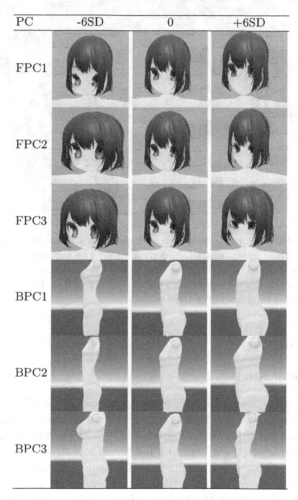

PC	-6SD	0	+6SD
FPC1			
FPC2			
FPC3			
BPC1			
BPC2			
BPC3			

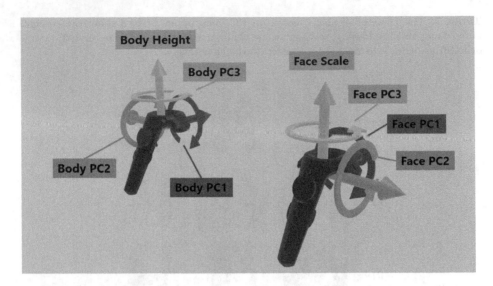

Fig. 6. The relation between controller and attributes. The left hand relates body deformation, the right hand relates face deformation. The left rotation axes correspond to PC1, PC2, PC3 of body, and the vertical position corresponds to the height of the avatar. The rotation 3 axes correspond to PC1, PC2, PC3 of face, and the vertical position correspond to the scale of the avatar.

5   User Study

5.1   Pipeline of Study

An evaluation study was conducted with 10 participants. The participants are composed of 9 males and 1 female, all of them are after graduates students. The participants operated VRoid Studio [21], a 3D avatar creation software with many parameters, as a conventional interface. After using VRoidStudio, the participants operated our application. Through the study, we order the participants to create their avatars a female protagonist in a video game. This is because, due to the bias of the training data, feminine avatars are created in almost all of the cases. After performing both operations, a participant were asked the following questions to verify the effectiveness of the interface.

1. Have you experienced 3D software such as Blender, Maya?
2. Have you experienced character making system in video game?
3. Is it more effective to operate few attributes than operate many parameters?
4. Is is more effective to operate in 3D VR space than with 2D monitor?

We set 5 levels of Likert scale in Q3, Q4.

6   Result

The result are below Table 4 (Table 3).

Table 3. The result of the questionnaire

Participant	Q1	Q2	Q3	Q4
1	Yes	No	5	5
2	Yes	Yes	4	5
3	No	Yes	4	5
4	No	Yes	4	5
5	No	Yes	4	5
6	No	Yes	4	5
7	Yes	Yes	4	5
8	Yes	Yes	5	5
9	No	Yes	4	5
10	No	No	2	4

Table 4. Time to complete work

Participant	2D-UI (sec)	VR-UI (sec)	dif
1	120	80	−40
2	120	90	−30
3	240	110	−130
4	270	50	−220
5	300	60	−240
6	650	110	−540
7	150	50	−100
8	460	100	−360
9	230	80	−150
10	290	100	−190

We got a mean score of 4.0 in Q3 and a mean score of 4.9 in Q4. Almost all participants gave a rating of 4 or higher for Q3 (more effective to operate few attributes) and Q4 (effective to operate in 3D VR space). The median time to complete in 2D-UI was 255 s and the median of VR-UI was 85 s, and the median of time difference was -170 s (Fig. 7). The time to complete was shorter for all participants when our application.

No relationship was found between the two conditions of Q1 (experienced 3D software) nor Q2 (experienced character making system in video game) and the evaluation nor the time.

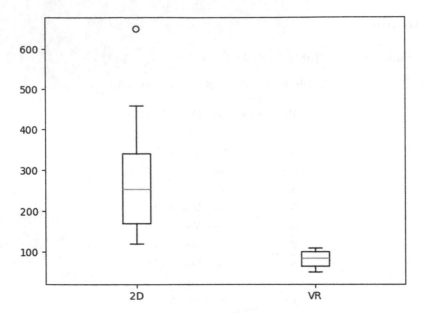

Fig. 7. Comparison of the time to complete. The left is 2D-UI and the right is VR-UI.

7   Discussion

In all participants, they completed the task in shorter time in our application. It indicates that an interface like our application is effective to reduce the time of modeling.

The effectiveness of modeling in the VR space was clearly rated highly, with 9 participants evaluated it 5 and 1 participant rating 4. Positive comments from the participants were that, they could get a better sense of the model by viewing it from various angles with a three-dimensional view, and that they could model with a sense of realism because they could feel the height difference.

The simplification of operation by extracting attributes was also considered to be effective to a certain extent, as 9 participants evaluated 4 or higher. The participants generally responded positively, but we got the following negative responses.

- When it came to millimeter-level adjustments, precision of this application was not enough. It was impossible to create perfectly what I wanted to create.
- I could not predict how will the operation change the avatar's shape. Some change was against my intention.

These reactions suggest that our application is suitable for global level adjustments in a short time, while the conventional system using many parameters adjusting is suitable for detailed adjustments after the completion of such coarse adjustments. This suggests that it would be ideal if both operations could be completed within VR space. But it is difficult due to the following limitations.

First, it is difficult to point to a precise position or make millimeter-level adjustments via the VR controller [22]. Therefore, if the number of parameters is increased to dozens, it is almost impossible to manipulate them in the VR space.

It is also difficult to do other things when user wear HMD, for example, to refer to the sample or to take a break. Such operations require the removal of the HMD, but frequently taking off the HMD is time-consuming and psychologically stressful [23].

The above points are not only limitations of the system, rather limitations of the HMDs and controllers at now.

In the future, as the performance of VR devices improves and the interface of VR applications more sophisticated, it is expected that some of these issues will be resolved. But at present, when manipulating parameters in the VR space, we need do all work in VR space, and the number of parameters that can be handled is limited to a few.

From these reasons, the interface for modeling in VR space should be used to quickly determine the direction of the model, and detailed adjustment should be done by adjusting parameters with conventionally tools.

8   Conclusion and Limitations

8.1   Conclusion

This research established a system that a user can easily create an avatar that will serve as an alter ego in metaverse. We revealed that the Subdivision Shrink method can extract attributes from anime-like avatars keeping the same topology.

In addition, this study developed an application for creating avatars while manipulating a few parameters in VR space. Through the user study, we revealed that such system is more intuitive and has many advantages than conventional character making systems that require operating a large number of parameters.

These results show that interfaces like our system can be a powerful tool for many users. On the other hand, the interface is limited by the performance of the HMD and controller. We believe that, until the limitations on the device are resolved, it is the best to combine the advantages of both methods.

8.2   Limitations

Dataset. This study used $N = 40$ of 3D models as the dataset. This is a small number for training, but budgetary limitations forced us to limit this number. Since this study showed that the proposed method is effective to a certain extent. We hope further studies use more number of dataset.

However, this would require an impractically huge budget. Therefore, it may be important to develop some means of data augmentation to improve the accuracy of the proposed method.

In addition, the proposed method requires manual adjustment for template matching. In this study, we adjust 90 landmarks. Though we took less than 5 min per 1 model, it should be a non-negligible effort as the dataset expands. Therefore, automation of template matching by automatic landmark estimation would be an effective enhancement to the proposed method.

Analysis Method. This study used principal component analysis for attributes extraction. This is a powerful method for extracting a large number of parameters into few attributes. But it has the disadvantages that it can only perform linear transformations. Many of the fine details of anime-like avatars should be expressed as nonlinear transformations.

The features obtained using principal component analysis are considered to be smoothly averaged, especially for areas with irregular changes (e.g., the sharp eyebrow). Non-linear methods like deep-learning could improve the quality, but this would increase the computation time when applied to VR application.

In our application, we applied deformations based on features as shape keys in Unity. This enabled linear but fast deformation with an instant time. In the future, when applying nonlinear deformations to applications, optimization will be necessary to reproduce the detail of the training data without excessive high-polygonization.

Extension to Texture Material. The deformations implemented in this study are limited to face and body shapes. However, the details in the training data include texture images. By extending the application of template matching to texture images, the range of avatars that can be generated will be increased dramatically.

References

1. Ministry of Economy Trade and Industry. Survey and analysis project on future possibilities and issues of virtual space (2021). https://www.meti.go.jp/press/2021/07/20210713001/20210713001.html
2. The Japan Research Institute Limited. Overview and trends of metaverse - for application in business scenes (2022). https://www.jri.co.jp/page.jsp?id=103031
3. Shi, T., Yuan, Y., Fan, C., Zou, Z., Shi, Z., Liu, Y.: Face-to-parameter translation for game character auto-creation. In: Proceedings of the IEEE/CVF International Conference on Computer Vision, pp. 161–170 (2019)
4. Bao, J., Chen, D., Wen, F., Li, H., Hua, G.: CVAE-GAN: fine-grained image generation through asymmetric training. In: Proceedings of the IEEE International Conference on Computer Vision, pp. 2745–2754 (2017)
5. Gatys, L.A., Ecker, A.S., Bethge, M.: Image style transfer using convolutional neural networks. In: Proceedings of the IEEE Conference on Computer Vision and Pattern Recognition, pp. 2414–2423 (2016)
6. Loper, M., Mahmood, N., Romero, J., Pons-Moll, G., Black, M.J.: SMPL: a skinned multi-person linear model. ACM Trans. Graph. (TOG) **34**(6), 1–16 (2015)

7. Ichim, A.E., Bouaziz, S., Pauly, M.: Dynamic 3D avatar creation from hand-held video input. ACM Trans. Graph. (ToG) **34**(4), 1–14 (2015)
8. Li, Z., Yu, T., Pan, C., Zheng, Z., Liu, Y.: Robust 3D self-portraits in seconds. In: Proceedings of the IEEE/CVF Conference on Computer Vision and Pattern Recognition, pp. 1344–1353 (2020)
9. Radford, A., et al.: Learning transferable visual models from natural language supervision. In: International Conference on Machine Learning, pp. 8748–8763. PMLR (2021)
10. Hong, F., Zhang, M., Pan, L., Cai, Z., Yang, L., Liu, Z.: AvatarCLIP: zero-shot text-driven generation and animation of 3D avatars. ACM Trans. Graph. (TOG) **41**(4), 1–19 (2022)
11. Niki, T., Komuro, T.: Semi-automatic creation of an anime-like 3D face model from a single illustration. In: 2019 International Conference on Cyberworlds (CW), pp. 53–56. IEEE (2019)
12. Li, R., Nakayama, M., Fujishiro, I.: Automatic generation of 3D natural anime-like non-player characters with machine learning. In: 2020 International Conference on Cyberworlds (CW), pp. 110–116. IEEE (2020)
13. Choy, C.B., Xu, D., Gwak, J.Y., Chen, K., Savarese, S.: 3D-R2N2: a unified approach for single and multi-view 3D object reconstruction. In: Leibe, B., Matas, J., Sebe, N., Welling, M. (eds.) ECCV 2016. LNCS, vol. 9912, pp. 628–644. Springer, Cham (2016). https://doi.org/10.1007/978-3-319-46484-8_38
14. Peng, S., Niemeyer, M., Mescheder, L., Pollefeys, M., Geiger, A.: Convolutional occupancy networks. In: Vedaldi, A., Bischof, H., Brox, T., Frahm, J.-M. (eds.) ECCV 2020. LNCS, vol. 12348, pp. 523–540. Springer, Cham (2020). https://doi.org/10.1007/978-3-030-58580-8_31
15. Qi, C.R., Su, H., Mo, K., Guibas, L.J.: PointNet: deep learning on point sets for 3D classification and segmentation. In: Proceedings of the IEEE Conference on Computer Vision and Pattern Recognition (CVPR) (2017)
16. Kato, H., Ushiku, Y., Harada, T.: Neural 3D mesh renderer. In: Proceedings of the IEEE Conference on Computer Vision and Pattern Recognition, pp. 3907–3916 (2018)
17. Mildenhall, B., Srinivasan, P.P., Tancik, M., Barron, J.T., Ramamoorthi, R., Nerf, R.N.: Representing scenes as neural radiance fields for view synthesis. In ECCV (2020)
18. Park, J.J., Florence, P., Straub, J., Newcombe, R., Lovegrove, S.: DeepSDF: learning continuous signed distance functions for shape representation. In: Proceedings of the IEEE/CVF Conference on Computer Vision and Pattern Recognition, pp. 165–174 (2019)
19. Genova, K., Cole, F., Sud, A., Sarna, A., Funkhouser, T.: Local deep implicit functions for 3D shape. In: Proceedings of the IEEE/CVF Conference on Computer Vision and Pattern Recognition, pp. 4857–4866 (2020)
20. Pixiv Inc. BOOTH. https://booth.pm/ja
21. Pixiv Inc., Vroid studio. https://vroid.com/studio
22. Alexandrovsky, D., et al.: Examining design choices of questionnaires in VR user studies. In: Proceedings of the 2020 CHI Conference on Human Factors in Computing Systems, CHI 2020, New York, NY, USA, pp. 1–21. Association for Computing Machinery (2020)
23. Knibbe, J., Schjerlund, J., Petraeus, M., Hornbæk, K.: The dream is collapsing: the experience of exiting VR. In: CHI 2018, New York, NY, USA, pp. 1–13. Association for Computing Machinery (2018)

A Study on Color Schemes for Nostalgic Illustrations

Ryuta Motegi[1](✉), Kai Lenz[2], and Kunio Kondo[2]

[1] Tokai University, Kanagawa 259-1292, Japan
motegi@tsc.u-tokai.ac.jp
[2] Tokyo University of Technology, Tokyo 192-0982, Japan

Abstract. Recently, many illustrations have been published mainly on social media, making it easier to appreciate a variety of illustrations on a daily basis. Among them are illustrations that evoke a sense of nostalgia, with tags such as "nostalgic", "natsukasii" and "emo". These often choose people and landscapes as motifs, and everyone seems to be able to feel the same nostalgia, despite cultural differences. Illustrations are still images, and like photographs, they have composition, three-dimensionality, and color. Therefore, we believe that illustrations that make people feel "nostalgic" have something in common. The purpose of this study is to clarify the components of illustrations that make people feel nostalgic. For this purpose, we collected 678 nostalgic illustrations of people and landscapes, and investigated whether there were any commonalities in terms of color scheme. The method of the research was to obtain the color of all pixels of each illustration.

Keywords: Nostalgic Illustrations · Color Schemes · Component of illustration

1 Introduction

Advances in network services have increased opportunities for artists to freely publish their works. In Japan, illustration works are published and shared using social media such as pixiv [2] and pinterest [3]. Among them, one of the popular genres in recent years is something that makes you feel nostalgia. In Japan, it is sometimes expressed as "Emoi". In Japan, nostalgia is perceived as nostalgia and melancholy, but it is also perceived positively, such as moving people's emotions. And nostalgia is said to be an experience and emotion felt all over the world, including Japanese people, although there are differences in cultures and ways of feeling it are slightly different [1]. Illustrations that make people feel nostalgia are popular in Japan, but it is not clear why they feel nostalgia from illustrations, but the phenomenon of feeling nostalgia has been confirmed. Emotional studies of nostalgia have been conducted, but few have focused on illustrations and animations. By conducting research on illustrations that feel nostalgia, the development of production support methods will advance and lead to the expansion of nostalgic content. The authors collected illustrations that felt nostalgia and investigated composition and depth expression based on basic photography techniques [4]. As

J. Y. C. Chen and G. Fragomeni (Eds.): HCII 2023, LNCS 14027, pp. 182–191, 2023.
https://doi.org/10.1007/978-3-031-35634-6_13

a result, I discovered the characteristics of illustrations that make me feel nostalgia. In this study, we collected illustrations that also felt nostalgia and investigated their color schemes.

2 Related Work

Nostalgia, which is the subject of this study, is a feeling of nostalgia, longing, and longing for the past. According to Horiuchi's research [5], nostalgia is classified into two categories: personal nostalgia and historical nostalgia. Personal nostalgia is a distillation of only the pleasant aspects of one's past, while historical nostalgia is caused by feelings for historical stories and historical figures from the good old days before one's birth. Nostalgia seems to be present in all cultures, but it is not known exactly what evokes it.

Much research has been conducted on color schemes and color harmony in the fields of interior design, clothing design, and image processing. Research on color schemes for interiors has revealed that warm and cold colors have an effect on human emotions, and that color harmony changes the impression people have on others [6]. Research has also been conducted to extract representative colors from textile images and illustrations and change the color harmony to suit the purpose [7]. However, no research has been conducted to analyze the color schemes of illustrations that evoke a sense of nostalgia. In this study, we collect 678 nostalgic illustrations and clarify the characteristics of their color schemes.

3 Color Scheme Analysis for Nostalgic Illustration

The purpose of the color scheme analysis was to find the characteristics of the color scheme of illustrations that evoke nostalgia. Illustrations were collected using social media such as pixiv and pinterest, as well as Google image search. The search was conducted using the Japanese words "Nosutarujiku" and "Natsukashii," and 678 illustrations were collected. The collected illustrations were analyzed according to the procedure shown in Fig. 1. The collected illustrations were resized to 500 pixels on the long side without changing the aspect ratio. The resizing was done to reduce the amount of data processed by the computer.

The next step was to analyze the color schemes of the resized illustrations using the k-means method of the clustering algorithm. The color scheme information was converted to the HSL color space, which is easy for humans to understand. Then we generated three charts as Hue Stacked Bar Chart, Saturation / Lightness Scatterplot and Mean Colors Pie Chart. The following three charts are explained.

The chart in Fig. 2 was created to give an idea of the hues used in the illustrations. The number of pixels of each color hue is counted and stacked as a bar graph. This allows us to see which hues are used more and which are not used in the illustration. The reason for selecting 36 hues instead of 360 is based on the painting materials used by humans and on the condition that point colors can be extracted when analyzing the illustration. This allows the hues used to be clearly distinguished as in a histogram.

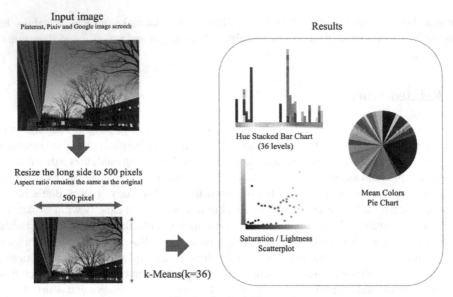

Fig. 1. Analysis Process

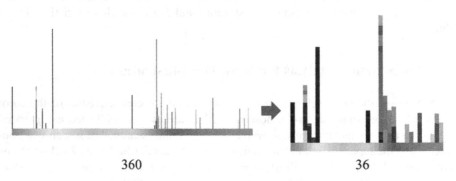

Fig. 2. Hue Stacked Bar Chart

The left side of Fig. 3, the Saturation and lightness distribution chart, is explained below. The vertical axis of this chart shows the saturation scale of the most commonly used hue. The horizontal axis is lightness. By looking at this division chart, the characteristics of the color scheme for each illustration can be confirmed.

The right side of Fig. 3, the Mean Colors Pie Chart, is explained below. This chart is used to show the ratio of colors in an illustration. The chart shows the average color reduction to 36 colors, but you can check which colors are used and how much.

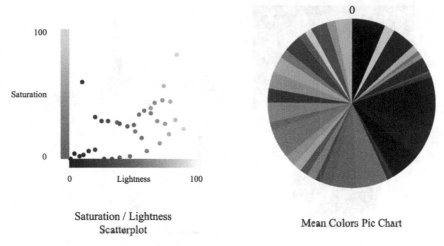

Saturation / Lightness
Scatterplot

Mean Colors Pie Chart

Fig. 3. Saturation / Lightness Scatterplot and Mean Colors Pie Chart

4 Results and Discussion

4.1 Results of Color Scheme

The results of the analysis of the illustrations are shown in Figs. 4, 5, 6, 7, 8 and 9. All illustrations used in the example results are blurred for copyright protection purposes.

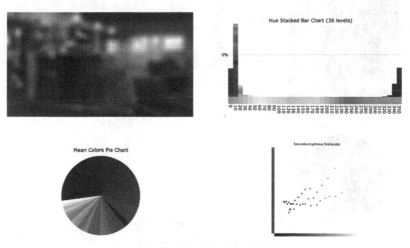

Fig. 4. Analysis Example 01

The illustration in Fig. 4 depicts the interior of a coffee shop. It can be seen that it is drawn using hues of 340–20°.

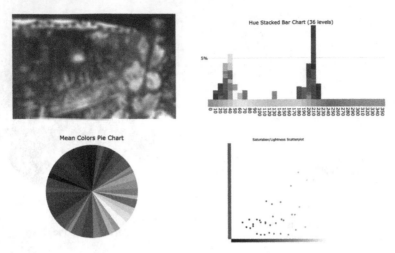

Fig. 5. Analysis Example 02

The illustration in Fig. 5 shows that it is drawn mainly using hues around 40 and 210°. This illustration depicts shopping at an imaginary store.

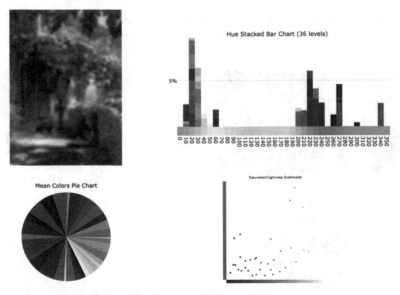

Fig. 6. Analysis Example 03

The illustration in Fig. 6 depicts a cityscape. Hues around 20 and 230° are mainly used. The mean color pie chart shows that although the color area is small, the point color of the person is well captured.

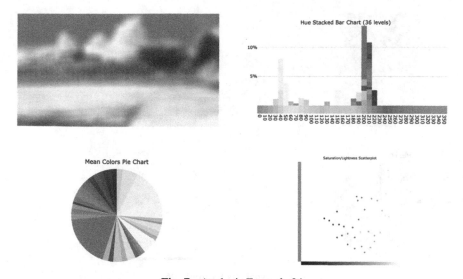

Fig. 7. Analysis Example 04

The illustration in Fig. 7 depicts a schoolyard of a Japanese junior or elementary school. As can be seen from the hue chart, the colors used in the illustration are mainly the colors of the ground and the sky of the schoolyard.

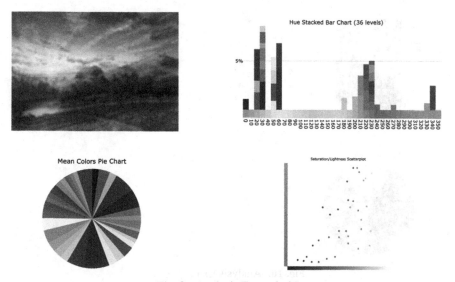

Fig. 8. Analysis Example 05

The illustration in Fig. 8 depicts a landscape of fields and houses in a mountainous region of Japan. As in Fig. 7, two hue regions are mainly used.

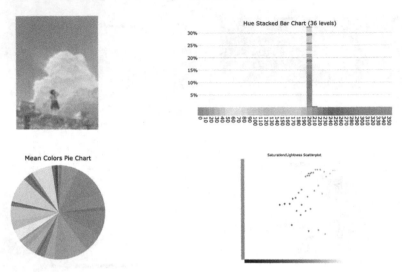

Fig. 9. Analysis Example 06

The illustration in Fig. 9 depicts a scene looking up at the sky from under the surface of a swimming pool in a Japanese junior or senior high school. As can be seen from the hue chart, the illustration uses only hues in the 2° range, so that it is safe to say that all the colors are blue.

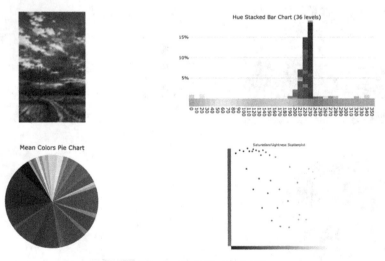

Fig. 10. Analysis Example 07

The illustration in Fig. 10 depicts the Japanese countryside just after sunset. As in Fig. 9, this illustration uses almost the same hues, but as can be seen from the chart of lightness, the impression of the same hue at lower lightness can be seen to have changed.

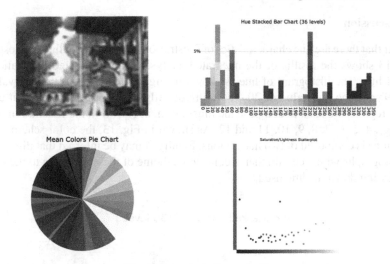

Fig. 11. Analysis Example 08

The illustration in Fig. 11 depicts a bus stop in a residential area in Japan. This illustration uses a wide range of hues to depict a residential area. However, the wide range of hues does not give the illustration a sense of unity. Therefore, a sense of unity is created by reducing the saturation.

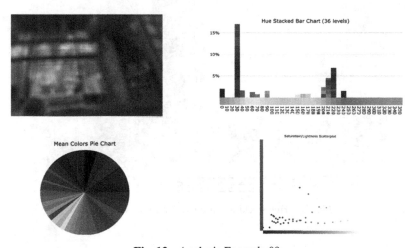

Fig. 12. Analysis Example 09

The illustration in Fig. 12 is composed of a traditional wooden Japanese house looking up at the sky from the floor.

Since the illustration depicts a room in a wooden Japanese house, a wide range of hues are used. However, as in Fig. 11, the saturation is lowered to create a sense of unity in the room and a clear contrast with the sky seen through the window.

4.2 Discussion

It is clear that there are hue characteristics of illustrations that evoke feelings of nostalgia. Figure 13 shows the results of the integrated analysis of the collected illustrations in terms of hue. The histogram of hue as shown in Fig. 13 reveals that the hue value of 210–229° and the hue value of 20–39° are frequently used. This indicates that one or two hue regions are used to compose the illustration, as shown in the illustration results from Figs. 4, 5, 6, 7, 8, 9, 10, 11 and 12. As shown in Fig. 13, the color scheme of the illustrations is composed of two hue regions. Finally, it may be inferred that illustrations and photographs with a certain theme convey the theme of the illustration to the viewer by narrowing down the hue used.

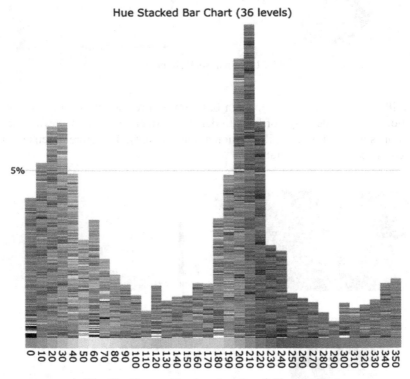

Fig. 13. Hue stacking bar chart for all illustrations

5   Conclusion

In this study, we collected 678 nostalgic illustrations to investigate the color scheme characteristics of nostalgic illustrations. The hue, lightness, and representative colors were extracted from the color schemes of these illustrations using the k-means clustering algorithm. As a result, it became clear that there was a certain trend in the hues used in the illustrations. Although the hues varied depending on the motif including the theme of the illustration and the time of day, it also became clear that illustrations that evoke a sense of nostalgia are drawn using red and blue pigments and in a single hue range. We believe that this can be used as an indicator of the color scheme used by creators when drawing illustrations.

Future work will require comparison with illustrations that do not evoke a sense of nostalgia. It is also necessary to analyze the relationship with the composition and motifs. As a future development, it is necessary to develop tools and methods for drawing support using these results.

References

1. Nagamine, M., Toyama, M.: Do Japanese people experience nostalgia?: focus on the side of "bitter sweetness" of nostalgia. Japan. J. Res. Emotions **24**(1), 22–32 (2016)
2. https://www.pixiv.net. Last accessed 10 Jan 2022
3. https://www.pinterest.com. Last accessed 10 Jan 2022
4. Motegi, R., Kondo, K.: Analysis of nostalgic illustrations based on photography techniques. In: Proceedings of the 13th Asian Forum on Graphic Science (AFGS 2021), pp. 43–48 (2021)
5. Horiuchi, K.: Consumer's Nostalgia: An Examination of Previous Studies and Future Research Themes, vol. 201, pp. 179–198. The Seijo University Arts and Literature Quarterly (2007)
6. Kobayashi, S.: The aim and method of the color image scale. Color Res. Appl. **6**(2), 93–107 (2009). Summer 1981
7. Ishii, M., Kondo, K.: Extraction system of kansei information for patterns. In: Proceedings of the 8th ICECGDG, vol.2, pp. 405–410 (1998)

An Approach for Visual Realism Complexity Classification of 3D Models in Virtual and Augmented Reality

Rahel Schmied-Kowarzik[✉] [ID], Pia Reisewitz, Lina Kaschub[ID], Rebecca Rodeck, and Gerko Wende

German Aerospace Center, Institute of Maintenance, Repair, and Overhaul, Hein-Saß-Weg 22, 21129 Hamburg, Germany
rahel.schmied-kowarzik@dlr.de

Abstract. 3D models are at the core of every virtual and augmented reality application. They appear in varying degrees of visual realism complexity, depending on the intention of use and contextual as well as technical limitations. The research concerning the effects induced by different degrees of visual realism complexity of 3D models can be used to define in which fields and applications a high visual realism is needed.

This paper proposes a classification of 3D models in extended reality applications, according to their visual realism complexity. To identify the aspects of realism classification this work considers how past studies defined the virtual realism complexity of 3D models and looks into approaches of diverse disciplines.

After defining the visual realism complexity scale, the paper validates the method in a user study. The study was conducted with 24 participants that viewed 16 different 3D models in virtual reality and rated them with the proposed scale.

The collected data shows a significant correlation between subjective realism and the proposed scale. Next to depicting visual realism, the scale also improves the explicitness of realism ratings.

The classification enables scientists to specify the level of visual realism complexity of their used 3D models. At the same time, this opens up opportunities to conduct comparable research about visual realism complexity.

Keywords: Human factors · Visual Realism · Extended Reality · Performance measurement · Visualization and image rendering

1 Introduction

3D models are at the core of every virtual and augmented reality (VR/AR) application. They appear in varying degrees of visual realism complexity, depending on the intention of use and contextual as well as technical limitations. Software developers aim to fit the degree of visual realism complexity of a 3D model to the task at hand. Knowing the effects of a specific degree of visual realism complexity is needed to decide when high visual realism is needed or when a low visual 3D model is sufficient or even better.

J. Y. C. Chen and G. Fragomeni (Eds.): HCII 2023, LNCS 14027, pp. 192–202, 2023.
https://doi.org/10.1007/978-3-031-35634-6_14

A lot of extended reality (XR) research focuses on the difference between high and low visual realism complexity of virtual environments throughout many different fields (use cases) [1–5]. This research produces a different solution to the question of how to define the difference between high and low realism complexity.

Huang & Klippel [2] and Hvass et al. [4] compare the visual realism complexity of two environments in XR by changing the number of polygons of the 3D models, stating that a lower number of polygons correlates with lower realism. While true in some cases, this assumption is not always valid. It is possible to have a cube or plane with just a few polygons and one with many and their surface is visually the same in both configurations. This is further discussed by Ramanarayanan et al. [6], who analyze how an object with fewer polygons can visually look the same to save computing power.

In Schmied-Kowarzik & Paelke [5] CityGML 2.0 [7] defines a city's visual realism complexity in VR. The CityGML 2.0 defines different Levels of Detail (LoD) of a building, starting with a wireframe of an object all the way to a furnished building with colors. Although it is possible to fit 3D objects of houses to this concept and define their LoD, this approach does not cover the entire realm of visual realism complexity since its focus is reduced to a specific kind of 3D model. Furthermore, CityGML 2.0 [7] does not give a big enough spectrum to classify 3D houses in every case.

Due to the lack of a universal classification for visual realism complexity in 3D models, research is incomparable, and conducting studies in this field is always inherent with the author's definition of what a low or a high realism 3D model looks like.

To address this problem, this work investigates how past studies chose factors that define the differences in realism between different XR objects. Additionally, a broader investigation in the field of visual realism is done. Looking into approaches of diverse disciplines allows getting an overview of the perception of visual realism complexity.

This overview is used to propose a classification of 3D models in XR applications, according to their visual realism complexity. Furthermore, the classification approach is validated with a user study.

2   Visual Realism Classification Scale

The level of realism, that a subject experiences in XR, is mostly investigated by collecting data on the level of immersion in a complete or partial virtual environment. Schwind et al. and Slater et al. for example show a higher presence in more realistic environments [1, 8]. Lead by the assumption that a high level of immersion correlates with a high level of realism, Stevens and Jerrams-Smiths [9] also collect data on presence to investigate the realism experience. However, this correlation assumption is not always true. Schmied-Kowarzik et al. [5] showed that factors like certain emotions can influence the level of immersion, decoupling it from the level of realism.

Alternative methods include scoring visual realism using binary classification (real or not real) [10] or introducing a point system, where realism can be evaluated more accurately [11, 12]. These subjective methods can lead to great variance in the answers and are therefore insufficient for conducting comparable research or using them as definitions in scientific work.

The visual realism classification scale (VRCS) defined in this chapter sets the foundation for measurable visual realism. To propose a classification scale for visual realism, the core elements which influence visual realism in XR need to be identified.

Other research papers which compare visual realism complexity such as Mel Slater [1], Lee et al. [3], Huang & Klippel [2], and Hvass et al. [4], often focus on geometry, texture, and in some cases on lightning.

Rademacher et al. examine the perception of visual realism in images. The two factors that were found to significantly impact perceived visual realism are shadows and structure. [13].

Taking these factors into account, the VRCS, shown in Table 1, combines the elements shadow, light, texture, and form complexity of 3D models. These elements each combine several items which can be mapped to the 3D object. For each element, the items have specific scores between 0–2 based on the scientific foundation.

In the research of Rademacher et al., soft shadows seem more realistic than hard shadows. In the VRCS the shadow element includes the items *no shadow* (0 pts.), *hard shadow* (1 pt.), and *soft shadow* (2 pts.).

Closely related to the shadow element is the light element, in which the VRCS distinguishes between *no light* (0 pts.), *general environment light* (1 pt.), and *directional light* (2 pt.).

In the studies of Huang & Klippel [2] and Hvass et al. [4] realism is changed by reducing texture quality and the number of polygons. Textured objects usually give a better impression of the look of an object, compared to objects that are intentionally colored without a pattern. The texture of a 3D model is described by the items *no intentional color* (0 pts.), *intentional color* (1 pt.), and a *color that shows a pattern* (2 pts.). When texturing a 3D model, one must also consider surface texture, which can be realized by adding a normal map, among other things. The texture element of the VRCS, therefore, has another item described if the *texture appears 3D*. This item can be true (1 pt.) or false (0 pts.).

Reduction of polygon count is a rather good method to get to objects with lower visual realism, however, it is not sufficient as a definition for visual realism as explained in the introduction of this paper. The VRSC element For, therefore, defines the form complexity in 3 states. An object is either *unintentionally shaped* (0 pts.), *intentionally shaped* (1 pt.), or *includes detailed form adjustment* (2 pts.).

The total value assigned to the 3D model is calculated by adding up the scores for each element. The score defines the visual realism complexity, from not looking like the real object at all (0) to very realistic (10).

3 Validation Study

To validate the VRCS, a study was conducted to test its reliability and validity. The general concept of the study is to show participants different objects in a virtual environment and have them rate those objects with the help of the proposed items. While the main aim is to see how the participants judge different objects and how similar the objects get rated, it also helps to see if the items were understood and how easy it is to use the scale. By doing a between-object comparison of the ratings of the objects, the reliability can

Table 1. Visual Realism Classification Scale

Element	Item Value	Explanation
Shadow	No Shadow	Shadows refer to dark areas around and on an object where the object blocks the light
	Hard Shadow	If the object has no dark areas around and on it, there are **no shadows**
	Soft Shadow	If the dark areas have sharp edges separating them from the light areas, the shadows are called "**hard**"
		If the edges between the light and dark areas are diffused, the shadows are called "**soft**"
Light	No Light	Light refers to the complexity of light sources shown by the object's light reflections
	General Environment Light	If the object is lit in a general, diffused way, the light is called "**general environment light**"
	Directional Light	The second option, "**directional light**", is true if the object is lit from one or multiple distinct directions
	Reflections	Reflection means the return of light from an object
		If the object has intentional reflections throughout the complete object, the option Reflections is true
		Intentional hereby means that the surface of the object reflects light like one would expect it to
Texture	Seemingly Unintentional	Texture here refers to the appearance of the surface of an object and its color
	One Intentional Color	If the color and surface of the object seem unrelated to the real object that should be displayed, the texture is "**seemingly unintentional**"
	A Texture that Shows a Pattern	If the texture has a color that relates to the real object that should be displayed, it has "**intentional color**"
	Texture Depth	If the texture also shows a pattern, the third option is true
		If the surface structure shows intentional depth information (appears 3D) then the item Texture Depth is true
Form	Seemingly Unintentionally Shaped	If the form/shape of the object seems unrelated to the object, the form is "**seemingly unintentionally shaped**"
	Intentionally Shaped	If the shape of the object relates to the object, it is "**intentionally shaped**"
	Includes Detailed Form Adjustment	If the object includes fine adjustments and displacements in form, the third option is true

be shown, as matching scores are an indicator of the VRCS being an objective measure to classify objects.

The study took between 30–50 min where the participants examine the objects in a virtual environment and subsequently answer the VRCS items on a computer. Before the participants looked at the actual objects they had to fill out a few questionnaires and were shown an exemplary video on the computer. This allowed the participants to get familiar with the questions and know what to look for in the VR environment.

3.1 Implementation

The main part of the study was implemented using the Game Engine Unity3D, where a virtual reality environment was built. A neutral scene was created, to not distract the participant and influence their judgment of the realism of the objects. Within the scene, the objects were placed on a grey cube, which allowed for a top-frontal view of the objects. The participants were able to explore the space freely and inspect the object from all perspectives to get a thorough impression. All the objects were scaled to fit on the cube, to allow the participants an easier inspection.

Using the HTC Vive Pro, participants were able to look at the objects without a time limit. They then set down the head-mounted display (HMD) to answer the VRCS questions on the computer. While rating the objects, they were allowed to reenter VR as often as they wanted.

3.2 Object Selection

Multiple factors played a role in the process of object selection. First participants needed to be familiar with the objects to accurately determine how realistic these objects are. Thus, only objects that are part of day-to-day life were chosen. Secondly, objects which display different levels of realism were required. To achieve that, without including personal opinions of realism, the objects were downloaded from the internet collection Turbosquid. After determining what kind of objects to show, the first four free objects were chosen (with the exception that objects that resembled each other too closely were not considered), to get a selection without any personal bias. Having four different groups of objects (shoes, bananas, house plants, and cars) with four objects each leads to a pool of 16 different objects.

Lastly, the shadow and lighting needed to be modified, as this is independent of the 3D model itself. To avoid personal biases on the association of shadows to objects, a shadow was randomly assigned to each object, while making sure that "soft", "hard" and "no shadow" were equally distributed.

3.3 Demographic Information

At the beginning of the Study, the participants had to answer some demographic questions, concerning age, gender, profession, and visual impairment, as well as questions about their media experience. Using 5-point scales they were asked to indicate how often they come in contact with virtual 3D models (never – almost every day), how often they experience VR (never heard of it – regularly), and how often they play video games (never – every day).

3.4 Immersive Tendencies Questionnaire (ITQ)

As the study takes place in a virtual environment the personal predisposition regarding immersion was additionally collected. Using the Immersive Tendency Questionnaire (ITQ) by Witmer and Singer (1994) [14] each participant is scored on how high their propensity is to feel immersed in different situations.

3.5 NASA-TLX

After rating all objects in a randomized order, the participants were asked to fill out the NASA-TLX [15], which was developed to measure the workload of a task, looking at mental demand, physical demand, temporal demand, performance, effort, and frustration.

3.6 Subjective Realism

In this paper, the investigation of the experience of realism was similarly based on the point system used in Elhelw et al. [12] and Zhu et al. [11] as participants had to rate the objects on a scale of 0 to 10 (not realistic at all to very realistic). Comparing this simple realism score with the VCRS score visualizes if the VRCS is measuring the concept of visual realism.

4 Results

The study was conducted with 24 participants (10 female, 14 male) between 20 and 60 years old. The majority ($n = 17$) were between 20 and 34 years old.

Sixteen Participants work as research associates. The other participants were students or employees. All participants except four had worn a VR HMD at least once before (Fig. 1).

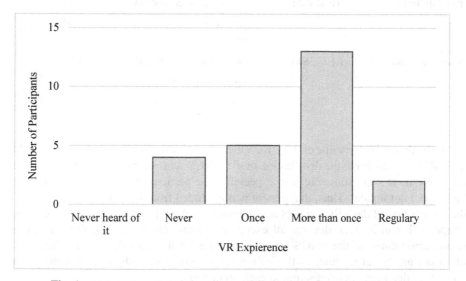

Fig. 1. Distribution of virtual reality experience throughout the participants

The experience with 3D models is similar, six people state no contact with 3D models, eleven come in contact with 3D models sometimes, four monthly, and five about once a week to almost every day.

On average the ITQ score was 70.75 ranging from a minimum of 41 points to a maximum of 97, with a standard deviation of 15.85. A higher score in the ITQ is indicative of a higher level of immersive tendencies.

The subjective realism score for each of the 16 objects was calculated as the mean from all the participants' judgments giving an average impression of the realism of the objects. These scores ranged between 0.71 and 8.08. The ratings show that *Object 4* was scored as the least realistic (0.71 points) and *Object 1* (8.00 points) and *Object 5* (8.08 points) were scored most realistic.

Evaluation of the VRCS is done by summing up the individual scores for each item. To get an average value for each item the mean for every object was calculated from the individual participants' scores. The worst score was achieved by *Object 4* (1.71 points), while *Object 1* (8.92 points) and *Object 5* (8.5 points) scored the highest, similar to the subjective realism score.

Correlating the subjective realism score with the VRCS score for each item shows a significant positive correlation for both a Kendall-Tau-b correlation ($\tau b = 0.70$, $p < 0.001$) and for Spearman-Rho ($r(14) = 0.83$, $p < 0.001$), as can be seen in Table 2. A positive correlation means that objects that ranked higher in the VRCS also had a higher perceived realism score.

Table 2. Correlation between the subjective realism score and the VRCS (** sig. For $p < 0.001$)

			VRCS
Kendall-Tau-b	REALISM	Correlation coefficient	,695**
		Sig. (two-sided)	,000
		N	16
Spearman-Rho	REALISM	Correlation coefficient	,834**
		Sig. (two-sided)	,000
		N	16

To further show the value of the VRCS the subjective realism scores are compared to the VRCS scores. First, the distribution of the VRCS scores for each object was looked at. While there were some outliers, especially one participant showed scores that are far off and not logical. Thus, that person was excluded from further analysis. In Fig. 2 the distribution of the VRCS scores are compared to the subjective realism scores using boxplots. It can be seen that for all except 2 objects (*Object 11* and *Object 12*) the interquartile range of the VRCS scores is smaller. That means that the medium 50% of values are closer together in the VRCS score than in the subjective realism score, indicating that rater scores resembled each other more.

It can further be seen that for a few objects the scores between VRCS and subjective realism vary from each other, for example, *Object 8* and *Object 10*. These objects both have a higher VRCS score than realism score.

The workload as given by the NASA-TLX can be looked at per factor or in total. The total is calculated by adding the individual scores up and averaging them. The total

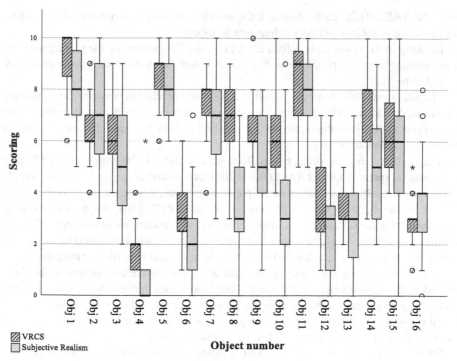

Fig. 2. Distribution of the VRCS scores compared to the subjective realism scores

workload has a mean score of 32.2 out of 100 (*min* = 5.5, *max* = 67.0, *SD* = 13.0). Looking at prior work the NASA-TLX scores can be interpreted in different ranges corresponding to different levels of workload. According to Prabaswari et al. [16] the mean score of 32.2 would be a *somewhat high* workload (30–49 points). Analyzing the NASA-TLX by factors the mental demand has the highest influence on workload with a mean of 53.1 points (*min* = 16, *max* = 100, *SD* = 21.2), followed by effort (*mean* = 40.9, *min* = 0, *max* = 88, *SD* = 25.9). Categorizing them, one gets a *high* (50–79 points) and the other one *somewhat high* workload respectively. The other factors all fall into the category of *medium* workload (10–29 points), which is only followed by *low* workload with (0–9 points). The performance scores a mean of 28.3 (*min* = 6, *max* = 67, *SD* = 12.8), the frustration is at a score of 24.9 (*min* = 0, *max* = 66, *SD* = 20.8), the temporal demand is slightly lower with a mean of 24.2 (*min* = 0, *max* = 84, *SD* = 24.4) and lastly, there is the physical demand with the score of 21.8 (*min* = 0, *max* = 85, *SD* = 20.3).

5   Conclusion

The results show that most of the participants were research associates. Most participants had at least some experience with 3D models and virtual reality. The participants in this study fit the application area of the VRCS, this is the first requirement to receive relevant data. The NASA-TLX scores show that the workload is only *somewhat high*, indicating that the scale is not too mentally exhausting in its use.

Looking at the research of Rózsa et al. [17], the ITQ scores of the participants are in the average range for people, which is at 73.14, and the average value from this study is just below that.

The study was able to show a significant positive correlation between the subjective realism scale and the VRCS score. This indicates that the VRCS measures the visual realism perceived by a subject, as objects with higher VRCS scores also score higher in the subjective realism score.

The objects were the subjective realism scores and VRCS scores showed higher discrepancies (namely *Object 8* and *Object 10*) were looked at in detail. To have a scale that reflects the subjective realism participants experience, it is important to look at those objects, in particular, to infer improvements to the VRCS. First, the item concerning reflections sticks out. Participants often scored visible reflections as true, regardless of whether the reflections of the object were appropriate or not. This could be solved by clearer instructions or examples for the VRCS elements and in particular the reflections. A clearer instruction and the examples could also help reduce the outliers in the data. Secondly, the elements light and shadows could have a too large influence. As they are closely related to one another, a high score in one item usually means a high score in the other. Additionally, *no light* is a scenario were nothing would be visible. In future research, the elements light and shadow should be revisited.

Further, it was explored how the VRCS ratings are distributed, as ratings close to each other are indicative of the scale being able to objectively capture the visual realism of objects. Looking at Fig. 2, the scores of the VRCS are closer to each other than the subjective realism scores for the same object. As two objects do not fit that pattern, it is important to look at those more closely. It can be seen that the shadows of *Object 11* are not illustrated correctly, which might affect how people scored the item regarding shadows and *Object 12* has a similar problem with textures, as it has one detailed part, while the rest is just colored plainly. This is one aspect, that could be explored in future work, as objects with indicators of different levels of realism, are difficult to be captured by the VRCS. However, these objects are usually not the norm and rather an edge-case scenario.

In conclusion, the results show that the scale not only captures visual realism but also contributes a more consistent rating than when asking for simple realism judgment. The classification enables scientists to define the level of visual realism complexity of their used 3D models and with further research to choose the visual realism complexity according to task etc. At the same time, this opens up opportunities to conduct comparable research about visual realism complexity.

References

1. Slater, M., Khanna, P., Mortensen, J., Yu, I.: Visual realism enhances realistic response in an immersive virtual environment. IEEE Comput. Graphics Appl. **29**, 76–84 (2009). https://doi.org/10.1109/MCG.2009.55

2. Huang, J., Klippel, A.: The effects of visual realism on spatial memory and exploration patterns in virtual reality. In: Teather, R.J., et al. (eds.) 26th ACM Symposium on Virtual Reality Software and Technology. VRST '20: 26th ACM Symposium on Virtual Reality Software and Technology, Virtual Event Canada, 01 11 2020 04 11 2020, pp. 1–11. ACM, New York, NY, USA (2020). https://doi.org/10.1145/3385956.3418945

3. Lee, C., Rincon, G.A., Meyer, G., Höllerer, T., Bowman, D.A.: The effects of visual realism on search tasks in mixed reality simulation. IEEE Trans. Visual Comput. Graphics **19**, 547–556 (2013). https://doi.org/10.1109/TVCG.2013.41

4. Hvass, J., Larsen, O., Vendelbo, K., Nilsson, N., Nordahl, R., Serafin, S.: Visual realism and presence in a virtual reality game. In: 2017 3DTV Conference: The True Vision – Capture, Transmission and Display of 3D Video (3DTV-CON). 2017 3DTV Conference: The True Vision – Capture, Transmission and Display of 3D Video (3DTV-CON), Copenhagen, 07.06.2017–09.06.2017, pp. 1–4. IEEE (2017). https://doi.org/10.1109/3DTV.2017.8280421

5. Schmied-Kowarzik, R.L., Paelke, V.: Examining the importance of realism in virtual reality therapy environments for people with specific phobias. In: Weier, M., Bues, M., Wechner, R. (eds.) GI VR/AR Workshop. Gesellschaft für Informatik e.V (2021). https://doi.org/10.18420/vrar2021_16

6. Ramanarayanan, G., Bala, K., Ferwerda, J.A.: Perception of complex aggregates. ACM Trans. Graph. **27**, 60 (2008). https://doi.org/10.1145/1360612.1360659

7. Löwner, M.-O.. Benner, J., Gröger, G., Gruber, U., Häfele, K.-H., Schlüter, S.: CityGML 2.0 – Ein internationaler Standard für 3D-Stadtmodelle. Teil 1: Datenmodell. ZFV – Zeitschrift fur Geodasie, Geoinformation und Landmanagement **137**, 340–349 (2012)

8. Schwind, V., Knierim, P., Haas, N., Henze, N.: Using presence questionnaires in virtual reality. In: Brewster, S., Fitzpatrick, G., Cox, A., Kostakos, V. (eds.) Proceedings of the 2019 CHI Conference on Human Factors in Computing Systems. CHI'19: CHI Conference on Human Factors in Computing Systems, Glasgow Scotland Uk, 04 05 2019 09 05 2019, pp. 1–12. ACM, New York, NY, USA (05022019). https://doi.org/10.1145/3290605.3300590

9. Stevens, B., Jerrams-Smith, J.: The sense of object-presence with projection-augmented models. In: Brewster, S., Murray-Smith, R. (eds.) Haptic HCI 2000. LNCS, vol. 2058, pp. 194–198. Springer, Heidelberg (2001). https://doi.org/10.1007/3-540-44589-7_21

10. Fan, S., et al.: Image visual realism: from human perception to machine computation. IEEE Trans. Pattern Anal. Mach. Intell. **40**, 2180–2193 (2018). https://doi.org/10.1109/tpami.2017.2747150

11. Zhu, J.-Y., Krahenbuhl, P., Shechtman, E., Efros, A.A.: Learning a Discriminative Model for the Perception of Realism in Composite Images. In: 2015 IEEE International Conference on Computer Vision (ICCV). 2015 IEEE International Conference on Computer Vision (ICCV), Santiago, Chile, 07.12.2015 – 13.12.2015, pp. 3943–3951. IEEE (122015). https://doi.org/10.1109/iccv.2015.449

12. Elhelw, M., Nicolaou, M., Chung, A., Yang, G.-Z., Atkins, M.S.: A gaze-based study for investigating the perception of visual realism in simulated scenes. ACM Trans. Appl. Percept. **5**, 3 (2008). https://doi.org/10.1145/1279640.1279643

13. Rademacher, P., Lengyel, J., Cutrell, E., Whitted, T.: Measuring the perception of visual realism in images. In: Gortler, S.J., Myszkowski, K. (eds.) EGSR 2001. E, pp. 235–247. Springer, Vienna (2001). https://doi.org/10.1007/978-3-7091-6242-2_22

14. Witmer, B.G., Singer, M.J.: Measuring presence in virtual environments: a presence question-naire. Presence: Teleoperators Virtual Environ. **7**, 225–240 (1998). https://doi.org/10.1162/105474698565686
15. Hart, S.G.: Nasa-task load index (NASA-TLX); 20 years later. Proc. Hum/ Factors Ergon. Soc. Annu. Meeting **50**, 904–908 (2006). https://doi.org/10.1177/154193120605000909
16. Prabaswari, A.D., Basumerda, C., Wahyu Utomo, B.: The mental workload analysis of staff in study program of private educational organization. IOP Conf. Ser.: Mater. Sci. Eng. **528**, 012018 (2019). https://doi.org/10.1088/1757-899X/528/1/012018
17. Rózsa, S., et al.: Measuring immersion, involvement, and attention focusing tendencies in the mediated environment: the applicability of the immersive tendencies questionnaire. Front. Psychol. **13**, 931955 (2022). https://doi.org/10.3389/fpsyg.2022.931955

Bow Device for Accurate Reproduction of Archery in xR Environment

Masasuke Yasumoto[✉]

Tokai University, 4-1-1 Kitakaname, Hiratsuka City 259-1292, Kanagawa Prefecture, Japan
m.yasumoto@tsc.u-tokai.ac.jp

Abstract. The purpose of this study is to develop an accurate bow device that can be used in an xR environment. The bow device is designed to be accurate enough to be used in actual archery training. The bow device measures the amount of string pull with a strain gage. In this study, to improve the accuracy of the bow device, experiments were conducted to measure the initial velocity of the arrow using multiple arrows and limbs. Reflecting the results of these experiments and the findings from previous bow device research, we developed new bow device hardware and software that can more accurately reproduce and measure bow behavior. The ultimate goal is to realize physical e-sports, in which players can use their real-life physical abilities and play by moving their bodies widely. Therefore, we created new contents using the bow device developed in this research.

Keywords: Bow Device · xR · Physical eSports · HCI

1 Introduction

The objective of this research is to realize a bow device that is equivalent to real life archery. This is to realize physical e-sports, a new category of sports involving intense physical activity in which physical abilities can be used in an xR environment. In the case of archery devices, this means that the use of individual archery devices can be used for real-life archery training, requiring skills equivalent to those required to handle a real-life bow.

In recent years, virtual sports have been increasingly introduced in shopping malls [1], and some digital sports machines combine video images with actual sports equipment [1]. Some of these machines use bows, but they simply use real bows and arrows and use the position of the arrow's hit. There are archery xR contents that use HMDs and game controllers, as well as consumer game consoles that use bows, but they are not dedicated bow and arrow devices, so the accuracy and reproducibility of bows and arrows are not as high.

On the other hand, for greater precision, we have produced various devices as bow devices. In the research and development of The Light Shooter [2], an electronic bow that uses a traditional Japanese bow and its contents, we incorporated strain gauges and 6-axis inertial sensors into a Japanese bow to estimate the amount of string pull and the direction in which the bow is aimed. The Light Shooter, the content of this project, uses

J. Y. C. Chen and G. Fragomeni (Eds.): HCII 2023, LNCS 14027, pp. 203–214, 2023.
https://doi.org/10.1007/978-3-031-35634-6_15

this information to send arrows flying in the direction of the target on a large screen using a projector. The Third Electronic Bow[3], developed later, uses a higher-precision 9-axis inertial sensor and is equipped with a small computer and laser projector inside to project a virtual image in that direction in all 360-degree directions, enabling the arrow to fly. In recent years, the company has incorporated guns as well as bows, and has also conducted research and development of a system that uses a smartphone screen instead of a projection system. This system, which uses HTC Vive Tracker and other devices, is capable of tracking not only direction but also position. VAIR Field [4] is a system that allows multiple shooters to move around a field of up to 10 m square and shoot at the same time, by reflecting this information to the smartphones attached to the individual devices. The bow device in this system is the VAIR Bow, of which two different versions have been produced so far, but there have been some problems.

One is that the inertial sensor inside the HTC Vive Tracker cannot withstand a bow shot. For this reason, improvements have been made to reduce direct impact transmission. The other problem is related to conventional bow devices. The power of an arrow fired from a bow has been changed according to the size of the strain gauge value, which is a relative but not an absolute measure. Therefore, accurate simulation was not possible.

In subsequent research [5], we have clarified the relationship between the amount of bowstring pull and the force applied to the bowstring, and have conducted research comparing real bow shooting with bow device shooting through changes in body movement and eye movement. Although this clarified the relationship between the bow and the string, it was unclear how these relationships would be reflected when the arrow was actually used. Therefore, this study clarifies the relationship between bow strength, string pull, and arrow velocity, and finally simulates arrow behavior based on strain gauge values. This will allow us to reconstruct a bow device that is accurate enough to be used for bow training. We also created contents using the new bow device.

2   VAIR Bow v3 System

Previous research [6] have shown that the force required to pull a bowstring is proportional to the distance it is pulled. It has also been found that the force required to do so is proportional to the value of the strain gage attached to the aluminum bow grip in the vicinity of the limbs. From these results, it is possible to determine the amount of force applied to the string and the amount of pull from the strain gage values. However, since it is unknown how much force or velocity an arrow will have when actually shot, there was not enough information to simulate it on the computer. Therefore, we first experimented to see what would happen to the arrow's velocity when the limbs strength and arrow type were changed and the amount of reduction in pull was varied.

2.1   Experiments on Arrow Velocity

The measurement device shown in the Fig. 1 was produced. The bow is fixed to this device, and the amount of string pull can be checked on a scale attached to the frame. A nocking point is attached to the position where the bow string is pulled, allowing the string to be pulled at the same position each time. A special releaser is used to pull the string. A velocity meter is fixed at approximately 55 cm from the bow's leading position to measure the arrow's velocity. This device has two gates, and the arrow speed can be measured from the passage time of these two gates. At the end of these gates, arrow stoppers are installed to safely stop the arrows (Fig. 3).

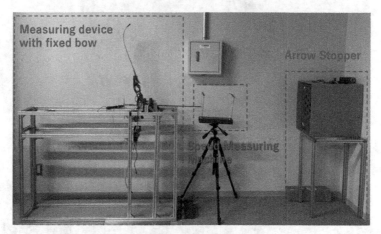

Fig. 1. Experimental equipment for measuring string pull and arrow velocity

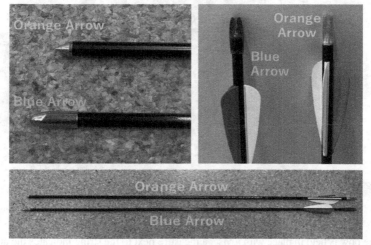

Fig. 2. Orange and blue arrows used in the experiment. They differ in length, weight, arrowhead, and arrow feather position.

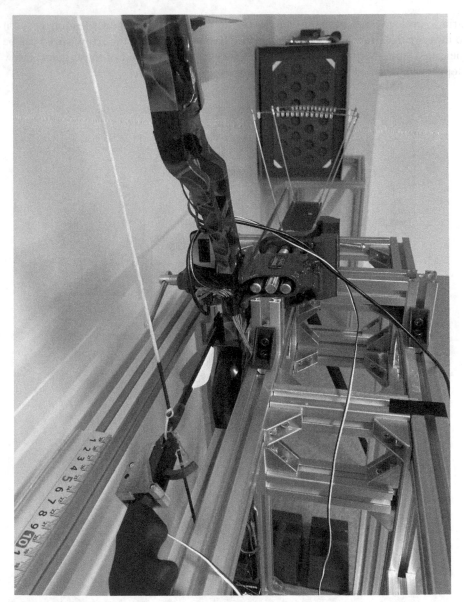

Fig. 3. The bow is held in place with a vise, a measure next to the string indicates the amount of pull, and the string has a green nocking point, which is clipped with a releaser to pull the string

Two limbs and two arrows were used for each measurement. The rims were ISO standard, a set of 68" 36 lb. and 66" 38 lb. and a set of 66" 14 lb. and 64" 16 lb. A set of 36" 36 lb. and 66" 38 lb. and a set of 66" 14 lb. and 64" 16 lb. The arrow is 72.4 cm, 22.3 g orange arrow and a 73.0 cm, 35.3 g blue arrow (Fig. 2).

First, the strings were fired 10 times each in 10 cm increments from 10 cm to 50 cm of string pull, and the velocity of each was recorded. The Fig. 4 shows. Arrows in this experiment were lightweight orange arrows.

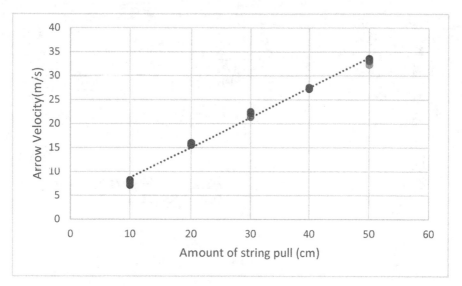

Fig. 4. Relationship between string pull and arrow velocity.

Next, the string pull was fixed at 50 cm, and the results of shooting with two types of arrows are shown in Fig. 5.

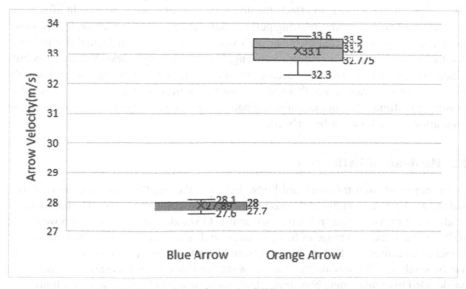

Fig. 5. Comparison of speeds of different weight arrows

Finally, the string pull was fixed at 30 cm and the results were compared by shooting 10 times with strong 36–38 lbs limbs and weak 14–16 lbs limbs, and the results are shown in the Fig. 6.

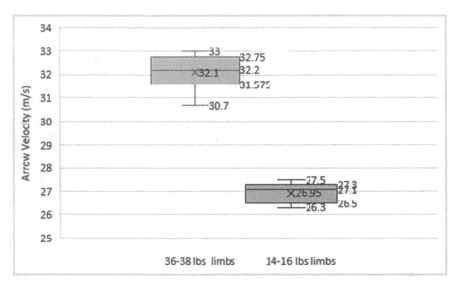

Fig. 6. Comparison of arrow velocity when using different strength limbs

These results show that in the case of the recurve bow, the amount of string pull and arrow velocity are almost proportional to each other. This relationship is similar to the relationship between the amount of string pull and strain gauges in previous researches. The weight of the arrow also affects the arrow velocity, because the weight affects the conversion of energy from the string pull into kinetic energy of the arrow. On the other hand, a stronger limb increases the arrow's velocity, but the experimental results show that the strength is more than twice as strong, but the velocity is less than twice as fast. When the bow device is actually used as a controller rather than for measurement, only the strain gauges' values are obtained as sensor data in real time. From this data, it is possible to estimate the amount of string pull and arrow velocity, and a highly accurate simulation of the bow can be realized.

2.2 Hardware of VAIR Bow v3

The experiment used ISO-standard limbs, but even the smallest ones are large in size, and the weakest one weighs 14 lb, making it difficult for children to use. The bow devices produced in previous research have used non-ISO standard bows, which are weaker at 10 lb and have the advantage of being smaller. In this research, we have two objectives: to increase accuracy so that the bow can be used for training, etc., and to make it easy to handle safely in a VR environment as a bow device that does not use arrows. Therefore, we decided to create a new bow device that can be used with either standard limb.

Previous research has shown that the string pull position can be estimated by attaching strain gauges directly under the upper and lower limbs, but a normal recurve bow is asymmetrical in that the arrow must be nocked and the grip must be attached. Therefore, even if the strain gauges are attached at the same position on the top and bottom, the values will not be the same. Since this device does not use arrows, there are few restrictions on the shape of the bow, and for greater accuracy, the shape of the bow was made symmetrical vertically. The ability to move freely in 360 degrees by attaching a smartphone to a bow device like the VAIR Bow is attractive, but it also has the disadvantage of a small screen and narrow viewing angle, which makes it difficult to handle. Therefore, the screen is projected in a large size using a projector, reducing the need for extra shapes and attachments.

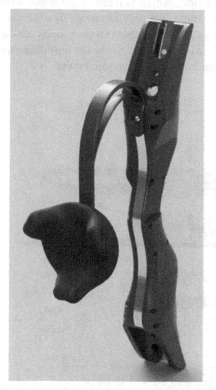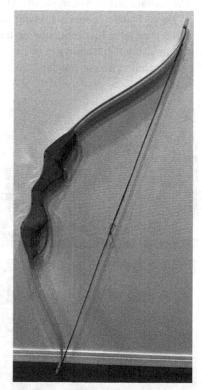

Fig. 7. VAIR Bow v3 Device. On the left is a CAD-designed model, and on the right is the actual bow device produced.

The new bow device in Fig. 7. is named VAIR Bow v3. As shown in the Fig. 8, the center is milled from 10 mm a6061 aluminum to ensure strength and to make it as light as possible. The perfect vertical symmetry makes it easy to compare the strain gauges of the upper and lower parts. As shown in the Fig. 9, the strain gauges are mounted directly under the limb, which is subjected to load when the bowstring is pulled, for greater accuracy and stability.

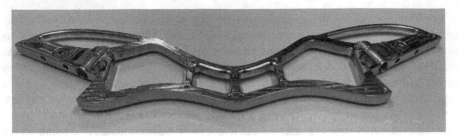

Fig. 8. Aluminum frame that forms the backbone of VAIR Bow v3, perfectly symmetrical vertically, and can be fitted with two types of limbs

The metal surround is made of 3D printed nylon, which is fixed to the metal with bolts. These plastic covers are asymmetrical in shape, but they are more flexible than metal, so they have less influence on the strain gauges. The same strain gauges can be used to measure different types of limbs. As shown in Fig. 10. Since the bolt diameter differs depending on the standard, an adapter can be attached for adjustment.

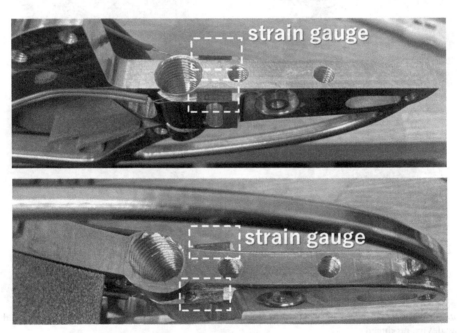

Fig. 9. The upper figure shows the surface and the lower figure shows the back surface, each of which has four strain gauge application surfaces, with cavities in between to facilitate distortion.

The M5 Stick microcomputer is built into the upper part of the unit to acquire strain gauges' values and transmit them wireless to a PC. The strain gages at eight locations in total on the top and bottom are wired inside the grip, and the signals are sent to M5 via two amplification circuits HX711. A Vive Tracker is attached to the top of the bow to acquire positional information. This is to prevent the sensor from malfunctioning for a certain period of time due to rapid acceleration when the impact of the bow is directly transmitted to the sensor. The bend of the mounting part is used to prevent this shock from being transmitted, but this has the disadvantage that the positional information is not exact because of the constant shaking. This is an area for future improvement.

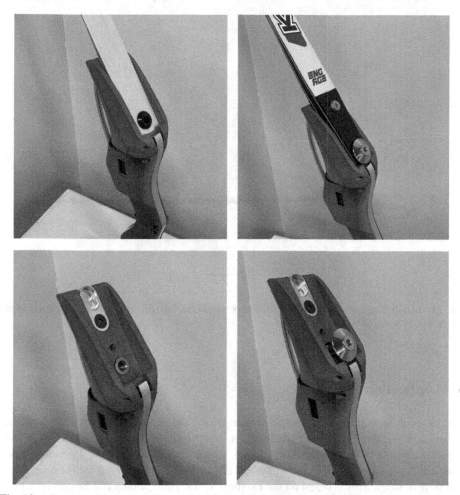

Fig. 10. The right side is the ISO standard limb and the left side is the limb of other standards. Although the diameters are different, the limbs can be fixed with the same holes.

2.3 Software of VAIR Bow v3

The performance of the v3 Bow was evaluated by measuring the strain gauge values simultaneously up and down. Five hundred frames were measured from pulling the bowstring to releasing it, and the results are shown in Fig. 11. The point where the value is rising is with the string being pulled, and then just before the sudden drop in value is the moment of shooting when the string is released. Compared to the past [2], it is clear that the strain values are stable. The values do not freeze before and after shooting, which causes sudden strain on the bow, and are stable at a certain value after shooting. Although some noise is always present, there are no large spikes, so the results are sufficient to estimate the moment of shooting and the amount of string pull from the strain values.

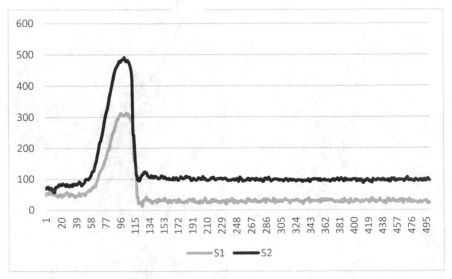

Fig. 11. Strain gauge values before and after shooting at the top (S1) and bottom (S2), horizontal axis at 80 for 1 s

3 Application

The xR is an archery tag-like competition in which two teams can shoot at each other. This is a physical eSport that is safe and involves physical activity and reflects real-life physical abilities by using the VAIR Bow v3, which does not use arrows. Previously, the company has created VAIR Field, a physical eSport that can be played with similar guns and bow devices. This is based on the existing VAIR Field, which can be played while walking around in a space up to 10 m square. However, the screen is not a smartphone, but a projector projecting images on a wall in front of the player. Although the system is capable of recognizing all directions in 360 degrees, the image exists only in front of the screen. Also, since the system is designed to be used by multiple people, the viewpoints of the images are fixed, and the immersive and three-dimensional feeling that has been achieved so far is lost. Until now, it was possible to play in two teams on the same field, but it is difficult to achieve this with only the front screen.

As shown in the Fig. 12 two teams could freely move around the entire virtual field. The new system divides the field into two fields, circled in red, and only one of these red fields corresponds to real space. In other words, it is not possible to enter the opponent's field. The image is that there is a screen on the border of these fields. Since the player is always looking at the opposing team, it is possible to play without any discomfort even if there is only one screen in front of the player. In terms of the system, what used to be one is now separated into two, each of which is connected by a network.

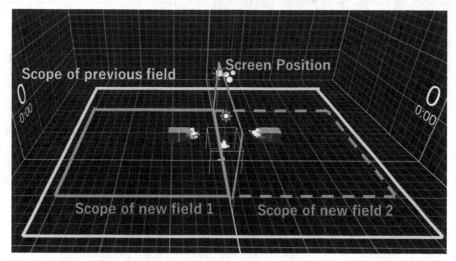

Fig. 12. VAIR Field being developed in Unity, defining the area in which the player can move and the image projected on the screen.

4 Future Works

At the present stage, only one VAIR Bow v3 device exists, making it difficult to conduct verification experiments with the new VAIR Field, but in the future, we would like to produce multiple units and conduct experiments by connecting these systems via a network. In the future, we would like to produce multiple units and conduct experiments by connecting these systems via a network. We would also like to continue development of this system as a system that can be played in a normal way by implementing it in society as well as in research.

Acknowledgment. This work was supported by JSPS KAKENHI Grant Number JP21K11345.

References

1. Air Digital: https://www.heroes-park.com/pages/4319778/page_202010161651
2. Yasumoto, M., Ohta, T.: The Electric Bow Interface. In: Shumaker, R. (ed.) VAMR 2013. LNCS, vol. 8022, pp. 436–442. Springer, Heidelberg (2013). https://doi.org/10.1007/978-3-642-39420-1_46

3. Yasumoto, M., Teraoka, T.: Electric bow interface 3D. In: SIGGRAPH Asia 2015, Emerging Technologies (SA 2015), p. 11:1–11:2 (2015)
4. Yasumoto, M., Teraoka, T.: Physical e-Sports in VAIR field system. In: SIGGRAPH Asia 2019 XR (SA 2019), pp. 31–33. ACM, New York (2019)
5. Yasumoto, M.: Evaluation of the Difference in the Reality of the Bow Device with and Without Arrows. In: Soares, M.M., Rosenzweig, E., Marcus, A. (eds) Design, User Experience, and Usability: Design Thinking and Practice in Contemporary and Emerging Technologies. HCII 2022. Lecture Notes in Computer Science, vol. 13323. Springer, Cham (2022). https://doi.org/10.1007/978-3-031-05906-3_32
6. Yasumoto, M., Shida, K., Teraoka, T.: Possibility of using high-quality bow interface in VAIR field. In: Marcus, Aaron, Rosenzweig, Elizabeth (eds.) HCII 2020. LNCS, vol. 12201, pp. 605–619. Springer, Cham (2020). https://doi.org/10.1007/978-3-030-49760-6_43

Realtime-3D Interactive Content Creation for Multi-platform Distribution: A 3D Interactive Content Creation User Study

Gareth W. Young[1]([✉]) [iD], Grace Dinan[2], and Aljosa Smolic[3] [iD]

[1] TRANSMIXR, Trinity College Dublin, Dublin, Ireland
YoungGa@tcd.ie
[2] RTÈ, Donnybrook, Dublin, Ireland
Grace.Dinan@RTE.ie
[3] TRANSMIXR, Hochschule Luzern, Lucerne, Switzerland
aljosa.smolic@hslu.ch

Abstract. With the recent reinvigoration of extended reality (XR) technology, including augmented and virtual reality (AR/VR), the potential of immersive technology to impact early adopters and the next generation of users is apparent. When combined with 3D visual content, real-time interactive tools can be applied across various media industries, from entertainment to studio set design. With this latest development, interest has been expressed in introducing new real-time 3D pipelines into multiple areas of the media industry. Likewise, the modern classroom employs various novel technologies to educate and inform tomorrow's industry leaders. In the presented study, we explore the opinions of expert and novice users towards using XR technology, recording their previous experiences and knowledge of 3D technology, gathering information about their current needs and requirements, and reporting on the potential future XR. Furthermore, we provide further details on the current conditions and provisions of contemporary 3D visual artists and the perceived possible future of 3D content creation from a creative media industry and educational perspective. It is expected that this user-type-focused study will inform the design of new educational software for novice users and create new pipelines for real-time interactive content creation fro real-world applications.

Keywords: Extended Reality · Virtual Reality · 3D Content Creation · Industry User Study

1 Introduction

3D interactive technologies in the form of extended reality (XR), such as augmented and virtual reality (AR/VR), are reestablishing themselves as powerful tools for multimedia content creation [6]. With the recent reinvigoration of XR (AR/VR) [2], the potential of this technology to influence the next generation

© The Author(s), under exclusive license to Springer Nature Switzerland AG 2023
J. Y. C. Chen and G. Fragomeni (Eds.): HCII 2023, LNCS 14027, pp. 215–229, 2023.
https://doi.org/10.1007/978-3-031-35634-6_16

of users and disrupt current content-creation pipelines is potentially vast [22]. In the last decade alone, AR and VR technology have exploded back onto the media technology scene in a way that will permanently disrupt home media consumption and current production workflows. With this latest wave of growth, interest has been expressed in introducing new real-time 3D pipelines into multiple areas of the media industry. For example, 2D visual media and real-time 3D interactive tools can be seen and applied across various emergent "metaverse" applications. When combined with 2D visual media, real-time 3D interactive tools can find application across various broadcast-industry sectors, from content creation to studio set design.

At the same time, the modern classroom is beginning to employ these novel technologies to educate and inform tomorrow's industry leaders and provide further training and support for the existing workforce [24]. In higher education, industry partnerships are fundamental for creating a pipeline of skilled operators for future studio productions and maintaining a suitably educated workforce. Thus, with the latest XR technologies, interest has been expressed in introducing emergent real-time 3D pipelines into multiple areas of the media training sector. However, how advanced and soundly these tools fit within current industry workflows is still debatable.

Human-computer interaction (HCI) and XR technology need further combined discussions to provide more informed guidelines for creative practices via 3D technology. While the potential of IVEs for co-creation is quickly becoming established, user-focused presentations via XR technologies fail to account for user perceptions of this technology's past, present, and future in learning and industry practices. Therefore, we seek to explore the current differences observed between XR users and emergent 3D content creation tools, focusing on user-type-specific experiences when undertaking tasks with 3D animation and modeling software. The motivation for collecting this data was to provide the XR industry with an enhanced understanding of the potential future of this technology. Moreover, this data collection approach gave our XR application creators and developers a more empathetic understanding of the people they are designing for and their attitudes toward using this technology.

In the presented study, we aim to discover more about the experiences and familiarity of 3D technology by users in the field, gather information about the current requirements of contemporary 3D visual artists, and report on the potential future of 3D content creation from a broadcast industry perspective "in the wild" [16]. It is expected that this cohort will provide insight to inform current and future XR practices. Moreover, this paper explores real-time XR immersive content creation tools as an alternative to traditional desktop hardware and software for future 3D digital artists and industry creatives, revealing the nascent opinions of this cohort of new users towards this budding technology. As such, we present our findings from the standpoint of different users – novices, end-users, and advanced users – and report on their perceived impact on the current and future media industry trajectory.

2   Background

Immersive VR technology has been around since the early 1980s [6] and presents users with digital computer-generated 3D environments that simulate the physical world via audio, visual, and even haptic stimuli [1]. This technology has been observed in educational contexts [19], gamified medical experiences [20], empathy building [23] and aircraft training [21]. Milgram and Kishino's virtuality continuum [10] presents a seminal field taxonomy that outlines mixed reality (MR) technology classification. In most modern XR systems, the user wears a head-mounted display (HMD) and holds a hand controller that facilitates interactions with 3D content in an immersive virtual environment (IVEs). The synchronicity between the IVE and the users' movements is critical in creating immersion and a sense of "being there" [15].

Currently, shared IVEs facilitated via AR/VR technology allow users to interact, collaborate, create, and manipulate virtual objects using familiar hand-based apparatuses [4]. The flexibility of such systems allows them to be easily used for new and existing design applications within standing media industries. Applying simple, instinctive interfaces makes these applications easy to use and facilitates constructivist and exploratory learning by building knowledge and understanding through applied practices [24]. Currently, XR enables the creation of artistic content (e.g., Tilt Brush, Quill, Medium, Blocks, etc.) and aids many new forms of creativity and interaction. Although artistic creation via XR can be similar to classical arts practices such as painting and sculpting, others diverge to produce new and unique interactive features. Today, AR and VR are both accepted novel mediums for artistic expression that can effectively deliver intangible cultural heritage content [13,14,25].

3D creation tools in XR often rely on intuition and are designed for both novices and advanced users in animation and modeling. This low-entry approach enables creative storytellers without 3D animation software experience to prototype their concepts quickly. Furthermore, XR also involves complete body movements stimulating and embodying physical experiences, allowing artists to "step" into their creations and completely immerse themselves in the creative practice [3]. However, immersive devices also present specific constraints concerning user interface design [5,18]. For example, the user must recognize the utility of a 3D tool and how to carry out a task with it. Furthermore, locomotion in an immersive environment must be carefully considered to prevent motion sickness [7,9]. These factors present many novel opportunities and challenges to the realtime-3D interactive content creation field.

3   Methodology

An inquiry process is presented here that involved engaging with different users applying new 3D tools "in the wild" to better understand their experiences in an emergent application context. Thus, a methodology is presented that targets both novice and advanced users with 3D animation and modeling pipelines using XR in various practices. We explore these users' attitudes and previous experiences regarding animation, 3D modeling, and motion capture involving observing, engaging, and empathizing with creative technologists to gather data on their experiences and motivations to use new tools and build a personal understanding of their concerns, requirements, and challenges when using XR technology in real-world practices. Thus, a heuristic experiment is presented that exposed both novices and advanced digital technology users to innovative animation, 3D modeling, and motion capture technologies designed for traditional screen-based media and XR.

3.1 Participants

Recruitment took place in the Republic of Ireland. A general call for participation was made via the project website, the university network, and an institute of technology. Volunteers were sought across a broad spectrum of potential user types; therefore, this call specifically targeted a 3D modeling and animation group. In total, 33 participants responded to contribute to this research.

Participants were first invited to report demographic information via an online questionnaire. This data included age, gender, education level, and employment sector. The participants were then asked to identify on 5-point Likert scales their general competencies with digital technologies (1 = Unskilled to 5 = Excellent); their familiarity with 3D modeling and animation (1 = Unfamiliar to 5 = Extremely Familiar); and their expertise using 3D modeling and animation technologies (1 = Novice to 5 = Expert). Professional employment status was polled to ascertain at which point in their career these users were currently situated. Participants were then categorized as "Novices", "End-users", and "Advanced Users" by the authors, as described by Nielsen [11]. Depending on user-type profiling, job title, and industry experience, participants were asked to attend a day-long practical workshop on using 3D modeling, animation, and motion capture (MOCAP) in an applied classroom workshop or to attend the RTÉ studios in Donnybrook, Dublin (Ireland's national broadcast headquarters) for exploratory discussions around tech in the industry.

In total, 11 participants attended the classroom workshop, identifying as 6 Males, 3 Females, and 2 Non-binary users with an average age of 21.08 (SD = 1.83). According to the Irish National Framework of Qualifications (NFQ), the education profile of the cohort consisted of levels 6 (n = 5) and 5 (n = 6). All members of this cohort were currently enrolled at an undergraduate level and contributed to the study. In total, 22 participants attended the professional studio session. Eleven contributed to the survey (response rate = 50%), identifying as 9 Males and 2 Females with an average age of 36.73 (SD = 8.81). According to the Irish National Framework of Qualifications (NFQ), the education profile of this cohort consisted of levels 10 (n = 5), 9 (n = 4), and 8 (n = 2). According to the professional Nomenclature of Economic Activities (NACE), the group's employment sectors were Education (n = 7) and Scientific and Technical Activities (n = 4); this included researchers, Ph.D. students, lecturers, directors, consultants, graphic designers, and tech company CEOs.

3.2   Apparatus and Material

Both sessions were in-person, pre-scheduled, and implemented strict Covid-19 social distancing and hygiene protocols. The novice cohort was invited to workshop XR technology in a classroom setting. Participants were given 3D modeling, animation, and MOCAP tutorials to complete that were delivered via prerecorded videos. They were shown first-hand how to use MOCAP technology for real-time animation using Unreal Engine. The cohort was then asked to model a 3D apple and animate the apple falling down stairs using VR. A lecturer was present at all times to demonstrate and provide additional support if needed.

The industry cohort was invited to experience animation, 3D modeling, and motion capture technology during a group visit to the RTÉ studios. A MOCAP device was demonstrated to the group, including real-time rendering and animation on a large-screen LCD wall display. Participants were encouraged to interact with the demo and ask questions. Following this, participants were debriefed and allowed to ask further questions. Two VR stations (Meta Quest 2 Link) were also set up for experiencing animation and 3D modeling. For these purposes, Tvori and Masterpiece Studio were used as exemplar applications. More information about the core technologies explored is presented below.

Perception Neuron (www.neuronmocap.com): The Perception Neuron Studio is a motion capture solution from Noitom. It boasts industry-leading sensor technology and an innovative sensor-processing algorithm, giving users the potential to explore new approaches to motion capture. This system includes inertial body sensors for full-body tracking, a transceiver, and gloves containing six 9-DOF IMU sensors. The system is self-contained with inertial trackers that provide a precise MOCAP experience.

Masterpiece Studio (www.masterpiecestudio.com): Masterpiece Studio Pro is a fully immersive 3D creation pipeline. It provides a suite of professional, intuitive, and easy-to-use immersive tools. Users can create high-fidelity 3D models and animations using easy-to-use and intuitive tools. The application allows users to create 3D concepts within VR, sculpt 3D assets, and prepare meshes for many different professional workflows.

Tvori (www.tvori.co/tvori): Tvori is an animation and prototyping software for VR and AR that can be used for previsualizations, animatics, or VR films. The application makes designing for both AR and VR simple. This software package can be used collaboratively to prototype interfaces, products, and experiences for XR. It is easy to learn, provides animations for design transitions and user interactions, and can be used collaboratively by remote teams.

After each session and to reduce face-to-face time during the pandemic, the different cohorts were asked to complete an online questionnaire to capture their impressions of these technologies in real-world practical situations. Qualitative data was recorded to add depth of knowledge and explore previous knowledge and experiences, potential benefits and problems of the technology, and future industry-focussed needs. Quantitative data were also recorded to highlight usability issues after the task-based exercises in the classroom.

Fig. 1. Studio visit workshop and discussion

Fig. 2. Students collectively experiencing VR

The following questionnaires operationalized these inquiries. The UMUX-Lite was used to identify usability issues in task-based situations; open-ended questions were then used to expand upon these data: "What previous knowledge or experiences have you had with the animation, 3D modeling, and motion capture technologies you have experienced today?"; "What benefits or problems do you see arising from using animation, 3D modeling, and motion capture technology in this way?"; and "What do you think you would need from future animation, 3D modeling, and motion capture technology like this?".

4   Results

Empirical data was collected and analyzed. Quantitative data was used descriptively to report on the cohort demographic. Qualitative data were coded and used to enrich and add depth of knowledge to our aims and objectives. The analyses of open-ended questions took a thematic approach guided by the frequency and fundamentality of the issues raised by the participants [8, 12].

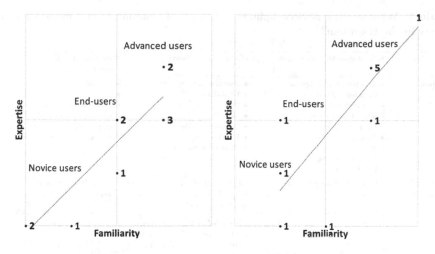

Fig. 3. User types: Workshop participants (left); Professional studio session (right)

4.1 Novice Workshop Results

All participants (n = 11) self-reported having a "Good" ability to use digital technology (M = 3.92; SD = 0.79). Data relating to their familiarity or knowledge of 3D animation and modeling (M = 3.00; SD = 1.13) and their expertise or experience in using 3D animation and modeling technologies (M = 2.58; SD = 1.08) were captured to identify their specific user types [11]. The distribution of user types was weighted towards Novice users (n = 6), with three potential End-users and two Advanced users (see Fig. 3 - left).

All members of the group completed the individual tasks (see Fig. 2. The cohort described the usability of the 3D modeling and animation software in practice as follows. The group reported a mean UMUX-Lite score of 78.47 (SD = 21.75). This result was converted to a raw System Usability Score (SUS) to help benchmark the collected data (M = 73.91; SD = 14.14). The percentile rank for the raw SUS score was calculated as 60%, or "above average", where a percentile above 50% is, by definition, above average [17]. ToT data calculated the average task completion time for 3D modeling and animation as M = 29 min (SD = 10.92).

Previous Knowledge and Experience: An overall breakdown of the qualitative data analysis for the workshop cohort can be seen in Table 1. Members of this group identified themselves as having little or no practical previous experience with 3D modeling software. Those with some experience listed Blender, Mudbox, Solidworks, 3DsMax, Auto CAD, Procreate, and Dragon Frame on the PC and generally had a mix of 3rd Year, 3D Design, Model-Making, and Digital Art level of expertise. None had previously used VR for these purposes.

Table 1. What are the novices' opinions on using 3D animation and modeling technology in the classroom?

	Knowledge & Experience	Good & Bad Features	New Features & Requirements
Themes	• Mostly knowledge of: - Blender - Mudbox - Solidworks - 3DsMax - Auto CAD - Procreate - Dragon Frame • Experiences with: - 3D Design - Model-Making - Digital Art	• Cybersickness • Usability • Fun • Novel • Industry skills • Learnability • User experiences	• Ubiquity • Accessibility • Tech integration • Learning materials • Improved usability • Scalable UIs
Example Answers	*"I have had no previous experiences like this"* *"No VR knowledge. I've used Mudbox, Solidworks, 3DsMax before"* *"Animating in Procreate and Dragon Frame"*	*"Some students may get headaches or feel unwell after using VR"* *"It's a lot of fun, and you get details you couldn't translate easily on regular digital modeling"* *"The industry is very much digital heavy"*	*"More VR headsets and a designated VR area"* *"ZBrush, Screen Tablets should be supplied..."* *"It should have a simpler interface"* *"Better layout structure and button configurations"*

Good and Bad Features: The group highlighted some of the benefits of using VR were that it was easy to use, a lot of fun, and they could see additional details that would not translate easily on traditional 2D PC modeling platforms. The ease of use that was experienced enhanced the accessibility of the medium and could potentially attract more people to the industry. It was recognized that the industry climate was very digital-orientated and tech-heavy, so the group felt it needed to know how to use new software and hardware for future employment. Although a lot of time would be required to learn how to use the software efficiently, the visualization of 3D data was thought to be much more enhanced and showed a lot more detail on the final output. The additional use of projection mapping and internal lighting spotlights for the 3D modeling object was considered advantageous for learning as a "visual experience". This advantage allowed our novices to model and contextualize their work much more quickly than with traditional 2D PC software.

Additionally, it was highlighted how physical modeling and animation projects could easily be damaged in the real world; therefore, a 3D digital model was more mobile and easier to transport between different locations and digital platforms. Ultimately, the group thought that VR for 3D modeling and animation could potentially be a cost-efficient, fast, safe, and an easy way to save their learning progress. While the group offered several advantageous scenarios for the use of XR in the classroom, it was also noted that there might be other disadvantages as well. As one participant commented:

> "It's easy to use and could allow a wide range of people to get into it, but it could potentially lead to less student-to-student feedback and collaboration".

Table 2. What are the experts' opinions on using contemporary animation, 3D modeling, and motion capture technology in practice?

	Knowledge & Experience	Good & Bad Features	New Features & Requirements
Themes	• Industry, lab-based, and educational knowledge • Commercial software as well as custom-built software experiences • Familiar with the presented technologies • Had applied similar techniques in practice	• Natural movement • 3D from conception • Real-time visualization • Low entry usability • Comfortable to use • Faster data collection • Lack of training • Equipment hygiene • Accuracy of the data	• Financial investment • Upskilling • Follow industry trends • Learnability • Usability • Provide robust data • Classroom to stage education pipeline • More use-cases
Example Answers	*"I am experienced using Maya, Cinema 4D, and Unity for 3D modeling and animation"* *"We build 3D reconstruction algorithms and do markerless motion capture"* *"I have knowledge of this technology from the gaming and movie industry"*	*"One major benefit is a natural movement for animation and ease of use"* *"It can be good to think and create in 3D"* *"You need someone familiar with the tech on hand"* *"Lack of external camera tracking/noise of the sensors"*	*"Creative ideas on how to use it"* *"A good training course would be useful"* *"3D modeling software which allows not only artists but other enthusiasts"* *"Virtual production will need further development"*

The problems listed by the workshop group highlighted typical issues that novice users might face when learning to use such software. User-type-specific issues included how some learners might suffer from VR sickness and "get headaches or feel unwell" when using VR for the first time. For some, the user interface or "layout of buttons" was also highlighted as problematic for ease of use. Furthermore, the task was particularly challenging for those inexperienced with such programs. These issues were thought to be easily overcome with accessible tutorials and a more-knowledgeable-other present to help novice users better understand the task scenarios. Interestingly, it was believed that this technology could potentially lead to reduced face-to-face collaboration.

New Features and Requirements: For VR to be more prominent in the future, our workshop users highlighted that more VR headsets would have to be made available for general use. This suggestion also included designated VR areas to be included in classroom spaces. Additional technology integration was also recommended, such as ZBrush and Screen Tablets. Some students highlighted usability problems and that future software would require enhanced "ease of use" features for novices, where the user interface would be scalable in difficulty for different user types. For example, a simple interface for beginners and a more complex one for advanced users—"There should be more straightforward layout selections, for example, cut lines, extrude, etc." For more streamlined interactions with other classroom software, it was suggested that future iterations have a layout that matches other programs for cross-platform use and "hot-key" shortcuts for fluid switching between platforms. For example:

"A better layout structure that matches other software, nearly cross-platform in terms of use, and hot-key shortcuts to be more fluid when switching between modeling software".

Although, it was suggested that this could be avoided if software selection existed. It was also recommended that tutorials be delivered inside the HMD and made more straightforward and accessible for entry-level users. Although, this was contradicted as some students preferred to bo made "aware of their surroundings" and alerted if someone was approaching them while wearing an HMD. This suggests that "mixed reality" would be an attractive feature for the classroom - a feature released by Meta for the Quest Pro after the workshops had taken place.

4.2   Industry Expert Results

All participants (n = 11) self-reported having an "Excellent" ability to use digital technology (M = 4.73; SD = 0.47) and attended the full session (see Fig. 1). Data relating to their familiarity or knowledge of animation, 3D modeling, and motion capture (M = 3.45; SD = 1.04) and their expertise or experience in using animation, 3D modeling, and motion capture technologies (M = 3.18; SD = 1.33) can be seen in Fig. 3 (Right). The distribution of user types was weighted toward End-users (n = 2) and Advanced users (n = 6) of animation, 3D modeling, and motion capture technologies, with three novices in the cohort.

Previous Knowledge and Experience: A breakdown of the qualitative data analysis can be seen in Table 2. Expectedly, this cohort reported much more industry, lab-based, and educational experiences in 3D modeling and animation using Maya, Cinema 4D, 3D Studio Max, and Unity 3D, and familiarity with more bespoke content creation approaches such as volumetric capture and other 3D reconstruction techniques. Most cohort members had previously experienced different versions of the presented technologies and platforms at exhibitions and conferences or had applied them in some way in their place of work. They also conveyed some real-world experiences with motion capture, although it was the first time some had seen a real-time motion capture and rendering pipeline first-hand. Traditional platforms for content creation were described, PCs, laptops, etc., and some group members were intimately familiar with VR development pipelines. This cohort was knowledgeable of the gaming and movie industry and was more familiar with the technology, terminology, and leading companies involved in the field than the previous group. The more advanced users within the group were skilled in 3D reconstruction algorithms, markerless motion capture, content creation experience in VR, and knew of the Perception Neuron Kickstarter.

Advantages and Disadvantages: One of the significant benefits identified by the industry user group was the use of natural movement for animation and the technology's overall ease of use; for example, "As part of a complete pipeline, it could allow for quicker pre-visual and broadcast-quality animation". Each platform experienced and discussed was also advantageous for three-dimensional thinking and creating throughout a project's lifecycle. This approach to a 3D rationale was expected to benefit the creation of new content that could be produced quicker and more realistic representations of human movement. After experiencing 3D modeling in VR, some participants thought that creating 3D models in a fully immersive 3D environment was more intuitive and ergonomic for the artist than building via traditional 2D screen-based desktop media. As one participant described:

> "It feels more natural, like drawing or physically sculpting with physical materials (e.g., stone or wood), than drawing with a mouse. I also like that it encouraged me to stand up while working, which I feel is healthier than constantly sitting at a desk".

Low entry usability and "comfort-of-use" were considered an advantage for novice industry users, making the business more accessible for more "casual" creatives, for example, more agile and mobile motion capture approaches instead of stricter fixed MOCAP suites. The Perception Neuron Studio captured data from multiple sensors, ensuring precise motion tracking in line with other studio-based operations. The technology pipeline's quick capture and display capabilities enhanced this feature: "Which means you can solve many problems in real-time".

The featured technology was also considered beneficial from a research perspective as it facilitates faster and more accessible data collection, allowing users to create more extensive and diverse datasets, which are essential to current machine learning technologies. Another benefit was the production speed, where making television shows with a real-time virtual host could be realized quickly. As one participant reported:

> "Integrating the 3D model with Unreal or Unity and the motion capture suit appears very easy and will lead to a more rapid workflow. The motion capture suit is more portable than traditional approaches that use many cameras to track the actor".

Disadvantages were also acknowledged. Notably, the requirement is to have someone trained and familiar with the technology to guide and troubleshoot potential issues at every production stage. Another drawback was the requirement for high-end computer systems to process data efficiently. Some participants also believed that VR modeling would not be a suitable replacement for working in a traditional 2D environment and would be more useful as a viewing tool or for making minor adjustments to preexisting content. As a product of the Covid-19 pandemic, it was also highlighted that virus transmission could occur when using communal VR equipment and the constant need to sanitize equipment before and after use.

It was also reported that VR and MOCAP technology may still be too expensive. The initial costs to train, set up, and operate and the technical and hardware requirements would continue to make it difficult for general day-to-day use. Specific to the complete 3D modeling, MOCAP, and reconstruction pipeline, participants thought problems might arise concerning the accuracy of tracking live actors within a studio with multiple wireless technologies running simultaneously. In this case, signal quality may suffer due to the lack of external camera tracking and the inherent noise of the different wireless sensors being used. However, it was acknowledged that this potential problem might be addressed through training and familiarity with the system in question.

The Future of Technology: Fundamentally, all participant group members commented on financial costs, a general lack of technology-specific expertise, and the requirement of effective teaching materials for continued growth and acceptance within the industry—"A good set of tutorials as well as someone with expertise that can troubleshoot". Moreover, although the cohort reported that the technology they experienced looked promising, the rise of virtual production tools will need further development concerning the availability of future skilled operators. On the one hand, a financial investment would be required to replace established traditional studios with next-generation real-time sensors and immersive virtual environments. On the other hand, operating such systems would also require industry-specific training. Therefore, a streamlined course should be created for advanced users to become fully accustomed to 3D control panels and the various available tools.

The group recognized that future growth in this area would require increased access to 3D modeling and motion capture pipelines to be integrated into the classroom to train the next incoming group of studio operators. Thus, the technology would need to be learnable, easily calibrated, and provide a robust data capture process reflective of the era's industrial applications. The pipeline would also require data to be captured in an open and streamable format to create and drive virtual 3D characters across multiple platforms. However, it was expressed that this technology's usability, affordability, and accessibility should not be detrimental to its accuracy. By achieving these goals, artists and other enthusiasts would have powerful 3D modeling, animation, and MOCAP capabilities. Future animation, 3D modeling, and motion capture technology (including mobile and wearable devices) will also facilitate and drive creativity and develop new ideas for using them effectively.

5   Discussion and Future Work

Firstly, the study participants could accurately describe and group themselves using a user cube approach [11]. In this way, we could provide a practical workshop for those with no substantial industry or education background in real-time 3D animation. Likewise, we could offer an informative breakdown of current and emergent technologies to the more advanced participants without having to infringe upon their working time with a task-based analysis. The novice cohort of learners reported a favorable usability score and sufficient ToT times.

On the one hand, the novice group had limited previous experience and knowledge of the VR platform they used during the workshop. Conversely, the advanced users had extensive professional experiences with the presented technology. This finding highlights a potential disconnect between the 3D software and media development pipeline between novices and advanced users. A more informed education and industry partnership should be formed to address this lacuna to ensure that new graduates, as novice users, have the correct skills to enter the professional domain.

The most notable similarity between cohorts was the identification of positive usability and user experiences of real-time visualization and creating media in 3D. This finding included complementary factors of learnability, comfort in use, and the naturalness of the creative process as a 3D-from-conception approach to creativity. At the same time, the technology was fun and novel for learners, and the speed and accuracy of the 3D data created were also considered professional standards. However, the disconnect between the novices' desire for industry-specific skills and advanced users' also identified a lack of training in new practices. Furthermore, issues relating to cyber-sickness and hygiene were commented upon by both groups.

Likewise, further improvements need to be made to increase accessibility for future integration of this technology in both contexts. This future requirements alignment was apparent from an awareness of both cohorts on the potential ubiquity of the technology and the need for more use cases. For this to happen effectively, there needs to be more work done to integrate existing 3D technologies into new design and creation workflows. Admittedly for both parties, this will require upskilling and financial investment from the industry and new learning materials in the educational domain. By addressing this future requirement, a classroom-to-stage education pipeline will be provided.

6   Conclusion

Within this paper, we explored the application of 3D media technologies by industry creatives and XR developers to develop an empathic understanding of the people these technologies are designed for and their attitudes toward using them in practice. Interests in AR and VR have disrupted the 3D media technology scene in a way that might permanently alter industry-recognized production workflows. In higher education, industry partnerships are fundamental for creating a pipeline of suitably skilled operators for future studio productions. It is the finding of this analysis that there currently exists a disconnect between the educational experiences of novice users and industry professionals concerning the use of this emergent technology. However, recommendations should be garnered regarding how this goal can be achieved moving forward.

Acknowledgments. The authors would like to thank John Buckley (IADT) for facilitating the use of XR and MOCAP in the classroom. We would also like to thank all members of the IBC Accelerator Programme for their support and feedback throughout the research. This publication has emanated from research conducted with the financial support of the Science Foundation Ireland (SFI) under Grant Number 15/RP/2776, EPSRC-SFI grant number EP/T03324X/1, and the Horizon Europe Framework Program (HORIZON), under the grant agreement 101070109.

References

1. Biocca, F., Delaney, B.: Immersive virtual reality technology. Commun. Age Virtual Reality **15**(32), 10–5555 (1995)
2. Evans, L.: The Re-emergence of Virtual Reality. Routledge (2018)
3. Freeman, D., et al.: Virtual reality in the assessment, understanding, and treatment of mental health disorders. Psychol. Med. **47**(14), 2393–2400 (2017)
4. Greenwald, S.W., Corning, W., Maes, P.: Multi-user framework for collaboration and co-creation in virtual reality. In: International Conference on Computer-Supported Collaborative Learning (CSCL). International Society of the Learning Sciences (ISLS) (2017)
5. Kamińska, D., Zwoliński, G., Laska-Leśniewicz, A.: Usability testing of virtual reality applications—the pilot study. Sensors **22**(4), 1342 (2022)
6. Lanier, J.: Dawn of the New Everything: A Journey Through Virtual Reality. Random House (2017)
7. Lewis-Evans, B.: A short guide to user testing for simulation sickness in virtual reality. Games User Research (2018)
8. Lunt, A.A.P., Cairns, P.: A qualitative approach to HCI research. In: Research Methods for Human-Computer Interaction, Cambridge, pp. 138–157 (2008)
9. McCauley, M.E., Sharkey, T.J.: Cybersickness: perception of self-motion in virtual environments. Presence Teleoper. Virtual Environ. **1**(3), 311–318 (1992)
10. Milgram, P., Kishino, F.: A taxonomy of mixed reality visual displays. IEICE Trans. Inf. Syst. **77**(12), 1321–1329 (1994)
11. Nielsen, J.: Usability Engineering. Morgan Kaufmann (1994)
12. Nowell, L.S., Norris, J.M., White, D.E., Moules, N.J.: Thematic analysis: striving to meet the trustworthiness criteria. Int. J. Qual. Methods **16**(1), 1609406917733847 (2017)
13. O'Dwyer, N., Young, G.W., Johnson, N., Zerman, E., Smolic, A.: Mixed reality and volumetric video in cultural heritage: expert opinions on augmented and virtual reality. In: Rauterberg, M. (ed.) HCII 2020. LNCS, vol. 12215, pp. 195–214. Springer, Cham (2020). https://doi.org/10.1007/978-3-030-50267-6_16
14. O'dwyer, N., Zerman, E., Young, G.W., Smolic, A., Dunne, S., Shenton, H.: Volumetric video in augmented reality applications for museological narratives: a user study for the long room in the library of trinity college Dublin. J. Comput. Cult. Heritage (JOCCH) **14**(2), 1–20 (2021)
15. Riva, G., Baños, R.M., Botella, C., Mantovani, F., Gaggioli, A.: Transforming experience: the potential of augmented reality and virtual reality for enhancing personal and clinical change. Front. Psych. **7**, 164 (2016)
16. Rogers, Y., Marshall, P.: Research in the wild. Synthesis Lectures on Human-Centered Informatics **10**(3), i–97 (2017)
17. Sauro, J., Lewis, J.R.: Quantifying the User Experience: Practical Statistics for User Research. Morgan Kaufmann (2016)
18. Sutcliffe, A.G., Kaur, K.D.: Evaluating the usability of virtual reality user interfaces. Behav. Inf. Technol. **19**(6), 415–426 (2000)

19. Timoney, J., Faghih, B., Gibney, A., Korady, B., Young, G.: Singing-blocks: considerations for a virtual reality game to create chords and progressions. In: Computer Simulation of Musical Creativity (CSMC) (2018)

20. Vagg, T., Tan, Y.Y., Shortt, C., Hickey, C., Plant, B.J., Tabirca, S.: MHealth and serious game analytics for cystic fibrosis adults. In: 2018 IEEE 31st International Symposium on Computer-Based Medical Systems (CBMS), pp. 100–105. IEEE (2018)

21. Vora, J., Nair, S., Gramopadhye, A.K., Duchowski, A.T., Melloy, B.J., Kanki, B.: Using virtual reality technology for aircraft visual inspection training: presence and comparison studies. Appl. Ergon. **33**(6), 559–570 (2002)

22. Wu, W.C.V., Manabe, K., Marek, M.W., Shu, Y.: Enhancing 21st-century competencies via virtual reality digital content creation. J. Res. Technol. Educ. 1–22 (2021)

23. Young, G.W., O'Dwyer, N., Smolic, A.: Exploring virtual reality for quality immersive empathy building experiences. Behav. Inform. Technol. **1**(1), 1–17 (2021)

24. Young, G.W., Stehle, S., Walsh, B.Y., Tiri, E.: Exploring virtual reality in the higher education classroom: using VR to build knowledge and understanding. J. Univ. Comput. Sci. **26**(8), 904–928 (2020)

25. Zerman, E., O'Dwyer, N., Young, G.W., Smolic, A.: A case study on the use of volumetric video in augmented reality for cultural heritage. In: Proceedings of the 11th Nordic Conference on Human-Computer Interaction: Shaping Experiences, Shaping Society, pp. 1–5 (2020)

Multimodal Interaction in VAMR

Inner Voices: Reflexive Augmented Listening

Andreas Kratky[✉] and Juri Hwang

University of Southern California, Los Angeles, CA 90089, USA
akratky@cinema.usc.edu, jurihwan@usc.edu

Abstract. This paper discusses the concept of reflexive augmented listening using three sound art projects realized by the authors as examples. Presenting a new take on the traditional soundwalk experience, two of the projects are location-specific and engage with historic events, and one of them employs machine learning to create an emergent form of location-specificity that adapts to the place where the audience is located. Facilitated by the custom-developed hardware platform of a combined sensor and transducer headset, the projects use a form of augmented reality that is focused on listening and the experience of sound and body movement in service of a reflexive engagement with historic events, space and sound. The paper discusses the conceptual, aesthetic and technological developments made in the realization of these projects. It contrasts the author's approach with augmented reality experiences of current, predominantly visual, forms.

Keywords: Augmented Reality · Soundwalk · Wearables

1 Introduction

1.1 A Subsection Sample

In the following, we discuss what we call reflexive augmented listening as a means to connect listeners to historic events and phenomena. Our approach is developed across three different art projects that use sound to stimulate an imaginative engagement with past events in the location where the events actually took place. The projects have been developed over the course of three years and explore a particular approach to the augmentation of human perception, focused mainly on listening. Each project engages with a specific historic and perceptual setting, relying on compositional and sound design techniques informed by site-specific research. We developed a dedicated technological platform to convey a complex, layered sound experience in response to the location and the listener, her movements and body. With these projects we are exploring an alternative concept to augmented reality that is focused on reflexive contemplation rather than fast and efficient consumption.

Our focus on sound diverges from the predominantly visual implementations of the augmented reality experiences that currently exist. All three projects employ a technique of listening in – and to – the environment via a combination of air- and multi-channel bone-conducted sound. This experience blends the spatio-temporal nature of the surrounding environment with a superimposed – and notably distinct – spatio-temporality

© The Author(s), under exclusive license to Springer Nature Switzerland AG 2023
J. Y. C. Chen and G. Fragomeni (Eds.): HCII 2023, LNCS 14027, pp. 233–252, 2023.
https://doi.org/10.1007/978-3-031-35634-6_17

evoked by the sound experience. It is conveyed through internal, bone-conducted sounds that resonate within the body of the listener. The technology for this experience has been developed in several iterations specifically for each of the three projects and the desired experience qualities. Using the approach of a soundwalk, these pieces formulate a position on embodied experience, memory, and augmented perception that critically reflects on how we perceive our surroundings, what we know, and how we can relate to the hidden historic layers, which are absent, but inform our being in a place.

The first project, Weeping Bamboo, engages with the invisible presence of indigenous memory in today's city of Manizales in Colombia; the second project, Ghost Letters, conveys the memory traces of patients of a mental asylum on the island of San Servolo in the Venetian Lagoon, formerly known as the Island of the Mad. Both experiences are site-specific and evoke multiple historic layers in the imagination of the listener through interactive, geo-located soundscapes. By traversing the sites, listeners explore the soundscapes, which intermix in various ways with the sounds of the cur-rent environment. The third project is an emergent experience generated by the movements and gestures of the listener. The movement and behavioral patterns create a site-specific experience that records a sonic trace of the interactions of the listener with the space. The soundscape is adaptive and uses machine learning to interpret the listener's behavior in respect to the surrounding space.

The three projects taken together formulate both a distinct approach to the concept of augmented reality and present a new take on the soundwalk as an art-historic phenomenon. The following text is structured in three parts, in which we discuss the notion of augmented listening and augmented reality (AR) and then connect this discussion to the art-historic context of the soundwalk as an art-form. Finally, we describe the specific implementation of the three projects and their contributions to our new take on the soundwalk.

2 Augmented Listening

Augmented listening is a listening-focused subset of "augmented reality," a set of techniques to enhance human perception of the surrounding natural environment by presenting additional, superimposed layers of information through media-display devices. While, in this context, the term "display" can refer to the rendering of information to the entire range of sense modalities of the human sensory apparatus, we are looking here specifically at auditive rendering. Most instances of augmented listening are implemented as a form of support for imperfect human senses: hearing aids, for example, aim to help people with hearing impairments restore their hearing abilities; augmented listening devices for people with normal hearing aim to improve auditive performance in noisy situations through customized filtering and amplification. Combinations of noise-cancellation, equalization and adaptive amplification built into wearable headphones and earbuds promise to tune the surrounding sounds according to personal preferences, to produce "improved situational awareness," [1] and to "hear and be heard like never before" [2]. These augmentation techniques rely on mobile technologies that sense the environment and then superimpose the supplemental information on the environment-data they gather. Most of these application types consider the human sensory apparatus as lacking in efficiency and aim to use technological means to remedy the insufficiencies and augment the senses to make them more efficient.

2.1 AR'S Focus on the Visual Sense

The same idea of the human sensory system in need of augmentation exists in the visual approaches to augmented reality (AR). Most of the AR experiences today are based on visual information, overlaid on the reality around the viewer. This is either done using smartphones with video cameras that composit supplemental information correctly registered with the images from the camera stream of the surrounding environment. More complex solutions employ AR headsets with glasses that present a visual overlay superimposed on what the viewer actually sees. Microsoft's HoloLens [3] is one example for this, as is the Magic Leap headset [4]. So far, research on the human sensory apparatus has had a strong focus on the visual sense, which occupies an important position in how humans relate to the world [5]. The fact that most AR applications also focus on the visual sense is therefore not surprising.

The first application of human sensory augmentation techniques that carried the name "augmented reality" was conceived in support of the visual sense, with the intention to make human action more precise, fast and efficient. T.P. Caudell and D.W. Mizell, both engineers at Boeing Company, strived to develop a technical solution to alleviate the tremendous effort of manufacturing and assembling aircraft. In a paper published in 1992, they describe their ideas for a solution to make the assembly workers more efficient by augmenting their visual perception. Guidance of workers assembling the aircraft was so far relying on plans, lists and other documentation mostly on paper that had to be consulted while working in-situ in the airplane. The exact positions of drill holes, wire connections etc. had to be determined from those plans. According to Caudell and Mizell, many errors, delays, and expenses could be prevented if the workers had access directly to the digital data from the computer aided design system, in which the airplane was constructed. To facilitate this, they built a headset, a so-called "heads-up see-through display head set," which was able to sense the position of the worker and the direction of view, and based on this information, indicate the mounting locations and orientations for parts. "This technology is used to 'augment' the visual field of the user with information necessary in the performance of the current task, and therefore we refer to the technology as 'augmented reality' (AR)." [6].

Following this principle, many applications have been developed to make humans perform tasks more efficiently. Applications like Blippar's AR City uses a smartphone to overlay precisely registered roadmaps over the camera image of the real environment to show people where they have to go, so that they do not have to decipher maps anymore to understand where they are and where they need to go.

2.2 Efficiency Goal and Disengagement with Space

Departing from a perspective of imperfect human sensory capabilities, most AR development goes toward the use of technology to streamline human behavior and increase task-efficiency. While this may, in many situations, be a desirable goal, we also have to see that the efficiency focus cuts off many other forms of engagement with the environment. If, for example, the goal is smooth and efficient navigation, a more individualized and serendipitous involvement with the city becomes impossible. Encounters and discoveries, as they were sought out by artists, poets, critics, urbanists and others to understand the relationship between human and environment, are prevented in this form of navigation. The art of walking, the aimless falling from one foot on the other, as Franz Hessel described in his essay "On the Difficult Art of Taking a Walk," [7] does not have a place in sensory augmentation for the purpose of efficiency. Artists and philosophers like Guy Debord and the movement of the Situation-ists around him [8], or Lucius Burkhard, a sociologist who developed the theory of strollology [9], practiced city walking as a poetic, analytical, and inspirational method, while poets like Franz Hessel or Victor Fournel [10] used it importantly as a form of entertainment.

Besides a large number of AR applications for efficiency optimization, some entertainment applications exist as well. The most well-known examples for this genre are probably Niantic's AR game "Ingress" and its successor AR game "Pokémon Go", developed by Niantic on the same platform as "Ingress," and distributed by Nintendo. "Pokémon Go" has been downloaded more than 1 billion times [11] and had 147 million active players in 2018 [12]. These numbers indicate the tremendous popularity of AR gaming. Nevertheless, as some of the criticism the game received shows, the genre suffers from similar difficulties as the efficiency-oriented AR applications in general. Despite the entertainment character of outdoor activities of AR games, the players are similarly disconnected from the environment and the game obscures important characteristics of the real environment. As Pokémon Go was built on the same platform as "Ingress," the players who played the earlier game created the map for Pokémon Go and determined in this way in which areas portals or "PokéStops" would be located. Portals, or PokéStops, are the real world locations to which virtual portals are referenced, and which players have to find in the real world. These maps thus reflect the demographic of the early adopters of the AR game and how they map their world. Locations they did not visit do not exist in the universe of Pokémon Go either. Rather quickly after the Pokémon Go game was launched, criticism of redlining and an uneven distribution of PokéStops, favoring affluent white neighborhoods, surfaced [13–15]. Another indicator of a disengagement of the players from their real environment was the concern about the number of accidents in the real world caused by distracted players [16].

2.3   Representation of Dominant Perspective

Augmented reality adheres to a principle of streamlined perception. In the examples we have discussed so far, AR appears as a form of augmented perception, in which more information is made available than the viewer would normally be able to access without technological aid. AR is, in this sense, akin to a telescope or a microscope, which extends the range of information available to the human sensory apparatus under certain conditions. AR presents a fusion of the views of normal reality and additional information, which is fused in such a way that information access is tailored specifically for the task at hand. This is a form of streamlining, which tends to remove or obscure unwanted information that may inhibit or clutter, for instance, the navigation of a certain environment, or in any other way distract from the task at hand. Obstructing objects are removed, as the example of MINI's AR Driving application literally shows by making parts of the car transparent so that the driver can see through them [17].

The environment is conformed to what the user wants to see, or what is considered most useful or important for the user to see at a certain point and in light of a certain task. This concept of streamlined perception explains why players of Pokémon Go may have accidents, because the traffic-reality is inhibiting the goal of getting to a certain PokéStop and therefore tuned out – if not from the rendition of the environment offered by the AR device, so, at least, it is tuned out by the channeled attention of the player. While this kind of streamlined attention and perception may be useful for engineering tasks such as the assembly of a complex airplane, we also understand how blind-spots and misperceptions are created and how redlining takes place when this behavior becomes the norm for navigating our every-day environment: other pedestrians become obstacles in the task of reaching the destination; places that do not part-take in a certain demographic are not perceived and removed from the map offered to the perception of the user. The pathway between origin and destination, between actual and desired state, is tuned out, because it does not contribute to the efficient way of reaching the desired state.

By these means, augmented reality tends to represent the dominant perspective, which, in a given environment and with a given task, will often be the most efficient way to get to the desired state or location. People will be directed to those restaurants and tourist attractions that the majority of people have deemed worthwhile going to, or they will look at the world in terms of portals to be reached, but they will not be open for a serendipitous encounter along the way. This kind of selective perception is not a new phenomenon, but AR devices are prone to making it significantly more prevalent.

3   Reflexive Listening

For the three projects discussed in this paper, our experience goal was the opposite of this form of streamlined augmented reality. The topics of our experiences are removed from mainstream awareness already, indeed they are intentionally eliminated and repressed from the surface of the reality we see in those places.

In the case of Weeping Bamboo, the aim is to make the layers of the past that are missing from the current situation perceivable. The architecture of the city of Maniza-les shows traces from the Spanish conquest and later Spanish-inspired architecture, as well as the concrete and steel structures of modern buildings – but no evidence of the indigenous cultures who used to inhabit the area exists in the current city-scape. This absence is not only due to the colonial development, political power structures and the exploitation of the area through mining and coffee cultivation, it is also due to very different forms of knowing and transmission of cultural heritage of the indigenous cultures.

The native cultures of the Quimbaya and Carrapa in the Manizales area had a high degree of cultural development and entertained trade activities with various native nations who spoke different languages. Despite the flourishing cultural establishments and a sophisticated agricultural and technical knowledge, the native cultures had an entirely different approach in respect to the materiality of their habitats and their environment. As chronicler Cieza de León notes, the indigenous people did not put much work to into their houses [18]. White, a British anthropologist, mentions that this aspect of the native cultures in the Manizales area is consistent with the indigenous cultures throughout the North-Western provinces of South America: they did not build monuments and lasting buildings as European cultures would have considered foundational for the transmission and preservation of cultural identity and heritage.

White argues that this material avoidance is not due to a lack of sophistication of the civilization, but to the collective wish to hand down memories to future generations in respect of their cultural origins [33]. These origins are profoundly linked to what the indigenous peoples consider sacred nature locations and the close kinship between human culture and nature. Preservation of nature is essential to their cultural identity. Cultural rituals are performed to communicate with nature and to continually reinstate and embody the relationship. Sacred locations are the depository of the knowledge and memories that are essential to continue their heritage to future generations.

It is this latter aspect that we are interested in communicating with the project Weeping Bamboo. Our aim is to enable users to get an understanding for the difference and practical incompatibility of the forms of knowledge preservation and transmission practiced by the indigenous cultures and those following the Spanish settlements. Since these knowledge structures are so fundamentally different from Western forms of commemoration and mediated communication, we decided to develop a fundamentally different approach to augmented reality. There are no real objects remaining from the aboriginal cultures – nor have they ever existed in the Western material sense – that could be the registration points or subjects for any augmentation. As Karsten Schoellner points out, the term "augmented reality" is blurring a very important distinction, which is that what is considered virtual information, displayed to augment the "real," is also "real:" The speed displayed on a heads-up speedometer, the roadmap to a certain destination, all these pieces of information are real, not virtual. "Augmented Reality [...] should only augment 'my reality' with more information about reality. A dysfunctional Heads-Up Display would give me a falsehood, and a virtual reality display would give me a fiction; but a properly functioning Augmented Reality display is entirely constrained by reality and nothing else" [19]. Our new approach to augmented reality copes with the absence of real existing information by transferring it into the head of the listener and registering it with her own body (Figs. 1 and 2).

A similar invisibility is the topic of our second project, Ghost Letter. This project engages with the mental asylum of San Servolo, an Island in the Venetian Lagoon. Use of the island as a mental asylum began in 1725 and it was reserved only for the rich in-habitants of Venice who could afford treatment in a facility. Until the 18th Century mental issues were not considered a treatable disease and people with such issues were simply locked away in asylums. Asylums were dumping grounds for all those whose behavior did not correspond to the norm. Even though San Servolo was not the same kind of dumping ground, mental disease was something that was separated from the normal life of the city. As Franco Basaglia, an Italian psychiatrist and neurologist, who is one of the pioneers of the modern concept of mental health and credited with the dismantling of the traditional insane asylums in Italy, wrote: "As long as we are within the system our situation will remain contradictory: the institution is managed and denied at the same time, illness is 'put into brackets' and cured, therapeutic acts are refused and carried out [...] We are destined to inhabit the contradictions of the system, managing

Fig. 1. Walking on the Plaza Simon Bolivar in Manizales, Colombia in "Weeping Bamboo"

Fig. 2. Looking at landmarks and imaginary sceneries at the plaza

an institution which we deny" [20]. This duality of norm and ab-norm, visibility and invisibility, acceptance and denial is the topic of the Ghost Letter project (Figs. 3 and 4).

Our interest in the third project, the Sonic Flaneur, is to think about an invisible landscape, which is constituted by the sonic phenomena the listener encounters while walking, and their inscriptions based on resonances and attentions the listener pays to the

Fig. 3. San Servolo Island, Italy

Fig. 4. Exploring the gardens of the former mental asylum

space and its sonic properties. The walking activity we are focusing on for this project is not the more or less directed navigation of a real terrain, but rather the gradual production of a terrain as a mental landscape. This landscape is not a geographical space but one of attention and memory. We are not interested in x/y coordinates or traditional forms of geographic mapping, the space we are interested in is a conceptual structure shaped through the interplay of listeners movements and the space. This is realized as a growing database of sonic phenomena and their spatial registration in terms of relative location and orientation collected through the engagement of the listener with the surrounding space (Figs. 5 and 6).

Fig. 5. Exploring an interior space with "Sonic Flaneur"

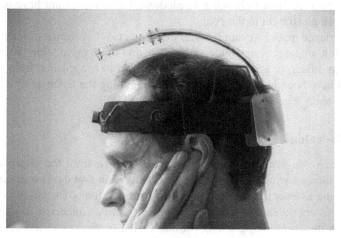

Fig. 6. Focusing on bone-conducted sound by closing the ears

4 Poetic Extension of Reality

As an approach to rendering these complexities of invisibility and absence, we decided, instead of following the visual paradigm of augmented reality, to create an audio-based experience that makes its point through the use of soundscapes and narrative text, aiming for a poetic extension of reality that is rooted in an act of listening rather than in a regime of visuality.

To understand our notion of poetic extension, we turn again to Schoellner, who discusses a similar idea of poetry as an augmentation of reality. He makes the point that "poetic imagination is a mediation upon reality rather than a willed recombination of ideas unconstrained by reality." This, we argue, fulfills a similar function as augmented reality, in that it provides the user – and in this case the listener – with a new perspective on reality, and this new perspective modifies reality inasmuch as the listener relates to the new perspective and adopts it as a viable representation of reality or a viable way to refer to reality. The augmentation as a modification or extension of reality therefore becomes part of reality, extending beyond a single person's whim or desire. By reaching a degree of intersubjective resonance it becomes a meaningful and shareable part of reality.

It is important for this kind of poetic augmentation to be communicated in a medium that allows a constitutive participation of the listener: it needs deciphering and interpretation; it needs the possibility for the poetic augmentation to resonate with the listener, otherwise it does not reach the level of intersubjectivity that makes it a real modification of reality. According to Schoellner, this can work through poetic words; in our case we use sound in order to achieve a similar result. It is essential for us to move away from the visual regime and make the listener a part of a physical and mental elaboration of the meaning. This elaboration invites swaying, deviation off the most efficient path and an active pondering. Exactly this labor necessary for deciphering and the construction of new meaning is what AR normally is there to avoid. Traditional AR makes navigating the city effortless, it presents all information necessary for a certain task in a certain place at a certain moment right when needed, so the user does not have to hesitate or ponder and can go straight to the goal.

The experience model we aim for with our projects is to obstruct efficiency, complicate navigation, make people wonder, take time, and loose orientation. We are inviting the listener to reflect, to access the hidden layers that have vanished from today's surface, or that have been banished from it. We are inviting the listeners to withstand the efficiency of today's goal-oriented society.

4.1   Why Listening

Our choice of sonic augmented reality is not only born from the absence of visible traces of the topics we are engaging with. It is a decision that uses sound as a medium that touches the listener directly and provides the opportunity for physical resonances between the listener's experience and the projects. It is a medium that connects the listeners with the surrounding space, rooting their experiences in the place, and that forgoes the visual regime of direct correspondence employed by AR. The experience does not have to be "in front of the eyes" or "seen with my own eyes" – as some of the common denominators of truth and reality suggest. Instead, sound connects to a more open concept of knowledge that does not necessarily only accept "truth" as its main objective. Expressions like "rumor," the Latin word for noise, stands for uncertainty and even doubtful truth. Our point is not to destabilize the notion of truth, but to provide a degree of uncertainty that stimulates the listener to question and engage in the form of constitutive participation discussed earlier.

The particular form of sound transmission we are employing establishes a duality between interiority and exteriority, with two different spatialities of sounds being constituted on one hand through the air-conducted environmental sound and on the other hand through bone-conducted internal sound. This connection between external reality and internal reality is a quality particular to sound. As media scholar Frances Dyson writes, "sound is the immersive medium par excellence [...] – the fact that it is invisible, intangible, ephemeral, and vibrational – coordinate with the physiology of the ears, to

create a perceptual experience profoundly different from the dominant sense of sight."
[21].

The close physical connection of sound and the body of the listener is a welcome characteristic for our projects, which we explore as an expressive possibility. We know what it feels like when a low bass tone vibrates our stomach and how this is subconsciously interpreted as dark and foreboding – an effect time and time again utilized in movies. Beyond those listening habits we are interested in relating the body movement through space, head positions and gestures to the experience. Walking and traversing specific places, for example, is an inherent part of the memory practice of the Quimbaya or the mental note-taking process of the flâneur – and in our projects we are establishing a metaphorical reference to this kind of physical relationship to space. On another level, we are exploring the physiognomy and materiality of the heads of listeners by experimenting with different positions of sound transducers on their heads. Each position makes the sound propagate differently through the bone structure of the listener's skull. This kind of internal spatiality also becomes part of the experiences we created.

The devices we developed for our projects also integrate gross body movement and orientation in space into the experience through locational tracking and inertial measurement units. All three projects are occurring in actual locations which allows the listeners to have a visual connection to the surrounding environment – this means every experience is always also visual. Nevertheless, the visual aspect, while important to our projects, plays a subordinate role to the sound. The actual traversal and aspects of way-finding and orientation through sound cues play central roles in the aesthetic concept of our projects.

5   Walking and Soundwalking as Cultural and Artistic Activities

Even though our projects employ custom developed hardware to realize a complex form of experience, they stand in the historic context of the tradition of walking as an artistic endeavor. Without the aim of being exhaustive, it seems appropriate to briefly discuss this context in order to situate the different forms of walking that we are modeling in the three projects; besides the specific forms of spatial traversal, all three experiences also partake in the art-historic line of the sound-walk.

Each one of the three projects discussed in this paper engages with a different kind of walking. The walking of Weeping Bamboo makes reference to early walking, to a culture in which walking was the normal means of transportation; walking as a means of carrying goods, hunting, gathering, traveling etc. was a normal activity and basic necessity of survival. As we know from interviews with some of the living representatives of the Quimbaya, it was normal to walk long distances as a means of travel. Today's tribes are living in locations that are difficult to access other than on foot and from there, they travel to come to cities such as Manizales at certain occasions. Along with walking as a daily necessity, it was also part of a close connection with nature; certain walks were done at certain times of the year to visit a network of sacred nature locations in which the close kinship between the human culture and nature was remembered and 'celebrated' (this term is an interpretation and may not exactly describe the relationship to the actions carried out in those places). Accessing those sacred locations is a way of renewing and performing the memory of the community in harmony with nature and handing it down to new generations. There is a hierarchy in who can access which locations that corresponds to age and the degree of initiation in the practices of communicating with nature. This relationship to the nature and practices of embodied knowledge through sacred locations, rituals and oral traditions are characteristic of the surviving aboriginal tribal communities such as Kogi and U'wa in contemporary Colombia.

The title Weeping Bamboo is inspired by the indigenous burial culture, in which the tombs were fenced with bamboo poles with holes cut into their stems. As aeolian instruments, they were humming and weeping evocative whistles to the winds, as we know through the written records of colonial witnesses. The songs of the Aeolian instruments relied on the wind as most of the myths and narratives relied on oral transmission and a spiritual enactment in sacred sites. Walking and ritual movements thus play an important role in the cultural life of the aboriginal communities and are both normal practice of every-day life as well as expression of cultural knowledge of the community.

The historical development of walking as cultural expression of the aboriginal cultures is very different from that in Western societies, where the need to walk came to be seen as a marker of lower class. People of higher class and those with wealth could afford to sit and be carried or transported. Thus walking had negative connotations with the exception for church processions or pilgrimages [22]. Only in the era of Enlightenment, in the 18th century, walking became an activity of choice for people of the upper classes. As Joseph Amato writes in his cultural history of walking, this kind of walking.

> required the correct place, the right occasion, and the proper surface. The court, the garden, or the newly rebuilt squares were the right venues for one's select walking. [...] Elaborate marble floors, spacious stairs, or finely graveled garden paths, the very opposite of the narrow, filthy, congested, rutted, mundane lane or common street, fit the movement of the proper and privileged. The path of somebody of importance had to be open, dry, firm, clean, safe, perhaps elevated, and as free as possible of obstacles, stomping and awkward peasants, foul crowds, and other unsightly and intrusive things. [22].

This means that walking takes place in prepared environments, nature has to be cleaned up, with graveled paths and the stride of the noble walker has to be unencumbered by obstacles. In this description we see a few parallels to the characteristics of the AR navigation efficiency; but we also clearly see a degree of detachment from nature and walking as natural activity. From this state on we can see how walking can become an elaborate exercise and a form of art that certain people, such as the poets like Fournel or Hessel, practice. Nevertheless, in a society in which walking is a necessity only for the less privileged, if walking is performed in a context that is not carefully prepared for it, it may be perceived as inappropriate or suspect. Franz Hessel describes in his essay The Suspect how he attracts suspicion: "I attract wary glances whenever I try to play the flaneur among the industrious; I believe they take me for a pickpocket" [23].

This duality between correct, orderly walking that corresponds to the norm, and the suspect, unruly act that does not, is what we are interested in in our second project, Ghost Letter. The small island of San Servolo has beautiful landscaping with winding graveled pathways across the island and the duality of walking on the path and deviating from it is easily choreographed. Being there today, we can imagine how the patients may have wandered across the island, kept from leaving the facility by the fact that it is an island, with only one pier and a boat leaving from the main building of the mental institution.

At least since Jean-Martin Charcot's photographic studies of walking styles of the mental patients in the Salpêtrière hospital in Paris, we are familiar with the focus on walking as a diagnostic tool to distinguish those with mental issues from those without [24]. In our project we implemented a system of guidance that invites the listener to perform the dialectic between order and chaos: walking on the pathways and off, away from them; being in control and getting lost; following the guiding narrative and losing orientation.

The third project, Sonic Flaneur, looks at walking as a form of memory construction. Walking is an act of observing and pacing out a terrain, a physical act that correlates physical activity with the mental activity of noticing things along the way, paying attention and perceiving in both a visual and acoustical sense. For us the relationship between the physical matters of the body, the muscle activity of engaging with the space and the vibrational impressions of the sounds we are exposed to in the space, were of primary interest. This set of questions arose from the previous projects as an attempt to understand better how the physical activity of traversing space correlates to the acts of perception and meaning constitution. The headset we developed for this experience measures motion, position, and orientation and in response to these physical activities records and preserves sounds that are salient and that the listener pays attention to. The recorded sounds are retrieved by revisiting the places where they have been recorded; in this case a superimposition of the previous sound and the current surrounding sound is created. By accumulating sounds and their specific locations a sonic terrain is emerging that is determined by the gestural interaction of the listener with the space.

Close to the original concept of the flâneur, the urban wanderer, the experience is about encountering unconscious memories in the cityscape and of finding reflexes of the past in the present. As Deborah Parsons writes, the flâneur "registers the city as a text to be inscribed, read, rewritten, and reread. The flâneur walks idly through the city, listening to its narrative" [25]. What Parsons describes as an act of listening has often also been described as a media inscription either in text, such as Baudelaire's poems, or by photography. In her book On Photography Susan Sontag likens the act of taking street photographs to the flâneur, who is collecting mental notes and observations in the street: "The photographer is an armed version of the solitary walker re-connoitering, stalking, cruising the urban inferno, the voyeuristic stroller who discovers the city as a landscape of voluptuous extremes" [26].

In the case of our project, walking is supported by a different form of technical mediation, our headset, which collects a specific kind of sonic inscription to build an emergent sonic space directed by the attention of the listener. This particular connection to sound transpires not only from the noise experience of the modern city walker as described by Walter Benjamin in his analysis of the metropolis, the description of the city-experience as a sonic experience is not uncommon. In the introduction of Lauren Elkin's book Flaneuse, she writes that "the flâneur, attuned to the chords that vibrate throughout his city, knows without knowing [27]."

5.1 Soundwalk as an Expressive Form

The three projects discussed here partake in both the activity of walking as an art form in general and the expressive form of the soundwalk in particular. Walking as an art form in this context is an act of performance or gesture, which is part of a haptic and aural engagement with the surrounding space. It functions as a source of inspiration, it inspires thoughts, allows scrutiny and creates perspectives. Walking played an important role in the poetry of artists like Baudelaire, Hessels or John Gay's Trivia: or the Art of Walking the Streets of London [28], it served Walter Benjamin as an analytical tool [29], and provided a structure of criticism to Debord, the Situationists and Ian Sinclair [30].

Our focus on listening as dominant part of the walking activity connects our projects more specifically to the artistic tradition of the soundwalk. Soundwalks are walks during which listening is directed to environmental sounds, an artistic discipline that appeared only in the 1960s. The term "soundwalk" was coined by Murray Schafer as part of his soundscape research. Schafer noted that in modern industrialized societies the acoustic environment has changed fundamentally, and the soundscape project aimed to pay attention to these changes, analyze them and take action in many ways, reaching from noise pollution abatement to the preservation of endangered soundmarks [31]. Sound artist Hildegard Westerkamp, who worked with Schafer on the Sound-scape Project, criticized that, in today's world, we are trained to selectively listen and desensitize our aural faculties to tune out unwanted sounds, which blinds our attention and perception away from aspects and phenomena that are not part of what we are trained by our environment to attend to. She further cautioned that "unless we listen with attention, there is a danger that some of the more delicate and quiet sounds may pass unnoticed by numbed ears and among the many mechanized voices of modern soundscapes and may eventually disappear entirely." [32] This kind of critical sensitivity to sounds, voices and signals that are not perceived, that are generally tuned out, is very close to the intentions of our projects and informed our decision to turn to the medium of the soundwalk. Westerkamp's almost activist call to "climb out of our bubbles now, emerge from behind our screens, walls, loudspeakers and headphones and open ears directly to the environment. Let's go for another soundwalk" [32] is particularly resonating with the critical reflexive practice and our attempt to get away from the screens and mediations that normally filter our image of the world around us.

While Westerkamp's notion of soundwalk was mostly a shift in attention to our sensory input coming from the current environment that did not use any mediating technology, our approach employs custom developed technology to contrast the current soundscape with a recorded version of sounds that are reminiscent of bygone soundscapes that used to exist in the place. To maintain the direct aural experience with the current soundscape, Westerkamp's analytical 'tool', is an important conceptual decision in our projects and the reason why we favored the open-ear listening model over conventional headphones. In the sense that we use hardware specifically developed for our projects, our projects also stand in conversation with the work of artists such as Christina Kubisch and her "Electric Walks" or Bernhard Leitner and his "Hand-Sound-Objects," who also have developed their own hardware platforms to enable certain listening situations.

6 Technological Platform

The technological platform we developed for the three projects discussed in this article is based on the same foundation. It combines computing (Teensy 3.2 board), various sensors, a geo-positioning (GPS) unit, amplifiers and sound transducers into a wearable headset unit. Listeners can wear the unit on their head while walking around in the areas dedicated for the experiences of Weeping Bamboo and Ghost Letter. In the case of the Sonic Flaneur project, no particular space is referenced, since the experience is emergent in any space the viewer decides to move in (Figs. 7 and 8).

Fig. 7. Headset for "Weeping Bamboo"

Fig. 8. Headset for "Sonic Flaneur"

6.1 Bone-Conduction Sound Transmission

The headset provides a four-channel sound experience consisting of pre-recorded, synthesized, real-time, and real-time recorded and synthesized sounds. All sounds are part of a composition that is mixed in reference to the space and the movement and gestures of the listener. The sounds are transmitted to the listener's head through bone-conduction transducers, which are placed on the skin of the listener in well-defined positions. The bone-conduction transducers are working like bare voice-coils of speakers without a diaphragm. Instead of transmitting the sound vibrations with a cone to air molecules, the vibration is here directly applied to the bone structure of the listener's head. The sound travels through the head to the inner ear, where it is perceived as sound by the same nerve cells in the cochlea as is air-conducted sound. Due to the fact that the sound from the headset travels through the bone structure no headphones are needed, and the ears remain open to perceive the surrounding sounds transmitted through the air, which are then layered in the cochlear with the bone-conducted sounds. This technique allows us to realize the layering described above and keep the listener's ear open to the current soundscape.

The transducers are placed in different locations on the forehead, the back of the head and right and left temples. We have experimented a lot with the positions of the transducers and they vary between the different incarnations of the platform. Each placement creates a different spatial feeling for the bone-conducted sounds and amplifies or attenuates them differently. The placement on the temples gives a strong and very well discernible directional sound, an effect we use for the voice-over parts in Weeping Bamboo and Ghost Letter. Sonic Flaneur has all transducers placed in a line around the head, so that the left and right transducers a placed above the temples. This placement attenuates their sound more and evens them with the other front and back transducers (Fig. 9).

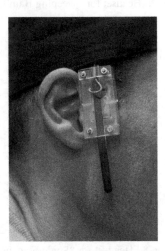

Fig. 9. Transducer on right temple in the "Weeping Bamboo" headset

The use of multi-channel bone-conducted sound allows us to establish a very particular spatiality in the sound experience of the listener. Roughly listeners hear a front, sides, and back spatial distribution of the sounds, but the sense of distance and exact location remains somewhat mysterious, because, despite all clearly decipherable spatiality of the sounds, they still sound as if they were coming from within the head-space. Modulated by the individual structure of the listener's head, the bone-conducted sounds are registered with the external space – i.e. when the listener turns the head, the sounds rotate accordingly as if they were fixed in the surrounding space – but seem at the same time to be coming from an internal source. We use this effect to evoke a sense of "thought-" or "memory-sound."

The headset is fixed with an elastic strap to the head to make close contact to the head surface, which is necessary for the bone-conduction transducers to have enough contact with the head surface to transmit the sound vibrations.

6.2 Sensor-Units and Computation

The placement and composition of sounds such as the voice overs in Weeping Bam-boo and Ghost Letter are controlled in accordance with GPS coordinates, direction, and the head inclination. The corresponding measurement units are placed above the head. In the headsets for Weeping Bamboo and Ghost Letter, the housing of the sensors also accommodates the computation and amplifier units, audio boards, charging electronics, and the battery. For the Sonic Flaneur only compass, inertial measurement unit, and a microphone are placed above the head, mounted on a curved bar, the rest of the electronics is placed at the back of the head. In this headset we are also using two bone-conduction transducers in the front and back, respectively, to be able to apply a stronger vibrational force (Figs. 10 and 11).

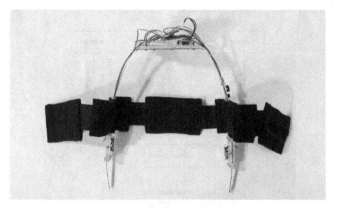

Fig. 10. Headset construction used in the "Weeping Bamboo" and "Ghost Letter" projects with electronics platform mounted above the head and adjustable temple-pieces

The computing unit we are using in all of the headsets is an extremely small, arduino-compatible processor board that can play, record, filter, and mix sounds, as well as create new, synthetic sounds. These sound manipulation capabilities are used to play and record sounds, apply effects such as echo or reverb (in the Ghost Letter project) to real sounds listeners hear at the same time through air conducted sound. Synthesized sounds are used in particular in the Sonic Flaneur to create a sonic inscription of the surrounding room

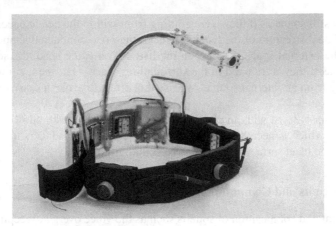

Fig. 11. Headset for "Sonic Flaneur" project with dual transducers in the back and front and distance sensors distributed around the head

characteristics and listener's movement within that space. As sensors, the headset used for Sonic Flaneur does not use a GPS unit for the determination of position, because these would only work in appropriate external locations. For the Sonic Flaneur concept we wanted to be able to create a sense of an emergent space that is not determined by geographic coordinates, but by attention and specific environment of the listener. To make this possible we are using an array of distance sensors in conjunction with a compass (Fig. 12).

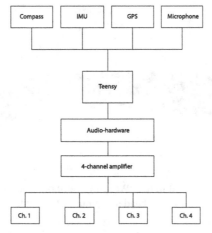

Fig. 12. Functional diagram of the headsets

7 Conclusions

We built one of each version of the headsets as prototypes to fathom what kinds of listening possibilities they would enable. Born from a conceptual thought and a creative discovery process, the three experiences, which we staged as part of three different events, give a sense of what "reflexive augmented listening" could be. The entire experience, including the act of putting on and fitting the headsets and the first experience of bone-conducted sound layered with normal sound is surprising and markedly different from other forms of listening and media technologies aimed at augmenting our sense of space. This difference puts listeners into a state of heightened awareness and shifts their perspective in respect to their normal environment. This perceptual attitude turned out to be extremely useful and satisfying for our intentions.

In all three experiences listeners were in an explorative mode: In Weeping Bamboo they were keen on hearing more of the narrative and explore more areas of the sonic environment; in Ghost Letters they were trying to chase ghost voices and understand what happened in the place, being drawn to a blurred boundary between reality sounds and their distortions and echoes emanating from an imaginary environment; and finally in Sonic Flaneur listeners attempted to read the patterns of sounds in order to correlate them to the movement through space and to revisit places that had been encountered previously.

While there is much room for experimentation with the format of bone-conducted multi-channel sounds and the real-time composition of real and synthetic sounds, the three experiences gave us a good sense of what this mode of listening is able to evoke in the listener and the perceptual attitudes it can foster.

References

1. Sennheiser: Sennheiser – Headphones & Headsets – Microphones – Business Communications (2019)
2. Bose: Smart Noise Cancelling Headphones 700 Bose (2019)
3. Microsoft: Microsoft HoloLens Mixed Reality Technology for Business (2019)
4. Magic Leap: Home Magic Leap (2019)
5. Stokes, D., Matthen, M., Biggs, S. (eds.): Perception and Its Modalities. Oxford University Press (2014). https://doi.org/10.1093/acprof:oso/9780199832798.001.0001
6. Caudell, T.P., Mizell, D.W.: Augmented reality: an application of heads-up display technology to manual manufacturing processes. In: Presented at the Proceedings of the Twenty-Fifth Hawaii International Conference on System Sciences (1992). https://doi.org/10.1109/hicss.1992.183317
7. Hessel, F.: Flâneries parisiennes. Rivages, Paris (2013)
8. Debord, G., Chetglov, I.: Theory of the Derive. Actar/Museum of Contemporary Art, Barcelona, Barcelona (1899)
9. Burckhard, L.: Why is Landscape Beautiful?: The Science of Strollology by Lucius Burckhardt (1-May-2015) Paperback. Birkhauser (2015)
10. Fournel, V.: Ce Qu'on Voit Dans Les Rues De Paris. HardPress Publishing (2019)
11. Webster, A.: Pokémon Go spurred an amazing era that continues with Sword and Shield (2019)

12. Phillips, T.: Pokémon Go active player count highest since 2016 summer launch • Eurogam-er.net (2019)
13. Hill, D.M.: Kashmir: How Pokémon Go changes the geography of cities (2019)
14. Kooragayala, S., Srini, T.: Pokémon GO is changing how cities use public space, but could it be more inclusive? (2016)
15. McClatchy: There are fewer Pokemon Go locations in black neighborhoods, but why? (2019)
16. Revell, T.: Did Pokémon Go really kill 250 people in traffic accidents? (2019)
17. Prasuethsut, L.: Taking Mini's augmented reality glasses for a test drive. (2015)
18. Valencia, L., Lano, A.: Manizales en la din√/°mica Colonizadora 1846–1930. Universidad de Cal-das, Manizales (1990)
19. Schoellner, K.: Augmented reality and augmented perception. In: Ariso, J.M. (ed.) Augmented Reality: Reflections on Its Contribution to Knowledge Formation. Berlin, De Gruyter, Boston, pp. 171–192 (2017)
20. Foot, J.: The Man Who Closed the Asylums: Franco Basaglia and the Revolution in Mental Health Care. Verso, London; Brooklyn, NY (2015)
21. Dyson, F.: Sounding New Media: Immersion and Embodiment in the Arts and Culture. University of California Press (2009)
22. Amato, J.: On Foot: A History of Walking. NYU Press, New York (2004)
23. Hessel, F.: Walking in Berlin: A Flaneur in the Capital. The MIT Press (2017)
24. Charcot, J.-M.: Nouvelle Iconographie de la Salpêtrière. Masson et Cie, Paris (1898)
25. Parsons, D.L.: Streetwalking the Metropolis : Women, the City and Modernity: Women, the City and Modernity. OUP Oxford (2000)
26. Sontag, S.: On Photography. Macmillan (2001)
27. Elkin, L.: Flâneuse: Women Walk the City in Paris, New York, Tokyo, Venice, and London. Farrar, Straus and Giroux (2017)
28. John, G.: Trivia: Or, the Art of Walking the Streets of London. By Mr. Gay. printed for Bernard Lintot (1730)
29. Benjamin, W.: The Writer of Modern Life: Essays on Charles Baudelaire. Harvard University Press (2006)
30. Coverley, M.: Psychogeography. Pocket Essentials (2006)
31. Schafer, R.M.: The Soundscape. Simon and Schuster (1993)
32. Westerkamp, H.: Soundwalking. Sound Heritage. 3, (1974)
33. White, R.B.: Notes on the Aboriginal Races of the North-Western Provinces of South America. The J. Anthropol. Inst. Great Brit. Ireland **13**, 240 (1884). https://doi.org/10.2307/2841890

Pseudo-haptic Feedback Design for Virtual Activities in Human Computer Interface

D. S. Lee, K. C. Lee, H. J. Kim, and S. Kim

Samsung Research, Seoul 06765, South Korea
{ds.james.lee,kenfe.lee,hakjungs.kim,su_yong.kim}@samsung.com

Abstract. Digital world such as Metaverse requires a fully multimodal integrated cognitive interface to provide realistic and immersive interaction that boosts user engagement. In this paper, cross-modality (visual and audio, and/or haptic) driven pseudo haptic interface has been investigated in AR environment. In-house haptic platform named "Haptic Signal Processing Platform" (HSPP) has been implemented to detect any modalities in real-time. For user test, five primitive virtual activities including click, scroll, object manipulation, zoom-in and zoom-out are considered using visual & audio and multimodal (visual & audio, and haptic) feedbacks. Cross-modality feedback using HSPP has been psychophysically evaluated in terms of three categories; intuitiveness, attractiveness and immersiveness. To evaluate above three qualitative categories, NASA-TLX has been implemented. This evaluation method is recommended to measure the performance of a particular individual in a task; mental, physical, temporal, performance, effort and frustration. The results clearly show that the cross-modality based pseudo-haptic with HSPP can produce higher performance in terms of intuitiveness, attractiveness and immersiveness.

Keywords: Human Computer Interaction · Multimodal interaction · Multimodal mixed reality interfaces · Tactile and haptic interaction · Pseudo-Haptic Feedback

1 Introduction

Human Computer Interaction (HCI) has been become the core technology to open an integrated application environments such as Virtual Reality (VR), Augmented Reality (AR) and further to Metaverse. Metaverse requires a fully multi-modal integrated cognitive interface [1, 2]. It boosts visual, audio and haptic feedbacks engaging with human sensory channels including seeing listening and intuitive touching interaction. Pseudo haptic based cross-modality has been studied to enhance the immersion of applications in VR, AR [3, 4]. However, the haptic feedback for virtual activities is still lacking in these environments especially in AR. Current virtual inter-faces only generate simple sounds and/or tactile feedback for user interaction.

Studies about pseudo-haptic have been conducted to improve the reality of interaction with virtual objects in VR and AR [5–7]. Haptic devices of the glove type [8], ring type [9], band type [10, 11], and fingertip type [12] have been developed to render

© The Author(s), under exclusive license to Springer Nature Switzerland AG 2023
J. Y. C. Chen and G. Fragomeni (Eds.): HCII 2023, LNCS 14027, pp. 253–265, 2023.
https://doi.org/10.1007/978-3-031-35634-6_18

the high-fidelity haptic feedback. Maereg et al. proposed a ring-type wearable haptic device and pseudo-haptic method with visual feedback [13]. Displacement of the spring generated by the pressing or releasing force is visually rendered, and pseudo-haptic is generated while changing the vibration amplitude according to the virtual stiffness. It is shown that the just-noticeable difference of stiffness discrimination using pseudo-haptic is decreased by 15% compared to rendering only visual feedback. Kronester et al. developed a band-type haptic device equipped with four Eccentric Rotating Mass (ERM) motors [14]. Vibration patterns to enhance realism of the electrical force, gravity, and spring force is studied by combining vibration amplitude, interval, rhythm, and the number of operating motors. Choi et al. proposed a visuo-haptic illusion method to improve perceived stiffness [12]. Virtual objects have a constant volume, and displacements in the x, y, and z directions are visually rendered depending on the interaction force and the stiffness of object. At the same time, the stiffness is represented using the vibration frequency of the finger type haptic device. Pezent et al. developed a band-type haptic device using six Linear Resonant Actuators (LRA) and squeezing mechanism [15, 16]. Discrete contact is rendered using LRAs, and continuous force is rendered using squeezing mechanism. Visual illusion and haptic feedback are used together to render stiffness, surface texture, and object inertia.

Pseudo-haptic with auditory and visual feedback enhance immersive experience in AR and VR [17–21]. Bernard et al. showed that providing both audio and haptic rendering of surface texture reduces the perception threshold of recognizing rhythm compared to providing only audio or haptic [22]. Turchet et al. proposed Musical Haptic Wearables for Audiences (MHWAs) for better immersion when enjoying live concerts [23]. Chrysanthakopoulou et al. developed a museum experience simulation based on VR for educational purposes. Realistic experience is provided using high-quality visual, auditory and haptic feedback using glove-type device [24]. Cheng et al. proposed a method of generating an audio using the haptic information calculated in the rigid-fluid interaction [25]. Wei et al. proposed a method of generating a haptic signal by extracting features from video and audio [26]. Multi-modal feedback is provided using the generated haptic signal. However, research on pseudo-haptic based cross-modality for essential motions in AR is insufficient.

In this paper, cross-modality (visual & audio, and/or haptic) driven pseudo haptic interface has been developed for fundamental virtual activities in AR environment. To increase immersive interaction, this interface considers five fundamental virtual activities including click, scroll, object manipulation, zoom-in and zoom-out. Details of primitive virtual interactions will be described in Sect. 2.2. The paper is organized as follows; Sect. 2 illustrates HSPP and definition of primitive interactions. And also this section includes haptic renders for virtual activities. Section 3 presents in-house haptic device; Wrist-worn Tactile Device (WTD). Psychophysical user test on augmented pseudo haptic experience are presented in Sect. 4. Finally, Sect. 5 delivers discussion and conclusion.

2 Haptic Signal Processing Platform

Cross-modality cognitive interface is integrated into in-house platform named Haptic Signal Processing Platform (HSPP) as shown in Fig. 1. HSPP has been developed for immersive experience on music, movie, game and ambient sound in android OS.

HSPP can be easily connected with AR glasses and in-house Wrist-worn Tactile Display (WTD). HSPP is capable to convert digital cross-modality signal obtained from AR glasses to analog signal and compresses to haptic signal activating WTD as shown in Fig. 1.

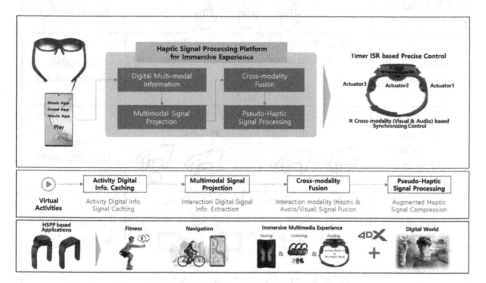

Fig. 1. Working diagram of cross-modality based HSPP and applications.

Multimodal Signal Projection collects all digital signals for virtual activities. Then *Cross-modality Fusion* carries out the followings;

- recognizes what sort of virtual activity is currently happening with which hand
- verifies what activities on left and right hand if there are more than one activity
- identifies which stage of interactions including *Touch, Press, Grab, Hover*
- runs audio manager handling audio feedback corresponding to the start, middle and end of gesture interactions

Pseudo-Haptic Signal Processing module renders and compresses haptic signal data corresponding to the detected interaction. In following subsections, what kinds of interaction are considered and how haptic feedback is rendered to provide effective multimodal feedback.

2.1 Definition of Primitive Virtual Interactions

In this paper, five primitive virtual activities are considered as shown in Table 1. Every primitive virtual activity starts with *"Touch"* and ends with *"Release"* interaction. Click gesture is consisted of three interactions including *Touch, Press* and *Release*. The *Press* interaction will activate button type of UI. For movable and scalable interactions, virtual activity is consisted of four interactions in order of *Touch, Grab, Hover* and *Release* interactions. The proposed method activates the audio feedback when *Touch* interaction is detected. And then *Release* interaction is the end of audio feedback.

Table 1. Fundamental virtual activities.

V. Activities	Gesture Interaction Definition	Functionality
Click/Select	*Touch → Press → Release*	Activating UI, Select Object
Scroll/Slider (Movable)	*Touch → Grab → Hover → Release* (Either horizontal or vertical displacement)	Navigating UI component
Object Manipulation (Movable)	*Touch → Grab → Hover → Release* (any direction of x, y and z-axis)	Navigating UI component
Zoom-in (Scalable)	*Touch → Grab → Hover → Release*	Zoom-in the selected object
Zoom-out (Scalable)	*Touch → Grab → Hover → Release*	Zoom-out the selected object

2.2   Haptic Rendering System for Primitive Virtual Activities

Haptic rendering is a computational model or system generating the reaction forces responding to user's virtual activities. The computed reaction forces will be sent to haptic device that creates a realistic touch sensation through WTD. The virtual activities shown in Table 1, can be clustered as static/instant and dynamic interactions. The instant interactions are *Touch* and *Grab* gestures while *Press* and *Hover* gestures are belongs to the dynamic interaction. None of haptic feedback is applied for *Release* interaction.

Touch Interaction. In this paper, *Touch* sensation of all fingers are generated using hybrid phantom sensation. Phantom sensation is a tactile illusion also known as passive tactile spatiotemporal illusion. A sequential taps at two separated skin locations can create another tap perception at intervening skin regions. The Wrist-worn Tactile Display (WTD) as shown in Fig. 2 b) includes three actuators that cannot generate touch sensations for all five fingers. So passive tactile spatiotemporal illusion technique is implemented to generate another two sensations by manipulating two actuators. The conventional methods for haptic illusion are in terms of linear, logarithm and power scale functions [27, 28]. In this paper, trigonometric scaled illusion method is developed and applied to generate all five (left handed) sensations as shown in Fig. 2 a). The main reason is that WTD is in the circular shape and trigonometric is the right method to depict the centrifugal vectors. For right hand, the sensation system will be symmetrical as Fig. 2 a). It can been that either one of actuators A1, A2 and A3 will be activated if there is *Touch* interaction by either thumb, middle or pinky finger. For index and ring fingers, either two actuators (A1 and A2 or A2 and A3) will be activated at the same time to generate haptic illusion. For *Touch* and *Grab* interactions, the first touch finger and grab fingers will be identified at the first step. Then the haptic rendering system will provide one or multiple instant haptic feedbacks corresponding to the detected interaction. For *Touch* interaction, haptic rendering system will generate the minimum amplitude (A_{min}) defined as PWM 150.

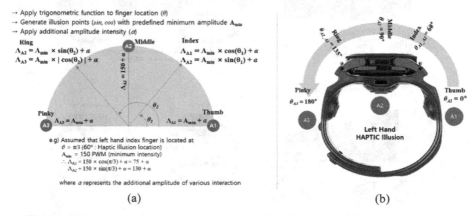

Fig. 2. a) Phantom sensation algorithm (left hand), b) Haptic illusion vs. finger mapping

Ten fingers are tracked using visual recognition method, but only the index finger on each hand is used as a collider for the interaction. In Mixed Reality Toolkit (MRTK) document, it is recommended to use only the index finger as the collider because unexpected collisions may occur if all ten fingers are used as the collider [29]. Due to this recommendation, the first *Touch* interaction is solely applied to the index finger in this paper.

Haptic Rendering for Virtual Interaction. For virtual activities, the haptic rendering system will generate dynamic (spatiotemporal) haptic illusion feedbacks as shown in Fig. 3.

Haptic feedback for *Click/Select* activity starts at the minimum amplitude (same as *Touch* interaction) and then the amplitude value of haptic feedback will be moderately increased to the maximum amplitude. For *Scroll/Slider* and *Zoom-In/Out* activities, the haptic illusion described in Fig. 2 is applied to express the directions such as towards to left or right and up or down. For instance, the location of horizontal slider is predefined from the minimum value as zero to the maximum value as one. This location value will be converted in to radian value to activate trigonometric haptic illusion. For *Object Manipulation* activity, the distance between user and object is applied; when the object is getting closer to the predefined distance, the maximum amplitude is applied. The

258   D. S. Lee et al.

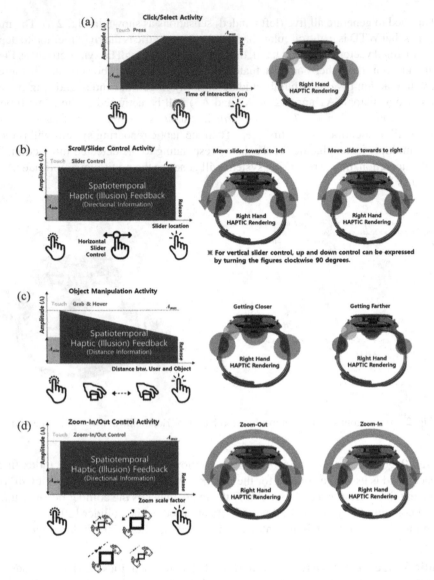

Fig. 3. a) Click/Select (top), b) Scroll (second from the top), c) Object Manipulation (second from the bottom) and d) Zoom-In/Out (bottom).

amplitude will be gradually decreased to the minimum amplitude when the distance is far enough.

3 Wrist-worn Tactile Display (WTD)

In this paper, in-house WTDs shown in Fig. 4 are used to generate augmented pseudo-haptic feedbacks. There are two types of WTDs; the first one is with smartwatch core (Galaxy Watch 5 in this case) while the second one is without core. These bands can be used for many applications; navigation, fitness, multimedia (music, movie, and game) and AR immersive feedback device. Each WTD provides multichannel haptic signal processing with three actuators; left, mid and right actuators activating based on predefined cross-modality haptic patterns as shown in Fig. 2. WTD has CPU: ARM® Cortex®-M0 + 32bit 48 MHz microcontroller (SAMD21G18) with 256 KB Flash, 32 KB SRAM. The center-to-center distance of ERM actuators is 35 mm that user can verify any spatiotemporal stimulation using cutaneous perception [30, 31]. The performance of applied ERM is similar to the motor shown in reference [32].

Left handed band shown in Fig. 4 a) will be activated if HSPP detects left hand virtual activity. The same system is applied to the right handed WTD. HSPP will activates both left and right handed WTDs with different haptic feedbacks if there are bimanual activities. For example, left hand is on selecting item while right hand is on controlling vertical slider. HSPP will generate two gesture interaction including *Select* (*Touch-Press-Release*) for left hand and *Slider* (*Touch-Grab-Hover-Release*) for right hand WTDs.

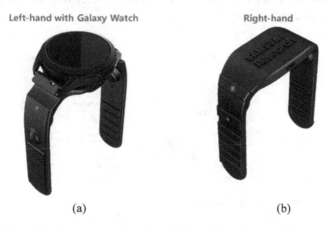

Left-hand with Galaxy Watch   Right-hand

(a)   (b)

Fig. 4. a) WTD with Galaxy watch core (left-hand) and b) without watch core (right-hand).

4 Psychophysical Test for Augmented Pseudo Haptic

In this section, psychophysical user test are defined. There are two user tests using the conventional (visual and audio feedbacks) and the proposed multimodal (visual & audio and haptic feedbacks) methods. The conventional method (M1) is interaction without haptic rendered multichannel signal processing. On the other hand, the proposed method (M2) counts all modalities including visual & audio and touch sensation as multimodal feedback. M2 provides the audio and haptic feedbacks exactly the same duration as the virtual activity. The psychophysical tests are conducted with two hypothesis as follows;

- Hypothesis 1: The magnitude of perceived virtual interaction can be clearly expressed with the manipulation of three actuators' amplitude of WTDs for all primitive virtual activities. (Validation of WTD)
- Hypothesis 2: The proposed multimodal (visual & audio and haptic) feedback provides more natural interaction (as realistic virtual activities) when compared to the conventional method. (Validation of HSPP multimodal rendering algorithm)

4.1 Psychophysical Test Environment

Psychophysical tests for immersive experience with AR glass, have been conducted to evaluate the performance of HSPP with/without cross-modality based augmented pseudo-haptic feedback. Test environment is shown in Fig. 5. For the user test, nReal light AR glass is used due to its light weight. The brief specifications of nReal AR glass are; weight 106 g, 52 degrees of Field of View (FoV), 6 DoF head tracking, hand tracking, image tracking and plane detection. The details of nReal light can be found in reference [33]. Algorithms for the interaction such as collision detection, object manipulation, visual and audio rendering are developed based on MRTK [34]. In addition, hand-tracking algorithm is developed based on MRTK-NrealHandTracking [35]. Galaxy S20 Ultra 5G (SM-G988N) are used, and two WTDs are connected to the smartphone using Bluetooth low energy.

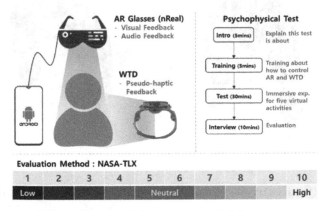

Fig. 5. User test (UT) environment (left), test process (right) and quantitative evaluation.

For psychophysical immersive experience, participants will wear AR (nReal) glass and left and right handed WTDs to get all multimodal (visual & sound and vibrotactile haptic) feedbacks for five virtual activities. The nReal application will be run on Galaxy S20 Ultra 5G. Ten people (aged 20 s–50 s, two female and eight male) are participated. This test is organized with four sessions including introduction, training, test and interview in total 50 min to one hour. During training session, users will learn how to make a proper gesture interaction under virtual environment. A simple virtual application will be activated during test session performing five virtual activities. During interview session, cross-modality cognitive interface with HSPP is evaluated in terms of three categories; intuitiveness, attractiveness and immersiveness with five questions. To evaluate above three qualitative categories, NASA-TLX [36, 37] has been implemented to get quantitative results. This evaluation method is recommended to measure the performance of a particular individual in a task; mental, physical, temporal, performance, effort and frustration (Fig. 6).

[Intuitiveness] How easy to feel the audio and haptic feedbacks?

1	2	3	4	5	6	7	8	9	10
Low				Neutral					High

[Attractiveness] How well match all multimodal feedback?

1	2	3	4	5	6	7	8	9	10
Low				Neutral					High

[Immersiveness: effort] How much mental/physical effort did you put?

1	2	3	4	5	6	7	8	9	10
High				Neutral					Low

[Immersiveness: stress] How much mental/physical stress did you get?

1	2	3	4	5	6	7	8	9	10
High				Neutral					Low

[Immersiveness] Immersiveness with visual (& audio) and haptic feedbacks?

1	2	3	4	5	6	7	8	9	10
Low				Neutral					High

Fig. 6. Questionnaire for intuitiveness, attractiveness and overall satisfaction using NASA-TLX.

4.2 Psychophysical Test Result

It can be seen that the results obtained by M1 (visual and audio feedback) and M2 (visual & audio and haptic) are statistically different especially for intuitiveness, attractiveness and immersiveness as shown in Table 2. Since all p-value is less than $\alpha = 0.05$, it can be concluded that there were sufficient evidence to say that not all of the group means are equal.

Figure 7 depicts the performance comparison between the conventional method M1 and the proposed method M2 in terms of intuitiveness and attractiveness. It can be seen that intuitiveness and attractiveness of the proposed method are 78% and 60% higher when compared to the conventional method. It means that the proposed method can produce better multimodal feedback to feel the virtual activity as realistic immersiveness.

Figure 8 compares the immersiveness obtained by the conventional method (M1) and the proposed method (M2). M2 produces higher immersiveness by 48% with less effort and stress by 26% and 10% respectively. The results clearly show that the cross-modality based pseudo-haptic with HSPP can produce higher performance in terms of intuitiveness, attractiveness and immersiveness when compared to the conventional feedback method.

Table 2. One-way ANOVA Analysis between M1 and M2.

Questionnaire	P-value	F-value	F-crit
Intuitiveness	2.44E−09	118.15	4.41
Attractiveness	7.01E−07	55.09	4.41
Effort	9.03E−05	26.88	4.49
Stress	4.03E−02	4.88	4.41
Immersiveness	6.63E−06	39.20	4.41

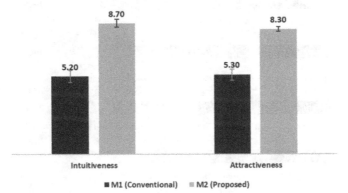

Fig. 7. Performance comparison between M1 and M2 in terms of intuitiveness (left) and attractiveness (right).

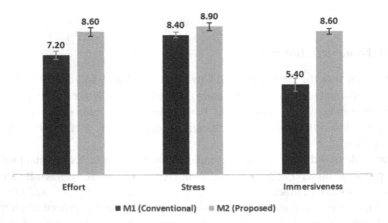

Fig. 8. Immersiveness between M1 and M2 in terms of effort, stress and immersive experience.

During interview session, it has been proven why the multimodal feedback (M2) produces better and clear interaction when compared to the conventional (visual and audio) M1.

1. Multimodal feedbacks deliver a clear status of virtual interaction (start/ middle/ end point of interaction).
2. Manipulation of amplitude and haptic illusion feedback can clearly describe the interactions especially three activities *Slider*, *Object Manipulation* and *Zoom-In/Out*.
3. In overall, majority of users have mentioned that multimodal feedback can provide a more natural (including immersive) interaction.

Even though the proposed method M2 produces immersive interaction, both M1 and M2 still needs a learning curve to make a correct interaction. During training session most of users had a difficulty to pose the right gesture at certain position in FoV. The main reason is that the gesture interaction at certain angle/position should be shown clearly to two outer cameras. Otherwise, the gesture recognition system will not catch what activity it is. This gesture learning curve will be a challenge for both AR and AI researchers.

5 Conclusion

This paper clearly demonstrated immersive system using multimodal feedback based wrist-worn tactile display. It can be seen that the proposed method; HSPP generating augmented pseudo-haptic with WTD, can deliver a natural virtual activities for immersive experience. In addition, the activities based on distance based and directional information can be well described by spatiotemporal haptic feedbacks with various amplitude. In near future, spatiotemporal haptic authoring tool-kit especially for WTD will be applied to Haptic Signal Processing Platform. For long-term future work, the physics-informed AI in haptic interface will be investigated to present a more realistic and natural interaction between human-to-human as well as human-to-robot.

References

1. Kozinets, R.V.: Immersive netnography: a novel method for service experience research in virtual reality, augmented reality and metaverse contexts. J. Serv. Manage. **34**, 100–125 (2022)
2. Park, S.-M., Kim, Y.-G.: A metaverse: taxonomy, components, applications, and open challenges. IEEE Access **10**, 4209–4251 (2022)
3. Pusch, A., Lécuyer, A.: Pseudo-haptics: from the theoretical foundations to practical system design guidelines. In: Proceedings of the 13th international conference on multimodal interfaces – ICMI'11, pp. 57–64 (2011)
4. Verona, E.D., Brum, B.R., Oliveira, C., Sanches, S.R.R., Corrêa, C.G.: Pseudo-haptic perception in smartphones graphical interfaces: a case study. In: Chen, J.Y.C., Fragomeni, G. (eds.) Virtual, Augmented and Mixed Reality HCII 2021. Lecture Notes in Computer Science LNCS, vol. 12770, pp. 203–222. Springer, Cham (2021). https://doi.org/10.1007/978-3-030-77599-5_16
5. Ozioko, O., Dahiya, R.: Smart tactile gloves for haptic interaction, communication, and rehabilitation. Adv. Intell. Syst. **4**(2), 2100091 (2021)

6. Caeiro-Rodríguez, M., Otero-González, I., Mikic-Fonte, F.A., Llamas-Nistal, M.: A systematic review of commercial smart gloves: current status and applications. Sensors **21**(8), 2667 (2021)
7. Adilkhanov, A., Rubagotti, M., Kappassov, Z.: Haptic devices: wearability-based taxonomy and literature review. IEEE Access **10**, 91923–91947 (2022)
8. Zhu, M., et al.: Haptic-feedback smart glove as a creative human-machine interface (HMI) for virtual/augmented reality applications. Sci. Adv. **6**(19), eaaz8693 (2020). https://doi.org/10.1126/sciadv.aaz8693
9. Sun, Z., Zhu, M., Shan, X., Lee, C.: Augmented tactile-perception and haptic-feedback rings as human-machine interfaces aiming for immersive interactions. Nat. Commun. **13**(1), 5224 (2022)
10. Kim, T., Shim, Y.A., Lee, G.: Heterogeneous stroke: using unique vibration cues to improve the wrist-worn spatiotemporal tactile display. In: Proceedings of the 2021 CHI Conference on Human Factors in Computing Systems (2021)
11. Liao, Y.-C., Chen, Y.-L., Lo, J.-Y., Liang, R.-H., Chan, L., Chen, B.-Y.: EdgeVib: effective alphanumeric character output using a wrist-worn tactile display. In: Proceedings of the 29th Annual Symposium on User Interface Software and Technology (2016)
12. Choi, I., Zhao, Y., Gonzalez, E.J., Follmer, S.: Augmenting perceived softness of haptic proxy objects through transient vibration and visuo-haptic illusion in virtual reality. IEEE Trans. Visual Comput. Graphics **27**(12), 4387–4400 (2021)
13. Maereg, A.T., Nagar, A., Reid, D., Secco, E.L.: Wearable vibrotactile haptic device for stiffness discrimination during virtual interactions. Front. Robot. AI **4**(42), 1–9 (2017)
14. Kronester, M.J., Riener, A., Babic, T.: Potential of wrist-worn vibrotactile feedback to enhance the perception of virtual objects during mid-air gestures. In: Extended Abstracts of the 2021 CHI Conference on Human Factors in Computing Systems (2021)
15. Pezent, E., O'Malley, M.K., Israr, A., Samad, M., Robinson, S., Agarwal, P., Benko, H., Colonnese, N.: Explorations of wrist haptic feedback for AR/VR interactions with Tasbi. In: Extended Abstracts of the 2020 CHI Conference on Human Factors in Computing Systems (2020)
16. Pezent, E., Agarwal, P., Hartcher-OrBrien, J., Colonnese, N., O'Malley, M.K.: Design, control, and psychophysics of Tasbi: a force-controlled multimodal haptic bracelet. IEEE Trans. Rob. **38**(5), 2962–2978 (2022)
17. Remache-Vinueza, B., Trujillo-León, A., Zapata, M., Sarmiento-Ortiz, F., Vidal-Verdú, F.: Audio-tactile rendering: a review on technology and methods to convey musical information through the sense of touch. Sensors **21**(19), 6575 (2021)
18. Frid, E., Lindetorp, H.: Haptic music: exploring whole-body vibrations and tactile sound for a multisensory music installation. In: Sound and Music Computing Conference, pp. 68–75. Torino, 24th–26th June 2020
19. Pezent, E., Cambio, B., O'Malley, M.K.: Syntacts: open-source software and hardware for audio-controlled haptics. IEEE Trans. Haptics **14**(1), 225–233 (2021)
20. Sigrist, R., Rauter, G., Riener, R., Wolf, P.: Augmented visual, auditory, haptic, and multimodal feedback in motor learning: a review. Psychon. Bull. Rev. **20**(1), 21–53 (2012)
21. Turchet, L., Burelli, P., Serafin, S.: Haptic feedback for enhancing realism of walking simulations. IEEE Trans. Haptics **6**(1), 35–45 (2013)
22. Bernard, C., Monnoyer, J., Wiertlewski, M., Ystad, S.: Rhythm perception is shared between audio and Haptics. Sci. Rep. **12**(1), 4188 (2022)
23. Turchet, L., West, T., Wanderley, M.M.: Touching the audience: musical haptic wearables for augmented and participatory live music performances. Pers. Ubiquit. Comput. **25**(4), 749–769 (2020)
24. Chrysanthakopoulou, A., Kalatzis, K., Moustakas, K.: Immersive virtual reality experience of historical events using haptics and locomotion simulation. Appl. Sci. **11**(24), 11613 (2021)

25. Cheng, H., Liu, S.: Haptic force guided sound synthesis in multisensory virtual reality (VR) simulation for rigid-fluid interaction. In: 2019 IEEE Conference on Virtual Reality and 3D User Interfaces (VR) (2019)
26. Wei, X., Shi, Y., Zhou, L.: Haptic signal reconstruction for cross-modal communications. IEEE Trans. Multimedia **24**, 4514–4525 (2022)
27. Alles, D.: Information transmission by phantom sensations. IEEE Trans. Man-Mach. Syst. **11**(1), 85–91 (1970)
28. Kato, H., Hashimoto, Y., Kajimoto, H.: Basic properties of phantom sensation for practical haptic applications. In: Kappers, A.M.L., van Erp, J.B.F., Tiest, W.M.B., van der Helm, F.C.T. (eds.) Haptics: Generating and Perceiving Tangible Sensations, pp. 271–278. Springer Berlin Heidelberg, Berlin, Heidelberg (2010). https://doi.org/10.1007/978-3-642-14064-8_39
29. Caseymeekhof: Direct manipulation with hands – mixed reality. Mixed Reality | Microsoft Learn. https://learn.microsoft.com/en-us/windows/mixed-reality/design/direct-manipulation. Accessed 06 Feb 2023
30. Cholewiak, R.W., Collins, A.A.: Vibrotactile localization on the arm: effects of place, space and age. Percept. Psychophys. **65**(7), 1058–1077 (2003)
31. Tsai, H., Liao, Y., Tsai, C.: Impactvest: rendering spatio-temporal multilevel impact force feedback on body in VR. In: 2022 CHI Conference on Human Factors in Computing System (2022)
32. Precision Microdrives: Model No. 310–103 Product Data Sheet (2021)
33. Nreal.ai. https://www.nreal.ai/specs/. Accessed 06 Feb 2023
34. Microsoft: Releases · Microsoft/MixedRealityToolkit-Unity. GitHub. https://github.com/microsoft/MixedRealityToolkit-Unity/releases. Accessed 06 Feb 2023
35. Yoshinaga, T.: Takashiyoshinaga/MRTK-profiles-for-nreallight. GitHub. https://github.com/TakashiYoshinaga/MRTK-Profiles-for-NrealLight. Accessed 06 Feb 2023
36. Hart, S.G., Staveland, L.E.: Development of NASA-TLX (Task Load Index): results of empirical and theoretical research. Adv. Psychol. **52**, 139–183 (1988)
37. Khan, M., Sulaiman, S., Said, M.D., Tahir, M.: Exploring the quantitative and qualitative measures for haptic systems. In: 2010 International Symposium on Information Technology (2010)

Effect of Repulsive Positions on Haptic Feedback on Using a String-Based Device Virtual Objects Without a Real Tool

Kairyu Mori, Masayuki Ando, Kouyou Otsu, and Tomoko Izumi[✉]

Ritsumeikan University, Kusatsu 525-8557, Shiga, Japan
is0527rp@ed.ritsumei.ac.jp, {mandou,k-otsu,
izumi-t}@fc.ritsumei.ac.jp

Abstract. Virtual reality (VR) is a growing field of research, which includes visual, auditory, and haptic feedback generation. Haptics, or the sense of touch, is one of the important factors in making a VR experience more realistic. A string-based haptic feedback device was developed to connect with a real tool having the same shape as the virtual tool in the VR environment. This device provides haptic feedback when the virtual tool interacts with other virtual objects. However, this approach requires a real tool in the real space, which can be costly and unrealistic. In this study, using a string-based haptic device connected to a VR controller instead of a real tool to create haptic feedback for touching virtual objects with a rod-shaped tool in VR is proposed. Further, the manner in which the virtual tool's length affects the user's suitability and haptic feedback when using a string-based device connected to the controller is investigated. In the verification, a comparison is made between the suitability and haptic feedback of using a string-based haptic feedback device with a real tool or with a VR controller for the virtual tool lengths of 25 cm, 50 cm, and 100 cm. The results show that a virtual tool length of around 50 cm can provide similar suitability and the haptic feedback with and without a real tool.

Keywords: haptic feedback · string-based haptic feedback device · virtual reality

1 Introduction

Virtual reality (VR) is an expanding field of research that has a variety of applications. It aims to create an immersive experience using visual, auditory, and tactile elements. Haptic feedback is a technique used to enhance immersion in virtual reality. To provide haptic feedback, commercial VR devices such as the Oculus [1] and HTC Vive [2] have built-in vibration motors in their controllers. However, they give simple feedback, therefore, they have limitations in providing realistic haptic feedback. To overcome this limitation, researchers are developing new devices that can provide more realistic haptic feedback to improve the physical interaction with virtual objects.

Wire-type haptic feedback devices are used in virtual reality to interact with stationary virtual objects, such as walls [3]. These devices involve attaching multiple wires to

© The Author(s), under exclusive license to Springer Nature Switzerland AG 2023
J. Y. C. Chen and G. Fragomeni (Eds.): HCII 2023, LNCS 14027, pp. 266–277, 2023.
https://doi.org/10.1007/978-3-031-35634-6_19

the hand or controller, which restrict the movement of the hand and arm in real space when the user touches an object in the virtual space. Achberger et al. have developed a string-based haptic feedback device called "STRIVE" that utilizes wires to provide haptic feedback when touching objects with a tool in virtual reality [4]. The user handles the same tool in the real world and wires from STRIVE are attached to the tool's tip to provide the same haptic feedback of the tool touching objects in the VR space. However, this approach is costly as real tools need to be constructed for the user to have the same tools in real space as the virtual ones. Therefore, there is a requirement for a method that can provide haptic feedback without relying on real tools.

In this study, a method to provide the haptic feedback of the tool touching objects in the VR space without corresponding real tools is proposed. The feedback of the tool touching other objects in situations where a rod-shaped tool is swung down from above is targeted. This method uses a string-based haptic feedback device [4] attached to the VR controller instead of a real tool that creates resistance when the user's tool in VR touches another object. However, it is not clear that the proposed method provides effective feedback for any tools. For example, when the virtual object is long rod-shaped, the tension from the string is only felt on the controller, not on the rod's tip. That is, the difference between the repulsive positions of real and virtual space can cause unsuitability and poor haptic feedback. Thus, the length of a virtual rod affecting the suitability and haptic feedback when using the string-based haptic feedback device connecting to a VR controller is verified. **Suitability is the ability for a user to have the same feeling as when touching an object with an actual tool, and haptic feedback is evaluated as the physical feeling experienced when touching an object.** As a result, it is found that using a virtual tool of less than about 50 cm in length is equivalent for participants and provides the same haptic feedback as the real tool. This implies that realistic haptic feedback can be provided from virtual tools with the string-based device attached to the VR controller without needing any real tools.

2 Related Research

Several novel methods which can provide more realistic haptic feedback to improve the physical interaction with virtual objects have been proposed. Haptic gloves are commonly used to create haptic feedback in virtual reality [5, 6]. They are worn on the hand and have wires connecting to the user's fingers, allowing them to mimic the sensation of holding objects. Fang et al. created a device called "Wireality" that provides haptic feedback when touching walls or larger objects in virtual reality [3]. The device is worn on the user's shoulder and provides feedback to the entire hand when touching objects in VR and allows touching with complex shapes. Achberger et al. created a string-based haptic feedback device called "STRIVE" using the "Wireality" technology [4]. It uses a single string to give haptic feedback by connecting the wire to a real tool and can be combined with multiple devices installed from walls or ceilings to mimic the haptic feedback when touching virtual objects with a virtual tool. In this study, it is assumed that a user handles the real tools as the virtual ones to provide realistic haptic feedback by limiting the movement of the real tool.

Similar to the research of Achberger et al., other researchers have been working on providing haptic feedback through real tools, assuming a case of using a virtual tool in

VR space. Studies have developed devices such as a pen-shaped haptic feedback device [7], a chopstick-shaped haptic feedback device [8], and a device that simulates using nails, screws, and saws in a VR space [9]. However, realistically, it is not enough to express all elements of the haptic sensation which is composed of various factors.

In contrast to these studies, this study aims to create the feeling of objects touching in VR without using real tools. Instead of real tools, a VR controller is utilized, which is common in VR activity. Additionally, the suitability and haptic feedback are verified when the string is attached to the VR controller. One study that provides high realism and immersion without needing real tools is that of Lim et al. [10]. They created a device called the "Hap tug," which allows for haptic feedback when poking and pulling virtual objects with virtual tools. In contrast, this study targets situations where a rod-shaped tool is swung down from above, and thus the targeted situation of the study is different.

Furthermore, the different lengths of the virtual tool affecting the haptic sensation is considered. This is because visual information can affect haptic feedback. That is, if the visual information in VR is very different from reality, the level of haptic feedback may be lower. In contrast, it may be possible to create the illusion of realistic haptic feedback from visual information in the VR space if the difference between the virtual and real situations is only slight. Botvinick et al.'s study showed that visual information could significantly affect the sense of touch by using an illusion of a rubber hand as part of the participant's body [11]. Kilteni et al.'s study considered how the arm length affects the touch sensation in VR and found that visual illusions can extend up to three times the arm's length [12]. Takakura et al. created a fishing game that uses haptic illusions [13]. They created a sensation of pulling when catching a fish using a linear actuator, making it feel like fishing in a real river. According to the results of these studies and in this current study, it can be concluded that even tools with longer lengths may provide realistic haptic feedback.

3   VR Environment and String-Based Haptic Feedback Device

An evaluation environment is implemented and a haptic feedback device is developed for creating haptic feedback in virtual reality without corresponding real tools in the real world. The evaluation environment consists of two synchronized systems: a VR object touch detection system and a string-based haptic feedback device. When the virtual tool touches the virtual object in the VR space, the string-based haptic feedback device in the real space activates, and the string is pulled tight. As the device string is connected to the VR controller, the user's ability to move their arm forward is limited. If there is no object detection in the VR space, the string is loose, and the user does not feel resistance.

In this study, a three-part setup is used consisting of the VR environment, middleware environment, and device environment. The VR environment, built in Unity, features a 3D space with virtual tools and objects for the user to interact with. The middleware environment receives signals from the VR environment whenever the virtual tool touches objects and sends them to the device environment. The device environment controls the string-based haptic feedback device and provides haptic feedback to the user.

First, the objects in the VR environment are explained. As a VR device, the Oculus Quest2 by Meta Inc is used. Figure 1 shows the VR environment, including the virtual tool and objects. In this evaluation environment, the focus is on the situation where the participants use the red virtual rod-shaped tool to touch the yellow object. The target objects to touch are a cube and a cylinder with a curved surface on top. Participants pick up the tool by holding the button on the Oculus controller. When the tool touches the object, it will stop moving on the surface of the object. Hence, the participants understand that the tool is touching the object visually. A pre-defined signal is sent to Arduino when the tool touches an object, and a different signal is sent when it does not.

Next, the string-based haptic feedback device worn by the participants is explained. The proposed string-based device was created based on Cathy Fung's Wireality and Alexander Achberger's STRIVE (Fig. 2). Considering the durability of the 5V solenoid operation in continuous use, the proposed device uses a servo motor instead of a solenoid to control the stopper that limits the movement of the string, which differs from Wireality and STRIVE. The device uses an Arduino board to receive signals. When the virtual tool touches the virtual object in VR, the servo motor rotates clockwise to stop the movement of the string and creates a resistance that the user feels (Fig. 3). When the virtual tool is not touching the virtual object, the servo motor rotates counterclockwise, and the restriction is released. The device is attached to the user's shoulder, and its string is connected to the VR controller or the real tool. It provides haptic feedback of the virtual tool touching the object.

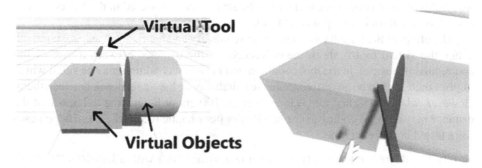

Fig. 1. Touching the virtual objects with the virtual tool in the VR environment.

Fig. 2. Structure of our sting-based haptic feedback device.

Fig. 3. The servo motor is activated, and the stopper stops the gear from rotating.

4 Verification Experiment

4.1 Aim of the Experiment and Hypotheses

This study evaluated suitability as the degree of appropriateness of the feeling when touching an object, and haptic feedback was evaluated as the physical feeling experienced when touching an object. An experiment is conducted to prove that there is no significant difference in suitability and haptic feedback between using a virtual tool with or without a real tool in the VR space. The feedback obtained when using virtual rod-shaped tools of three different lengths (25 cm, 50 cm, and 100 cm) are compared in two different conditions; where the string of the string-based haptic feedback device was connected to a real tool (tool condition), and where the string was connected to the VR controller instead of a real tool (non-tool condition).

The effect of the virtual tool's length on suitability and haptic feedback is examined. When the virtual tool is short, the differences in the distance between a user's hand and repulsion position in the tool condition and non-tool condition may be small which implies there would be no difference in the suitability or haptic feedback between them. However, when the virtual tool is long, such as 100 cm or longer, the difference of the distance may be large leading to unsuitability or poor haptic feedback. These hypotheses were tested in this experiment.

H 1.1: The degree of suitability when using a virtual tool with a length of 25 cm or 50 cm in the VR space will be the same whether a real tool is used or not.
H 1.2: The degree of suitability when using a virtual tool with a length of 100 cm in the VR space will be lower when a real tool is not used than when it is used.
H 2.1: The degree of haptic feedback when using a virtual tool with a length of 25 cm or 50 cm in the VR space will be the same whether a real tool is used or not.
H 2.2: The degree of haptic feedback when using a virtual tool with a length of 100 cm in the VR space will be different when a real tool is used compared to when it is not used.

4.2 Experimental Conditions

The proposed hypotheses are tested by conducting experiments in three different conditions. In addition to the tool and non-tool conditions, an experiment called the real-space condition was conducted where participants used a real tool to touch existing objects in real space. This was carried out to confirm the feedback when using a rod-shaped tool to touch objects in real space before conducting experiments in the VR space using the tool and non-tool conditions. Figure 4 shows the three experimental conditions.

Real-space condition: Participants touch the real objects using the rod-shaped tools in real space.

Tool condition: Participants holds the rod-shaped tool in the real space, the tip of which is attached to the string-based haptic feedback device's string; then, they touch the virtual objects in the VR space.

Non-tool condition: Participants holds the controller connecting the string of the string-based haptic feedback device. Then, they touch the virtual objects in the VR space.

Figure 5 shows the different rod-shaped tools of lengths 25 cm, 50 cm, and 100 cm used in this experiment. The tools on the left in Fig. 5 are used in the real-space condition. The tools on the right in Fig. 5 have been modified to embed the VR controller and are used in the tool condition.

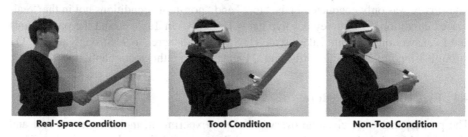

Real-Space Condition   **Tool Condition**   **Non-Tool Condition**

Fig. 4. The three experimental conditions.

Fig. 5. (Left) Real tools used in real-space condition, (Right) Real tools used in tool condition.

In this study, the effects of using a real rod-shaped tool are investigated on the suitability and haptic feedback in a VR experience. The participants experienced the three conditions: "real-space," "tool," and "non-tool." First, the real-space condition is conducted to become familiar with touching an object with the rod-shaped tool of three lengths. Then, three different lengths of tools are used in the tool and non-tool conditions to compare the experience. To avoid order effects, there are two different patterns of experimental order, with one pattern being the tool condition followed by the non-tool condition and the other being the non-tool condition followed by the tool condition. The order of the tool lengths used in each condition is randomized for each participant.

Table 1. Questionnaire

	Questionnaire items
Q1	There was suitability as I imagined it would feel visually when touching the virtual object
Q2	There was suitability for the position where the tool and the virtual object were touching
Q3	There was suitability in how my wrist felt when putting pressure on the virtual object
Q4	I felt haptic feedback when touching the virtual object with the tool
Q5	When touching the virtual object with the tool, I felt as if I was restricted to my arm

4.3 Evaluation Items

In this study, the participants were asked to answer a survey about their suitability and haptic feedback while experiencing VR using a string-based haptic feedback device. The survey was only conducted in the "tool" and "non-tool" conditions not in the "real-space" condition. The survey has five items, as shown in Table 1, and the participants had to answer on a 7-point Likert scale (1: Strongly disagree to 7: Strongly agree). Q1 through 3 inquire about suitability, and Q4 and 5 inquire the about haptic feedback.

4.4 Experimental Procedure

The participants were given an overview of the experiment, including using real and virtual tools and their consent was obtained through an informed consent form. They were instructed on how to wear the VR goggles and use the VR controller in the VR space and the string-based haptic feedback device. They were further required to wear a special vest during the experiment to install the device (Fig. 6).

Before the experiment, the participants practiced using the VR goggles and controllers in the training environment with objects that could be grabbed (Fig. 7). They were asked to pick up the red objects in the practice phase. This practice phase aims to help participants become more familiar with moving and grabbing objects in the VR space.

First, in the real-space condition, the participants practiced using different tools of lengths 25 cm, 50 cm, and 100 cm. Subsequently, the experiment was conducted in the tool condition and non-tool condition using the different tool lengths. Before the experiment, the participants were instructed to swing the tool down slowly from top to bottom, touch the object as if pushing it in, touch the object on the tip of the tool, and hold the end of the tool. The participants wore VR goggles and a special vest, held the VR controller, and used the string-based haptic feedback device. They touched a cube and cylinder object in the VR space five times for each tool and non-tool condition. After completing the VR task, the participants answered a questionnaire and repeated this process with different tool lengths, a total of six times.

Fig. 6. Special vest to install the device.

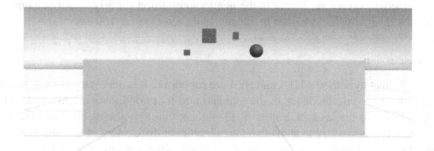

Fig. 7. Training VR environment

5 Experimental Results and Discussion

5.1 Experimental Results

In this section, the results of the survey responses from the experiment conducted with 24 participants (16 males and 8 females) are presented. The box-and-whisker plots are used to display the data and analyze it using the t-test and equivalence test. The two one-sided t-tests (TOST) test is used to determine if there is no difference between the means [14]. In this evaluation, the threshold is set for validating the equivalence in the TOST method to 0.7, corresponding to the 95% confidence interval. This parameter was determined by taking 10% of the maximum value on the Likert scale.

Table 2 shows the mean values and standard deviations of the survey results in the tool and non-tool conditions with three different lengths (25 cm, 50 cm, and 100 cm). Further, the table presents the results of the t-tests and equivalence tests, comparing the results with the same length of virtual tools in both conditions. Figure 8 presents the results of the survey in box-and-whisker plots.

In this study, the suitability for Q1, 2, and 3 between the tool and non-tool conditions using the same tool length are compared. The results from the t-test show no significant difference across all cases of using the 25 cm, 50 cm, and 100 cm tool lengths. However, the equivalence test results show that although the results are not the same for 25 cm, the results are the same for 50 cm. The box plots in Fig. 8 show that the mean and median values for suitability are slightly higher in the non-tool condition, and the variance is smaller for 25 cm. For the 100 cm virtual tool length, the mean and median values for Q1 and 2 were higher in the non-tool condition and participants reported a higher level of suitability for Q3 in the tool condition.

From the results of Q4 and 5, the haptic feedback results of Q4 and 5 are compared for the tool and non-tool conditions using the same tool length. The results from the t-test show no significant difference across all cases of using the 25 cm, 50 cm, and 100 cm tool lengths. However, the results from the equivalence test show that although the results are not the same for 50 cm and 100 cm in Q4 and 25 cm and 100 cm in Q5, the results for 25 cm in Q4 and 50 cm in Q5 are the same, respectively. Figure 8 shows that the validity of the results for Q4 and Q5 are similar. For 25 cm, the mean value is lower in the tool condition than the non-tool condition for Q4, but Q5 reverses this result. For Q4, the median values are higher in the non-tool condition for 50 cm and 100 cm, and in Q5, the median value is higher in the non-tool condition for 100 cm.

5.2 Discussion

To confirm that hypotheses H1.1 and H2.1 are supported, it is necessary to show that the suitability and haptic feedback in the tool and non-tool conditions are the same when using a 25 cm or 50 cm tool. Similarly, to confirm that hypotheses H1.2 and H2.2 are supported, it is necessary to show there are significant differences in the suitability and haptic feedback between the tool and non-tool conditions when using a 100 cm tool. Looking at the p-values in Table 2 and Fig. 8, for a 50 cm tool, there is equivalence for all the questions, which supports H1.1 in 50 cm. However, for a 25 cm tool, there is equivalence for Q3 but not for Q1 and 2, so H1.1 in 25 cm is rejected. For H2.1, the equivalence test results for Q4 with a 25 cm tool and Q5 with a 50 cm tool partially support the hypothesis. However, H1.2 and H2.2 are rejected as the t-test results for the 100 cm tool did not show a significant difference between the conditions.

For suitability, the reason that there was no equivalence for a 25 cm tool in the two conditions is the larger variance, especially in the tool condition, in Q1 and 2. This might be because some of the participants expected stronger haptic feedback when using a shorter tool, however, the feedback in the tool condition was not as strong. Subsequently, they felt in suitability with the feedback. In the 100 cm condition, the results for both the tool and non-tool conditions are lower, and the variances are bigger. These results might be caused by the difficulty in imagining the correct feedback, leading to varying expectations and diverse answers.

Regarding the haptic feedback, the results show that there is equivalence in the tool and non-tool conditions in Q4 or Q5 when the virtual tool is 25 cm and 50 cm in length. However, for Q4, which asks for haptic feedback, the participant felt the mean value is higher for the non-tool condition than the tool condition for all lengths. This may be because as the length of the real tool increases, the haptic feedback may decrease due to the distance between the string-based haptic feedback device attached to the user's shoulder and the repulsive part from the real tool. This result suggests the possibility of providing strong haptic feedback by connecting a string-based haptic device to a controller without using real tools.

From these results, it can be concluded that when using a virtual tool of 50 cm in length, the suitability and haptic feedback in both the tool and non-tool conditions are the

Table 2. The results of the survey, including t-tests and equivalence tests (TOST) for the different tool lengths and conditions with and without tools.

Question	Tool length	Tool		Non-tool		t-test	Equivalence test (TOST)	
		Mean	SD	Mean	SD	p-value	Confidence interval	p-value ($\varepsilon = 0.7$)
Q1	25 cm	4.875	1.676	5.125	1.569	0.596	−1.036, 0.536	0.171
	50 cm	4.916	1.380	4.875	1.329	0.916	−0.614, 0.698	0.049**
	100 cm	4.291	1.573	4.541	1.559	0.583	−1.009, 0.509	0.162
Q2	25 cm	5.250	1.539	5.583	1.282	0.419	−1.020, 0.353	0.187
	50 cm	5.500	1.179	5.416	1.282	0.816	−0.513, 0.680	0.044**
	100 cm	5.000	1.817	5.125	1.727	0.808	−0.984, 0.734	0.133
Q3	25 cm	5.166	1.340	5.083	1.380	0.833	−0.576, 0.742	0.061*
	50 cm	5.000	1.179	5.000	1.383	1.000	−0.623, 0.623	0.032**
	100 cm	5.041	1.267	4.666	1.372	0.331	−0.265, 1.015	0.199
Q4	25 cm	5.750	1.032	5.875	1.261	0.709	−0.684, 0.434	0.045**
	50 cm	5.500	1.474	5.833	1.129	0.384	−0.970, 0.303	0.169
	100 cm	5.208	1.318	5.708	1.301	0.193	−1.134, 0.134	0.299
Q5	25 cm	5.333	1.239	5.041	1.601	0.484	−0.403, 0.986	0.164
	50 cm	4.916	1.248	4.916	1.442	1.000	−0.653, 0.653	0.039**
	100 cm	4.958	1.428	5.458	1.284	0.209	−1.158, 0.158	0.306

*: p-value < 0.1, **: p-value < 0.05

same. This suggests that it may be possible to provide haptic feedback through a string-based device connected to the VR controller without using a real tool if the virtual tool is around 50 cm long. However, when the length of the virtual tool is 25 cm, the suitability

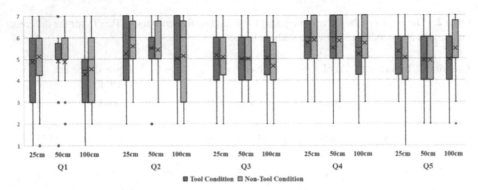

Fig. 8. Box-and-whisker plot of survey results

and haptic feedback are not the same in both conditions, although the suitability is the same in Q3. In Q3, we asked about the user's feeling in the wrist when putting pressure on the objects. As this feeling is easy to confirm in a real-space condition, which was conducted before the tool or non-tool condition, we believe that the participants could easily imagine what they were being asked. That is, this suggests that by confirming haptic feedback in real space before the experiment, it may be possible to get similar answers for suitability and haptic feedback in both the tool and non-tool conditions when the virtual tool is short, that is, less than about 50 cm.

6   Conclusion

For an activity with a virtual tool in VR, this study aimed to investigate the possibility of providing haptic feedback without using a real tool. In this study, using a string-based haptic feedback device connected to a VR controller was proposed and the suitability and haptic feedback experienced by participants in both the "tool condition" where the real tool is used, and the "non-tool condition" where the real tool is not used were compared. The results showed that when the virtual tool was 50 cm in length, equivalent suitability and haptic feedback were provided in both conditions. In the case of the 25 cm tool length, the tendency of equivalence was shown in terms of feeling when force was applied to the hand. Therefore, the experimental results indicated that when using the short virtual tool less than about 50 cm in length, the string-based haptic feedback device connecting to a VR controller may provide similar feedback as if real tools were being used.

In future research, the effects of combining the proposed haptic feedback method with other VR modalities such as varying object touch postures will be considered and the realism and satisfaction of the VR experiences will be enhanced by integrating other senses such as sound effects.

References

1. Meta Quest2 Homepage: https://www.meta.com/jp/quest/. Last accessed 6 Jan 2023
2. Vive Homepage: https://www.vive.com/jp/. Last accessed 6 Jan 2023
3. Fang, C., Zhang, Y., Dworman, M., Harrison, C.: Wireality: Enabling complex tangible geometries in virtual reality with worn multi-string haptics. In: Proceedings of the 2020 CHI Conference on Human Factors in Computing Systems, pp. 1–10 (2020)
4. Achberger, A., Aust, F., Pohlandt, D., Vidackovic, K., Sedlmair, M.: STRIVE: string-based force feedback for automotive engineering. In: The 34th Annual ACM Symposium on User Interface Software and Technology, pp. 841–853 (2021)
5. Blake, J., Gurocak, H.B.: Haptic glove with MR brakes for virtual reality. IEEE/ASME Trans. Mechatronics **14**(5), 606–615 (2009)
6. Caeiro-Rodríguez, M., Otero-González, I., Mikic-Fonte, F.A., Llamas-Nistal, M.: A systematic review of commercial smart gloves: Current status and applications. Sensors **21**(8), 2667 (2021)
7. Kataoka, K., Otsuki, M., Shibata, F., Kimura, A.: Evaluation of ExtickTouch: an advanced extendable virtual object touching device. Comput. Vision Image Media (CVIM) **2021**(20), 1–6 (2021)
8. Yang, J., Horii, H., Thayer, A., Ballagas, R.: VR Grabbers: Ungrounded haptic retargeting for precision grabbing tools. In: Proceedings of the 31st Annual ACM Symposium on User Interface Software and Technology, pp. 889–899 (2018)
9. Strandholt, P.L., Dogaru, O.A., Nilsson, N.C., Nordahl, R., Serafin, S.: Knock on wood: combining redirected touching and physical props for tool-based interaction in virtual reality. In: Proceedings of the 2020 CHI Conference on Human Factors in Computing Systems, pp. 1–13 (2020)
10. Lim, J., Choi, Y.: Force-feedback haptic device for representation of tugs in virtual reality. Electronics **11**(11), 1730 (2022)
11. Botvinick, M., Cohen, J.: Rubber hands 'feel' touch that eyes see. Nature **391**(6669), 756 (1998)
12. Kilteni, K., Normand, J.M., Sanchez-Vives, M.V., Slater, M.: Extending body space in immersive virtual reality: a very long arm illusion. PloS One **7**(7), e40867 (2012)
13. Takamoto, S., Amamiya, T., Ito, S., Gomi, Y.: Expression and application of the traction illusion in VR fishing. The Trans. Hum. Interface Soc. **18**(2), 87–94 (2016)
14. Stanton, J.M.: Evaluating equivalence and confirming the null in the organizational sciences. Organ. Res. Methods **24**(3), 491–512 (2021)

A Head Mounted Display Attachment Olfactory Display to Offer Multimodal Sensory Information for Advertisements in Metaverse

Noriko Takimoto[2], Koichi Onuki[2], Yohei Seta[1], Yuichi Bannai[2], and Motofumi Hattori[2(✉)]

[1] Graduate School of Science and Engineering, Chuo University, Bunkyo, Japan
a15.s845@g.chuo-u.ac.jp
[2] Department of Information Media, Kanagawa Institute of Technology, Atsugi, Japan
hattori@ic.kanagawa-it.ac.jp

Abstract. In order to offer many kinds of scent to a human nose (a user's nose), the authors developed olfactory displays using piezo-electric elements. In order to offer scent to the user who immerses a VR space in metaverse, the authors had developed an olfactory display which can be attached to a Head Mounted Display. This HMD attachment olfactory display is controlled by a Unity project. Thus we can offer scent which is appropriate to the graphics which can be seen through Head Mounted Display.

Keywords: metaverse · advertisement · VR · olfaction · vision · multimodal sense

1 Introduction

Metaverses are developing on world wide internet spaces. Many kinds of business are developing in metaverses. In metaverses, many consumers can enjoy virtual shopping and seek many objects to buy. Such buyers seek goods based on advertisement posters in virtual spaces. Many advertisement posters appear in virtual spaces of metaverse. Since a buyer see many advertisement posters, the buyer cannot determine what to buy.

In such circumstances, the seller must display an advertisement poster which can attract many buyers' interest. Brilliant lighting and loud voices will attract buyers' interest. In addition to such kinds of information, the authors think that appropriate scent is also effective to attract buyers' interest on advertisement posters.

In this research, the authors make a VR space by Unity project as shown in Fig. 2. A user can immerse such a VR spaces by wearing a Head Mounted Display (HMD) as shown in Fig. 1. The advertisement posters as shown in Fig. 3 are displayed in a VR space for virtual shopping.

In order to offer many kinds of scent to a human nose (a user's nose), the authors had developed olfactory displays using piezo-electric elements. These olfactory displays will be explained in the Sect. 3. In order to offer scent to a user's nose who immerses a VR

J. Y. C. Chen and G. Fragomeni (Eds.): HCII 2023, LNCS 14027, pp. 278–294, 2023.
https://doi.org/10.1007/978-3-031-35634-6_20

Fig. 1. Immersing metaverse using the HMD attachment Olfactory Display and the Head Mounted Display

Fig. 2. An example of an advertisement VR in space (for metaverse) constructed by Unity.

space by wearing a Head Mounted Display, the authors developed an olfactory display which can be attached to a Head Mounted Display. Such HMD attachment Olfactory Display will be explained in the Sect. 4.

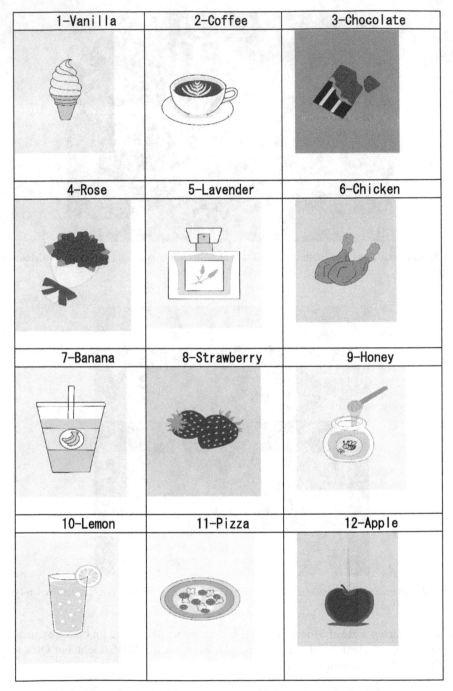

Fig. 3. Example of advertisement posters which are shown in the VR space.

2 Related Researches

In order that a user can immerse a VR space with high presence feeling, it is very effective to offer olfactory information (scent) in addition to visual information (3 dimensional computer graphics) and auditory information (sound). Although visual information and auditory information are transported to human sensory organs (a user's eyes and ears) indirectly by light and air pressures, olfactory information is transported to human sensory organ (a user's nose) directly by matters. Thus, a user can immerse a VR space with high presence feeling when the user is offered olfactory information (scent) [1].

Tomono et al. [2] had created a VR shopping street in an immersive screen VR system. In this system, when a walking user passes by an advertisement poster, this system offers appropriate scent from a scent diffuser. The diffused scent attracts the user to the advertisement poster. The users looked at the advertisement poster for long time when appropriate scent was offered. The time length was about 2 times by comparing the time length when no scent was offered.

The concept of Tomono et al. [2] is expected to be effective for VR shopping system in metaverse. Since users immerse metaverse space trough Head Mounted Displays, the authors apply the concept of Tomono et al. [2] to the Head Mounted Display systems. In order to offer scent to user, the author developed an olfactory display which can be attached to a Head Mounted Display in the following Sect. 4.

Nakano et al. [3] had studied how users perceive direction of wind (direction of air flow) at the user's head. Since matters which cause scent are transported to users' nose by air flow (wind), there is possibility that users feel direction of scent by the direction of wind which is offered to the users. Air flow affects haptic sense of users. The authors expect multimodal effect by olfactory sense (scent) and haptic sense (wind).

Saito et al. [4] had studied the multimodal effect by visual sense (video through Head Mounted Display), auditory sense (sound by earphone), and haptic sense (wind). Saito et al. [4] discusses that multimodal effect increase the presence feeling of the user who immerses the VR space.

By inspired Saito et al. [4], the authors also studies the multimodal effect by olfactory sense (scent by olfactory display), visual sense (graphics through Head Mounted Display), and haptic sense (wind by bladeless fan by Dyson Limited).

3 Developed Olfactory Displays using Piezo-Electric Elements

In order to offer appropriate scent according to an object in a VR space, the authors' had developed olfactory displays. An example is shown in Fig. 4. When the user immerses a VR space, appropriate scent is offered from an olfactory display. As shown in Fig. 5. When a banana appears in the VR space, the scent of banana is offered from the olfactory display. When a lemon appears in the VR space, the scent of lemon is offered from the olfactory display.

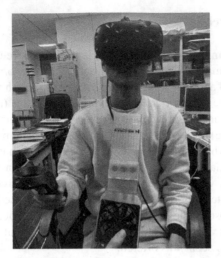

Fig. 4. Scent is offered from an olfactory display.

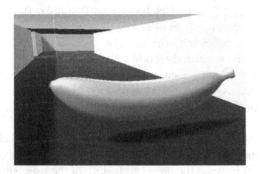 

Fig. 5. Each scent is offered according to each object in a VR space made by Unity.

Figure 6 shows the structure of olfactory displays which the authors had developed. Figure 7 shows an example of olfactory displays which the authors had developed. As Fig. 6 shows, aroma liquid tank ejects aroma spray into air flow in a flow channel of the olfactory display. Aroma spray is vaporized into aroma gas. Aroma gas is transported to a human nose (a user's nose) by the air flow in the flow channel of the olfactory display. Since there are 3 aroma liquid tanks on the olfactory display which is shown in Fig. 7, three kinds of scent are offered from 3 aroma liquid tanks on this olfactory display. A photograph and a CAD figure of an aroma tank are shown in Fig. 8.

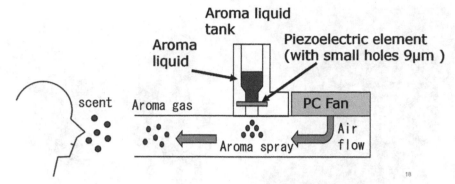

Fig. 6. The structure of Olfactory Displays using Piezo-electric elements.

Fig. 7. A photograph of an Olfactory Display using Piezo-electric elements.

There is a piezo-electric element in the bottom of the aroma liquid tank. Aroma spray is dripped from the bottom of the aroma liquid tank into the air flow channel of the olfactory display during electric voltage is applied to the piezo-electric element. Aroma spray is dripped from many holes whose diameters are 9 μm (9 micro meters) into the air flow channel of the olfactory display. Since these. holes are very small, aroma spray is never dripped when we do not apply electric voltage to the piezo-electric element. By the effect of molecular force between aroma liquid and the piezo-electric element, aroma spray is never dripped from the above small holes when we do not apply electric voltage to the piezo-electric element (Fig. 9).

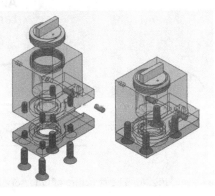

Fig. 8. The Aroma Liquid Tank which ejects Aroma Spray. (The left is a photograph and the right is a CAD.)

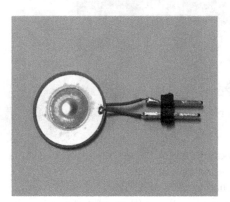

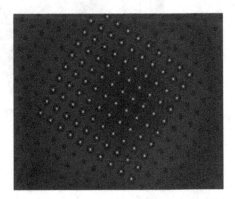

Fig. 9. The piezo-electric element which has many small holes. (The left shows the whole and the right shows the part.)

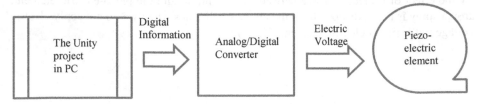

Fig. 10. The Unity project control the electric voltage to the piezo-electric elements.

Fig. 11. D/A converter which controls the voltage to the piezo-electric elements.

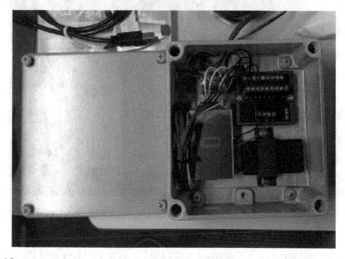

Fig. 12. D/A converter which controls the voltage to the piezo-electric elements.

In order to control the electric voltage which is applied to the piezo-electric element as shown in Fig. 10, the authors had developed a Digital/Analog converter as shown in Fig. 11 and Fig. 12. By controlling time length of applied voltage, the strength of scent is controlled. If we apply electric voltage to the piezo-electric element long time, scent becomes strong. If we apply electric voltage to the piezo-electric element short time, scent becomes weak. Such time length is controlled from the Unity C# script of the Unity project which makes a VR space through Head Mounted Displays (HMDs). The authors use Vive Pro Eye (by HTC Corporation) as the Head Mounted Display which makes VR spaces.

4   An Olfactory Display is Attached to the Head Mounted Display with Eye Tracking System

In order to offer 3 kinds of scent to a user who immerses a VR space, an olfactory display of the authors' laboratory is attached to the Head Mounted Display as shown in Fig. 13. We call these olfactory displays as HMD attachment Olfactory Displays. A HMD attachment Olfactory Display is shown in Fig. 14.

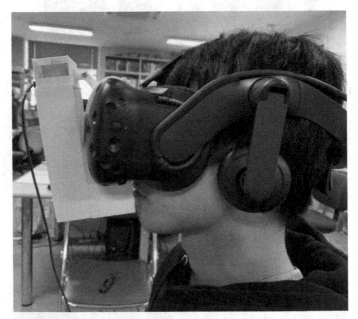

Fig. 13. The Olfactory Display is attached to the Head Mounted Display.

When a user immerses a VR space by the HMD Vive Pro Eye and the HMD attachment Olfactory Display, the 3 dimensional position and 3 dimensional orientation are measured in real time by two infrared measurements (Base Stations by HTC Corporation) as shown in Fig. 15. Thus, the VR space and the real physical space overlap accurately.

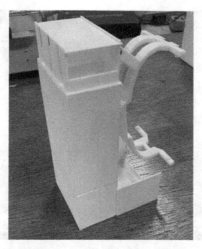

Fig. 14. The HMD attachment Olfactory Display.

Fig. 15. The position and the orientation of the Head Mounted Display is measured by the infra-red measuring system.

Further, The Head Mounted Display Vive Pro Eye (by HTC Corporation) has Eye Tracking System. Thus, we can compute 3 dimensional position of the point at which the user is looking in real time. Figure 16 is a demonstration video of this Eye Tracking System of Vive Pro Eye (by HTC Corporation).

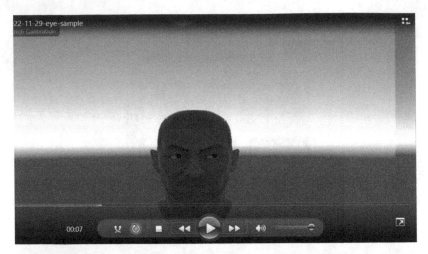

Fig. 16. The Eye Tracking System of the Head Mounted Display.

Fig. 17. Physical real space.

5   Experiment 1: Offering Only Wind (With No Graphics, With No Scent)

In order to judge that a user can recognize the direction from where wind blows, the authors created wind to a user. This wind was created by bladeless fan by Dyson Limited as shown in Figs. 17 and 18. The authors created wind to each user from 8 directions i.e. north, northeast, east, southeast, south, southwest, west, and northwest as shown in

Fig. 18. The user feel wind immersing a VR space.

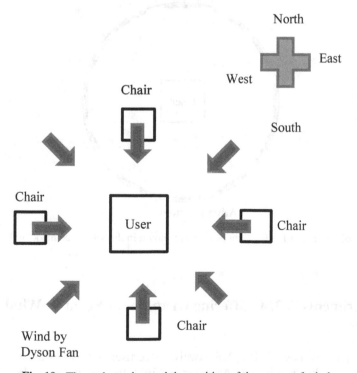

Fig. 19. The authors changed the position of the source of wind.

Figs. 18 and 19. Each user wore a blindfold and a Head Mounted Display as shown in Fig. 18. Nine users who wore blindfolds and Head Mounted Displays had judged the directions from where winds blow. It was difficult for many users to judge the true directions. But most users can judge the direction within 45 degrees margin error. The Table 1 shows numbers and the rates who judged directions truly among 9 users who attended this experiment.

Table 1. The numbers and the rates of true judgements for wind direction

	north	east	south	west
numbers	8	9	9	9
rates[%]	88.9	100	100	100
	northeast	southeast	southwest	northwest
numbers	8	9	9	8
rates[%]	88.9	100	100	88.9

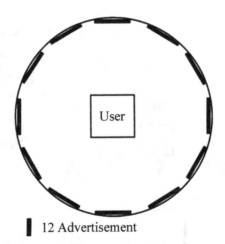

■ 12 Advertisement

Fig. 20. Twelve advertisement posters are shown in the VR space made by Unity.

6   Experiments 2, 3, 4: Offering Graphics or Scent or Wind in a VR Space

In the VR space as shown in Fig. 2, the twelve advertisement posters as shown in Fig. 3 are displayed as shown in Fig. 20. As shown in Fig. 1, the user wearing a Head Mounted Display immerse the VR space and looks at the advertisement posters. The Eye Tracking System of the Head Mounted Display measure 3 dimensional position of the point at which the user is looking in real time.

The authors conducted the following 3 experiments in the Sects. 7, 8 and 9. The user wearing the Head Mounted Display sit on the chair which exists the center of the physical real space which is shown in Figs. 17 and 18. The bladeless fan by Dyson Limited created wind toward the user. The case with wind and the case with no wind were compared.

Many users immersed the above VR space. These users were divided into the following three cases (which are described in the Sect. 7, the Sect. 8, the Sect. 9). Each user looked at the 12 advertisement posters as shown in Figs. 3 and 20. Through the Head Mounted Display. Further, some kinds of scent (banana's scent, or lemon's scent) were offered by the HMD attachment olfactory display as shown in Figs. 13 and 14. Further, wind was offered from the bladeless fan by Dyson Limited as shown in Figs. 17, 18 and 19. Each user was not informed the kind of scent by the authors. Each user was not informed the position of the bladeless fan by Dyson Limited which was the source of wind. When banana's scent was offered from the HMD attachment olfactory display, the wind was offered from the position of the banana's advertisement poster which is the Number 7-Banana in the Fig. 3. When lemon's scent was offered from the HMD attachment olfactory display, the wind was offered from the position of the lemon's advertisement poster which is the Number 10-Lemon in the Fig. 3.

7   Experiment 2: Offering only Graphics (with no Scent, with no wind)

Case 1. Each user only looked at the 12 advertisement posters as shown in Figs. 3 and 20. Through the Head Mounted Display. No scent was offered by the HMD attachment olfactory display as shown in Figs. 13 and 14. No wind was offered from the bladeless fan by Dyson Limited as shown in Figs. 17, 18 and 19. Five users attended this Case 1 experiment.

Table 2 shows the average of time length on which the users looked at each h advertisement poster.

Table 2. The average of time lengths

advertisemant	time length [sec]
1-Vanilla	4.46
2-Coffee	3.52
3-chocolate	2.40
4-Rose	2.04
5-Lavender	2.84
6-Chicken	3.10

(*continued*)

Table 2. (*continued*)

advertisemant	time length [sec]
7-Banana	3.44
8-Strawberry	4.38
9-Honey	7.06
10-Lemon	5.26
11-Pizza	3.18
12-Apple	4.50
sum	46.18

8 Experiment 3: Offering Graphics and Scent (With No Wind)

Case 2. Each user looked at the 12 advertisement posters as shown in Figs. 3 and 20 through the Head Mounted Display. Further, some kinds of scent (banana's scent, lemon's scent, or rose's scent) were offered by the HMD attachment olfactory display as shown in Figs. 13 and 14. But, no wind was offered from the bladeless fan by Dyson Limited as shown in Figs. 17, 18 and 19. Each user was not informed the kind of scent by the authors. Ten users attended this Case 2 experiment.

Table 3 shows the average of time length on which the users looked at each h advertisement poster. In Table 3, the scent of a rose is offered to the users.

Table 3. The average of time lengths

advertisement	time length [sec]
1-Vanilla	0.00
2-Coffee	0.00
3-chocolate	0.00
4-Rose	1.30
5-Lavender	8.90
6-Chicken	15.10
7-Banana	9.70
8-Lemon	5.60
9-Honey	2.50
10-Strawberry	2.50
11-Pizza	1.30
12-Apple	0.00
sum	46.90

9 Experiment 4: Offering Graphics, Scent, and Wind

Case 3. Each user looked at the 12 advertisement posters as shown in Figs. 3 and 20 through the Head Mounted Display. Further, some kinds of scent (banana's scent, or lemon's scent) were offered by the HMD attachment olfactory display as shown in Figs. 13 and 14. Further, wind was offered from the bladeless fan by Dyson Limited as shown in Figs. 17, 18 and 19 Each user was not informed the kind of scent by the authors. Each user was not informed the position of the bladeless fan by Dyson Limited which was the source of wind. When banana's scent was offered from the HMD attachment olfactory display, the wind was offered from the position of the banana's advertisement poster which is the Number 7-Banana in the Fig. 3. When lemon's scent was offered from the HMD attachment olfactory display, the wind was offered from the position of the lemon's advertisement poster which is the Number 10-Lemon in the Fig. 3. Seven users attended this Case 3 experiment.

Table 4 shows the average of time length on which the users looked at each h advertisement poster. In Table 3, the scent of a lemon is offered to the users.

Table 4. The average of time lengths

advertisement	time length [sec]
1-Vanilla	2.60
2-Coffee	1.65
3-chocolate	1.20
4-Rose	1.95
5-Lavender	1.45
6-Chicken	1.75
7-Banana	6.20
8-Strawberry	6.45
9-Honey	8.60
10-Lemon	11.10
11-Pizza	7.15
12-Apple	4.40
sum	54.5

10 Results of the Experiments 2, 3, 4 (Case 1, 2, 3)

Based on the measurements of the Eye Tracking System of the Head Mounted Display, the authors computed each time length on which a user looked at each advertisement poster.

In the Case 1 experiment described in the above Sect. 7, there were little differences between the 12 time lengths of the advertisement posters at which each user looked. Since there were no scent and no wind, each user looked at the 12 advertisement posters equally.

In the Case 2 experiment described in the above Sect. 8, there were some differences between the 12 time lengths of the advertisement posters at which each user looked. Each user looked at some advertisement posters for long time, but other advertisement posters for short time.

In the Case 3 experiment described in the above Sect. 9, the same tendency was obtained as the Case 2 experiment described in the above Sect. 8. Some users looked at the posters which were near the source of the wind for long time. But, some users looked at the posters which are not near the source of the wind for long time.

In order to attract users to a particular advertisement poster on VR shopping in metaverse space, we can expect the effect of scent. We must research the effect of the wind more and more in future.

11   Conclusions

In order to offer many kinds of scent to human nose (a user's nose), the authors developed olfactory displays using piezo-electric elements. In order to offer scent to the user who immerses a VR space in metaverse, the authors had developed an olfactory display which can be attached to a Head Mounted Display. This HMD attachment olfactory display is controlled by Unity project. Thus we can offer scent which is appropriate to the graphics offered through Head Mounted Display.

The multimodal effect by olfactory sense (scent), visual sense (graphics), and haptic sense (wind) will be researched more and more in future.

References

1. Okada, K.: A VR space and scent. J. Virtual Reality Soc. Japan 9(3), 149–153 (2004)
2. Tomono, A., Otake, S.: The eye catching property of digital-signage with scent and a scent emitting video display system. J. Inst. Electr. Eng. Japan, Section C 130(4), 668–675 (2010)
3. Nakano, T., Yanagida, Y.: Measurement and evaluation of wind direction perception at the whole head. Trans. Virtual Reality Soc. Japan 24(1), 53–59 (2019)
4. Saito, Y., Murosaki, Y., Ono, R., Nakano, A., Hada, H.: Measurement of wind direction perception characteristics with head mounted display. In: Proceedings of the Entertainment Computing Symposium (Information Processing Society of Japan, pp.138–144 (2017)

A Humanoid Saxophone-Playing Robot Based on Instrument-Centered Design

Sound Improvement with Fingers Using Hybrid Soft Materials

Jun Uchiyama[1,2](✉) ⓘ, Tomoyuki Hashimoto[1] ⓘ, Hina Ohta[2] ⓘ, Jia-Yeu Lin[2] ⓘ,
Sarah Cosentino[2] ⓘ, and Atsuo Takanishi[2]

[1] Advanced Institute of Industrial Technology, Tokyo 140-0011, Japan
uchiyama-jun@aiit.ac.jp
[2] Waseda University, Tokyo 169-8050, Japan
contact@takanishi.mech.waseda.ac.jp

Abstract. We will develop a saxophone-playing robot that enables human-robot interaction. Our previous generation of robots was larger and more complex to achieve higher performance, which made human interaction difficult. Therefore, we began developing the Waseda Anthropomorphic Saxophonist robot X (WAS-X), redesigned to simulate a saxophonist playing in a seated posture. In the early stages of development, the robot was created by a product designer using Design Thinking. The robot was designed with the saxophone centered. The design reference points are integrated and organized to restructure the robot, resulting in a small and simple configuration and a stable blowing range. This approach, Instrument centered design, is a fundamental development concept for WAS-X. However, the performance of WAS-X has not yet reached the level of beginners. In addition, the sound quality of WAS-X was comparable to that of previous robots, even though a neck strap held it. The cause of these problems probably involves the condition of the blown air and the contact points with many instruments. Thus, this research focused on the keys and fingers, the contact points between the saxophone and the robot. As a result, the lower sound quality was improved using a hybrid soft material for the fingers. These fingers are flexible plastic fingers with silicone rubber tips. Furthermore, a fingering control system was also implemented to adjust the initial values efficiently.

Keywords: Humanoid Robot · Soft Materials · Instrument-Centered Design

1 Introduction

We have been researching and developing humanoid musician robots since 1990 [1]. The ultimate model for robots is the human being. Our goal is to pursue the mechanisms of the human mind and body through the development of robots. Musical performers have high-performance skills and bring empathy to people through performance. Therefore, developing and researching music performer robots is one of the optimal robotics research projects. First, we started research on an artificial flutist robot [2]. Since 2008,

J. Y. C. Chen and G. Fragomeni (Eds.): HCII 2023, LNCS 14027, pp. 295–306, 2023.
https://doi.org/10.1007/978-3-031-35634-6_21

we have focused on developing anthropomorphic saxophonist robots [3]. These robots have gradually clarified the mechanisms of the human body and mind [4, 5]. These findings have added more depth to our research.

The saxophone is one of the most popular musical instruments often used in various genres of music, such as classical, jazz, and pop. Nevertheless, few robots have been developed to play the instrument as a professional saxophonist performs. Playing the saxophone requires modeling the intricate coordination of lips, tongue, lungs, and fingers. Other than our research team, other saxophone-playing robots include a tenor saxophone-playing robot developed by Hosei University (APR-SX2) [6].

We aim to develop a saxophone-playing robot that can communicate emotionally with musicians and attract audiences to their performances. As previously described, we have been developing a 31-DoF Waseda Anthropomorphic Saxophonist robot No.5 (WAS-5), an alto saxophone-playing robot. We have achieved results by simulating human organs and improving their performance in the past. The Robot's complexity also disables Human-Robot Interaction [7]. The conflict between improved music performance and human interaction has created complex and difficult robots. Future interaction research should be facilitated by downsizing and simplification. In conclusion, a true saxophonist robot should be redesigned using human performance as a model through a backcasting approach in addition to the previous forecasting approach.

Therefore, the Waseda Anthropomorphic Saxophonist robot X (WAS-X) was developed using the new approach described above [8]. WAS-X was designed with the saxophone at the center. The design reference points are integrated and organized to restructure the robot, resulting in a small and simple configuration and a stable blowing range. We called this design approach "Instrument-centered design." Details are discussed in Sect. 2.

Meanwhile, soft materials are expected to contribute significantly to Instrument-centered design. Because the saxophonist is human, all the points of contact with the saxophone are mostly soft biomaterials; the lips on the mouthpiece, the fingers on the keys, the neck on the neck strap et al.. Air passages, such as the cheeks, lungs, and airways, also contribute to the sound. Additionally, the diaphragm generates blowing pressure. Even hard teeth and nails are supported by soft biomaterials. WAS-X also utilizes soft materials in various parts of the robot; on the lips, the oral cavity, the diaphragm material in the pump for generating blowing pressure, piping, et al.

The WAS-X is smaller and has a simpler configuration and a larger stable blowing range than the previous WAS-5. However, the performance of the WAS-X has not yet reached the level of beginners. The sound quality was similar to previous robots, despite being held by a neck strap. The cause of these problems is probably the condition of the blown air and the contact points with many instruments. This research, therefore, focused on the keys and fingers, the points of contact between the saxophone and the robot. As a result, the lower sound quality has been improved by using a hybrid soft material for the fingers. New WAS-X fingers are flexible plastic fingers with silicone rubber tips. A finger control system was also implemented to adjust the initial values efficiently.

This paper is organized as follows. Section 2 reviews current issues and shows the WAS-X development concept. We discuss how to improve the finger part, which is the focus of this project, as well as the development goals of the control system and the demonstration methods. Section 3 analyzes and discusses the implementation details and evaluation results. Section 4 presents conclusions and future work.

2 Materials and Methods

As described above, our previous robots made human interaction difficult due to their complexity and increased size to achieve higher performance. Thus, our previous predictive approaches would create complex and difficult robots. A backcasting approach would be required. To achieve this, we needed to make some breakthroughs in our research (Fig. 1).

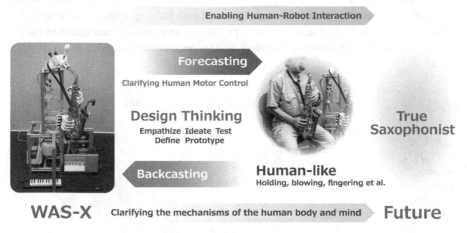

Fig. 1. WAS-X Design Concept

2.1 Instrument-Centered Design

Design Thinking is a designer's way of thinking. Moreover, IDEO's "The five phases of Design Thinking (1. Empathize, 2. Define, 3. Ideate, 4. Prototype, 5. Test)" are well known. Hence, Design Thinking was applied to solve the problem. Deep understanding through empathy is critical to problem-solving [9]. Although, Design Thinking is not limited to a process.

Design Thinking solves apparent and inapparent problems by empathizing with the user through observing and experiencing the user experience. In this case, instruments and systems would be designed user-centered. User-centered design is also known as human-centered design because the most valuable human is the user.

Meanwhile, saxophonists treat the instrument respectfully, like a human being. The empathic target is not a human being but an alto saxophone. Therefore, WAS-X has designed an Alto saxophone-centered, Instrument-centered design (Fig. 2).

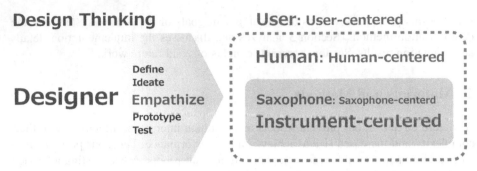

Fig. 2. Empathetic Targets in Design Thinking

The product designer on our team with experience in developing entertainment robots [10, 11] observed and experienced saxophone playing while designing WAS-X. Saxophonists manipulate instruments to produce sound. WAS-X manipulates instead of saxophonists. The Instrument-centered design perspective provides many insights (Fig. 3).

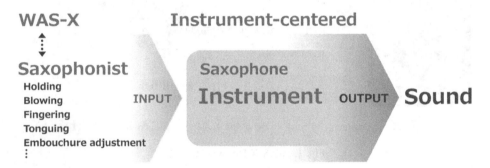

Fig. 3. Instrument-centered design conceptual diagram

Based on the following fundamental findings, the preconceptions were eliminated, and the WAS-X was developed. Figure 4 shows the overall view of previous WAS-X and WAS-5 before the finger improvement [8].

- The mouthpiece is held by the upper anterior teeth and lips
- The neck strap ring hangs by the neck strap
- The right thumb supports the thumb hook
- The left thumb supports the thumb rest
- The other fingers support the Major keys

As previously described, WAS-X has significantly improved, although many issues still need to be addressed. In this research, we focused on the contact point between the keys and fingers as one of the factors that greatly affect sound quality and made improvements based on the concept of Instrument-centered design.

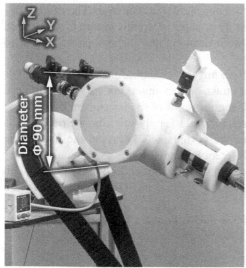

(a) WAS-X lip and oral cavity

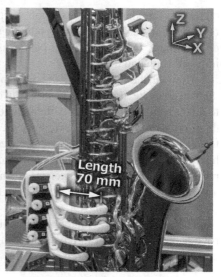

(b) WAS-X fingers without tips

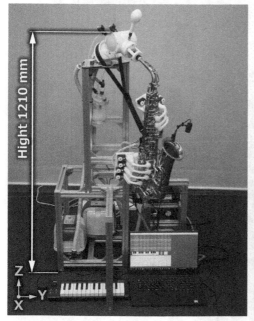

(c) WAS-X with fingertips

(d) WAS-5 (left) and WAS-X (right)

Fig. 4. Waseda Anthropomorphic Saxophonist (WAS)

2.2 Fingers Using Hybrid Soft Materials

The saxophone's characteristic overtone attracts the audience [12]. For this reason, saxophonists take great care not to constrain the instrument redundantly [13]. WAS-X sound quality was similar to previous robots, despite being held by a neck strap. Therefore, a significant improvement in blowing sound quality is required. In this research, we focused on the finger, the contact point between the instrument and the saxophone player, to improve sound quality.

Although the current WAS-X has 1 DoF per finger, the flexible plastic material allows them to adapt flexibly to the keystroke. In contrast, human fingers not only allow the keys to adapt flexibly but also relax the redundant constraints of the instrument by covering them with soft biomaterials. We have therefore tried to apply soft silicone rubber pads to the finger, the point of contact between the saxophone's keys and the finger. The hybrid combination of soft materials of different hardness improves the sound quality performance (Fig. 5). The fingertips are made of silicone rubber (Ecoflex™ 00–30) with a softness similar to the cheek. The finger frame is made of 3D-printed PP-like resin (Stratasys's Rigur; RGD 450).

The research on soft materials in robotics is mostly done for two reasons; developing robotic parts to perform soft manipulation and soft actuators [14]. The studies of WAS-X are a unique applied research approach.

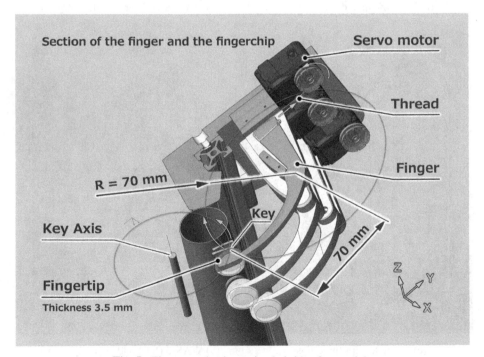

Fig. 5. Finger mechanism using hybrid soft materials.

2.3 Fingering Control System

The current WAS-X control system is simple, mainly for checking finger movements. The Instrument-centered design has greatly improved the hardware adjustment performance of WAS-X. However, the string tension adjustment in the open position and the setpoint adjustment in the closed position are still manual adjustments.

As a next step, we aimed to simplify the initial setup by knowing the servo motor torque value (Fig. 6). Each servo target value is controlled by command control from the Windows PC. The servo target value is reflected in the initial setting by examining the servo value when the key reaches the servo torque value to be closed.

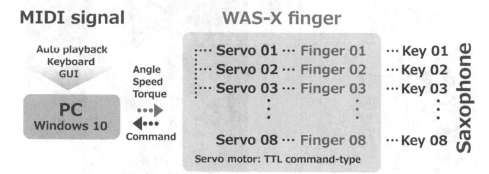

Fig. 6. Fingering control system

2.4 Experimental Protocol for Evaluating Sound Quality

To confirm the sound improvement with fingers using hybrid soft materials, fingers with and without silicone rubber tips must be compared. This experiment compares the open note (E4), which has the least fingering influence, with the fully closed note (E-flat 3), which has the most fingering influence. The same pitch is blown at the same sound pressure for a period and recorded.

The alto saxophone is a YAMAHA YAS-475, the mouthpiece is an AS4C, and the reed is a Legere Alto sax studio cut 2. Audio-Technica's ATM35 condenser microphone and Zoom's UAE-2 USB audio converter are used for recording. Adobe's Audition and Audacity 3.2.4 (Audacity®) are used for recording and analysis. MATLAB is also used for analysis. The servos are Futaba RS303MR command-type servos, and a 60 mm long aramid fiber thread is used to tension the finger mechanism through the pulley.

3 Result and Discussion

3.1 Soft Material Fingertips Implementation

We designed and fabricated fingertips made of soft silicone rubber with a hardness similar to that of the cheek (Fig. 7). As a result, WAS-X blew two octaves from E-flat 3 to E flat 5. In addition, the new WAS-X had a wider range of adjustments and more stable blowing in the lower octaves than without the fingertips. PTC Creo parametric was used to create the 3D CAD data.

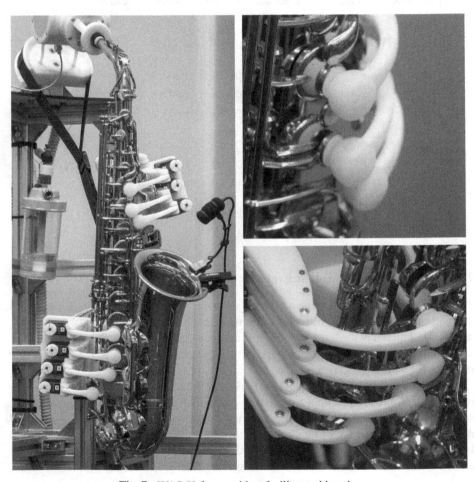

Fig. 7. WAS-X finger with soft silicon rubber tips

3.2 Fingering Control System Implementation

A fingering control system was implemented. As a result, the system enables the following. Figure 8 shows the graphical user interface of the fingering control system.

- Playback with MIDI keyboard and GUI keyboard
- Automatic playback of prepared music
- Target value setting of open and close for each servo motor
- Dynamic visualization of the status of each servo motor

The servo values at the appropriate torque for each finger at closing were studied and used as a guide to determine the target values. We plan to use this algorithm for initial calibration in the future.

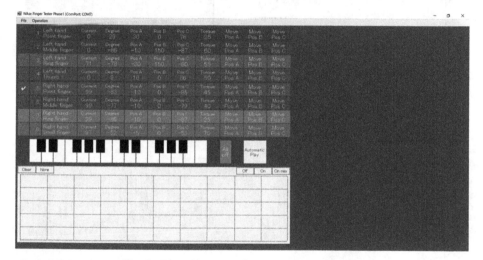

Fig. 8. Fingerling control graphical user interface

3.3 Sound Quality Analysis

To compare the sound quality with and without the soft silicone rubber tips, the open note (E4), which is least affected by fingering, and the fully closed note (E-flat 3), which is most affected by fingering, were compared by visualizing the overtone components using the amplitude spectrum. Data at 1.0 s intervals are used, and edges are processed with a Hamming window. After recording each note for more than 10 s and confirming that the results are similar throughout the period, representative data are shown. The intraoral pressure at the time of blowing was about 3 kPa, the same level as normal blowing [15].

The E4, with all the keys opened, has no significant difference in the attenuation of the overtone component observed between the two. If anything, it is moderately affected by the silicone rubber-covered fingers that touched the keys (Fig. 9).

The E-flat 3, with the basic keys closed, showed a noticeably moderate and natural attenuation of overtones in the bass range. The actual listening clearly showed rich overtones (Fig. 10).

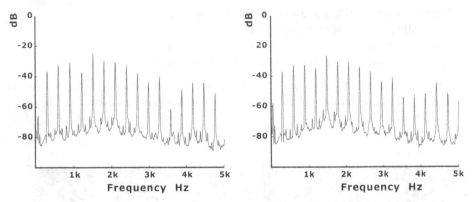

Fig. 9. E4 audio frequency analysis: without tips (left) and with tips (right).

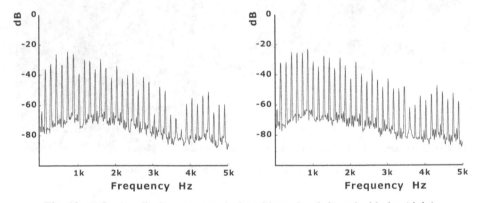

Fig. 10. E-flat 3 audio frequency analysis: without tips (left) and with tips (right).

3.4   Discussion

For the Instrument's resonance to remain intact, silicone rubber tips are implemented on the plastic fingers. As a consequence, the sound quality of low-pitched notes improved. At least, there is room for performance improvement by optimizing the finger shape and materials. Furthermore, the fingering control system allows the simple adjustment of the initial setting. Automatic setup and integration with oral cavity and lip control are also expected.

In other aspects of fingering, the order, speed, and strength of closing are also found to affect the stability of the blowing. We will investigate these effects in detail to improve fingering control performance.

4 Conclusion

The methodology of Instrument-centered design will provide many insights into the concept of WAS-X and has been successful in its development. As a result, the contribution of the fingers with hybrid soft materials resulted in improved sound quality and blowing stability. Design thinking eliminated preconceptions, and awareness of Instrument-centered design led to innovation.

However, WAS-X is still far from professional saxophonists in every way. Many challenges remain, especially for use in interactive research with humans. In the future, it will be necessary to balance backcasting and forecasting in the development process.

Acknowledgments. The authors would like to thank Tokyo Women's Medical University/Waseda University Joint Institution for Advanced Biomedical Sciences (TWIns), Humanoid Robotics Institute (HRI), Parametric Technology Corp., Microsoft, Dassault Systèmes and Yamaha Corp. For supporting this work. The authors would also like to thank Dr. S. Wesugi from Waseda Univ. And Mr. K. Omori from Sony Electronics Inc. For their useful insights.

This study was conducted with the support of the Research Institute for Science and Engineering, Waseda University; Center for Advanced Biomedical Sciences (TWIns), Waseda University; Future Robotics Organization, Waseda University, and as part of the humanoid project at the Humanoid Robotics Institute, Waseda University. Advanced Institute of Industrial Technology also supported the present work.

References

1. Sugano, S., Kato, I.: WABOT-2: Autonomous robot with dexterous finger-arm--Finger-arm coordination control in keyboard performance, vol. 4, pp. 90–97 (1987)
2. Takanishi, A., Sonehara, M., Kondo, H.: Development of an anthropomorphic flutist robot WF-3RII. In: Proceedings of IEEE/RSJ International Conference on Intelligent Robots and Systems. IROS'96, vol. 1, pp. 37–43 (1996)
3. Chida, K., et al.: Development of a new anthropomorphic flutist robot WF-4. In: IEEE International Conference on Robotics and Automation, 2004. Proceedings. ICRA'04. vol. 1, pp. 152–157. IEEE (2004)
4. Yi-Hsiang, M.A., et al.: A synchronization feedback system to improve interaction correlation in subjects with autism spectrum disorder. In: 2018 9th International Conference on Awareness Science and Technology (iCAST), pp. 285–290 (2018)
5. Han, Y., et al.: A human-robot interface to improve facial expression recognition in subjects with Autism Spectrum Disorder, pp. 179–184 (2018)
6. Miyawaki, T., Takashima, S.: Control of an automatic performance robot of saxophone: performance control using standard midi files. In: The Proceedings of JSME annual Conference on Robotics and Mechatronics (Robomec), vol. 33 (2003)
7. Cosentino, S., Takanishi, A.: Human–robot musical interaction. In: Miranda, E.R. (ed.) Handbook of Artificial Intelligence for Music: Foundations, Advanced Approaches, and Developments for Creativity, pp. 799–822. Springer International Publishing, Cham (2021)
8. Uchiyama, J., et al.: Development of an anthropomorphic saxophonist robot using a human-like holding method. In: The 2023 IEEE/SICE International Symposium on System Integration Atlanta, USA (2023)
9. Meinel, C., von Thienen, J.: Design thinking. Informatik-Spektrum **39**(4), 310–314 (2016). https://doi.org/10.1007/s00287-016-0977-2

10. Qrio, the robot that could. IEEE Spectr. **41**, 34–37 (2004)
11. Fujita, M.: On activating human communications with pet-type robot AIBO. Proc. IEEE **92**, 1804–1813 (2004)
12. Cottrell, S.: The Saxophone. Yale University Press, New Haven, United States (2013)
13. Teal, L.: The Art of Saxophone Playing. Summy-Birchard (1963)
14. Elango, N., Faudzi, A.A.M.: A review article: investigations on soft materials for soft robot manipulations. The Int. J. Adv. Manuf. Technol. **80**, 1027–1037 (2015)
15. Rossing., N.F.T.: The Physics of Musical Instruments. Springer, New York, New York (1998)

Multimodality: Exploring Sensibility and Sense-Making Beyond the Metaverse

Gareth W. Young[1]([⊠])(iD) and Oliver Dawkins[2](iD)

[1] TRANSMIXR, School of Computer Science and Statistics,
Trinity College Dublin, Dublin, Ireland
YoungGa@tcd.ie
[2] Data Stories, Maynooth University Social Sciences Institute,
Maynooth University, Maynooth, Ireland
oliver.dawkins@mu.ie

Abstract. Immersive technologies are increasingly integrated into creative practice and various aspects of everyday life as augmented and virtual reality (AR/VR). These extended reality (XR) technologies are particularly relevant for researchers exploring human-computer relationships where users intend to interact with 3D objects and real-time multimedia in a spatial context. XR is being researched, developed, and deployed for communicating and building knowledge around what is being called the metaverse. The present trajectory for creating metaverse experiences strongly tends toward attaining heightened realism. Here we discuss the various factors of multimodality that challenge the idea that research in interaction for mixed realities should narrowly converge on or limit itself to developing applications intended to captivate users in these realist environments. We emphasize advancements in multimodality to further experimentation with human sensory modalities. To this end, we discuss the recent aesthetic theory proposed by Fuller and Weizman (2021), which is oriented to the attunement of the senses to further our capacities for sensing and sense-making. Building on Fuller and Weizman's references to notions of memory, synaesthesia, kinaesthetics, and chronesthesia, we consider multimodality within mixed realities beyond realism to raise users' sensibility and discernment toward both virtual and physical environments via new forms of experimentation with the senses.

Keywords: Multimodality · Metaverse · Sensibility · Sense-making

1 Introduction

Immersive technologies are increasingly being integrated into creative practice and various aspects of everyday life, including social networking [1], data visualization [24], healthcare [16], creative storytelling [49], classroom interventions [46], and many other areas of contemporary lifestyle routines. Immersive technologies like augmented and virtual reality (AR/VR) have been grouped under

J. Y. C. Chen and G. Fragomeni (Eds.): HCII 2023, LNCS 14027, pp. 307–322, 2023.
https://doi.org/10.1007/978-3-031-35634-6_22

the umbrella term "extended reality" (XR). These technologies are particularly relevant for researchers exploring human-computer relationships in contexts where users intend to interact with 3D objects and real-time multimedia in a spatial computing context, including digitizing the activities of machines, people, objects, and physical environments to enable and optimize actions and interactions.

AR and VR use similar enabling technologies and computational techniques to generate immersive user experiences. However, AR and VR interfaces also have different affordances that fundamentally influence those experiences' nature. The most immediate difference between AR and VR is the degree to which the digital content they present is integrated with the user's immediate physical environment. As the technologies enabling XR platforms and devices afford different degrees of integration between digital content and the physical environment, there is no sharply discrete divide between the experiences afforded by AR and VR interfaces. Instead, they provide access to a continuum affording different degrees of mixed reality (MR) [27]. In what follows, our use of XR will refer to the various technologies vendors provide that enable immersive experiences. MR will refer to the experience and affordances enabled through different degrees of blending between a user's physical environment and digital content made possible using XR technologies.

The affordances of VR tend toward one extreme of this continuum by presenting artificial or "virtual" environments that substitute for the user's immediate physical environment. Immersion in virtual environments is achieved by providing believable and consistent sensory feedback to the user's interactions [39]. With the help of specialized multisensory equipment, such as head-mounted displays (HMDs), immersive virtual environments (IVEs) are amplified through stereoscopic vision, ambisonic sound, haptic displays, real-time movement tracking, and physical-world-like interaction with purely virtual objects.

AR technology applies similar technologies but is targeted toward creatively augmenting physical spaces and site-specific performance [31]. AR is used to superimpose digital artifacts, as virtual objects, into the physical world. It is spatially accurate and merges the physical with the virtual world. AR facilitates the integration of digital information with the users' environment in real-time, usually enabled by devices such as mobile phones, smart glasses, and other HMD devices. Hence, by providing real-time sensory stimulation, users can be immersed in a VR simulation, like the New York Times using VR tech for storytelling in *Seeking Pluto's Frigid Heart* (2016) or have their physical space enhanced by spatially anchored AR, such as *Pokémon GO* (2016) or *Snapchat* (2011).

Commercial XR technology providers have long studied the application of user-interaction metaphors for IVEs [8,20,33]. These metaphors are based on visual conventions, actions, and processes already familiar to users, such as voice assistants like Alexa and Siri, and touch and multitouch interactions like those used on mobile phones and tablets. These metaphors are helping XR technologies gain penetration into fields ranging from health care and digital heritage to

CAD and film production, where the use of IVEs provides advantages over traditional screen-based visualization methods through the integration of multiple communication modalities for interaction and sensory feedback. These modalities mainly include our Aristotelian senses of sight, hearing, touch, and in some cases, simulated gustatory and olfactory feedback.

Multimodality in the context of Milgram & Kishino's definition of MR refers to the integration of multiple sensory modalities – typically sight and hearing but sometimes touch in more contemporary XR technology – as a means to enhance a user's experience of immersion [27]. Multimodal interaction combines multiple inputs and outputs, typically delivered by specially designed devices, to facilitate more intuitive and natural interactions that mutually accommodate the affordances of human bodies and their perceptual systems to digitally mediated content and environments. Multimodal interaction helps to captivate the user by stimulating both attentive and pre-attentive engagement with a particular activity or experience. In this way, multimodality enhances immersive technologies by increasing the subjected user's sense of embodiment, presence, and agency, their ability to affect and be affected by the digital objects or virtual environments presented to them.

In the architecture, engineering, and construction sectors, geospatial technology providers like Cesium are collaborating with computer graphics and game engine companies like NVIDIA, Epic, and Unity to enable the construction of global-scale IVEs for training and simulation applications under the banner of the "Open Metaverse". IVEs have also long been used for education and training [26] via early CAVE and more modern HMD systems [25]. While IVEs provide safe environments in which mistakes have low consequences, the development and use of multimodal interaction aim to confer ecological validity while encouraging the user's embodied sense of value and risk to reinforce negative feelings expressed during the experience [21].

Various entertainment and media companies, notably social media giant Meta (formerly Facebook), have appropriated the metaverse concept. For Meta, their appropriation of the metaverse moniker provides brand distinction while leveraging their acquisition of headset manufacturer Oculus in 2014 to encourage a new, younger user base onto its platform by enriching the social media experience with the immersiveness of emergent social VR platforms. Ball's definition of the metaverse captures the technical aspirations for such environments:

"A massively scaled and interoperable network of real-time rendered 3D virtual worlds that can be experienced synchronously and persistently by an effectively unlimited number of users with an individual sense of presence, and with continuity of data, such as identity, history, entitlements, objects, communications and payments" [2, p. 29].

Meeting these requirements promises the ability to build highly detailed worlds but offers little direction regarding the nature and quality of users' experiences. It begs the question – what will it be like exploring and interacting in these worlds? Smaller 3D blockchain-based platforms like Decentraland, Sandbox, Cryptovoxels, and Somnium Space combine gamification elements with developing cryptocurrency-backed markets, driving the commercialization of digital worlds where users can play games but also buy and sell plots of virtual land on which to build. Often resembling the cartoon-like worlds of platforms like SecondLife from the 2000s,s, many of the current metaverse offerings have been criticized for the lack of quality of experience in aesthetics and the interactions they offer. They have also been condemned for their unscrupulous marketing strategies.

The present trajectory for developing XR technology as immersive VR and AR experiences strongly tends toward attaining heightened realism through computer-generated imagery (CGI) and visual effects (VFX). The ongoing development of advanced real-time rendering techniques and computational improvements in lighting and physics simulation facilitates this. Increased physical realism drives the development of new haptic feedback devices, binaural audio, and olfactory technology. Particularly in VR, by monopolizing the users' sensorium, multiple channels of synthetically produced stimuli that are mutually consistent in their response to user interaction heighten immersion through the experiential immediacy and immanence, which allows users to overlook their artifice [5]. Immersion creates feelings of presence for the user when their interactions with the digital content of a mixed-reality experience align with their expectations for comfort, immediacy, responsiveness, and prior experiences of interacting with their physical environment. In this context, developments in multimodality are geared toward the instrumental engagement and captivation of new users through multimodal interactions by which XR technology enables immersion, creates more profound feelings of presence in IVEs, and conveys the authenticity of the experience [37].

In this paper, we challenge the idea that research in multimodal interaction for mixed realities should narrowly converge on or limit itself to developing metaverse applications intended to captivate users in realist environments typically designed to capture their time, attention, and money. Instead, we emphasize advancements in multimodality to further experimentation with human sensory modalities. To this end, we discuss the recent aesthetic theory proposed by Fuller and Weizman [13], which, developed in the context of 3D forensics, is oriented to the attunement of the senses and their sensitivity to different forms of stimuli but also to our ability to make sense of those stimuli and produce meaning from them. They are fundamentally concerned with enhancing human sensibility to new objects and environments and their capacity for sense-making. In this way, their theory has implications beyond their immediate field of application.

Building on Fuller and Weizman's references to notions of memory, synaesthesia, kinaesthetics, and chronesthesia, we consider multimodality within mixed realities beyond realism to raise users' sensibility and discernment toward both virtual and physical environments via new forms of experimentation with the senses. We hypothesize that this may contribute to a new appreciation and enhanced ability to respond to complex physical, aesthetic, and emotional experiences utilizing emergent XR technologies. This discussion is intended to provide a platform for dialogue around new ways to interact and engage with mixed realities to further our ability to engage meaningfully with our shared physical realities.

2 The Metaverse and Criticisms

The term "metaverse" was first popularized in science fiction literature of the early 90s [40]. However, it can be linked to both the prior notion of "cyberspace" [14] and to the visual arts concept of "sensory spaces", which describe the idea of technology and cybernetics as pervasive and interconnected environments [22]. Stephenson defines the metaverse as a single, persistent, three-dimensional (3D) environment constructed from digital information as software and running on infrastructure analogous to the emerging Internet [40]. Personal HMD devices project the virtual world, and users use avatars to access the metaverse from a first-person perspective. While initially a thing of science fiction, we have more recently appropriated the practices of interface, interaction, and experience design using XR technology—"If it works for an audience, some part will work for all users" [38, p. 310].

It is now possible to facilitate real-time communications in both human-human and human-computer interactions using contemporary XR technology. Social VR platforms, such as VR Chat and the recently sunsetted AltspaceVR, have been developed to provide more natural embodied interaction between participants represented by three-dimensional avatars. However, it is also essential to explore how non-verbal communication can be supported using multimodality in these spaces to further MR's social interaction. Within the metaverse, multimodality is currently used to replicate natural interactions from the physical world. While real-time multimodal interaction is possible in most metaverse applications, there are still limitations in reproducing the full range of interactions involved in daily communication. One example is the lack of subtle cues associated with gaze and eye-to-eye contact, which XR device providers are attempting to address through the introduction of eye-tracking.

It is also notable that many experiences are limited in how interactions can be effectively staged such that when one person speaks, the others must all stop and listen. They must take turns without the possibility of whispering and limited opportunity for side conversations. In this way, the limitations of the technology can require modified behaviors and etiquette. These interactions also tend to be staged in simulations of familiar and uninspired office and boardroom settings. While the underlying technology enables real-time co-presence, it is not always clear that the XR solution provides further convenience than a simpler and more immediately expressive video chat. It is principally technology vendors like Microsoft, with their Mesh platform and concept of *holoportation*, who drive the idea that users would want to intermingle in IVEs as avatars during online meetings.

On the one hand, interactions via this technology may alleviate Zoom fatigue, the exhaustion felt after long-term videoconferencing; On the other hand, it is equally possible that users will experience discomfort wearing an XR HMD and working with associated peripherals for long periods. After all, the current generation of HMDs are cumbersome, the avatars are uncanny or child-like in appearance, volumetric video is grainy and low-fidelity, and CGI office spaces may be sparse and dismally depressing or overly distracting depending on the quality of their design. Commercial applications of social VR such as these may fail to help users communicate effectively and get their intended jobs done as efficiently as other technological means.

While the synchronous nature of the metaverse is built upon real-time telepresence technologies, its innate latencies between the physical and digital worlds are no longer a technological hurdle to be overcome, such as is demonstrated in popular massively multiplayer online games (MMOs). However, the technology applied to bring people together from all over the world online is built upon vastly different technologies. While able to interact with each other in real time, users may not be sharing the same digital space or physical server, further compounding the requirements for multiplatform communication devices.

The early metaverse was conceptualized to track entitlements, objects, communications, and payments over time anywhere within it. However, due to current limitations that result from particular vendors' attempts to lock users into their platforms to gain the most significant market share, interoperability between different platforms is limited or lacking altogether. Moving from one platform to the next has an overhead for users in that it typically requires the creation of new user accounts and avatars, learning new interaction metaphors, and adopting different etiquettes which may be platform specific. Interoperability is lost, while synchronous communication is widely available, creating islands of users who cannot communicate immediately outside their immediate IVE without swapping platforms to do so. This development departs considerably from popular aspirations derived from 90s web culture, which conceived of the metaverse, cyberspace, and virtual realities as seamlessly integrated worlds, free from the physical constraints associated with the human body and free from the territorial conditions related to architecture, cities, and the borders of nation-states [3]. This goal of which was the far-out promise of Sutherland's "ultimate display":

> "There is no reason why the objects displayed by a computer have to follow the ordinary rules of physical reality with which we are familiar. [...] The ultimate display would, of course, be a room within which the computer can control the existence of matter. A chair displayed in such a room would be good enough to sit in. Handcuffs displayed in such a room would be confining, and a bullet displayed in such a room would be fatal" [42, p. 2].

The metaverse has more recently been described as a "post-reality" space, manifest as a "perpetual and persistent" multiuser IVE [28]. As per Ball's definition of the metaverse quoted in our introduction, the concept of a single overarching system that provides a unified experience and identity presupposes persistence and continuity of data, precisely, as persistent state worlds (PSWs) that continue "to exist and develop internally even when there are no people interacting with it" [4]. PSWs frequently reference massively multiplayer online role-playing games (MMORPGs) and MMOs, but they are not limited to this gaming style. PSWs support hundreds or thousands of users simultaneously, and gaming continues to lead these novel metaverse developments, whether users are role-playing as imaginary characters or just being themselves.

In the metaverse today, the illusion that a PSW is always available is often simulated between players via modern Information and Communications Technology (ICTs), such as voice, instant messaging, and community forums. A "World Server" provides the PSW data for game instances or "bubbles", created on-demand as players are matched to interact together. The PSW generates world events offline regardless of a player's online presence. The players' presence and interactions drive the narrative, run the economy, and direct the content of the virtual world from the bottom up [11, 35]. While their existence is technically viable, as demonstrated by SecondLife, these platforms are subject to the organizations that own them and may disappear (as seen with the sunsetting of AltspaceVR in 2023) even when they have vast numbers of users and online communities.

As more users worldwide gain access to and become fully immersed in online PSW gaming worlds using HMDs and avatars, it's natural that monetization will creep in, and cryptocurrencies are playing a more prominent industry role. While monetizing online video games is nothing new, the introduction of blockchain technology has created crypto gaming. This Play to Earn (P2E) model facilitates software developers in adding elements of real-world economics to their games. Crypto gamers can earn non-fungible tokens (NFTs) or other cryptocurrencies by playing online games, creating digital assets that become the player's property. There are various P2E business models in crypto gaming, including advertising or selling in-game items, such as unique or rare weapons, character "skins", and virtual lands. Other P2E platforms allow crypto investors to gamble on casino-like games, such as BitStarz, 7bitcasino, and mBitcasino. According to CoinMarketCap (2022), the highest-value gaming crypto coin and token projects have a total market capitalization value of $7.9 billion. For example, as of November 2022, the top cryptocurrencies are ApeCoin (APE) with a Market Cap of $1.1 billion; Sandbox's (SAND) Market Cap is $1 billion; Decentraland's (MANA) Market Cap is worth $994 million. Accordingly, there are various risks associated with crypto games and token-based P2E platforms, such as supply and demand dynamics and hacking.

NFTs are digital records of ownership stored on a distributed database or ledger as a cryptocurrency. Each NFT points to unique digital content that the owner can trade. NFTs are a centerpiece of Web 3.0, the latest iteration of the World Wide Web. Unlike other virtual currencies, such as Bitcoin or Ethereum, NFTs can represent various items, such as physical property, digital assets, music, and art. The most developing NFT markets are in digital art collections. Many applications for generative art creation, artistic analyses, and text-and-image approaches combining AI processes have appeared in creative use cases [23]. While purely vision based in recent years, text-to-image frameworks can also be used for multimodal applications and IVE metaverse creation tools across different platforms. By combining generated artwork with multimodal outputs, 3D assets may have more commercial value due to the input applying multiple datasets, which results in items that have better interaction with users. These multimodal generative arts can also create unique NFT-based capital for commercial advantages in the emergent metaverse marketplace. Multimodal NFTs are "interactive, reactive, and intelligent" [32]. As they exist today, the various metaverse platforms are essentially becoming storehouses for user NFTs and a marketplace for extracting or inflating their value.

Pursuing extreme realism and monetization may not be justified without considering the broader implications of multimodality, as physical realism and simulation realism do not always compute [7]. Focusing on IVE realism implies that virtual worlds are evaluated by their similarity to the corresponding physical world. However, realism is also an art movement, meaning IVE simulation realism could also be considered an aesthetic category. Something perceived as reality does not have to perfectly represent physical reality in an IVE [48]. Therefore, the perceived authenticity of an IVE rests on four main aspects of realism — scene realism, audience behavior realism, audience appearance realism, and sound realism — connections that have been verified between realism, immersion, presence, and aesthetics over many years [34, 48]. Although these are familiar concepts in discussions around virtual experiences, immersion, presence, co-presence, flow, and simulation realism are often given cursory attention in commercial software developments for P2E gaming and the negative impact of pursuing the physical world authenticity in IVEs for PSW gaming.

The metaverse we are currently presented with is a misappropriated concept that lacks critical appreciation. It serves as a buzzword for attempts to establish and expand networks of IVE's with varied aims, including the promotion of online social connectivity, participation, and engagement, productivity, digital marketing, but also inherently involving the capture of user attention, time, the value they create, or money they are actively willing to spend. The more the metaverse replicates the physical world, the less its claim to autonomy can be substantiated. In the case of AR, AR overlays digital content on the physical world; therefore, the content may be autonomous, but it must also refer to the world around the user. While VR fails to provide complete user autonomy from the physical world, AR aggressively engages with it. Nonetheless, the social aspects of metaverse environments are promising. The most successful platforms have pursued mixed realities' social and participatory elements. Companies like Meta have seized on this as their primary means for expanding their services and user base.

Following Ball's definition, our current aspirations and criticisms for the metaverse include concerns for scale, interoperability, synchronicity, persistence, presence, and continuity of data encompassing the identity, history, entitlements, objects, communications, and payments of users [2]. Still, it facilitates its users to engage with physical space and place narratives within a digital realm, presenting many challenges for cross-platform community engagement [10]. Although problematic in their current state, multimodal interactions in XR can combine sensory displays of the metaverse, provide a richer set of interactions for embodied interaction, and enhance our sense-making abilities when experiencing IVEs in the metaverse.

3   Aesthetics, Sensibility, and Sense-Making

In contemporary art theory, aesthetics is typically associated with ideas of beauty and judgment, with the beautification of the art object, the production of ornament, and the cultivation of "good taste". In these terms, aesthetic appreciation emphasizes the subjective pleasure taken in the reception of art. In Fuller and Weizman's recent work, they explore an alternative concept of aesthetics deriving from the ancient Greek term "aisthesis", which describes much more broadly and inclusively 'that which pertains to the senses' [13, p. 33]. Here aesthetics concerns not just the passive reception of stimuli but also the active construction of experience: sensing and sense-making. Here sensing is "the capacity to register or be affected" while sense-making is "the capacity for sensing to become knowledge". Furthermore, they argue that "to aestheticise something is not to prettify or decorate it, but to render it more attuned to sensing" [13, p. 33]. Strikingly their theory of aesthetics and aestheticization is not limited to the refinement and augmentation of human capacities for sensing but also extends to the capabilities of non-human entities, such as plants, animals, inorganic substances and materials, computational sensors, and larger-scale digital infrastructures to register traces of events and encode information:

> "...the environment captures traces. Unpaved ground registers the tracks of long columns of armoured vehicles. Leaves on vegetation receive the soot of their exhaust while the soil absorbs and retains the identifying chemicals released by banned ammunition. The broken concrete of shattered homes records the hammering collision of projectiles. Pillars of smoke and debris are sucked up into the atmosphere, rising until they mix with the clouds, anchoring this strange weather at the places the bombs hit" [13, p. 1].

Aesthetics as sense-making is more than passive sensing. It involves conceiving what is being sensed as part of a global worldview. Therefore, making our senses productive requires "constructing means of sensing" [13, p. 34]. The link between this theory of aesthetics and multimodality is how multimodal technologies provide these means of sensing by enabling and modulating a user's capacity to interact and be affected by digital media in immersive environments. If someone using a VR headset loses power to the headset display while body tracking continues, they become blind. They can remove the headset and stop the simulation, or they can proceed to try to use other available devices and associated modalities to try and make sense of that experience.

Fuller and Weizman's concept of aesthetics benefits those working in multimedia environments as it focuses on developing different kinds of sensory "attunement" or "sensitization" to digital objects and their environments. By way of illustration, the context for developing their theory is the spatially informed research, advocacy, and activism of the Forensic Architecture (FA) group, which specializes in using architectural visualization and spatial analysis to support the investigation of state violence and human rights violations. What distinguishes their work is the extensive modeling of architectural and urban spaces in 3D, which then act as spatiotemporal references for the analysis of different evidentiary media such as photographs, audio, and video to verify eye-witness testimony.

FA does not create metaverse-like applications; instead, each 3D environment they build functions as an operative "device" or "model" that acts as a "navigational platform" and a "way of inhabiting an environment of simultaneous media" [13, p. 6]. What matters in this approach is the process of sensing and sense-making, both by human users and by way of different interaction technologies and modeled features of the depicted environments. By virtue of the range of media they work with, FA's analyses and outputs are inherently multisensory. And while their analyses often focus on visibly or audibly perceptible evidence, their forensic approach also seeks to reveal and communicate evidential traces of processes that human perception could not register.

One case they investigated using these methods was the Saydnaya torture prison in Syria. At the time, there were no images of the prison in the public domain, and the prisoners who survived their experiences had typically been kept in the dark or blindfolded. Nonetheless, the FA team created a three-dimensional representation of the facility in 2016 by drawing on interviews with surviving prisoners. In particular, they used the surviving prisoner's heightened recollections of sound to reconstruct a model of the prison interior with the aid of architectural and acoustic modeling techniques. The prisoners' auditory memories provided a fundamental means of sensing and retrospective sense-making as they worked with FA to piece together the model from each of their solitary but overlapping experiences. As they worked with researchers to refine the prison model, they also recalled new memories activated through the combination of recognizable sounds in the context of the reconstructed prison model. Virtual reality was subsequently used to communicate carefully curated aspects of their experience as part of a campaign led by Amnesty International, which called on the Syrian government to allow independent monitors into its prisons.

4   Memory, Synaesthesia, Kinaesthetics, and Chronesthesia

In discussing virtual art, Grau proposes that the end of artistic work and play with new media is "self-reflection, the awareness of inner distance and perception" [15, p. 347]. This awareness is a form of sensing and sense-making, though principally aimed at the self. According to Grau, telepresence has led us to a turning point in the "cultural history of our sensorium" whereby we can actively begin to experience the limitations and enrichment of the dominant visual sense through the incorporation of the other senses in immersive multimodal experiences [15, p. 345]. While the importance of presence is enhanced through the "maximization of realism" [15, p. 14], the development of immersion is not exclusively dependent on it. From a critical perspective, Grau sees the efficacy and motive of the technology in its power to deceive the senses to maximize suggestion and erode the user's crucial distance through the immediacy of the experience. However, interactive and multisensory environments are also performative and gamic spaces. They provide ideal settings for exploring the senses and developing aesthetic sensibility in the manner described by Fuller and Weizman as attunement to the capacities for both sensing and sense-making.

Humans typically experience the world from a first-person perspective, which is conducive to many XR experiences. Via multimedia, we can also share events from a third-person perspective, as an observer might see us. This approach to memory-building is already leveraged in education and therapy. First and third-person perspectives have been shown to directly influence the formation of memories [17] and positively impact long-term memories in older adults [45]. Therefore, XR applications can enable people to memorize items for test preparation, using visual mental aids for remembering. As a recent example of this potential, *Librarium* has launched a VR memory palace platform on the Meta Quest 2, a visual cognitive memory aid that can improve memory retention using the method of loci. Furthermore, lifelike IVEs are potentially helpful in retraining spatial awareness following a stroke by using third-person perspectives to enhance spatial memory [6]. VR may also improve memory function by enhancing focused attention [29].

Synesthesia is a perceptual and spatial phenomenon where an attribute of a stimulus, such as a sound, shape, meaning, etc., leads to the conscious experience of an additional attribute [47]. Several real-time VR techniques and applications have been explored for sound and music visualization, localization and visualization, and digital environments versus photographic [19,30,36]. Similarly, the Synesthesia Suit provides an immersive embodied experience in an IVE by applying vibrotactile sensations on the user's body [18]. *Richie's Plank* demonstrates the power of six-degrees-of-freedom navigability and synesthesia in VR. Multimodal stimulus is used for entering an elevator to press a button physically. The experience applies spatial audio to shift the user's focus from the external CGI urban environment to the elevator's interior. The elevator then ascends, giving the user a glimpse of the world through a crack in the door, providing an upward motion sensation. Once it reaches its final destination, the elevator opens to reveal a wooden plank that reaches out from the door with a sheer drop below, inducing a sense of height and vertigo. If the user steps or falls off the plank, the visual field shifts upward, giving the user the sensation of rushing toward the ground.

Kinesthetics is the study of body motion, including the conscious and unconscious perception of bodily movements. VR is often lauded as a platform that affords embodied learning due to its immersiveness, use of natural user interfaces, and body-tracking capabilities. For example, the natural affordances of VR can be leveraged as a platform for language education, connecting language and body to enhance the way we learn [44]. Another prominent example of kinesthetics can be seen in OSMOSE, a VR experience that applied breath and balance with a visual aesthetic based on transparency and spatial ambiguity [9]. The "immersant" in Osmose wears a vest of sensors that controls the experience while the HMD provides visual feedback. The experience was inspired by sea diving and used the unconscious physical process of breathing to enhance immersion. The sense of embodied presence is heightened by music and sound. Davies hoped virtual environments like Osmose would enable people to explore their experience of "being-in-the-world" [15, p. 199]. Solitude was felt to be a prerequisite for immersion in Osmose to avoid distraction. Davies's artistic intention was to embody mental models or abstract constructs through kinesthetic and synaesthetic interaction. The user's virtual embodiment in three dimensions was felt to be the best means to achieve this sense of full-body immersion. The user's emotional involvement reduced their recognition of the experience as a construction. Despite its strengths, Osmose also raised concerns regarding participants' susceptibility to visual suggestion and invoked phobic reactions to immersion in water. Instead of aiming at realism, Grau analogically likens the effect of Osmose to the painterly technique of sfumato, which is a softening of the transition between colors similar to that experienced by the human eye at the edges of focus [15]. In a more frenetic register recent rhythm-driven triple-A game Beat Saber uses the rhythm of a musical track to guide physical body motions.

Chronesthesia, or mental time travel, is the capacity to mentally reconstruct past personal events and imagine possible future scenarios [41,43]. Academic studies have been undertaken in which researchers gave participants the ability to travel backwards in time using VR to relive a sequence of events in which they could intervene and to change history to resolve a moral dilemma [12]. Their findings indicated that participants were able to feel the illusion of "time travel" provided that they also experienced a sense of presence and agency over their avatar. They found that the experience of time travel also produced an increase in moral responses. More gamic experiences may reference past or imagined future events but typically these are experienced linearly. However, The Last Clockwinder is a VR experience in which the player records multiple motions kinesthetically which are then carried out on their behalf by avatars who replay those motions synchronously with each other in order to collaboratively undertake a task. In this way the player must project themselves forward in time to imagine the required actions of each avatar and then wait to see the result before trying again. While not strictly chronesthetic another game that plays with time as a mechanic is Superhot. In this first-person shooting game, players interrupt the forward passage of time to protect themselves from attack by holding still. When the player stops moving, the flow of game time stops. When the player moves game time speeds up proportionally. In this way, this game also incorporates kinesthetics as a mechanism for controlling the action.

The presented experiences show how a new approach to multimodality might look. However, our discussion of Fuller and Weizman's aesthetics suggests an alternate understanding of what those experiences can do and how they might be used. By focusing on the possibilities of MR concerning this aesthetics, we hope to suggest alternative paths for the development of MR beyond current trends, which converge on the production of metaverse applications oriented toward maximizing realism. Instead, we wish to promote alternatives engaging a more comprehensive range of experiences, such as those suggested by Fuller and Weizman's allusions to memory, kinesthetics, synesthesia, and chronesthesia.

5   Conclusions

The metaverse being marketed is based on the misappropriation of a concept that lacks critical appreciation. The metaverse serves as a buzzword for attempts to establish and expand commercial networks of IVE's with varied aims, including the promotion of online social connectivity, participation, and engagement, productivity, digital marketing, but also typically involving the capture of user attention, time, the value they generate through their activities on each platform, or money they are actively willing to spend there. The most successful putative metaverse platforms have pursued mixed realities' social and participatory elements. Providing social experiences has become the primary means for companies like Meta to expand their services, gain market penetration and extend their user base; whether achieved or not, they typically aim at providing heightened graphical realism and realistic experiences.

In distinction to commercial applications of 3D immersive technologies, the work of Forensic Architecture explores more meaningful uses of virtual environments. The theory of aesthetics that Fuller and Weizman derive from this work indicates broader potential for using virtual environments with multimodal technologies to develop sensibility and sense-making capacities. Their work also suggests how memory-related experiences and synaesthesia, kinaesthetics, and chronesthesia supported by multimodal technologies can help further sensing and sense-making in an immersive environment.

One of the great promises of VR adopted from science fiction, and its founding figures has always been the possibility of gaining autonomy from the physical world. However, in the founding vision of Ivan Sutherland, this autonomy would not be achieved by transcending physical matter but rather by gaining the ability to create it. Existing XR falls short of this fatal possibility. Instead, it should offer us a playground for the imagination, allowing the senses to be played with and experimentally manipulated.

Acknowledgments. This publication has emanated from research conducted with the financial support of the Science Foundation Ireland (SFI) under Grant Number 15/RP/2776, EPSRC-SFI grant number EP/T03324X/1, European Research Council (ERC) via the Data Stories project grant no. 101052998, and the Horizon Europe Framework Program (HORIZON), under the grant agreement 101070109.

References

1. Appel, G., Grewal, L., Hadi, R., Stephen, A.T.: The future of social media in marketing. J. Acad. Mark. Sci. **48**(1), 79–95 (2020)
2. Ball, M.: The Metaverse: And How It Will Revolutionize Everything. Liveright Publishing, New York (2022)
3. Barlow, J.P.: A declaration of the independence of cyberspace. Duke L. Tech. Rev. **18**, 5 (2019)
4. Bartle, R.A.: Designing Virtual Worlds. New Riders, Indianapolis (2004)
5. Blascovich, J., Loomis, J., Beall, A.C., Swinth, K.R., Hoyt, C.L., Bailenson, J.N.: Immersive virtual environment technology as a methodological tool for social psychology. Psychol. Inq. **13**(2), 103–124 (2002)
6. Borrego, A., Latorre, J., Alcañiz, M., Llorens, R.: Embodiment and presence in virtual reality after stroke: a comparative study with healthy subjects. Front. Neurol. **10**, 1061 (2019)
7. Bowman, D.A., McMahan, R.P.: Virtual reality: how much immersion is enough? Computer **40**(7), 36–43 (2007)
8. Burdea, G.C., Coiffet, P.: Virtual Reality Technology. Wiley, Hoboken (2003)
9. Davies, C.: OSMOSE: notes on being in immersive virtual space. Digital Creativity (1998)
10. Dawkins, O., Young, G.W.: Engaging Place with mixed realities: sharing multisensory experiences of place through community-generated digital content and multimodal interaction. In: Chen, J.Y.C., Fragomeni, G. (eds.) HCII 2020. LNCS, vol. 12191, pp. 199–218. Springer, Cham (2020). https://doi.org/10.1007/978-3-030-49698-2_14
11. DiPietro, J.C., Black, E.W.: Visual analysis of avatars in gaming environments. In: Handbook of Research on Effective Electronic Gaming in Education, pp. 606–620. IGI Global (2009)
12. Friedman, D., Pizarro, R., Or-Berkers, K., Neyret, S., Pan, X., Slater, M.: A method for generating an illusion of backwards time travel using immersive virtual reality—an exploratory study. Front. Psychol. **5**, 943 (2014)
13. Fuller, M., Weizman, E.: Investigative Aesthetics: Conflicts and Commons in the Politics of Truth. Verso Books, New York (2021)
14. Gibson, W.: Burning Chrome. Hachette, UK (2017)
15. Grau, O.: Virtual Art: From Illusion to Immersion. MIT press, Cambridge (2004)
16. Hsieh, M.C., Lee, J.J.: Preliminary study of VR and AR applications in medical and healthcare education. J. Nurs. Health. Stud. **3**(1), 1 (2018)
17. Iriye, H., St. Jacques, P.L.: Memories for third-person experiences in immersive virtual reality. Sci. Rep. **11**(1), 4667 (2021)
18. Konishi, Y., Hanamitsu, N., Outram, B., Minamizawa, K., Mizuguchi, T., Sato, A.: Synesthesia suit: the full body immersive experience. In: SIGGRAPH 2016 VR Village, pp. 1–1. ACM (2016)
19. Kose, A., Tepljakov, A., Astapov, S., Draheim, D., Petlenkov, E., Vassiljeva, K.: Towards a synesthesia laboratory: real-time localization and visualization of a sound source for virtual reality applications. J. Commun. Softw. Syst. **14**(1), 112–120 (2018)
20. Krueger, M.W.: Environmental technology: making the real world virtual. Commun. ACM **36**(7), 36–37 (1993)
21. Lavoie, R., Main, K., King, C., King, D.: Virtual experience, real consequences: the potential negative emotional consequences of virtual reality gameplay. Virtual Reality **25**, 69–81 (2021)

22. Lillemose, J., Kryger, M.: The (re) invention of cyberspace. Kunstkritikk Nordic Art Review (2015). https://kunstkritikk.com/the-reinvention-of-cyberspace/
23. Liu, V., Chilton, L.B.: Design guidelines for prompt engineering text-to-image generative models. In: Proceedings of the 2022 CHI Conference on Human Factors in Computing Systems, pp. 1–23 (2022)
24. Lugmayr, A., Lim, Y.J., Hollick, J., Khuu, J., Chan, F.: Financial data visualization in 3D on immersive virtual reality displays. In: Mehandjiev, N., Saadouni, B. (eds.) FinanceCom 2018. LNBIP, vol. 345, pp. 118–130. Springer, Cham (2019). https://doi.org/10.1007/978-3-030-19037-8_8
25. Mestre, D.R.: Cave versus head-mounted displays: ongoing thoughts. Electron. Imaging **29**, 31–35 (2017)
26. Mikropoulos, T.A., Natsis, A.: Educational virtual environments: a ten-year review of empirical research (1999–2009). Comput. Educ. **56**(3), 769–780 (2011)
27. Milgram, P., Kishino, F.: A taxonomy of mixed reality visual displays. IEICE Trans. Inf. Syst. **77**(12), 1321–1329 (1994)
28. Mystakidis, S.: Metaverse. Encyclopedia **2**(1), 486–497 (2022)
29. Optale, G., et al.: Controlling memory impairment in elderly adults using virtual reality memory training: a randomized controlled pilot study. Neurorehabil. Neural Repair **24**(4), 348–357 (2010)
30. Outram, B.I.: Synesthesia audio-visual interactive-sound and music visualization in virtual reality with orbital observation and navigation. In: 2016 IEEE International Workshop on Mixed Reality Art (MRA), pp. 7–8. IEEE (2016)
31. O'dwyer, N., Zerman, E., Young, G.W., Smolic, A., Dunne, S., Shenton, H.: Volumetric video in augmented reality applications for museological narratives: a user study for the long room in the library of trinity college Dublin. J. Comput. Cult. Heritage (JOCCH) **14**(2), 1–20 (2021)
32. Pacella, D.: NFT 2.0: Building fan communities and creating user engagement (2021). https://www.verizon.com/about/news/nft-20-building-fan-communities-and-creating-user-engagement
33. Pimentel, K., Teixeira, K.: Virtual Reality Through the New Looking Glass. CUMINCAD (1993)
34. Poeschl, S., Doering, N.: The German VR simulation realism scale-psychometric construction for virtual reality applications with virtual humans. Annu. Rev. Cyberther. Telemed. **11**, 33–37 (2013)
35. Qian, Y.: 3d multi-user virtual environments: promising directions for science education. Sci. Educ. **18**(2), 25–29 (2009)
36. Ross, M.: Virtual reality's new synesthetic possibilities. Telev. New Media **21**(3), 297–314 (2020)
37. Seth, A., Vance, J.M., Oliver, J.H.: Virtual reality for assembly methods prototyping: a review. Virtual Reality **15**, 5–20 (2011)
38. Shedroff, N., Noessel, C.: Make it So: Interaction Design Lessons from Science Fiction. Rosenfeld Media, New York (2012)
39. Slater, M., Sanchez-Vives, M.V.: Enhancing our lives with immersive virtual reality. Front. Robot. AI **3**, 74 (2016)
40. Stephenson, N.: Snow Crash: A Novel. Spectra, California (2003)
41. Suddendorf, T., Addis, D.R., Corballis, M.C.: Mental time travel and shaping of the human mind, pp. 344–354. M. Bar, Karnataka (2011)
42. Sutherland, I.E., et al.: The ultimate display. In: Proceedings of the IFIP Congress, vol. 2, pp. 506–508. New York (1965)
43. Tulving, E.: Memory and consciousness. Can. Psychol./Psychol. Can. **26**(1), 1 (1985)

44. Vázquez, C., Xia, L., Aikawa, T., Maes, P.: Words in motion: kinesthetic language learning in virtual reality. In: 2018 IEEE 18th International Conference on Advanced Learning Technologies (ICALT), pp. 272–276. IEEE (2018)
45. Wais, P.E., Arioli, M., Anguera-Singla, R., Gazzaley, A.: Virtual reality video game improves high-fidelity memory in older adults. Sci. Rep. **11**(1), 2552 (2021)
46. Wang, X., Young, G.W., Mc Guckin, C., Smolic, A.: A systematic review of virtual reality interventions for children with social skills deficits. In: 2021 IEEE International Conference on Engineering, Technology & Education (TALE), pp 436–443. IEEE (2021)
47. Ward, J.: Synesthesia. Annu. Rev. Psychol. **64**, 49–75 (2013)
48. Witmer, B.G., Singer, M.J.: Measuring presence in virtual environments: a presence questionnaire. Presence **7**(3), 225–240 (1998)
49. Young, G.W., O'Dwyer, N., Smolic, A.: Volumetric video as a novel medium for creative storytelling. In: Immersive Video Technologies, pp. 591–607. Elsevier (2023)

Robots and Avatars in Virtual and Augmented Reality

Detecting Swarm Degradation: Measuring Human and Machine Performance

August Capiola[1]([✉]), Dexter Johnson[1], Izz aldin Hamdan[2], Joseph B. Lyons[1], and Elizabeth L. Fox[1]

[1] Air Force Research Laboratory, Wright-Patterson AFB, OII 45433, USA
august.capiola.1@us.af.mil
[2] General Dynamics Information Technology, Dayton, OH 45431, USA

Abstract. Swarms comprise robotic assets that operate via local control algorithms. As these technologies come online, understanding how humans interact with these systems becomes more important. The present work replicated a recent experiment aimed at understanding humans' competence in identifying when and the extent to which swarms experience degradation (defined as assets breaking from consensus), as asset loss is expected in deployed swarm technologies. The present work also analyzed cluster formation in swarm simulations and explored its relationship with actual degradation. The present work replicated past findings showing people are not competent in detecting and estimating swarm degradation in flocking tasks. However, the cluster analysis showed clusters formed in simulations correlate with swarm reliability. Future work ought to expand investigations of methods to optimize cluster analysis techniques for real-time use. The implications of this work provide suggestions to interface designers on features to display to operators in human-swarm interaction.

Keywords: Human Factors · Human Performance · Human Swarm Interaction

1 Introduction

Robots are gaining ground in both capability and implementation. One domain that can benefit from the addition of robots is Urban Search and Rescue (USAR; [1]). USAR domains require rapid response to dynamic constraints; high-fidelity understanding of one's environment and the conditions of things like buildings, terrain, and human teams; and high-consequence decision-making where lives are at stake. In 2021, aerial drones were deployed to support rescue teams during the Florida Surfside Collapse. Drones provided access routes to human teams, monitored emergent fires, and provided 3-Dimensional terrain mapping capabilities. In all, drones were used in over 300 flights, making this the largest use of robots for a rescue mission in history [2]. Operators noted the immense challenge of coordination between the drone pilots, ground teams, and other emergency responders. Thus, imagine a world where one could send in a swarm of drones that could self-manage with the assistance of a human partner. While this proposition is future-oriented, research is needed today to understand factors that shape a human's ability to monitor and manage swarm technologies.

J. Y. C. Chen and G. Fragomeni (Eds.): HCII 2023, LNCS 14027, pp. 325–343, 2023.
https://doi.org/10.1007/978-3-031-35634-6_23

Robotic swarms are a unique class of robots that comprise autonomous assets functioning through local control algorithms [3]. Single robots flock and forage while being shaped by others' location and heading direction as well as environment features. Robotic swarm behaviors are based on emergent behaviors of natural swarming organisms like birds, fish [4], and sheep [5]. Researchers interested in human-swarm interaction (HSwI) often prioritize the investigation of human situation awareness on [6], comprehension of, and trust toward swarms [5]. The reason for this is that assuming swarming technologies are deployed for tasks from USAR to unmanned aerial partnerships in defense contexts [7], human understanding, perception, and action with swarming technologies ought to be explicated to facilitate appropriate human-autonomy partnerships [8]. Researchers have leveraged what is known about biological swarming systems and investigated not only how robots can emulate these decentralized complex movements to remain robust to perturbations but also how humans can(not) intuit these complex emergent behaviors [9].

We replicated work [10] that investigated human competence estimating when and to what extent swarms experience degradation (defined as a proportion of assets diverging from overall swarm consensus) in a flocking task, as well as their confidence in their estimates. As this aspect is a replication, we pose the following research question:

RQ_1: Is there a relationship between swarm asset degradation and human degradation detection accuracy, estimation of degradation, and confidence in those estimates?

We expand our investigation by testing the efficacy of cluster analysis and its relationship to objective degradation.

RQ_2: Is there a relationship between swarm asset degradation and clusters formed and asset outliers?

1.1 Human-Swarm Interaction

Human-centered research on swarms investigates HSwI. Experiments often train participants about the gist of swarming technologies, present goals for the swarm in a particular simulation, and ask people to interact with the swarm in some way [11–13]. Others have investigated peoples' interaction with swarms to find targets in an occluded environment [14]. Still, other studies show that people can be trained to intuit some swarming behaviors based on visual features, and interface affordances facilitate better human-swarm coordination [15]. Others focus on human situation awareness in HSwI [16] and display features to bolster swarm transparency [17].

There is evidence that people have trouble understanding swarm behavior [18]. Unlike human-automation scenarios or human-robot interaction (HRI) studies wherein a human would typically interact with one entity, HSwI involves interactions with multiple robots. Hayes and Adams [19] explicitly demarcate swarms ($\geq$ 50 robots) from multi-robot systems ($<$ 50 robots). Increasing the number of robots in HSwI increases uncertainty, specifically the human operators' understanding of the swarm system, and investigating human(s) supervision of large multi-robot teams in a variety of search and rescue contexts has been a goal of HRI research for decades [20].

Regardless of whether the referent is multiple individual robots or abstracted to the swarm as a whole, HSwI is a unique class of HRI. Researchers have investigated metrics inspired by biological swarms that may afford human understanding of swarm state, harkening back to differences between traditional HRI and HSwI as well as illustrating challenges of humans understanding swarm performance. Harriott et al. [21] called for more work on HSwI, particularly in reference to human performance in offering appropriate inputs in HSwI and maintaining situation awareness. In HSwI contexts, there are both the individual assets themselves as well as the overall swarm that needs to be considered. This makes the overall reliability of the swarm opaque relative to both human-automation interaction and HRI scenarios. As swarms will eventually be deployed alongside human operators, it will be important to determine when and how people appraise swarm behavior. Laboratory studies show this understanding can be trained in the lab on small swarms [13], and recent work has used simulation testbeds comprising hundreds of swarm assets to find that peoples' intuition versus actual swarm degradation does not follow the expected linear relationship [10].

In a novel within-subjects design, Capiola et al. [10] manipulated swarm asset degradation and had participants estimate when and to what extent swarms degraded, as well as their confidence in those estimates. Degradation was instantiated as a proportion of assets falling out of communication with functional assets adhering to a flocking algorithm; that is, degraded assets were no longer influenced by neighboring functional assets, but they could affect functional assets by pulling them away from the overall swarm, thus perturbing consensus. Participants in the experiment were explicitly told that degraded assets deviate from the swarm's overall flocking pattern, and degraded assets could pull functional assets away from their ongoing trajectory. This proportion of degraded assets continued in the trajectory they were on immediately before the onset of degradation until the end of each 30-s simulation.

Capiola et al. [10] found that asset degradation did affect aforementioned criteria, but this effect was not linear. Moreover, these estimations were plagued with false alarms, estimates of degradation proportion hovered around 50%, and participants' confidence in their estimates was around 5 on a 9-point scale. Taken together, Capiola et al. showed people are inaccurate in judging when and the extent to which swarms experience degradation, and they lack confidence in such perceptions. However, Capiola et al.'s analyses were limited in that they were unable to account for the unique features of assets within each block. Researchers have discussed that people may use more holistic features to determine whether assets are clustered or outlie most of the swarm [22]. These visual features may cue humans to detect swarm degradation at a nuanced level which may be undetected through Capiola et al.'s [10] lens of analysis. A reason that this is important is that identifying these features (and displaying them appropriately) may facilitate human degradation detection and ultimately improve HSwI outcomes as swarming technologies come online in defense and commercial contexts.

In the present research, we developed a novel cluster analytic method based on work from statistics [23] and cognitive architecture research [24]. We replicated the methods in Capiola et al. [10] to explore the relationship between swarm degradation and cluster formation. Through this process, we offer analytic techniques to isolate cluster and outlier formation and discuss how display designers may use these granular features to facilitate peoples' degradation detection competence in HSwI.

1.2 Cluster Analysis

First, we explain how we chose the cluster analysis techniques as candidates to provide insight into how people perceive swarms. The six major types of clustering algorithms are Connectivity-, Distribution-, Fuzzy-, Constraint-, Centroid-, and Density-based [25]. From an initial evaluation of these methods, we further evaluated centroid- and density-based algorithms. We begin with the unchosen methods and explain why they were not pursued further. For more detail on (un)chosen methods, see Prasad [25].

Connectivity-based algorithms are hierarchical. In the present study, there is no hierarchy to the cluster as all assets work together: one asset is no more important/weighted than others. Hence this method was jettisoned. With *distribution*-based algorithms, data points are placed into distributions based on the probability of them belonging. A downside is that the data must be synthetic or have defined clusters. Otherwise, if the data points are too dense, the algorithm will group them into one distribution. If the data points are spread out, then it will create many small clusters; it assumes that the data supplied has a complex underlying mathematical model controlling it. As the present study comprises swarms that are dense, non-synthetic, and follow a simple underlying mathematical model, we discarded this method. (Relative to the mathematical model controlling the swarm, complex structures may arise in flocking swarms, but the underlying model remains the same.) *Fuzzy*-based algorithms work by assigning membership values to each data point. The membership value is the likelihood that members will be within a cluster based on its relationship with the centroid, but the boundaries between clusters are not distinct because of the membership value [26]. As we wanted to account for distinct boundaries in clusters of assets, we did not pursue this method. *Constraint*-based algorithms are supervised, meaning the user can set more constraints and influence the clusters' size, location, and amount more easily which would not be useful in this application as we do not want to bias the data [25].

Centroid-based algorithms like k-means attempt to divide the data points into a predefined number of clusters. k-means selects random centroids at first and then as a cluster pulls in points, it will average the centroid so that it stays in the center of the cluster. Points can only be in one cluster, and clusters will not overlap. Researchers choose a method to determine the "optimal" number of clusters for k-means (e.g., Elbow, Silhouette). In R [27], there is a package called Nbclust [28], which provides 30 metrics researchers can run and select the cluster count that is the majority solution. Once selected, k-means will take that number and will keep cycling through the points until all points are in a cluster, and the centroids have been moved to the center of their respective clusters. However, the limitations of this method include: 1) the algorithm cannot predict the optimal number of clusters, 2) the clusters that are produced are uniform (in our experiment, the dispersion, cohesion, and alignment of assets change with the introduction of degradation; assuming or quantifying uniform clusters here is inappropriate), and 3) this method does not identify outlying data points. Hence, we chose a density-based algorithm method which we explain next.

DBSCAN stands for *density*-based spatial clustering of applications with noise. DBSCAN can identify arbitrary clusters and identify noise points in a dataset [29]. The algorithm uses two parameters: *eps*, the max distance between neighbors, and *minimum points,* the number needed for a group to be considered a cluster. The points are grouped into three categories: 1) core points, which are points that have the minimum points in their radius; 2) border points, in which there are fewer than the minimum points in their radius, but are still reachable by the core points; 3) outliers are any points that are not reachable by the core points [29]. First, the algorithm selects a random point and checks neighbors if minimum points are not present. Then, it is marked as an outlier and keeps going until the first cluster is formed. From there, it will group and add the core points and border points to the cluster. Points that are marked as outliers can be pulled into clusters if they are near enough; just because a point is marked as an outlier does not mean it will remain an outlier. This will continue until all points are visited. One downside to DBSCAN is that you do need to have some metrics for determining *eps*, otherwise you will have to tweak until the specifics you want are achieved. In our case, the simulator has a set of *eps* for controlling the assets in the swarm. We used that to determine clusters. For minimum points, one should select an amount that is greater than or equal to the dimensions $+ 1$. We chose 4 because it was the default value for 2-dimensional data [30, 31]. Other downsides to DBSCAN are that it is inefficient computationally. If you were trying to execute this, say, in real-time, then it will cause a noticeable lag spike. Also, the order of the data matters: unordered data is better as it is selecting and reading random points. The order could bias the algorithm. If the clusters are similar in density, then the algorithm will struggle with that data.

1.3 Summary

In summary, we evaluated several clustering algorithm types and selected one that fit the needs of our research question (i.e., DBSCAN). We ran this clustering method on each of the 21 unique swarm recordings comprising a unique degradation percentage to explore whether clusters and outliers emerge differently at various times over the course of each trial. From there, we could compare the clusters and outliers at the time of a) actual degradation, b) participant degradation detection response, c) 10-s after degradation onset, and d) trial end and leverage this data to discuss how people might use this visual cue in attributing degradation toward swarms (see Table 1).

2   Method

2.1 Participants

We leveraged Amazon's Mechanical Turk (MTurk), an online platform where participants (i.e., workers) self-enroll in Human Intelligence Tasks (HITs) and are paid for participation. Workers completed this study's HIT at a time and location of their choosing. We also used CloudResearch [32], a platform that integrates MTurk with online research protocols to facilitate data collection.

An *a priori* power analysis in the *WebPower* package [33] in RStudio [34] showed we needed 336 participants. With the wp.anova function, we estimated this sample assuming a medium effect size ($f = .25$), with 80% power ($\alpha = .05$) and one group (within-subjects) over 21 measurements, and a satisfied sphericity assumption.

We collected data from 394 workers. After data cleaning, we found 338 usable participants (49.4% female), aged 18–75 years ($M = 38.89$, $SD = 11.36$), accepted the

HIT, and participated for $5 remuneration plus a monetary bonus for their performance in the task. Most participants were White (76.3%), followed by Black (10.7%), Asian (7.1%), and other (5.9%). The study was approved by the Air Force Research Laboratory Institutional Review Board (protocol # FWR20200168E, v1.02).

The pros of MTurk are that we could obtain a well-powered sample. The cons, however, were that we could not monitor that participants were attending to the training, practice trials, and experiment trials, nor could we answer questions they may have had. We attempted to sidestep these limitations by assessing a slew of careless responding metrics (see Data Cleaning) and comprehension checks before participants could proceed to the experiment. This was our next-best option compared to running several hundred subjects in person, particularly during the COVID-19 Pandemic.

2.2 Experiment

We leveraged a custom swarm platform [15] constructed in Microsoft Visual Studio 2017 to record simulations of swarms flocking via consensus in a topographically barren space. We recorded each simulation with the Xbox Game Bar in Windows 10. The degradation percentage and time were specified in a text file. Each simulation comprised 256 assets within a virtual landscape sized at 500 m (meaning length and width; m^2). Non-degraded assets adhered to a particular density, cohesion, and dispersion criteria based upon preset weights in the configuration file. Only degraded assets violated these parameters. The swarm achieves a convex hull via consensus and flocks throughout the environment. In this simulation, degraded assets can draw functional assets away from the majority swarm and lead to further perturbations in the overall swarm consensus by influencing their nearest neighboring assets still flocking via consensus. Degraded assets were no longer influenced by functional assets and instead continued in the direction they were going, up until they were degraded, through the end of the trial. Though degraded assets lose their cohesive properties and can fly outside the simulation area, both degraded and functional assets are always visible as 30 s was never long enough for assets to leave the virtual environment. Assets were depicted as white triangles and originated in the center of the virtual environment. When a simulation commenced, the swarm oriented and began flocking. Each simulation comprised a different percent of asset degradation (i.e., 0–100% in increments of 5%) which degraded 10–20 s into a 30-s trial. Simulations were presented in a randomized order. Each trial began when participants pressed the *Play Video* button. They monitored the swarm and clicked *Swarm Degraded* when they perceived degradation. After each trial, participants estimated the percentage of degradation the swarm experienced and rated their confidence in that estimate. For an illustration of a trial timeline, Fig. 1 depicts a swarm experiencing 60% degradation a) 0 s into the 30-s trial, b) at the actual time of degradation (i.e., 12 s), c) at the average time participants responded *Swarm Degraded* (i.e., 18.38 s, excluding FAs and misses), and d) at trial end (i.e., 30 s).

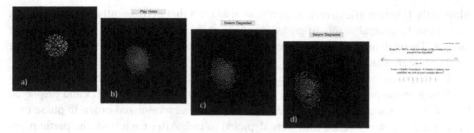

Fig. 1. Experiment trial, 60% degradation.

2.3 Measures

Response Time. During each trial, we recorded the time (milliseconds) at which participants clicked *Swarm Degraded*, denoting the time they perceived the swarm experienced degradation.

Degradation Estimates. After each trial, participants answered the question "From 0%–100%, what percentage of the swarm do you perceive has degraded?" They slid an indicator along a line (in 5% increments) to estimate the percentage of degraded assets.

Confidence. Participants answered the question "From 1 (totally uncertain) – 9 (totally certain), how confident are you in your estimate above?" indicating their confidence in their degradation estimate.

Comprehension Checks. Before the experiment, participants were quizzed on their comprehension of the task. Two sample multiple choice questions read "What does it mean when a swarm degrades?" (*answer*: assets within the swarm deviate from the overall flocking pattern of the swarm) and "True or False: if one asset degrades then the entire swarm is faulty" (*answer*: false).

2.4 Procedure

Participants completed a demographics survey followed by a PowerPoint introduction and a high-level explanation of robotic swarms. Importantly, participants learned that a swarm's goal in the present experiment was to stay together and move as a cohesive unit, and their (i.e., the participant's) goal was to detect if/when a degradation occurred in the swarm and the severity of this degradation. Degraded swarms were explained as comprising assets deviating from the consensus flocking pattern.

In training, participants read that swarms can experience problems and become degraded. Specifically, assets that are degraded go off in a direction away from the rest of the swarm, and since swarms consist of assets whose speed and heading direction are influenced by their nearest neighbors, degraded assets can affect their nearest neighbors, which can have a negative effect on the overall swarm. Training went on to describe that degraded assets deviate from a swarm's overall flocking pattern and can pull functional assets away from consensus ongoing trajectory. Degradation can lead to minor issues, in which the overall swarm of functional assets eventually recover and ultimately function effectively, or severe degradation that permanently disrupt a swarm and cause functional assets to go askew without the ability to return to the collective swarm. Throughout, participants were shown pictures of swarms experiencing varying levels of degradation.

Participants completed three training phases, each comprising five trials of swarms exploring an unspecified landscape. In all phases, each video lasted 30 s and displayed 0%–100% of assets degrading in increments of 25 in a randomized order. In phase one, the degraded assets in each trial were depicted in red. After each trial, the participants received feedback on the percentage of assets that degraded. In phase two, degraded assets were not displayed in red. However, participants were instructed to observe the *Swarm Degraded* button automatically click when the swarm degraded to train them on how to respond when they perceived degradation. Participants then estimated the percentage of assets that degraded between 0–100% in increments of 25 and rated their confidence in that estimate. Afterward, participants received feedback on their estimates. In phase three, participants pressed the *Swarm Degraded* button themselves, estimated the percentage of degradation, rated their confidence in that estimate, and received feedback. Then, they completed eight comprehension check questions.

Before the experiment trials commenced, participants learned they would receive $0.10 each time they estimated the time of degradation within 3 s following the actual degradation. They would also receive $0.10 every time their degradation estimate fell within 5% of the actual degradation. Participants then completed the 21 randomized experimental trials. After the last trial, participants received their MTurk code to claim their payment.

2.5 Data Cleaning

To ensure data quality, we assessed an attention check in phase two of the training (i.e., ensuring participants estimated 0% degraded assets after they were shown explicitly and informed that no assets degraded in the 0% trial of phase two), completion time (i.e., ensuring task engagement fell within 2.5 standard deviations of the mean completion time), and consecutive identical responses (i.e., ensuring participant did not offer the same response for any one criterion on more than 50% of trials) [35]. If participants were flagged on two or more indices, they were removed from the dataset. A total of 63 participants removed, resulting in a final sample of 371. Sphericity was violated for the degradation estimate criterion; however, a post hoc power analysis with the updated correction ($\varepsilon = 0.87$) revealed we obtained an adequately powered sample.

3 Results

First, we replicated analyses conducted in Capiola et al. [10]. Linear mixed-effects analysis was conducted in the *lme4* package [36]. Repeated-measure analysis of variance (RM ANOVA) analyses were performed using the *afex* package [37]. Post hoc comparisons were made across all 21 trials by assessing the estimated marginal means and using Tukey's method of *p*-value adjustment in the *emmeans* package [38]. Then, we explored the results of the cluster analyses. Partial correlation tests were conducted using the pcor.test function in *ppcor* [39]. All analyses were performed in RStudio [34].

3.1 Response Time

The data were first assessed for false alarms (i.e., responding a degradation occurred before one took place) and misses (i.e., withholding a response when in fact a swarm did degrade). A total of 7,791 trials (371 participants * 21 trials) were evaluated. Of these trials, 3,791 were false alarms (48.7%) and 871 were misses (11.1%), which were removed to avoid obfuscating the effect of asset degradation on response time. This led to an unequal number of cases across conditions. Therefore, we conducted a linear mixed effects analysis. Response time was regressed onto condition (percent degraded), with participant set as a random effect. Results indicated a significant effect of asset degradation on response time, $F(20, 2878.7) = 42.12, p < .001$. Indeed, 122 comparisons were significant, $ts(2913.41) \geq 3.58, ps < .05$.

The mean response times, indicating the time at which participants responded by pressing *Swarm Degraded*, were compared to the time when an *actual* degradation took place to demonstrate the accuracy of peoples' degradation detection in each trial. As mentioned, degradation onset took place between 10 and 20 s in each trial. To account for this and compare responses across trials, we calculated the difference between the actual time of swarm degradation onset and the average response time in each trial. We removed the 0% trial in the subsequent correlation analysis since any response was a false alarm. The correlation between a) actual degradation onset and b) the average difference from the actual onset of degradation and participants' responses was not significant, $r = -0.06, p = .8$. Thus, we did *not* find evidence that as actual degradation increased so too did participants' degradation accuracy increase.

3.2 Degradation Estimates

We analyzed the effect of actual degradation on participants' estimates of swarm degradation with RM ANOVA. There was a significant effect of actual degradation on estimated degradation, $F(17.31, 6404.98) = 169.43, p < .001, \eta^2 = .314$. Post hoc comparisons of means (i.e., degradation estimates in each trial) showed 164 comparisons were significant, $ts(7791) > 3.64, ps < .05$.

We used the following formula to determine the discrepancy between the *estimated* from *actual* percent of degradation for each trial:

$$Deviation\ from\ Actual\ Degradation = |Estimated\ \%\ of\ Assets\ Degraded\ -\ Actual\ \%\ of$$
$$Assets\ Degraded|$$

(1)

The absolute value of the difference was taken to determine how far off the estimates of degradation were from the actual percent of degradation while ignoring the directionality of the difference in the estimate (see Fig. 2). The value on each bar represents the number of clusters and outliers, respectively, present at the end of each trial (see Table 2). We found a positive correlation between the deviation from actual degradation and the percent of assets degraded, $r(18) = [.639], p = [.002]$. Figure 2 illustrates the discrepancy between participants' perception of and actual degradation in each trial, allowing us to observe over and underestimation of degradation. Together, participants' proficiency in estimating the percent of degradation diminishes as actual degradation increases.

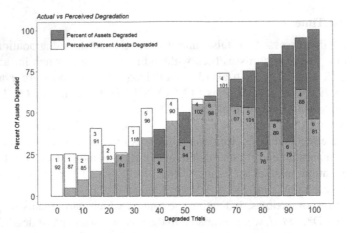

Fig. 2. Actual versus perceived degradation.

3.3 Confidence

The effect of asset degradation on participants' confidence in their estimates of degradation was analyzed with RM ANOVA. Asset degradation had a significant effect on confidence, $F(17.29, 6398.14) = 13.70$, $p < .001$, $\eta^2 = .036$. Post hoc comparisons showed 72 significant comparisons, $ts(7791) > 3.064$, $ps < .05$. This replicates the results found in [10]: when we inspected the mean values of confidence, participants' confidence was about 5 on the 9-point scale. This may indicate people are unsure of their predictions or that participants' confidence fluctuates greatly resulting in a central mean score per trial.

3.4 Cluster Analysis

We investigated the number of clusters and outliers present at a) the time of degradation, b) the average *perceived* time of degradation (i.e., when participants pressed *Swarm Degraded*), c) 10-s after degradation onset, and c) the end of each of the 21 trials both with and without false alarms and misses excluded from analysis (see Tables 1 and 2). The number of clusters and outliers at the time of degradation did not fluctuate much. When a degradation occurred, the swarm comprised one or two clusters and anywhere from 31–79 outliers. Based on the data in Table 2, it seems that there is not a linear relationship between the number of clusters or outliers and the percent of degraded assets *at the time* a degradation occurs. This is expected because when a degradation occurs, the swarm does not immediately disperse; it takes a few seconds for the degraded assets to diverge from consensus.

We investigated the number of clusters and outliers at the time participants perceived a degradation (Table 1). To do this, we removed false alarms and misses, then we took the average time for each trial that participants pressed *Swarm Degraded*. At the average time of perceived degradation, the swarm comprised anywhere from 1.21–4.41 clusters and 46.11–94.46 outliers. There did not seem to be a pattern between the number of clusters and outliers present during each trial at the time participants perceived a degradation to have occurred, and this did not appear to change when false alarms and misses were included.

Lastly, we investigated the number of clusters and outliers present at the end of each trial, at which time swarms consisted of one to eight clusters and 76–118 outliers. Based on Table 2, it seemed there was a positive relationship between the number of clusters at the end of each trial and the percent of assets that degraded. Conversely, there does not seem to be a linear relationship between the number of outliers at the end of each trial and the percent of degraded assets. To further investigate the utility of cluster analyses, we ran a linear regression to quantify the relationship between the number of clusters formed at the end of each trial and the *actual* percentage of asset degradation at the end of each trial. The results showed this relationship was significant, $t(19) = 4.249$, $r = .70$, $p < .001$. As actual asset degradation increases so too does the number of clusters identified with the selected DBSCAN method. The time swarms could degrade was different for each trial (i.e., degradation took place between 10 and 20 s in each trial, except for the 0% trials). Statistically controlling for the time at which the swarm experienced a degradation, we still find that this relationship is strong, $r = .69$, $p < .001$, using a partial correlation test. To further account for the variance in degradation onset in each trial, we investigated the correlation between the clusters formed 10 s after degradation occurred (not including the 0% degradation trial as there was no value for degradation time) and the actual percentage degraded and found this relationship remained significant, $t(18) = 2.64$, $r = .528$, $p = .0166$.

Table 1. DBSCAN Cluster Analysis and Human Responses.

Actual		Percieved Degradation (Full)					Percieved Degradation (No FA or Misses)				
Percent of Assets Degraded	Time	Time	Time Relative to Actual Degradation	Number of Clusters	Number of Outliers	Percent of Assets Degraded	Time	Time Relative to Actual Degradation	Number of Clusters	Number of Outliers	Percent of Assets Degraded
0	0	21.03	NA	1.23	63.91	25.03	NA	NA	NA	NA	0
5	20	18.22	-1.78	1.17	57.21	25.43	23.14	3.14	1.21	78.21	21.96
10	18	18.71	0.71	2.00	59.06	24.66	21.53	3.53	1.74	69.66	23.49
15	10	16.33	6.33	2.08	51.91	40.66	16.91	6.91	2.19	54.28	41.22
20	13	20.36	7.36	2.71	58.59	30.67	20.64	7.64	3.29	59.40	34.48
25	15	20.43	5.43	2.53	62.18	26.11	23.14	8.14	2.72	68.48	27.58
30	16	17.58	1.58	1.92	74.90	41.67	22.11	6.11	2.38	94.46	38.06
35	19	15.31	-3.69	1.73	52.94	52.80	23.02	4.02	2.08	82.08	48.78
40	13	21.08	8.08	3.13	66.07	22.96	21.39	8.39	3.57	67.39	31.14
45	13	14.08	1.08	1.91	37.90	58.49	16.86	3.86	2.21	46.11	56.73
50	20	17.20	-2.80	1.98	58.76	32.08	22.92	2.92	2.80	70.08	27.64
55	10	15.10	5.10	2.29	50.29	58.03	15.70	5.70	2.34	52.91	58.59
60	12	15.93	3.93	3.02	61.55	57.26	18.38	6.38	3.41	71.08	55.83
65	13	14.99	1.99	1.96	53.11	73.72	18.44	5.44	2.36	63.69	72.00
70	19	16.98	-2.02	1.37	57.99	53.48	23.55	4.55	1.89	77.11	50.48
75	14	16.01	2.01	2.82	60.91	52.94	19.16	5.16	3.68	71.84	52.76
80	17	17.21	0.21	2.17	56.64	27.96	22.99	5.99	2.58	70.06	32.88
85	18	16.40	-1.60	3.00	65.15	45.23	23.24	5.24	4.41	84.05	46.42
90	20	18.48	-1.52	2.49	53.36	32.30	25.80	5.80	2.19	70.01	29.48
95	15	17.34	2.34	2.41	64.50	63.85	20.60	5.60	2.55	76.30	64.66
100	18	15.59	-2.41	1.95	62.41	45.94	22.43	4.43	1.81	84.33	42.94

Table 2. DBSCAN Cluster Analysis Utility.

Percent of Assets Degraded	Actual Degradation				10 Seconds After Degradation				End Degradation		
	Time	Number of Clusters	Number of Outliers	Assets in Each Cluster	Time	Number of Clusters	Number of Outliers	Assets in Each Cluster	Number of Clusters	Number of Outliers	Assets in Each Cluster
0	0	NA	NA	NA	NA	NA	NA	NA	1	92	164
5	20	1	64	181	30	1	87	168	1	87	168
10	18	2	51	190_2	28	3	79	169_3_5	2	85	166_5
15	10	1	47	226	20	1	64	192.00	3	91	153_8_4
20	13	2	60	224_2	23	3	72	173_7_4	2	93	180_4
25	15	1	46	208	25	3	72	179_3_2	4	91	154_4_4_3
30	16	1	77	179	26	2	107	145_4	1	118	138
35	19	1	62	194	29	5	97	145_2_6_3_3	5	96	138_3_7_3_9
40	13	2	36	217_3	23	6	77	159-4-5-4-3-4	4	92	150-4-6-4
45	13	1	38	218	23	4	68	176-4-4-4	4	90	135-20-9-2
50	20	2	67	87_2	30	4	94	152-4-4-2	4	94	152-4-4-2
55	10	2	31	223_2	20	3	67	175-8-6	4	102	139-7-3-5
60	12	1	47	209	22	6	80	151-4-5-6-6-4	6	98	132-9-4-6-4-3
65	13	1	42	218	23	6	82	4-153-2-4-7-4	4	101	134-16-2-3
70	19	1	69	187	29	1	99	157.00	1	97	159
75	14	1	58	198	24	8	90	139_4_7_3_4_2_3_4	5	104	132_7_7_3_3
80	17	1	64	192	27	5	74	169_5_3_2_3	5	76	158_8_5_5_4
85	18	2	73	179_4	28	5	96	143_5_4_4_4	8	89	102_38_8_4_4_4_3_4
90	20	1	64	192	30	6	79	157_5_4_4_4_3	6	79	157_5_4_4_4_3
95	15	1	66	190	25	4	83	155_7_7_4	4	88	156_4_4_4
100	18	2	79	175_2	28	4	91	155_3_3_4	6	81	149_10_5_4_5_2

4 Discussion

Humans make attributions toward robotic swarms that are not necessarily part and parcel with that system's performance [40]. Though humans can be trained (to some extent) to recognize swarm performance [13], it will become necessary to keep operators in the loop when HSwI becomes commonplace as a capability for commercial and military missions and these systems behave in unexpected ways [41]. Humans may struggle to understand swarm performance due to their lack of transparency [18], and recent work has shown this to be the case in contexts where humans monitor simulations of flocking swarms [10]. The present work sought to perform analyses of swarm clusters to explore how these features might be used as cues to facilitate the detection of asset degradation in HSwI.

Replicating findings from Capiola et al. [10], the results of the present work show that people are not incredibly competent at detecting swarm degradation and estimating the proportion of asset degradation in a flocking simulation. We found no evidence that people are differently (in)competent at *detecting* swarm degradation at different levels of degradation. However, after a swarm simulation concluded, people were worse at *estimating* the extent of swarm degradation at higher degrees of actual asset degradation. With the high prevalence of false alarms and low confidence in performance, it is clear people need some kind of decision support system (DSS) to aid their detection of swarm perturbations.

We incentivized participants to detect degradation onset during each trial. However, as there was no penalty for false alarms, participants may have simply offered a response even when they did not perceive a degradation. This may explain the high false alarm rate in the present study. Over time, degradation becomes more detectable as the swarm increases in spread. Degraded assets continue a trajectory and are not influenced by functional assets, but functional assets are influenced by these offline nearest neighbors. Though the correlation was still significant 10 s after degradation onset, even the results of our cluster analysis were more strongly related to actual degradation when implemented at the end of the 30-s trial. Hence, humans may perform better at estimating degradation onset and degree if they could view the swarm forage for a longer period.

The novel approach to evaluating and leveraging density-based cluster analysis showed such analytic approaches may be useful. Indeed, the strong correlation between actual swarm degradation and cluster formation provides evidence that this method could be a useful aide for humans in HSwI. In situations where operators wish to monitor friendly robotic swarms, these tools may help track perturbations in swarm cohesion seconds after degradation occurs. In other situations, operators wishing to monitor unknown or enemy swarms may leverage these tools to monitor status reports on swarms to track the effects of forces (e.g., targeted attack, weather disruption) on those swarms' cohesion. As the present research was a laboratory-based simulation, the researchers had privileged access to swarm dynamics such as control algorithm details and pre-defined degradation time. Still, a process by which clustering analysis selects an appropriate method and tracks swarm features based on a rolodex of parameters (e.g., values, weights) is one novel way operators might leverage DSS tools in HSwI. *If* we could track clusters in real-time, *then* we could provide feedback to operators. We hope that applied research initiatives use these methods for developing real-time cluster analysis techniques as DSSs in HSwI.

4.1 Implications and Future Research

The work highlights the need for transparency in HSwI. Transparency remains a critical element of human-machine interaction [42] and these benefits will apply to HSwI as well, though different methods are likely needed. For instance, Chen et al.'s [43] model of transparency was inspired by Endsley's [44] work on situation awareness and has been applied to thinking about transparent HSwI. Indeed, Hepworth et al. [45] have prioritized instantiating the tenets of transparency (i.e., interpretability, explainability, and predictability) in HSwI and have proposed a human-swarm-teaming transparency and trust architecture, or HST3-Architecture, which facilitates trustworthy HSwI.

Transparency methods for human-agent interaction can include methods for establishing awareness, understanding, and projection of the agent [43]. HRI researchers have emphasized the need for human-centered design in HRI, leveraging best practices from human factors in interface design to account for and facilitate human situation awareness and decision-making (among other things; [16]). Adams et al. [9] discuss the difficulties facilitating transparency of robotic swarm systems, as humans struggle to intuit swarm performance without the ability to ground appropriately to any one point of a swarm's state. For instance, Hussein, Elsawah, and Abbass [17] manipulated features (reliability, transparency) of small swarms comprising 20 robots and investigated their effects on trust and reliance criteria (see also [46]). They showed that in a target collection task, participants' trust toward swarms was positively related to reliance and negatively related to response latency. Moreover, reliability-based trust was associated with fewer correct rejections, while transparency-based trust was positively associated with this criterion. These results show the importance of swarm transparency shaping HSwI outcomes, particularly trust calibration and appropriate reliance.

Methods focused on human-automation interaction (e.g., DSSs) provide rationale to support recommendations [47]. Transparency approaches for swarms may need to be developed at the swarm-level versus at the level of each individual asset. Related work from Roundtree et al. [6] investigated the effect of displaying swarms comprising 200 assets as abstract collectives or individual assets much like the present work. Their rationale was that the latter may overload operators' understanding of the swarm state. Participants were instructed to aid swarms (displayed as collective or individual assets) in selecting high-value targets sequentially in a best-of-n search decision task. Collective swarms led to better performance, lower decision time, and greater situation awareness compared to individual swarm displays. However, collective displays led to more information requests from operators, which may indicate more engagement but less trust toward the swarm displayed as a collective. We provided a solution for a limitation of Capiola et al.'s [10] research by tracking clusters at the time of a) degradation onset, b) participant response time, and c) the end of each trial, as well as after 10-s of degradation onset in each simulation. Extending this analytic process—that is, tracking cluster fluctuation based on an evaluation of parameters and values in real-time—is the next step for software engineers to optimize and interface designers to display, respectively. Still, the value added in the current work comes from showing cluster analysis *could* be used in degradation detection, as detected clusters were strongly correlated with actual degradation.

In a battlespace where communication/connectivity between friendly (and possibly foe) assets cannot be verified, cluster analysis may provide a useful tool humans can intuit to estimate the percentage of degradation of robotic swarms. In a future congested airspace, the cluster analysis methods discussed herein could provide a practical quick assessment of swarm health. Cluster analysis could also provide a method to detect low and slow cyber-attacks which may be otherwise too subtle for human detection [48]. Researchers have investigated different display visualizations to facilitate effective HSwI [49], unsurprisingly showing that contextual constraints and task goals affect which swarm visualization to obtain human situation awareness is preferred. In the present experiment, humans were not accurate judges of swarm reliability; thus, operators will need assistance from DDSs.

If a tool were able to (in real-time) either identify that a cluster is getting wider than a specified parameter, or that a large number of assets are beyond a range specified *a priori*, then such a tool would allow operators to recognize possible issues or areas of interest. Consider an example: a signal jammer in the field causes assets to lose communication with their overall swarm. If operators notice that the assets are becoming corrupted and drifting away from the swarm in a specific area, it will allow them to gain intelligence that there may be a signal disrupting device in the area. In the case of future real-time application studies, if one were able to, say, train a decision tree to take previous runs of cluster analysis, swarm flight patterns, their encounters, and how the swarm reacted, one could give the swarm greater autonomy, helping it speed up response time and the ability to notify the operator of what it has encountered. Then, operator intervention would only be necessary as swarms encounter new stimuli, which would result in fewer assets being lost and greater information being gathered.

Identifying when and the extent to which perturbations affect swarm coherence is important *even before* asset loss detracts from swarm performance. Even though minor asset degradation (as defined in the current experiment) may not substantively affect the goals of a flocking swarm, users would not want to "wait until something goes wrong" to react; observing gradual degradation of asset functionality will prepare operators to update their perceptions in time. Thus, we believe the utility of cluster algorithms as DSSs is one option to leverage to help humans stay in the loop in HSwI.

4.2 Limitations

The current study is not without limitations. We were unable to show the variance accounted for by cluster analysis in criteria of interest (i.e., response times, degradation proportion estimated, and confidence) beyond the effect of the independent variable, *actual* degradation proportion. This is because the former is nested within the latter: clusters formed and actual degradation in each trial were *not* orthogonal. However, as clusters formed strongly correlated with actual degradation, we still insist clusters are a useful heuristic for approximating degradation. Some findings seemed anomalous which could raise concerns regarding the linearity of the effect of swarm degradations on clusters. This was most notable in the 30% and 70% degradation trials.

Running several simulations over and again, for instance, the 30 and 70%, trials which resulted in only one cluster at the end of the trial, might offer a more accurate assessment of cluster algorithm utility. In a subsequent follow-on, one might run the simulation with varying degrees of degradation (i.e., 0–100%) multiple times to quantify the utility of these algorithms at detecting degradation in general. Assuming that you could run through meaningful parameters, for example, an *eps* value (as in the current case), a density-based method could identify clusters in real-time when communication and tracking of individual assets are not possible (e.g., a friendly force has degraded sensor communication; an unfriendly force is detected in an area surveyed by friendly swarms). Though real-time use of the present DBSCAN method would lead to lag, future work may wish to optimize a method to cycle through evaluations thereby making cluster analysis desirable for intelligence, surveillance, and reconnaissance.

On this note, this approach using cluster analysis as a DSS is a first step toward assisting humans to detect and comprehend swarm performance in HSwI, necessitating replication and extension. There most certainly are other alternatives, and future work should test these alternatives as well as compare their efficacy with our proposed method in more ecologically valid simulations and real-world environments.

The final parameters we chose were conservative and grounded mostly based on the parameters in the swarm simulator platform and real-world application. This afforded greater experimental control. We did explore a few other steps to observe *how* or *if* they would affect the results. Specifically, we lowered the minimum points from four to three. We ultimately chose four because the literature [30, 31] and practice [50] note that if points are 2-dimensional, four should be used to mimic real-world values. Since reality is 3-dimensional, using the smaller minimum point value resulted in smaller, more numerous clusters and fewer outliers; however, the smaller clusters were nearly indiscernible in the simulator.

From there, we proceeded to alter the *eps* but we discovered between 3.5 and 5.0, there are little, if any, notable differences. To make the cluster analysis tool more useful, we explored implementing a marker that could raise the *eps* according to time and distance. We implemented this change in Python to alter the *eps* based on the coordinates the swarm covers as it spreads and contracts so that the "optimal" *eps* could be determined for a given simulation, reducing the number of outliers, but there were still some strange cases where outliers exceeded expectations. Future work should explore processes to select and test varying parameters and values in density-based cluster analysis, as well as other software languages to run test cases on cluster analysis methods. A process by which cluster analysis is implemented and iterated in real-time is beyond the scope of the current work but ought to be investigated in future iterations.

We did not assess colorblindness in our sample. Ishihara colorblindness tests are not as reliable when assessed online, and although our experiment trials comprised white assets foraging on a black background, we should have assessed self-reported colorblindness as 1 in 12 men experience some degree of colorblindness. Finally, we did not give participants a reason as to why the swarm degraded, and future work should investigate this as some causes (e.g., weather events) may lead to different human perceptions of and reliance on the swarm compared to others (e.g., system hack, direct attack from an enemy).

4.3 Conclusions

Swarms offer the potential to bring mass effects through emergent control parameters enabling individual assets to work collectively toward an objective, yet swarms come at a risk. We replicated a now semi-robust finding that humans have difficulty judging the reliability of simulated swarms flocking via consensus. HSwI requires unique solutions for elements such as transparency. Cluster analysis may serve as a cue to human operators to signal swarm degradation. While the current results are encouraging, additional research is warranted to clarify and replicate these effects.

Acknowledgements. Distribution A. Approved for public release; distribution unlimited. AFRL-2022-0735; Cleared 17 February 2022. The views, opinions, and/or findings contained in this article are those of the author and should not be interpreted as representing the official views or policies, either expressed or implied, of the U.S Air Force, Air Force Research Laboratory, or the Department of Defense. This research was supported, in part, by the Air Force Research Laboratory (contract # FA-8650-16-D-6616).

References

1. Chiou, E.K., et al.: Towards human–robot teaming: Tradeoffs of explanation-based communication strategies in a virtual search and rescue task. Int. J. Social Robot. **14**(5), 1117–1136 (2022)
2. Murphy, R.R.: How robots helped out after the surfside condo collapse. In: IEEE Spectrum, pp. 1–2. IEEE, New York, NY (2021)
3. Kolling, A., Walker, P., Chakraborty, N., Sycara, K., Lewis, M.: Human interaction with robot swarms: A survey. Trans. Hum.-Mach. Syst. **46**(1), 9–26 (2016)

4. Brambilla, M., Ferrante, E., Birattari, M., Dorigo, M.: Swarm robotics: a review from the swarm engineering perspective. Swarm Intell. **7**, 1–41 (2013)
5. Abbass, H.A., Hunjet, R.A.: Smart shepherding: towards transparent artificial intelligence enabled human-swarm teams. In: Shepherding UxVs for Human-Swarm Teaming An Artificial Intelligence Approach to Unmanned X Vehicles, Part of the Unmanned System Technologies book series (UST), pp. 1–28. Springer, Manhattan, NY, (2021)
6. Roundtree, K.A., Cody, J.R., Leaf, J., Onan Demirel, H., Adams, J.A.: Visualization design for human-collective teams. In: Proceedings of the Human Factors and Ergonomics Society Annual Meeting, vol. 63, no. 1, pp. 417–421. SAGE Publications, Los Angeles, CA (2019)
7. Chung, T.H.: DARPA Offensive Swarm-Enabled Tactics (OFFSET): advancing swarm capabilities. Presented at the Autonomy Community of Interest Scalable Teaming of Autonomous Systems Working Group, DARPA (2020)
8. Lewis, M., Li, H., Sycara, K.: Chapter 14 – Deep learning, transparency, and trust in human robot teamwork. In: Trust in Human-Robot Interaction, pp. 321–352. Academic Press, Cambridge, Massachusetts (2020)
9. Adams, J.A., Chen, J.Y., Goodrich M.A.: Swarm transparency. In: Companion of the 2018 ACM/IEEE International Conference on Human-Robot Interaction, pp. 45–46. IEEE, New York, NY (2018)
10. Capiola, A., Hamdan, I., Fox, E.L., Lyons, J.B., Sycara, K., Lewis, M.: "Is something amiss?" Investigating individuals' competence in estimating swarm degradation. Theor. Issues Ergon. Sci. **23**(5), 562–587 (2021)
11. Hamdan, I., et al.: Exploring the effects of swarm degradations on trustworthiness perceptions, reliance intentions, and reliance behaviors. In: Proceedings of the Human Factors and Ergonomics Society Annual Meeting, vol. 65, no. 1, pp. 1141–1145. SAGE Publications, Los Angeles, CA (2021)
12. Walker, P., Lewis, M., Sycara, K.: The effect of display type on operator prediction of future swarm states. In: 2016 IEEE International Conference on Systems, Man, and Cybernetics (SMC), pp. 002521–002526. IEEE, New York, NY (2016)
13. Nagavalli, S., Chien, S.Y., Lewis, M., Chakraborty, N., Sycara, K.: Bounds of neglect benevolence in input timing for human interaction with robotic swarms. In: Proceedings of the Tenth Annual ACM/IEEE International Conference on Human-Robot Interaction, pp. 197–204. IEEE, New York, NY (2015)
14. Capiola, A., et al.: The effects of asset degradation on human trust in swarms. In: International Conference on Human-Computer Interaction, pp. 537–549. Nova, Hauppauge, New York (2020)
15. Walker, P., Nunnally, S., Lewis, M., Kolling, A., Chakraborty, N., Sycara, K.: Neglect benevolence in human control of swarms in the presence of latency. In: 2012 IEEE International Conference on Systems, Man, and Cybernetics (SMC), pp. 3009–3014. IEEE, New York, NY (2012)
16. Adams, J.A.: Critical considerations for human-robot interface development. In: Proceedings of 2002 AAAI Fall Symposium, pp. 1–8. AAAI Press, Washington, DC (2002)
17. Hussein, A., Elsawah, S., Abbass, H.A.: The reliability and transparency bases of trust in human-swarm interaction: principles and implications. Ergonomics **63**(9), 1116–1132 (2020)
18. Roundtree, K.A., Goodrich, M.A., Adams, J.A.: Transparency: transitioning from human-machine systems to human-swarm systems. J. Cogn. Eng. Decis. Mak. **13**(3), 171–195 (2019)
19. Hayes, S.T., Adams, J.A.: Human-swarm interaction: Sources of uncertainty. In: 2014 9th ACM/IEEE International Conference on Human-Robot Interaction (HRI), pp. 170–171. IEEE, New York, NY (2014)
20. Adams, J.A.: Human-robot interaction design: understanding user needs and requirements. In: Proceedings of the Human Factors and Ergonomics Society Annual Meeting, vol. 49, no. 3, pp. 447–451. Sage Publications, Los Angeles, CA (2005)

21. Harriott, C.E., Seiffert, A.E., Hayes, S.T., Adams, J.A.: Biologically-inspired human-swarm interaction metrics. In: Proceedings of the Human Factors and Ergonomics Society Annual Meeting, vol. 58, no. 1, pp. 1471–1475. SAGE Publications, Los Angeles, CA (2014)
22. Walker, P., Lewis, M., Sycara, K.: Characterizing human perception of emergent swarm behaviors. In: 2016 IEEE International Conference on Systems, Man, and Cybernetics (SMC), pp. 002436–002441. IEEE, New York, NY (2016)
23. Im, H.Y., Zhong, S.H., Halberda, J.: Grouping by proximity and the visual impression of approximate number in random dot arrays. Vision. Res. 126, 291–307 (2016)
24. Lindstedt, J.K., Byrne, M.D.: Simple agglomerative visual grouping for ACT-R. In: Proceedings of the 16th International Conference on Cognitive Modeling, pp. 68–73. ACS Publications, Washington, DC (2018)
25. Prasad, S.: Different types of clustering methods and applications. Analytix Labs (2022) https://www.analytixlabs.co.in/blog/types-of-clustering-algorithms/
26. Fuzzy c-means clustering algorithm, Data Clustering Algorithms (2020) https://sites.google.com/site/dataclusteringalgorithms/fuzzy-c-means-clustering-algorithm
27. R Core Team: The R Project for Statistical Computing, R Foundation for Statistical Computing (2022)
28. Charrad, M., Ghazzali, N., Boiteau, V., Niknafs, A.: NbClust: an R package for determining the relevant number of clusters in a data set. J. Stat. Soft 61(6), 1–36 (2014)
29. Yildirim, S.: DBSCAN clustering - explained. Medium (2020) https://towardsdatascience.com/dbscan-clustering-explained-97556a2ad556
30. Ester, M., Kriegel, H.P., Sander, J., Xu, X.: A density-based algorithm for discovering clusters in large spatial databases with noise. In: KDD proceedings, pp. 226–231, KDD, Portland, Oregon (1996)
31. Sander, J., Ester, M., Kriegel, H.P., Xu, X.: Density-based clustering in spatial databases: the algorithm gdbscan and its applications. Data Min. Knowl. Disc. 2(2), 169–194 (1998)
32. Litman, L., Robinson, J., Abberbock, T.: TurkPrime.com: a versatile crowdsourcing data acquisition platform for the behavioral sciences. Behav. Res. Methods 49(2), 433–442 (2016). https://doi.org/10.3758/s13428-016-0727-z
33. Zhang, Z., Yuan, K.H.: Practical Statistical Power Analysis Using Webpower and R. ISDA Press, New York, NY (2018)
34. RStudio Team: Open source & professional software for data science teams. RStudio: Integrated Development for R, RStudio, PBC (2022)
35. Curran, P.G.: Methods for the detection of carelessly invalid responses in survey data. J. Exp. Soc. Psychol. 66, 4–19 (2016)
36. Bates, D., Mächler, M., Bolker, B., Walker, S.: Fitting linear mixed-effects models using lme4". J. Stat. Soft. 67(1), 1–48 (2015)
37. Singmann, H., Bolker, B., Westfall, J., Aust, F., Ben-Shachar, M.S.: afex: analysis of factorial experiments. R Package Version 1.0-1 (2015)
38. Length, R.V., et al.: Estimated marginal means, aka least-squares means. R Package Version 1.7.2 (2022)
39. Kim, S.: ppcor: an R package for a fast calculation to semi-partial correlation coefficients. Commun. Stat. Appl. Methods 22(6), 665–674 (2015)
40. Nam, C., Li, H., Li, S., Lewis, M., Sycara, K.: Trust of humans in supervisory control of swarm robots with varied levels of autonomy. In: IEEE International Conference on Systems, Man, and Cybernetics (SMC), pp. 825–830. IEEE, New York, NY (2018)
41. De Visser, E.J., Pak, R., Shaw, T.H.: From 'automation' to 'autonomy': the importance of trust repair in human–machine interaction. Ergonomics 61(10), 1409–1427 (2018)
42. Chen, J.Y.C., Flemisch, F.O., Lyons, J.B., Neerincx, M.A.: Guest editorial: agent and system transparency. IEEE Trans. Hum-Mach. Syst. 50(3), 189–193 (2020)

43. Chen, J.Y.C., Lakhmani, S.G., Stowers, K., Selkowitz, A.R., Wright, J.L., Barnes, M.: Situation awareness-based agent transparency and human-autonomy teaming effectiveness. Theor. Issues Ergon. Sci. **19**(3), 259–282 (2018)
44. Endsley, M.R.: Toward a theory of situation awareness in dynamic systems. Hum. Factors **37**(1), 32–64 (1995)
45. Hepworth, A.J., Baxter, D.P., Hussein, A., Yaxley, K.J., Debie, E., Abbass, H.A.: Human-swarm-teaming transparency and trust architecture. IEEE/CAA J. Autom. Sin. **8**(7), 1281–1295 (2020)
46. Hussein, A., Elsawah, S., Abbass, H.A.: Trust mediating reliability–reliance relationship in supervisory control of human–swarm interactions. Hum. Factors **62**(8), 1237–1248 (2020)
47. Lyons, J.B., Koltai, K.S., Ho, N.T., Johnson, W.B., Smith, D.E., Shively, R.J.: Engineering trust in complex automated systems. Ergon. Des. **24**(1), 13–17 (2016)
48. Mancuso, V., Funke, G.J., Finomore, V., Knott, B.A.: Exploring the effects of "low and slow" cyber attacks on team decision making. In: Proceedings of the Human Factors and Ergonomics Society Annual Meeting, vol. 57, no. 1, pp. 389–393. SAGE Publications, Los Angeles, CA (2013)
49. Manning, M.D., Harriott, C.E., Hayes, S.T., Adams, J.A., Seiffert, A.E.: Heuristic evaluation of swarm metrics' effectiveness. In: Proceedings of the tenth annual ACM/IEEE international conference on human-robot interaction extended abstracts, pp. 17–18. IEEE, New York, NY (2015)
50. Mullin, T.: DBSCAN parameter estimation using python. Medium (2020)

Relevance-Aware Question Generation in Non-task-Oriented Dialogue Systems

Amika Chino[1](✉) and Takehiro Teraoka[2]

[1] Graduate School of Engineering, Takushoku University, Tokyo, Japan
198444@st.takushoku-u.ac.jp
[2] Department of Computer Science, Faculty of Engineering, Takushoku University,
815-1 Tatemachi, Hachioji, Tokyo 193-0985, Japan
tteraoka@cs.takushoku-u.ac.jp

Abstract. In recent years, there has been a growing interest in dialogue systems as spoken agents and communication robots become available for practical use. Much research has been conducted on non-task oriented dialogues, in which the goal is for the dialog system to interact naturally with a person. However, at present, it cannot be said that the system and people are sufficiently able to have a natural dialogue.

Therefore, this study focuses on question generation and aims to develop natural dialogue between the system and people by generating questions that take into account the relevance of the dialogue.

Here, the topic of an utterance is extracted, and related words are obtained on the basis of information associated with the extracted topic and their literal co-occurrence. Interrogative word is selected with the utterance information considering the context, and a question is generated using the acquired related word and interrogative word.

The experimental results show the effectiveness of the proposed method in generating contextualized question.

Keywords: Non-task oriented dialogue · relevance · question generation

1 Introduction

With the development of information technology, spoken dialogue agents and communication robots have been put to practical use, and interest in dialogue systems has increased. Dialogue systems can be classified into two types: task-oriented dialogue and non-task-oriented dialogue. Task-oriented dialogue is dialogue that aims to solve a problem, while non-task-oriented dialogue is so-called chat dialogue that does not aim to solve a problem. There is a survey result showing that about 60% of human-to-human dialogues are casual conversations [1]. Furthermore, the development of non-task-oriented dialogue systems is indispensable for the practical use of communication robots. Therefore, research on non-task-oriented dialogue systems has been actively conducted. However, it is difficult to say that these systems and the people that use them are having a sufficiently natural dialogue, and many issues remain to be solved.

J. Y. C. Chen and G. Fragomeni (Eds.): HCII 2023, LNCS 14027, pp. 344–358, 2023.
https://doi.org/10.1007/978-3-031-35634-6_24

In this study, we focused on one of the issues: question generation. In non-task oriented dialogue, it is necessary to elicit personal information from the user. Until now, it has been thought that dialogue will be lively if the system asks questions [2,3]. However, focusing on asking questions leads to unnatural dialogue. Generating context-sensitive questions is important for developing natural dialogue. Therefore, Katayama et al. [4] attempted to generate questions that correctly delve deeper into the utterances of the other party. The questions were acquired from Twitter data, and questions were generated by using deep learning to generate questions considering the context. They acquired question sentences from Twitter and used speech generation technology based on a neural network that applied a neural translation model using the encoder-decoder described by Vinyals et al. [5]. The problem in this study is that only the Twitter corpus was used for the training data, which differs from actual dialogues, and the transition in topics is small. In addition, because the focus is on the relationship of replies, the dialogues are in a question-and-answer format, making it difficult to understand the flow of the dialogues. By contrast, Horiuchi and Higashinaka [6] attempted response generation for generating certain questions in chat-oriented dialogue systems. First, a question guidance corpus for learning was created, and an utterance generation model was constructed that generates utterances. The question guidance corpus was created by extracting the dialogue context along with a list of target questions. The problem in this study is that the context lacks naturalness because Reddit, PersonaChat, and DailyDialog were used as training data, which is in a chat format and differs from actual dialogue.

Therefore, in this study, we aim to generate questions that develop natural dialogues by considering the relevance of the dialogues. We extract the topic of utterances and obtain related words on the basis of information associated with the extracted topic and lexical co-occurrence. An interrogative word is selected from utterance information by considering the context, and question sentences are generated using the acquired related word and interrogative word. By acquiring related word and using them in question sentence, we aim to improve the accuracy of related question generation.

2   Related Work

2.1   Dialogue System

So far, research on non-task-oriented dialogue has been conducted from a variety of approaches. In this section, we take up utterance generation, question answering, and question generation.

In utterance generation, there is study by Iulian Vlad Serban et al. [7]. This study uses a method of generating utterances with restrictions on Decode. However, it is not intended for generating questions.

Studies on question-answering include those by Iulian Vlad Serban et al. [8], Boyuan Pan et al. [9], and Stephen Roller et al. [10]. Iulian Vlad Serban et al. created a question-and-answer corpus and used a neural network to generate questions.

On the other hand, the method used in the study by Boyuan Pan et al. is based on the degree of relevance between a dialogue history consisting of questions and responses and the rationale sentences for each response.

Stephen Roller et al. built open domain chatbots that provide compelling storytelling and maintain consistent personas while appropriately displaying knowledge, empathy, and personality. These studies, like Iulian Vlad Serban et al., emphasize responses and do not aim to generate them.

Studies on question generation include research by Katayama et al. [4] and research by Horiuchi and Higashinaka [6]. Katayama et al. tried to generate questions that correctly dig deep into the utterances of the other party. However, only the Twitter corpus was used as training data, so there was a problem in that it was difficult to understand the flow of dialogue because it is in a question-and-answer format. On the other hand, Horiuchi and Higashinaka's study attempted to generate utterances to ask specific questions such as "What did you do?" However, the problem is that the context lacks naturalness.

In this study, we focused on generating question. To improve the above problems, we aim to improve accuracy by generating questions that are relevant to the topic.

2.2 Dialogue Corpora

2.2.1 Osaka University Multimodal Dialogue Corpus Hazumi

Osaka University Multimodal Dialogue Corpus Hazumi (hereinafter referred to as Hazumi) [15] is a collection of dialogues between dialogue agents and people. It is a corpus that records how a person and an agent converse on a number of topics without a specific purpose. The Wizard-of-Oz method is used for agents. It is a method in which a person called a wizard pretends to be the system and interacts with the user. Hazumi has both face-to-face and online recording versions.

2.2.2 Nagoya University Conversation Corpus

The Nagoya University Conversation Corpus (hereinafter referred to as Meidai corpus) [16] is a collection of chats of 30 min to one hour in length, mainly for graduate students. The majority of conversations are conducted in common language, but dialects are also used. The participants were informed in advance that they would be recorded. However, there are no restrictions on the content of the chat. One of the problems with the Meidai corpus data is that it is sometimes difficult to identify dialects. There are also some problems with the transcription, such as difficulty in judging the given responses, misalignment with actual pronunciation, and inaccurate transcription of unfamiliar words (place names, names of people, dialects, young people's words, etc.).

Since this study is about non-task oriented dialogues, only the data of the dialogues are used.

2.3 Associated Concept Dictionary (ACD)

2.3.1 Verb-ACD

Verb-ACD consists of three elements: stimulus words, associated words from the stimulus words with semantic relations, and word distances among the two. An association experiment was conducted on a large scale on the Web to collect information on verb associations. Stimulus words are assumed to be basic verbs with ten semantic relations corresponding to deep cases: Agent, Object, Source, Goal, Duration, Location, Tool, Aspect, Reason, and Purpose. These verbs were selected from Japanese elementary school textbooks, and the entries were prioritized as in basic Japanese dictionaries.

Linear programming method is used to quantify the word distance between a stimulus word and an associated one. As shown in Eq. 1, the distance $D(x, y)$ between a stimulus word x and associated word y is expressed with Eqs. 2–4

$$D(x, y) = \frac{7}{10} F(x, y) + \frac{1}{3} S(x, y) \tag{1}$$

$$IF(x, y) = \frac{N}{n(x, y) + \delta} \tag{2}$$

$$\delta = \frac{N}{10} - (N \geq 10) \tag{3}$$

$$S(x, y) = \frac{1}{n(x, y)} \sum_{i=1}^{n(x,y)} s_i(x, y) \tag{4}$$

2.3.2 Noun-ACD

Noun-ACD also consists of stimulus words, i.e., nouns, associated words with semantic relations, and word distances among these words. Table 2 lists semantic relations and examples when the stimulus word is the Japanese word "jisho", meaning "dictionary". Currently, the number of stimulus words in Noun-ACD is 1,100, and there are over 5,000 participants. There are proximately 280,000 associated words. After eliminating all overlapping words, there are approximately 64,000 associated words.

Table 1. Example of associated words in Verb-ACD (stimulus word: 運ぶ (hakobu) "convey")

Deep case	Associated words (Word distance)
Agent	I (3.60), Mover (4.21)
Object	Package (1.36), Furniture (7.78)
Source	House (1.45), School (3.81)
Goal	House (1.92), Station (3.73)
Duration	Morning (2.71), Midnight (5.88)
Location	Warehouse (3.73)
Tool	Car (1.62), Hands (3.47)
Aspect	Desperately (3.17)

Table 2. Example of associated words in Noun-ACD (stimulus word: 辞書 (jisho) "dictionary")

Semantic relation	Associated words (Word distance)
Hypernym	Book (1.17)
Hyponym	English-Japanese dictionary (2.31)
Part/Material	Paper (1.23), Page (3.31)
Attribute	Heavy (2.00), Difficult (5.54)
Synonym	Encyclopedia (5.60)
Action	Consult (1.63), Investigate (1.86)
Situation	Library (1.66), Book store (2.22)

3 Proposed Method

In this study, first, we create a question corpus and extract a topic word from the utterances using the TF-IDF method. Next, related words are calculated from the extracted topic word using an associative concept dictionary [11,12] and literal usage representation (LUR) [13,14]. Finally, the interrogative word is selected from the context of utterance using BERT, and a question sentence including the related word and the interrogative word is generated using the created corpus. In this study, we aim to generate questions that take relevance into account and to create a more natural dialogue.

3.1   System Flow

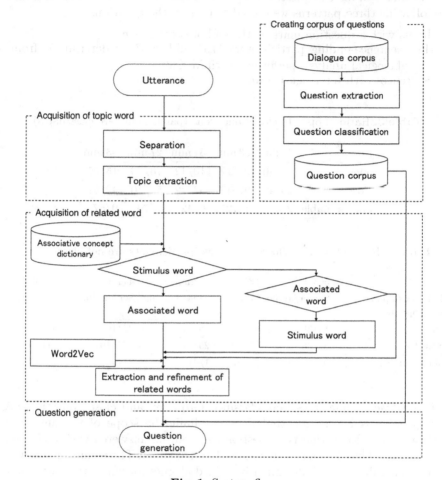

Fig. 1. System flow

Figure 1 shows the process flow of the proposed method. The detailed procedure of the method is shown below.

   i. Extract question sentences from an existing dialogue corpus
  ii. Classify the extracted question sentences into open questions and closed questions
 iii. Create a corpus of open questions only
  iv. Extract a topic word with the flow of dialogue
   v. Extract a related word using an associative concept dictionary and LUR
  vi. Select the appropriate interrogative word with the flow of dialogue using BERT
 vii. Generate a question including the related word using the created corpus

3.2   Creating Corpus of Questions

Hazumi was used for the question corpus, and questions were extracted from it. The following three patterns were used to extract the questions.

  i. Items with a question mark at the end of the sentence
 ii. The sentence-ending particle were "ka" and "no" as determined from a morphological analysis performed with MeCab
iii. Sentences with interrogative words.

Table 3. Ratio of open to closed questions (participants are classmates)

time	43 min	53 min	31 min	27 min	33 min
open	12/40	29/127	10/42	16/70	15/57
closed	26/40	97/127	32/42	53/70	42/57
unclassifiable	2/40	1/127	0/42	1/70	0/57

Table 4. Ratio of open to closed questions (participants are not classmates)

| time | 56 min | 35 min | 84 min | 44 min | 31 min |
Relationship of participants	Senior/Junior	Friends	First meeting	Senior/Junior	Colleague
open	14/38	36/97	15/41	22/198	3/25
closed	24/38	56/97	25/41	175/198	21/25
unclassifiable	0/38	5/97	1/41	2/198	1/25

The extracted questions were classified into open and closed questions. An open question is a question that does not limit the scope of the answer. In contrast, a closed question is a question that can be answered with a choice of "yes" or "no". The Meidai corpus was used for the study. The results are shown in Table 3 and Table 4. Table 3 summarizes the dialogues for which the participants were of the same class, and Table 4 summarizes those for which they were not of the same class. Open questions serve to broaden, deepen, and develop dialogue, and closed questions have been found to have a role in keeping the dialogue going. We aimed to improve the accuracy of the question corpus by classifying the questions before creating the corpus. The corpus of questions to be created included not only target questions but also target questions and the parts of speech of the words in the questions. Since the aim of this study was to develop rather than continue the topic, only open questions were extracted from the classified questions and included in the corpus. Open and closed questions were categorized as follows. Open questions were those that included an interrogative word, and closed questions were those that included other questions. For those that could not be classified, a questionnaire was administered. Three respondents answered per questionnaire. If two or more persons judged the question to be an open question, the question was considered to be an open question.

3.3   Acquisition of Topic Word and Related Word

3.3.1   Topic Word

We judged what the topic of dialogue was from the utterances of the Hazumi. We defined an extracted topical word as a topic word. The TF-IDF method was used to obtain topic word. To obtain word-based topics, only "verbs", "nouns", and "adjectives" excluding function words were judged using the TF-IDF method. The word with the highest TF-IDF value was the topic word.

3.3.2   Verb-ACD

An associative concept dictionary was used for the extracted topic word. Only "verbs" and "nouns" were extracted as related words. If the topic word was included as a stimulus word in the associative concept dictionary, the associated word with the shortest associative distance was obtained and taken as the related word. If a topic word was not included as a stimulus word in the associative concept dictionary but was included as an associative word, the stimulus word with the shortest associative distance was obtained as the related word. If the topic word was neither a stimulus nor an associative word in the associative concept dictionary, Word2Vec [17] was used to extract words with high cosine similarity and treat them as related words. In all cases, five related words were extracted here.

3.3.3   Refinement of Related Words

The five related words extracted in 3.3.2 were narrowed down to one. The LUR proposed by Liu et al. was used to narrow down the related words. LUR is a method that creates a set of vectors using co-occurring words and determines the meaning of an expression on the basis of the degree of similarity between the set and the words in the target sentence. In this study, LUR was used to narrow down related words, and one appropriate related word was extracted.

3.4   Question Generation

Question text including the extracted related word was generated, and a template was used for the generation. To create a template, we used the question corpus created in 3.2. The following describes the procedure for creating a template. First, we selected interrogative word from the question corpus using BERT [18]. Questions corresponding to the selected interrogative word was extracted. The target word and its part of speech were extracted from the extracted question text. If the part of speech of the related word and that of the target word matched, the cosine similarity between the related word and the target word was calculated. Question sentences were extracted that contained words with the highest cosine similarity. The target word was replaced with the related word, and a question was generated.

4   Evaluation Experiment

4.1   Experimental Data

Two, four, and six utterances were extracted from the dialogues in the Hazumi, and these were used as input for the experiment. For each utterance, a question was generated. In this study, the number of turns was all utterances that appeared just before question generation and was the range in which the related word was acquired. To compare the generated questions with the actual dialogues, Hazumi was used as the input for evaluation. Here, a total of 240 sentences were prepared, 40 sentences each from the Hazumi (source utterance) and 40 sentences from the generated question (generated sentence), and they were rated on a 5-point scale using a questionnaire. The evaluation items were given on a 5-point scale: "5: in context", "4: a little in context", "3: undecided", "2: not very much in context", and "1: not in context".

Questionnaire evaluations were conducted with students in their 20 s, and five students rated each questionnaire. Since Hazumi contains dialogues by young people in their 20 s and 30 s, we evaluated the same age groups. Since 60% of human interaction is chatting, it is possible to obtain valid evaluation results even if the evaluation is conducted on students in their 20 s.

4.2   Results

The results of the questionnaire are shown in Table 5. From the top, the results are for topic word, related word, generated question, and utterance in the corpus (source utterance). This table shows that the topic word exceed 90% in turns two and six. The worst rated was 80% in four turns. From this we can see that the appropriate topic word could be acquired regardless of the number of turns. For related words, we see that 90% for two turns, 80% for four turns, and 78% for six turns. Even the lowest exceeded 70%, indicating that the related word could be acquired also obtained correctly. As the number of turns increases, the evaluation is getting worse. For generated questions, two turns received a good evaluation, with more than 70% judged to be in context. However, four and six utterances did not receive a good rating of about 50%. In contrast, source utterances were judged to be in context arround 80% in all turns. These results indicate that even human-to-human dialogue is a difficult task for the system since a third party's assessment of contextualization is never uniform.

Table 6 shows the input utterances, extracted topic word, extracted related word, and generated question. Each of the five output examples is assigned an ID. ID 1 and ID 2 show examples in which the topic word, related word, and generated question were all rated well. ID 3 shows an example of a good evaluation for the topic and related word but a poor evaluation of the generated question. ID 4 shows an example of a good evaluation of the topic word but a poor evaluation of the related word and generated question. Because the related word "room" was not appropriate, our system output the incorrect question "What kind of room do you have?". ID 5 shows an example where the topic word, related word, and generated question were all rated poorly. In fact, our system output "you know" as a topic word which is different from the content of the dialogue, therefore all phases were poor results.

Table 5. Results of evaluation

Phase	Number of turns	Good	Fair	Poor
topic word	2 turns	0.90 (36/40)	0	0.10
	4 turns	0.80 (32/40)	0.02	0.18
	6 turns	0.95 (38/40)	0.02	0.03
related word	2 turns	0.90 (36/40)	0	0.10
	4 turns	0.80 (32/40)	0	0.20
	6 turns	0.78 (31/40)	0.02	0.20
generated question	2 turns	0.72 (29/40)	0.03	0.25
	4 turns	0.55 (22/40)	0.15	0.30
	6 turns	0.58 (23/40)	0.15	0.27
source utterance	2 turns	0.83 (33/40)	0.02	0.15
	4 turns	0.88 (35/40)	0.10	0.02
	6 turns	0.83 (33/40)	0.07	0.10

Table 6. Input and Output Example (A and B indicate speaker's utterances. S(A) indicates system output questions instead of speaker A.)

ID	"Japanese utterances" English utterances	topic word	related word
1	A：'カラオケは好きですか？ B：大好きです. A：カラオケで歌ったりするのですか？ B：はい歌いますよ. 習いに行って楽しく 　　新しい歌を教えてもらってます.' S (A)：'何を歌うんですか？' A：Do you like karaoke? B：I love it. A：Do you sing at karaoke? B：Yes, I do. I go to lessons 　　and enjoy learning new songs. S (A)：What do you sing?	'カラオケ' karaoke	'歌う' sing
2	A：'最近ゲームはしますか？ B：しません.' S (A)：'何をして遊ぶんですか？' A：Do you play games these days? B：No, I don't. S (A)：What do you play?	'ゲーム' game	'遊ぶ' play
3	A：'コンサートとかには行きますか？ B：行きます. A：となたのコンサートとかに行きますか？ B：行ったのうんコブクロとか行きました' S (A)：'いつコンサートを聴きますか？' A：Do you go to concerts and such? B：Yes, I do. A：Who do you go to concerts with and such? B：I went to one of Kobukuro's concerts. S (A)：When will you listen to a concert?	'コンサート' concert	'コンサート' concert
4	A：'日本で開催されるオリンピックを 　　見に行く予定はありますか？ B：今のところはないです. A：そうですか. テレビでの観戦はなされるんですか？ B：はい. テレビでの観戦はしたいと思ってます.' S (A)：'とんな部屋なんですか？' A：Do you plan to go to the Olympics in Japan? B：Not at the moment. A：I see. Will you watch the games on TV? B：Yes, I will. S (A)：What kind of room do you have?	'テレビ' TV	'部屋' room
5	A：'最近では人工知能を搭載した家電が 　　注目されているようですね. ご存知ですか？ B：ええ炊飯器とか電子レンジとか 　　すごいと思います.' S (A)：'何をええになりたいですか？' A：Recently, there seems to be a lot of interest 　　in home appliances with artificial intelligence. 　　Did you know that? B：Yes, I think rice cookers 　　and microwave ovens are great. S (A)：What would you like to be Yeah?	'ご存知' you know	'ええ' yes

5   Discussion

5.1   Acquisition of Topic Word and Related Word

Table 5 shows that more than 80% of the respondents judged the topic word to be appropriate. Therefore, it can be said that this study was able to obtain the correct topic word. From this result, it can be said that the use of the TF-IDF method to obtain the topic word was effective. When using this method, we narrowed down to verbs and nouns and also removed functional verbs, which allowed us to remove irrelevant words in the dialogues, and thus obtained good results. To determine the degree of relevance of a topic word and its related word, Table 7 shows whether the related word was also judged to be appropriate if the topic word was judged to be appropriate. Table 5 shows that the number of related word judged to be appropriate as a whole was about 70% in six turns, and as shown in Table 7, the accuracy was about 80%. If the topic word was correct, the acquisition rate of the related word also increased. This indicates that topic word plays a significant role in the acquisition of related word. The reason the appropriate related word was obtained is that an associative concept dictionary was used. This was effective in calculating the related words in the dialogue because the information was actually associated by humans. In addition, when narrowing down the related words, the topic words were not included among the related words when a negative utterance was made, which allowed the topic to be shifted, thus ensuring that the relevant word was obtained appropriately.

However, there are many issues to be addressed. In this study, since only the TF-IDF method was used to acquire the topic word, only words contained in the utterances were considered. Therefore, as the number of turns increased, the amount of information increased, making it difficult to properly acquire the information. In the future, it will be necessary to obtain a sentence vector for each utterance and consider the context in relation to the word vector. Further improvement in accuracy can be expected by considering not only words but also context.

Table 7. Accuracy of related words when the topic word is correct

	Good
2 turns	0.92 (33/36)
4 turns	0.84 (27/32)
6 turns	0.81 (31/38)

5.2   Question Generation

The results of the overall question generation are shown in Table 5. Table 5 shows that the percentage of two turns is over 70%, while the percentage of four turns and six turns is about 50%. Table 8 shows the results of question generation when the topic word and related word are taken correctly. The Table 8 shows that in two turns the questionnaire is 85% appropriate. On the other hand, from Table 5, it can be seen that the evaluation result for actual human questions is 83%. From the two results, it can be said that in two turns, this system is able to obtain the same level of evaluation as a human. In four and six turns, the accuracy is around 70%, indicating that the accuracy is higher than the overall accuracy. This confirms the effectiveness of the method of generating question using related word. Also, as can be seen from ID 3 of Table 6, the choice of interrogative word is correct in a dialogue situation. The reason for this correct selection may be due to the use of BERT.

However, there were many issues to be addressed in question generation. As the number of turns increased, it was found that fewer contextual questions were generated, even when the related word was properly retrieved. In the example of ID 3 in Table 6, the sentence "いつコンサートを聴きますか？" ("When will you listen to a concert?") was generated. In this example, the topic word and related word were properly acquired, but the Japanese in the sentence generation part was incorrect. If the sentence were "いつコンサートに行きましたか？" ("When did you go to the concert?"), then this would have been a natural question based on context. The reason why such natural question text could not be generated is related to the use of a template for question generation. Templates were few except for "How" and "What", so when a noun was substituted, the correct verb was not used. In the future, this is expected to be improved by generating questions with related words and words that co-occur with those words.

As the number of turns increased for the "How" and "What" generation results, a question was sometimes asked regarding the content of the immediately preceding utterance. This is due to the fact that context was not taken into account. In the future, by taking the context into account, we can expect to generate better interrogative sentences even when the number of turns increases. Furthermore, in Japanese, some questions in which are used with "How" or "What" determine their interrogative words by understanding their answers. Therefore, we implicate our system to improve the accuracy of question generation by using the relations between questions and their answers.

Table 8. Accuracy of generated sentence when the related word is correct

	Good
2 turns	0.85 (28/33)
4 turns	0.74 (20/27)
6 turns	0.68 (21/31)

Table 9. Results by interrogative word

	What	How	When	Where	Why	Who
2 turns	28/38	1/2	–	–	–	–
4 turns	20/34	1/3	1/2	1/1	–	–
6 turns	20/35	2/2	–	0/1	0/1	1/1

6 Conclusion

In this study, we focused on question generation in non-task oriented dialogues, and we aimed for question generation that considers the relevance of dialogues and allows natural dialogues to develop. The topics of utterances were extracted, and related words were obtained on the basis of information associated with the extracted topics and their lexical co-occurrences. In addition, BERT was used to select interrogative words. The obtained related words and interrogative words were used to generate questions. In this way, it was possible to generate questions that were consistent with the context of the dialogue.

The results of an experiment showed that the acquired topic words and related words were highly rated. However, when generating questions from related words, it was not possible to generate correct Japanese after the substitution because of the use of templates.

Future work is needed to take into account the entire sentence in the generation process since humans understand not only words but also whole sentences when they interact. When acquiring related words, it is necessary to obtain a sentence vector for each utterance and to consider the context on the basis of the relationship with the word vector. In addition, using not only related words but also words that co-occur with related words in question generation is expected to generate better question sentences. With these improvements, contextualized utterance generation can be expected even when the number of turns increases.

Acknowledgement. This work was supported by JSPS KAKENHI Grant Numbers JP18K12434, JP18K11514, and JP22K00646.

References

1. Koiso, H., et al.: Toward construction of a large-scale corpus of conversational Japanese: on methodology of recording naturally occurring conversations. Trans. Jpn. Soc. Artif. Intell. **5**, 37–42 (2015). (in Japanese)
2. Yoshino, K., Suzuki, Y., Nakamura, S.: Information navigation system with discovering user interests. In: Proceedings of the 18th Annual SIGdial Meeting on Discourse and Dialogue, pp. 356–359. Association for Computational Linguistic (2017)
3. Li, J., Galley, M., Brockett, C., Gao, J., Dolan, B.: A diversity-promoting objective function for neural conversation models. In: Proceedings of the 2016 Conference

of the North American Chapter of the Association for Computational Linguistics, pp. 110–119, San Diego, California (2016)

4. Katayama, T., Otsuka, A., Mitsuda, K., Saitou, K., Tomita, J.: Question generation to deepen your talk. In: 32nd Annual Conference of the Japanese Society for Artificial Intelligence, 4G103–4G103, pp. 1–4 (2018). (in Japanese)

5. Vinyals, O., Quoc, V.L.: A neural conversational model. In arXiv preprint arXiv:1506.05869 (2015)

6. Horiuchi, S., Higashinaka, R.: Response generation for generating certain questions in chat-oriented dialogue systems. In: The 35th Annual Conference of the Japanese Society for Artificial Intelligence, p. 2Yin5-02, pp. 1–4 (2021). (in Japanese)

7. Xing, C., et al.: Topic aware neural response generation. In: Proceedings of AAAI, pp. 3351–3357 (2017)

8. Serban, I.V., et al.: Generating factoid questions with recurrent neural networks: the 30M factoid question-answer corpus. In: Association for Computational Linguistics, pp. 588–598 (2016)

9. Pan, B., Li, H., Yao, Z., Cai, D., Sun, H.: Reinforced dynamic reasoning for conversational question generation. In: Association for Computational Linguistics, pp. 2114–2124 (2019)

10. Roller, S., et al.: Recipes for building an open-domain chatbot. In: Association for Computational Linguistics, pp. 300–325 (2021)

11. Teraoka, T., Yamashita, T.: Construction of associative vocabulary learning system for Japanese learners. In: Proceedings of the 34th Pacific Asia Conference on Language, Information and Computation, pp. 294–301 (2020)

12. Okamoto, J., Ishizaki, S.: Construction of associative concept dictionary with distance information, and comparison with electronic concept dictionary. J. Nat. Lang. Proc. 8(4), 37–54 (2001). (in Japanese)

13. Liu, C., Hwa, R.: Heuristically informed unsupervised idiom usage recognition. In: Proceedings of the 2018 Conference on Empirical Methods in Natural Language Processing, pp. 1723–1731 (2018)

14. Funato, H., Teraoka, T.: Disambiguation of Japanese idiomatic expressions using bias in occurrence of verbs. In: International Conference on Technologies and Applications of Artificial Intelligence, pp. 114–118 (TAAI) (2020)

15. Komatani, H., Okada, S., Nishimoto, H., Araki, M., Nakano, M.: Multimodal dialogue data collection and analysis of annotation disagreement. In: International Workshop on Spoken Dialogue System Technology, vol. 714 (IWSDS) (2019)

16. Fujimura, I., Chiba, S., Ohso, M.: Lexical and grammatical features of spoken and written Japanese in contrast: exploring a lexical profiling approach to comparing spoken and written corpora. In: Proceedings of the VIIth GSCP International Conference. Speech and Corpora, pp. 393–398 (2012)

17. Mikolov, T, Chen, K., Corrado, G., Dean, J.: Efficient estimation of word representations in vector space. In arXiv preprint arXiv:1301.3781 (2013)

18. Devlin, J., Chang, M.-W., Lee, K., Toutanova, K.: BERT: pre-training of deep bidirectional transformers for language understanding. In: Proceedings of the 2019 Conference of the North American Chapter of the Association for Computational Linguistics: Human Language Technologies, vol. 1 (Long and Short Papers), pp. 4171–4186 (2019)

Embedding Self-Assessment Manikins in Mobile Augmented Reality Applications

Leonie Lübbing[1], Tanja Kojić[1]([✉]), Sebastian Möller[1,2],
and Jan-Niklas Voigt-Antons[2,3]

[1] Quality and Usability Lab, Technische Universität Berlin, Berlin, Germany
tanja.kojic@tu-berlin.de
[2] German Research Center for Artificial Intelligence (DFKI), Berlin, Germany
[3] Immersive Reality Lab, University of Applied Sciences Hamm-Lippstadt,
Lippstadt, Germany

Abstract. Augmented Reality (AR) applications have been widely investigated over the past decades, however, due to the simultaneous advancements in technology, the research has to be constantly evolving, too.

Specifically, if looking at aspects that influence User Experience (UX) and Usability, newer technologies in AR-hardware, as well as in evaluation methods, offer promising features that could have a positive influence but might also uncover new challenges.

The following paper is going to propose a prototype for the assessment of emotional responses to provided stimuli with Self-Assessment Manikin (SAM) to be integrated within an AR application. For that, the first important aspects of AR will be introduced, defined, and at times complemented and compared with known concepts from Virtual Reality.

After assessing the current state-of-the-art by investigating related literature, the motivation behind an integrated approach will be explained in more detail and the implementation of the SAM prototype with the UI design platform Figma will be introduced. Results from the conducted user study will provide valuable insight into how the three-dimensional SAM was received and consider the opportunities and limitations of the implemented design.

Keywords: Augmented Reality · SAM · Mobile UX

1 Introduction

Over the past decades, Augmented Reality (AR) technology has developed rapidly, and with that, the need for more precise vocabulary and definitions has increased. Understanding AR as a medium rather than a technology can emphasize the wide range of technological innovations it comprises and through which it is realized [7]. A widely referenced visualization in the context of virtually altered environments is the *"Virtuality continuum"*, ranging from a fully

© The Author(s), under exclusive license to Springer Nature Switzerland AG 2023
J. Y. C. Chen and G. Fragomeni (Eds.): HCII 2023, LNCS 14027, pp. 359–371, 2023.
https://doi.org/10.1007/978-3-031-35634-6_25

real environment to a fully virtual one. With AR, it does not depend on a fully synthetic virtual world but takes place in real environments, with added virtual objects [19].

With Mobile Augmented Reality (MAR) becoming accessible to the majority of people owning mobile devices, most user experiences happen outside of controlled laboratory environments and often without in-depth knowledge about the technology. The question that motivated this paper is whether user experience and usability of MAR-applications can be improved by integrating questionnaires. One indicator of that is the highly interactive experience and user involvement offered by AR. In contrast, paper-pencil evaluations or digital versions thereof can be tedious. Therefore creating embedded self-assessments could remove challenges caused by the transition and adjustment from the application to the questionnaire, improving the workflow and maintaining the participants' sense of presence [28]. Integrated questionnaires also offer the prospect to experience and evaluate AR applications simultaneously. This may have several advantages due to the inherent bias of retrospective ratings [6].

2   Related Work

While there has been substantial research into AR over the past decades, the evaluation of UX is complicated due to the wide spectrum of AR applications as well as variation in hardware, e.g. smartphones versus Head-Mounted Displays (HMD) [8]. There have been efforts to adapt AR-specific evaluation methods for UX. [3] However, these mainly include post-hoc evaluations, and most are completed on either a computer or as paper-pencil questionnaires. Retrospective evaluation can distort results due to the so-called *Memory-Experience-Gap*, a discrepancy between the degree of emotional responses collected retrospectively and the actual degree of emotional responses during an experiment [6].

To the authors' knowledge, there has been no previous research into questionnaires integrated within Mobile AR and data is limited on integrated approaches in AR. More research exists for the evaluation of questionnaires embedded within VR applications (In-VR), and even though a direct translation of findings from VR research to AR applications is not possible, they can provide valuable insight.

2.1   Usability in AR

Presence and Immersion. Presence in the context of AR applications describes a participant's feeling of being inside the combined virtual and real space. It requires the virtual information to create stimuli that blend in with and behave like the real environment [12]. Therefore, inconsistencies within the virtual environment can lead to the realization that the perceived and actual location of a subject is misaligned. This abrupt change has been coined *Break in Presence* [25].

Furthermore, for the evaluation of virtual environments, the concept of immersion is commonly used. While various definitions exist [24,27,30], immersion as *the participant's willing suspension of disbelief* to be *"inside"* a *virtually enhanced environment* does not rely on fully virtual environments, thus can be applied to AR applications [9].

Usability. Despite the fact that technology components of AR have been extensively researched in recent decades, research into the assessment of Usability within AR is limited [28]. However, as an important aspect of UX, Usability can impact the success of a system and thus is recommended to be prioritized during the development and evaluation of a system [14]. Further, the Usability and UX of an AR application as well as the sense of presence and immersion are closely linked to a user's interaction with the application in question. Emotional states caused by presence and immersion or breaks thereof can effect User Experience. Moreover, insufficient Usability can impact to what degree a state of presence occurs. Due to this intersecting influence, they are looked at separately.

2.2   Self-Assessment Manikin (SAM)

The Self-Assessment Manikin (SAM) is a non-verbal graphic scale based on the idea that complex emotional reactions can be assessed in three dimensions: Pleasure, arousal, and dominance [4]. The Arousal scale describes perceived alertness and ranges from boredom or sleepiness to a state of arousal and excitement. The pleasure scale investigates positive or negative feelings and ranges from feeling unhappy or annoyed to feelings of happiness and joy. The dominance scale evaluates the perceived control over a situation and ranges from the feeling of being controlled to the sensation of being in control of the situation [13].

2.3   Related Work in Augmented Reality (AR)

A systematic review of 10 years of Augmented Reality Usability studies found HMDs and handheld devices to be dominating research. Since 2011, publications on AR with handheld displays outnumbered HMD [10]. Despite being published in 2018, the study focused on publications published between 2005 and 2014. This before, for example, the 2016 introduction of the HoloLens[1]. Research into the Usability of Augmented Reality was reported to be less than 10% of publications on AR technology [10]. Another review on Mixed and augmented reality literature from 2009–2019 examined 458 papers and found around 248 that conducted user-studies scenarios, out of which approximately 21% (53/248) specifically looked at Usability and approximately 15% (36/248) investigated participants' emotions [18].

For the evaluation of Augmented Reality applications, different heuristics have been proposed. A checklist based on ISO 9241-11 [14] and an adapted version of the *Ten Usability Heuristics* [21], specifies the latter within the context of AR. While details on all of them would be beyond the scope of this paper,

---

[1] https://news.microsoft.com/europe/features/microsoft-hololens-comes-to-europe/.

the following can be noted: *1. Visibility* was extended by requirements for quick and reliable tracking systems; *2. Match of system and real world* in context of AR needs to include criteria for presence [12]. Additionally it emphasized the need for comprehensive error detection and correction mechanisms for AR. The inclusion of ISO 9241-11 [14] resulted in three further heuristics for (the interaction with) AR applications: High accuracy, simple environment setup, and satisfaction. The checklist proved to be a reliable evaluation tool for AR systems, while also promoting more consistency [8]. A similar proposal also based on the *Ten Usability Heuristics* [21] further highlighted the need for virtual objects to be adaptive to changes in location and/or perspective of users [11].

While not for Mobile Augmented Reality (MAR), research towards the integration of surveys into AR for optical see-through HMDs has been conducted. The questionnaire was presented as two-dimensional, with a tangible pen to enter input. The main reason for the integrated approach was the cumbersome calibration process of the HMD, if taken off during an experiment. However, a decreased chance of a break in Presence was noted. It was further reported that participants returned positive feedback specifically for the In-AR questionnaire [15].

2.4 Related Work in Virtual Reality (VR)

One study investigated UX and presence for questionnaires integrated into VR compared to paper-pencil questionnaires. To evaluate presence the *iGroup Presence Questionnaire (IPQ)* [1] was used. Results showed no significant differences for the global and spatial presence or experienced realism. However, the lower variance of presence for the In-VR questionnaire indicated it to be more reliable [22]. This can be linked to the *Memory-Experience Gap* [6] of post-hoc questionnaires. Evaluation for Usability reported mostly positive results. Participants reported a preference for In-VR questionnaires, linked to the sense of presence/immersion and convenience.

A similar study used three presence questionnaires, namely *iGroup Presence Questionnaire (IPQ)* [1], *A Presence Questionnaire* [30], and the *Slater-Usoh-Steed*² [26]. For the VR environments, two different levels of realism/abstractness were included. There were no significant changes to the mean scores of the questionnaires. However, the variance of scores increased with increased abstractness for Out-VR, but not In-VR questionnaires. This indicated a break in presence caused by the Out-VR questionnaires. Moreover, the concern of altered ratings in post-hoc testing caused by recalled experiences was raised [23].

A literature review on In-VR questionnaires identified differences in design, implementation, realization, and extent of various studies as problematic. Additionally, the lack of comprehensive reports on the use of integrated questionnaires was criticized and a need for guidelines and standards was expressed. A subsequent user study compared Out-VR to In-VR questionnaires. Most participants

---

² In literature commonly abbreviated as SUS, however in this paper SUS solely refers to the System Usability Scale [5].

experienced the In-VR questionnaire as enjoyable and around 45% as easy to use. However, there were mentions of frustration due to the UI not always responding [2].

Another paper looked at various degrees of integration. After an expert study concluded significantly higher User Experience for an intradiegetic setup, a subsequent user study compared it to a paper-pencil questionnaire, with the use of *A Presence Questionnaire* [30]. While most participants preferred the In-VR questionnaire and reported higher feelings of joy, the completion time was significantly longer. There were no significant differences for Usability and acceptance. Yet participants reported lower Usability and feelings of irritation for In-VR questionnaires due to difficulties with the User Interface and spatial tracking. Positive feedback noted not having to remove the HMD, which is on par with previously discussed findings [22].

3   Method

Self-Assessment Manikins are widely being used in the context of evaluating User Experience to rate emotional responses to provided stimuli. Conventionally this assessment happens in 2D, either online or as paper-pencil questionnaires. To realize an integrated Self-Assessment Manikin prototype in Mobile Augmented Reality applications, the first task was to transform the SAMs illustrations into three-dimensional graphic characters. These SAMs were then implemented in a mock-up smartphone application, where they could also be viewed in 3D. A within-subject user study was then conducted to get a first impression of how this type of scale would be received.

3.1   Design and Implementation

For the design of the prototype, several factors had to be considered. Due to the ongoing Covid-19 pandemic, it was decided to conduct the experiment remotely. Therefore the AR element would be displayed through handheld devices, namely smartphones. Since the user study would be voluntary and without reimbursement, it had to be easily accessible.

Figma. The prototype was designed with Figma[3], a free online User Interface design-tool for creating designs and prototypes. As it is web-based, there was no download of a separate application needed to access the prototype. Moreover, there were fewer compatibility limitations due to it not being limited or tied to a specific operating system. With Figma, AR elements can be embedded through a plugin offered by Vectary[4]. The prototype included a mockup smartphone layout, with the 3D-SAM graphics above a 5-point scale for the rating. The AR

---

[3] https://www.figma.com/ui-design-tool/.
[4] https://www.vectary.com/3d-modeling-blog/figma-3d-vectary-plugin.

manikins were linked to the corresponding images using a Figma Reference file [16].

As Figma does not allow for videos to be played within prototype mode, the video stimuli were uploaded to YouTube as 360° Videos and linked to the Figma prototype. The videos were based on research from the Virtual Human Interaction Lab at Stanford University. As the video database was only partly available, chosen were *50: Puppies host SourceFed for a day, 68: Jailbreak 360* and *69: Walk the tight rope* [17]. To get a more complete picture on whether the SAM reference values were reproducible in the three-dimensional implementation, a repeated measurement design was decided on.

Vectary. Vectary is a browser-based 3D modeling tool. Most 3D file formats are supported and designs can be imported or created from scratch and then be directly integrated into Figma. The graphic characters were converted to .svg files, uploaded to Vectary and modeled into three dimensional objects. Settings for lighting and the material and texture were consistent for all 15 characters. Since the dominance scale includes varying sizes of the manikin, the 3-point manikin matched the pleasure and arousal scales in size, while the other items were adjusted proportionally. For the AR-environment the field of view was manipulated, as the AR-object appears at a different place or distance dependent on where a surface is scanned: the higher the SAM-rating the narrower the view thus the visible area decreased and the SAM seemed closer to the viewer. As the ability to see the environment through the manikin made it seem less artificial in AR, but factors like changes in lighting or different smartphone models impacted the visibility, the opacity and color was chosen accordingly.

Examples of the In-AR SAM are shown in Fig. 1 and Fig. 2. All images depicted were screen recorded with a Huawei Mate 20 Pro[5] at different locations of the central library at TU Berlin library. The distinction between Fig. 1a and the other figures is made clearer by the fact that Fig. 1b and Fig. 1c have backgrounds that are less neutral. However, Fig. 1b and Fig. 1c were captured within seconds of one another and without any evident changes to the surroundings. Despite this, the colors in Fig. 1b seem to have a lower saturation, and the contrast appears to have reduced and it is possible to tell the difference. Similarly, in Fig. 2 where Fig. 2b and 2c are shown in a setting where the light levels have been adjusted. Figure 2c seems to have a substantially brighter illumination than Fig. 2b, despite the fact that both figures were captured sequentially. This is because of differences in perspective and angle. In addition, the opacity seems to be considerably better within a more scattered background and under various lighting.

---

[5] EMUI 12 operating system.

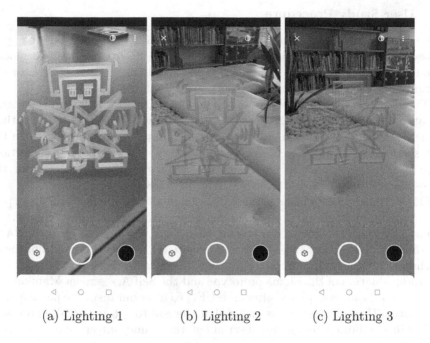

(a) Lighting 1   (b) Lighting 2   (c) Lighting 3

Fig. 1. Arousal scale item 5

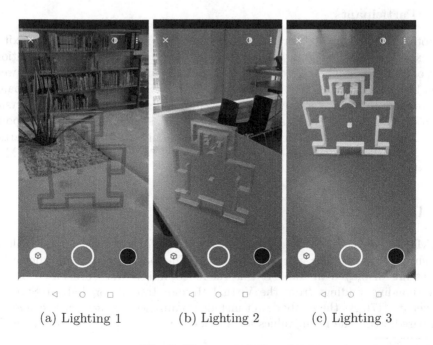

(a) Lighting 1   (b) Lighting 2   (c) Lighting 3

Fig. 2. Pleasure scale item 1

3.2   User Study Procedure

The questionnaire was created with Google forms[6] and consisted of a pre-survey examining age, gender, level of education, occupation, phone model, vision impairment, previous experience, and included the short version of the "Affinity for Technology Interaction Scale" (ATI-S)[7] [29].

The main survey contained three subsequent QR codes linked to the Figma prototype, followed by SAM scales. Participants were asked to re-enter their rating, as the prototype changed according to input but did not save it. In the next section, participants were asked to fill out the User Experience Questionnaire (UEQ) twice, once in regard to the Figma prototype and once for the three-dimensional SAM character in Augmented Reality.

Due to the implementation of the Self-Assessment Manikin with Figma in prototype mode, multiple platforms were necessary (the online questionnaire, the Figma prototype, the 360° video stimuli, then back to Figma to open the SAM-scale in AR). As it was repeated three times, this was a lengthy process. Implementing the UEQ twice, asking for separate ratings intended for the data to be separated into the evaluation of the Figma prototype and the Self Assessment Manikin.

A trap question was placed after each UEQ to filter out insincere participants. The System Usability Scale was included at the end to get an overall impression of Usability, followed by one question about the sound output and a free text section for comments.

3.3   Participants

In total, 20 participants were recorded by Google Forms, however, one exited the experiment prematurely and thus could not be included in the evaluation. Out of 19 participants 9 were female, 8 were male and 2 non-binary. They were aged between 23 and 34 years old (M = 26.53 years SD = 3.08). All participants were either students at a university (68.4%) or had graduated from a university (31.6%). Participants were asked to rate their previous experience on a 5-point scale ranging from no experience (1) to very experienced (5) however, no participant rated their experience higher than 3 (M = 1.74, SD = 0.81) (ATI-S: M = 3.5, SD = 0.92)

4   Results

SAM. The collected SAM-scale values were transformed to a 9-point scale to match the results of the video database [17]. The mean and standard deviation values are displayed in Table 1. The reference values (RV) are based on the corresponding findings from the Virtual Human Interaction Lab at Stanford University [17]. As the study didn't include dominance ratings, those cannot be compared. Still, the mean values for all videos were close to the middle of the

---

[6] https://www.google.com/forms/about/.

[7] https://ati-scale.org/wp-content/uploads/2019/09/ati-s-scale-short-version.pdf.

scale, and therefore overall, the degree of control was perceived as neither being controlled nor being in control. For video number 50 with the title *"Puppies host SourceFed for a day"* [17], the values of the AR-SAM are close to the reference values, but for videos 68: *"Jailbreak 360"* and 69: *"Walk the tight rope"* were both lower. Additionally, the standard deviation was high for all values recorded by the participants.

Table 1. M, SD and RN for Self-Assessment Manikin

	SAM (M)	SAM (SD)	(RV)
Arousal Video 50	5.95	2.86	5.35
Pleasure Video 50	7.00	2.11	7.47
Dominance Video 50	5.53	2.89	0.00
Arousal Video 68	5.11	2.16	6.70
Pleasure Video 68	4.79	1.62	4.40
Dominance Video 68	4.58	1.84	0.00
Arousal Video 69	4.79	2.20	6.91
Pleasure Video 69	5.32	2.14	6.46
Dominance Video 69	4.47	2.57	0.00

SUS. The total System Usability Scale score of all participants returned a value of 61.58 (SD = 12). There was no significant correlation found between SUS score and results from the ATI-S, or between SUS score and previous experience. However, the participants with no previous experience had the lowest mean SUS score and highest standard deviation (1: M = 58.89, SD = 11.26), while participants with little to medium amount of previous experience had similar mean values yet differed in standard deviation (2: M = 65.83, SD = 15.06; 3: M = 61.25 SD = 9.46) (Fig. 3) While results indicated, higher ratings were given by male

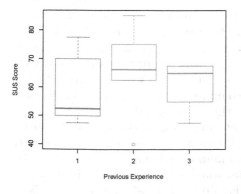

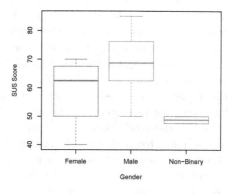

Fig. 3. SUS score by previous experience

Fig. 4. SUS score by gender

participants on the System Usability Scale, there was no significant correlation between both variables. (Female: M = 58.89, SD = 11.26; Male: M = 65.83, SD = 15.06; Non-Binary: M = 61.25, SD = 9.46) (Fig. 4)

User Experience Questionnaire. As previously discussed, the results from the UEQ-S can be split into (i) pragmatic and (ii) hedonic quality, to get more details on (i) how functional and (ii) how enjoyable the use of the system was perceived. The pragmatic quality was rated higher than the hedonic quality, as seen in Fig. 5 and Fig. 6.

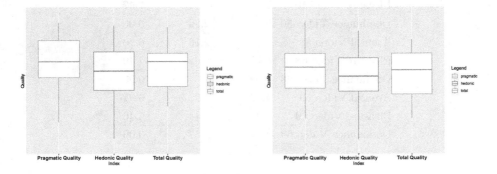

Fig. 5. UEQ results prototype   **Fig. 6.** UEQ results SAM

5   Discussion and Conclusion

One of the items of interest in this paper was whether Self-Assessment-Manikins integrated into Augmented Reality were a reliable method to evaluate AR applications. Results of the In-AR SAM only reproduced the reference values for one of the videos from the database [17]. However, while Video 50 was the first to be listed in this paper, it was the last video in the questionnaire. It could have been expected for the ratings to decrease with time due to repeating the same process for the third time. On the other hand, by the third time, participants had gotten used to the prototype and thus could focus more on the video. Combined with the higher level of pleasure Video 50 had compared to the other two videos, may have resulted in more accurate ratings for the stimuli itself.

After the study, feedback reported confusion about Video 68 the *Jailbreak*, as one participant described "rooting for the escapee to get away" but worried about the misunderstanding. A perceptual map of pleasure x space locates the reference value for that video in the Unpleasant-Excited quadrant with descriptions like "overwhelmed" or "defiant" [20]. While there were no strong outliers within the ratings for SAM, this kind of feedback provides valuable insight as to why the results didn't correspond to the reference values, with explanations beyond the integrated questionnaire approach.

The results of the System Usability Scale compared to the User Experience Questionnaire show lower ratings for the functional aspect of the prototype in both cases. However, two participants reported to be unsure which UEQ referred to which part of the design. Since this study was conducted in Germany, English likely was not the native language for some participants. As the word "manikin" is not commonly used, there might have been a language barrier in understanding what part the SAM is. Additional feedback mentioned the process being to complicated and lengthy. One participant desired the ability to zoom out. Another comment described the SAM as "cute".

While it was designed as a prototype and not intended as a full implementation, the complicated procedure may not have been ideal for a user study with mostly novice AR users. Because of this, it is likely that participants started but did not finish the questionnaire. Furthermore, feedback where the AR could not be displayed despite the smartphone supposedly supporting AR. Additionally, the low number of participants and narrow age group within the study were likely limiting factors and reasons why the data yielded little significant results. Over half of the participants being students further limits the validity.

Another factor that could have influenced the experiment was the remote conduction which offers less control over the participants as well as fewer ways for participants to ask for clarification when needed. There was a free-text comment section towards the end, but if participants exited before, they possibly didn't reach out to provide feedback. Within a laboratory, this would have been a valuable opportunity to learn what specific aspects need to be improved.

This paper was intended to provide an overview of aspects to consider when attempting to integrate questionnaires within AR while also proposing a practical approach to three-dimensional Self-Assessment Manikin. While the study left room for improvement, it would be interesting to implement these findings in future work and also test the approach on a larger, more varied group of participants.

References

1. i-group presence questionnaire (IPQ) overview. http://www.igroup.org/pq/ipq/index.php
2. Alexandrovsky, D., et al.: Examining design choices of questionnaires in VR user studies, pp. 1–21. Association for Computing Machinery (2020). https://doi.org/10.1145/3313831.3376260
3. Arifin, Y., Sastria, T.G., Barlian, E.: User experience metric for augmented reality application: a review. Procedia Comput. Sci. **135**, 648–656 (2018). https://doi.org/10.1016/j.procs.2018.08.221, https://www.sciencedirect.com/science/article/pii/S187705091831514X
4. Bradley, M.M., Lang, P.J.: Measuring emotion: the self-assessment manikin and the semantic differential. J. Behav. Ther. Exp. Psychiatry **25**(1), 49–59 (1994). https://doi.org/10.1016/0005-7916(94)90063-9, https://www.sciencedirect.com/science/article/pii/0005791694900639

5. Brooke, J.B.: SUS: A 'quick and dirty' usability scale (1996)
6. Bruun, A., Ahm, S.: Mind the gap! comparing retrospective and concurrent ratings of emotion in user experience evaluation. In: Abascal, J., Barbosa, S., Fetter, M., Gross, T., Palanque, P., Winckler, M. (eds.) INTERACT 2015. LNCS, vol. 9296, pp. 237–254. Springer, Cham (2015). https://doi.org/10.1007/978-3-319-22701-6_17
7. Craig, A.B.: Understanding Augmented Reality. Morgan Kaufmann, Boston (2013). https://doi.org/10.1016/C2011-0-07249-6, https://www.sciencedirect.com/book/9780240824086/
8. De Paiva Guimaraes, M., Martins, V.F.: A checklist to evaluate augmented reality applications (2014). https://doi.org/10.1109/svr.2014.17
9. Dede, C.: Immersive interfaces for engagement and learning. Science **323**, 66–69 (2009)
10. Dey, A., Billinghurst, M., Lindeman, R.W., Swan, J.E.: A systematic review of 10 years of augmented reality usability studies: 2005 to 2014. Front. Robot. AI **5**, 37 (2018)
11. Endsley, T.C., Sprehn, K.A., Brill, R.M., Ryan, K.J., Vincent, E.C., Martin, J.M.: Augmented reality design heuristics: designing for dynamic interactions. Proc. Hum. Fact. Ergonom. Soc. Ann. Meet. **61**(1), 2100–2104 (2017). https://doi.org/10.1177/1541931213602007
12. Gall, D., Latoschik, M.E.: The effect of haptic prediction accuracy on presence. In: 2018 IEEE Conference on Virtual Reality and 3D User Interfaces (VR), pp. 73–80 (2018). https://doi.org/10.1109/VR.2018.8446153
13. Irtel, H.: PXLab: the psychological experiments laboratory. version 2.1.11. (2007). http://www.pxlab.de
14. ISO 9241–11, q.: ISO 9241: Ergonomics of human-system interaction - Part 11: Usability: Definitions and concepts. Standard, International Organization for Standardization (2018)
15. Kahl, D., Ruble, M., Krüger, A.: The influence of environmental lighting on size variations in optical see-through tangible augmented reality. In: 2022 IEEE Conference on Virtual Reality and 3D User Interfaces (VR), pp. 121–129 (2022). https://doi.org/10.1109/VR51125.2022.00030
16. Kengadaran, S.: View in 3D - Reference File. https://www.figma.com/community/file/947832835915257827. licensed under CC BY 4.0
17. Li, B.J., Bailenson, J.N., Pines, A., Greenleaf, W.J., Williams, L.M.: A public database of immersive VR videos with corresponding ratings of arousal, valence, and correlations between head movements and self report measures. Front. Psychol. **8**, 2116 (2017). https://doi.org/10.3389/fpsyg.2017.02116, https://www.frontiersin.org/articles/10.3389/fpsyg.2017.02116
18. Merino, L., Schwarzl, M., Kraus, M., Sedlmair, M., Schmalstieg, D., Weiskopf, D.: Evaluating mixed and augmented reality: a systematic literature review (2009–2019) (2020). https://doi.org/10.1109/ismar50242.2020.00069
19. Milgram, P., Kishino, F.: A taxonomy of mixed reality visual displays. IEICE Trans. Inf. Syst. **77**, 1321–1329 (1994). https://web.cs.wpi.edu/~gogo/courses/imgd5100/papers/Milgram_IEICE_1994.pdf
20. Morris, J.D.: Observations: SAM: the self-assessment manikin. J. Advert. Res. **35**(6), 63–68 (1995)
21. Nielsen, J.: Ten usability heuristics (2006)
22. Regal, G., et al.: Questionnaires embedded in virtual environments: reliability and positioning of rating scales in virtual environments. Qual. User Exp. **4**(1), 1–13 (2019). https://doi.org/10.1007/s41233-019-0029-1

23. Schwind, V., Knierim, P., Haas, N., Henze, N.: Using presence questionnaires in virtual reality (2019). https://doi.org/10.1145/3290605.3300590
24. Slater, M.: Measuring presence: a response to the Witmer and singer presence questionnaire. Presence **8**, 560–565 (1999). https://doi.org/10.1162/105474699566477
25. Slater, M., Steed, A.: A virtual presence counter. Presence: Teleoperators Virtual Environ. **9**(5), 413–434 (2000). https://doi.org/10.1162/105474600566925
26. Slater, M., Steed, A., McCarthy, J.D., Maringelli, F.: The influence of body movement on subjective presence in virtual environments. Hum. Factors: J. Hum. Factors Ergon. Soc. **40**, 469–477 (1998). https://doi.org/10.1518/001872098779591368
27. Slater, M., Wilbur, S.: A framework for immersive virtual environments (five): speculations on the role of presence in virtual environments. Presence: Teleoperators Virtual Environ. **6**, 603–616 (1997). https://doi.org/10.1162/pres.1997.6.6.603
28. Verhulst, I., Woods, A., Whittaker, L., Bennett, J., Dalton, P.: Do VR and AR versions of an immersive cultural experience engender different user experiences?. Comput. Hum. Behav. **125**, 106951 (2021). https://doi.org/10.1016/j.chb.2021.106951, https://www.sciencedirect.com/science/article/pii/S0747563221002740
29. Wessel, D., Attig, C., Franke, T.: ATI-S - an ultra-short scale for assessing affinity for technology interaction in user studies (2019). https://doi.org/10.1145/3340764.3340766
30. Witmer, B.G., Singer, M.J.: Measuring presence in virtual environments: a presence questionnaire. Presence: Teleoperators Virtual Environ. **7**(3), 225–240 (1998). https://doi.org/10.1162/105474698565686

The Development of Mix-Reality Interface and Synchronous Robot Fabrication for the Collaborative Construction

Yang-Ting Shen and Jia-Shuo Hsu[✉]

Department of Architecture, National Cheng Kung University, Tainan City, Taiwan
{10808028,n76094142}@gs.ncku.edu.tw

Abstract. The construction field in Taiwan is facing the serious issues about the worker shortage and low birthrate. The intervention of collaborative robots brings one of the possible ways to solve those problems. In this paper, we propose the ROCOS system (Robot Collaboration System) to integrate the mix-reality interface and robot fabrication for the collaborative construction between the designer and the robotic arm. ROCOS system consists of three parts including (1) Mix-reality interface, (2) Iterative design, and (3) Collaborative construction. In the MR interface, the designer builds the BIM-based environment before the collaborative design with the robot. The ROCOS system provides a MR layout method that the designer can use the Oculus handles and MR glasses to layout the real space and turn it into MR space. After the MR layout is built, the designer starts the iterative design through the ROCOS's design interface. The designer uses the MR handles to draw multiple virtual sticks to build the stick-weaving structure. The ROCOS system simulates the assembly path of robotic arm for each stick to make sure no confliction during the fabrication process. Then the ROCOS system translates the simulation into robotic arm's commands and deliver it to the robot control system. Finally, the robot control system drives the robotic arm to grip the real stick and assemble it to the corresponding position. This process can be run multiple times until the designer finish his iterative design. The loop of iterative design and robot fabrication achieves the collaborative construction between designer and robot.

Keywords: Iterative Design · Human–Robot Collaboration · Mixed Reality · Robotic Arm · Digital Fabrication · Build Information Model

1 Introduction

The construction field in Taiwan is facing the serious issues caused from the labor shortage and low birthrate. The construction industries still stay in the relatively backward fields which are used to apply labor intensive methods [8]. However, in recent years, a shrinking labor population caused by low birth rate companies with unstable quality and quantity in the construction market. In addition, the labor's safety issue is also fatal and inevitable due to the uncertainly dangerous construction environment. It further decreases the will of potential human resource to join. Those labor issues not only

© The Author(s), under exclusive license to Springer Nature Switzerland AG 2023
J. Y. C. Chen and G. Fragomeni (Eds.): HCII 2023, LNCS 14027, pp. 372–381, 2023.
https://doi.org/10.1007/978-3-031-35634-6_26

cause the increase of construction cost in short term, but also causes the stagnation of construction industry in long term.

The construction industries need a disruptive innovation to sole the dilemma. The intervention of robots brings one of the possible ways to solve those problems fundamentally. The environments of the automation and manufacturing industries are well arranged for the use of robots, which have been successfully performing high speed and high precision tasks to increase process productivity and product quality. The construction industry can leverage the achievements of automation and manufacturing industries to improve safety, efficiency, productivity, and even creativity.

The emerging field of human-robot collaboration has significant potential applications in construction defining the responsibilities of both humans and robots during collaborative work [14]. Inagaki et al. propose that humans and robots can have a common goal and work cooperatively through perception, recognition and intention inference [13]. For construction application, natural human-robot collaboration is necessary because it is almost not possible to ask complex robot coding or manipulating from workers. Human or robot would be able to infer the intentions of the other from natural language or intuitive behavior during collaborative process. In addition, all the communication should carry the spatial referencing for the collaboration in the working space. It means we need an interface which can communicate, record, analyze, and visualize the information through spatial modeling. Building Information Model (BIM) and Mixed Reality (MR) may provide the potential environment which has the spatial-information-rich interface. The BIM model becomes the bridge to translate the spatial intention or result between humans and robots. BIM-based models including geometry, material type, and component parameters, are extracted and used for planning the robot-aided construction process [9]. Moreover, when the full-scale BIM model is placed in the immersive environment based on MR, it facilitates the effective spatial representation for the human's cognition and robot's recognition in real-scale construction.

In this research, we propose the ROCOS system (Robot Collaboration System) to integrate the MR interface and robot fabrication for the collaborative construction between human and robot.

2 Literature Review

2.1 The Immersive Technology for Spatial Engagement

The immersive technology can provide spatial cues for human-robot collaboration. It contains three categories including Virtual Reality (VR), Augmented Reality (AR), and Mixed Reality (MR). VR is a simulated experience that employs pose tracking and 3D near-eye displays to give the user an immersive feel of a virtual world [6]. AR is a technology that facilitates the overlay of computer graphics onto the real world. AR differs from VR in that in a virtual environment the entire physical world is replaced by computer graphics, AR enhances rather replaces reality [10]. MR and AR share the common agreement that engages the physical environment to increase the mixed experience both in real world and virtual world. However, in the field of human-robot collaboration, an implementation closer to a true MR approach merges physical and virtual sensor readings, allowing a robot or device to sense physical and virtual objects or activities at the same time [7, 11]. It means MR should contain more environmental data or instant feedbacks to merge or blur the boundary between physical and virtual worlds.

The HoloLens MR device launched by Microsoft was a head-mounted device (HMD) that focuses on MR mixed reality technology. In addition to capturing the real environment through the depth camera, it also used hand movement information as the main input method on the system. Among the various MR design systems developed on HoloLens, Fologram developed by Cameron Newnham has also been widely used in recent years. Titled "Steampunk" and made from steam-bent timber, the voluptuous pavilion was designed by UCL's Barlett School of Architecture, in collaboration with Fologram facilitated the construction of complex designs. The timber elements were prefabricated and assembled following holographic construction information viewed in MR (Fig. 1).

Fig. 1. Steampunk project uses MR to assemble the complex timber shape. (photo from https://soomeenhahm.com/portfolio-item/steampunk-pavilion/)

Daniela Mitterberger (ETH Zurich) and Kathrin Dörfler (TUM) developed the Augmented bricklaying system based on object-aware MR [16]. They used the depth awareness HMD to create the immersive environment that a worker could lay and adjust bricks through the augmented hints. The immersive environment provided the spatial mapping information to assist a worker's precise and intuitive work flow. According to these cases, we can further understand the immersive environment created via MR provides not only the mixed spatial senses, but also the inter-operability to assist or enhance the spatial activities.

2.2 The Alternating Control for Collaborative Fabrication

Human-robot collaboration (HRC) is defined as human and robot interact with each other to establish a dynamic system for accomplishing tasks in the environment [1, 2]. With the development of robot-aided manufacturing and sensing technologies, design thinking to quickly intervene in manufacturing becomes possible and presents a valuable work process to HRC [3, 15]. Wei proposed the concept of robot aware fabrication, which meant robot-aided manufacturing was no longer just a close procedure but enabled the robot to perceive the environment and co-work with human [18]. This method was essentially different from the traditional digital fabrication, but instead represented the digital craft of HRC making the results more diverse and unpredictable.

Brugnaro and his group was inspired from bird's nesting behaviors and developed an adaptive robotic fabrication system for woven structures called Robotic Softness [4, 5]. Brugnaro used depth camera to scan the undergoing woven structures. Based on the instant figure of structures, the computer could predict the next appropriate structure and drove the robotic arm to weave it into whole structures. The adaptive fabrication process needs to combine depth camera, adaptive fabrication algorithm, and robot control system to achieve the real-time woven structures. In this case, although the design decision was made by the computer, the adaptable process still showed the potential of the non-linear manufacturing method.

The interactive manufacturing system FormFab [17] proposed by Mueller et al. integrated the real-time human control with the actual robot manufacturing. It enabled the designer to continuously change the appearance of the product during the process of robot fabrication. In the operation of FormFab, the designer used his finger to select the thermoplastic sheet area where needed to be reshaped, and then the robotic arm held the heat gun to heat the area. When the material reached the appropriate temperature, the pneumatic system would blow air pressure retraction to change the shape of target area. Based on this novel method, FormFab's system could explore various possibilities under the relationship among human controls, robot fabrications, and material changes.

Atanasova et al. proposed a robotic timber structure collaboration system that could provide design suggestions and options during the fabrication process. The Prototype-as-Artefact system [2] was designed for one robot and two humans, facilitated by a shared AR workspace. In this AR workspace, humans manually placed the first timber element in one of orthogonal dimensions. The cooperating robots continued the assembly cycle by placing two elements in other two orthogonal dimensions to complete the basic structure unit. Then the alternating loop between human and robot started over to expend the aggregation of units (Fig. 2).

Fig. 2. Left- Robotic Softness: an adaptive robotic fabrication process for woven structures [5]. Mid-FormFab enables the designer to continuously change the appearance of the product during the process of robot fabrication [17]. Right- Prototype-as-Artefact: a robotic timber structure collaboration system [2].

The projects mentioned above shows varying proportions of HRC, with an emphasis on unpredictable outcomes and creative processes. It keeps the precision of robotic-assisted manufacturing while allowing designers' creativity. Through this iterative design based on human-machine collaboration, it may propose a new possibility of digital craftmanship.

3 ROCOS System

ROCOS (Robot Collaboration System) aims to develop the collaborative construction method which allows one designer and one robotic arm co-working in MR environment. It proposes a stick-weaving construction method based on the iterative design. The designer can continuously simulate the stick placement in a MR environment while working synchronously with the robotic arm. Every time when the designer finishes a simulated placement of virtual stick, the robotic arm will immediately grip and assemble the actual stick to the correct position. In the process of simulation and assembly between the designer and the robot arm, the ideal stick-weaving design is gradually completed.

The ROCOS system consists of three parts including (1) Mix-reality Interface, (2) Iterative design, and (3) Collaborative construction.

3.1 Mix-Reality Interface

The layout is the beginning of every construction site. In our research, the correct layout which digitalizes the physical environment is the essential function to build the BIM-based platform for the collaboration between the designer and the robotic arm.

ROCOS provides the MR interface that the designer can use the Oculus handles and glasses to layout the real space and turn it into MR space. The designer with MR glasses can see the real world and use the MR handles to measure the space size. All the measuring data will be documented and translated into virtual spatial model. In the end, the full-scale BIM-based model which mirrors the real space will be built automatically along with the layout process. In addition, MR interface also allows the designer to create the additional virtual objects which are not existed in the real world to be the augmented reference for spatial design clues. After the MR layout is done, the designer and the robotic arm can start collaborating on this BIM-based platform (Fig. 3).

Fig. 3. ROCOS MR interface can create the BIM-based model and additional virtual objects to build the MR layout.

3.2 Iterative Design

In this research, we propose the stick-weaving construction method based on the iterative design between the designer and the robotic arm. There are two reasons we develop this design method. First, we try to explore the potential design method using simple element to aggregate complex shape through iterative design process. Too functional elements such as pillars, windows, doors or walls may limit the design possibility or diversity in full-scale design process. We choose the stick shape as the basic element which allows free-dimension aggregation to gradually shape the complex form. The designer can add and modify his design stick by stick instead of placing the correct configuration immediately. In addition, the stick-weaving structure facilitates the robot-assisted construction because of the iterative assembly process [12]. The operation of robotic arm only needs to focus on the correctness of the assembly path and position. It reduces the difficulty of construction while maintaining the design complexity and makes the robot-assisted construction more feasible.

ROCOS provides the BIM-based platform which engages the designer and robotic arm collaborating the stick-weaving construction. First, the designer uses the MR handles to draw the virtual line (Fig. 4). The virtual line can be presented in MR and examined the appropriateness immediately. For example, if the line conflicts to the MR space boundary, the extra part will be highlighted as red to remind the designer. In addition, the designer also can judge whether sticks are overlapped with each other appropriately by watching from different MR angles. Once the designer confirms the design, the ROCOS system with virtual robotic arm will simulate and present the assembly paths automatically. The designer can observe the simulated path animation to find out the ideal one. If the simulated path passes the designer's evaluation, ROCOS will send the instructions to execute the real robot construction.

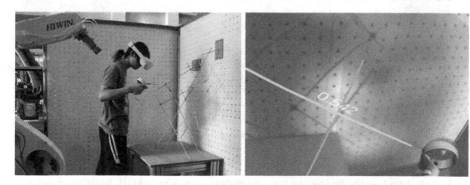

Fig. 4. The immersive design method and interface of ROCOS

3.3 Collaborative Construction

The collaborative construction aims to synchronously execute the stick structure assembly according to the designer's design. In the last iterative design part, the designer places and confirms one stick position in MR. Then the virtual robotic arm in ROCOS system will simulate the assembly path and finally drive the real robotic arm to assemble it. To achieve the process, we need to overcome two problems. (1) the confliction between design model and fabrication paths. (2) the translation and communication between simulation and fabrication.

(1) **the confliction between design model and fabrication paths.**

During the design process, each time the designer will creates one spatial line and its weaving relationship to other lines. We call the design model including spatial relationship as the BIM-based model. According to the BIM based model, the ROCOS system abstracts the spatial information of target line such as position, vector, and shape to plan the virtual assembly path of robotic arm (Fig. 5). The ROCOS system uses the Grasshopper (GH) and Python to develop the visualized interface which can present the dynamic relationship between virtual robotic arm and BIM-based model. Based on the BIM-based relationship, the ROCOS system can simulate and examine the confliction between robotic arm's assembly path and existing BIM-based model. If the conflictions occur during the simulating animation, the collided parts will be highlighted in red and re-simulate the assembly path until all the conflictions are solved.

(2) **the translation and communication between simulation and fabrication**

The correct simulation will be auto-translated into robotic arm assembly paths via our translation program in GH. In the translation program, the data format called HRSDK will be generated from assembly path simulation to fit the robotic arm's control commands. The HRSDK is synchronously delivered to robot control system embedded in robotic arm via Ethernet. Once receiving the HRSDK commands, the robot control system will activate the real robotic arm to execute the assembly motions.

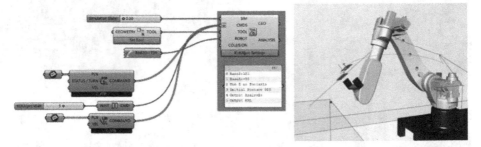

Fig. 5. Left-the auto-translated robotic arm's assembly path program in GH. Right-the visual path simulation in the ROCOS MR interface.

4   The Practice of ROCOS

ROCOS finally achieves the stick-weaving design-to-fabrication process which integrates the MR interface (Fig. 6 left) and synchronous robot fabrication (Fig. 6 right). A complete process loop is as follows: In the beginning, the designer creates one virtual stick in MR. The ROCOS system simulate the assembly path of robotic arm to ensure no confliction. Then the simulation is translated into robotic arm's command and deliver to the robot control system. The real robotic arm grips and assembles the physical stick to the corresponding position. Here the designer and robotic arm have completed single design-to-fabrication collaborative process. This process can be run multiple times until the designer stops it.

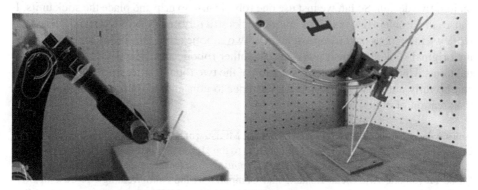

Fig. 6. Left-the MR interface. Right-the robot fabrication

In Fig. 7, we present the serial design-to-fabrication photos to demonstrate the process of iterative design based on the collaboration between the designer and the robotic arm. We can see how the robotic weave the stick structure according to the designer's plan step by step.

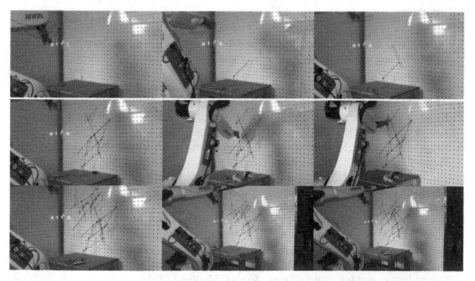

Fig. 7. The weaving process with the mix-reality Interface and synchronous robot fabrication.

5 Conclusion

In this research, we develop the ROCOS system which integrates the MR interface and synchronous robot fabrication for stick-weaving structure. It not only demonstrates the collaborative construction, but also presents the possibility of digital craft creation based on iterative design. So far, we just use one robotic arm to grip and place the stick units. It causes the problem that the joints among sticks still rely on human's assistance. The next work we may focus on the improvement of two robotic arms. One robotic arm maintains the original stick placement work, and the other robotic arm is responsible for welding the joints. Under the cooperative operation of the two robotic arms, the assembly process can be fully automated, allowing the designer to concentrate on immersing himself in the creation of digital craftsmanship.

Acknowledgement. Gratefulness is given to the Ministry of Science and Technology and Higher Education Sprout Project, Ministry of Education to the Headquarters of University Advancement at NCKU for project support: (1) Adaptive Computing: The Development of Self-Standing Wall Based on Robotic Arm Metal-Bending and Computer Vision Auto-Welding - A Case of Steel Mesh Wall Construction (Project No.: 111-2221-E-006 -050 -MY3). (2) Smart Construction: The Integration of Computer Vision and Robot Arm Apply to the Human-Robot Collaboration in the Building Construction-A Case of Curve Rebar Grid (Project No.: 110-2221-E-006 -049-). (3) IP (Island Performance): The Creation Plan Based on the Translation of Techno Art Scene and Cross-disciplinary Collaboration - Matsu Islands as a Demo Site (Project No.: 112-2420-H-006-002-)
.

References

1. Ajoudani, A., Zanchettin, A.M., Ivaldi, S., Albu-Schäffer, A., Kosuge, K., Khatib, O.: Progress and prospects of the human–robot collaboration. Auton. Robot. **42**(5), 957–975 (2017). https://doi.org/10.1007/s10514-017-9677-2
2. Atanasova, L., Mitterberger, D., Sandy, T., Gramazio, F., Kohler, M., Dörfler, K.: Prototype As Artefact (2020)
3. Bauer, A., Wollherr, D., Buss, M.: Human–robot collaboration: a survey. Int. J. Humanoid Rob. **5**(1), 47–66 (2008)
4. Brugnaro, G., Hanna, S.: Adaptive robotic training methods for subtractive manufacturing. In: Proceedings of the 37th Annual Conference of the Association for Computer Aided Design in Architecture (ACADIA), pp. 164–169. Acadia Publishing Company (2017)
5. Brugnaro, G., Baharlou, E., Vasey, L., Menges, A.: Robotic softness: an adaptive robotic fabrication process for woven structures (2016)
6. Burdea, G.C., Coiffet, P.: Virtual Reality Technology. John Wiley & Sons (2003)
7. Chen, I.Y.H., MacDonald, B., Wunsche, B.: Mixed reality simulation for mobile robots. In: 2009 IEEE International Conference on Robotics and Automation, pp. 232–237 (2009)
8. Chu, B., Jung, K., Lim, M.T., Hong, D.: Robot-based construction automation: an application to steel beam assembly (Part I). Autom. Constr. **32**, 46–61 (2013)
9. Ding, L., Jiang, W., Zhou, Y., Zhou, C., Liu, S.: BIM-based task-level planning for robotic brick assembly through image-based 3D modeling. Adv. Eng. Inform. **43**, 100993 (2020)
10. Green, S.A., Billinghurst, M., Chen, X., Chase, J.G.: Human-robot collaboration: a literature review and augmented reality approach in design. Int. J. Adv. Rob. Syst. **5**(1), 1 (2008)

11. Hoenig, W., et al.: Mixed reality for robotics. In: 2015 IEEE/RSJ International Conference on Intelligent Robots and Systems (IROS). IEEE, pp. 5382–5387 (2015)
12. Hsu, J.S., Shen, Y.T., Cheng, F.C.: The development of the intuitive teaching-based design method for robot-assisted fabrication applied to bricklaying design and construction. In: International Conference on Human-Computer Interaction, pp. 51–57. Springer, Cham (2022)
13. Inagaki, Y., Sugie, H., Aisu, H., Ono, S., Unemi, T.: Behavior-based intention inference for intelligent robots cooperating with human. In: Proceedings of 1995 IEEE International Conference on Fuzzy Systems, vol. 3, pp. 1695–1700 (1995)
14. Liang, C.J., Wang, X., Kamat, V.R., Menassa, C.C.: Human–robot collaboration in construction: classification and research trends. J. Constr. Eng. Manag. **147**(10), 03121006 (2021)
15. Mitterberger, D., Atanasova, L., Dörfler, K., Gramazio, F., Kohler, M.: Tie a knot: human–robot cooperative workflow for assembling wooden structures using rope joints. Constr. Robot. **6**, 1–16 (2022)
16. Mitterberger, D., et al.: Augmented bricklaying. Constr. Robot. **4**(3), 151–161 (2020)
17. Mueller, S., et al.: FormFab: continuous interactive fabrication. In: Proceedings of the Thirteenth International Conference on Tangible, Embedded, and Embodied Interaction. pp. 315–323 (2019)
18. Wei, L., et al.: RAF: Robot Aware Fabrication-Hand-motion Augmented Robotic Fabrication Workflow and Case Study (2019)

Mixed Reality Applications for Manipulating Robots and Rovers: ARSIS 6.0

Digno J. R. Teogalbo[✉], David Auner, Natalie Ayala, Charles Burnell, Trice Dayrit, Gamma Gamel, Nick Lotspeich, Alex Smith, Steve Swanson, Elias Willerup, Brady Williamson, and Ben Villanueva

Boise State University, Boise, ID 83725, USA

Abstract. Augmented Reality Space Informatics System (ARSIS) 6.0 is a software prototype that envisions mixed reality usage for astronauts. Designed in accordance with the 2023 NASA SUITS (National Aeronautics and Space Administration) (Spacesuit User Interface Technologies for Students) Challenge, ARSIS 6.0 is a modular system of interactables for the Microsoft HoloLens 2. The mixed reality (MR) user interfaces are intended to enhance the efficiency and autonomy of a user navigating hazardous terrain and manipulating a rover for geological sampling and data collection. This system additionally concentrates on improving and aiding the completion of lunar mission objectives in conjunction within an XR (extended reality) environment. The XR environment is enriched with displays, beacons, utility tool belt, virtual reality (VR) mission control, telemetry data, and an arm bar to support an operator in a given scenario to navigate toward a point of interest, perform mission objectives, and operate an autonomous rover to extract geological data. In addition to the heads up display (HUD), the application works with a rover assistant to navigate lunar terrain and understand points of interest for missions. ARSIS 6.0 supplements the operational capacity and functionality of a spacesuit information system with a designed XR environment.

Displays in the ARSIS XR environment are virtual control panels that provide visual indicators for haptic controls. The user manipulates these windows virtually to perform operations in software. In practice users are aided by using the XR user interface (UI) in obtaining mission objectives and procedures, space suit biometrics, rover controls, spectroscopy data, software help and usage, and software settings. Displays additionally include audio, visual, and tactile affordances. Finally, text-based UI in the heads up display (HUD) provides information quickly to the astronaut user in order to notify them of situations or scenarios that require immediate attention. Pop up text UI is designed to alert astronaut users on information related to emergencies for the user or mission objective.

In addition to HUD UIs, the system includes wayfinding and navigation beacons. The beacons act as markers the user can place to designate a point of interest. They also represent places of interest for the astronaut or rover. These places include wayfinding elements for travel, a notation on hazardous locations to avoid, or a trail the user leaves as they navigate the terrain.

The ARSIS XR environment contains a utility tool belt which can be accessed through predetermined gestures or through the arm bar and other windows. These are virtual objects within the user's field of view which allow them to perform operations as if they were physical devices. These gadgets can be considered

© The Author(s), under exclusive license to Springer Nature Switzerland AG 2023
J. Y. C. Chen and G. Fragomeni (Eds.): HCII 2023, LNCS 14027, pp. 382–394, 2023.
https://doi.org/10.1007/978-3-031-35634-6_27

virtual replacements for physical tools such as compasses and measuring devices. Also, they may act as virtual implements to take the place of physical gadgets like maps, inventory for field notes and spectroscopy data, and controllers for a rover.

Telemetry data is a stream of information sent to the user and is interpreted by ARSIS 6.0 and displayed to the user in the appropriate section.

The arm bar is an interface anchored to the user's left arm. It allows for immediate access to frequently referenced information such as battery and oxygen levels, as well as the current mission objective.

Within an AR environment, studies have shown that users were able to retain and learn the subject matter more effectively versus traditional oral or visual methods. ARSIS 6.0 as a system takes advantage of this enhanced learning capability by immersing the user with AR interactables which gamifies the mission scenario and allows the operator to "play" by mimicking the operating procedures.

Additionally, ARSIS as a system aims to promote user autonomy by providing independent access to mission objectives and procedures. The user autonomy provided by ARSIS 6.0 will aid in reducing the necessity for ground station communication on extraterrestrial missions, which would otherwise be compromised due to informational delay or degradation. This prototypal system provides insight into the use cases of augmented reality as a means to enhance task performance, workload, and situational awareness. Overall ARSIS as an AR environment seeks to enable prolonged sustained missions through supporting operator autonomy and increasing mission success by providing enhanced technical support and ease of use.

Keywords: Gamification · Robots · Avatars and Virtual Human · UX (User Experience) · VR · AR · MR · XR and Metaverse

Abbreviations

AR	Augmented Reality
ARM	Arm Retained Menu
ARSIS	Augmented Reality Space Informatics System
EVA	Extra Vehicular Activity
HUD	Heads Up Display
MR	Mixed Reality
MRTK	Mixed Reality Toolkit
NASA	National Aeronautics and Space Administration
ROS	Robot Operating System
SUITS	Spacesuit User Interface Technologies for Students
UI	User Interface
UX	User Experience
VR	Virtual Reality
XR	Extended Reality

1 Introduction and Background

On November 16th, 2022, the National Aeronautics and Space Administration (NASA) launched Artemis 1 to orbit the moon. A successor of the Apollo missions, the Artemis program has prompted renewed interest in lunar and planetary exploration. Artemis 1 was the first of a series of missions to provide a foundation for future manned missions to the Moon and to Mars. Artemis' stated goal is that "NASA will land the first woman and first person of color on the Moon, using innovative technologies to explore more of the lunar surface than ever before." (nasa.gov, 2023).

To further this grand endeavor, the program started the NASA Spacesuit User Interface Technologies for Students (SUITS) challenge: a student designed project to generate ideas and prototypes of technologies to be used by the astronauts to meet the requirements of their missions. Due to the complexity of these missions, many challenges are posed to the teams. For example the current proposed landing site on the Moon is on the lunar south pole. The south pole presents a scientific opportunity as evidence suggests an abundance of ice there. However, working on the south pole would be particularly challenging. The sun shines from the horizon at all times causing maximum glare for the astronaut. With no atmosphere to diffuse light, there would be extreme visual contrast, causing bright surfaces flanked by long, very dark shadows.

This paper covers one of the proposed solutions for the 2022–2023 NASA SUITS challenge as depicted by the Boise State University NASA SUITS team. Additionally, this paper discusses the importance of gamified experiences in developing heads up display (HUD) user interfaces (UI).

ARSIS 6.0 is the sixth iteration of the mixed reality prototype designed and created by the Boise State University NASA SUITS research team for the NASA SUITS challenge. ARSIS 6.0 is used with the Microsoft HoloLens 2 and built in the Unity Game Engine with the Microsoft Mixed Reality Toolkit (MRTK). With Unity and Microsoft's Mixed Reality Toolkit working as cross-platform, it could hypothetically be built to other devices that have a parity of features with the HoloLens 2. Therefore, other hardware NASA may choose to develop in the future for the Artemis Mission is possible to use. The ARSIS 6.0 iteration builds upon the previous successes and innovations of the ARSIS 5.0 system with a focus towards implementing interfaces to manipulate an autonomous rover. Additionally, ARSIS 6.0 utilizes newly designed user interfaces, and the use of additional UI based tool sets such as the tool belt, redefined Arm Retained Menus (ARMs) and beacon systems.

The 2023 NASA SUITS challenge requires the user to execute procedures within a mission scenario in which the user navigates terrain in order to collect geological samples with a spectrometer with the assistance of a rover. The challenge goals are to enable long-duration missions with supplementary XR interfaces which promote user autonomy and increased situational awareness and safety during extraterrestrial missions. These supplementary XR interfaces are designed to facilitate ease of use and access, interface redundancy, and improve cognitive and technical capacity. Given the hypothetical base location at the lunar south pole, these objectives are incredibly demanding. Having a user interface that functions in high contrast light environments poses a unique challenge not experienced in normal terrestrial use. The rover must be able to map a new environment, as well as interpret commands from the user to autonomously navigate to locations of interest. Additionally, the environment is inherently unfamiliar, thus implying the rover's goal of navigation to those locations may be difficult.

2 Challenge and Design

2.1 Challenge and Design Purpose

As NASA pursues additional Artemis Missions, it is important astronauts participating in lunar spacewalks are equipped with technology that promotes autonomy and meet the demands of lunar exploration, navigation, and extreme terrain access. Astronauts' tasks may include exploring surface terrain, executing scientific and engineering research, and interacting with various types of assets and payloads. As such, astronauts need to manipulate and operate various resources such as spacesuits, life-support systems, rovers, geological tools, human landers, power systems, scientific payloads, and varying habitats in a reliable and safe manner. ARSIS 6.0 is the solution created by the Boise State University NASA SUITS research team to address these challenges.

2.2 Challenge Goals and Requirements

The requirements in the 2023 NASA SUITS Challenge state that the design must tolerate harsh lighting conditions and outdoor conditions at the proposed mission site. Additionally, the XR application must access and display telemetry data and provide a caution and warning system providing visual and auditory alerts to the user of any spacesuit anomalies. The telemetry data is responsible for providing the simulation data and spacesuit state, therefore this requirement ensures that the design can respond accordingly to the telemetry data and display the appropriate notifications and indicators. The design must not prohibit the user from performing procedures in the event of interruptions, this includes exceptions and errors. The design will provide assistance during navigation, display the task instructions for extravehicular activities, and should not distract the user or crowd them with non-critical information. ARSIS 6.0 aims to fulfill these requirements through the use of its ARM bar, beacons, utility belt, rover control, and various forms of data visualization in an AR environment.

2.3 Design Objectives

Our design philosophy for ARSIS 6.0 centers around three key principles: functionality, effectiveness, and autonomy. ARSIS 6.0 is designed to provide a concise and explicit interface with which a user is able to autonomously navigate and perform mission procedures. The XR environment produced by ARSIS 6.0 provides functionality to supplement and support the mission scenario and execution of procedures with respect to the requirements outlined. In order to successfully complete tasks autonomously, ground control has the ability to create a series of tasks to accomplish, referred to in ARSIS 6.0 as "Procedures". The procedures are sent to the astronaut's HUD to reduce the need for constant verbal communication with ground control to receive instructions. Additionally, these tasks may have associated images, videos, and animations with them, thus providing the astronaut with an intuitive idea of what their current task is and how to complete it, rather than relying on a series of verbal commands. Instructions for mission procedures are displayed through auditory and visual means, enabling the user to complete tasks more efficiently. These mission procedures, or changes to the procedures will be uploaded in real-time to the astronaut by Mission Control giving the astronaut more autonomy. The astronaut is able to transmit and receive data such as location, heading, resource conditions, and emergencies bi-directionally with Mission Control.

2.4 XR Environment

An XR Environment is the foundation of the ARSIS 6.0 project. The team aims to provide the astronaut access to vital information through an unobtrusive HUD, as well as giving quick access to information that is not needed immediately in the astronaut's field of view.

3 Displays

ARSIS 6.0 includes various windows to display information about the mission. These menus are planned to be accessible to the astronaut via the ARM Bar menu or voice commands. The menus are planned to include biometrics, navigation, rover controls, mission procedures, mission summary, and an informational log.

3.1 ARM Bar

Through gesture tracking, the arm bar tool gives the astronaut access to all of the integrated tools and menus needed for Extravehicular Activities (EVAs). The arm bar is planned to act as the user's central hub for accessing and navigating through the menus

Fig. 1. ARM Bar User Interface

in the HUD. When the user reveals the underside of their wrist to the HoloLens 2 field of view, the arm bar is planned to display next to the wrist of the user, thus allowing for navigation of menus. The arm bar is shown is Fig. 1.

3.2 Beacons

Beacons are waypoints placed in the XR environment by the astronaut to designate points of interest, navigational waypoints, or areas of caution. Beacons may also be used to direct the rover's movement, scout areas, or instruct the rover to avoid certain areas. The beacons are planned to have an assortment of colors to differentiate between their individual purposes. An example of the beacons is shown in Fig. 2.

Fig. 2. Beacons shown in the ARSIS 6.0 HUD

3.3 Utility Belt

The utility belt aims to give the astronaut access to a set of XR tools to aid in research and navigation during EVAs. The tool belt is planned to include a virtual ruler, virtual protractor, laser pointer, bearing halo, beacon compass, and mini-map. The utility belt is shown in Fig. 3. Once the astronaut selects a tool, it becomes active and is shown to the astronaut. For example, if the astronaut selects the beacon compass this will be shown on the back of their hand as represented in Fig. 4, with the bearing pointer pointed at the selected beacon.

3.4 Data Visualization

Within ARSIS 6.0, astronauts have access to various menus that display the status of different metrics about the suit and mission in order to alleviate sole reliance on ground

Fig. 3. Toolbelt User Interface

Fig. 4. Compass User Interface

control. The use of data visualization allows the astronaut to more easily interpret large, complex amounts of data. Biometric suit data will be available to the astronaut through the ARM Bar menus. In the event that suit metrics are outside of optimal ranges, the astronaut will be alerted via visual and auditory indicators.

3.5 Peripheral Equipment

To add the astronaut's vision in the very dark areas and to aid the AR system in its ability to perform the hand tracking function, the team has added high power lights to the top of the Hololens 2 and to the body of the astronaut. For testing our Hololens 2 will be equipped with an attachable sunshade to allow the astronaut to clearly see the hologram UI while looking into the sun's direction. For the scenario given by NASA SUITS, the astronaut will be able to use a compass heading to assist in their navigation. The Hololens 2 does have a magnetometer, however the team believes we can get more accurate compass data from an off-the-shelf compass system. The team's plan is to attach this compass to the Hololens 2 and send the data to the Hololens 2 through the telemetry server. The ARSIS 6.0 system also has a connection to a VR system in Mission Control. The VR user in Mission Control can annotate information on the astronauts Hololens 2 in real-time allowing Mission Control to easily help the astronaut if needed.

3.6 Autonomy and Improved Situational Awareness

Our goal is to give the astronaut ground-level management of assets, thus providing greater flexibility for both them and the ground control team. Through design choices, the team aims to give the astronaut an enhanced level of autonomy during EVAs. While ground control will still be able to monitor the astronauts, these built in systems will give the astronauts the ability to continue working in the event that communications with Mission Control are interrupted. Through this XR system, the astronaut will have access to a tremendous amount of data and functionality. This will allow the astronaut to have increased situational awareness and give the astronauts the ability to make many decisions without the need to contact MIssion Control. These abilities become very important in future missions on Mars where time delays can be as long as 40 min.

4 Gamification Procedures

Gamification means to include elements from games to improve a traditional design, such as allowing users on a message board to customize an avatar. Certain gamification techniques are proven to improve user engagement, sociability, information retention, among other benefits. In our case, we are interested in how gamification can benefit the workflow of the astronauts.

Because of the high pressure scenario and the general complexity of the Artemis missions, astronauts may benefit from a gamified system. Such a system can provide a more engaging and intuitive way to access information, use virtual tools, and complete objectives. This could help reduce cognitive workload, increase situational awareness, and improve overall mission performance.

An example of a gamified HUD is progress bars that could show astronauts their progress towards main objectives. Video games have demonstrated the benefits of tracking progress in completing an objective (O'Brien, 2016). A progress bar could be visible on the HUD displaying a comprehensive status of the mission objective for that day. This reminds the astronaut of the broader context of their tasks. During extravehicular activity (EVA's) it is vital to manage and track the progress of your procedures while managing assets like the rover. After the astronaut has assigned a task to the rover a progress bar will display the status of completion on the astronaut's HUD. The astronaut stays informed of the asset status and is informed in the event the asset is unable to complete the assigned task.

Another example of gamification can be seen in the ARSIS 6.0 utility belt. Good virtual tools are not just functional; they feel like real tools and provide a sense of satisfaction. The goal in gamifying virtual tools is for astronauts to use them subconsciously. If the astronauts have to think too hard it will cause stress. By gamifying the utility belt with visual and haptic feedback the astronauts may be more confident while completing procedures.

Training in a VR environment was used in a nurse training program involving catheter insertion. (Butt et al., 2017). The training allows for information retention which increases the success rate of live patient procedures. The team hypothesizes this element of efficiency can carry over to the ARSIS 6.0 scenario. In the scenarios associated with ARSIS 6.0 use, the application is the actual mission tool. However, during training for lunar spacewalks, astronauts may use an XR system many times, essentially training them on their procedures, rover function, and communication to Mission Control.

Research suggests efficient gameplay results in well designed user interfaces. For example, games such as Car Mechanic Simulator is a game where the player simulates technical tasks. (Car Mechanic Simulator, 2021). These simulator-type games let users play a gamified version of the job in preparation to perform it in real life. Similarly the objective of ARSIS 6.0's heads up display is to take procedures, and other information, and present them in ways to help the user perform them. In a study where a maintenance worker was assisted by a subject matter expert via HoloLens all maintenance workers reported that the HoloLens remote assistance was an improvement. In addition, all maintenance workers said it at least partially helped identify hazards. Maintenance workers felt safer taking advice through the HoloLens instead of over the phone. (Vorraber, Gasser, Webb, et al., 2020).

An additional study compared users utilizing paper plans versus a HoloLens to assist in an exercise where teams of 2 people would assemble pre-cut and labeled components in a mock-bathroom. Teams were separated into 2 groups, one with only paper plans, and one with HoloLens environments to assist with visualizing where components go in the finished assembly. Though the sample size of this study was small the HoloLens teams were 9% faster than the teams with only the paper plans. (DaValle and Azhar, 2020).

All of the improvements shown in these studies support the hypothesis that using the HoloLens with a link to subject matter expert improves user efficiency and confidence. Considering the effectiveness of games to convey meaning and intention through interactions, objectives, and context. ARSIS 6.0 utilizes the XR environment to populate the mission scenario with game-like aspects as a means to provide cohesion between the actions required to accomplish the mission objectives while maintaining the itinerary outlined within the operational and technical procedures.

5   Rover

The rover is a NANO-RT1 Robot. It has a 1080P camera and a Lidar sensor. Lidar is a time of flight sensor which measures distances by timing how long it takes to receive a reflection of light that it has emitted. In addition this Lidar has a rotating head allowing it to measure the distances to objects in the plane of its rotation. It uses the Robot Operating System (ROS) to coordinate its activity and will receive its commands through a websocket connection to a server that aggregates user commands. Through the same connection, data from the rover will be sent to the user after being processed in the telemetry server, which is part of our test environment. The rover will also have high powered lights to help illuminate the shadows in the harsh lighting environment of the lunar south pole (Fig. 5 and Fig. 6).

Fig. 5. Rover, image obtained from Amazon.com

The primary tool the astronauts will use to control the rover is the laser pointer. The laser pointer will allow the astronaut to select an area in their line of sight without needing to travel to it. When an area is selected the astronaut can send the rover to it to autonomously perform a task, for example collecting samples or taking pictures. When the astronaut sends the rover, a sphere shaped beacon will appear over the selected area in the astronaut's HUD. The sphere is color coded to indicate the current state the rover is in. Blue if the rover is still working, green when it completes its task, yellow if there is a problem (such as being stuck), red if there is an emergency (such a damage), or

Fig. 6. UI of Rover Cam as seen in the HUD

Fig. 7. Waypoint selecting using the Rover

purple if there is an issue or notification that falls outside of these categories. Selecting a waypoint for the rover is shown in Fig. 7.

The rover is an extension of the astronauts' awareness helping them achieve the mission's objectives. It will provide images, video, and lidar mapping data used to create a point cloud of terrain that it has seen. By using the extended reality tools provided by ARSIS 6.0 the user can use the rover to scout ahead in areas of low light and visibility, and can use the rover to light up an area for them to work. Scouting ahead may ensure there is a safe path for the astronaut to translate between work sites, ensuring the astronaut's resources are spent as efficiently as possible. When at a new work site the rover can ensure that all of the relevant terrain is mapped so the astronaut can have a full 360 degree map of where they are going to assist in their situational awareness. These capabilities should increase the astronauts ability to safely traverse the environment and assist the astronaut to perform their objectives efficiently and safely.

6 Conclusion

The Boise State University NASA SUITS research team envisions an informatic system which will increase productivity, safety, and autonomy of an astronaut on the lunar surface near the poles. By leveraging the unique capabilities of the HoloLens 2 mixed-reality environment in combination with the UI/UX components of the ARSIS 6.0 application, the team aims to provide solutions which have a meaningful positive impact to the Artemis missions. The team's proposed solution meets the goal of using innovation to assist in lunar exploration. Through the utilization of gamified techniques, digitized tools and user interfaces may thus reduce the overall payload to extra-terrestrial missions, providing a means to improve an astronaut's capabilities without requiring additional weight and maintenance.

Gamification inspired user interfaces utilized in previous ARSIS systems have proven effective in past application testing. Incorporating more elements of gamification into astronaut's procedures should encourage higher levels of engagement, information retention, situational awareness and reduce cognitive workload. Gamification elements should allow for easier understanding of mission objectives and assist the user in managing mission assets. Due to the effectiveness of gamification in other studies, the design of ARSIS 6.0 is reflected to take advantage of this phenomenon.

Utilizing autonomous rovers during exploration should enhance the efficiency of the mission and aid the astronaut in completing tasks effectively. By leveraging the rover's video, lights, and lidar systems to map and navigate terrain, the rover can create a safer environment during EVAs despite extreme conditions. In addition the rover could be used to help light locations of interest for the astronaut or even shuttle basic tools between astronauts.

The aspirational goal of the Artemis project of using lunar exploration as a way to prepare for a mission to Mars requires a herculean effort, needing epic amounts of innovation. The team's hypothesis is that ARSIS 6.0 may help with this endeavor. By providing a complete informatics system that allows an astronaut to be able to safely, and efficiently complete tasks, with streamlined communication channels to ground control, and leveraging autonomous rovers to assist astronauts, the team can say the system will meet the goals of the Artemis project.

References

Boise State University: Boise State Nurses, Gamers Win National Award for New Nursing Simulation Technology. Newswise (2015, September 17). https://www.newswise.com/art

icles/boise-state-nurses-gamers-win-national-education-award-for-developing-nursing-sim
    ulation-technology

Borgen, K.B., Ropp, T.D., Weldon, W.T.: Assessment of augmented reality technology's impact
    on speed of learning and task performance in aeronautical engineering technology education.
    The International Journal of Aerospace Psychology **31**(3), 219–229 (2021). Taylor Francis
    Online. https://doi.org/10.1080/24721840.2021.1881403. Author, F.: Contribution title. In: 9th
    International Proceedings on Proceedings, pp. 1–2. Publisher, Location (2010)

Breitkreuz, K.R., et al.: Nursing faculty perceptions of a virtual reality catheter insertion game: a
    multisite international study. Clinical Simulation in Nursing **53**, 49–58 (2021). ScienceDirect.
    https://doi.org/10.1016/j.ecns.2020.10.003

Butt, A.L., Kardong-Edgren, S., Ellertson, A.: Using game-based virtual reality with haptics for
    skill acquisition. Clinical Simulation in Nursing **16**, 25–32 (2017). ScienceDirect. https://doi.
    org/10.1016/j.ecns.2017.09.010

Red Dot Games: Car Mechanic Simulator [PC]. PlayWay S.A (2021)

DaValle, A., Azhar, S.: An investigation of mixed reality technology for onsite construction assem-
    bly. MATEC Web of Conferences, 312(2). ResearchGate (2020). https://doi.org/10.1051/mat
    ecconf/202031206001

Mitra, P.: Human Systems Integration of an Extravehicular Activity Space Suit Augmented Reality
    Display System. Theses and Dissertations. Mississippi State University Institutional Repository
    (2018). https://hdl.handle.net/11668/21103

NASA: ARTEMIS. NASA (2019). https://www.nasa.gov/specials/artemis/

O'Brien, C.: O'Brien: Get ready for the decade of gamification. The Mercury News (2016, August
    14). Retrieved 10 February 2023, from https://web.archive.org/web/20181015153249/https://
    www.mercurynews.com/2010/10/21/obrien-get-ready-for-the-decade-of-gamification/

Vorraber, W., et al.: Assessing augmented reality in production: remote-assisted maintenance with
    HoloLens. Procedia CIRP **88**, 139–144 (2020). ScienceDirect. https://doi.org/10.1016/j.procir.
    2020.05.025

Now Look Here! ⇓ Mixed Reality Improves Robot Communication Without Cognitive Overload

Nhan Tran[1,2(✉)], Trevor Grant[3], Thao Phung[2], Leanne Hirshfield[3], Christopher Wickens[4], and Tom Williams[2]

[1] Cornell University, Ithaca, NY 14853, USA
nt322@cornell.edu
[2] Colorado School of Mines, Golden, CO 80401, USA
twilliams@mines.edu
[3] University of Colorado Boulder, Boulder, CO 80309, USA
leanne.hirshfield@colorado.edu
[4] Colorado State University, Fort Collins, CO 80523, USA

Abstract. Recently, researchers have initiated a new wave of convergent research in which Mixed Reality visualizations enable new modalities of human-robot communication, including *Mixed Reality Deictic Gestures* (MRDGs) – the use of visualizations like virtual arms or arrows to serve the same purpose as traditional physical deictic gestures. But while researchers have demonstrated a variety of benefits to these gestures, it is unclear whether the success of these gestures depends on a user's level and type of cognitive load. We explore this question through an experiment grounded in rich theories of cognitive resources, attention, and multi-tasking, with significant inspiration drawn from *Multiple Resource Theory*. Our results suggest that MRDGs provide task-oriented benefits regardless of cognitive load, but only when paired with complex language. These results suggest that designers can pair rich referring expressions with MRDGs without fear of cognitively overloading their users.

Keywords: Mixed Reality · Cognitive Load · Deictic Gesture

1 Introduction

Successful human-robot interaction in many domains relies on successful communication. Accordingly, there has been a wealth of research on enabling human-robot communication through natural language [31,49]. However, just like human-human dialogue, human-robot dialogue is inherently multi-modal, and requires communication channels beyond speech. Human interlocutors regularly use gaze and gesture cues to augment, modify, or replace their natural language utterances, and will often use deictic gestures such as pointing, for example, to (1) direct interlocutors' attention to objects in the environment, (2) reduce the number of words that the speaker must use to refer to their target referents, and (3) lower the cognitive burden imposed on listeners to interpret those utterances.

Due to the prevalence and utility of deictic gestures in situated communication, human-robot interaction researchers have sought to enable robots to understand [30] and generate [39,40,42] deictic gestures as humans do. However, the ability to understand and generate deictic gestures comes with hardware requirements that can be onerous or unsatisfiable in certain use cases. While perceiving deictic gestures only requires a camera or depth sensor, generating deictic gestures requires a specific morphology (e.g., expressive robotic arms). This fundamentally limits gestural capabilities, and thus overall communicative capabilities, for *most* robotic platforms in use today. As examples, robots such as mobile bases used in warehouses, assistive wheelchairs, and unmanned aerial vehicles (UAVs) lack the morphologies needed to effectively communicate in this manner. Even for robots that do have arms, traditional deictic gestures have fundamental limitations. In contexts such as urban or alpine search and rescue, for example, robots may need to communicate about hard-to-describe and/or highly ambiguous referents in novel, uncertain, and unknown environments.

Consider, for example, an aerial robot in a search and rescue context. If the robot needs to generate an utterance such as "I found a victim behind *that tree*" (cf. [68]), the ability to precisely pick out the target tree using a gestural cue would be of great value, as the referring expressions the robot would need to generate without using gesture would likely be convoluted (e.g., "the fourth tree from the left in the clump of trees to the right of the large boulder") or not readily human-understandable (e.g., "the tree 48.2 m to the northwest").

Unfortunately, such a UAV would be unlikely to have an arm mounted on it solely for gesturing, meaning that physical gesture is not a realistic possibility, no matter its utility. Moreover, even in the unlikely case that the robot had an arm mounted on it, it is unlikely that a traditional pointing gesture generated by such an arm would be able to pinpoint a specific far-off tree. In this work, we present a solution to this problem that builds on recent collaborative work between the HCI subfields of Mixed Reality and Human-Robot Interaction, which have come together to initiate a new wave of convergent research in which Mixed Reality visualizations are used to enable fundamentally new modalities of human-robot communication. Specifically, we present a *Mixed Reality* solution that enables robots to generate effective deictic gestures without imposing any morphological requirements. Specifically, we present the first use of the Mixed Reality Deictic Gestures *MRDGs* proposed by Williams et al. [67] to be deployed in a rich, multimodal, task-based environment using real robotic and mixed reality hardware.

MRDGs are visualizations that can serve the same purpose as traditional deictic gestures, and which fall within the broad category of *view-augmenting* mixed reality interaction design elements in the Reality-Virtuality Interaction Cube framework [65]. Williams et al. [67] divide these new forms of visual gestures into *perspective-free* gestures that can be projected onto the environment, and *allocentric* gestures (visualized in the perspective of the listener) that can be displayed in teammates' augmented reality (AR) head-mounted displays.

Recent work on perspective-free gestures has focused on the *legibility* of projected gestures [54], while recent work on allocentric gestures has focused on gesture effectiveness when paired with different kinds of language (in virtual online testbeds) [63,64] and on effectiveness of *ego-sensitive allocentric* gestures such as virtual arms [7,14,16,18,20]. In this work we focus on this first, (non-egosensitive) allocentric category of MRDG.

In previous work, Williams et al. [64] (see also [63]), suggested that (non-ego-sensitive) allocentric MRDGs might increase communication accuracy and efficiency, and, when paired with complex referring expressions, might be viewed as more effective and likable. However, MRDGs have been primarily tested in video-based simulations [63,64], or in rigid experiments with low ecological validity [7,18,20]. In this paper, we present the first demonstration of MRDGs generated on actual AR Head-Mounted Displays (the Hololens) by commercial-grade robots, in rich, multi-modal, task-based environments.

Deploying MRDGs in these realistic task-based robotic environments allows us to how the dimensions of realistic task contexts and realistic robotic communication may or may not actually afford the effective use of such gestures. As previously pointed out by Hirshfield et al. [23], the tradeoffs between language and visual gesture may be highly sensitive to teammates' level and type of cognitive load. For example, Hirshfield et al. [23] suggest that it may not be advantageous to rely heavily on visual communication in contexts with high visual load, or to rely heavily on linguistic communication in contexts with high auditory or working memory load. These intuitions are motivated by prior theoretical work on human information processing, including the Multiple Resource Theory (MRT) by Wickens [57,58]. On the other hand, recent work conducted in rigid, non-task-based laboratory studies involving robots with *purely* gestural capabilities has demonstrated the extremely successful effectiveness of MRDGs at manipulating interactant attention in order to maximize object task-based metrics of interaction success [7,18].

It is thus unclear whether the success of MRDGs depends on the level and type of cognitive load that a user is under, or the type of multimodal communications strategies they are used in service of, or whether they might simply be broadly effective regardless of these factors. In this work, we thus analyze the use of MRDGs in the context of different multimodal robot communication strategies through a human-subjects experiment whose experimental design is grounded in rich theories of cognitive resources, attention, and multi-tasking, with significant inspiration drawn from *Multiple Resource Theory*.

Our results provide partial support for a *Universal Benefit Hypothesis*, which suggests that MRDGs provide task-oriented benefits regardless of what type of load users are under; our results show that MRDGs may only provide these benefits when paired with rich referring expressions. These results provide critical insights for designers, suggesting that designers operating in Mixed Reality Robotic domains can and should pair rich referring expressions with MRDGs without fear of cognitively overloading their users in certain cognitive contexts.

The rest of the paper proceeds as follows. In Sect. 2, we discuss related work on Mixed Reality HRI and the resource theories of attention and multitasking.

In Sect. 3, we present a human-subject experiment to study the effectiveness of different robot communication styles under different types of cognitive load. In Sect. 4, we present the results of this experiment. Our results show that MRDGs enhance the effectiveness of robot communication, regardless of how robots' verbal communication is phrased, and regardless of what level and type of mental workload interactants are under (at least under the phrasings and parameterizations used in this experiment). Finally, in Sects. 5 and 6 we conclude with general discussion, and recommendations for future research.

2 Related Work

2.1 AR for HRI

Mixed reality technologies that integrate virtual objects into the physical world have sparked recent interest in the Human-Robot Interaction (HRI) community [66] because they enable better exchange of information between people and robots, thereby improving mental models and situation awareness [47].

Despite significant research on augmented and mixed reality for several decades, [3–5,50,69] and acknowledgement of the potential for impact of AR on HRI [15,32], only recently has there been significant and sustained interest in the Virtual, Augmented, and Mixed Reality for Human-Robot Interaction (VAM-HRI) community [17,53,66]. Recent works in this area include approaches using AR for robot design [36], calibration [43], and training [46]. Moreover, there are a number of approaches towards communicating robots' perspectives [22], intentions [2,8,9,11,13], and trajectories [6,12,37,52].

Sharing perspectives is one of the best ways to improve human-robot interaction. Amor et al. [1] suggest that projecting human instructions and robot intentions in a constrained and highly structured task environment improves human robot teamwork and produces better task results [1,2,13]. Similarly, Sibirtseva et al. [44], enable robots receiving natural language instructions to reflexively generate mixed reality annotations surrounding candidate referents as they are disambiguated [44]. Finally, several researchers [7,14,19,20,63,64] investigate AR augmentations as an *active* rather than passive communication strategy, generated as gestures accompanying verbal communication.

2.2 Resource Theories of Attention and Multitasking

The previous section outlines the current state of AR for HRI, especially with respect to active and passive communication. We argue that future robots must tailor visual cues to the contextual needs of human teammates. As the first step towards enabling adaptive multimodal interfaces for human-robot communication, this study aims to unravel the interaction between MRDGs, human mental workload, and the nature of the multimodal interface in which gestures are generated, to determine whether mental workload and multimodality should be accounted for in future adaptive systems. The theoretical foundation for our investigation is supported by theories of attention and multitasking, especially as they pertain to mental workload and multiple resources [58–60].

First, resource theory posits limits to multitasking related to the difficulty or mental workload imposed by a task, and the relation between the resources demanded by the task (MWL) and the cognitive resources available to the user [61]. In a dual task context, when one (primary) task is increased in difficulty, the resources available for a secondary task decrease, along with performance on that task, in a *reciprocal* fashion. This is the foundation of *single resource theory* [25,35]. In our experiment, we assess the MWL demands of a primary robotics task by a standardized scale, the NASA Task Load Index (TLX).

Second, the theory of resources in multi-task contexts has been expanded to assume *multiple resources* [34] defined on the basis of neurophysiological structures such as the auditory versus visual cortex or the spatial and verbal cerebral hemispheres [59,60,62]. As applied to multitasking, the existence of multiple resources implies that the perfect reciprocity between the demands of one (primary) task, and a concurrently performed (secondary) task no longer holds, to the extent that the two tasks employ different resources (e.g., auditory presentation on one, visual on the other). Performance on one task can still be preserved, despite higher demands on the other. This high time-sharing efficiency when separate resources are used, forms the basis of our empirical work, and our envisioned future adaptive interfaces: to switch the modality of information provided in a dialogue, as a function of the higher demands of a primary task. In the next two subsections, we provide further detail on relevant prior work on both Multiple Resource Theory and on Theories of Dual-Tasking.

2.3 Multiple Resource Theory

The Multiple Resource Theory (MRT) proposed by Wickens [57,58] states that people have different cognitive resources for processing information. These resources can process different information at the same time and can be categorized along three dimensions: 1) early vs. late processing stage, 2) spatial vs. verbal processing code, and 3) visual vs. auditory modality [58].

The complexity of the tasks determines how these resources are utilized. For example, if the various tasks need to tap the same pool of resource, it will process the information sequentially. If the tasks need to access different resources, information will be processed in parallel. Additionally, the task performance indicates how these resource limits are reached. When two or more tasks that require a single resource are performed at the same time, a supply and demand occurs. Task error and performance decrement occur when a task that requires the same resource causes excess workload. Furthermore, MacDonald et al. [28] suggests that there is a complex relationship between workload and job performance: An increase in workload does not always result in a decrease in performance and performance can be affected by both high and low workload [28]. If the users are under low workload, also known as underload, they might become bored, lose situation awareness, and reduce alertness.

Applying MRT in the context of collocated human-robot teaming, it is even more crucial for robots to communicate using the appropriate modalities and context-aware methods that do not overload the mental resources of the human operator. Wickens' MRT framework can be used to evaluate: (1) when tasks can be carried out simultaneously, (2) how tasks interfere with each other, and (3) how increasing in one task's difficulty may impact other task's performance [58]. Our current work is motivated by a vision of future MRT-inspired robotic communication systems that could be used in scenarios involving multitasking by human operators and multimodal presentation of information. Such adaptive systems can potentially lead to more efficient use of resources, more task-relevant presentation of information, increased task performance, improved perception of the robot, and safer environment for collocated human-robot collaboration.

2.4 Dual-Tasking

Many researchers have used dual-tasking to study the limitations of human ability to process information [41,45]. In the dual-task method, subjects perform two tasks concurrently; often one of thee is designated primary and the other secondary. It is assumed (and instructed) that the participant will allocate necessary resources to the primary task, so that it does not deteriorate in the presence of the secondary task. The results then provide insights into how tasks can be carried out together and how they contribute to the workload. A classic example is driving a car and talking with passengers. This dual-task situation becomes challenging when the demand for driving task increases in poor road conditions, or if the secondary task involves a heated argument [45].

Wickens [58] demonstrated how performance decreases under dual-task condition and provides theoretical implications for resource allocation. For example, two tasks requiring the same modality will produce lower performance compared to when modalities differ. During an intense car drive that requires the driver to increase demand in processing the primary task spatially, it would be much easier to verbally process a secondary task (e.g., additional navigation instructions). Taking into account the impact of dual-task performance on mental workload, we designed a dual-task experiment that systematically varies cognitive load by changing the input modality (visual vs. auditory presentation of task structure) and the central processing code (spatial annotation over the target object vs. verbal instruction describing where the target object is located).

3 Experiment

We experimentally assessed whether the level and type of cognitive load and/or the multimodal communication strategies into which MRDGs are integrated mediate the effectiveness of those mixed-reality deictic gestures. To do so, our experiment used a 4×3 within-subjects experimental design (as described below), in which four levels and types of cognitive load (high visual perceptual load, high auditory perceptual load, high working memory load, and low overall load) were crossed with three different multi-modal communication strategies (MRDGs paired with complex vs simple language, as well as vs complex language alone without the use of mixed-reality deictic gestures). This design is

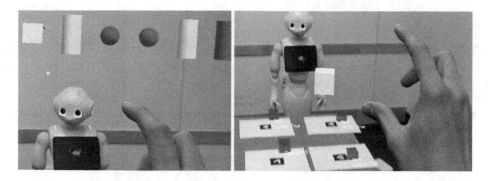

Fig. 1. During the experiment, participants play a mixed reality game using the Microsoft HoloLens. The Pepper robot is positioned behind the table, ready to interact.

based on the assumptions that there are different perceptual resources, that MRDGs employ visual-spatial resources in accordance with MRT, and that the linguistic dimensions of different communication strategies differentially employ auditory resources in accordance with MRT. Our experiment was designed to contrast two overarching competing hypotheses.

The first hypothesis, the *Cognitive Contextual Benefit Hypothesis*, formalizes the intuitions of Hirshfield et al. [23]:

H1.1 Users under high **visual perceptual load** will perform quickest and most accurately when robots rely on complex language without the use of MRDGs.

H1.2 Users under high **auditory perceptual load** will perform quickest and most accurately when robots rely on MRDGs without the use of complex language.

H1.3 Users under high **working memory load** will perform quickest and most accurately when robots rely on MRDGs without the use of complex language.

H1.4 Users under **low overall load** will perform quickest and most accurately when robots rely on MRDGs paired with complex language.

The second hypothesis, the *Universal Benefit Hypothesis*, instead would suggest that due to the substantial task-oriented benefits provided by mixed reality decitic gestures (as observed in experimental work on real robotic and MR hardware published after that Hirshfield et al. [23], e.g. [18]), MRDGs will be universally beneficial, regardless of cognitive load.

H2 Mixed-reality deictic gestures will be equally effective regardless of level and type of cognitive load.

3.1   Task Design

We will now describe the design of the experimental task designed to assess these two competing hypotheses. Participants interacted with a language-capable

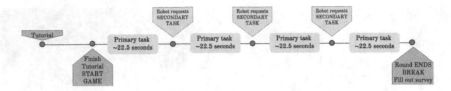

Fig. 2. After completing the tutorial and familiarizing themselves with the HoloLens, participants engage in each of the twelve trials. Their primary task is to pick-and-place the target block into the target bin. Throughout a 90-s experiment trial, the robot Pepper interrupts every 22.5 s with a secondary task.

robot while wearing the Microsoft HoloLens over a series of trials, with the robot's communication style and the user's cognitive load systematically varying between trials. The experimental task ensemble employed a dual-task paradigm oriented around a tabletop pick-and-place task. Participants view the primary task through the Microsoft HoloLens, allowing them to see virtual bins overlaid over the mixed reality fiducial markers on the table, as well as a panel of blocks above the table that changes every few seconds. As shown in Fig. 1, the Pepper robot is positioned behind the table, ready to interact with the participant.

Primary Task

The user's *primary task* is to look out for a particular block in the block panel (selected from among *red cube, red sphere, red cylinder, yellow cube, yellow sphere, yellow cylinder, green cube, green sphere, green cylinder*[1]). These nine blocks were formed by combining three colors (red, yellow, green) with three shapes (cube, sphere, cylinder). Whenever participants see this target block, their task is to pick-and-place it into any one of a particular set of bins. For example, as the game starts, the robot might tell a user that whenever they see a *red cube* they should place it in bins *two or three*.

Two additional factors increase the complexity of this primary task. First, at every point during the task, one random bin is marked as unavailable and greyed out (with the disabled bin changed each time a block is placed in a bin). This forces users to remember all target bins. Second, to create a demanding auditory component to the primary task ensemble, the user hears a series of syllables playing in the task background, is given a target syllable to look out for, and is told that whenever they hear this syllable, the target bins and non-target bins are switched. In other words, the bins they should consider to place blocks in should be exchanged with those they were previously told to avoid. For example, if the user's target bins from among four bins are bins two and three, and they hear the target syllable, then future blocks will need to be placed

---

[1] These block colors were chosen for consistent visual processing, as blue is processed differently within the eye due to spatial and frequency differences of cones between red/green and blue. This did mean that our task was not accessible to red/green colorblind participants, requiring us to exclude data from colorblind participants.

instead into bins one and four. The syllables heard are selected from among (*bah, beh, boh, tah, teh, toh, kah, keh, koh*). These nine syllables were formed by combining three consonant sounds (b,t,k) with three vowel sounds (ah,eh,oh).

Secondary Task

As shown in Fig. 2, three times per experiment trial, the participant encounters a secondary task, in which the robot interrupts with a new request, asking the participant to move a particular, currently visible block, to a particular, currently accessible bin. Depending on experiment trial condition, this spoken request was sometimes accompanied by a MRDG. Unlike the long-term primary task that requires participants to remember the initial target block and keep track of the continuously changing target bins during the 90 s round, in the secondary task the robot asks participants to pick a different target block and place it in a different target bin, after which participants can continue the primary task.

3.2   Experimental Design

We used a Latin square counterbalanced within-subjects design with two within-subjects factors: Cognitive Load (4 loads) and Communication Style (3 styles).

Cognitive Load

Our first independent variable, cognitive load, was manipulated through our primary task. Following Beck and Lavie [27], we manipulated cognitive load by jointly manipulating memory constraints and target/distractor discriminability (cp. [26]), producing four load profiles: (1) all load considered low, (2) only working memory load considered high, (3) only visual perceptual load considered high, and (4) only auditory perceptual load considered high.

Working memory load was manipulated as follows: In the high working memory load condition, participants were required to remember the identities of three target bins out of a total of six visible bins, producing a total memory load of seven items: the three target bins, the target block color and shape, and the target syllable consonant and vowel. In all other conditions, participants were only required to remember the identities of two target bins out of a total of four visible bins, producing a total memory load of six items.

Visual perceptual load was manipulated as follows: In the high visual perceptual load condition, the target block was always difficult to discriminate from distractors due to sharing one common property with all distractors. For example, if the target block was a red cube, all distractors would be either red or cubes (but not both). In the low visual perceptual load condition, the target block was always easy to discriminate from distractors due to sharing no common properties with any distractors. For example, if the target block was a red cube, no distractors would be red or cubes.

Auditory perceptual load was manipulated as follows: In the high auditory perceptual load condition, the target syllable was always difficult to discriminate from distractors due to sharing one common property with all distractors.

For example, if the target syllable was *kah*, all distractors would either start with *k* or end with *ah* (but not both). In the low auditory perceptual load condition, the target syllable was always easy to discriminate from distractors due to sharing no common properties with any distractors. For example, if the target syllable was *kah*, no distractors would either start with *k* or end with *ah*.

Communication Style

Our second independent variable, communication style, was manipulated through our secondary task. Following Williams et al. [63,64], we manipulated communication style by having the robot exhibit one of three behaviors:

1. During experiment blocks associated with the **complex language** communication style condition, the robot referred to objects using full referring expressions needed to disambiguate those objects (e.g., "the red sphere").
2. During experiment blocks associated with the **MR + complex language** communication style condition, the robot referred to objects using full referring expressions (e.g., "the red sphere"), paired with a MRDG (an arrow drawn over the red sphere).
3. During experiment blocks associated with the **MR + simple language** communication style condition, the robot referred to objects using minimal referring expressions (e.g., "that block"), paired with a MRDG (an arrow drawn over the object to which the robot was referring).

Following Williams et al. [63,64], we did not examine the use of simple language without MR, which precludes referent disambiguation, resulting in the user needing to ask for clarification or guess between ambiguous options.

3.3 Measures

We expected performance improvements to manifest in our experiment in four ways: task accuracy, task response time, perceived mental workload, and perceived communicative effectiveness. These were measured as follows:

Accuracy was measured for both tasks by logging which object participants clicked on, determining whether this was the object intended by the task or by robot, and determining whether this object was placed in the correct bin.

Response time (RT) was measured for both primary and secondary tasks by logging time stamps at the moment participants interacted with virtual objects (both blocks and bins). In a primary task, whenever participants see a target block, their task is to pick-and-place it into any one of a particular set of bins. Thus, response time was measured as the delay between when the target block is first displayed and when the placement is completed because a new target block is immediately placed in a different location within the shown panel after a completed placement by the participant. In the secondary task, response time was measured as the time between the start of Pepper's utterance and the placement of the secondary target block.

Perceived mental workload was measured using a NASA Task Load Index (TLX) survey [21]. At the end of each experiment block, participants were asked to fill out a NASA TLX Likert 7-point scale survey across six categories: mental demand, physical demand, temporal demand, performance, effort, and frustration.

Perceived communicative effectiveness was measured using the modified Gesture Perception Scale [42] previously employed by Williams et al. [63,64]: Participants were asked at the end of each experiment block to answer three 7-point Likert items on the effectiveness, helpfulness, and appropriateness of the robot's communication styles.

3.4 Procedure

Upon arriving at the lab, providing informed consent, and completing demographic and visual capability survey, participants were introduced to the task through both verbal instruction and an interactive tutorial.

The use of this interactive tutorial was motivated by several pilot tests that were run before conducting official trials. The initial pilot testers were given verbal instructions on how to use the HoloLens, how to complete their tasks in each round, and then were asked to start the 12 rounds. Feedback from these pilot tests showed that participants were not confident in their understanding of the HoloLens or game, so they struggled in the first couple rounds and improved with trial and error. This caused the participants' performance to be lower in the first few rounds than the later rounds, which made it hard to tell how the variations in the 12 rounds affect performance. To correct this, our team designed a tutorial scene that each participant completes at the start of the experiment, which further pilot studies demonstrated as addressing those concerns.

The tutorial scene walks the participant through a sample experimental round. When the participant starts the tutorial, they see a panel with text-instructions, a row of blocks, and four bins. Participants are walked through how to use the HoloLens air tap gesture to pick up blocks and put them in bins through descriptive text and an animation showing an example air tap gesture, and informed of task mechanics with respect to both target/non-target bins and temporarily disabled grey bins. Participants then start to hear syllables being played by the HoloLens. When the target syllable *teh* plays, the target and non-target bins switch. Each bin on screen is labeled as a 'target' or 'non-target', in order to help the participant understand what is happening when the target syllable plays. These labels are only shown in the tutorial and participants are reminded that they will have to memorize which bins are targets for the actual game. At the end of the tutorial the participant has to successfully put a target block in a target bin three times before they can start the experiment.

After completing this tutorial, participants engaged in each of the twelve (Latin square counterbalanced) experimental trials formed by combining the four cognitive load conditions and the three communication style conditions, with surveys administered after each experiment block. The length of the experiment, including surveys and breaks between each trial, was around 30 min.

3.5 Participants

36 participants were recruited from Colorado School of Mines (31 M, 5 F), ages 18–32. None had participated in previous studies from our laboratory.

3.6 Analysis

Data analysis was performed within a Bayesian framework using JASP 0.11.1 [48], using the default settings as justified by Wagenmakers et al. [51]. For each measure, a repeated measures analysis of variance (RM-ANOVA) [10,33,38] was performed, using communication style and cognitive load as random factors. Inclusion Bayes Factors across matched models (BF$_{Incl}$ [29]) were then computed for each candidate main effect and interaction. BF$_{Incl}$ for candidate effect E represents the ratio between two probabilities: the probability of our data being generated under models that included E, and the probability of our data being generated under models that did not include E. Therefore, this BF$_{Incl}$ represents the relative strength of evidence for an effect E, i.e.

$$\frac{\sum_{m \in M | e \in m} P(m|data)}{\sum_{m \in M | e \notin m} P(m|data)},$$

where e is an effect under consideration, and m is a candidate model in the space of candidate models M. When sufficient evidence was found for a main effect, the results were further analyzed using a post-hoc Bayesian t-test [24,55] with a default Cauchy prior (center $= 0$, $r = \frac{\sqrt{2}}{2} = 0.707$).

The task accuracy was calculated as the ratio between the number of correct block placement and the total number of block placements, with 0 being complete failure and 1 being correct placement for each placed block within a trial.

Finally, transformations were applied to response time data. Since response time distributions are often not Gaussian (normally distributed) but rather have a long right-tail, logarithmic $log(RT)$ transformations are often used by researchers to handle such data [56].

A Shapiro-Wilk test of normality indicated ($p < .01$) that data in all conditions was non-normally distributed. While an assumption of normal distribution is not necessary for our analyses due to our use of a Bayesian analysis framework, the reason for non-normality in our data was asymmetry, with a long right tail and a number of extreme positive outliers. These considerations together suggested the need for data transformation, regardless of analysis framework. To reduce sensitivity to non-normally distributed outliers and induce a more normal data distribution, we applied a log transformation on all response time data.

4 Results

4.1 Response Time

Strong evidence was found against any effect of communication style or imposed cognitive load on primary task response time, with all BFs$_{Incl} < 0.028$ for an effect. These results fail to support either hypothesis, with no benefit of MRDGs observed in *any* condition. Our results provided strong evidence for an effect of communication style ($\text{BF}_{Incl} = 17.860$) on secondary task response time, as shown in Fig. 3, but evidence against an effect of imposed workload ($\text{BF}_{Incl} = 0.017$), or of an interaction between workload and communication style, on response time ($\text{BF}_{Incl} = 0.018$). A post-hoc Bayesian t-test analyzing the effect of communication style revealed extreme evidence ($\text{BF} = 601.460$) for a difference in response time between the complex language condition ($\mu = 2.095$, $\sigma = 0.325$; untransformed $\mu = 8.877$ s, $\sigma = 4.072$ s) and the MR + complex language condition ($\mu = 1.955$, $\sigma = 0.323$; untransformed $\mu = 7.779$, $\sigma = 3.877$), weak evidence ($\text{BF} = 1.551$) for a difference in response time between the complex language condition and MR + simple language condition ($\mu = 2.006$, $\sigma = 0.436$; untransformed $\mu = 8.764$, $\sigma = 6.203$), and moderate evidence ($\text{BF} = 0.203$) *against* a difference between the MR + complex language and MR + simple language conditions. In other words, when you use MR, language makes little difference. And when you use complex language only, having MR is a big help. The evidence against an effect of workload but for an effect of communication style provides partial support for the *Universal Benefit Hypothesis*, as MRDGs do indeed provide task-oriented benefits regardless of level and type of cognitive load, but only when paired with rich referring expressions.

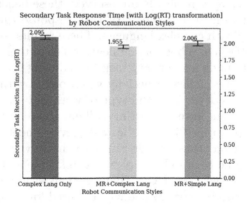

Fig. 3. Effect of communication styles on participant's secondary task log(RT). Error bars represent standard errors.

4.2   Accuracy

Strong evidence was found *against* effects of communication style or imposed cognitive load on primary or secondary task accuracy (All $\text{BFs}_{Incl} < 0.033$ for an effect). Mean primary task accuracy was 0.706 ($\sigma = 0.261$). Mean secondary task accuracy was 0.984 ($\sigma = 0.074$). These results fail to support either hypothesis, with no benefit of MRDGs observed in *any* condition.

4.3 Perceived Mental Workload

Strong evidence was found *against* any effects of communication style or imposed cognitive load on perceived mental workload (BF_{Incl} between 0.006 and 0.040 for an effect). Aggregating across conditions, TLX score sums had a mean of 21.109 out of 42 points ($\sigma = 5.443$). Thus, most participants' perceived workload data was almost perfectly centered around "medium load". These results fail to support either hypothesis, with no benefit of MRDGs observed in *any* condition.

4.4 Perceived Communicative Effectiveness

Anecdotal to strong evidence was found *against* any effects of communication style or cognitive load on perceived communicative effectiveness (BF_{Incl} between 0.049 and 0.117 for an effect on all questions). Participants' perceived communicative effectiveness had a mean of 5.611 out of 7 ($\sigma = 1.208$). These results fail to support either hypothesis, with no benefits observed in *any* condition.

5 Discussion

Our results provide partial support for the *Universal Benefit Hypothesis*: while the types of task-oriented benefits of MRDGs previously observed in some recent laboratory studies [7,18] were largely unobserved, these benefits *were* observed, *regardless* of cognitive load, for secondary task response time; but *only* when MRDGs were paired with complex language. These results suggest that the primary benefit of MRDGs in robot communication lies in their ability to increase users' speed at performing a secondary task by reducing the time taken to perform constituent visual searches (especially when paired with complex referring expressions), regardless of the level and type of workload users are experiencing.

Moreover, our results have interesting (albeit non-identical) parallels with previous work *not* performed in realistic task environments [64], which found that participants demonstrated slower response times when complex language alone was used, with no clear differences between simple and complex language when pairing language with MRDGs. That previous study also suggested that people found a robot to be more likable when it used longer more natural referring expressions. When combined with the results of our own experiment, this suggests that robots can likely pair complex referring expression with mixed reality gestures without worrying about cognitively overloading their interlocutors.

Our results overall provide evidence against the four Cognitive Contextual Benefit Hypotheses, casting doubt on the potential of adaptive automation to provide benefits in mixed reality human robot dialogue. While this hypothesis would have predicted that the differences between communication styles under different cognitive load profiles would primarily be grounded in whether communication style was overall visual or overall auditory, in fact what we observed is that visual augmentations, especially when paired with complex referring expressions, may *always* be helpful for a secondary task (when paired with complex language), regardless of level and type of imposed workload.

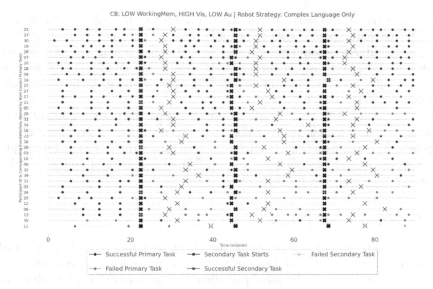

Fig. 4. Visualization of participant performance in the *Complex Language Only/High visual perceptual load* condition. Each row depicts the performance of one participant, with participants presented in decreasing order of primary task accuracy. Green and red dots represent primary task block placement times, with green dots indicating successful placement and red dots indicating unsuccessful placement (i.e., placement involving an incorrect block or incorrect bin). Xes represent secondary task instruction and completion times, with dark Xes indicating when the robot started uttering a secondary task request, blue Xes indicating when participants successfully completed that secondary task, and pink Xes indicating when participants failed a secondary task (i.e., placement involving an incorrect block or incorrect bin). (Color figure online)

Similarly, we found no effect of imposed workload or gesture on perceived workload or perceived effectiveness. This may have been for at least three reasons. First, secondary response time differences might simply not have been large enough for participants to notice: the observed differences were on the order of one second of response time when overall secondary task response time was around 7.5 s, representing only a 15% secondary task efficiency increase.

Second, the benefits of mixed reality were only seen on speed of response to the relatively rare secondary tasks, and not to the much more frequent primary tasks. Participants may have primarily – or only – considered their primary task when reporting their perceived workload and perceived effectiveness.

Finally, while participants' TLX scores had a mean of 21.109 out of 42 points in all conditions (i.e., the data was nearly perfectly centered around "medium" load), analysis of individual performance trajectories demonstrates that the task was sufficiently difficult that many participants experienced catastrophic primary task shedding. Consider Fig. 4, which shows the results of each participant within one of the twelve conditions, with participants listed in decreasing order of primary task accuracy. As shown in this figure, and described in the caption, the bottom 50% of participants experienced large numbers of failures, with many of these participants experiencing a failure that they never recovered from immediately after a secondary task, perhaps due to missing an auditory cue during that secondary task. While Fig. 4 shows only one condition (the *complex language/High visual load* condition) for the sake of space, in fact all twelve condition plots show similar results.

This suggests it may be too early to cast doubt on the potential use of adaptive automation in human-robot dialogue, as our results may have been due to subtle aspects of our experimental or task design rather than universal principles of human cognition. Moreover, our experiment had a number of limitations that further motivate the need for future work.

5.1   Limitations and Future Work

While our study provides evidence of the effect of MRDGs on human's task response time, it has key limitations to address in future work. Given the catastrophic errors experienced by some participants, and given that all twelve condition plots show similar results, our experimental setup should be reconsidered. For example, some participants failed early into the game and completely lost track of what block to place in what bin. Providing real-time, directive cues might help participant recover from errors. However, the purpose of a challenging primary task is to impose high workload on the participants and to observe how different communication styles can help enhance human task performance under cognitive overload. The poor performance observed in our experiment demonstrates the effect of the cognitive demanding primary task, but the catastrophic primary task shredding complicated our effort to unravel the impact on accuracy, response time, and perceived workload. Additional consideration is needed to design ways that recovery hints can be presented (visual or auditory) without interfering with the imposed workload profiles during the experiment.

Additionally, we received feedback from some participants during the debriefing that they felt the series of syllables playing in the task background (e.g., *bah, beh, boh, tah, teh, toh, kah, keh, koh*) could easily be misheard. After missing the auditory cue that signals the switch of the target and non-target bins, they started to guess the target bins to attempt to proceed with the primary task. We recommend in future research to use distinguishable sounds instead of these syllables in order to improve auditory discrimination.

Another direction for future research is to use eye- or hand-tracking (e.g., through the HoloLens 2) to more precisely capture response time. For example, it would have been advantageous to capture the delay between when a target block first appeared and when participants first gazed at it, or the time between the block's first appearance and the participants movement of their hands to commit to a new target goal. Rather than measuring response time as *TimeBlockPlaced - TimeBlockAppeared* in this experiment, researchers could use hand trajectories and movement data to infer the underlying cognitive processes, such as mental processing time and midflight corrections (i.e., when participants initially move their hands towards an incorrect block, and then perhaps under the suggestion of the robot, switch their target to the correct block).

Furthermore, devices such as HoloLens 2 enable new input modalities that allow completely natural hand gestures rather than the simple gaze-and-commit (e.g., air tap) interaction of the Hololens 1. In our experiment, participants were given time and tutorials to become acquainted with the headset and practice the air-tap hand gesture. Even though most participants expressed that they felt comfortable with the headset and interaction to start the experiment, some still struggled to pick-and-place the virtual blocks, affecting the measurement of response time, interfering with the load placed by the primary task. Accordingly, the system's limitations led to issues in differentiation between the delay participants took to figure out how to use the gesture vs. the true delay caused by the cognitively taxing primary task.

Another limitation of our experiment was the number of participants recruited. We were able to recruit 36 participants pre-COVID 19, and while our current analysis provided evidence against effects of workload profiles on task time, a larger participant pool would have allowed for more decisive conclusions.

6   Conclusion

We examined the effectiveness of different combinations of natural language reference and MRDG under different types of mental workload, through a 36-participant Mixed Reality Robotics experiment. We found that, for our verbal and nonverbal communication strategies and workload manipulations, MRDGs improve the effectiveness of users by shortening their response time in a secondary visual search tasks, regardless of underlying level and type of cognitive load, providing partial support for a *Universal Benefit Hypothesis*. Moreover, we found this to be especially true when MRDGs were paired with complex referring expressions rather than concise demonstrative pronouns. These results will help inform future efforts in mixed reality robot communication by demonstrating how MRDGs and natural language referring expression should be paired to best enhance the effectiveness of robots' human teammates.

Acknowledgement. This research was funded in part by NSF grants IIS-1909864 and CNS-1823245.

References

1. Amor, H.B., Ganesan, R.K., Rathore, Y., Ross, H.: Intention projection for human-robot collaboration with mixed reality cues. In: International WS on Virtual, Augmented, and Mixed Reality for HRI (VAM-HRI) (2018)
2. Andersen, R.S., Madsen, O., Moeslund, T.B., Amor, H.B.: Projecting robot intentions into human environments. In: International Symposium on Robot and Human Interactive Communication (RO-MAN), pp. 294–301 (2016)
3. Azuma, R.: A survey of augmented reality. Presence: Teleoperators Virtual Environ. **6**, 355–385 (1997)

4. Azuma, R., Baillot, Y., Behringer, R., Feiner, S., Julier, S., MacIntyre, B.: Recent advances in augmented reality. IEEE Comput. Graph. Appl. **21**, 34–47 (2001)
5. Billinghurst, M., Clark, A., Lee, G., et al.: A survey of augmented reality. Found. Trends® Hum.-Comput. Interact. **8**(2–3), 73–272 (2015)
6. Meyer zu Borgsen, S., Renner, P., Lier, F., Pfeiffer, T., Wachsmuth, S.: Improving human-robot handover research by mixed reality techniques. In: International WS on Virtual, Aug, and Mixed Reality for Human-Robot Interaction (VAM-HRI) (2018)
7. Brown, L., et al.: Best of both worlds? Combining different forms of mixed reality deictic gestures. ACM Trans. Hum.-Robot Interact. **12**, 1–23 (2022)
8. Chakraborti, T., Sreedharan, S., Kulkarni, A., Kambhampati, S.: Alternative modes of interaction in proximal human-in-the-loop operation of robots. arXiv preprint arXiv:1703.08930 (2017)
9. Cheli, M., Sinapov, J., Danahy, E.E., Rogers, C.: Towards an augmented reality framework for k-12 robotics education. In: International WS on Virtual, Augmented, and Mixed Reality for HRI (VAM-HRI) (2018)
10. Crowder, M.J.: Analysis of Repeated Measures. Routledge, Milton Park (2017)
11. Dudley, A., Chakraborti, T., Kambhampati, S.: V2V communication for augmenting reality enabled smart huds to increase situational awareness of drivers (2018)
12. Frank, J.A., Moorhead, M., Kapila, V.: Mobile mixed-reality interfaces that enhance human-robot interaction in shared spaces. Front. Rob. AI **4**, 20 (2017)
13. Ganesan, R.K., Rathore, Y.K., Ross, H.M., Amor, H.B.: Better teaming through visual cues: how projecting imagery in a workspace can improve human-robot collaboration. IEEE Robot. Autom. Mag. **25**(2), 59–71 (2018)
14. Goktan, I., Ly, K., Groechel, T.R., Mataric, M.: Augmented reality appendages for robots: design considerations and recommendations for maximizing social and functional perception. In: International WS on Virtual, Augmented and Mixed Reality for HRI (2022)
15. Green, S.A., Billinghurst, M., Chen, X., Chase, J.G.: Human-robot collaboration: a literature review and augmented reality approach in design. Int. J. Adv. Robot. Syst. **5**(1), 1 (2008)
16. Groechel, T., Shi, Z., Pakkar, R., Mataric, M.J.: Using socially expressive mixed reality arms for enhancing low-expressivity robots. In: International Conference on Robot and Human Interactive Communication (RO-MAN), pp. 1–8. IEEE (2019)
17. Groechel, T.R., Walker, M.E., Chang, C.T., Rosen, E., Forde, J.Z.: Tokcs: tool for organizing key characteristics of VAM-HRI systems. Rob. Autom. Mag. (2021)
18. Hamilton, J., Phung, T., Tran, N., Williams, T.: What's the point? Tradeoffs between effectiveness and social perception when using mixed reality to enhance gesturally limited robots. In: Proceedings of the HRI (2021)
19. Hamilton, J., Tran, N., Williams, T.: Tradeoffs between effectiveness and social perception when using mixed reality to supplement gesturally limited robots. In: International WS on Virtual, Augmented, and Mixed Reality for HRI (2020)
20. Han, Z., Zhu, Y., Phan, A., Garza, F.S., Castro, A., Williams, T.: Crossing reality: comparing physical and virtual robot deixis. In: International Conference HRI (2023)
21. Hart, S., Staveland, L.: Development of NASA-TLX (task load index): results of empirical and theoretical research, pp. pp 139–183. Amsterdam (1988)
22. Hedayati, H., Walker, M., Szafir, D.: Improving collocated robot teleoperation with augmented reality. In: International Conference on Human-Robot Interaction (2018)

23. Hirshfield, L., Williams, T., Sommer, N., Grant, T., Gursoy, S.V.: Workload-driven modulation of mixed-reality robot-human communication. In: ICMI WS on Modeling Cognitive Processes from Multimodal Data, p. 3. ACM (2018)
24. Jeffreys, H.: Significance tests when several degrees of freedom arise simultaneously. Proc. R. Soc. Lond. Ser. A Math. Phys. Sci. (1938)
25. Kahneman, D.: Attention and effort (1973)
26. Lavie, N.: Perceptual load as a necessary condition for selective attention. J. Exp. Psych.: Hum. Percept. Perform. $21(3)$, 451 (1995)
27. Lavie, N.: The role of perceptual load in visual awareness. Brain Res. 1080, 91-100 (2006)
28. MacDonald, W.: The impact of job demands and workload on stress and fatigue. Aust. Psychol. $38(2)$, 102-117 (2003)
29. Mathôt, S.: Bayes like a baws: interpreting Bayesian repeated measures in JASP [blog post]. cogsci.nl/blog/interpreting-bayesian-repeated-measures-in-jasp (2017)
30. Matuszek, C., Bo, L., Zettlemoyer, L., Fox, D.: Learning from unscripted deictic gesture and language for human-robot interactions. In: AAAI (2014)
31. Mavridis, N.: A review of verbal and non-verbal human-robot interactive communication. Robot. Auton. Syst. 63, 22-35 (2015)
32. Milgram, P., Zhai, S., Drascic, D., Grodski, J.: Applications of augmented reality for human-robot communication. In: International Conference on Intelligent Robots and Systems (1993)
33. Morey, R., Rouder, J.: Bayesfactor (version 0.9. 9) (2014)
34. Navon, D., Gopher, D.: On the economy of the human-processing system. Psychol. Rev. $86(3)$, 214 (1979)
35. Norman, D.A., Bobrow, D.G.: On data-limited and resource-limited processes. Cogn. Psychol. $7(1)$, 44-64 (1975)
36. Peters, C., Yang, F., Saikia, H., Li, C., Skantze, G.: Towards the use of mixed reality for HRI design via virtual robots. In: International WS on Virtual, Augmented, and Mixed Reality for HRI (VAM-HRI) (2018)
37. Rosen, E., et al.: Communicating robot arm motion intent through mixed reality head-mounted displays. In: Amato, N.M., Hager, G., Thomas, S., Torres-Torriti, M. (eds.) Robotics Research. SPAR, vol. 10, pp. 301-316. Springer, Cham (2020). https://doi.org/10.1007/978-3-030-28619-4_26
38. Rouder, J.N., Morey, R.D., Speckman, P.L., Province, J.M.: Default Bayes factors for ANOVA designs. J. Math. Psychol. $56(5)$, 356-374 (2012)
39. Salem, M., Eyssel, F., Rohlfing, K., Kopp, S., Joublin, F.: To err is human (-like): effects of robot gesture on perceived anthropomorphism and likability. Int. J. Soc. Robot. $5(3)$, 313-323 (2013)
40. Salem, M., Kopp, S., Wachsmuth, I., Rohlfing, K., Joublin, F.: Generation and evaluation of communicative robot gesture. Int. J. Soc. Rob. $4(2)$ (2012)
41. Sanders, A.: Dual task performance (2001)
42. Sauppé, A., Mutlu, B.: Robot deictics: how gesture and context shape referential communication. In: International Conference on Human-Robot Interaction (HRI) (2014)
43. Schönheits, M., Krebs, F.: Embedding AR in industrial HRI applications. In: International WS on Virtual, Augmented, and Mixed Reality for HRI (VAM-HRI) (2018)
44. Sibirtseva, E., et al.: A comparison of visualisation methods for disambiguating verbal requests in human-robot interaction. In: International Symposium on Robot and Human Interactive Communication (2018)

45. Siéroff, E.: Attention: multiple resources (2001)
46. Sportillo, D., Paljic, A., Ojeda, L., Partipilo, G., Fuchs, P., Roussarie, V.: Learn how to operate semi-autonomous vehicles with extended reality (2018)
47. Szafir, D.: Mediating human-robot interactions with virtual, augmented, and mixed reality. In: International Conference on Human-Computer Interaction (2019)
48. J Team: JASP (version 0.8.5.1) [computer software] (2018)
49. Tellex, S., Gopalan, N., Kress-Gazit, H., Matuszek, C.: Robots that use language. Ann. Rev. Control Robot. Auton. Syst. **3**, 25–55 (2020)
50. Van Krevelen, D., Poelman, R.: A survey of augmented reality technologies, applications and limitations. Int. J. Virtual Reality **9**(2), 1–20 (2010)
51. Wagenmakers, E., Love, J., Marsman, M., Jamil, T., Ly, A., Verhagen, J.: Bayesian inference for psychology, Part II: example applications with JASP. Psychon. Bull. Rev. **25**(1), 35–57 (2018)
52. Walker, M., Hedayati, H., Lee, J., Szafir, D.: Communicating robot motion intent with augmented reality. In: International Conference on Human-Robot Interaction (2018)
53. Walker, M., Phung, T., Chakraborti, T., Williams, T., Szafir, D.: Virtual, augmented, and mixed reality for human-robot interaction: a survey and virtual design element taxonomy (2022). https://arxiv.org/abs/2202.11249
54. Weng, T., Perlmutter, L., Nikolaidis, S., Srinivasa, S., Cakmak, M.: Robot object referencing through legible situated projections. In: International Conference on Robotics and Automation (ICRA) (2019)
55. Westfall, P.H., Johnson, W.O., Utts, J.M.: A Bayesian perspective on the Bonferroni adjustment. Biometrika **84**(2), 419–427 (1997)
56. Whelan, R.: Effective analysis of reaction time data. Psychol. Rec. **58**(3), 475–482 (2008)
57. Wickens, C.D.: Processing resources and attention. Multiple-task performance (1991)
58. Wickens, C.D.: Multiple resources and performance prediction. Theor. Issues Ergon. Sci. **3**(2), 159–177 (2002)
59. Wickens, C.D.: Multiple resources and mental workload. Hum. Factor **50**(3), 449–455 (2008)
60. Wickens, C.D., Santamaria, A., Sebok, A.: A computational model of task overload management and task switching. In: Human Factors and Ergonomics Society Annual Meeting, vol. 57, pp. 763–767. SAGE Publications, Los Angeles (2013)
61. Wickens, C.D., Tsang, P.: Handbook of Human-Systems Integration. APA (2014)
62. Wickens, C.D., Vidulich, M., Sandry-Garza, D.: Principles of SCR compatibility with spatial and verbal tasks: the role of display-control location and voice-interactive display-control interfacing. Hum. Factors **26**(5), 533–543 (1984)
63. Williams, T., Bussing, M., Cabrol, S., Boyle, E., Tran, N.: Mixed reality deictic gesture for multi-modal robot communication. In: International Conference on HRI (2019)
64. Williams, T., Bussing, M., Cabrol, S., Lau, I., Boyle, E., Tran, N.: Investigating the potential effectiveness of allocentric mixed reality deictic gesture. In: International Conference on Virtual, Augmented, and Mixed Reality (2019)
65. Williams, T., Szafir, D., Chakraborti, T.: The reality-virtuality interaction cube. In: International WS on Virtual, Augmented, and Mixed Reality for HRI (2019)
66. Williams, T., Szafir, D., Chakraborti, T., Ben Amor, H.: Virtual, augmented, and mixed reality for human-robot interaction. In: International Conference on Human-Robot Interaction (LBRs), pp. 403–404. ACM (2018)

67. Williams, T., Tran, N., Rands, J., Dantam, N.T.: Augmented, mixed, and virtual reality enabling of robot deixis. In: Chen, J.Y.C., Fragomeni, G. (eds.) VAMR 2018. LNCS, vol. 10909, pp. 257–275. Springer, Cham (2018). https://doi.org/10. 1007/978-3-319-91581-4_19
68. Williams, T., Yazdani, F., Suresh, P., Scheutz, M., Beetz, M.: Dempster-Shafer theoretic resolution of referential ambiguity. Auton. Robots **43**(2), 389–414 (2019)
69. Zhou, F., Duh, H.B.L., Billinghurst, M.: Trends in augmented reality tracking, interaction and display: a review of ten years of ISMAR. In: International Symposium on Mixed and Augmented Reality, pp. 193–202. IEEE (2008)

VAMR in Medicine and Health

Virtual Reality Immersion: Enhancing Physician Communication to Promote Ethical Behavior at the Bedside

Lea Brandt[1]([⊠]) [iD] and Sara Mostowfi[2]

[1] School of Medicine, University of Missouri, Columbia, MO, USA
brandtlc@health.missouri.edu
[2] Industrial and Manufacturing System Engineering, University of Missouri, Columbia, MO, USA
2sm3yp@umsystem.edu

Abstract. The goal of this project was to examine communication between physicians and patients or their surrogates, in order to optimize clinical interventions and reduce ethically problematic actions related to overuse. An immersive virtual environment (IVE), including use of a virtual human, was developed to explore the relationship between communication techniques, ethical intent and ability to navigate difficult conversations in the face of external pressure to offer inappropriate medical interventions. Unlike self-efficacy measures or other tools designed to assess knowledge acquisition or intention, IVE allowed researchers to assess the behavioral skills necessary to optimize provider-patient communication and subsequent treatment decisions. Virtual human enactment depicting external pressures to offer inappropriate treatments also provided the researchers insight regarding the qualitative relationship between these pressures and the clinician's ability to assist patients and surrogates in choosing treatments consistent with what is clinically appropriate and in line with the patient's values. After participating in the virtual immersion, providers expressed an enhanced understanding of patient and surrogate points of view and the scaffolding onto which effective communication skills can be continuously cultivated.

Keywords: Clinical Ethics · Effective Communication · Virtual Human · Simulation

1 Introduction

Even though there is acknowledgment of the complex skills required to navigate ethical conflicts in practice settings, much of the clinical ethics training uses normative theory-based teaching strategies that do not necessarily inform or shape future practice decisions nor actions [1–3]. This type of training and education does not significantly influence future ethical behavior [4]. Given these barriers, as well as difficulty in controlling for clinical variables and providing real-time feedback, it is important to explore other training tools which can produce professional behaviors reflective of ethical clinical

© The Author(s), under exclusive license to Springer Nature Switzerland AG 2023
J. Y. C. Chen and G. Fragomeni (Eds.): HCII 2023, LNCS 14027, pp. 419–429, 2023.
https://doi.org/10.1007/978-3-031-35634-6_29

practice. Specifically, optimal ethics training should provide opportunities for learners to reflect on inconsistencies between their intentions and actual behavior [4]. Virtual immersion allows for this type of real time feedback that can work to close gaps between ethical intent and actions in practice. Instructional methods incorporating IVE may provide an avenue to teach communication and other ethically relevant practice skills, which result in improved health care quality and a better patient experience [5].

Data has been collected within a midwestern academic medical center concerning cases of inconsistent communication that led to suboptimal clinical outcomes. Examples include lack of clarity regarding which actions to take due to confusion regarding Code Status and Limitations of Treatment. The confusion has resulted in patients receiving CPR when they did *not* wish to or could not benefit from the clinical intervention, and in patients not receiving interventions they wanted when they *should* have received them. In addition, it is not uncommon for medically futile interventions to be provided based on family demands and contrary to medical appropriateness. It is posited that cost reduction and improved patient experience can be achieved by standardizing communication across providers.

Challenges related to the introduction of new technology as well as epidemic social concerns increase the complexity of these conversations. There is a need to provide clinicians with the skills to limit procedures due to medical futility. With the advent of predictive analytics that give insight into mortality risk, there is an opportunity to increase access to palliative care services and improve quality of life for seriously ill patients [6]. Development of the virtual immersion as a training tool was predicated on related work in the field demonstrating the viability of this pedagogical approach in changing behavior.

There are multiple studies which show virtual immersion is significantly more effective than two-dimensional training in producing behaviors reflective of ethical decision making such as empathetic response, social perspective taking, and reduction of bias [7–9]. This project aimed to develop an innovative way to increase vital clinician knowledge, develop an under-discussed skill set, and change clinician behavior to improve the patient experience and meet goals related to value-based care.

The goal of this project was to examine communication in a virtual setting between physicians and patient surrogates, in order to optimize clinical interventions consistent with patient values and medical effectiveness. The secondary organizational goal was to promote value-based care by addressing the problem of performing procedures that are not only inconsistent with patient values, but are also unnecessary, inappropriate, ineffective, and costly [10–13]. The following specific aims guided the study.

Specific Aim #1: To evaluate clinician behavior using immersive virtual environments reflective of complex clinical encounters which may result in inappropriate clinical recommendations.

Specific Aim #2: Compare the medically indicated treatment to observed IVE clinical recommendation in order to assess gaps between clinician intention and behavior.

2   Methods

An immersive virtual environment (IVE) was developed to explore the relationship between communication techniques, ethical intent and ability to navigate these difficult conversations in the face of external pressure to offer inappropriate medical interventions. Unlike self-efficacy measures or other tools designed to assess knowledge acquisition or intention, IVE allowed researchers to assess the behavioral skills necessary to optimize provider-patient communication. The differing variables depicting external pressures to offer inappropriate treatments also provided the researchers insight into development of the scenario and standardized patient/surrogate roles. The project was based on conceptual models aimed at understanding influences on medical recommendations and acceptance of appropriate medical interventions to limit overtreatment [14]. Figure 1. Depicts the adapted conceptual model outlining intervention and outcomes variables.

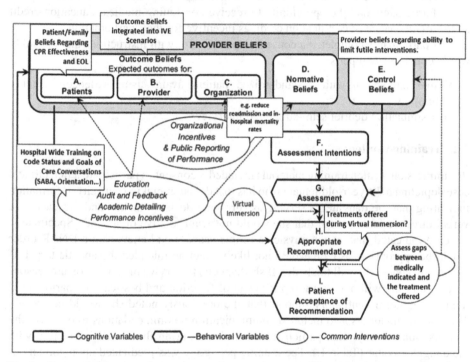

Fig. 1. Conceptual framework to understand appropriateness of recommendations to reduce futile interventions through use of IVE (Adapted from Powell, Bloomfield, Burgess, Wilt, & Partin, 2013).

The immersion was predicated on recognition of the influence of outcomes beliefs, both provider and patient, that can influence acceptance of medical recommendations. The secondary organizational goal to promote value-based care, reflective of organization beliefs to save money and improve clinical outcomes, was also integrated into the IVE scenario that depicted a patient who could not benefit clinically from certain treatments being requested by her surrogate.

2.1 Participants

Participants were recruited from a midwestern academic medical center. There were 10 participants in this study all of them were physicians, except for one fourth-year medical student in her last month of training prior to residency. Physicians in an acute care hospital setting were the target audience for this work, specifically on the general medicine floors and step-down units. Years of experience ranged from 0–41 years, with a majority of junior physicians having practiced less than 5 years. However, convenience sampling resulted in the majority of participants, who had additional training in palliative care, ethics, and/or breaking bad news. The study group consisted of 7 males, and 3 females. All participants were assigned the same scenario. Among participants, none had prior virtual human experience.

The study was reviewed and approved by the IRB at the level of exempt; approved documents included both the consent procedures and semi-structured interview questions. Participants had the opportunity to receive continuing medical education credit and/or maintenance of certification credit as incentive for their participation.

All participants completed a consent to participate, with instructions that the study would consist of two parts:

1. Virtual interaction with a standardized patient avatar using videoconferencing technology
2. Post-simulation debrief semi-structured interview.

2.2 Training Content

Pre-immersion written training materials included a consent to participate letter, clinical case depicting a 79-year-old female who has lost decision making capacity, information indicating that the daughter is serving as surrogate decision maker, and presence of a verbal directive from patient that she would not want to "live on a vent". Specifically, the case indicated that, as the physician in this case, "you believe that a DNAR order would be appropriate as CPR would not likely meet an intended therapeutic target. If the patient codes, she will likely die. If she happens to survive the code, you are reasonably certain she will not return to prior level of function and best-case scenario would require long-term ventilatory support that she previously noted she would not want". The training materials also included communication recommendations to optimize the conversation the physician participant would have during the virtual interaction with the daughter/avatar (Table 1.). The training pedagogy was predicated upon contemporary work in health communication focused on eliciting, discussing and understanding patient preferences and fears concerning goals of care, specifically burden and benefit of high-risk/low yield procedures, and conveying medical futility[15–17]. Participants were provided with the packet upon enrollment and again provided opportunities to review the case profile and communication strategies just before participating in the immersion.

From interaction with a specific, complex patient case through IVE, providers navigated the conversation in attempt to produce optimal outcomes consistent with the patient's values, the limitations of current medical interventions, and value-based care.

Table 1. Recommendations to optimize clinical encounter

1. Greet your patient and engage in conversation to establish rapport. Prepare your patient to receive bad news
2. Give your patient the bad news regarding their diagnosis and prognosis.
3. Check your patient's understanding of what you have said.
4. If your patient does not fully understand, reframe the unclear part of what you said in a different way. Repeat 3 & 4 as needed.
5. Give your patient your treatment recommendation and explain why you recommend it.
6. Check your patient's understanding of what you have said.
7. If your patient does not fully understand, reframe the unclear part of what you said in a different way. Repeat 6 & 7 as needed.
8. If your patient understands and agrees with your recommendation, then proceed to step 11.
9. If your patient disagrees with your recommendation although they appear to understand it, try to uncover the source of fear behind that decision and address it.
10. If your patient disagrees with your recommendation although they appear to understand it, try to uncover the values behind that decision and address them.
11. Confirm the decision with your patient and document (or make a plan to document) that decision.

2.3 Apparatus

The experience was conducted in a room with controlled light and no voice. The system hardware setup was consisted of apple iPhone 12, desktop capable gaming PC (Intel Core i7-9700K, Nvidia RTX2080 Ti, 32GB RAM) running Windows 10, webcam (Logitech). The scenario' scene including virtual avatar and patient's room were both developed in Unreal Engine 4.4. The digital human was created via metahuman creator in Unreal Engine 4.4 to act as a patient's daughter (see Fig. 2.)

Metahuman Creator

Virtual Daughter's patient developed using Metahuman

Actor acting as virtual daughter

Live Link Face (LLF) and Unreal Engine (UE) for acquiring facial expression from actor

Fig. 2. Overview of involved devices and virtual human and physician

To promote communication, the facial expression equivalent to those of human has been reproduced. The virtual avatar was also integrated with "Faceware Studio" facial recognition software to mimic the facial motion of the actor who acted and communicated in the role of the patient's daughter. Live Link Face (LLF) is a software which can acquire the facial expression form an actor to virtual avatar.

2.4   Experiment Procedure

Before the experiment the participants were provided with the patient case, recommendations on how to optimize the conversation, and a list of the questions they would be asked in the post-immersion semi-structured interview. In the developed scenario there were two roles: a patient's daughter and a physician. The physicians (participants) were contacted one week before the experiment to find a time which worked best for them. The conversation was done and recorded over a zoom call between physician and virtual human. Each zoom call lasted about 30 min. During the conversation, the person who played the role of the patient's daughter was acting as surrogate decision maker during a goals of care conversation that included discussion of procedures that would meet criteria for medical futility.

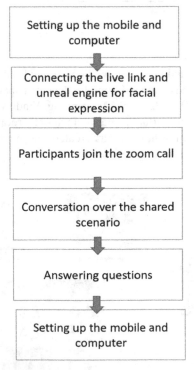

Fig. 3. The experiment procedure

At the end of the simulation the physicians participated in a semi-structured interview to discuss their experience, including if there was concordance between the clinical interventions they were recommending and what the daughter accepted. (See Fig. 3).

Each encounter conducted via Zoom technology was recorded. Video recordings were saved under deidentified markers based on date of recording. The video and audio files were electronically submitted to Rev, professional audio transcription services, deidentified by the service and coded based on sequence of recordings. The video, audio and transcribed sessions were saved onto a secure, password protected server accessible by the lead researcher. An IRB approved research student reviewed, cleaned and ensured transcripts were deidentified, then uploaded into Dedoose, a web-based cross-platform app for analyzing qualitative and mixed methods research with text, photos, audio, videos and spreadsheet data. Dedoose uses encryption technologies to secure data. Passwords and access to Dedoose for approved members of the research team were acquired in congruence with industry guidelines and IRB requirements.

3 Data Analysis

Ten sessions were held, however only data from nine out of the ten sessions resulted in recordings that could be used for the study secondary to technical difficulties with Zoom recording uploads. Transcripts and video data from each of the nine viable virtual immersion sessions were independently reviewed by two researchers for congruence between appropriate treatment recommended and acceptance by the daughter.

Transcripts were also reviewed to assess for the participants use of recommended communication strategies during the session. Communication strategy categories were developed using extant literature review serving as the basis for training content materials. Categories aligned with the recommendations for optimizing communication including, rapport building, giving bad news in clear terms, closing gaps in understanding of prognosis, ongoing clarification, providing a clear recommendation and rationale, uncovering fears and values, and limiting medical jargon. Researchers met via Zoom to resolve incongruencies between reviews.

Findings were exported from Dedoose into an Excel document and coded for concordance. For outcomes variables, concordance related to matching medical appropriate recommendations with avatar acceptance. Communication strategies were coded as either occurring or not occurring. Once exported the data were transformed into binary classifications to complete quantitative operations using IBM SPSS Statistics software.

4 Results

A review of the data showed that two sessions resulted in discordance between code status recommendations and acceptance, in that the physician kept the patient a Full Code, incongruent with their medical recommendations to the contrary. While in eight out of 10 sessions the physicians were able to reach concordance in code status recommendations and daughter acceptance of a Do Not Attempt Resuscitation (DNAR) order, in only 2 of the 10 sessions was a goals of care conversation successful in matching the plan of care with treatments consistent with medical recommendations, including change in code status and a transition to comfort care with clear limitations of treatment orders written based on medical futility. Four sessions resulted in introduction of palliative care and a referral to that service for ongoing conversations.

Data were recoded into 0 for didn't occur and 1 for order written that was consistent with clinical appropriateness. Categorical predictor variables include Code status (CPR v. DNAR), transition to Comfort Care/Hospice, and Palliative Care Consult. These variables were recoded with a 0 for CPR and 1 for DNAR. Comfort Care was coded as a 0 when disease-oriented treatment was continued and 1 for transition to comfort care or hospice. Palliative Care consult was coded as a 0 when not ordered and 1 when a referral was made. Using SPSS software frequency tables indicating frequency of outcomes and percent were created (Table 2.)

Table 2. Frequencies and Percentages (N = 09)

Variable	Category	Frequency	Percent
Code Status	0 (Full Code)	2	22.2
	1 (DNAR)	7	77.8
	Total	9	100
Comfort Care/Hospice	0 (Full Tx.)	7	77.8
	1 (Comfort)	2	22.2
	Total	9	100
Palliative Care Consult	0 (No consult)	4	44.4
	1 (Referral)	5	55.6
	Total	9	100

While frequencies and descriptive statistics could be run using SPSS, secondary to the small data set, statistically significant conclusions related to the relationship between outcomes and communication strategies could not be drawn secondary to limitations of variability. However, the data were reviewed qualitatively to determine if any insights could be drawn related to best practices in physician communication strategies when discussing limitations of treatment.

Using the themes identified through literature review and compilation of training material, certain distinct characteristics emerged related to effective and ineffective communication strategies employed by physicians when the surrogate pressed for treatment interventions that were either medically inappropriate or incongruent with the patients prior stated wishes.

As part of the training materials participants were encouraged to give "bad news regarding their diagnosis and prognosis" and continue to provide clarifying information as needed to close gaps in understanding. There were distinct differences in communication strategies resulting in either increased requests for inappropriate treatment or increased understanding regarding the clinical situation. Communication that resulted in confusion included use of statistics to explain prognosis as even a small chance of recovery was seen by the daughter as a reason for pursuing treatment. Examples included the following statements:

- "if chance of death goes above 20-30%, that's a very bad prognosis"
- "chances of getting a meaningful life after CPR is about 30-40%"
- "chances of [CPR] working are less than 5%"

Other communication pitfalls were being too vague with regard to prognosis or medical effectiveness.

- "it's unlikely that her heart would restart"
- "it's highly likely she would be on a ventilator for a long time"
- "when your heart stops beating, obviously we can do compressions to try and keep blood flowing, but all the potential consequences of having that happen and the further damage that could happen to the kidneys, happen to the brain and stuff, we don't know that beforehand"

Conversely, using plain terms and clear statements regarding death improved understanding.

- "The outlook right now is that she is going to die, and that it will probably be pretty soon, in the near future. We don't know when, but the prognosis...with all of the organ failure that she has, and the heart failure which is the underlying cause of most of this, not all of it but most of it, if we can't fix that, then we cannot turn this around and so yes, she is going to die."

While there didn't appear to be any one communication strategy that aligned with increased concordance in acceptance of medically appropriate interventions, offering clear recommendations that were paired with understanding patient values, uncovering surrogate fear regarding limitations of treatment, and shouldering the burden of the decision was very effective. Some of the following excerpts illustrate this approach.

- "I wouldn't want to do something she expressed desire against."
- "In your mom's condition, where there are a lot of irreversible conditions, there's multi organ failure, a lot of organs are not working, so most of the people will not opt for CPR; and that is what I would suggest in this situation as well."
- "Doing CPR, putting her through a code situation, will only serve to potentially cause injury and greater suffering. And we just shouldn't do that."

During the debrief, all participants expressed an enhanced understanding of patient points of view and the scaffolding onto which effective provider-patient communication skills can be continuously cultivated. The majority of participants commented on how much more difficult it was to accomplish concordance than what they had originally anticipated. Also noted, was the realistic nature of the immersion and that interacting with the virtual human evoked the same or similar emotions as having difficult conversations in real life.

5 Discussion

While this study was limited in scope, it piloted how virtual immersion training can be utilized to optimize communication between patients, their surrogates, and physicians as well as promote care consistent with patient values and medical effectiveness. While the study did not identify specific communication skills that would result in concordance between medically appropriate interventions and acceptance of medical recommenda tions by the physician, it did produce preliminary evidence that when multiple strategies designed to close gaps in understanding are used together to provide a clear recommendation, there is a greater likelihood of concordance. Review of the encounters also revealed clear pitfalls in communication that lead to overuse and inappropriate use of futile medical interventions. In addition, encounters revealed that barriers related to patient/surrogate beliefs and provider beliefs both influence concordance between medical effectiveness and acceptance of recommended medical procedures and plans of care.

The debrief sessions give credence to the claim that virtual immersion can support the development of cognitive empathy by increasing understanding of other perspectives.

6 Limitations

As a pilot study this research initiative was limited in scope. There was only one academic medical center from which participants were recruited. With convenience sampling and limited resources for recruitment, participants were individuals already interested in promoting better end of life care conversations. In addition, the sample was reflective of physicians with additional training in ethics, palliative care, and serious illness conversations. Data were only collected on nine encounters, further limiting scope and generalizability. The intrinsic biases of the standardized patient/surrogate that served as the virtual human impacted the encounters. While the responses of the individual playing the role of the patient daughter were predicated on extant literature and 20 years of experiential knowledge in the field as a clinical ethicist, her portrayal may not be reflective of many family members making similar decisions in real life scenarios. Ongoing research is needed to increase understanding of the range and likelihood of responses to these types of situations and varying communication strategies.

7 Conclusion

There is a considerable opportunity to expand current clinical ethics learning environments, both professional and academic, to incorporate virtual immersion and specifically, virtual human interaction. Virtual immersion is a safe and accessible way to shift clinical ethics training towards a behavior-based model, which has greater potential than traditional methods to influence future practice decisions. Virtual immersion provides opportunities for clinicians to develop essential skills such as empathetic response, perspective taking, and navigating complex belief structures to promote ethical practice and maximize medical decisions consistent with value-based care.

References

1. Crutchfield, P., Johnson, J.C., Brandt, L., Fleming, D.: The limits of deontology in dental ethics education. Int. J. Ethics Edu. **1**(2), 183–200 (2016). https://doi.org/10.1007/s40889-016-0018-7
2. Brandt, L., et al.: Health care ethics ECHO: Improving ethical response self-efficacy through sensemaking. Int. J. Ethics Edu. (2021)
3. Brandt, L., Popejoy, L.: Use of sensemaking as a pedagogical approach to teach clinical ethics: an integrative review. Int. J. Ethics Edu. (2020)
4. Bazerman, M., Gino, F.: Behavioral ethics: toward a deeper understanding of moral judgment and dishonesty. Annual Review of Law and Social Science **8**(1), 85–104 (2012)
5. Alexandrova, I.V., et al.: Enhancing medical communication training using motion capture, perspective taking and virtual reality. Medicine Meets Virtual Reality **19**, 16–22 (2012)
6. Pierce, R.P., et al.: A comparison of models predicting one-year mortality at time of admission. J. Pain and Symptom Manage. (2021)
7. Ahn, S.J., Bailenson, J.N., Park, D.: Short- and long-term effects of embodied experiences in immersive virtual environments on environmental locus of control and behavior. Comput. Hum. Behav. **39**, 235–245 (2014)
8. Gehlbach, H., et al.: Many ways to walk a mile in another's moccasins: Type of social perspective taking and its effect on negotiation outcomes. Comput. Hum. Behav. **52**, 523–532 (2015)
9. Oh, S.Y., et al.: Virtually old: Embodied perspective taking and the reduction of ageism under threat. Comput. Hum. Behav. **60**, 398–410 (2016)
10. Celso, B.G., Meenrajan, S.: The triad that matters: palliative medicine, code status, and health care costs. Am J Hosp Palliat Care **27**(6), 398–401 (2010)
11. Kazaure, H.S., Roman, S.A., Sosa, J.A.: A population-level analysis of 5620 recipients of multiple in-hospital cardiopulmonary resuscitation attempts. J Hosp Med **9**(1), 29–34 (2014)
12. Marcia, L., et al.: Advance Directive and Do-Not-Resuscitate Status among Advanced Cancer Patients with Acute Care Surgical Consultation. Am. Surg. **84**(10), 1565–1569 (2018)
13. Zhang, B., et al.: Health care costs in the last week of life: associations with end-of-life conversations. Arch Intern Med **169**(5), 480–488 (2009)
14. Powell, A.A., et al.: A conceptual framework for understanding and reducing overuse by primary care providers. Med Care Res Rev **70**(5), 451–472 (2013)
15. Crawford, G.L., Kloepper, K.D.: Exit Interviews: laboratory assessment incorporating written and oral communication. J. Chem. Educ. **96**(5), 880–887 (2019)
16. DuPré, A.: Communicating about health : current issues and perspectives. Fifth edition. Oxford University Press (2017)
17. Lo, B., Quill, T., Tulsky, J.: Academia and clinic. Discussing palliative care with patients. Annals of Internal Medicine **130**(9), 744–749 (1999)

Multimodal Approach to Assess a Virtual Reality-Based Surgical Training Platform

Doga Demirel[1]($\boxtimes$) iD, Hasan Onur Keles[2] iD, Chinmoy Modak[1],
Kubranur Kara Basturk[2], Jacob R. Barker[1], and Tansel Halic[3] iD

[1] Florida Polytechnic University, Lakeland, FL, USA
{ddemirel,cmodak9952,jbarker}@floridapoly.edu
[2] Ankara University, Ankara, Turkey
hokeles@ankara.edu.tr, kubranur.kara@tootech.com.tr
[3] Intuitive Surgical, Peachtree Corners, GA, USA
tansel.halic@intusurg.com

Abstract. Virtual reality (VR) can bring numerous benefits to the learning process. Combining a VR environment with physiological sensors can be beneficial in skill assessment. We aim to investigate trainees' physiological (ECG) and behavioral differences during the virtual reality-based surgical training environment. Our finding showed a significant association between the VR-Score and all participants' total NASA-TLX workload score. The extent of the NASA-TLX workload score was negatively correlated with VR-Score ($R^2 = 0.15$, P < 0.03). In time-domain ECG analysis, we found that RMSSD ($R^2 = 0.16$, P < 0.05) and pNN50 ($R^2 = 0.15$, P < 0.05) scores correlated with significantly higher VR-score of all participants. In this study, we used SVM (linear kernel) and Logistic Regression classification techniques to classify the participants as gamers and non-gamers using data from VR headsets. Both SVM and Logistic Regression accurately classified the participants as gamers and non-gamers with 83% accuracy. For both SVM and Linear Regression, precision was noted as 88%, recall as 83%, and f1-score as 83%. There is increasing interest in characterizing trainees' physiological and behavioral activity profiles in a VR environment, aiming to develop better training and assessment methodologies.

Keywords: Virtual Reality · Skill assessment · ECG · Mental workload

1 Introduction

Virtual Reality (VR) is becoming a more widely used teaching and learning aid in several fields, such as medical training and robotics. Conventional training methods are hard to grasp, non-reusable, non-repeatable, and costly. VR allows students and teachers to interact in a real-time learning environment, which would be nearly impossible to do in the physical world. Trainees face trouble obtaining skills in this unnatural environment. Training with VR simulators established benefits, however, methods for skill assessment in VR, particularly in real-time, are still undeveloped and unknown. Virtual reality simulators are computer-based systems that generate output data, which is very helpful for skill assessment [1, 2].

© The Author(s), under exclusive license to Springer Nature Switzerland AG 2023
J. Y. C. Chen and G. Fragomeni (Eds.): HCII 2023, LNCS 14027, pp. 430–440, 2023.
https://doi.org/10.1007/978-3-031-35634-6_30

In general, skill assessment approaches can be found in technical, non-technical, and mental workload assessments. For mental workload assessment, questionnaires and physiological measurements can be useful tools, and for non-technical skill assessment, all methods (questionnaires, expert-rating and physiological measurement) can be utilized [3]. In critical fields such as surgical education and healthcare, learning is based on an apprenticeship model [4]. In this model, the proficiency assessment is the responsibility of the trainers. However, their assessment is subjective. Objective assessment is essential because performance in training and performance are difficult to correct without objective feedback. Psychophysiological measures allow a more objective assessment and can provide an uninterrupted evaluation [5].

Technological advances in wearable sensor technology make objective assessment less intrusive and capable of delivering continuous, multimodal information. Electroencephalogram (EEG) and Electrocardiogram (ECG), including Heart Rate (HR), Heart Rate Variability (HRV), have also been correlated with NASA-TLX scores as well as task complexity, performance and expertise in surgery [5, 6]. Studies also indicate that such descriptors correlate with the overt performance of human operators [7]. For example, mental workload gauged by a standard self-reporting tool was proportional to the rate of errors committed and suture quality in laparoscopic surgery training [8]. However, efforts to characterize mental status descriptors and their effect on individual and team performance face a significant challenge: the descriptors are not directly observable. To quantify them, researchers traditionally resort to physiological variables (e.g., ECG, EEG, skin conductance), behavioral indicators (e.g., secondary task performance), or survey results (e.g., NASA-TLX questionnaire). Few studies focused on combining VR environments and physiological sensors during training approach [9–12].

Previous gaming experience helps get accommodated to this training environment faster, increases visual attention capacity, and makes multitasking easier. Thus, it helps the trainees to facilitate these obstacles and acquire skills more quickly. Video gamers and surgeons have similarities in skill acquisition [13, 14]. Video gamers have superior eye-hand coordination, faster reaction times, superior spatial visualization skills, and a high capacity for visual attention and spatial distribution. Both laparoscopic surgery and computer games require eye-hand coordination, visuospatial cognitive ability, attention, and perception skills. Individuals who interact or play video games tend to have better visuospatial ability when compared to non-gamers [15, 16].

Grantcharov et al. [17] demonstrated the effect of video game experience on the MIST-VR® surgical simulator and found that surgeons with previous video game experience made significantly fewer errors than non-gamers. Therefore, this project aims to assess how the gaming experience gives advantages to the new trainees and makes the learning process more accessible on the VR-based surgical training platforms. Demand for the safety of patients has prompted the need for efficient and affordable training for preparing surgeons. Several VR-based simulators have recently been developed to fulfill this need, and VR applications, simulation, and e-learning have improved the learning metrics [18]. Conventional human and animal models, cadavers, and mannequin-based training for surgeons can be risky, non-reusable, subjective, and expensive. VR-based simulators measure several characteristics or metrics for objectively assessing the trainee's performance.

According to Enochsson et al. [19], video game players were more efficient and faster than non-gamers performing the simulated colonoscopy. There were also no gender-specific differences in performance. Jalink et al. [20] suggested that video games could be used to train surgical residents in laparoscopic skills. Based on these findings, one might expect that gaming will facilitate and improve the training of novice surgeons.

where the performance requires a firm reliance on spatial orientation and the recognition of various visual inputs.

We aim to investigate trainees' physiological and behavioral differences during the virtual reality-based surgical training environment. This paper shows multimodal information collected from a VR + ECG system for skill assessment during a surgical training game. We hypothesize that multimodal information can lead to a more accurate assessment than single modality-based measurement approaches. In addition, we also showed how the game experience could affect performance and behavioral measures (task load). To our knowledge, the studies to date which investigated these links exclusively utilized overt performance and behavioral measures. However, given the complexity of skill assessment, multimodal approaches are required.

2   Methods

2.1   Participants

Our dataset consisted of 30 participants with varying levels of gaming experience (from 0 to 60 h per week). It was subsequently divided into two groups according to their previous gaming experience as gamers and non-gamers. The Research Ethics Board of Ankara University approved this study (2021/435), which was performed in agreement with the Declaration of Helsinki. All participants signed informed consent and could withdraw from the study at any time.

2.2   Study Design

For this experiment, we created a simple VR environment where the users were asked to bounce a balloon and keep it in a proper range while in the air. To achieve a high score in this environment, the trainee must keep the balloon between the planes while bouncing for as long as possible with fewer impacts while causing no damage to the balloon. A VR score is calculated by the amount of time between the planes. This environment assesses the gentleness of a surgeon [21]. We used a Meta Quest 2 as the VR headset.

The participants were given two minutes to get accommodated with the scene (resting state), and then the next three minutes were used to capture data. In this study, we recorded physiological signals such as ECG while using a VR device. After subjects completed the training in VR headsets, they completed the NASA task load index (NASA-TLX) questionnaire. Nasa-TLX is a multidimensional rating scale that provides an overall index of mental workload and the relative contributions of six subscales: mental, physical, and temporal task demands: effort, frustration, and perceived performance. VR-Score, jerk, velocity, and acceleration were recorded for all participants using a VR headset. RMSSD, pNN50, and pNN20 were used for heart rate variability (HRV) analysis.

Fig. 1. A(a) VR-ECG Setup and (b) VR Racket Game

2.3 Physiological Signal Recording and Processing

The ECG data were obtained through the ExG Explorer device (wearable wireless) (Mentalab, Germany). One channel was recorded by placing the electrodes on the designated body locations. Raw ECG signals were digitalized with a sampling rate of 250 Hz and filtered by a low pass Gaussian filter with a cut-off frequency of 40 Hz, while IIR Zero-Phase Filter was used to attenuate baseline wander with a cutoff frequency of 0.5 Hz. Time domain analysis was used to process the preprocessed ECG signals. The HRV time domain parameters (RMSSD, pNN 50, and pNN 20) were chosen in the current study as the assumed assessment indicators for the later analysis.

2.4 Statistical Analysis

When conducting a regression analysis comparing two numerical variables, linear fit with analysis of variance was used. The descriptive results comparing two groups, NASA-TLX, and total VR score, contained non-paired data. To assess the statistical significance of the difference between two groups of non-paired results, we used the non-parametric Kolmogorov test. We did not utilize null hypotheses whose rejection would have required corrections for multiple comparisons or false discovery. The statistical significance of the results were interpreted based on p values, and $p < 0.05$ was set as the level of statistical significance.

3 Result

3.1 VR Results

According to our results, gamers had an average VR score of 3581.86, over two times higher than non-gamers average VR score of 1748.8. The time gamers kept the balloon between the planes (66.36) is almost two times higher than the non-gamers (34.96).

Also, gamers popped the balloon times above the top plane (24.21) was significantly higher than the non-gamers (12.8). The mean jerk was 40.9%, the mean acceleration was 29.1%, and the mean velocity was 7% more in non-gamers than gamers. While for mean path length, gamers had 7.1% more than non-gamers. For standard deviation results, gamers had a lower standard deviation in path length (7.6%), velocity (30.1%), acceleration (27.8%), and jerk (23.6%). These findings indicate that gamer's hand and spatial movement were gentler, with a minor standard deviation, than non-players.

The results of the features of the compared groups are illustrated in Fig. 2. The gamer's hand position (Fig. 2a) and path length (Fig. 2b) while moving the tennis racket are more scattered than the non-gamers. Figure 2b also shows that gamers had a longer mean path length showing that they were more decisive and knew what they were doing. This finding implies gamer has better hand-eye coordination as they perform better and produce better result than non-gamers. However, from Fig. 2c, we can see that non-gamers had more velocity meaning that gamers used more positive force. As gamers have less acceleration (Fig. 2d) and jerk (Fig. 2e), their movement is more stable than the non-gamers.

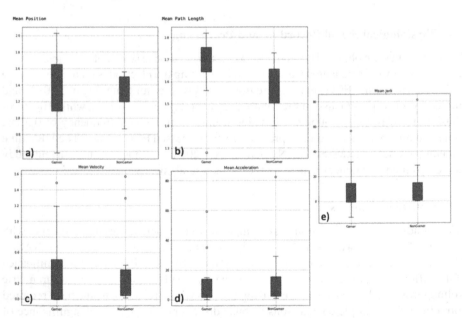

Fig. 2. A(a) Mean Position, (b) Mean Path Length, (c) Mean Velocity, (d) Mean Acceleration, and (e) Mean Jerk box plots comparing Gamer and Non-gamer results.

3.2 Clustering Results

After selecting the features from the data set, we used multiple metrics to measure the difference between the data groups. We used the Davies Bouldin score, Silhouette Score, and the Mutual Information Index metrics with the K-Means, Mean Shift, and

Spectral Clustering algorithms for clustering. We got the optimum score at the number of clusters (n) = 2. Figure 3 shows the graphs for the metrics score of the clustering algorithms. Normalizing the data, other better results over Spectral Clustering and Mean Shift algorithm. Though there are variations in the results, Mean-Shift performed the best, achieving an 80% success rate in classifying the users based on their previous gaming experience. However, since the range of data is smaller, the Mutual Information Index dropped in almost all instances.

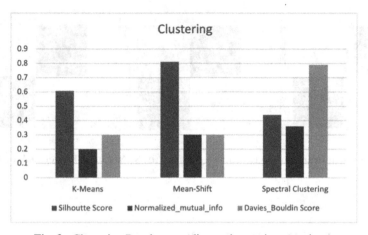

Fig. 3. Clustering Results according to the gaming experience

3.3 Classification Results

After the clustering, we passed the data through classification algorithms such as Logistic Regression and Support Vector Machine with linear kernels. We looked at those classification algorithms' precision, recall, F1 score, and average accuracy. We normalized the data the same way as above and obtained massive improvements in the Logistic regression algorithm. We could classify the performance between the gamers and non-gamers at best 83% of the time.

Table 1. Classification results according to the gaming experience

Algorithms	Precision	Recall	F1 Score
Logistic Regression	80%	67%	62%
SVM Linear	88%	83%	83%
AdaBoost	88%	83%	83%

Table 1 lists the Precision, Recall, and F1 Scores of different classification algorithms. We achieved at best, 88% of the average score for those algorithms. The distribution of the observed values is displayed more clearly in Fig. 4. We predicted that the gamers would perform than the participants with no gaming experience, and in the case of all classification algorithms, the True Positive (TP) is significantly higher. Logistic regression successfully classified gamers with 82% accuracy and non-gamers with 86% accuracy (Fig. 4a). Logistic regression successfully classified gamers with 82% accuracy and non-gamers with 86% accuracy. Figure 4b shows SVM Linear classified gamers with 91% accuracy and non-gamers with 86% accuracy. Adaboost Classifier classified both gamers and non-gamers with 100% accuracy (Fig. 4c).

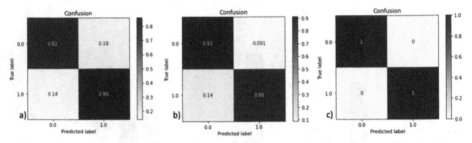

Fig. 4. Confusion matrix for (a) Logistic Regression, (b) SVM Linear Kernel, and (c) AdaBoost classifier

3.4 Behavioral and Physiological Results

We present the behavioral and subjective metrics and physiological measurement (ECG) of non-gamer and gamers, measured while performing virtual training tasks using a VR headset. Thirty participants (mean age 23.25 ± 8.5 years) were enrolled in the study. The participants' experience with gaming varies. Fifteen participants have no experience with gaming. The rest of the participants have an experience with gaming (mean: 12.4 h per week ± 11.4 years).

Figure 5a shows that gamers have greater VR scores when compared to non-gamers. A significant difference in VR Score was noted between gamers and non-gamers ($P < 0.05$), confirming the difference between the two groups. Figure 5b, through regression analysis, we found a significant association between the VR score and Nasa-TLX total score for all participants. The extent of the Nasa-TLX score (MW) was negatively correlated with the VR performance score ($R^2 = 0.14$, $P < 0.05$). Although gamers have a higher Nasa-TLX score, the difference between gamers and non-gamers did not reach significance during the racket game.

In time-domain ECG analysis, we found that RMSSD ($R^2 = 0.16$, $P < 0.05$) and pNN50 ($R^2 = 0.15$, $P < 0.05$) scores correlated with significantly higher VR-score of all participants (Fig. 6). There were similar trends for pNN20, although group differences were not statistically significant.

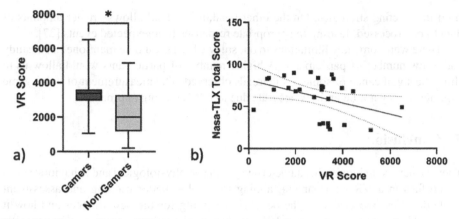

Fig. 5. A(a)VR Performance of non-gamer students (gray, circle indicates the median) vs. gamer students (black). Error bars indicate sample standard deviations (*p < 0.05; **p < 0.01). (b) Nasa-TLX Total Score vs. VR Score

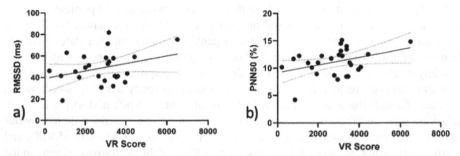

Fig. 6. A(a) VR score vs RMSSD ($R^2 = 0.14$ P < 0.05). (b) VR Score vs PNN50 ($R^2 = 0.16$ P < 0.05). In the scatter plots, the solid black lines indicate the linear best fit to the data points, and the dotted lines indicate the 95% confidence interval.

4 Discussion

Our main results suggest a relationship between VR performance scores and the ECG time domain parameters of trainees. To our knowledge, this is the first study that includes physiological and performance metrics (multimodal approach) during a VR environment using a VR headset. Time-domain approach for ECG has been widely used to investigate the cardiovascular outcome of mental work. Several studies showed that mental workload leads to a decrease in the time domain measure of ECG [22, 23]. This supposes a predominant increase in sympathetic activity or a predominant decrease in para sympathetic activity [24, 25].

Our results showed a significant negative correlation between cognitive load and gaming experience in all participants. This outcome is important because previous research has demonstrated that scores from NASA-TLX can accurately predict future performance [6, 26]. Furthermore, playing VR games that have high levels of cognitive demand may result in being easily distracted, having limited options to consider, or being rigid in selecting strategies. On the other hand, a low load allows greater amounts of data to be processed, leading to appropriate responses to unexpected events [27].

There were some key limitations to our study which should be mentioned. Our study had a low number of participants. A higher number of participants would allow us to show the significance of some of the trends observed. The measurement of video game experience may not be entirely accurate due to self-reporting approach.

5 Conclusion

There is increasing interest in characterizing trainees' physiological and behavioral activity profiles in a VR environment, aiming to develop better training and assessment methodologies. We evaluated the benefits of gaming for the new trainees and how it improves learning accessibility on VR-based surgical gentleness training platforms. We conducted investigations involving human subjects primarily to establish content and construct validations. We used different kinematics data, such as position, path length, acceleration, jerk, and velocity, collected from the subject's interactions with the virtual reality environment. The dataset for this project consisted of 30 participants, who were then divided into groups based on their prior gaming experience. We depicted that gamer's hand and spatial movement were gentler, with a minor standard deviation, than non-players. Then, we distinguished between gamers and non-gamers by utilizing a variety of clustering and classification algorithms. We applied clustering algorithms such as K-means, Mean-shift, and Spectral Clustering to verify the difference between the data. Though there are variations in the results, Mean-Shift performed the best, achieving over an 80% success rate in classifying the users based on their previous gaming experience. Using Logistic Regression, Support Vector Machine (SVM), and AdaBoost classifier, we were able to classify over 80% of the performance between the gamers and non-gamers and achieved 88% accuracy at best. Gamer's subjective performance and situation awareness correlated more positively with task performance than the non-gamers.

Acknowledgement. This project was made possible by NIH/NIAMS 5R44AR075481- 03 and the Arkansas INBRE program, supported by the National Institute of General Medical Sciences (NIGMS), P20 GM103429 from the National Institutes of Health (NIH), and partially supported by NIH/NIBIB 1R01EB033674-01A1, 5R01EB025241–04, 3R01EB005807-09A1S1, and 5R01EB005807–10.

References

1. Yu, P., et al.: Quantitative influence and performance analysis of virtual reality laparoscopic surgical training system. BMC Med. Educ. **22**(1), 1–10 (2022)
2. Ota, D., Loftin, B., Saito, T., Lea, R., Keller, J.: Virtual reality in surgical education. Comput Biol Med. **25**(2), 127–137 (1995). https://doi.org/10.1016/0010-4825(94)00009-f. PMID: 7554831

3. Dias RD, Ngo-Howard MC, Boskovski MT, Zenati MA, Yule SJ. Systematic review of measurement tools to assess surgeons' intraoperative cognitive workload. Br J Surg. 2018 Apr;105(5):491–501. doi: https://doi.org/10.1002/bjs.10795. Epub 2018 Feb 21. PMID: 29465749; PMCID: PMC5878696
4. Beard, J.D.: Assessment of surgical skills of trainees in the UK. Ann R Coll Surg Engl. 90(4), 282–285 (2008). https://doi.org/10.1308/003588408X286017.PMID:18492389; PMCID:PMC2647187
5. Zakeri, Z., Mansfield, N., Sunderland, C., et al.: Physiological correlates of cognitive load in laparoscopic surgery. Sci Rep 10, 12927 (2020). https://doi.org/10.1038/s41598-020-695 53-3
6. Keleş, H. O., Cengiz, C., Demiral, I., Ozmen, M. M., & Omurtag, A., (2021). High density optical neuroimaging predicts surgeons's subjective experience and skill levels. PLOS ONE , vol.16, no.2
7. van Merriënboer, J.J., Sweller, J.: Cognitive load theory in health professional education: design principles and strategies. Med Educ. 44(1), 85–93 (2010). https://doi.org/10.1111/j. 1365-2923.2009.03498.x. PMID: 20078759
8. Yurko, Yuliya Y. MD; Scerbo, Mark W. PhD; Prabhu, Ajita S. MD; Acker, Christina E. BA; Stefanidis, Dimitrios MD, PhD. Higher Mental Workload is Associated With Poorer Laparoscopic Performance as Measured by the NASA-TLX Tool. Simulation in Healthcare: The Journal of the Society for Simulation in Healthcare 5(5):p 267–271, October 2010
9. Suárez, J.X., Gramann, K., Ochoa, J.F., Toro, J.P., Mejía, A.M., Hernández, A.M.: Changes in brain activity of trainees during laparoscopic surgical virtual training assessed with electroencephalography. Brain Res. 1783, 147836 (2022)
10. Yu, P., Pan, J., Wang, Z., Shen, Y., Wang, L., Li, J., Hao, A. and Wang, H., 2021, March. Cognitive load/flow and performance in virtual reality simulation training of laparoscopic surgery. In 2021 IEEE Conference on Virtual Reality and 3D User Interfaces Abstracts and Workshops (VRW) (pp. 466–467). IEEE
11. Tremmel, C., Herff, C., Sato, T., Rechowicz, K., Yamani, Y., Krusienski, D.J.: Estimating Cognitive Workload in an Interactive Virtual Reality Environment Using EEG. Front Hum Neurosci. 14(13), 401 (2019). https://doi.org/10.3389/fnhum.2019.00401.PMID:31803035; PMCID:PMC6868478
12. Aspiotis, V., et al.: Assessing Electroencephalography as a Stress Indicator: A VR High-Altitude Scenario Monitored through EEG and ECG. Sensors (Basel). 22(15), 5792 (2022). https://doi.org/10.3390/s22155792.PMID:35957348;PMCID:PMC9371026
13. Nahum, M., Bavelier, D.: Video games as rich environments to foster brain plasticity. Handb Clin Neurol 168, 117–136 (2020)
14. Rosser JC Jr, Lynch PJ, Cuddihy L, Gentile DA, Klonsky J, Merrell R (2007) The impact of video games on training surgeons in the 21st century. Arch Surg 142(2):181–186; discusssion 6
15. Datta, R., Chon, S.H., Dratsch, T., Timmermann, F., Muller, L., Plum, P.S., et al.: Are gamers better laparoscopic surgeons? Impact of gaming skills on laparoscopic performance in "Generation Y" students. PLoS ONE 15(8), e0232341 (2020)
16. Chalhoub, E., et al.: The role of video games in facilitating the psychomotor skills training in laparoscopic surgery. Gynecol. Surg. 13(4), 419–424 (2016). https://doi.org/10.1007/s10 397-016-0986-9
17. Grantcharov, T.P., Bardram, L., Funch-Jensen, P., Rosenberg, J.: Impact of hand dominance, gender, and experience with computer games on performance in virtual reality laparoscopy. Surg. Endosc. Other Interv. Tech. 17, 1082–1085 (2003)
18. Thijssen, A.S., Schijven, M.P.: Contemporary virtual reality laparoscopy simulators: quicksand or solid grounds for assessing surgical trainees? The American Journal of Surgery 199(4), 529–541 (2010)

19. Enochsson, L., et al.: Visuospatial skills and computer game experience influence the performance of virtual endoscopy. J. Gastrointest. Surg. **8**, 874–880 (2004)

20. Jalink, M.B., Goris, J., Heineman, E., Pierie, J.P.E., Henk, O.: The effects of video games on laparoscopic simulator skills. The American Journal of Surgery **208**(1), 151–156 (2014)

21. Farmer, J., et al.: Systematic approach for content and construct validation: case studies for arthroscopy and laparoscopy. The International Journal of Medical Robotics and Computer Assisted Surgery **16**(4), e2105 (2020)

22. Fan, X., Zhao, C., Zhang, X., Luo, H., Zhang, W.: Assessment of mental workload based on multi-physiological signals. Technol Health Care. **28**(S1), 67–80 (2020). https://doi.org/10.3233/THC-209008.PMID:32364145;PMCID:PMC7369076

23. Yu, D., Antonik, C.W., Webber, F., et al.: Correction to: Multi-modal physiological sensing approach for distinguishing high workload events in remotely piloted aircraft simulation. Hum.-Intell. Syst. Integr. **3**, 201–211 (2021). https://doi.org/10.1007/s42454-021-00033-3

24. Weippert, M., Behrens, K., Rieger, A., Stoll, R., Kreuzfeld, S.: Heart rate variability and blood pressure during dynamic and static exercise at similar heart rate levels. PLoS ONE **8**(12), e83690 (2013). https://doi.org/10.1371/journal.pone.0083690.PMID:24349546;PMCID:PMC3862773

25. McCraty, R., Shaffer, F.: Heart Rate Variability: New Perspectives on Physiological Mechanisms, Assessment of Self-regulatory Capacity, and Health risk. Glob Adv Health Med. **4**(1), 46–61 (2015). https://doi.org/10.7453/gahmj.2014.073.PMID:25694852;PMCID:PMC4311559

26. Adapa, K., Pillai, M., Das, S., Mosaly, P., Mazur, L.: Predicting Objective Performance Using Perceived Cognitive Workload Data in Healthcare Professionals: A Machine Learning Study. Stud Health Technol Inform. **6**(290), 809–813 (2022). https://doi.org/10.3233/SHTI220191. PMID: 35673130

27. Carswell, C.M., Clarke, D., Seales, W.B.: Assessing mental workload during laparoscopic surgery. Surg Innov **12**(1), 80–90 (2005)

Effect of Tactile Affordance During the Design of Extended Reality-Based Training Environments for Healthcare Contexts

Avinash Gupta[1](✉), J. Cecil[2], Mahdiyeh sadat Moosavi[3], Jacob Williams[2], and Frédéric Merienne[3]

[1] University of Illinois Urbana-Champaign, Champaign, USA
avinashg@illinois.edu
[2] Oklahoma State University, Stillwater, USA
[3] Arts Et Metiers Institute of Technology, Chalon-Sur-Saone, France

Abstract. In this paper, the effect of tactile affordance during the design of Extended Reality (XR) based environments is presented. Tactile affordance is one of the Human eXtended Reality Interaction (HXRI) criteria which help lay the foundation for human-centric XR-based training environments. XR-based training environments developed for two surgical procedures have been used to study the role of tactile affordance. The first XR environment is developed for the Condylar plating surgical procedure which is performed to treat the fractures of the femur bone and the second XR environment is developed to train users in endotracheal intubation. Three studies have been conducted to understand the influence of different interaction methods to elevate tactile affordance in XR-based environments. The studies and the results of the studies have been exhaustively discussed in this paper.

Keywords: Affordance · Tactile Affordance · Human eXtended Reality Interaction · HXRI · Virtual Reality · Extended Reality (XR)

1 Introduction

Extended Reality (XR) is an umbrella term used to collectively describe Virtual Reality, Mixed Reality, Augmented Reality, and other supporting technologies such as haptic technology. The Healthcare domain has benefited from the use of XR technologies in the last two decades. There has been an exponential technological advancement, especially in the last five years, with the introduction of low-cost VR headsets such as Vive and Quest, AR-capable smartphones and tablets, and Mixed Reality headsets such as Hololens and Magic Leap. Such advancements have enabled designers to create VR, MR, and AR-based training simulators for a wide range of applications ranging from less invasive laparoscopic surgery to complex procedures such as brain and cardiac surgery [1–15].

As more researchers invest time and resources towards technological advancements, the research focusing on the human-centric aspects of an XR-based environment has

J. Y. C. Chen and G. Fragomeni (Eds.): HCII 2023, LNCS 14027, pp. 441–452, 2023.
https://doi.org/10.1007/978-3-031-35634-6_31

taken a backseat. This paper explores the impact of a Human eXtended Reality Interaction (HXRI) criterion during the design and development of XR-based environments. HXRI can be defined as the application of current HCI-based principles and the formulation of novel principles for the creation of effective XR-based applications. Only a few researchers have focused on understanding the HCI-centric aspects of the XR platforms and devices [6, 16–19]. In this paper, the HXRI criteria termed tactile affordance is being described and its impact on both VR and MR-based environments developed for two healthcare-related training scenarios is being studied. The word affordance was first coined in [20] by psychologist James J. Gibson who defined it as what the environment offers to the individual. In the context of Human-Computer Interaction, the term affordance was defined by Norman as action possibilities that are perceivable readily by an actor [21]. Gaver delineated affordances as the world's properties, which are defined with respect to how people interact with them. Gaver provided an analysis of the relationship between affordance and perceptual information about the information which led to four possible combinations viz. Perceptible affordance, false affordance, hidden affordance, and correct rejection [22].

While designing and developing XR-based applications, designers focus on spatial, manipulation, and feedback affordances. Head-mounted XR-based displays provide natural movement of the head and body, enabling users to sense the depth of images intuitively, creating a sense of presence. Researchers, in the past, have studied affordances related to the XR-based environments. A test for objective assessment of judgment and action-based measures to measure perceptual fidelity in AR using HoloLens [23]. A similar study in which HoloLens-based XR environment was used to understand the effect of varying wide and deep gaps on users was presented in [24]. During the interactions with XR-based environments for surgical training, a user has to perform complex tasks; however, past researchers focused on how basic tasks such as passing through a door, or an aperture, and observing gaps affect affordance in virtual and augmented reality [25–27]. There has been a lack of research focusing on tactile affordance during complex tasks. As most XR environments, especially in the surgical domain, are designed such that users can perform complex tasks, it is important to understand how tactile affordance affects the users when such tasks are being performed. Other researchers have elaborated on the learning affordance in an XR environment using various subjective and objective questionnaires [28, 29]. These affordance questionnaires only serve as basic knowledge-based questions regarding the process without highlighting the importance of understanding the relationship between various objects of interest (OOIs) and various interaction methods in the XR environment.

In a previous publication [31], affordance was classified into two main categories (Visual and Tactile Affordance). In this paper, the focus is on understanding the impact of tactile affordance during the design of XR-based simulators. Tactile Affordance (TA) can be defined as the function of a scene's ability to support comprehension through the sense of touch.

XR-based training environments developed for two surgical procedures have been used to study the role of tactile affordance in knowledge and skills acquisition. The first XR environment is developed for the Condylar plating surgical procedure which is performed to treat the fractures of the femur bone and the second XR environment is developed to train users in endotracheal intubation. Three studies have been conducted to understand the influence of different interaction methods to elevate tactile affordance in XR-based environments.

The rest of the paper is organized in the following manner. In Sect. 2, the design of the XR-based environments is presented. The design of the study is elaborated in Sect. 3. In Sect. 4, the results from the studies are presented and discussed.

2   Design of XR Based Environments

The HCI-based XR environments were designed for using Virtual, Mixed and Haptic-based technologies. Orthopedic surgical training. The VR-based environments were developed for Vive Pro immersive platform and the MR-based environments were developed for the HoloLens 2 platform. The VR and MR environments were developed using the Unity 3D engine. Steam VR tool kit was used for the development of VR environments and Mixed Reality Toolkit (MRTK) was used for the development of MR environments. Training environments were developed for Condylar plating surgery and endotracheal intubation.

2.1   Condylar Plating Training Environment

The HCI-based XR environments were designed for using Virtual, Mixed and Haptic-based technologies. Orthopedic surgical training. The VR-based environments were developed for Vive Pro immersive platform and the MR-based environments were developed for the HoloLens 2 platform. The VR and MR environments were developed using the Unity 3D engine. Steam VR tool kit was used for the development of VR environments and Mixed Reality Toolkit (MRTK) was used for the development of MR environments. Training environments were developed for Condylar plating surgery and endotracheal intubation.

Dynamic Plate Compression Environment. The dynamic Plate compression environment is the most complex training environment among the three environments. In some critical femur fractures, dynamic plate compression is performed to reduce the bones and complete the treatment. In dynamic plate compression, the two fractured bones are transfixed by exerting dynamic pressure between the bone fragments. Figure 1 shows the views of VR and MR-based training environments developed for dynamic plate compression. During the training, the users learn to complete a complex set of procedures including plate positioning, drilling, and screw insertion. During the training, the users first insert the plate in the correct position and orientation based on the location of the fracture. Secondly, the users fix the plate in the position using clamps. Subsequently, an eccentric drill guide is used to drill holes in the bone. Finally, screws are inserted, that compress the bone segment together and transfix them. For the VR-based training, the users interacted with the environment using Vive Pro fully immersive headset. Wireless handheld controllers were used to perform the training activities. For the MR-based training, the users interacted wearing the HoloLens 2 platform. The users interacted with the physical mockup of the training tool and equipment by following the MR-based instructions on the HoloLens 2 headset. The users can be seen interacting with the VR and MR-based training environments in Fig. 4.

Fig. 1. VR and MR based Training Environments for Dynamic Plate Compression

2.2 Endotracheal Intubation Training Environment

Performing an endotracheal intubation is a complex and challenging medical procedure. An extensive amount of training is required in order to acquire the skills necessary to perform endotracheal intubation. As part of the medical procedure, an endotracheal tube is commonly inserted into the patient's trachea to provide artificial respiration to the patient by optimizing the airway. In the process of inserting the endotracheal tube, scrapes can occur in the esophagus. Consequently, the patient is at an increased risk of infection. In order to reduce the risk, a laryngoscope will be used to help the doctor place the endotracheal tube. By using a laryngoscope, the doctor is able to see the vocal cords more clearly and place the endotracheal tube more safely and consistently. In order for the endotracheal tube to function correctly, the doctor will secure the tube and clear the airway of obstructions [17]. The virtual environment (Fig. 2) allows users to perform each step of the procedure providing visual cues and feedback during each step.

Fig. 2. VR-based Training Environments for Endotracheal Intubation

3   Design of Studies

Three studies were conducted in the two training environments (condylar plating and endotracheal intubation) to understand how various interaction methods impact the tactile affordance of an XR-based training environment. A discussion of the three studies follows.

3.1   Comparison of Haptic and Non-haptic VR Environments

The goal of this study is to compare haptic-based interactions and non-haptic-based interactions in a VR environment. The VR environment developed for the condylar plating surgical procedure was used for such comparison. The users were provided two types of interaction capabilities in this study. The users were able to use a haptic device that provided tactile vibration during the interaction in the first case. In the second case, the users interacted with the environment using the non-tactile Vive controller. The views of users interacting with the haptic device and Vive controller are shown in Fig. 3.

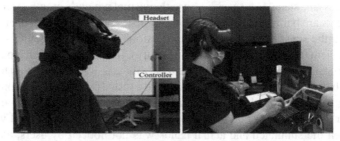

Fig. 3. Users interacting with controller-based non-haptic environment and haptic-based environment

3.2   Comparison of Non-haptic VR and Fully Haptic MR Environments

The goal of this study is to compare non-haptic interactions and fully haptic (using the physical tools and equipment) in an XR environment. Both VR and MR environments developed for the condylar plating surgical procedure were used for such comparison. The users were provided two types of interaction capabilities in this study. In the first case, the users interacted with the environment using the non-tactile Vive controller, and the users interacted with physical tools and equipment in the second case. The views of users interacting with the vive controller and physical tools are shown in Fig. 4.

For studies 3.1.1 and 3.1.2., assessments were conducted to assess the impact of interaction methods on users' knowledge and skills acquisition to understand how such interactions affect the tactile affordance of an XR environment. A complete description of the knowledge and skills assessment used in this paper is presented in [32].

Fig. 4. Users interacting with VR and MR-based Training Environments

3.3 Use of Visual-Propreoception Feedback

The objective of this study is to create a VR learning simulation that provides accurate hand movements and real-time feedback during endotracheal intubation. Endotracheal intubation can be performed in a realistic virtual reality scenario using a laryngoscope and other necessary steps. However, because the virtual patient's mouth is small and the Vive controllers are bulky, the controllers will bump together in the virtual environment. This will ruin the sense of presence and immersion. A haptic retargeting solution can solve this problem (reference omitted for anonymity). In this study, visual input primarily influences proprioception feedback. Ultimately, this was what enabled us to solve the bumping problem, thus resolving it. We introduced a visual proprioception conflict model by offsetting the virtual hands from the real hands. By using this model, virtual hands can be closer together rather than separated by a small distance in the real world. This offset between the simulated and actual hands was not noticed by users, as they were not aware of it. There are two different scenarios which were designed to measure the effectiveness of the haptic retargeting model in order to evaluate the results.

Reference condition

Visual proprioception conflicts were not perceived in this condition. The virtual hands of the participants were aligned with the actual hands of the participants. Real hand offset equaled virtual hand offset. This condition was perceived as conflict-free by participants.

Conflict condition

As a result of this condition, the virtual hand will have an offset of six centimeters from the real hand. It has been found that when this value is applied to a subject, he or she is unable to distinguish their virtual hand from their actual hand. It is important to emphasize that although the virtual hand moved with the same speed as the actual hand, its position was different from that of the actual hand As a measure of the effectiveness of the haptic retargeting model in our experiment, we used the presence questionnaire to gauge its effectiveness.

4   Results and Discussion

The assessment activities were conducted at two medical centers and a university. The results of the three studies follow.

4.1 Comparison of Haptic and Non-haptic VR Environments

A total of eighty participants interacted with two environments (task 1: plate insertion and task 2: dynamic plate compression) in this study (Table 1).

Table 1. Participants' categorization for comparison of haptic and non-haptic environments

	Haptic Device	Vive Controller
Task 1	Subject 1–40	Subject 41–80
Task 2	Subject 41–80	Subject 1–40

The result of the comparison study is shown in Fig. 5. According to the result of the t-test, the group interacting with the Vive controller (M = 66.3, SD = 9.38) received significantly higher score compared to the group interacting with the haptic device (M = 53.25, SD = 10.5), t (158) = 8.3, p = 0.001.

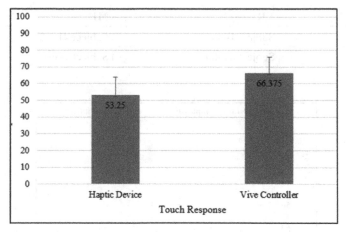

Fig. 5. Results for comparison of haptic and non-haptic environments

Although the haptic device provided the sense of touch, there is a limitation in motion during the interaction. The Vive controller, on the other hand, provides the users with unrestricted motion. This could be the main reason behind the result. However, when asked about their preference during force-based tasks such as drilling, more than 80% of the participants preferred the haptic device over the Vive controller. The haptic-based interface through vibrations and force feedback provides a more realistic replication of the actual drilling procedure.

The statistical results which favor the vive controller do not completely justify the role of haptic interfaces in surgical training. The substantial preference for the haptic interfaces shown by the users is a confirmation of the need for haptic interfaces. Haptic interfaces can be very useful in surgical procedures where force feedback becomes necessary such as drilling, and fracture reduction, among others. Currently, haptic devices are widely used in laparoscopic and orthopedic simulators [1, 2, 7] despite the restricted motion associated with the haptic interfaces. Haptic interfaces have the potential to co-exist in an integrated manner with other XR interfaces.

4.2   Comparison of Non-haptic VR and Fully Haptic MR Environments

A total of eighty participants interacted with MR and VR environments with two levels of complexity. The low complexity task was plate assembly, and the high complexity task was dynamic plate compression. The design of the experiment is shown below. The participants were divided into groups of nursing students and practicing nurses. The participants performed low complexity task first; subsequently, they performed high complexity task (Table 2).

Table 2. Participants' categorization for comparison of non-haptic VR and fully haptic MR environments

	VR	MR
Task 1	Subject 1–40	Subject 41–80
Task 2	Subject 41–80	Subject 1–40

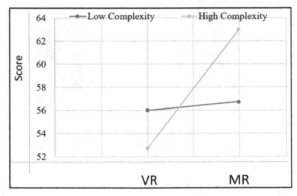

Fig. 6. Results for comparison of non-haptic VR and fully haptic MR environments

The results of the experiment for comparison of MR and VR environments are shown in Fig. 6. It can be seen from the figure that the difference in score depended on the complexity of the environment. Two t-tests were performed to further analyze the results. For the low complexity environments, no significant difference was observed in scores between the group interacting with VR (M = 56, SD = 11.26) and the group interacting with MR environment (M = 56, SD = 8.88), t (78) = 0.33, p = 0.37. However, for the high complexity environments, a significant difference was observed in scores between the group interacting with VR (M = 52.75, SD = 8.65) and the group interacting with MR environment (M = 63, SD = 87.81), t (78) = 5.56, p = 0.001.

The results indicate that the interaction methods do not contribute much when the users are performing a low-difficulty task. However, the interactions with the physical tools and equipment become crucial when the users are trying to learn a more complex procedure. After the interactions with the MR and VR-based training environments, the eighty participants responded to a NASA Task Load Index (TLX) [31] survey. In the survey, the participants were asked to rate the MR and VR environments in terms of effort, frustration, mental, physical, and temporal demand they faced during the interactions. The results of the NASA TLX survey show that the experienced nurses preferred MR environments whereas the nursing students preferred VR environments for the interactions. This leads to the understanding the experience level also impacts the choice of interaction method. As nurses are more used to interacting with physical tools and equipment compared to the students, they preferred the MR environment which provided higher tactile affordance compared to the VR environment.

4.3 Use of Visual-Proprioception Feedback

A total of seven participants interacted with the VR-based endotracheal intubation environment to assess the effectiveness of the haptic retargeting model.

It is shown in Fig. 7 that the mean value of the presence questionnaire was calculated for different 7 participants. Compared to the reference condition, the image below shows that subjects perceive more realism under conflict conditions than they do in the reference condition. Additionally, the subjects perceived that they had a greater possibility of acting in the conflict condition. It is important to note, however, that the quality of the interface was almost the same for both conditions. The group also estimated that they had a better performance in conflict conditions compared to non-conflict conditions.

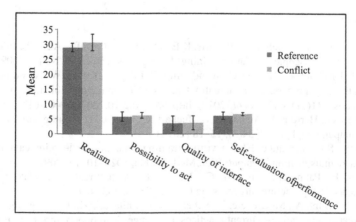

Fig. 7. Analysis of the presence questionnaire in different conditions, Y-axis indicates the mean value of 7 participants while the x-axis shows the calculated features from the presence questionnaire

Endotracheal Intubation Simulation suffered from a significant quality and usability problem. Simulation has a problem where controllers bump into each other and cause immersion to break. This problem was caused by two major factors. One of the main limitations of the simulation is that both hands must be placed in the patient's mouth at the same time. A second issue is that HTC Vive controllers are significantly larger than human hands. While it is still possible to complete the simulation in spite of this problem, it is much more difficult and strenuous than before. To solve the problem, a no-fee, simple coding base solution was proposed. The solution presented here is a great alternative to highly expensive solutions such as virtual reality robotic hand gloves. Virtual reality applications and fields may benefit from the use of this method. By using this method, VR developers can enhance the sense of presence of the user without requiring additional devices and equipment.

5 Conclusion

In this paper, the effect of tactile affordance during the design of Extended Reality (XR) based environments was presented. Tactile affordance is one of the Human-Computer Interaction criteria which help lay the foundation for human-centric XR-based training environments. Two XR-based training environments were used to understand the effect of tactile affordance viz (i) VR and MR-based Condylar plating training environment and (ii) VR-based endotracheal intubation training environment. Three studies have been conducted to understand the influence of different interaction methods to elevate tactile affordance in XR-based environments. The first study focused on the comparison of haptic and nonhaptic interactions in VR, the second study compared nonhaptic VR and fully haptic MR and the third study was related to the use of proprioception feedback. The results of the study underscore the importance of having proper tactile affordance during the interactions with the XR environments.

References

1. Panait, L., Akkary, E., Bell, R.L., Roberts, K.E., Dudrick, S.J., Duffy, A.J.: The role of haptic feedback in laparoscopic simulation training. J. Surg. Res. **156**(2), 312–316 (2009)
2. Huber, T., Paschold, M., Hansen, C., Wunderling, T., Lang, H., Kneist, W.: New dimensions in surgical training: immersive virtual reality laparoscopic simulation exhilarates surgical staff. Surg. Endosc. **31**(11), 4472–4477 (2017). https://doi.org/10.1007/s00464-017-5500-6
3. Echegaray, G., Herrera, I., Aguinaga, I., Buchart, C., Borro, D.: A brain surgery simulator. IEEE Comput. Graph. Appl. **34**(3), 12–18 (2014)
4. Choi, K.S., Soo, S., Chung, F.L.: A virtual training simulator for learning cataract surgery with phacoemulsification. Comput. Biol. Med. **39**(11), 1020–1031 (2009)
5. Pedersen, P., Palm, H., Ringsted, C., Konge, L.: Virtual-reality simulation to assess performance in hip fracture surgery. Acta Orthop. **85**(4), 403–407 (2014)
6. Ashtari, N., Bunt, A., McGrenere, J., Nebeling, M., Chilana, P.K.: Creating augmented and virtual reality applications: current practices, challenges, and opportunities. In: Proceedings of the 2020 CHI Conference on Human Factors in Computing Systems, pp. 1–13, April 2020
7. Tabrizi, L.B., Mahvash, M.: Augmented reality-guided neurosurgery: accuracy and intra-operative application of an image projection technique. J. Neurosurg. **123**, 206–211 (2015)

8. Botden, S.M., Buzink, S.N., Schijven, M.P., Jakimowicz, J.J.: ProMIS augmented reality training of laparoscopic procedures face validity. Simul. Healthc. **3**(2), 97–102 (2008)
9. Botden, S.M., de Hingh, I.H., Jakimowicz, J.J.: Suturing training in augmented reality: gaining proficiency in suturing skills faster. Surg. Endosc. **23**(9), 2131–2137 (2009)
10. Lu, S., Sanchez Perdomo, Y.P., Jiang, X., Zheng, B.: Integrating eye-tracking to augmented reality system for surgical training. J. Med. Syst. **44**(11), 1–7 (2020). https://doi.org/10.1007/s10916-020-01656-w
11. Ogawa, H., Hasegawa, S., Tsukada, S., Matsubara, M.: A pilot study of augmented reality technology applied to the acetabular cup placement during total hip arthroplasty. J. Arthroplasty. **33**, 1833–1837 (2018)
12. Shen, F., Chen, B., Guo, Q., Qi, Y., Shen, Y.: Augmented reality patient-specific reconstruction plate design for pelvic and acetabular fracture surgery. Int. J. Comput. Assist. Radiol. Surg. **8**, 169–179 (2013)
13. Cho, H.S., Park, Y.K., Gupta, S., et al.: Augmented reality in bone tumour resection: an experimental study. Bone Joint Res. **6**, 137–143 (2017)
14. Elmi-Terander, A., Nachabe, R., Skulason, H., et al.: Feasibility and accuracy of thoracolumbar minimally invasive pedicle screw placement with augmented reality navigation technology. Spine (Phila pa 1976) **43**, 1018–1023 (2018)
15. Wang, H., Wang, F., Leong, A.P.Y., Xu, L., Chen, X., Wang, Q.: Precision insertion of percutaneous sacroiliac screws using a novel augmented reality-based navigation system: a pilot study. Int. Orthop. **40**(9), 1941–1947 (2015). https://doi.org/10.1007/s00264-015-3028-8
16. Sutcliffe, A.G., Poullis, C., Gregoriades, A., Katsouri, I., Tzanavari, A., Herakleous, K.: Reflecting on the design process for virtual reality applications. Int. J. Hum.-Comput. Interact. **35**(2), 168–179 (2019)
17. Moosavi, M.S., Williams, J., Guillet, C., Merienne, F., Cecil, J., Pickett, M.: Disassociation of visual-proprioception feedback to enhance endotracheal intubation. In: 2022 International Conference on Future Trends in Smart Communities (ICFTSC), pp. 233–236. IEEE, December 2022
18. Moosavi, M.S., Raimbaud, P., Guillet, C., Plouzeau, J., Merienne, F.: Weight perception analysis using pseudo-haptic feedback based on physical work evaluation. Front. Virtual Reality **4**, 13 (2023)
19. Menekse Dalveren, G.G., Cagiltay, N.E., Ozcelik, E., Maras, H.: Insights from pupil size to mental workload of surgical residents: feasibility of an educational computer-based surgical simulation environment (ECE) considering the hand condition. Surg. Innov. **25**(6), 616–624 (2018)
20. Gibson, J.J.: "The concept of affordances." Perceiving, acting, and knowing 1 (1977)
21. Donald, N.: The Design of Everyday Things. ISBN: 0–465–06710–7. Originally published under the title The Psychology of Everyday Things (often abbreviated to POET)
22. Gaver, W.W.: Technology affordances. In: Proceedings of the SIGCHI Conference on Human Factors in Computing Systems, pp. 79–84, March 1991
23. Pointon, G., Thompson, C., Creem-Regehr, S., Stefanucci, J., Bodenheimer, B.: Affordances as a measure of perceptual fidelity in augmented reality. In: 2018 IEEE VR 2018 Workshop on Perceptual and Cognitive Issues in AR (PERCAR), pp. 1–6, March 2018
24. Wu, H., Adams, H., Pointon, G., Stefanucci, J., Creem-Regehr, S., Bodenheimer, B.: Danger from the deep: a gap affordance study in augmented reality. In: 2019 IEEE Conference on Virtual Reality and 3D User Interfaces (VR), pp. 1775–1779. IEEE, March 2019
25. Regia-Corte, T., Marchal, M., Cirio, G., Lécuyer, A.: Perceiving affordances in virtual reality: influence of person and environmental properties in perception of standing on virtual grounds. Virtual Reality **17**(1), 17–28 (2013)

26. Van Vugt, H.C., Hoorn, J.F., Konijn, E.A., de Bie Dimitriadou, A.: Affective affordances: Improving interface character engagement through Interaction. Int. J. Hum. Comput. Stud. **64**(9), 874–888 (2006)
27. Gagnon, H.C., Rosales, C.S., Mileris, R., Stefanucci, J.K., Creem-Regehr, S.H., Bodenheimer, R.E.: Estimating distances in action space in augmented reality. ACM Trans. Appl. Percept. (TAP) **18**(2), 1–16 (2021)
28. Koutromanos, G., Mavromatidou, E., Tripoulas, C., Georgiadis, G. Exploring the educational affordances of augmented reality for pupils with moderate learning difficulties. In: 9th International Conference on Software Development and Technologies for Enhancing Accessibility and Fighting Info-exclusion, pp. 203–207, December 2020
29. Thompson, C.J., Hite, R.: Exploring the affordances of computer-based assessment in measuring three-dimensional science learning. Int. J. Learn. Technol. **16**(1), 3–36 (2021)
30. Hart, S.G., Staveland, L.E.: Development of NASA-TLX (Task Load Index): results of empirical and theoretical research. In: Advances in Psychology, North-Holland, vol. 52, pp. 139–183 (1998)
31. Gupta, A., Cecil, J., Pirela-Cruz, M., Shamsuddin, R., Kennison, S., Crick, C.: An Investigation on the role of affordance in the design of extended reality based environments for surgical training. In: 2022 IEEE International Systems Conference (SysCon), pp. 1–7. IEEE, April 2022
32. Gupta, A., Cecil, J., Pirela-Cruz, M.: A cyber-human based integrated assessment approach for Orthopedic surgical training. In: 2020 IEEE 8th International Conference on Serious Games and Applications for Health (SeGAH), pp. 1–8. IEEE, August 2020

Treatment of Anorexia Nervosa Through Virtual Reality-Based Body Exposure and Reduction of Attentional Bias

Jose Gutierrez-Maldonado[1]([⊠]), Natalia Briseño[1], Mariarca Ascione[1], Franck Meschberger-Annweiler[1], Bruno Porras-Garcia[2], Marta Ferrer-Garcia[1], Eduardo Serrano[3], and Marta Carulla[3]

[1] Department of Clinical Psychology and Psychobiology, Institute of Neurosciences, University of Barcelona, Paseo Valle de Hebrón, 171, 08035 Barcelona, Spain
jgutierrezm@ub.edu
[2] Department of Population Health Sciences, School of Medicine, University of Utah, 295 Chipeta Way, Room 1N490, Salt Lake City, UT 84108, USA
bruno.r.porras@hsc.utah.edu
[3] Department of Child and Adolescent Psychiatry and Psychology, Hospital Sant Joan de Déu, Passeig de Sant Joan de Déu, 2, Esplugues de Llobregat, 08950 Barcelona, Spain
eserrano@sjdhospitalbarcelona.org

Abstract. Anorexia nervosa (AN) is a severe disorder. It has higher mortality rates than other eating disorders (ED) and is increasingly being diagnosed in younger patients. One of the main fears among individuals with AN is the fear of gaining weight (FGW). Patients with AN also display dysfunctional behaviors that aim to avoid weight gain by drastically reducing food intake, vomiting, using laxatives and diuretics, or doing intense exercises. AN patients engage in frequent conduct of checking and scrutinizing those parts of their body directly related with weight, which suggests attention focused on the body that has a dysfunctional nature. Although research on the presence of attentional biases in ED is extensive, very little has been done up to the present to apply the information gathered in those studies with the purpose of improving the efficacy of the available treatments. One of our recent projects aimed to provide evidence of the efficacy of a virtual reality-based body exposure therapy in AN in directly targeting the FGW through a randomized controlled clinical trial. We are currently developing a new clinical trial to test whether the addition of a component aimed at reducing the attentional bias towards the body serves to intensify the effect of the exposure treatment. It is expected that the reduction of the attentional bias will facilitate the control of visual avoidance behaviors during exposure sessions, increasing the efficacy of the treatment.

Keywords: Attentional Bias · Body Dissatisfaction · Anorexia Nervosa · Virtual Reality · Body Image

J. Y. C. Chen and G. Fragomeni (Eds.): HCII 2023, LNCS 14027, pp. 453–463, 2023.
https://doi.org/10.1007/978-3-031-35634-6_32

1 Introduction

Eating disorders (ED) are usually characterized by dysfunctional eating patterns and/or disordered behaviors directed towards weight control that negatively affect the person's physical and mental health. Anorexia Nervosa (AN) is specifically characterized by persistent food intake restriction, an intense fear of gaining weight, and a dysfunctional body self-perception (BIDs). These characteristics are reflected in a refusal to maintain body weight at least at a minimally normal level, which in turn results in high rates of morbidity and mortality.

AN is a severe disorder, affecting approximately 1–4% of women and 0.3–0.7% of men [1]. It has higher mortality rates than other eating disorders (ED), and is increasingly being diagnosed in younger patients, with a typical age of onset of around 14 and 19 years. One of the main fears among individuals with AN is the fear of gaining weight (FGW); an overconcern of the possibility of gaining weight in the whole body or in some specific body parts. Patients with AN also display dysfunctional behaviors that aim to avoid weight gain by drastically reducing food intake, vomiting, using laxatives and diuretics, or doing intense exercises.

Several therapies have been recommended for the treatment of AN; Cognitive Behavioral Therapy (CBT) is recommended in several international guidelines for the psychological management of patients with ED. Other alternatives also supported by the available literature would be interpersonal psychotherapy or family-based treatment, the last one specially indicated for teenagers. However, there is a significant number of ED patients that do not improve after treatment, and this is particularly relevant for those with AN; they have lower rates of recovery and experience fewer long-term effects on weight gain or psychological symptom improvements than other ED patients. This increased difficulty in the recovery of AN means that it is still necessary to either search for better alternatives to the interventions that are currently in use or to look for ways to improve them.

Patients with AN frequently experience anxiety and avoidance behaviors (such as food restriction) in response to certain stimuli (such as food or their own bodies). As a result, incorporating components that target the anxiety experienced by patients in relation to eating and weight gain can strengthen the treatment of AN. It is for this reason that exposure techniques have been proposed as an effective treatment for this disorder. Exposure techniques are included frequently in the treatment of anxiety and related disorders, such as phobias, and they are often combined with other CBT components. The conceptualization of some of the core elements of AN can effectively explain the rationale of the addition of exposure therapy to the treatment of this disorder. As mentioned earlier, two of the core aspects of AN are BIDs and FGW. There is a possible explanation that links these two factors: the over-evaluation of weight and shape would come from the fear of imagined negative outcomes or consequences resulting from violating the thin ideal (such as being seen as disgusting, being rejected, or losing control). This belief of the negative consequences of gaining weight would come with safety and compulsive behaviors around eating and the body that appear in EDs. In AN, the restricted food intake would momentarily reduce the anxiety generated by the FGW, thus reinforcing the avoidance behavior (in this case, restriction). The fear and anxiety processes are a driving force for the problematic behaviors that maintain disordered eating. Another reason to pay special attention to these elements is that BIDs frequently persist even after treatment and recovery, and they are reliable predictors for relapse.

There are several treatments in which different forms of exposure are included as components. Among the exposure-based procedures using body image cues, mirror exposure therapy (MET) has been widely used, reducing negative body-related emotions and cognitions through habituation [3]. In severe cases of AN, in-vivo mirror exposure techniques may be contraindicated, due to the risk of eliciting habituation toward a very skinny body shape.

Imaginal exposure might help patients with AN confront their core FGW, which is impractical to do with in-vivo exposure. However, some patients who undergo imaginal exposure might report difficulties maintaining a visualization over time, due to attentional fatigue, and may also display avoidance-based strategies while they imagine a progressive weight gain. The application of virtual reality (VR) offers an innovative solution to these problems since it does not rely on the visualization ability of the patient. In addition, this technology can significantly reduce avoidance-based behaviors by using eye-tracking (ET) devices to control the patient's gaze patterns towards their own body.

Some studies have connected BIDs with the presence of attentional bias (AB), and even suggested that this connection may be bidirectional. AN patients engage in frequent conduct of checking and scrutinizing those parts of their body directly related with weight, which suggests attention focused on the body that has a dysfunctional nature. Analyzing attentional biases related with specific parts of the body, several studies have found that patients with ED, and particularly those with AN, pay more attention to the parts of their own body that they define as unattractive, while individuals who do not have ED show a broader distribution of attention, that is unbiased, and includes the entire body [2]. Biased attention to body stimuli has been shown to influence the development and maintenance of ED symptoms and is a mediator of the relationship between body mass index and body dissatisfaction. Also, body-related AB may reduce the efficacy of body exposure therapy in patients with AN. Hence, this leads to turning the modification of AB into a potentially important target, as it can directly affect BIDs and improve the efficacy of current treatments.

Numerous methods have been used to assess attention bias in patients with ED. The most frequent are based on modified Stroop tasks, dot-probe, visual search and eye-tracking (ET). Albeit to a lesser extent, other methods have been used, such as dichotic listening tasks, lexical decisions and spatial signaling. Of all of these techniques, ET is the only one with which it is possible to record a continuous measurement of attention devoted to different stimuli. On another note, and with few exceptions, most cognitive tasks involve verbal stimuli, while ET techniques facilitate analysis of behavior most directly related with the stimuli that in natural situations trigger the dysfunctional responses. Therefore, this technique facilitates the objective, direct measurement of attention biases, while with cognitive tasks, such as those previously mentioned, those biases can only be inferred through response latencies.

Although research on the presence of attentional biases in ED is extensive, very little has been done up to the present to apply the information gathered in those studies with the purpose of improving efficacy of the available treatments.

One of our recent projects aimed to provide evidence of the efficacy of a VR body exposure therapy in AN in directly targeting the FGW through a randomized controlled clinical trial [4]. We are currently developing a new project to test whether the addition of a component aimed at reducing the attentional bias towards the body serves to intensify the effect of the exposure treatment. It is expected that the reduction of the attentional bias will facilitate the control of visual behaviors during exposure sessions, increasing the efficacy of the treatment.

To bring about a reduction in attentional bias, we apply a training based on an adaptation of the Smeets, Jansen and Roefs [5] bias induction procedure. This procedure has proven its efficacy in triggering changes in the attentional biases of participants with varying levels of body dissatisfaction. The procedure is adapted to produce a reduction of the bias, instead of a bias induction toward any given parts of the body. Therefore, the result is a balanced distribution of attention among the different parts of the body. Furthermore, the procedure is adapted for use with VR devices featuring built-in ET devices, so that the training is carried out while the patient observes an avatar through immersive VR that is a simulation of their own image reflected in a virtual mirror.

The synergies between these two technological resources offer opportunities of great interest to study, through objective indicators (such as those offered by ET instruments) in highly-controlled situations and with high ecological validity (such as those that can be achieved with VR techniques) of basic processes that are altered in eating disorders, and in a relevant manner for the design of new treatment components that could enable an improvement in the efficacy of the interventions currently available for eating disorders, especially anorexia nervosa.

Based on the relationships between FGW, BIDs, and AB, it is possible to hypothesize that by decreasing the AB, there will be a strengthening of the effects of the interventions to decrease both FGW and BIDs. While this will have to be repeatedly contrasted in the future, with samples of patients, the current study aims to verify the observed AB decrease after a body-related AB modification training intervention using ET and VR technology in healthy individuals. The body-related AB modification training is based on a VR exposure to the person's own body (simulated with a virtual avatar) with a task designed to alter AB by forcing the participants to look at the different parts of the body for an equal amount of time, in order to habituate them to this pattern of looking at their body. The hypothesis is that, after this task, the AB values would become more balanced, that is, the participants will spend an equal amount of time looking at weight-related and non-weight-related body areas. If this attentional bias reduction procedure were effective, it could be used in the treatment of patients with anorexia nervosa.

2 Method

2.1 Participants

The participants were psychology students (Universitat de Barcelona) who accepted to participate in the experiment. The study was approved by the bioethics committee of the University of Barcelona. The initial number of participants was 108. Since some studies have indicated a possible gender difference in the expression of AB [4]. And the sample was mostly female, it was decided for men to be excluded (totaling 17), thus resulting in a sample of 91 adult women. Those participants with missing data were not taken into account, which left a final working sample of 80 adult women.

Exclusion criteria were severe mental disorders with psychotic or manic symptoms, a current diagnostic of ED, visual impairments that actively prevented or obstructed completing the tasks, and epilepsy.

2.2 Measures and Instruments

Eating Disorders Inventory (EDI-3; Garner, 2004) was used to obtain a measure o body dissatisfaction. EDI-3 is a self-report inventory consisting of 12 scales and 91 items, in which the answers are provided on a 6-point Likert scale. In the current study, the Spanish version of the Body Dissatisfaction subscale (EDI-BD) was used. The EDI-BD scale, with 10 items, measures the negative attitude or evaluation of one's body or specific body areas, including their shape, weight, and fitness.

Regarding the AB measures, the ET device within the VR headset recorded the gaze behavior, allowing to later derive two measures from the raw ET data: Complete Fixation Time (CFT) and Number of Fixations (NF). CFT refers to the sum of the fixation time at the specified area of interest (AOI), either weight-related (W-AOI) or non-weight-related body parts (NW-AOI), measured in milliseconds. NF is the total number of fixations in the areas of interest (again, weigh-related and non-weight-related body parts).

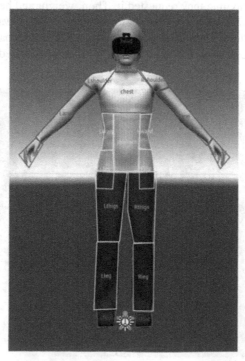

Fig. 1. Visual representation of the weight-related Areas of Interest (in yellow) and non-weight related Areas of Interest (in blue) in the virtual avatar. (Color figure online)

Using the Physical Appearance State and Trait Anxiety Scale (PASTAS [7]), two areas of interest (AOI) were defined: weight related AOIs, and non-weight related AOIs. The weight-related AOIs were defined as the thighs, buttocks, hips, stomach, legs, and waist, while the remaining areas were defined as non-weight-related AOIs; A visual representation of this division can be observed in Fig. 1, with the yellow forms specifying the weight-related AOIs and the blue forms delimiting the non-weight-related AOIs.

All participants used the same VR headset to complete the task: a VR IITC-VIVE PRO Eye head- mounted display (HTC Corporation, New Taipei City, Taiwan), with 2 controllers and two trackers to follow the hand movements of the participants and their feet movements. The VR training task and environment were developed in Unity 2021.x (Unity Technologies, San Francisco, CA, USA). The environment consisted of a room with a large mirror in the wall, facing the participants' avatar. Besides that, some boxes were placed on the floor, next to the avatar's feet, as neutral stimuli. The avatar was designed to have a simple white tank-top with jeans and black trainers (the top and the jeans' colors could be changed to match the participants' clothing), while the hair was covered by a hat (Fig. 2).

2.3 Procedure

Each participant was informed of the procedure, read, and signed the informed consent after an explanation of the usage of the data, the non-compulsory participation and that they could stop anytime they requested it. Then, weight and height measures were taken, alongside a frontal and a sideways photo, to create a virtual avatar. The researchers adjusted the avatar to have a similar silhouette to that of the participants. Once ready, the trackers and VR headset were put on the participant and calibrated. Then, visuomotor

Fig. 2. Avatar simulating the reflected image of the participant

and visuotactile stimulations were conducted to evocate the FBOI, feeling the virtual body as the participants' own body (Fig. 3).

Fig. 3. Visuomotor and visuotactile stimulation for FBOI production

Next, the first ET measures were taken, camouflaged as a calibration of the sensors to avoid any bias due to knowledge of the real objective (it was explained after the completion of the procedure). After the measurements, the attentional bias modification task (ABMT) started.

The ABMT was a VR adaptation of the procedure developed by Smeets, Jansen & Roefs [5], and it consisted of staring for 4 s at the places where geometrical figures appeared on the avatar's reflection, following this distribution: 45% of the figures appeared on non-weight related body parts, 45% appeared on weight related body parts, and the remaining 10% appeared on neutral stimuli (boxes on the floor). They repeated this search-and-stare task for 90 trials (Fig. 4).

When the ABMT finished, the ET measures were taken again. Then the VR headset and trackers were removed, and the researchers explained the concealment of the ET and cleared any remaining doubts.

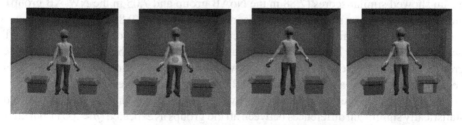

Fig. 4. Atentional Bias Modification Task (ABMT)

2.4 Data Analysis

To prepare the compiled ET data for the analysis, the Open Gaze and Mouse Analyzer (OGAMA) software was used. All the following analyses were done with SPSS (version 27). An additional data transformation was conducted by subtracting the difference between W-AOI and NW-AOIs (e.g., in fixation points: 25 (W-AOIs) − 10 (NW-AOIs) = 15). Therefore, a positive score would mean that the participant had been looking more at the weight-related body parts than at the non-weight-related body parts, while a negative outcome would mean the opposite.

The participants were divided into three groups for the analysis, based on the baseline body-related AB (CFT measures). Thus, the total sample was split in three, according to the percentile distribution of the first CFT measure: women past the percentile 75 (2133.5 ms) were assigned to the weight-related AB group (WR-AB; n = 20), those under the percentile 25 (−3183.5 ms) to the non-weight-related AD group (NW-AB; n = 20), and those with CFT values between those percentiles were put into the no AB group (n = 40).

A two-way mixed ANOVA analysis was conducted to assess whether there was a statistically significant interaction between time (pre-post ABMT assessment times) and the defined groups. Regarding the analysis for CFT, six outliers were detected by inspecting a boxplot for values greater than 1.5 box-lengths from the edge of the box, but as their values didn't significantly affect the results, it was decided to keep them for the analysis.

3 Results

The participants were all women, with a mean age of 23.76 years (SD = 3.52, age range: 20–41 years), and a mean Body Mass Index (BMI) of 21.77 (SD = 2.93, range: 17.40–30.94). Age and BMI were similar in the three groups: mean age NoAB group was 23.53, mean age WR-AB group was 22.95, and mean age NW-AB group was 23.32; BMI NoAB group was 21.6, BMI WR-AB group was 21.75, and BMI NW-AB group was 21.5. As expected, since attentional biases to weight body parts are associated with body dissatisfaction and other ED characteristics, some differences between the groups were found in the body dissatisfaction level (EDI-BD): the NoAB group and the NW-AB group showed similar scores (7.88 in the NoAB group and 7.05 in the NW-AB group), but the WR-AB group showed a higher score in this variable (9.84).

A statistically significant interaction between the intervention and group on CFT was found, $F(2, 73) = 7.66$, p < .001, partial $\eta^2 = .174$. As can be seen in Fig. 5, those groups with AB (be weight-related on non-weight-related) showed a tendency towards neutral values, that is, a reduction of the AB after the ABMT intervention.

When the simple effects of the group were explored, the pre-assessment showed statistically significant differences between all the groups as expected ($p < .001$), but after the intervention, only the groups NW-AB/WR-AB maintained a significant difference ($p = .005$), while the differences between groups NW-AB/No AB and WR-AB/No AB were not significant ($p > .05$). For the simple effects of time, the only group that showed a statistically significant difference between the two assessments was the WR-AB group ($p < .001$).

When accounting for the mixed ANOVA conducted for the NF measures, there was a significant interaction between group and time $F(2, 73) = 4.21, p < .019$, partial $\eta^2 = .103$. Figure 6 shows how the tendencies are similar to those seen with the CFT, with both AB groups getting closer to the No AB group after the intervention.

Regarding the simple effects of the group, the results mimic those from the CTF: while the differences are statistically significant between the groups during the first

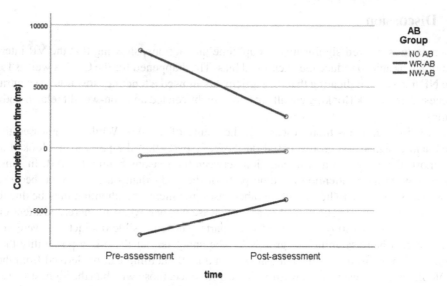

Fig. 5. CFT time*group interaction. Pre-assessment is the CFT before the ABMT, and Post-assessment is the CFT after the ABMT

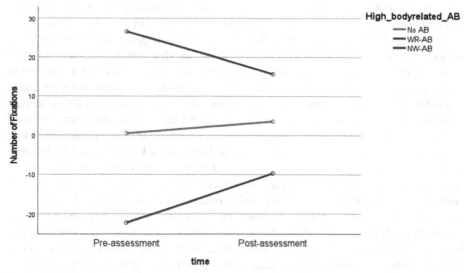

Fig. 6. NF time*group interaction. Pre-assessment is the NF before the ABMT, and Post-assessment is the NF after the ABMT

assessment ($p < .001$), the only statistical significance maintained after the ABMT intervention is the one between the WR-AB and NW-AB groups ($p = .005$). For the simple effects of time, the NW-AB group is the only one with a statistically significant difference ($p < .05$) between the two assessment points, while the WR-AB group showed a marginally significant difference ($p = .058$).

4 Discussion

ET measures showed significative group*time interactions, showing that the VR intervention was able to reduce the attentional bias. This happened for the CFT as well as for the NF measures, indicating that the participants showed a tendency towards the neutral values after the task (looking equally at both weight-related and non-weight related body parts).

A point that needs more research is the nature of the AB. While we assessed the CFT and assigned the groups based on the body parts that the participants looked at the most, there was not a differentiation between the reasons behind the AB. In some cases, paying more attention to some parts of the body than others may be because those parts are more to her liking. In other cases, the increased attention may be due to avoiding the other parts, because they are not pleasant to her. Also, the increased attention may come from scrutiny of the least liked parts. These possible distinctions were not considered when assigning the groups for the analysis, but there is a possibility that some variability in the results may stem from this. Something can be derived from the EDI-BD descriptives: albeit it wasn't a huge difference, those who had the highest scores on body dissatisfaction were in the WR-AB group. This was expected, since attentional biases to weight body parts are associated with body dissatisfaction and other ED-like characteristics, even in healthy individuals. Thus, it could be thought that those in the WR-AB group showed a tendency to pay more attention on the parts of their body that they do not like, and, therefore, their AB would be the result of scrutiny behaviors.

This study has some limitations. The silhouette was adjusted to be similar to the participant's, but there were many aspects of the avatar that didn't look alike (the most obvious differences stemmed from the only personalization available for the clothes being the option to change colors, or the hair of the avatar being covered with a grey beanie for all participants), and this could very well be an impediment for the participant to identify the avatar as his own body, which can be relevant for these interventions. Another important limitation is suggested by comments from some participants, who indicated that they found the attentional bias modification task too long and boring after the first few trials. Anticipating that this could happen, different types of geometric figures were used in the design of the task, which could also vary in color. However, it would be necessary to explore in future studies other ways of maintaining the motivation to perform the task. One possibility would be to gamify it, proposing objectives and offering rewards for reaching them. Another possibility would be to study the minimum duration of the task to obtain the results sought in reducing attentional bias, so that the participants performed only the necessary and sufficient number of trials to do so, without prolonging the task beyond what was strictly necessary.

The results of this study show that the task designed to reduce attentional biases towards the body is effective when applied to healthy individuals. In a subsequent phase, it would be necessary to verify if this efficacy is also demonstrated when applied to patients with AN. If so, this training in reducing attentional bias towards certain parts of the body could be incorporated as a component in the treatments currently used to intervene on this disorder. For example, as a preliminary phase in order to increase the effect of the exposure to the body. However, before moving on to studies with patients, it would be necessary to improve some aspects of the task, to establish the minimum time necessary to achieve the bias reduction effect without producing fatigue that could reduce adherence to treatment or its effectiveness.

Funding. This study was funded by the Spanish Ministry of Science and Innovation (Agencia Estatal de Investigación, Ministerio de Ciencia e Innovación, Spain). Grant PID2019-108657RB-I00 funded by MCIN/AEI/10.13039/501100011033.

References

1. Keski-Rahkonen, A., Mustelin, L.: Epidemiology of eating disorders in Europe: prevalence, incidence, comorbidity, course, consequences, and risk factors. Curr. Opin. Psychiatry **29**, 340–345 (2016)
2. Kerr-Gaffney, J., Harrison, A., Tchanturia, K.: Eye-tracking research in eating disorders: a systematic review. Int. J. Eat. Disord. **52**(1), 3–27 (2019)
3. Vocks, S., Wächter, A., Wucherer, M., Kosfelder, J.: Look at yourself: can body image therapy affect the cognitive and emotional response to seeing oneself in the mirror in eating disorders? Eur. Eat. Disord. Rev. **16**, 147–154 (2008)
4. Porras-Garcia, B., et al.: AN-VR-BE. A randomized controlled trial for reducing fear of gaining weight and other eating disorder symptoms in anorexia nervosa through virtual reality-based body exposure. J. Clin. Med. **10**(4), 682 (2021)
5. Smeets, E., Jansen, A., Roefs, A.: Bias for the (un) attractive self: on the role of attention in causing body (dis) satisfaction. Health Psychol. **30**(3), 360 (2011)
6. Porras-Garcia, B., et al.: The influence of gender and body dissatisfaction on body-related attentional bias: an eye-tracking and virtual reality study. Int. J. Eat. Disord. **52**(10), 1181–1190 (2019). https://doi.org/10.1002/eat.23136
7. Thompson, J.K.: Physical Appearance State and Trait Anxiety Scale. APA, Washington, DC (1999)

Preliminary Experiment for Measuring the Anxiety Level Using Heart Rate Variability

Haochen He[✉], Chen Feng, Peeraya Sripian, Tipporn Laohakangvalvit, and Midori Sugaya

Shibaura Institute of Technology, 3-7-5 Toyosu, Koto-Ku, Tokyo 135-8548, Japan
{AM20003,i042370,peeraya,tipporn,doly}@shibaura-it.ac.jp

Abstract. Anxiety is one of the most significant health issues. Generally, there are four levels of anxiety: mild anxiety, moderate anxiety, severe anxiety, and panic level anxiety. While mild anxiety may not significantly impact a person's daily life, severe anxiety can be debilitating and affect their ability to carry out normal activities. People with moderate, severe anxiety and panic level anxiety cannot be relieved through common relaxation methods. However, psychology-based therapeutic intervention such as Virtual Reality therapy has been shown to be effective in alleviating anxiety. To develop an efficient VR therapy system for anxiety relief, it is necessary to measure and understand a person's anxiety state using a wearable device, which can be easily equipped without the need to be interrupted during the therapy session. The aim of this study is to investigate the methods to accurately measure periodic anxiety and to find the reliable physiological indexes that can be used in anxiety research. We conduct a flicker task experiment by constantly flickering two images with subtle differences to induce anxiety. The results showed that LF/HF ratio, RMSSD, and SDNN can effectively be used to detect anxiety levels.

Keywords: Anxiety · Virtual Reality · Heart Rate Variability

1 Introduction

The global prevalence of anxiety disorders has increased by 25% because of Covid-19, according to the World Health Organization report [1]. On the other hand, the number of adolescents with varying degrees of depression due to impaired peer relationships or self-esteem, family conflicts and other issues has been increasing in recent years. According to WHO data survey estimates [2], about 8.6% of adolescents ages (10–19 years old) have anxiety disorders or the tendency to anxiety. Anxiety is one of the most significant health issues that could lead to difficulty sleeping or being extremely sad, which could lead to suicide in severe cases. Generally, there are four levels of anxiety: mild anxiety, moderate anxiety, severe anxiety, and panic level anxiety. Mild and moderate anxiety could be relieved by relaxation in many ways, such as listening to music, taking a bath, or taking a nap. However, individuals with moderate to severe, or panic anxiety may find that standard relaxation methods are no longer effective. In

J. Y. C. Chen and G. Fragomeni (Eds.): HCII 2023, LNCS 14027, pp. 464–477, 2023.
https://doi.org/10.1007/978-3-031-35634-6_33

such cases, psychology-based therapeutic interventions, such as Virtual Reality therapy, can help alleviate psychological problems such as depression, phobias, or anxiety. To establish an effective system for mitigating anxiety during therapy, it is significant to accurately assess an individual's preexisting level of anxiety and continuously monitor their progress towards reducing it.

For the majority of the anxiety research, the common method for assessing anxiety levels is to use a self-assessment questionnaire. State-Trait Anxiety Inventory (STAI) [3], a psychological inventory, that overall have 40 self-report items on a 4-point Likert scale, which are 1: not at all, 2: sometimes, 3: from time to time, and 4: very much so. The anxiety score scale ranges from 20 to 80, with a higher score indicating a higher level of anxiety. There are two forms of the questionnaires, questionnaire Y-1 and questionnaire Y-2. The score of questionnaire Y-1 indicates how you feel right now. The score of questionnaire Y-2 indicates how your general feel. It should be noted that the validity of the self-assessment questionnaire is open to question, as it may be impacted by individual characteristics such as personality or prior knowledge and other subjective issues. However, there are limitations in some of the existing research on the elicitation and objective measurement of anxiety states. Most previous studies have relied solely on self-reported measures such as questionnaires or interviews, which may not provide a comprehensive assessment of anxiety. In this case, physiological indexes such as heart rate variability (HRV) and brain waves could be used for a more objective evaluation of level of anxiety [4, 5].

2 Background

A variety of methods existed in the past that could be used to measure anxiety. In 1998, researchers have used several indexes for measuring different emotions, such as skin conductance level (SCL) or short-duration skin conductance responses (SCRs), or heart rate variability (HRV) [6]. Researchers have found that by using physiological signals like heart rate variability, it is possible to classify different emotions [7]. Previous researchers were using pNN50, RMSSD and SDNN which were calculated from heart rate variability, as indexes that can be used in emotion estimation [4]. Moreover, LF, HF ratio (LF/HF ratio), calculated by heart rate variability, is also widely approaching to emotion study [8]. In other words, heart rate variability (HRV) may be a potential reliable physiological signal in using anxiety measurement.

Heart rate variability is a measure of the degree of change in continuous heart rate. Heart rate variability (HRV) is a well-established index for evaluating the dynamic changes in heart rate over time. N-N intervals are typically obtained from HRV analysis, and they are a fundamental measure of HRV. The N-N interval refers to the normal-to-normal interval in an electrocardiogram (ECG), which represents the time between consecutive heartbeats (Fig. 1). The N-N interval is used to calculate various heart rate indexes. From N-N intervals, a number of HRV indices, such as Mean NN interval, pNN50, RMSSD, SDNN, LF, HF and LF/HF ratio, are commonly used to quantify the balance between sympathetic and parasympathetic nervous system activity and assess autonomic regulation, which can be used in our study. In this work, we will be using four indexes as follows.

- **PNN50**

    PNN50 is expressed as a percentage, quantifies the frequency of N-N intervals that differ by more than 50 milliseconds. It provides insight into the short-term variability of heart rate and reflects the activity of the parasympathetic nervous system.
- **Root Mean Square of Successive Differences (RMSSD)**

    RMSSD measures the root mean square of successive differences in N-N intervals and is used to reflect the parasympathetic nervous system activity.
- **SDNN**

    SDNN provides a measure of the overall HRV and reflects both sympathetic and parasympathetic nervous system activities.
- **The LF/HF ratio**

    Low Frequency Power (LF) and High Frequency Power (HF) are frequency domain measures of HRV and reflect the balance between sympathetic and parasympathetic nervous system activity, respectively. The LF/HF ratio provides a quantifiable measure of this balance.

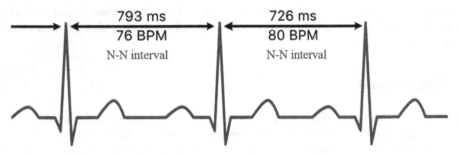

Fig. 1. N-N interval

3 Research Objective

The objective of the study is to investigate the suitability of various indexes of heart rate variability, including pNN50, RMSSD, SDNN, and LF/HF, for the analysis of anxiety. In this work, we collect State-Trait Anxiety Inventory questionnaires as the subjective evaluation of the results and compare it with the physiological indexes. The results of this study could provide valuable insights into the use of heart rate variability as a tool for anxiety research and development in the future.

4 Experiment

4.1 Participants

In our study, 8 participants (5 male, 3 female) were recruited voluntarily ranging in age from 18 to 39. All participants had normal visual acuity and an absence of color blindness. These participants did not exhibit any prior medical history of epilepsy or report experiences of screen flashes. All participants gave informed consent prior to the experiment.

4.2 Stimuli

In our study, we chose twenty-four images from International Affective Image System (IAPS) [9], which were chosen based on the emotional valence score: eight images with the negative categories (mean valence score $= 1.92 \pm 0.20$), eight with positive categories (mean valence score $= 8.17 \pm 0.11$) and eight with the neutral categories (mean valence score $= 4.99 \pm 0.25$). The images that we chose were modified by Photoshop software, which makes researchers have two different versions of one image. Each image was modified differently in trivial detail, such as erasing the people on the beach, erasing the books from the bookshelf behind the characters, and so on. Figure 2. Shows the example (Similar content to IAPS) of original image (left) and modified image (right).

Fig. 2. The sample of the original neutral image (left) and the modified image (right)

4.3 Method and Apparatus

In this study, we employ a flicker task to evoke the anxiety. Flicker task is believed to induce the anxiety in the participants due to the pair of similar images being flickered at a very high speed. The images will keep flickering and reproduced original image and modified image in sequence, that alternated by a grey screen. The appearance of stimuli image was 240 ms, with 80 ms grey screen duration. When the participants indicate the difference between original and modified image, they are responsible to press spacebar on keyboard, that experiment will continue to next image.

Flicker task was divided into three blocks, each block contains eight images from the specific category: positive, negative, and neutral. In order to control for potential order effects, the presentation order of the three blocks was randomized, but the order of the images in each block remains the same. This means that participants could be presented with various arrangements of the categories, such as positive-negative-neutral, neutral-positive-negative, or any other combination.

The flicker task was shown on a 19 inches computer monitor. The response time for each stimulus in the flicker task experiment were recorded and programmed using Psychopy [10] on an PC with Intel Core i7 10750. Responses were collected from spacebar of keyboard. We collected response time from Psychopy [10] in order to find correlations between response time of each stimulus (positive, negative, neutral) and HRV indexes. The heart rate variability is recorded by Mybeat [11]. Considering the aim of our study, only Y-1 from State-Trait Anxiety Inventory (STAI) questionnaire was assessed in before the experiment and after the experiment.

5 Procedure

1. The participant wears the heart rate variability (HRV) measurement device (*mybeat*).
2. The participant answer State-Trait Anxiety Inventory (STAI Y-1) questionnaire. This process takes about 2–3 min.
3. The participant rest with their eyes closed for baseline measurement for 5 min.
4. The participant performs flicker task on the computer screen.

   4.1 Show original image for 0.24 s.
   4.2 Show blank grey screen for 0.08 s.
   4.3 Show modified image for 0.24 s.
   4.4 Repeat steps 4.1–4.3 until the participant notices the different by pressing the "spacebar" key. The time when the image pair is shown until the pressing of spacebar is then recorded as the response time for that image pair.

5. Finish HRV measurement.
6. The participant answer State-Trait Anxiety Inventory (STAI Y-1) questionnaire.

   The experimental procedure is shown in Fig. 3.

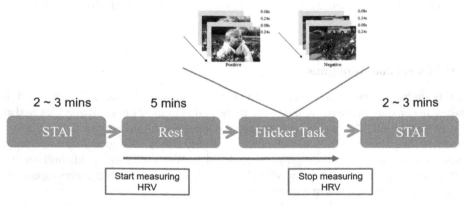

Fig. 3. Experiment Procedure

6   Result and Discussion

We analyzed the STAI questionnaire before and after the experiment to ensure that the participants felt stress from the experiment. The result of the comparison STAI score before and after the experiment is shown in Fig. 4. The results of the State-Trait Anxiety Inventory (STAI) questionnaire revealed a significant increase in the scores of all participants before and after the experiment was conducted. In addition, a paired t-test was conducted, the results of which indicate a significant difference in STAI scores before and after the intervention of the experiment (t (6) $= -5.689$, p < 0.01).

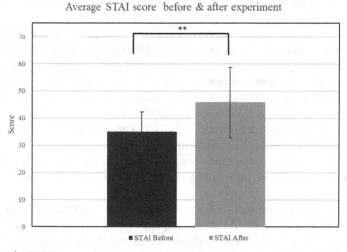

Fig. 4.   STAI Score of male participants (Left) and female participant (Right)

6.1   Correlation Analysis

We performed the correlation analysis of STAI scores and physiological indexes under different stimuli (positive images, negative images, neutral images), and the correlation analysis of participants' response times and physiological indexes under different stimuli (positive images negative images, neutral images) in the flicker task experiment.

The Correlation Between STAI and Physiological Indexes
We perform a correlation test on the different STAI scores (before – after) and the average of physiological indexes for each participant during each block (positive, negative, and neutral) and also the entire period. The results of the Spearman's correlation analysis revealed a significant negative correlation between the STAI score and LF/HF ratio during positive stimulus in the flicker task (r (8) $= 0.786$, $p < 0.05$) indicates that as the values of STAI score increase, the values of LF/HF ratio during positive stimulus tend to decrease. The scores from the STAI questionnaire revealed that all participants' STAI scores increased before and after the trial. As LF/HF ratio and STAI showed a negative correlation, with a decrease in LF/HF ratio and a predominantly parasympathetic dominance of the body, the participants mainly showed a tendency to a state of deep relaxation.

However, no significant correlation exists for other blocks with other physiological indexes.

The Correlation Between Response Time and Physiological Indexes
In addition, there is a significant positive correlation between the response time and SDNN (Standard Deviation of N-N Intervals) during positive stimulus (r (8) − 0.714, p < 0.05).

From the analysis of the response time and its correlation with SDNN, it is surprising that the longer the response time is, the higher SDNN values are. For SDNN, higher values indicate that the participants' emotional state tends to be relaxed. From this result, it can be implied that longer response times tend to give participants a more relaxed state when they viewed positive stimulus images response.

We also found a significant negative correlation between response time and Root Mean Square of Successive Differences (RMSSD) during negative stimulus in flicker task (r (8) = −0.714 p = < 0.05). The correlation shows that the value of RMSSD decreases as the response time to negative images becomes longer. As the lower RMSSD values indicated that participants gradually developed anxiety, tension, etc. in response to negative stimuli. However, there is no significant correlation for other heart rate variability such as pNN50, LF/HF ratio or SDNN. The reason for this situation may be due to the insufficient number of participants.

In addition, our study found that there's a significant positive correlation between the response time and LF/HF ratio during neutral stimulus in flicker task (r (8) = 0.714 p < 0.05).

During neutral stimulation of flicker task, participants' response time was positively correlated with the LF/HF ratio. As the participant's response time increased, the LF/HF ratio increased, thus the participant's body was dominated by sympathetic nerves, which would manifest characteristics such as tension and anxiety.

6.2   Time Series Analysis

The results of our correlation analysis did not yield many significant correlations. Therefore, we conducted an examination of the characteristic on the data of each participant time series analysis. Our analysis revealed that there were discernible differences between the data of different individuals. We selected a participant whose data could be used as a representative of the trends observed. To improve the visualization of the data, we applied a moving average to reduce noise in the physiological indexes. This was done for the data shown in Fig. 5, 6, 7, 8, 9, 10, 11 and 12. The plot was then used to demonstrate the correlation between the physiological indexes and the different affective stimuli.

Changes in pNN50. The results obtained from pNN50 revealed valuable insights and shown in Fig. 5 and Fig. 6, the window size for computing the moving average is 40 s.

For participant 1, the pNN50 displayed a declining trend in response to both negative and positive images as shown in Fig. 5. This trend can be attributed to the fact that longer response times and the affective content of negative images elicited anxiety and nervousness in the participants. Meanwhile, an increasing trend can be found in neutral images for participant 1. Meanwhile, for participant 2, all the images displayed a declining trend of pNN50, as shown in Fig. 6. It could be implied that extended experiment duration and multiple stimulations induced anxiety for this particular participant.

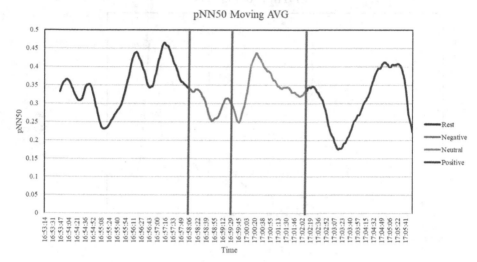

Fig. 5. The time series data of pNN50 for participant 1

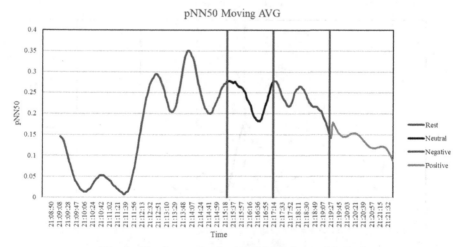

Fig. 6. The time series data of pNN50 for participant 2

Changes in LF/HF. The results obtained from LF/HF revealed valuable insights and shown in Fig. 7 and Fig. 8. The window size for computing the moving average is 40 s.

For participant 1, the graph shows a trend of decreasing LF/HF ratios associated with neutral stimuli, while LF/HF ratios associated with positive and negative stimuli increased simultaneously. These observations imply that the participants were subjected to feelings of anxiety and tension due to the emotional content of the negative stimuli, or also the long response time.

Surprisingly, the same results were obtained in another participant, as shown in Fig. 8.

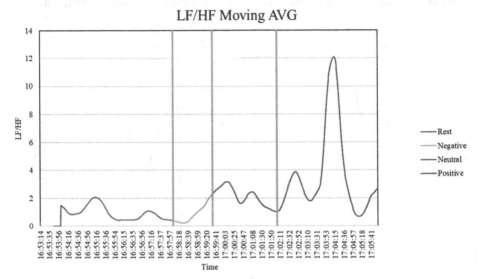

Fig. 7. The time series data of LF/HF for participant 1

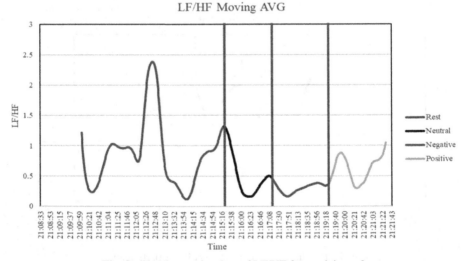

Fig. 8. The time series data of LF/HF for participant 2

Changes in RMSSD

The results obtained from LF/HF revealed valuable insights and shown in Fig. 9 and Fig. 10. The window size for computing the moving average is 30 s. For participant 1, the results revealed that RMSSD showed an increasing trend with increasing response time for negative images. Conversely, RMSSD showed a decreasing trend with increasing response time for neutral and positive images. These observations suggest that there are more relationships between RMSSD and response time than for images with different content. However, the RMSSD of participant 2 showed a decreasing trend with increasing negative image response time. The results from participant 2 showed that there was a relationship between participants presenting emotions such as anxiety and response time rather than stimulus content.

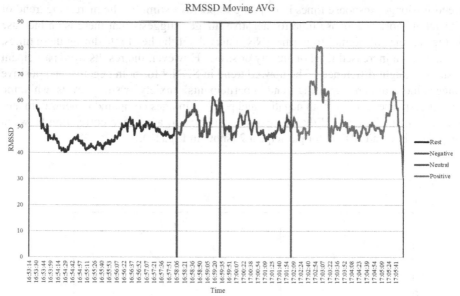

Fig. 9. The time series data of RMSSD for participant 1

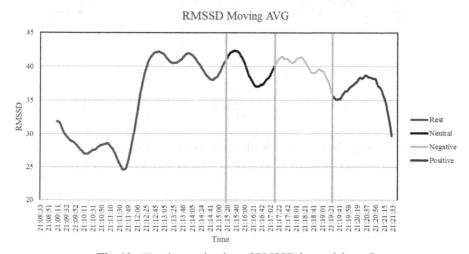

Fig. 10. The time series data of RMSSD for participant 2

Changes in SDNN

The results obtained from LF/HF revealed valuable insights and shown in Fig. 11 and Fig. 12. The window size for computing the moving average is 30 s.

The result of participant 1, as depicted in the Fig. 11, indicate that the trend of SDNN is comparable to that of RMSSD. In particular, the SDNN exhibits an upward trend for shorter response times in response to negative stimuli, while exhibiting a downward trend for longer response times in response to positive stimuli. The increasing trend of SDNN at shorter response time for negative images suggests that there is an increase in the variance of normal-to-normal (NN) intervals of the heart rate during these times, indicating an increased level of anxiety or stress. However, the results from participant 2 showed slight differences. The upward trend in SDNN for both negative and positive images indicated an increasing trend in participants' anxiety or stress levels, while the longer response time for both negative and positive images compared to neutral images for participant 2 indicated that the experiment showed a positive correlation between response time and SDNN for participant 2 (show in Fig. 12).

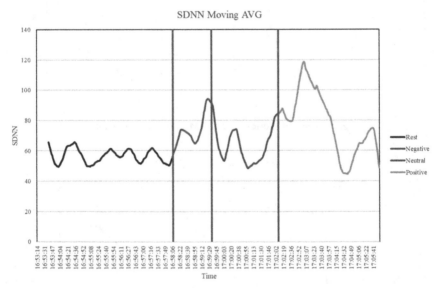

Fig. 11. The time series data of SDNN for participant 1

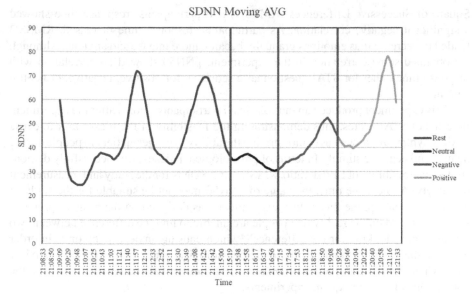

Fig. 12. The time series data of SDNN for participant 2

6.3 Discussion

There are several limitations to the current experiment. Firstly, the sample size is insufficient and narrow, with most of the participants between the ages of 18–24, and only one participant at 39 years old. This may not accurately reflect the variability in responses to anxiety-evoking stimuli across different age groups. Future experiments should consider a larger and more diverse sample size that includes a wider range of age groups. Secondly, the analysis of physiological indexes was limited to Heart Rate Variability (HRV) alone. While HRV is valuable, future experiments could benefit from the inclusion of additional indexes, such as brain waves, to obtain a more comprehensive understanding of the physiological response to anxiety-evoking stimuli. Finally, a more extensive analysis of HRV, including pNN20, pNN10, etc., would provide more detailed data for the experiment.

In conclusion, STAI questionnaire scores for physiological indexes and experimental response time for physiological indexes were correlated. For the STAI scores, all participants' scores increased after the experiment, and this increase proved that the flicker task has an arousing effect on anxiety. Also, we found a significant negative correlation between STAI scores and LF/HF ratio in response to positive stimuli. Response time of participants to each stimulus in the flicker task was also significantly correlated with different physiological indexes. With positive stimulus, SDNN showed a significant positive correlation with response time. Since SDNN increased with longer response time, it reflected that participant showed a deep relaxation emotional state under positive stimuli. With neutral stimuli, participants' response time and LF/HF ratio showed. a significant positive correlation. As the participants' response time to the stimulus became longer, the LF/HF ratio increased and sympathetic nerves dominated the participants' body, and the participants exhibited tension or anxiety. Under negative stimuli, Root Mean

Square of Successive Differences (RMSSD) and participants' response time showed a significant negative correlation. As participants' response time increased, RMSSD tended to decrease thus emotions gradually became more intense and anxious. Although we obtained some correlation in the experiment, pNN50 showed no correlation with response time either for STAI questionnaire scores or for positive, negative, or neutral stimuli.

This experiment produced an increase in all participants' scores after the experiment in terms of STAI scores, thus demonstrating the feasibility of the flicker task to cause anxiety symptoms, as well as demonstrating the ability to trigger anxiety in people during neutral and negative stimuli. In terms of physiological indexes, we successfully demonstrated the feasibility of LF/HF ratio, RMSSD and SDNN for the study and measurement of anxiety. At the same time, the value of pNN50 may not be suitable for the study of anxiety. To sum up, the flicker task experiment was designed on the basis of previous study and based on the reality that people are unable to find the difference between two images when "looking for the difference", which causing anxiety symptoms, in order to know the value or trend of a baseline physiological index of the patient's anxiety state when exploring the relief of anxiety symptoms in the future, which will be the cornerstone of the subsequent experiments.

7 Conclusion

This paper explores the use of physiological indexes and questionnaires to study periodic anxiety. The focus is on the potential of heart rate variability (HRV) indexes, including pNN50, RMSSD, SDNN, and LF/HF, in analyzing anxiety. In this work, we collect State Trait Anxiety Inventory questionnaires as the subjective evaluation of the results and compare it with the physiological indexes. In this study, we employ a flicker task to evoke the anxiety. The questionnaire survey revealed a significant increase in the scores of all participants before and after the experiment. Through correlation analysis we found that a significant negative correlation between the STAI score and LF/HF ratio during negative stimulus. In addition, there is a significant positive correlation between the response time and SDNN during positive stimulus. We also found a significant negative correlation between response time and RMSSD during negative stimulus. Not only that, but a significant positive correlation between the response time and LF/HF ratio also revealed during neutral stimulus.

Individual differences in time series data show different trends for all indexes. pNN50 shows a declining trend in response to both negative and positive images, attributed to longer response times and affective content eliciting anxiety and nervousness. LF/HF ratio decreases with neutral stimuli and increases with positive and negative stimuli for both participants. RMSSD exhibits a decreasing trend with increasing response time for neutral and positive images, suggesting a relationship between RMSSD and response time. SDNN shows an upward trend for shorter response times with negative stimuli and a downward trend for longer response times with positive stimuli, indicating increased anxiety or stress levels. However, the results from the other participant showed differences in the upward trend of SDNN for both negative and positive images, indicating a positive correlation between response time and SDNN.

There are several limitations to the current experiment. The sample size is insufficient and narrow. Moreover, future experiments could benefit from the inclusion of additional indexes such as brain waves. Finally, a more extensive analysis of HRV would provide more detailed data for the experiment.

Acknowledgement. We extend our sincere gratitude to all the participants who dedicated their valuable time and effort to this study. Additionally, we express our appreciation to Zhouhaotian Yang for his valuable technical guidance and unwavering support for the image processing involved in this experiment.

References

1. World Health Organization: Covid-19 pandemic triggers 25% increase in prevalence of anxiety and depression worldwide (2022). https://www.who.int/news/item/02-03-2022-covid-19-pandemic-triggers-25-increase-in-prevalence-of-anxiety-and-depression-worldwide
2. World Health Organization: Adolescent mental health (2021). https://www.who.int/news-room/fact-sheets/detail/adolescent-mental-health
3. Spielberger, C.D.: State-trait anxiety inventory for adults (1983)
4. Tsai, C.-F., Hsu, Y.-W., Huang, Y.-T., Hsu, W.-L., Chung, M.-H.: The effect of augmented reality and virtual reality on inducing anxiety for exposure therapy: a comparison using heart rate variability. J. Healthc. Eng. **2018**, 7 (2018)
5. Forte, G., Favieri, F., Tambelli, R., Casagrande, M.: Anxiety and attentional processes: the role of resting heart rate variability. Brain Sci. **11**(4), 480 (2021)
6. Mauss, I.B., Robinson, M.D.: Measures of emotion: a review. Cogn. Emot. **23**(2), 209–237 (2009)
7. Kawakami, Y., Hasegawa, S., Furukawa, R., Homma, R.: Preliminary study on color therapy effect evaluation by the emotion estimation method with biological signals. In: Di Bucchianico, G., Sethi, T., Lee, Y. (eds.) Advances in Industrial Design: Proceedings of the AHFE 2020 Virtual Conferences on Design for Inclusion, Affective and Pleasurable Design, Interdisciplinary Practice in Industrial Design, Kansei Engineering, and Human Factors for Apparel and Textile Engineering, 16–20 July 2020, USA, pp. 71–79. Springer (2020)
8. Appelhans, B.M., Luecken, L.J.: Heart rate variability as an index of regulated emotional responding. Rev. Gen. Psychol. **10**(3), 229–240 (2006)
9. Lang, P.J., Bradley, M.M., Cuthbert, B.N.: International affective picture system (IAPS): technical manual and affective ratings. NIMH Cent. Study Emot. Attention **1**, 39–58 (1997)
10. Peirce, J., Gray, A.A., Simpson, A., MacAskill, M.R.: PsychoPy: psychophysics software in Python. In: Bilgin, A.A., Kurbanoglu, S., Tonta, Y. (eds.) Proceedings of the 9th International Conference on Computer Science and Information Management, pp. 123–134. Springer (2019)
11. Union Tool. https://www.uniontool-mybeat.com/

A Participatory Design Approach to Develop a VR-Based Electrocardiogram Training Simulator

Harris Nisar[1]([✉]) , Arnav Shah[1], Avinash Gupta[1], and Abraham Kocheril[2]

[1] University of Illinois at Urbana-Champaign, Champaign, IL, USA
nisar2@illinois.edu
[2] OSF Heart of Mary Medical Center, 1400 West Park Street, Urbana, IL 61801, USA

Abstract. Virtual Reality (VR) allows complete immersion in virtual environments. VR is used in many applications including training healthcare professionals in a time and cost effective manner. Effectively incorporating clinical feedback into simulation design to ensure usability of the software is a challenge. In this paper, a discussion of a pipeline which was developed to allow for efficient participatory design for the creation of a VR-based electrocardiogram training simulator. Further, the results from the usability, content validity, and face validity which was conducted to assess the ECG simulator is presented. The results indicate that the proposed approach can be used to create and assess other VR-based medical training simulators.

Keywords: Virtual reality · extended reality · training simulator · participatory design approach · electrocardiogram · ECG

1 Introduction

Virtual reality (VR) enables users to become completely immersed in virtual environments by using a head-mounted display (HMD). The HMD tracks the position and rotation of the user's head and renders the environment from their viewing angle in the near-eye displays. A virtual environment is composed of computer-generated 3D objects with programmed behavior, and users can interact with these objects using various mechanisms, including handheld controllers or haptic devices. VR is currently being utilized in the gaming, education, and business industries [1–5].

More recently, there has been a rapid increase in the use of VR technology in the healthcare space. For example, medical imaging data of patients' hearts have been visualized in 3D using VR for surgical planning [6, 7]. VR is also utilized directly with patients in applications related to rehabilitation and therapy [8–12]. Additionally, several VR simulators of medical procedures have emerged to enhance the curriculum and improve training [13–16]. VR allows complete immersion of a learner in a virtual training environment enabling them to repetitively explore anatomical structures, medical procedures, and protocols in a risk-free environment where they can safely commit errors

J. Y. C. Chen and G. Fragomeni (Eds.): HCII 2023, LNCS 14027, pp. 478–489, 2023.
https://doi.org/10.1007/978-3-031-35634-6_34

and learn from them. This technology has proven beneficial, with studies demonstrating improved learning curves and retention after distributed practice with VR surgical simulators [17, 18]. In addition, training in virtual environments is cost-effective. For example, Rehman et al. calculated that it costs $672,000 to train 105 residents on basic competency in robotic surgery inside an operating room using animals. However, when a simulator was used, the cost was reduced to around $125,000 [19].

Currently, several challenges exist when developing and implementing VR for the healthcare domain. Baniasadi et al. conducted a literature review to determine common challenges in this space [20]. The authors found that challenges include creating education related to the appropriate use of VR technology, the costliness of hardware for implementation, the cost, time, and programming skills required to build the software, and effective validation of the usability of the software. Additionally, the authors highlight the challenges associated with designing VR simulators that are attractive and that encourage repetitive actions while providing immediate feedback. Furthermore, they emphasize the importance of user-centered design to build the simulations to satisfy end users. This naturally leads to the need for inter- and multidisciplinary collaboration between clinicians, engineers, and technical artists.

To address the challenges associated with designing VR simulations for medical education, a participatory design approach was followed to develop a VR simulator to train medical personnel on how to connect an ECG machine safely and correctly to a patient. Recent studies have shown that designers create more innovative concepts and ideas when working in a co-design environment than when creating ideas on their own [21, 22]. Moreover, including stakeholders in the simulation design can help ensure acceptance by those same stakeholders as users of the technology. The participatory design paradigm ensured that all stakeholders were part of the entire design, development, assessment, and implementation of the ECG simulation (not just at the beginning).

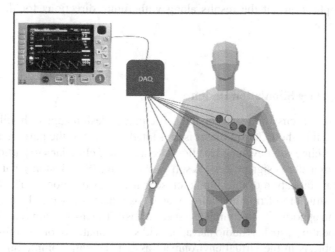

Fig. 1. Typical ECG setup. Ten electrodes are connected to the data acquisition (DAQ) unit which sends the information to the ECG monitor.

The ECG is a procedure to record the electrical signals in the heart and diagnose numerous cardiac abnormalities. It is a frequently performed, non-invasive procedure where a healthcare professional places 10 electrodes on specific locations of the patient's torso and limbs. Wires connect these electrodes to an ECG machine. As the heart pumps, the heart muscles depolarize, creating electrical activity that propagates to the skin. The electrodes read these electrical signals, and the lead wires transmit them to the ECG machine, where they are recorded for interpretation by cardiologists (see Fig. 1).

Electrode placement is crucial in correctly reading signals using the ECG. Bickerton et al. found that electrode placement accuracy varies from 16–90% because standards and guidelines were not followed. Poor electrode placement can lead to under- or over-diagnosis, leading to increased morbidity and mortality, or unnecessary treatment or hospitalization [23]. Electrode placement depends on tracking the error between the 3D position of the electrode and its known correct location. VR can serve as a useful tool to learn such electrode placement techniques.

The focus of this paper is to develop methods for rapid prototyping of an ECG VR simulator while still maintaining a participatory design paradigm. Our team consisted of a cardiologist, engineers, computer scientists, and technical artists contributing equally to the software's design and implementation. A pipeline was developed to create and modify the simulation scenarios to ensure that the engineering team members could easily implement feedback received from clinical team members. While this work focuses on developing an ECG simulator, the approach can be generalized to build other VR simulators for medical education. Additionally, we validated our software with experts in ECG placement to determine its usability, realism, and effectiveness as an educational tool.

The rest of the paper is organized as follows: In Sect. 2, the methods of designing and implementing the simulation are presented, along with techniques utilized to validate the software. In Sect. 3, the results from the validation study are presented. The discussion about the implications of the results along with future directions for this project is presented in Sect. 4.

2 Methods

2.1 Participatory Simulation Design

In this section, a discussion regarding the participatory design approach utilized during the development of the ECG simulator is presented. As part of the participatory design approach, a pipeline was developed to allow engineers and clinicians to participate effectively in the simulator design process. A software package (StepSystem) that allows easy creation and modification of the simulation scenarios was developed. The StepSystem abstracts the structure of training delivery as steps where users first hear instructions, followed by an opportunity to complete a specific task. The instructions can be delivered in various modalities, such as audio narration, videos, animations, or a combination. The state of the objects in the virtual environment associated with completing a particular step is maintained. Once the state reaches a specific configuration, the step is completed, and the user can move on to the next step. The StepSystem utilizes an event system to communicate with other assets in the virtual environment. These events fire at important points of the simulation, like when a step starts, when the instructions are complete, and when the task is completed, and can therefore trigger processes at these times. This allows designers to easily modify the virtual environment at various points of the simulation. The StepSystem also enables designers to quickly add or remove steps, change their order, and modify them without impacting the rest of the simulation.

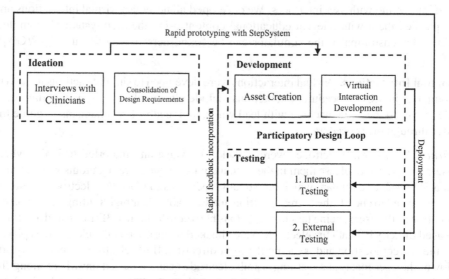

Fig. 2. Participatory design process.

The StepSystem allowed our team to maintain a participatory design approach since feedback from stakeholders can be easily incorporated into our simulation. To simplify the process for the clinicians, a table was created to document the ECG procedure and associated educational content. Clinicians can directly edit this document and can provide notes regarding how virtual interactions should be implemented. This table allowed the interdisciplinary team to remain aligned and led to an effective clinical knowledge transfer. Moreover, we created a script to parse this table to create the entire structure of a simulation scenario with one click. Using this approach, we collected the initial design requirements from the cardiologist and started implementing the simulation by developing the interactions necessary to simulate the ECG (discussed in Sect. 2.2). As the simulation was developed, we consistently created software builds that the cardiologist could test on their headset. Weekly meetings were conducted where that feedback was discussed. The engineering team then incorporated the clinical feedback, and the process was repeated until the prototype was ready for external testing. See Fig. 2 for our participatory design pipeline.

2.2 Simulator Implementation

We utilized the subject matter expertise obtained from cardiologists and the StepSystem to create a training simulator for the ECG procedure. The simulator contains two modes:

tutorial mode and walkthrough mode. In tutorial mode, users learn how to navigate and interact with the virtual environment. The walkthrough mode trains the user on how to place the ECG. This mode aims to instruct users on how to connect a 12-lead ECG to the patient. Unity 3D was used to create the simulator. We used the XR Interaction Toolkit Unity package to communicate with the Meta Quest 2 HMD. This package was also utilized to add common VR interactions to the simulator, such as grabbing and interacting with user interfaces. We developed all necessary virtual interactions and sequenced them with relevant educational content using the StepSystem. A complete video demonstration of the simulator can be found here: https://youtu.be/_zWG0qA 3P4o.

Virtual Interactions. Virtual interactions were developed to simulate actions needed to complete the ECG procedure. Interactions include placing electrodes, connecting those electrodes to the ECG machine with lead wires, and feedback mechanisms to guide the user through the procedure.

Virtual Electrodes. Electrodes were modeled in Maya and imported to Unity where users can grab and release them in the virtual environment. Several cutouts were created in a 3D mesh of a human, which are suitable locations to place the electrodes. Cutouts were created to encode the correct position and to enable clear highlighting of the correct location as the user is being taught. Collisions between the human 3D mesh and a collider placed directly beneath the electrode were checked to ensure that the electrode is placed in the correct location and is facing the right direction. If the electrode is placed upside down, the user receives a warning. Limb electrodes can be placed anywhere along the limb, so long as they are symmetric with the electrode on the opposite limb. After placing a limb electrode, its symmetric electrode's coordinates must be within a certain threshold. For example, the walkthrough simulation would only allow the user to move forward if the electrode was placed symmetrically in the approximate location on the left arm as the right arm (see Fig. 3).

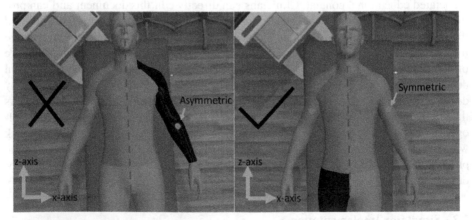

Fig. 3. Check for symmetry among limb electrodes. Left is incorrect as the electrodes do not share the same position along the z-axis.

Virtual Lead Wires. To give a more realistic feel of the simulation, we used Obi Rope to simulate the lead wires. Obi is a commercially available Unity package for creating advanced particle-based simulations of deformable materials, including ropes. Obi provides several parameters that we manually tuned to achieve the correct visual effect based on feedback from the clinicians (see Fig. 4). The damping factor was set so that the wires lost 50% of their velocity per second to settle down. Finally, we allowed the simulation to calculate seven times per frame for improved accuracy and convergence speed. This led to the creation of a realistic wire.

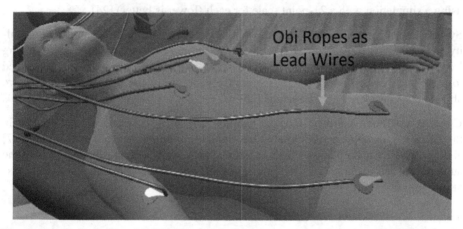

Fig. 4. A completed virtual ECG. The look of the ropes was confirmed to be realistic by the clinical team.

Snap Zones. We used XR Socket Interactors of the XR Interaction Toolkit to act as snap zones that attach ECG lead wires to electrodes. Snap zones create a zone in the virtual environment. When a subset of the objects in the virtual environment are placed in the zone, they will automatically "snap" to a particular position and orientation. The simulation allows the user to try and attach a lead wire to any of the electrodes. However, following the American Heart Association (AHA) color coding standards for a 12-lead ECG, it snaps in place if and only if the lead wire hovers over the correct electrode.

Feedback. In addition to the audio instructions, the user receives feedback from the software through audio-visual cues and haptic vibration. Realistic sounds like lead wires clamping onto the electrodes were also incorporated. The controllers provide haptic feedback as vibrations to the users as they reach out for the electrode and place it in the correct position.

2.3 Simulation Validation

To validate the simulation, experts (healthcare professionals who have placed at least 3 ECGs) were asked to complete the tutorial and walkthrough modes. They were then asked to complete several surveys to collect their feedback about the usability of the simulation in general and as a teaching tool. All surveys can be found in the appendix.

Demographics. Participants were asked to complete a demographic survey about their experience in healthcare, the number of ECGs they have placed, and their experience with VR.

SIM-TLX. SIM-TLX (based on NASA-TLX) aims to quantify nine types of cognitive loads (mental demands; physical demands; temporal demands; frustration; task complexity; situational stress; distraction; perceptual strain; task control; presence) while using a simulation with a 21-point scale for each (lower is better) [24].

System Usability Scale. The System Usability Scale (SUS) aims to quantify the usability of a system with a 10-question survey with questions on a 5-point Likert scale, ranging from strongly agree to strongly disagree. All the answers from a participant are processed to yield one number (0–100), representing the usability of the software. A SUS score above 68 is considered above average [25].

Content and Face Validity. Content validity [26] aims to quantify if the content in the simulation is appropriate for what the simulation aims to teach. Face validity [27] aims to quantify a simulation's realism. Participants rated several statements about the authenticity and genuineness of various aspects of the simulation and its effectiveness at teaching ECG were presented on a 5-point Likert scale.

3   Results

3.1   Demographics

5 nurses and 3 X-ray technicians (n = 8) were recruited to complete the study. 6 of the participants were female, and 2 were male. Their ages ranged from 22–58. They had 1–40 years of experience in healthcare. All participants had placed at least 3 ECGs. When asked about their familiarity with VR, six said they were completely unfamiliar, one said they were barely experienced, and one said they were strongly experienced.

3.2   Sim-TLX

Figure 5 shows the SIM-TLX results. The participants did not give a score higher than 4.5 on average for any of the load categories. Of the 9 categories, task control was rated to be the most (4.25 ± 4.03).

3.3   System Usability Scale

Figure 6 shows the SUS score for the ECG simulator (77.19 ± 13.260) compared to the score considered average [25]. As seen from the figure, the SUS score is greater than average.

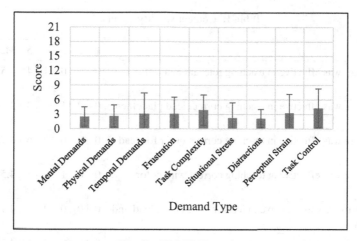

Fig. 5. SIM-TLX results.

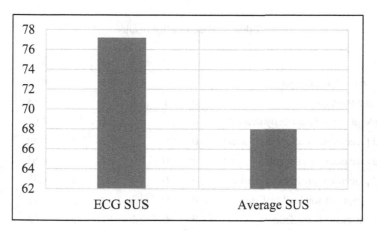

Fig. 6. System usability scale results.

3.4 Content Validity

Table 1 shows the content validity result. As seen in the table, the majority of the participants highly rated the simulator in terms of its content validity (provided a rating of 4 or 5 for each statement). Further, it can also be observed that none of the participants provided a low rating for the simulator (a rating of 1 or 2 for any of the statements).

3.5 Face Validity

Table 2 shows the face validity results. As seen in the table, the majority of participants highly rated the simulator in terms of its face validity (provided a rating of 4 or 5 for each statement). Further, it can be observed that none of the participants gave a rating of 1 for any statement. Three participants gave a score of 2 to statements regarding the graphical authenticity of the human, ribcage, and ECG leads.

Table 1. Content validity results.

Question	1	2	3	4	5	Mean	Std
The software was effective in teaching relevant anatomical landmarks	0	0	0	4	4	4.50	0.99
The software was effective in teaching correct lead placement locations	0	0	1	4	3	4.75	1.13
The software was effective in teaching correct order for lead placement	0	0	0	2	6	4.75	0.93
The software was effective at teaching correct wire color coding	0	0	1	2	5	4.50	0.76
The VR software was effective in teaching the entire lead and wire placement	0	0	0	2	6	4.75	0.52
Overall teaching utility	0	0	0	2	6	4.75	0.74

Table 2. Face validity results.

Question	1	2	3	4	5	Mean	Std
The human model is realistic	0	1	0	4	3	4.13	0.99
The ribcage is realistic	0	1	1	2	4	4.13	1.13
The Angle of Louis is correctly depicted	0	0	3	2	3	4.00	0.93
The lead placement locations are correct	0	0	1	2	5	4.50	0.76
The leads are placed in the correct order	0	0	0	3	5	4.63	0.52
The lead placement process is realistic	0	0	1	3	4	4.38	0.74
The wire snapping sounded realistic	0	0	2	3	3	4.13	0.83
The ECG machine is realistic	0	0	1	4	3	4.25	0.71
The leads are realistic	0	1	0	3	4	4.25	1.04
The cables are realistic	0	0	1	4	3	4.25	0.71
The environment is realistic	0	0	1	3	4	4.38	0.74

4 Discussion

The StepSystem enabled the rapid creation of a ECG VR training simulator while maintaining a participatory design paradigm. Since the entire structure of the software could be generated with a click of a button, the team had a working prototype in seconds. Further, the entire team was well versed with the simulator architecture leading to productive weekly meetings where the clinical team could provide feedback on exactly where to modify/improve the simulator. The StepSystem enabled the rapid integration of this feedback into the simulator.

The feedback collected during the design process led to the creation of a useful and compelling educational tool as seen from the promising results collected relating to the usability, realism, and educational capabilities of the simulator.

When asked about the load placed on the participant (SIM-TLX), the category with the highest score (most load) was related to task control. However, this score was still less than 5 out of 21. This could be because the group of participants was inexperienced in handling VR technology. Since the only tutorial they had regarding VR was the tutorial mode of the simulator itself, they may not have been as confident as they would have been had they had more time to experiment with VR (in future we are planning to conduct a distributed study to understand these results). Overall, the low SIM-TLX scores indicate that the interactions were designed in an intuitive manner.

The SUS score was greater than what is considered average, further proving the intuitiveness and useability of the simulator. Content validity focuses on whether the educational content in the simulator is correct and adequate. The high content validity scores indicate that the ECG VR simulator has potential to be useful as an educational tool in terms of content. Face validity focuses on the realism of the simulator. The high scores regarding face validity indicate that the ECG VR simulator is realistic. The lowest scores regarding face validity were about the graphical realism of the human model, ribcage, and leads. This feedback has been accounted for and the team is focused on improving the overall graphical realism of the simulator. While the pipeline followed here is not entirely perfect, any team that is striving to create VR simulators should focus on automation process to ease the development and testing of their simulator.

For future work, the team plans to conduct a more exhaustive study to confirm the findings in this paper with a larger group of ECG experts, clinicians, and other healthcare personnel. Additionally, the team plans to test the transfer validity of the simulator with a more inexperienced population set comprising of first year medical students and nursing students. Transfer validity aims to understand whether the knowledge presented in the simulator transfers from the virtual environment to the physical world. The transfer validity studies will further provide insights on the usefulness of the simulator in training learners for real world situations. The team also plans to utilize the StepSystem to create medical simulators for other protocols. The same approach can be replicated to create any educational tool step-based procedure for medicine. Additionally, the team plans to improve the StepSystem to make the development of such simulators effective so that clinicians can create the entire simulator without writing code. Easing the barrier of entry to develop VR simulators will in turn lead to a greater research effort to understand the efficacy of VR in the medical education space.

5 Conclusion

In this paper, a discussion was provided regarding the creation of an ECG training simulator in VR. The simulator was developed following a participatory design approach. To make this process more efficient, a novel pipeline (StepSystem) was created. This allowed for the rapid prototyping of the simulator as well as rapid integration of clinical feedback. Several studies were conducted to rate the usability, realism, and educational potential of the simulator. The results from the study indicate that the simulator can serve as a promising training tool for the ECG procedure. Further developments and studies are being conducted to understand the usefulness and importance of such simulators. This work highlights the importance of automating aspects in the development of VR software for medical education.

References

1. LaViola, J.J.: Bringing VR and spatial 3D interaction to the masses through video games. IEEE Comput. Graph. Appl. **28**(5), 10–15 (2008). https://doi.org/10.1109/MCG.2008.92
2. Slavova, Y., Mu, M.: A comparative study of the learning outcomes and experience of VR in education. In: 25th IEEE Conference on Virtual Reality and 3D User Interfaces, VR 2018 - Proceedings, pp. 685–686, August 2018. https://doi.org/10.1109/VR.2018.8446486
3. Freina, L., Ott, M.: A literature review on immersive virtual reality in education: state of the art and perspectives. http://www.google.com/patents/US3050870. Accessed 02 Feb 2023
4. Claudia, M., Dieck, T., Jung, T.: Progress in IS Augmented Reality and Virtual Reality The Power of AR and VR for Business. http://www.springer.com/series/10440. Accessed 02 Feb 2023
5. Lee, L., Nisar, H., Roberts, J., Blackford, J., Kesavadas, T.K.: Face and content validation of food safety training in Virtual Reality (VR). In: SeGAH 2022 - 2022 IEEE 10th International Conference on Serious Games and Applications for Health (2022). https://doi.org/10.1109/SEGAH54908.2022.9978588
6. Ong, C.S., et al.: Role of virtual reality in congenital heart disease. Congenit. Heart Dis. **13**(3), 357–361 (2018). https://doi.org/10.1111/CHD.12587
7. Sadeghi, A.H., et al.: Immersive 3D virtual reality imaging in planning minimally invasive and complex adult cardiac surgery. Eur. Heart J. Digit. Health **1**(1), 62–70 (2020). https://doi.org/10.1093/EHJDH/ZTAA011
8. Lewis, G.N., Rosie, J.A.: Virtual reality games for movement rehabilitation in neurological conditions: how do we meet the needs and expectations of the users? Disabil. Rehabil. **34**(22), 1880–1886 (2012). https://doi.org/10.3109/09638288.2012.670036
9. Steiner, B., Elgert, L., Saalfeld, B., Wolf, K.H.: Gamification in rehabilitation of patients with musculoskeletal diseases of the shoulder: scoping review. JMIR Serious Games **8**(3), e19914 (2020). https://games.jmir.org/2020/3/e19914, https://doi.org/10.2196/19914
10. Laver, K.E., Lange, B., George, S., Deutsch, J.E., Saposnik, G., Crotty, M.: Virtual reality for stroke rehabilitation. Cochrane Database Syst. Rev. **2017**(11) (2017)
11. Jack, D., et al.: Virtual reality-enhanced stroke rehabilitation. IEEE Trans. Neural Syst. Rehabil. Eng. **9**(3), 308–318 (2001). https://doi.org/10.1109/7333.948460
12. Laver, K., George, S., Thomas, S., Deutsch, J.E., Crotty, M.: Virtual reality for stroke rehabilitation. Stroke **43**(2) (2012). https://doi.org/10.1161/STROKEAHA.111.642439
13. Izard, S.G., et al.: Virtual reality as an educational and training tool for medicine. J. Med. Syst. **42**(3), 1–5 (2018). https://doi.org/10.1007/S10916-018-0900-2/FIGURES/5
14. Ruthenbeck, G.S., Reynolds, K.J.: Virtual reality for medical training: the state-of-the-art. J. Simul. **9**(1), 16–26 (2015). https://doi.org/10.1057/JOS.2014.14/FIGURES/2
15. Sankaran, N.K., et al.: Efficacy study on interactive mixed reality (IMR) software with sepsis prevention medical education. In: 26th IEEE Conference on Virtual Reality and 3D User Interfaces, VR 2019 - Proceedings, pp. 664–670, March 2019. https://doi.org/10.1109/VR.2019.8798089
16. Gupta, A., Cecil, J., Pirela-Cruz, M., Ramanathan, P.: A virtual reality enhanced cyber-human framework for orthopedic surgical training. IEEE Syst. J. **13**(3), 3501–3512 (2019). https://doi.org/10.1109/JSYST.2019.2896061

17. Andersen, S.A.W., Konge, L., Cayé-Thomasen, P., Sørensen, M.S.: Learning curves of virtual mastoidectomy in distributed and massed practice. JAMA Otolaryngol. Head Neck Surg. **141**(10), 913–918 (2015). https://doi.org/10.1001/JAMAOTO.2015.1563
18. Andersen, S.A.W., Konge, L., Cayé-Thomasen, P., Sørensen, M.S.: Retention of mastoidectomy skills after virtual reality simulation training. JAMA Otolaryngol. Head Neck Surg. **142**(7), 635–640 (2016). https://doi.org/10.1001/JAMAOTO.2016.0454
19. Rehman, S., et al.: Simulation-based robot-assisted surgical training: a health economic evaluation. Int. J. Surg. **11**(9), 841–846 (2013). https://doi.org/10.1016/J.IJSU.2013.08.006
20. Baniasadi, T., Ayyoubzadeh, S.M., Mohammadzadeh, N.: Challenges and practical considerations in applying virtual reality in medical education and treatment. Oman Med. J. **35**(3), e125 (2020). https://doi.org/10.5001/OMJ.2020.43
21. Trischler, J., Pervan, S.J., Kelly, S.J., Scott, D.R.: The Value of Co design, vol. 21, no. 1, pp. 75–100, July 2017. https://doi.org/10.1177/1094670517714060
22. Mitchell, V., Ross, T., May, A., Sims, R., Parker, C.: Empirical investigation of the impact of using co-design methods when generating proposals for sustainable travel solutions, vol. 12, no. 4, pp. 205–220, October 2015. https://doi.org/10.1080/15710882.2015.1091894
23. Bickerton, M., Pooler, A.: Misplaced ECG electrodes and the need for continuing training, vol. 14, no. 3, pp. 123–132, March 2019. https://doi.org/10.12968/BJCA.2019.14.3.123
24. Harris, D., Wilson, M., Vine, S.: Development and validation of a simulation workload measure: the simulation task load index (SIM-TLX). Virtual Real **24**(4), 557–566 (2020). https://doi.org/10.1007/S10055-019-00422-9/FIGURES/3
25. Brooke, J.: SUS-A quick and dirty usability scale. https://www.tbistafftraining.info/. Accessed 02 Feb 2023
26. Sireci, S.G.: /3, Validity Theory and the Methods Used in Validation: Perspectives from Social and Behavioral Sciences, vol. 45, no. 1, pp. 83–117 (1998)
27. Thomas, S.D., Hathaway, D.K., Arheart, K.L.: Face validity. West J. Nurs. Res. **14**, 109–112 (1992)

Research on Mixed Reality Visual Augmentation Method for Teleoperation Interactive System

Yueyang Shi, XiaoLing Li$^{(\boxtimes)}$, Long Wang, Zhangyi Cheng, Zeyu Mo, and Shiweng Zhang

School of Mechanical Engineering, Xi'an Jiaotong University, Xi'an 710000, China
{victories,xjtu_mzy,wang1521,3120101240,
zhangshiwen}@stu.xjtu.edu.cn

Abstract. Highly intelligent teleoperated robots are playing an increasingly important role in high-risk tasks. This paper proposed a teleoperation vision enhancement method in mixed reality scenarios, aiming at the problems of poor interactive telepresence at the control terminal of the teleoperation system and the difficulty for the operator to obtain real experience. By building the video stream transmission based on this method, the researchers realized the real-time presentation of the remote scene. This research carried out the interface visualization of the mixed reality visual enhancement interactive system by analyzing the target requirements in the teleoperation interaction task and improved the interactive control strategy in the mixed reality scene. This teleoperation interactive system effectively solves the problem of synchronous reproduction of remote operation scenes, improves operators' interaction efficiency and accuracy, and verifies the advantages and application prospects of mixed reality display technology.

Keywords: Teleoperation · Mixed reality · Immersive 3D display · Visual enhancement · Interaction design

1 Introduction

With the rapid development of automation control, natural human-computer interaction, information communication, and other technologies, highly intelligent and autonomous robot systems for teleoperation environments are increasingly important in high-risk tasks [1]. At the same time, teleoperation technology is also widely used in highly complex environments such as mine clearance, search and rescue, high-altitude operations, underwater exploration, and space exploration. In these application fields, robots often replace people in dangerous environments. The focus of research is how to endow robots with human-like sensory systems and cognitive abilities to intuitively reproduce remote scenes on the operator side [2].

Studies have shown that among the five human sensory systems, the number of neurons and information transmission rate of vision are much higher than those of other sensory modes [3]. To some extent, more than half of the human brain is directly or

J. Y. C. Chen and G. Fragomeni (Eds.): HCII 2023, LNCS 14027, pp. 490–502, 2023.
https://doi.org/10.1007/978-3-031-35634-6_35

indirectly used to process visual images, and the processing of visual information dominates the processing of information from other modalities. This shows the importance of correct feedback on visual information to humans [4]. At present, most remote operating systems provide visual feedback through 2D displays. In this case, the operator must infer the operation situation through two-dimensional image information [5]. In addition, the operating equipment used in traditional robot teleoperation methods limits the space for interaction, and usually, operation and feedback are independent of each other. In the actual operation and interaction process, the operator not only needs to pay attention to the camera image of the robot in real-time but also needs to obtain the motion posture of the robot in real-time. That is, the operator must constantly switch between the visual feedback area and the operation area, resulting in distraction. This approach needs to be more natural and efficient. Therefore, the traditional teleoperation scheme has problems such as limited observable field of view [6], lack of depth information [7], and unintuitive interactive operation [8]. Mixed reality technology can gradually replace the two-dimensional display interface with its advantages of immersion [9], realism [10], and intuition [11], which is convenient for remote operators to carry out safe and efficient operational feedback [12].

Based on the above research content and technical background, this paper focused on teleoperation application scenarios and studied mixed reality technology to study visual enhancement methods to improve the operator's sense of presence. The research starts with building a remote vision software and hardware platform to achieve real-time presentation and formulates the interaction process and interface layout principles of the remote operation main terminal. The solution provides a better visual environment for monitoring remote operating robot work sites. It solves the problems of low human-computer interaction efficiency in traditional remote operating systems and extensively promoted the security and stability of the system.

2   System Architecture Design

This research focuses on the critical technologies of the mixed reality interactive system. By taking the human-computer interaction channel as the research object and starting from the integration of multi-channel information, a detailed scheme of the human-computer interaction system for a specific teleoperation scene was proposed to realize the reproduction of the operating environment and the optimization of human-computer interaction. First, the visual enhancement method and real-time image acquisition and transmission were studied to realize real-time video stream, which showed multi-angle teleoperation and the mixed reality display based on Unity 3D. Secondly, this paper studied the interaction method of augmented information in space based on the mixed reality scene, analyzed the natural human-computer interaction technology based on the human sensory system, and proposed the human-computer interaction layout and specification of a mixed reality teleoperation interface. Finally, through the development of the virtual interface between the hardware, the application program, and the 3D scene was developed based on the unity platform. The processed image and scene information was displayed in real-time with the help of the mixed reality HMD to realize natural human-computer interaction.

According to the research focus summarized above, this study started from the existing problems and actual needs of teleoperation operations and summarized the overall functional framework as follows:

- Visual enhancement and real-time presentation of the scene
    In building an augmented reality scene, the user perceives the remote environment through real-time video stream information to achieve a natural and immersive visual experience.
- Natural interaction system
    In the process of human-computer interaction, the interaction behavior between the user and the scene includes selection, movement, grasping, and release. At the same time, different interaction states need to be distinguished through visual perception.
    This study helps contextual understanding during teleoperation by changing the traditional third-person perspective observation. On the other hand, this system can provide teleoperation users with a telepresence interface that accurately displays robot-side information to achieve a more immersive and natural interactive experience.

2.1 Visual Enhancement and Real-Time Presentation of Remote Vision

According to the actual operation scenarios and project requirements, this study built its interactive prototype based on analyzing the framework of the teleoperation visual enhancement method and the interactive characteristics of mixed reality to realize the immersive display and multi-channel interaction. Figure 1 shows how this research builds the interactive system prototype of the visually enhanced interactive system.

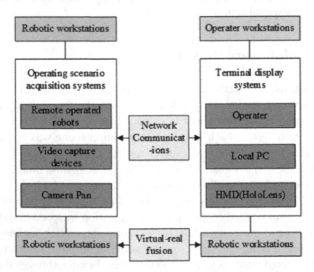

Fig. 1. The interactive system prototype of the visually enhanced interactive system

In the specific implementation process, since the built system solution will finally be applied to the remote operation work, the collection and transmission of remote scene information must also be considered. Therefore, it is divided into three aspects: scene acquisition equipment, communication equipment, and mixed reality display equipment to realize the vision enhancement interactive system solution.

Scene Acquisition Equipment. When arranging the interactive system, the observation angle is divided into the global angle of view and the hand angle of view according to the different observation angles. Among them, the global perspective needs to provide a complete working scene. So the resolution of the camera, which has a view of 110°, is set by 1080P, and the focal length is set by 3.6 mm.

Communication Equipment. For the medium and long-distance teleoperation involved in this research, a teleoperation communication system based on wireless communication modules is established, and a portable broadband IP ad hoc network station with a 300 m transmission distance is selected.

Mixed Reality Display Device. The HoloLens2 used in this study is an OST-HMD device with independent computing power, a wireless communication system, and assembled with multiple high-precision sensors that provide an excellent immersive experience [13]. Based on the sensors integrated into HoloLens2, a multi-channel interactive experience can be realized. Therefore, in the following research, HoloLens2 is selected as the display device so that the operator can consider the near-end environment and reduce the sensory load in viewing remote information. At the same time, the operator can realize the free interaction with the manipulator under the mixed reality system.

2.2 Real-Time Presentation of Remote Vision

The main function that the mixed reality visual enhancement interactive system needs to achieve is to capture or record the near-end task environment through the camera, and at the same time obtain real-time video streams on the remote HMD, that is, the real-time presentation of the remote scene based on end-to-end video transmission. The specific implementation method of video transmission is shown in Fig. 2 below. First, set the streaming media channel for publishing video output, video encoding and video streaming release, and finally use this video streaming channel in the holographic application to deploy to HoloLens 2.

In order to input the network camera from the outside world into the development environment, this research builds a scene that can play RTSP real-time video stream, uses scripts to control the playback of RTSP video stream, and designs and develops the corresponding program interface and software interface.

Running the program will open a new window on the local computer that provides the webcam image, as shown in Fig. 3, which indicates that the video encoder is receiving image data.

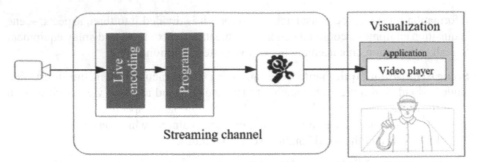

Fig. 2. End-to-end video transmission

Fig. 3. The webcam image is showed in HoloLens2.

3   Teleoperation Human-Computer Interaction Based on Mixed Reality

The gaze tracking or gesture interaction supported by the HoloLens device provides an intuitive and natural interaction channel for robot collaboration and realizes the operation method based on natural interaction. To further improve the accuracy of the operation, the conventional method is to combine eye gaze and gesture interaction to trigger the target, which can effectively solve the misoperation caused by staring at an object for a long time, reduce the fatigue of gesture interaction, and enrich the application scenarios and scope.

To combine the content area suitable for eyes to obtain information with the interaction area of hand operation, the interaction space will be divided into several parts in the mixed reality teleoperation scene to realize the layout design of the main terminal operation interface.

3.1 Main Interface Layout and Design

The human-computer interface is the primary medium for transmitting information between the operator and the computer, directly affecting the efficiency and experience of human-computer interaction [14]. On both the robot side and the operator's interactive side, corresponding information needs to be presented, and corresponding interactive actions should be completed according to the interaction requirements.

Hybrid Display Interface Layout Framework. Unlike the absolute size of a two-dimensional interface, the size of objects in space will be affected by depth information, so the impact of spatial depth should be fully considered in the layout design of mixed reality interfaces. In the actual test process, when the distance is less than 0.5 m, the human eye cannot focus. Between 1 m and 5 m, the human eye can strongly perceive the three-dimensional sense of the object and the sense of distance between elements. While the distance is more than 2 m, it is easier to get the attention that can avoid or minimize the discomfort caused by vergence-accommodation conflict.

The field of view and depth distance of the HoloLens 2 device determines the size and position of the scene. As shown in Fig. 6, HoloLens 2 has a field of view of 52° and a screen aspect ratio of 3:2 (Fig. 4).

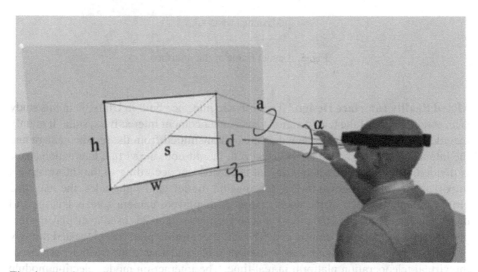

Fig. 4. The field of view and depth distance of the HoloLens 2 device determines the size and position of the scene.

From Eq. (1), it can be obtained that the optimal height of the picture at a distance of 2 m from the front of HoloLens 2 is 1.24 m, and the width is 1.87 m. At this time, the visible range of the picture in HoloLens 2 is 100%.

$$s = 2d \tan\frac{\alpha}{2} \tag{1}$$

where s is the diagonal length of the viewing area; α is the diagonal field of view; d is the distance from the viewing area.

Also, we can get the layout frame of the interface in Fig. 5, which is divided by the real-world coordinate system as the reference system. The dark gray area represents the canvas range in the static state; the middle area represents the most comfortable rotation range. The light gray area indicates the canvas extent at maximum head rotation. Through this framework, the structure of the mixed reality interface can be laid out according to the basis to ensure that users can interact easily and comfortably.

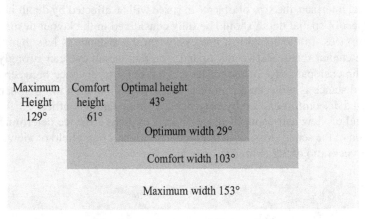

Fig. 5. Layout frame of the interface

Mixed Reality Interface Design. The software interface built in Unity3D in this study is an essential part of the teleoperation visual enhancement interactive system. It mainly includes two parts, the real-time video stream transmitted from the remote camera and the interactive object, which is 3D visualized. In addition, the virtual interaction space is divided, and the corresponding layout is carried out according to the information's importance level. As shown in Fig. 6 below, on the left and right sides, the real-time video streaming screen of the teleoperation is displayed, camera screen 1 is used to display the actual scene of the robot hand, and camera screen 2 is used to display the real global scene of the teleoperation end. The AR recognition platform is located directly in front of the field of vision and is used to track and locate the spatial position of the virtual teleoperation platform in real-time. The interaction mode selection module integrates functions such as performance analyzer, gesture interaction mode selection, AR platform selection, scene switching, and other functional components, respectively, responding to corresponding features. This interface is finally displayed by the operator through the HoloLens2 device, assisting the remote operating system in realizing natural human-computer interaction and immersive operations.

The interface calibration method used in the interactive system is environment-locked. However, in the actual application process, in order to adapt to different application scenarios and the individual needs of operators, an interface calibration method based on head tracking is provided for the operator to choose. This method can also

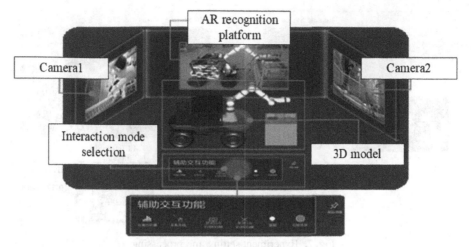

Fig. 6. The design of interactive system

Effectively avoid screen disappearance or frequent manual positioning caused by the operator's movement.

4 Experiment

Similar to other studies [15], this study conducted a comparative experiment between the mixed reality interface and two traditional HMIs and conducted usability tests after the task with two standard questionnaires: System Usability Scale (SUS) subjective evaluation scale [16] and NASA Workload Index (NASA-TLX) scale [17].

In the comparative experiment, the study set up three groups of different interfaces, which are 2D interface based on desktop display (Desktop-2D), 3D interface based on desktop display (Desktop-3D), and MR interface based on HoloLens2 display (Holo-MR). As shown in the figure below, the experiment carried out the robot teleoperation task under universal conditions, requiring the subjects to use the corresponding interface to operate the seven-axis robotic arm in different visual environments and guide the robotic arm to reach the designated position to grab different objects.

In the experiment, two different positions in the sand table were selected and marked to place the target object, and the subjects received feedback on the target position from the interface. Other systems provided the control of the robotic arm in this work, and a single experiment lasted approximately 15 min, including a 60-s tutorial video that provided a short explanation of robot operation. Before each main experiment, participants had two minutes to test each interface, giving participants time to familiarize themselves with the controllers, augmented reality images, and robot. In all experimental environments or test modes, subjects were asked to wear a HoloLens2 to control the possible effects of wearing a helmet. After the completion of each experiment, the participants were required to fill in relevant questionnaires. The experimental scene of the subjects is shown in Fig. 7.

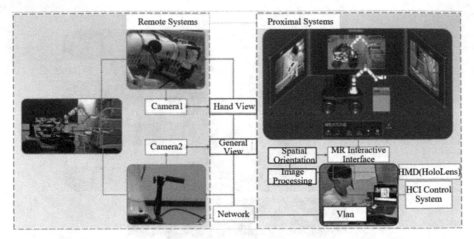

Fig. 7. Experiment setting and processing

Only from the experimental data of participants completing related tasks, compared with the traditional 2D visualization interface, the total time required to complete the task under the Holo-MR interface is below the average level, and the accuracy rate is above the average level, indicating that Holo-MR has clear advantages to the 2D visualization interface. It is calculated that the MR interface reduced task completion time by 17.3% and improved accuracy by an average of 7.4% compared to 2D displays. However, the MR system has specific problems. Compared with the mouse input and feedback in the desktop 2D interactive environment, the system's response time under the MR interface is relatively long, and the interaction fluency is reduced.

4.1 Analysis of System Usability Scale

SUS is a standardized evaluation form containing 10 questions in total and adopts the method of positive and negative cross-examination. This table measures users' subjective evaluation of the system to assess the overall usability and the *Learnability* and *Usability* of each interface. After completing a series of experimental tasks, participants will be asked to fill in the SUS evaluation form shown in Table 1. The scale used by the subjects uses a 5-point scale, the number 1 represents strongly disagree, and the number 5 represents very much agree. The scoring standard for odd items is the initial score minus 1. The score for the even-numbered items is 5 minus the initial test score. The initial score range of a single item is recorded as 0 to 4, and the maximum score of the scale is 40. Since the score range of the final SUS evaluation is 0 to 100, the total score of the 5-point scale needs to be multiplied by 2.5 in the process of data statistics to obtain the SUS score.

In addition, the *Learnability* subscale is composed of the 4th item and the 10th item, and the *Usability* subscale is composed of the other 8 items. In order to maintain the consistency of the overall SUS score, the final evaluation score range is between 0 and 100, and the original score must be converted. The final score for the learnability scale was the raw score multiplied by 12.5, and the final score for the usability scale was the raw score multiplied by 3.125.

Table 1. SUS subjective feeling evaluation form

Question	Score
1. I am willing to use the vision system frequently	⊓, 1⊓, 2⊓, 3□, 4□, 5
2. I find the vision system too complicated	□, 1□, 2□, 3□, 4□, 5
3. I think the vision system is easy to use	□, 1□, 2□, 3□, 4□, 5
4. I think I need help from a technician to use this vision system	□, 1□, 2□, 3□, 4□, 5
5. I found that the vision system integrates functions well	□, 1□, 2□, 3□, 4□, 5
6. In the process of using the vision system, I found that many operations were inconsistent with expectations	□, 1□, 2□, 3⊔, 4⊔, 5
7. I think most users can quickly learn to use the vision system	□, 1□, 2□, 3□, 4□, 5
8. I found the vision system awkward to use	□, 1□, 2□, 3□, 4□, 5
9. I am confident in mastering the vision system	□, 1□, 2□, 3□, 4□, 5
10. I need to learn many instructions before using this system	□, 1□, 2□, 3□, 4□, 5

After calculation, the average and standard deviation of the overall evaluation scores of SUS on the prototype of the mixed reality interactive system designed in this paper are 71.4 and 8.1. The mean and standard deviation of the *Usability* scores were 73.9 and 7.9. Judging from the evaluation results, the participants' subjective evaluation of the system is good, and they think it has good usability.

The overall *Learnability* score is relatively low, and the individual differences are large, but it is also above the general level of the overall score. This is mainly because most participants have no experience in VR/AR and robot-related operations.

4.2 Analysis of NASA-TLX

The NASA-TLX scale is mainly used to study the impact of different interfaces and evaluate the overall load on users. The table consists of 6 evaluation items including Mental Demand (MD), Physical Demand (PD), Time Demand (TD), Effort Level (EF), self-performance evaluation (PE) and Frustration Level (FR) [75]. The scale contains a detailed text description of each evaluation item, and is marked with a straight line of 100 equal divisions. The subjects must mark the position consistent with their true perception level.

Table 2 shows the scores of the Desk-2D, Desk-3D and Holo-MR interfaces in the NASA-TLX questionnaire, which are mainly used to analyze the performance of the teleoperation visual enhancement interactive system. Compared with the traditional teleoperation vision system, the Holo-MR interface has characteristics that other systems under test do not have, and can view the 3D model of the teleoperation platform. The information is more intuitive presented by Holo-MR. At the same time, due to the spatial properties of the MR interface, it can provide scenes that are more in line with the user's visual habits and enhance their spatial understanding.

Table 2. Analysis data of NASA-TLX Physiological Loading Project

Project	Desk-2D			Desk-3D			Holo-MR		
	scale mean	Weig-hts	Load	Scale mean	Weig-hts	Load	Scale mean	Weig-hts	Load
MD	31.03	0.03	0.93	51.23	0.22	11.27	41.71	0.20	8.14
PD	52.20	0.20	10.44	43.20	0.15	6.48	50.07	0.20	10.25
TD	70.75	0.29	20.52	65.51	0.26	17.03	46.93	0.19	8.72
EF	50.22	0.15	7.53	33.30	0.08	2.66	46.21	0.10	4.40
PE	55.80	0.20	11.16	50.28	0.20	10.06	27.29	0.29	7.80
FR	40.20	0.13	5.23	35.26	0.09	3.17	30.64	0.03	1.02
Total load	55.81			50.68			40.33		

From the above table, we can calculate the proportion of NASA-TLX physiological individual evaluation items under different interfaces. Based on this data, we can evaluate the key factors that affect user cognition and optimize based on this design.

Figure 8 shows that the user's time demand load on the Holo-MR interface has been significantly reduced. Compared with the Holo-MR interface, in the Desk-2D and Desk-3D interfaces, the cumbersome interface operation and interaction process will affect the user's cognitive load and mental state, causing users to spend more energy on performing tasks. It will also result in additional time consumption, resulting in a decrease in all points.

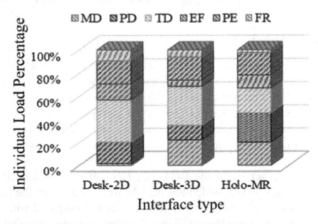

Fig. 8. Individual load percentage of different interface type

4.3 Discussion

The experimental results show that the MR interface design in this paper provides strong feedback for users to operate the robot remotely. The MR-based interface design is superior to the traditional 2D interface design in most indicators, and its interactive visual interface has significant advantages. The objective results show that the 3D interactive interface based on mixed reality designed in this paper can assist the operator to complete the task in a shorter time than the original inter-active interface, and has a higher task accuracy rate. Compared with the 2D display Compared, the MR interface reduced task completion time by 17.3% and increased accuracy by an average of 7%. From the statistical results of the subjective measurement table, the inconsistency between the visual reference frames will slightly affect the operator's motion perception and operation intention, resulting in deviations between interface evaluations. However, the mixed reality interactive system's comprehensive evaluation of usability and task load is still better than other traditional interfaces.

However, due to the inherent limitations of the MR display terminal, there will be the following problems in the process of visualizing and interacting with the MR scene:

The first problem is interface layout issues. Limited by the perspective of HoloLens 2, users tend to focus on smaller visual areas. When much information is displayed, the tiled layout will cause information overload, which will cause visual confusion and difficulty in understanding and increase the cognitive burden.

The second problem is the feedback on interactive instructions. Gesture interaction in three-dimensional physical space allows users to input operation commands without touching the physical interface. In this case, if the user does not get instant feedback, it is not easy to judge and confirm the input status, so the feedback design for interactive commands must be explicit.

The third problem is network communication. Due to the limitation of network bandwidth and rate, the degradation of communication quality will make the display of data view discontinuous, which objectively interferes with user interaction.

5 Conclusion

Based on human visual perception and cognition characteristics, this research explored the visual enhancement method of teleoperation, realized the master-slave real-scene telepresence and mixed reality display, solved the problem of remote communication, and completed the construction of a teleoperation visual enhancement interactive platform. Compared with the traditional visual feedback method, this method not only ensures real-time performance but also enhances the user's sense of presence and spatial perception.

The teleoperation interactive system based on the mixed reality visual enhancement method proposed in this study ensures that users can naturally interact with virtual objects to the greatest extent, reduces learning costs, effectively solves the problem of synchronous reproduction of remote operation scenes, and improves operational efficiency. It has significant application value for remote operation operations in dangerous environments.

References

1. Tachi, S., Inoue, Y., Kato, F.: TELESAR VI: telexistence surrogate anthropomorphic robot VI. Int. J. Hum. Rob. **17**(5), 1–33 (2020)
2. Han, L., Zheng, T., Zhu, Y., et al.: Live semantic 3D perception for immersive augmented reality. IEEE Trans. Vis. Comput. Graph. **26**(5), 2012–2022 (2020)
3. Kastner, L., Lambrecht, J.: Augmented reality based visualization of navigation data of mobile robots on the Microsoft HoloLens - possibilities and limitations. In: IEEE Conference on Cybernetics and Intelligent Systems, Robotics, Automation and Mechatronics. IEEE (2019)
4. Kent, D., Saldanha, C., Chernova, S.: Leveraging depth data in remote robot teleoperation interfaces for general object manipulation. Int. J. Robot. Res. **39**(1), 39–53 (2020)
5. Shin, M., Lee, S., Song, S.W., et al.: Enhancement of perceived body ownership in virtual reality-based teleoperation may backfire in the execution of high-risk tasks. Comput. Hum. Behav. **115**(52), 1–11 (2021)
6. Wang, B., Zhang, R., Xi, C., et al.: Virtual and real-time synchronous interaction for playing table tennis with holograms in mixed reality. Sensors **20**(17), 4857 (2020)
7. Puri, N., Alsadoon, A., Prasad, P.W.C., et al.: Mixed reality using illumination-aware gradient mixing in surgical telepresence: enhanced multi-layer visualization. Multimed. Tools Appl. **81**(1), 1153–1178 (2022)
8. Fang, D., Xu, H., Yang, X., et al.: An augmented reality-based method for remote collaborative real-time assistance: from a system perspective. Mob. Netw. Appl. **25**, 412–425 (2020)
9. Delmerico, J., Poranne, R., Bogo, F., et al.: Spatial computing and intuitive interaction: bringing mixed reality and robotics together. IEEE Robot. Autom. Mag. **29**(1), 45–57 (2022)
10. Ho, S., Liu, P., Palombo, D.J., et al.: The role of spatial ability in mixed reality learning with the HoloLens. Anat. Sci. Educ. (2021)
11. Malaweera, A., Jogi, R., Wright, M., et al.: A mixed-reality holographic viewing platform enabling interaction with 3D electroanatomical maps using the HoloLens. Eur. Heart J. (2021)
12. Hu, F., Deng, Y., Zhou, H., et al.: A vision of an XR-aided teleoperation system toward 5G/B5G. IEEE Commun. Mag. IEEE **59**(1), 34–40 (2021)
13. Sakr, M., Uddin, W., Loos, H.F.M.V.D.: Orthographic vision-based interface with motion-tracking system for robot arm teleoperation: a comparative study, pp. 424–426 (2020)
14. George, J.T., George, M.J.: Human-Computer Interaction Research and Development, pp. 287–300 (2022)
15. Muoz, A., Mahiques, X., Solanes, J.E., et al.: Mixed reality-based user interface for quality control inspection of car body surfaces. J. Manuf. Syst. **53**, 75–92 (2019)
16. Lewis, J.R.: The system usability scale: past, present, and future. Int. J. Hum.-Comput. Interact. **34**(9), 577–590 (2018)
17. Hart, S.G., Staveland, L.E.: Development of NASA-TLX (Task Load Index): results of empirical and theoretical research. Adv. Psychol. **52**(6), 139–183 (1988)

Designing and Evaluating a Virtual Reality Training for Paramedics to Practice Triage in Complex Situations

Paul Vogt[1,4(✉)], Rik Boer[1], Marieke de Boer[2], Hilco Prins[3], Joya Smit[2],
Daan Tuinstra[1], Nick Degens[1], Marike Hettinga[3], and Wolter Paans[2]

[1] Research Group Digital Transformation, Hanze University of Applied Science, Zernikeplein 7, 9747 AS Groningen, The Netherlands
p.a.vogt@rug.nl
[2] Research Group Nursing Diagnostics, Hanze University of Applied Science, Zernikeplein 7, 9747 AS Groningen, The Netherlands
[3] Research Group IT Innovations in Healthcare, Windesheim University of Applied Sciences, Postbus 10090, 8000 GB Zwolle, The Netherlands
[4] Bernoulli Institute for Mathematics, Computer Science and Artificial Intelligence, University of Groningen, Nijenborgh 4, 9747 AG Groningen, The Netherlands

Abstract. Paramedics are often the first to provide medical aid at mass-casualty incidents. These are complex stressful situations where the first paramedics' role is to provide rapid response and perform a triage to classify the urgency of victims needing to go to hospital. As these situations do not occur frequently, Virtual Reality provides a cost-effective manner to frequently train for these incidents. We present a user-centered design approach to design the training, which we evaluated with 32 paramedics and trainers. We integrated the design with developing a business model that we evaluated with ten training coordinators of ambulance services. The evaluation revealed that paramedics were highly motivated during the training and that they rated the training high on user-experience. Trainers indicated that the resulting training can be used in practice; not as a replacement but as an addition to current practices. To conclude, the study reveals that co-developing a VR training with paramedics and their trainers, can yield an effective platform to practice triage in complex situations. While further improvements are necessary, our study not only provides a set training, but also a roadmap for how to design VR training environments for paramedics and possibly other (medical) services.

Keywords: Mass-casualty incident training · Paramedic training · User-centered design

1 Introduction

Providing first medical aid at mass-casualty incidents (MCIs) is hard to train, because these incidents occur infrequently, are costly to simulate in the physical world and most other methods do not offer the immersion and presence that such training would benefit from [1]. Immersion and presence are essential because they provide paramedics the

J. Y. C. Chen and G. Fragomeni (Eds.): HCII 2023, LNCS 14027, pp. 503–522, 2023.
https://doi.org/10.1007/978-3-031-35634-6_36

experience and sensation that help them preparing well for acting effectively in such stressful situations [2]. One crucial aspect of providing emergency care at MCIs is to triage casualties to decide what first aid needs to be provided. In this paper we explain how we designed a training with VR elements and present our evaluation with professional paramedics, their trainers, and heads of training.

1.1 Challenges in Preparing Paramedics for MCIs

Highly complex emergency response situations have a major impact on those involved, bystanders, family members and the emergency services present. Paramedics are one of the first on the scene and must reassure victims and panicked bystanders. At the same time, medical assistance must be offered to victims and bystanders to prevent further incidents from occurring [3].

Incidents can arise from aggression and panic in highly complex situations, because of which people can act erratically and pose a danger to themselves and the environment [4]. The paramedics must have sufficient competences in these and similar situations. A commonly used training for nurses working in hospitals, mental health care, prisons, defense, rehabilitation centers and ambulance centers is simulation education and simulation training [5]. The aim of simulation education is to simulate practical situations, so that knowledge and practical skills can be translated into practice. Typically, these simulations take place in the real world. When situations occur infrequently, such as MCIs, professionals need to practice frequently how to act. Research has shown that re-training the triage at MCIs on a regular (yearly) basis improves preparedness of paramedics [6].

One of the simulation exercises is the re-enactment of major disasters, in which all emergency services are involved. The advantages of a re-enactment of disasters are practicing scenarios at different locations, collaborating with various disciplines, and taking a critical look at one's own actions by means of debriefing [7]. Practicing complex and unpredictable circumstances realistically is a costly affair and is sometimes not feasible with the resources available for education. One of the drawbacks of these practices is that they are costly in both time and resources and lotus victims rarely act like actual victims [1]. Also, not every situation can be simulated with high fidelity, which means that simulation training can feel unrealistic for the paramedic. However, fidelity of simulations plays a crucial role in the effectiveness of the training [8].

Alternatives to simulating major disasters in real-life include Virtual Simulations (VS). While VS may include simulations in VR using a headset, they more often refer to screen-based simulations [9–11]. While screen-based VS tend to be highly effective, they lack the level of immersion that can be achieved by VR headsets [12]. Various studies have investigated how VR may support training paramedics for their behavior at MCIs (e.g., [2, 12–14]). Most studies focused on training of the triage, and generally found little differences in the efficacy between standard simulation training and VR simulation training [1, 14]. Moreover, a meta-analysis found that VR was more effective than their controls in terms of knowledge-gain, while they performed similarly to their controls concerning skills, satisfaction, confidence, and performance time [15]. In addition, research has shown that learning in a virtual environment increases paramedics' motivation and attitude, which contributes to wanting to actively participate in training [16].

So, while these studies demonstrate that VR is an effective tool to simulate training of nurses and paramedics, the costs of carrying out a VR training is much lower than real-life training, especially with head-mounted displays becoming increasingly available [1, 17]. Since VR gives users a high sense of immersion and presence during simulation, making the training feel more real, this could become a mainstream method to train paramedics. The challenge remains how to design and develop a VR training that is acceptable, effective and has high fidelity. Also, important is the question how the VR can be implemented within the organization of the ambulance care.

1.2 Didactive Considerations

To design adequate education material for paramedics (or any other professional in general), it is important to have a good sense of the background and profession of the target population. Certified paramedics in the Netherlands are nurses with a bachelor's degree in nursing or in medical assistance supplemented with a specialized training of seven months. The Dutch Individual Health Care Professions Act[1] must promote the quality of care provided by professionals. The law also intends to protect patients or clients against improper or negligent actions by healthcare providers.

The profession of paramedics has been formally described in the Netherlands [18] and centers around the seven CanMEDS (Canadian Medical Education Directions for Specialists [19]) –a framework that describes the core competences a paramedic should have in terms of seven CanMEDS roles: Caregiver, Communicator, Collaborative Partner, Reflective Professional, Health Promoter, Organizer and Professional and Quality Promoter. These CanMEDS roles form the foundation of the further education of paramedics, and so it is essential that these competences can be trained within our VR training module.

It is also important to realize that older adults with professional experience learn differently from younger adults because they have an already built-up frame of reference, and they developed a professional identity [20]. Adult students experience different emotions while learning and combine their studies with work and/or family. The professional identity reflects how they see themselves as professionals, what values and norms they consider are important for practicing their profession and what image they have of themselves. The frame of reference of paramedics is shaped by previous experiences in education, work, and life, which ensures a critical look at training. Training should be of added value and in line with their (future) professional practice. Apart from the critical view, learning ability plays a major role in the composition of education for the adult target group.

Illeris's [21] learning theory describes different dimensions of learning and aligns with the adult's frame of reference. The following dimensions should be considered when designing good teaching: *learning content, interaction,* and *incentive.* Learning content includes that which is to be learned. The interaction dimension indicates how the adult student interacts with his social and societal environment during learning. The final dimension, incentive, involves the incentives, emotions, motivation, and resistance

---

[1] In Dutch: *Wet BIG.* https://www.igj.nl/onderwerpen/wetten-in-ons-toezicht/wet-big.

that plays a role in learning. Figure 1 provides a schematic representation of how these dimensions are connected and influence each other.

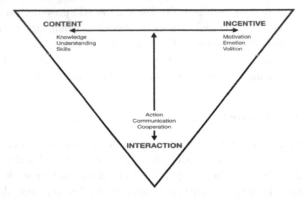

Fig. 1. Illeris' three dimensions of learning (adapted from [20]).

Besides shaping the learning content, how paramedics want to learn was examined. Knowles, Holton and Swanson's [22] model stemming from andragogy best aligns with how paramedics want to learn. Andragogy is a scientific discipline that focuses on adult education. This model indicates how the characteristics of adult learning affect the learning goals of the education offered. Knowles shifted the focus from the teacher to the student (learner). In addition, he uses learning principles that apply to adults. Self-direction or making their own choices that are in line with their experience (knowledge and skills) contribute to learning participation. Relevance, orientation and motivation are the final principles within andragogy in practice [22].

Because motivation is reflected in the learning theory of Illeris and the model of Knowles, it is important to give it a prominent place in the education to be developed. The educational model, called ARCS-model (attention, relevance, confidence, satisfaction) [23], is a learning motivation model and focuses on students' motivation and readiness [24]. The four components from the ARCS-model contribute to creating motivation.

1.3 Business Perspective

To develop a VR training that can be used in practice by ambulance services, the business perspective must also be considered. Lehoux et al. [25] show the close relationship between the business model, the value proposition of an innovation and the stakeholders for whom value is created and to whom value is offered. The business and technology development processes they observed were characterized by reciprocal adjustments. Technology development and business case development go hand in hand. That is why in this project from start to finish technology development and business case development formed input for each other, with mutual adjustments being made to each other.

In the remainder of this paper, we first outline the process and results of designing the VR training. Next, we present the methods and results of our evaluation study. This is followed by a discussion and concluding remarks.

2 Designing VR Training for Paramedics

We took a user-centered design (USD) approach to develop a prototype for this training, following the main principles of Design Thinking [26]. To achieve this, we applied a co-creation, scrum-like design cycle in which we iterated roughly in the following four steps (Fig. 2): 1) The project team (nurse educators, USD researchers, health-care IT researchers, and IT developers) and users (paramedics and their trainers) defined a joint vision on the end-product, resulting in a roadmap. 2) The project team and users agreed on concrete actions to take in the developmental phase, yielding a backlog list. 3) The project executed the developmental actions, while having multiple standups. 4) The users (i.e., paramedics and trainers) verified and (dis)approved the prototype during the sprint review.

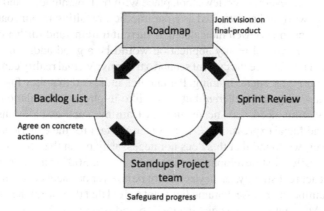

Fig. 2. The scrum-like design cycle to design the VR training for paramedics.

Because designers know that VR does not only work on the basis of literature and expert knowledge, we wanted to involve the user intensively and let their wishes be leading [27]. We took an agile approach and allowed the user to experience and test multiple prototypes. Eventually, this would save more time than the cost of an additional iteration, because it results in having the user become the owner of the decision process and the technology is thus not pushed.

It is, however, difficult for paramedics to indicate what they want when they have no expert knowledge about the possibilities in VR. Yet, building a prototype without the knowledge of what it is supposed to do is also hard. By taking time and space to develop and adjust prototypes, adding new functionality, and demonstrate these to the users, one can solve this chicken-and-egg issue faster than organizing many brainstorm sessions. The mindset of the developer should be "I'll quickly make something, so you can see …" During our design process, we realized that paramedics think in protocols, the creative industry thinks in possibilities, and developers think in tasks. These three worlds and the three languages that accompany them need to be translated. We gave ample attention to this during the development process.

We gave the users ownership of the development by asking them to direct the progress of the scrum-sprints and have the designers follow them. In the scrum-like design cycle, next steps were only taken after approval of the paramedics, yielding the end-product in five sprints of eight weeks each.

In the remainder of this section, we first detail the roadmap thus achieved, after which we explain the development of the business case, as this adds to some design requirements for the final training. We end by explaining the developed of the end-product. We mostly provide our explanations without referring to intermediate results of the individual sprints.

2.1 Constructing the Roadmap

Motivating paramedics is reflected in the requirements of the users of the VR education tool. To find out what the design criteria are from the mindset of the paramedics, for the VR education tool, several interviews took place with both paramedics and their trainers (who often also work or have worked as a paramedic), resulting in our roadmap.

All paramedics interviewed indicated that current training and further education are well established. A virtual reality application would be a good addition to the current offer and should not replace the current scenario training. Virtual reality can contribute to the realistic nature of scenario training. Paramedics indicated that they find it difficult to empathize in a setting that feels *real* but is not, like in physical simulations. Interviews indicate that victims need realistic features in training, such as emotions, behavioral expressions, and facial expressions. *Realness* is important for the experience of a virtual world. However, we found that this does not necessarily mean that the world should be photorealistic. After first developing a prototype using a 360° camera, paramedics felt they could not act realistically, as they could not bend over or kneel beside the victim, nor could they examine their pulse. Paramedics want to feel that they are at the location where the victim is. Ambient sounds, social interaction and haptic feedback contribute to this. Making the experience as real as possible contributes to the user's learning experience. Users need to experience the feeling of *being there* (presence) before acceptance of the virtual world as being real (suspension of disbelief) can take place. The realistic factor is what paramedics consider essential for training.

A study by Kampling [28] focusing on the role of individual learning with VR found that it can enhance learning if an immersive environment is used. The importance of environment is emphasized. Immersive environment can include the clinical image of a victim. Another systematic literature review [29] examines exercises in nursing education through human simulation. Here, the training environment is also emphasized. To make it as realistic as possible, these took place in a clinical setting, among others. This motivates students to respond to real-life situations. These outcomes support the importance of a realistic environment.

Another form of realism is returning to the method for clinical reasoning of the paramedic. The ABCDE model is a methodology used during primary assessment, focusing on life-threatening abnormalities [30], and used by Dutch paramedics. For proper primary assessment, the clinical picture of the victims is very important. A lot of information can be recalled from the clinical picture [31]. Paramedics indicated that they particularly want to see external features and symptoms that fit the clinical picture in the training. By using realistic clinical images, diagnosis can be well trained during virtual reality training.

Not all aspects of the training, however, should be realistic. Literature reveals that learning under time pressure does not benefit the mastery of new skills [32]. So, while paramedics are under a lot of time pressure in real-life situations, trainers and paramedics preferred not to have to operate within a given time while practicing.

Another requirement for use is that it is user-friendly, or in other words no complicated instructions for use. From a didactic point of view, people indicate that it should match their skill-level, so setting a difficulty level is desirable. Also the possibility of using the VR training tool for multiple purposes (individual, in duos or classroom) was considered important.

Paramedics indicated that they want to know why they need to learn something, understanding of importance is a key driver. Briefing the paramedic about the training and their learning goals –as set by the trainer, often in consultation with the trainee– is therefore instrumental to achieve this. Receiving effective and regular feedback is crucial to learning, encourages self-reflection, and stimulates the learner in their learning process [33]. Feedback can be given during the VR practice, but the question was how frequent this should happen. Tests revealed that this distracted the trainee when this occurred after each classification of a virtual patient. Showing feedback immediately after the final victim was classified was judged better, but in the implemented version this included visiting all victims again, which the paramedics did not like in the end. It was therefore decided to provide feedback after the session in VR, together with an opportunity for self-reflection and consulting with the trainer if so desired.

2.2 Developing the Business Case

In this study we investigated which factors contribute to the implementation and long-term use of VR training by ambulance services for their employees. At the start we held interviews with five heads of learning & development departments of ambulance services. We developed a questionnaire with 20 open questions based on the S(ervice)T(echnology)O(rganization)F(inance) model [34] in combination with phases of technology development for eHealth, the eHix [35]. The interviews were recorded and then analyzed by placing relevant comments and statements in the CANVAS business model [36].

Regarding the value proposition, respondents think that use of VR can contribute to the organizations' vision on ambulance care training. They strive for practice-based, personified, teacher-independent, blended learning, learning together and ownership to the learner. Practice based learning means learning in a realistic learning environment and going through the cycle of doing, experiencing, reflecting and feedback. Respondents would like to see that the VR training focuses on components that now receive less attention and situations that cannot easily be trained with other means, such as soft skills, rare situations, and upscaling. They also find dealing with distracting and dangerous circumstances extremely suitable for VR. Respondents find it important that the VR training can be embedded in working processes and linked to IT systems. Both in terms of terminology and in terms of content, the VR training must fit with professional requirements and tasks, the CanMEDS roles and learning objectives. It must be provided with teaching materials and lesson plan. For accreditation, it should be possible to automatically register the credits and training hours of employees. Insights and procedures are changing rapidly in the world of ambulance care, which means that maintenance and organization of updates will have to be a major part of the service.

Regarding the business case, a distinction should be made between individual, duo and team use. In the case of individual or duo (couple of nurse and ambulance driver) use, scarce ambulance personnel need to be scheduled less for training days, making them more employable. During the service, individuals or duos can train independently at times when no effort is required, even during evening, night, or weekend shifts. In the case of team use, savings can be made if it leads to substitution of more expensive training courses. With VR it should be possible to get more out of or save on expensive large-scale simulation exercises on location. It provides the opportunity for preparation, practice and repetition of all roles, thereby increasing learning outcomes. In addition, the respondents refer to the shortage of personnel. Learning with the help of new technology such as VR appeals to young people. This is strategically important in times of high staff shortages.

2.3   The Design of the VR Training

The design process resulted after five iterations in a prototype training that not only involved an immersive VR experience, but also a learning environment that facilitates a briefing and debriefing of the training that runs on a laptop computer or PC (Fig. 3). This system is designed such that 1) a trainee can take a lesson, 2) a trainer can provide feedback, and 3) a trainer can design a lesson. Lessons can be taken and designed for a single trainee, a duo, or a group of trainees. In the latter two cases, communication, observation, and group-based feedback can become a major part of the learning goals. To facilitate all this, the VR-experience relates to an online database containing the design of the lesson and a history of performance that is constructed during the VR-experience. This database thus takes input from the trainer and provides output for the debriefing.

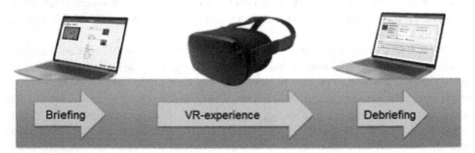

Fig. 3. The three phases in training.

The briefing module can be accessed with a personal account. Once inside, the trainee can choose a lesson, (re-)read feedback, rehearse the triage protocols, and gets informed about the lesson itself. The trainer can, prior to the trainee accessing the system, write feedback about the previous lesson, prepare a new lesson for the trainee, and write questions to be answered during debriefing. To develop a training, the following parameters can be set in the database:

- the specific environment (currently indoors/outdoors),
- the number of victims (1–6),
- type of symptoms per victim (heart rate, bleeding wounds, breathing, etc.),
- the number of bystanders (numeric),
- background noise from environment (on/off),
- background noise from sirens (on/off),
- background noise and visual images from an overhanging helicopter (on/off),
- presence of fog (on/off – outdoors only).

These settings are typically set by the trainer based on the trainee's skill level. The trainer can also specify the learning objectives, and whether the training is carried out by an individual, a duo or a group. The briefing module informs the trainee about the learning objectives.

After the briefing, the trainee experiences the VR exercise with the aim to correctly triage all victims and communicate this to the emergency center through a virtual transceiver, which is recorded in the database so trainees can listen to their own communication afterwards. When practicing in a duo or a group, communication may support collaboration. Prior to starting the practical exercise in VR, trainees can carry out a VR tutorial to learn about the controls, how to navigate the environment and how to perform the activities for carrying out the triage. This tutorial is essential for onboarding the trainees and can be done multiple times until the trainees is confident to practice. We also built in a start check to verify whether the trainee still masters the necessary skills in VR before they start their exercise.

To carry out the exercise, the trainee moves through the environment (either walking or using the joystick) searching for victims (Fig. 4). When a victim is found, the trainee can examine the victim by sight (visual injuries shown as bleeding wounds), by measuring the pulse (a vibration in the controller signals heartbeats when the wrist or neck is touched and a wristwatch indicates time; Fig. 5), or examining breathing (heard when ear is near the victim's mouth or seen by movements in the victim's chest). Based on this examination, the trainee decides whether a direct medical response should be taken (e.g. placing a tourniquet to stop bleeding or performing a chin lift to open the victim's airway), and what triage classification should be provided by placing the appropriate wristband or 'slapwrap' (choice between red/T1 –urgent to hospital, yellow/T2 –not urgent but to hospital, green/T3 –wounded but not to hospital, and white –death). After that, the trainee should communicate the location and classification through the transponder and move on to find the next victim.

When a bystander is visible, the paramedic can signal it to come over and stay with the victim. We decided against verbal communication to and from the virtual characters to avoid technical issues in natural language processing –something that various paramedics regretted. Instead they could "point and direct" bystanders to help, a solution we found after numerous iterations and which paramedics appreciated. Once the trainee believes all victims were triaged, they could stop the VR-experience.

After the exercise, the trainee would take the debriefing on the laptop. Here they receive feedback from the system about the correctness of the triage. They can also

Fig. 4. A 360° view of the virtual indoor environment.

Fig. 5. A paramedic examining the heart rate by 'touching' the victim's wrist, and feeling the controller vibrate with the heart rate's frequency while timing using his wristwatch.

listen to their own voice recordings, see the victim with classification, answer questions posed by the trainer, and provide a written self-reflection. Based on the written feedback, the trainer can provide additional feedback.

A didactive learning cycle is constructed that allows the trainee to redo the VR-experience in case they feel not yet competent. Paramedics considered it extremely important that trainers could only see their performance of the final practices after their own approval—trainees are in the lead of their training. However, the trainer can decide that the trainee should redo the training or decide to move on to a next level.

3   Evaluation Methods

The resulting VR training has been evaluated among professional paramedics and trainers from several ambulance service centers throughout the Netherlands. For this evaluation, we have set up one single lesson with 6 victims in an indoor setting. All noises were turned on, except the helicopter's sound. In addition, we evaluated our business model with training program representatives of different ambulance services. In this section, we describe the evaluation methods.

3.1 Participants

We recruited 32 paramedics (12 females) from five different regional ambulance services in the Netherlands to evaluate our training with VR elements (briefing, VR experience and debriefing). Five participants were also a trainer in their regional service organization. In total, four discontinued their training due to motion sickness. The remaining 28 participants completed the entire training and provided input for our evaluation.

3.2 Materials

To evaluate the training, we asked all participants to fill out a questionnaire composed of the Reduced Instructional Materials Motivation Survey (RIMMS) [37] and the short User Experience Questionnaire (UEQ-s) [38] on a 5-point scale (Cronbach alpha's > 0.72 for all categories). Additional questions probed for participants' behavioral intention and to provide free text comments.

The reason for using these tools was to obtain a good indication about the way paramedics were engaged in the training: the RIMMS is particularly suited to measure motivation that participants feel, and the UEQ measures the user-experience (UX) of working through the training. The RIMMS contains questions concerning the four different dimensions of the ARCS model, which formed the didactic basis of the training, to evaluate the participants' motivation in the training activity [23, 24].

The UEQ-s contains questions about five different dimensions (attractiveness, efficiency, novelty, perspicuity, and stimulation) that, combined, indicate how well users rate the application's use and feel. When the training has a positive UX, the motivation to engage in the training is high and helps to focus on the training itself rather than having to focus on how to use the application. High scores of both tools suggest that users are highly engaged with the training, which in turn tends to contribute to effective learning [21–23].

Trainer Perspective

To evaluate the trainer's perspective, we held semi-structured interviews with the five trainers that participated in this evaluation. These interviews were carried out using an interview-guide including questions about how trainers experienced the training method we developed; to what extent they would want to incorporate this training in their institute, and to what extent this training should become part of the standard training for paramedics.

3.3 Procedure

Trainee Test Procedure

Participating paramedics were mostly visited at their own organization-unit, but three of them visited our location. After obtaining informed consent, participants were asked to fill in a short survey about prior experiences with using VR and with carrying out triage in complex situations, and they were given some information about the procedure. After this, they started the briefing part of the training. Following this, we provided them with the VR headset and hand controllers and helped to start a short manual explaining them how to carry out the different elements withing VR. During this introduction, paramedics could ask all kinds of questions. When they finished the manual, they could start the VR experience part of the training. To provide all participants with the same situation, we had set the environment to indoors, the number of casualties to six and having six dynamic (i.e. moving) bystanders.

We instructed the participants to continue the training until they believed they have classified all six casualties in the building. They could also stop their training whenever they wanted, for example in case they would experience motion sickness. Once they finished the VR experience, they were asked to complete the training by going through the debriefing module.

Finally, after the entire training was completed, participants were asked to fill out the survey, consisting of the RIMMS, UEQ-s and behavioral intention surveys.

Trainer Procedure

The five trainers received an additional demonstration of the entire module prior to experience the VR training themselves. This demonstration included a presentation concerning the objective of the training tool and what kind of features the tool included, focusing especially on how the trainers can use them in their own practice. This also contained a hands-on practice to set up a training session for a random trainee.

After this demonstration, the trainers received the same training as described in the trainee procedure, including filling out the survey. Finally, this was followed by the semi-structured interview.

3.4 Evaluation Business Model

The VR-training was also evaluated from the business perspective. Based on the prototype, an estimate of financial costs and benefits was drawn up from a business perspective and interviews were conducted with ten program representatives individually after demonstration of the prototype. During the interviews, questions were asked about strengths and weaknesses of the VR training, and opportunities and threats for application within ambulance services. The business case was submitted for verification. Finally, questions were asked about implementation. This provided input for a 'definitive' business case and implementation roadmap.

4   Evaluation Results

4.1   Survey Results

Participants were highly motivated: on average, they scored high on all constructs in the RIMMS (Fig. 6, left), demonstrating that the participants felt that the experience raised their attention and confidence in the training, which they rated as being relevant and satisfactory. The scores for each construct were equal around 4 with standard deviations smaller than 1. This shows that participants rate the training higher than what would be expected at random.

Participants scored similarly high on the UEQ-s (Fig. 6, right), showing that they found the experience attractive, efficient, novel, perspicuous and stimulating. Here too, all participants scored around 4 on all constructs with standard deviations smaller than 1. We see a little bit more variation in the scores with novelty scoring highest and perspicuity lowest. However, these differences are not statistically significant.

On average, participants rated the behavioral intention questions whether they would like to take the training again with a score of 4.1 and whether they would recommend the training tool to colleagues a score of 4.2. This confirms their overall interest in using this tool to improve their triaging skills.

Responses to the final open-ended question confirmed these findings, highlighting that most paramedics perceived the training likeable, innovative, and instructive. Some stressed the importance of being guided by human trainers, while at the same time stressing the added value. As one respondent wrote "Very nice to do but decent guidance is necessary... according to me [this training] has an added value to the schooling within the ambulance care." Other participants indicated possible future improvements, such as adding more variability in ways to examine the virtual casualties and symptoms they can have. One example for improvement is the inclusion of verbal communication, as this allows the paramedic to examine whether the victim is conscious and communicative. Finally, one respondent who completed the training indicated to suffer from motion sickness, "so this [training] is totally not for me."

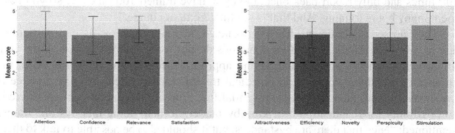

Fig. 6. Barplots showing the mean scores for each construct of the RIMMS questionnaire (left) and the UEQ-s (right). Error-bars indicate standard deviations.

4.2 Trainer's Views

Semi-structured interviews with trainers further confirmed the potential of this approach. They confirmed that the training is highly realistic, motivation inducing and instructive for learning the appropriate triage skills. This would be useful to train how to act in MCIs. They indicated that they would use it; not (yet) in replacement of practicing in the physical world, but as an additional format that can be utilized more frequently to keep up and improve their skills. In the physical world, you can for instance practice with a lotus subject or a manikin, which makes certain activities more realistic.

Multiple trainers stress the ability to train in small groups and for training during the waiting times between two responses, which makes the training more flexible. As one respondent said "It is just a new opportunity… [T]he nice thing is that you can now also practice in your own waiting times. You can then do this with two or three persons."

The advantage of training in duos or groups is stressed multiple times, because this way you can learn from each other. Although it is possible to see what the person doing the VR-experience sees through an external monitor, it is in the current product not possible to experience the VR part of the training by acting in a team. One trainer suggested that "[i]t would be nice if you could do this as a team. That you can see each other and that you can complement each other, because that is daily practice."

The trainers were also considering how they would incorporate this training into the education within their ambulance care service. "If I would apply this in our schooling, … I would train the scenarios in the morning … with a video monitor so [other trainees] can see how one reacts [in VR] … and then change [who works with VR]. Then you would have a very nice training."

The trainers also very much like the debriefing module. The fact that you receive effective feedback on performance and that you can listen to your own communication is much appreciated. However, one trainer indicated that not everyone is open to self-reflection. Some are very open and willing to improve, others are reluctant and not open to self-reflection, especially older paramedics as they have little experience and say 'we used to do this without self-reflection, so why should I bother'. One trainer also liked the ability to repeat the training before reporting back to the trainer: "Even if you train 100 times and only report back once, then you have trained 100 times … so you have spent many hours training. And that is the final goal, of course."

They do see some downsides. For instance, not every paramedic can participate due to motion sickness. Some functionalities do not work smoothly, such as the chin lift, which is hard to achieve and has no appropriate follow-up procedure. Also, the number of possible symptoms and medical treatments that often occur in practice is somewhat limited, though the most essential functions are there. For example, there is no possibility for reanimation or asking bystanders to help doing this. As one trainer mentioned: "Nice that there are bystanders, but it should also be possible to talk to them and give instructions (for example to help with reanimating victims, something that happens in practice)".

4.3 Business Case Evaluation

By providing input for the development of the VR training from a business perspective, it was possible (with greater certainty) to respond to the vision and views of training managers about the (future) training of ambulance service providers. Desired concepts in this context, such as flexible learning, personalized learning, blended learning, work-based learning, learning in a professional context, ownership by learners, more attention to 'soft' competences and training of rare situations that are otherwise difficult to simulate, were very recognizable in the chosen design. The possibility to deploy the training individually, as well as in duos and groups, was much appreciated and gives the opportunity to tailor the training to the organization.

Wishes collected at the beginning of the project were largely recognized in the prototype. After seeing the prototype, not only did they realize that the application fits their vision of learning, but also that the application can be an attractive means to give concrete shape to their vision of learning in practice. It is not always easy to break through existing ideas about learning and replace them with new ones. Applications that respond to changing vision can offer added value for decision makers.

It is also important that the effort can be raised from the budgets reserved for training. Substituting other, more costly forms of education, using downtime hours, saving on extra expenses such as travel and accommodation costs and obtaining extra resources or subsidies (e.g. in the context of innovation) can offer solace here. However, the managers have different view on the possibilities of saving costs through VR training. For example, not every manager sees much room to save on downtime hours.

For the purpose of implementation, it is also important, given the high costs and impact, to convince and align all stakeholders with regard to purchasing decisions: management, financial department/purchasing, ICT department and, very importantly, the trainers who have to work with it and to motivate their students. The trainers are key-users, and they must be enthusiastic, otherwise it has little chance of success. It is also important to embed VR training in training policy and program.

In addition, having a link to a Learning Management System and availability within one platform with other eLearning tools is desirable. Technically it should just work, too many hitches are disastrous for use. It should also require little preparation before working with it. Proper setup and testing at the place where it is used is therefore important.

5 Discussion

5.1 User-Centered Approach

We designed the training using a user-centered approach in a scrum-like manner with five design cycles that lasted eight weeks each. However, we did not focus too much on the users, but more on the collaborative aspect of the process. To achieve this, we gave the end-users, training coordinators, trainers and paramedics, the lead in our scrum-sessions. In our opinion, this facilitated deciding what was interesting to develop, and what were the necessary and desirable ingredients that the training should have. We as researchers and designers took a subordinate role in the scrum sessions to avoid directing the design too much. Moreover, we believe that visiting them at their ambulance care services, rather than asking them to visit our premises, was important to allow them to show their work and have them feel at ease during the design process, something they are not accustomed to.

Working with a multi-disciplinary design team involving nurse educators, user-centered design researchers, health-care IT researchers, and IT developers made that we could communicate well with the different stakeholders and translate the language from the world of paramedics to the world of VR design and back. To achieve the latter, we often rapidly designed some prototypical features to demonstrate what could be done in VR and what the consequence of certain design decisions would be in VR. This way, paramedics and their trainers not familiar with VR became aware of the possibilities and limitations of the VR technology.

5.2 Evaluation Findings

Results indicate that paramedics rate our VR training very high on motivation factors measured by the RIMMS and on user-experience measured by the UEQ-s. This may be surprising, but it is not because the training was carefully designed in a process where the users took the lead in what it should contain. Furthermore, we based our design for motivation in training on the ARCS model [23], which is also the basis for the RIMMS questionnaire [37]. Moreover, during the design we had iterations with rapid prototyping to demonstrate and test the look and feel of the training, focusing on the needs and desires of the paramedics and trainers involved in the process, which gave rise to the high user-experience rating. While this makes sense, some caution is in place, because for most participants in the evaluation, experience in VR –and our VR training in particular—was new. As a result, the high ratings might be caused by the novelty effect [39], and it is important to investigate whether similarly high rates are achieved when evaluating the training over multiple sessions. The reason we did not do this was a lack of resources from both the research team and the ambulance services.

We decided not to evaluate the training on achieving effectiveness in learning, because there is a lot of variation in experience and skills within the ambulance services that facilitated our evaluation study. While some studies demonstrated the potential of high learning gain using VR, these typically involved student paramedics in comparison to live training in classrooms [1, 14]. Koutitas and colleagues [13] found that VR training among professional paramedics improved their accuracy in first respondence and speed in executing tasks considerably in a real-world simulation training. Although we did not measure effectiveness, we are optimistic that our training is effective for improving the trained skills. The reason for this optimism is the didactic approach we took stimulating, among others, students' intrinsic motivations based on the ARCS model that was rated highly in the evaluation. However, a verification would be desirable in a future study, which should also involve evaluating the effectiveness on the long run with paramedics engaging in the training multiple times.

Paramedics and trainers were very enthusiastic about the training and indicated they would want to use it in practice but provided some suggestions for improvement. These focused on including more functionalities in terms of medical examination, improvements of existing functions like the hard-to-use chin lift, and the ability to communicate verbally with victims and bystanders. Trainers offered ideas how to incorporate the VR training in practice. One possibility would be that paramedics can practice the triage during waiting hours between calls. This would allow them to train for many hours, which would improve their skills. However, a potential downside is that immersion in VR may cause cybersickness or after-effects in the perceptuomotor system that could influence how well a person acts after their VR-experience [40, 41]. Such after-effects could prevent paramedics from acting effectively when called to an emergency during the VR-experience. Further research is required to investigate to what extent such after-effects of using VR would influence urgent responses in the real-world and how to remedy these, if possible. Allowing for dedicated training time –e.g., as part of the standard schooling– is therefore recommended for the moment.

5.3 Towards a Business Case

Simultaneously with the development of the VR application, we have started investigating the requirements from the business perspective so that this can serve as input for the development. This interactive method means that the implementation issue is still evolving. Important issue in the short term is ownership of the application and in the long-term multiplayer opportunities with other first responders such as police and firefighters.

As far as follow-up is concerned, it seems to be difficult to find a party that wants to continue the 'proof on concept' to a 'minimal viable product'. We are also dealing with the 'valley of death' phenomenon: the gap between academic-based innovations and their commercial application in the marketplace [42]. Ambulance services and partnerships between them do not see further development, maintenance, expansion, and associated services as their 'core business'. They naturally want to remain closely involved in further development. Ambulance services would therefore like to see a party that is already familiar with and already has a platform for digital learning resources within the industry as the 'publisher/supplier' of the product. Several innovative ambulance services could play a pioneering role in further development. Respondents suggest that the regional 'GHOR' (the Dutch 'Medical Assistance Organization in the Region') might want to contribute to investments if this would benefit large-scale medical assistance in disasters.

6 Conclusions

In this paper, we present a design study for developing and evaluating a training with VR elements for paramedics to practice triage in complex situations as occur in mass-casualty incidents. The system is designed such that trainers can construct training program personalized to individual paramedics. The development took a user-centered design approach with a multi-disciplinary team where the users (paramedics and trainers) took the lead in design during our scrum-like sessions with researchers, nurse educators, IT specialists and business developers took a more subordinate role in these sessions.

The evaluation of the training was received well by the users and other stakeholders, such as training coordinators and managers, both concerning the training itself and the business case around it. The training is rated high on motivation and user-experience. Although we did not measure effectiveness, these findings indicate a high potential for effective training. Moreover, our business model provides a framework for implementation in the professional education within the ambulance case services.

While further improvements are necessary, our study not only provides a set training, but also a roadmap for how to design VR training environments for paramedics and possibly other (medical) services.

Acknowledgements. This project, called VRAMBO, was funded by the Dutch Regieorgaan SIA with a RAAK public grant (nr RAAK.PUB05.037) and received additional funding from the AXIRA network of several ambulance services. We thank our consortium partners from WildSea BV and regional ambulance services Ambulancezorg Groningen, Kijlstra Personenvervoer & Ambulancegroep Fryslân, RAV IJsselland. We are also grateful for the invaluable contributions by Chris Dijksterhuis, Bram Oosting and Harmen de Weerd. Finally, we thank all other people who contributed to this study.

References

1. Mills, B., et al.: Virtual reality triage training can provide comparable simulation efficacy for paramedicine students compared to live simulation-based scenarios. Prehospital Emerg. Care **24**(4), 525–536 (2020)
2. Berndt, H., Wessel, D., Mentler, T., Herczeg, M.: Human-centered design of a virtual reality training simulation for mass casualty incidents. In: 2018 10th International Conference on Virtual Worlds and Games for Serious Applications (VS-Games). IEEE (2018)
3. Bosse, T., Gerritsen, C., de Man, J., Treur, J.: Towards virtual training of emotion regulation. Brain Inform. **1**(1–4), 27–37 (2014). https://doi.org/10.1007/s40708-014-0004-9
4. Pourshaikhian, M., Gorji, H.A., Aryankhesal, A., Khorasani-Zavareh, D., Barati, A.: A systematic literature review: workplace violence against emergency medical services personnel. Arch. Trauma Res. **5**(1) (2016)
5. Sanford, P.G.: Simulation in nursing education: a review of the research. Qual. Rep. **15**(4), 1006 (2010)
6. Dittmar, M.S., Wolf, P., Bigalke, M., Graf, B.M., Birkholz, T.: Primary mass casualty incident triage: evidence for the benefit of yearly brief re-training from a simulation study. Scand. J. Trauma Resuscitation Emerg. Med. **26**(1), 1–8 (2018)
7. Roes, L., De Schepper, S., Franck, E.: Naar een veiligere patiëntenzorg: Crew Resource Management tijdens urgenties (2017)
8. Wheeler, B., Dippenaar, E.: The use of simulation as a teaching modality for paramedic education: a scoping review. Br. Paramedic J. **5**(3), 31–43 (2020)
9. Verkuyl, M., Mastrilli, P.: Virtual simulations in nursing education: a scoping review. J. Nurs. Health Sci. **3**(2), 39–47 (2017)
10. Foronda, C.L., Fernandez-Burgos, M., Nadeau, C., Kelley, C.N., Henry, M.N.: Virtual simulation in nursing education: a systematic review spanning 1996 to 2018. Simul. Healthcare **15**(1), 46–54 (2020)
11. Dolan, H., Amidon, B.J., Gephart, S.M.: Evidentiary and theoretical foundations for virtual simulation in nursing education. J. Prof. Nurs. **37**(5), 810–815 (2021)
12. Farra, S.L., Miller, E.T., Hodgson, E.: Virtual reality disaster training: Translation to practice. Nurse Educ. Pract. **15**(1), 53–57 (2015)

13. Koutitas, G., Smith, S., Lawrence, G.: Performance evaluation of AR/VR training technologies for EMS first responders. Virtual Reality **25**(1), 83–94 (2020). https://doi.org/10.1007/s10055-020-00436-8

14. Wiese, L.K., Love, T., Goodman, R.: Responding to a simulated disaster in the virtual or live classroom: Is there a difference in BSN student learning? Nurse Educ. Pract. **55**, 103170 (2021)

15. Chen, F.-Q., et al.: Effectiveness of virtual reality in nursing education: meta-analysis. J. Med. Internet Res. **22**(9), e18290 (2020). https://doi.org/10.2196/18290

16. Park, Y.J.: Policy game, online game-simulated: applying the ecology of policy game to virtual world. Commun. Teach. **26**, 45–49 (2015)

17. Farra, S.L., et al.: Comparative cost of virtual reality training and live exercises for training hospital workers for evacuation. Comput. Inform. Nurs. **37**(9), 446 (2019)

18. V&VN Beroepsvereniging van beroepsprofessionals: Expertisegebied ambulanceverpleegkundigen (2015). ISBN/EAN 978-90-78995-21-0

19. Frank, J.R., Deborah, D.: The CanMEDS initiative: implementing an outcomes-based framework of physician competencies. Med. Teach. **29**(7), 642–647 (2007)

20. Bolhuis, S.M.: Leren en veranderen bij volwassenen: een nieuwe benadering (Ser. Volwasseneneducatie, dl. 2). Coutinho (1995)

21. Illeris, K.: How We Learn: Learning and Non-Learning in School and Beyond, 2nd edn. Routledge, Taylor & Francis Group (2017)

22. Knowles, M.S., Holton, E.F., Swanson, R.A.: The Adult Learner: The Definitive Classic in Adult Education and Human Resource Development, 6th edn. Elsevier (2015)

23. Keller, J.M.: Motivational Design for Learning and Performance: The ARCS Model Approach, 1st edn. Springer, New York (2010)

24. Shu, Y., Chen, Y.J., Huang, T.C.: Exploring the future of nursing education: an integrated motivation learning model based on virtual reality. J. Nurs. **66**(2), 22–28 (2019)

25. Lehoux, P., Daudelin, G., Williams-Jones, B., Denis, J.-L., Longo, C.: How do business model and health technology design influence each other? Insights from a longitudinal case study of three academic spin-offs. Res. Policy **43**(6), 1025–1038 (2014)

26. Brown, T.: Design thinking. Harvard Bus. Rev. **86**(6), 84 (2008)

27. Loup-Escande, E., Burkhardt, J.M., Christmann, O., Richir, S.: Needs' elaboration between users, designers and project leaders: analysis of a design process of a virtual reality-based software. Inf. Softw. Technol. **56**(8), 1049–1061 (2014)

28. Kampling, H.: The role of immersive virtual reality in individual learning. In: Proceedings of the 51st Hawaii International Conference on System Sciences (2018)

29. Brewer, E.P.: Successful techniques for using human patient simulation in nursing education. J. Nurs. Scholarsh. **43**(3), 311–317 (2011)

30. Klijn, A., Knarren, L., Nguyen, N., Olgers, T.J., Veldhuyzen, C.J.H.: Opvang instabiele patiënt - Het Acute Boekje (2017)

31. Bakker, M., van Heycop ten Ham, C.: Klinisch redeneren in zes stappen, 2de editie. Boom Lemma (2014)

32. Beck, J.W., Schmidt, A.M.: State-level goal orientations as mediators of the relationship between time pressure and performance: a longitudinal study. J. Appl. Psychol. **98**(2), 354 (2013)

33. Burgess, A., Mellis, C.: Feedback and assessment during clinical placements: achieving the right balance. Adv. Med. Educ. Pract. **6**, 373–381 (2015)

34. Bouwman, H., Faber, E., Haaker, T., Kijl, B., De Reuver, M.: Conceptualizing the STOF model. In: Bouwman, H., De Vos, H., Haaker, T. (eds.) Mobile Service Innovation and Business Models, pp. 31–70. Springer, Heidelberg (2008). https://doi.org/10.1007/978-3-540-79238-3_2

35. Menko, R.A., Visser, S., Janssen, R., Hettinga, M., Haaker, T.: Applying the STOF business model framework in eHealth innovations. Proc. eTELEMED 108–113 (2013)
36. Osterwalder, A., Pigneur, Y.: Business Model Generation. Wiley, Hoboken (2010)
37. Loorbach, N., Peters, O., Karreman, J., Steehouder, M.: Validation of the Instructional Materials Motivation Survey (IMMS) in a self-directed instructional setting aimed at working with technology. Br. J. Edu. Technol. **46**(1), 204–218 (2015)
38. Schrepp, M., Hinderks, A., Thomaschewski, J.: Applying the user experience questionnaire (UEQ) in different evaluation scenarios. In: Marcus, A. (ed.) DUXU 2014. LNCS, vol. 8517, pp. 383–392. Springer, Cham (2014). https://doi.org/10.1007/978-3-319-07668-3_37
39. Huang, W.: Investigating the novelty effect in virtual reality on stem learning. Doctoral dissertation, Arizona State University (2020)
40. Baniasadi, T., Ayyoubzadeh, S.M., Mohammadzadeh, N.: Challenges and practical considerations in applying virtual reality in medical education and treatment. Oman Med. J. **35**(3), e125 (2020)
41. Rizzo, A.A., Strickland, D., Bouchard, S.: The challenge of using virtual reality in telerehabilitation. Telemed. J. E Health **10**(2), 184–195 (2004)
42. Gbadegeshin, S.A., et al.: Overcoming the valley of death: a new model for high technology startups. Sustain. Futures **4**, 100077 (2022). https://doi.org/10.1016/j.sftr.2022.100077

Is Industrial Tomography Ready for Augmented Reality? A Need-Finding Study of How Augmented Reality Can Be Adopted by Industrial Tomography Experts

Yuchong Zhang[1]([✉])[iD], Adam Nowak[2][iD], Guruprasad Rao[2][iD],
Andrzej Romanowski[2][iD], and Morten Fjeld[1,3][iD]

[1] Chalmers University of Technology, Gothenburg, Sweden
zyc941030@gmail.com
[2] Lodz University of Technology, Lodz, Poland
[3] University of Bergen, Bergen, Norway

Abstract. Augmented Reality (AR) has grown into a well-established technique with a compelling potential for interactive visualization. In spite of its clear potential, this novel tool has not yet been widely embraced as an industrial solution. In this paper, we address AR for a specific domain: industrial tomography. Within this domain, we conducted a need-finding study featuring 14 surveyed participants, each with sufficient years of experience. A systematic survey study was designed as the main body of our approach. Using this survey, we collected answers helping us to establish findings and formulate novel insights. The study as a whole consisted of a pilot and a formal study for better robustness. Our findings uncovered the current status of AR being used in industrial tomography, and showed that the potential of AR in this domain was positively rated by the participants. Based on our findings, we present key challenges and propose potential for interdisciplinary synergies between AR and industrial tomography.

Keywords: Need-finding · Augmented reality · Industrial tomography · Visualization · Interactivity

1 Introduction

While having some common points with Virtual Reality (VR), Augmented Reality (AR) is an interactive technique where computer-generated perceptual information is visually superimposed on the real world [2,27]. On one hand, in VR, a user interacts with virtual objects in a fully artificial three-dimensional world. On the other hand, in AR, a user's view of the real environment is enhanced with virtual objects shown at the right time and position from the user's perspective [12,37]. AR technology has been effectively deployed in various applications within industry due to its high mobility and interactivity. For example, AR can

J. Y. C. Chen and G. Fragomeni (Eds.): HCII 2023, LNCS 14027, pp. 523–535, 2023.
https://doi.org/10.1007/978-3-031-35634-6_37

provide functional tools that support users undertaking domain-related tasks, especially helping them in data visualization and interaction because of its ability to jointly augment the physical space and the user's perception [7,8]. Taking devices and hardware as key parameters [8,27], AR can be classified into three categories:

- **Head-Mounted Displays (HMD) and wearable hardware:** These devices can be further categorized into optical see-through and video see-through [19], displaying information inside the device while allowing users to see the surrounding real world.
- **Hand-Held Displays (HHD):** These are mobile screens, smartphones, or tablets with embedded camera and screen. The device fits within the user's hands and can display virtual objects.
- **Spatial Augmented Reality (SAR):** These systems utilize digital projectors to display virtual information onto the physical objects.

Industrial tomography is a broad domain involving a number of measurement modalities applied to study process performance and analyzes multi-phase flow behavior across industrial branches [22,30,32]. It extracts qualitative and quantitative data regarding the ongoing processes, which is usually visualized in ways serving to understand the nature, to measure the critical process characteristics, and to implement process control in a feedback network. This information, for example, a 2D graph of the spectral information or a 3D reconstruction of the voxel data, if gathered interactively in real time by a related domain expert, can help in better understanding of the process [24]. Industrial tomography is found in many manufacturing units as well as in non-destructive or monitoring purposes [33–36]. Prominent examples are oil and gas [9], chemical engineering [29], seismology [17], nuclear waste processing [21], and flow inspection [20].

AR has successfully provided accessible and innovative solutions for various industrial application domains due to its capacity for interactive visualization through intelligent user interfaces. Given its proven success within the automotive industry [3], within shipbuilding [8], within mechanics [41], and within robotics [7], our driving question is whether AR is also able to bring useful facilitation to the domain of industrial tomography. Then research question is elicited: could AR effectively support process monitoring in industrial tomography? Both to capture the current status and to examine the potential of AR in this domain, we conducted a need-finding study in the form of a systematic survey to model the involved 14 participants. All were industrial tomography experts with at least three years of hands-on experience, whom we considered eligible to offer sufficiently in-depth insights and opinions. The main contributions of this paper are illustrated as follows.

- Give an overview of the present status of using AR by industrial tomography experts.
- Identify the potential need of using AR by industrial tomography experts to effectively support process monitoring.
- Illuminate the potential challenges in deploying AR into facilitating process monitoring in industrial tomography.

2   Related Work

In this section, we first review the usage of AR in various industrial scenarios as a visualization tool, then we introduce the current status of deploying AR in the context of industrial tomography.

2.1   AR Visualization in Industry

There is a body of research to reflect the growing interest of the deployment of AR in various industrial applications [5,10,11,25,31,40]. Cardoso et al. [27] wrote a systematic survey paper revealing the present status of industrial AR, where they concluded that most AR applications in the domain of industry are incremental as they offer a different and more efficient way to convey information needed. Bruno et al. [4] presented an AR application that industrial engineering data were visualized superimposed to the real object that represents a spatial reference, where the exploration is more natural compared to a traditional visualization software. A recently published paper by Noghabaei et al. [16] indicated that the utilization of AR in architecture, engineering, and the construction industry had a significant increase from 2017 to 2018. More specifically, according to the powerful visualization functionality provided by AR, Lamas et al. [8] pointed out that AR could be used to visualize the 2D location of products and tools as well as hidden installation areas in the shipyard industry. Mourtzis et al. [15] proposed an AR approach to visualize and showcase the industrial production scheduling and monitoring data which made people to supervise the incorporated components. Alves et al. [1] developed a comparative study to prove that the reliance on AR based visualizations obtained better results in physical and mental demand in production assembly. In robotics' industry, DePace et al. [7] found that AR can enhance a user's ability to understand the movement of mobile robots.

2.2   AR in Industrial Tomography

Regarding the domain of industrial tomography, AR has been investigated to provide novel visualization approaches although there is still a gap between AR developers and industrial tomography practitioners [39]. Early in 2001, Mann et al. [13] proposed to use AR to capture and visualize the dynamics of the mixture in stirred chemical reactors operated by Electrical Resistance Tomography (ERT). Soon after, Stanley et al. [28] harnessed AR visualization to display images for a desirable format while they pioneered the first example of ERT applied to a precipitation reaction process. Making use of the Microsoft HoloLens AR platform, Nowak et al. [18] demonstrated an innovative approach to visualize industrial tomography data and enable collaborative in-situ analysis. In addition, they also further investigated a prototype supporting complex data visualization and analysis in entire 3D surroundings within the same context [19]. Sobiech et al. [26] explored gestural interactions with 3D data by employing HMD AR within general industrial tomography visualizations. Recently, Zhang

Fig. 1. The three AR modalities presented to the participants. *a*): Head Mounted Display: These devices can be further categorized into optical see-through and video see-through [19], displaying information inside the device while allowing users to see the surrounding real world; *b*): Hand Held Display [6]: These are mobile screens, smartphones, or tablets with embedded camera and screen. The device fits within the user's hands and can display virtual objects; *c*): Spatial Augmented Reality [14]: These systems utilize digital projectors to display virtual information onto the physical objects. The clear description of each modality was provided for the participants.

et al. [38, 39] directed a study where they proposed a novel AR framework to support volumetric visualization in the context of industrial process tomography, especially to bring about high mobility and information richness. However, applying AR to handle industrial tomography related problems is not yet mature for widespread use. Thus, identifying the current position of AR and the potential demand and challenges in this designated domain is indispensable.

3   Method

Our aim was to gain a broad overview of what is now emerging as a prescient area of study in the field of AR usage by industrial tomography experts. In particular, we intended to model the domain users to obtain the link between interactive visualization of AR and effective working performance of the experts. To implement this proposition, we designed a survey study including a number of objective questions and several subjective narration parts (25 questions in total) which was divided into three sections: **general demographic section which included five questions** (age, gender, country of residence, place of work - industry or academia and size of organization); **visualization in tomography section with twelve questions** (years of experience in industrial tomography, modalities of industrial tomography and visualization techniques used in work along with their relevance and importance, and problems regarding visualization during daily work); and **a final part regarding AR with eight questions** (knowledge and experience with AR, recently involved projects, and possible usage with potential advantages and drawbacks of AR in the industrial tomography domain). Of the final section, the three AR settings: HMD, HHD, and SAR were presented to the participants, as shown in Fig. 1 (The three sub-figures were from internet). All collected responses were anonymous.

Table 1. The surveyed participants (P1–P4) involved in the pilot study. Abbreviations: Academia (I): Academia with tight collaboration of industry; ERT: Electrical resistivity tomography; EIT: Electrical impedance tomography; MWT: Microwave tomography; UST: Ultrasound Tomography.

	Working Status	Tomography Involved	Current Project with Tomography	Org. Size	Exp.
P1	Academia (I)	ERT and EIT	Industrial tomography in crystallization	University	6 yrs
P2	Academia (I)	MWT	Tomographic sensors for process control	University	6 yrs
P3	Academia (I)	ERT	Polymer foam with an MWT sensor	University	5 yrs
P4	Academia (I)	ERT and UST	Imaging the crystals using ERT	University	5 yrs

3.1 Participants

We invited 14 participants (10 self-identified male, 4 self-identified female) from our Europe-wide project (https://www.tomocon.eu/) network to complete the survey via emailing. Their ages ranged from 29 to 62 ($mean = 43.47$, $SD = 10.68$). The working status of the participants were categorized into working in academia with tight collaboration of industry, working in industry, and working in both academia and industry. All were either experienced researchers or industrial practitioners distributed across Europe. Furthermore, all had distinguished skills in industrial tomography for at least five years while some were outstanding researchers in this domain. To mitigate undesired biases as well as to make our study more robust, we carried out a small pilot study followed by the formal study. All participants approved a consent that the data collected from the survey will be kept confidential and merely used for research.

3.2 Pilot Study

We wanted to address issues of ambiguity or in response to new insights that emerged during our first contact with participants. Thus, we first requested the four most junior researchers to undertake a pilot study. The relevant information about these participants (**P1–P4**) is shown in Table 1. The survey containing in-depth questions was presented to these 4 participants to the test the studying usability and efficiency. Each participant was required to complete the survey and indicate the deficiencies regarding the questions. Based on their initial answers and comments, we concluded that some minor rewording and polishing of the survey were sufficient to acquire more valuable insights.

3.3 Formal Study

After revising and improving according to the feedback from the pilot study, we then carried out the formal survey study by inviting the remaining 10 senior

Table 2. The surveyed participants (P5–P14) involved in the formal study. Abbreviations: A&I: both academia and industry. ECT: Electrical capacitance tomography; MIT: Magnetic induction tomography; CT: Computed tomography; UDV: Ultrasonic doppler velocimetry; CIFT: Contactless inductive flow tomography.

	Working Status	Tomography Involved	Current Project with Tomography	Org. Size	Exp.
P5	Academia (I)	X-ray tomography	Flow visualization for liquid metals	1001–2000	10 yrs
P6	A&I	ECT	X-ray CT of rotating mixing drum	11–50	N.A.
P7	Academia (I)	ECT, MIT, and UST	N.A.	1001–2000	14 yrs
P8	Academia (I)	X-ray CT and Gamma-ray CT	N.A.	1001–2000	13 yrs
P9	Academia (I)	X-ray tomography	Phase distributions in technical devices	University	17 yrs
P10	Academia (I)	UDV and CIFT	X-ray tomography of bubble columns	University	10 yrs
P11	Industry	N.A.	Continuous casting control	Over 5000	N.A.
P12	Academia (I)	ERT, EIT, and ECT	Multiphase flow monitoring	University	23 yrs
P13	Industry	N.A.	Fluidised bed ECT	Over 5000	N.A.
P14	Academia (I)	ERT and ECT	Tomographic sensors for process control	University	14 yrs

participants (**P5–P14**) to concentratedly complete the more constructive questions. The formal study was fundamentally identical to the pilot study but with some improvements regarding the language expression and information presentation in some questions. Table 2 provides a summary of these senior participants' background and projects involving industrial tomography. For those answers where the participants did not provide their related information due to personal reasons, we used N.A. instead.

4   Findings

We organized our findings into four themes: **visualization in industrial tomography, current status of AR among the domain experts, potential use of AR**, and the **challenges to apply AR in industrial tomography**.

4.1   Visualization in Industrial Tomography

From the study, we noticed that visualization plays a dominant role in the experts' daily work. Most of the participants used mainly Line-based (e.g. line graph), Plot-based (e.g. 2D/3D scatterplot) or Map-based (e.g. heatmap) visual

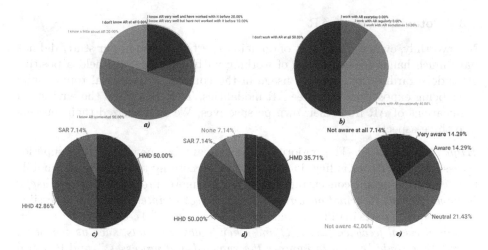

Fig. 2. The answers of how domain experts responded to the current AR status and the prospective usage. *a*): Q: How much do you know about AR? *b*): Q: Have you ever worked with any modalities of AR? *c*): Q: Comfort: Which AR scenario shown above looks most comfortable for you? *d*): Q: Usability: Which AR scenario shown above looks most usable for you (might help with your work)? *e*): Q: Are you aware of any ongoing AR applications in industrial tomography?

representations for analyses. Some difficulties pertaining to visualization were reported, such as low resolution, image reconstruction, and image segmentation. Notably, at least three participants encountered some problems with 3D visualization. P1 commented: *"Simultaneous visualization and image processing are difficult to handle."*.

4.2   Current Status of AR Among Domain Experts

Only two participants were familiarized with AR and had previous hands-on experience with it. Additionally, one participant claimed a profound knowledge of AR but no actual working experience. The remaining participants reported that either they knew about AR in some aspects (9 participants) or they were merely aware of it to a limited extent (two participants).

We presented the three modalities of AR (HMD, HHD, and SAR) to the participants and queried their opinions on their comfort and potential usability. Further, we investigated their awareness of ongoing AR applications and prospective AR usage in industrial tomography. The answers we obtained are illustrated in Fig. 2. From Fig. 2*a* and *b*, we summarized that most of the domain experts did not have much experience in harnessing AR for their daily work. From Fig. 2*c* and *d*, we concluded that most of them regard HMD and HHD AR as the most comfortable as well as the most advantageous modalities for use in industrial tomography. However, those who were aware of ongoing AR applications accounted for only a small percentage of the participants (4 out of 14, Fig. 2*e*).

4.3   Potential Use of AR

Noteworthily, even though most of domain experts engaged in our study did not have much hands-on experience of working with AR, they still held a positive attitude regarding its potential usage in the context of industrial tomography after being exposed to the three AR modalities. They described the envisioned applications of AR from their own perspectives. We summarized their answers into three aspects.

High Accessibility. The majority of participants acknowledged the superior accessibility of AR for aiding domain experts. According to P6, AR, as a mobile tool, can make people concentrate on the targets more directly: *"It is very useful to have relevant information directly at the object of interest."*. The accessible AR supports experts in different manners. For example, P9 commented: *"Combination of visual feedback (i.e. AR) and other feedback signals, such as acoustics, in real time could be used to improve the knowledge of processes."*, and P14 also praised: *"By using the functionality, AR is exceptional for object detection and identification when performing domain tasks."*.

See-Through Capability. Simultaneously, these experts spotted the huge potential of utilizing AR within industrial tomographic processes. As noted by P1, *"It is great for future development. It might also be beneficial in case of visualization which aims for "seeing" through the systems."*, AR might become one effective tool to support task resolution. Similarly, P5 came up with a comment regarding specific application cases: *"Especially, if you deal with the case where there are opaque fluids which you cannot see, AR could be used as a powerful tool for the interactive visualization."*.

3D Visualization Ability. Another significant potential of adopting AR is its 3D visualization ability based on a few participants. The interactive 3D visualization will help them with more precise task analytics. Especially, P10 emphasized this in his answer: *"In my opinion, AR would be advisable particularly for 3D visualization."*.

From the responses obtained from these experienced domain experts, we probed the opportunity of deploying the capability of AR into industrial tomography. The participants who were in favor of AR-tomography interplay claimed the prospective specific applications in terms of their hands-on projects. Most of them believed that AR could be unexpectedly beneficial for domain tasks pertaining to interactive visualization.

4.4   Challenges to Apply AR in Industrial Tomography

Although most of participants gave positive responses regarding the potential of AR, we have to realize that AR is still not prevalent in most industries [27]. To uncover how to apply AR appropriately into industrial tomography as well as understand its usability, we probed the latent challenges when working with AR according to the descriptions afforded by the participants. These findings should be well tackled to situate AR properly with in industrial tomography.

Ease of Use. The most common challenge posed by them is the easiness. Through the survey, participants got a fundamental conceptuation of AR while they mostly questioned the ease of use. For example, some experts were reluctant to wearing HMD AR for long-time inspection of a specialized process which would create unacceptable strain on human bodies: *"Yes, I think the headset is too difficult to wear for the industrial processes which have longer duration."*(P3); *"In many large reactors, the projection is possible. But for AR using head mounted display or other devices, it is difficult for hands-on operations and long time use."*(P7). Furthermore, P10 straightforwardly pointed out this problem by commenting: *"Ease of use is the biggest challenge for real-time application/visualisation/calculation."*.

Speed and Accuracy. Besides, participants suggested that the speed and accuracy of AR may become a core problem hindering the satisfactory exploitation in many application cases. As P1 said, *"I doubt the speed and accuracy of AR to satisfy the industrial-scale processes."*, it is thus critical to apply AR in domain tasks only of the speed and accuracy are qualified. P12 posed a more concrete appraisal: *"Industrial tomographic processes are often faster than human interaction and need automated control."*. It is challenging for AR to make human interaction achieve the pace of industrial processes or to properly visualize the vital information in the form of virtual elements.

Convertibility. *"There is no large application range of AR in this domain yet."*, indicated by P9, which implies that AR is still rarely used in industrial tomography due to its uncertainty on suitably converting domain-related data into desirable visualizations. P4, a researcher dealing with massive hands-on tomographic tasks marked: *"From my point of view, converting the output from the tomographic sensor to properly represent output (i.e., moisture distribution) by AR can be challenging."*. We have to realize that most of the domain experts lack the specialized knowledge of using AR devices, which is indispensable when adopting AR for visualization. It is then notable that obtaining content convertibility is definitely challenging for merging AR with industrial tomography.

5   Discussion

AR has become a renowned concept and technique with the rapid development of mobile smart devices. As AR provides immersive and interactive experience by presenting visualized information as virtual elements, it is increasingly being recognized for its potential as a powerful tool to support diverse domain applications. Although AR has not yet achieved widespread use in industries, with the incentives of the current research we conducted a systematic investigation into its existing status, future viability, and potential challenges for industrial tomography experts working with it. Distinct from [16] (specialized in understanding VR/AR in design and construction) and [27] (specialized in evaluating AR in industries), we specifically focused on exploring AR in the domain of industrial tomography.

We recruited 14 participants who each had at least three years of hands-on experience of industrial tomography. To make the results more robust and persuasive, we first carried out a pilot study with the four most junior researchers and incorporated their feedback and suggestions for the main study. Then, a calibrated formal study was implemented with regard to the remaining 10 senior participants. The consequential findings were organized into four themes: visualization in industrial tomography, current status of AR among the domain experts, potential use of AR, and challenges to apply AR in industrial tomography.

We found that for domain experts, visualization is a critical inclusion of their daily work, especially 3D visualization which aroused the most difficulties. As an interactive technique supporting immersive 3D visualizations, AR did not turn out to be a practical tool in the view of our experts. On the premise that Nowak et al. [18] had already identified regarding the effectiveness and usability of AR for visualization analyses of industrial tomography, we sought to dig out more about its prospects, especially in terms of data-driven and machine learning-driven applications [23]. According to our surveyed participants, HMD and HHD AR are considered to be favorable modalities which are able to bring comfort and effectiveness to benefit industrial tomography. Notably, almost all of our participants expressed a positive attitude towards the potential usage of AR due to its promising functionality such as interactivity and providing an extra platform for 3D visualization. On the other hand, we admit to the prospective challenges (hardware, ease of use, and speed & accuracy) raised by our experts.

Even though we have acquired satisfactory results, we have to admit that there still exists limitations of our study. One limitation is that our study was exclusively from the perspectives of a specific group of experts in industrial tomography. We do not know if we would gain similar findings for other modalities of tomography domains. Furthermore, we surveyed 14 Europe-wide participants, which is only a small sample of the domain practitioners. A larger number of samples would contribute more rigorous and persuasive conclusions. Last but not least, we did not control the entire influential factors of the survey, such as the time length of the survey, which might affect the answers obtained.

6   Conclusion

In this paper, we implemented a need-finding investigation into how some experienced industrial tomography experts could effectively work with AR, by means of modeling users through a systematic survey. We designed a logically-consistent survey study, recruited 14 domain experts with solid disciplinary backgrounds, then executed a pilot study and a formal study. We displayed the current status of the use of AR in industrial tomography. We found that the domain experts would be willing to adopt AR more in the future owing to the superiority in interactive visualization shown by this technique. Finally, we offered three significant challenges regarding the envisioned use of AR in the related domain. Through our study, we hope to broaden the horizon of deploying the advanced tool AR in industrial tomography to facilitate the interdisciplinary interplay.

In future work, we will concentrate on the development of real AR applications based on the intelligent user interfaces for supporting industrial tomography visualization analysis, using interactivity to advance the domain related tasks. Certainly, a larger scale and more comprehensive need-finding study may also be required for better prerequisite works.

Acknowledgment. This project has received funding from the European Union's Horizon 2020 research and innovation program under the Marie Sklodowska-Curie grant agreement No. 764902. This work has been supported by the Polish National Agency for Academic Exchange under the PROM programme co-financed by the European Social Fund.

References

1. Alves, J.B., Marques, B., Ferreira, C., Dias, P., Santos, B.S.: Comparing augmented reality visualization methods for assembly procedures. Virtual Reality **26**(1), 235–248 (2022)
2. Azuma, R.T.: A survey of augmented reality. Presence: Teleoperators Virtual Environ. **6**(4), 355–385 (1997)
3. Boboc, R.G., Gîrbacia, F., Butilă, E.V.: The application of augmented reality in the automotive industry: a systematic literature review. Appl. Sci. **10**(12), 4259 (2020)
4. Bruno, F., Caruso, F., De Napoli, L., Muzzupappa, M.: Visualization of industrial engineering data visualization of industrial engineering data in augmented reality. J. Vis. **9**(3), 319–329 (2006)
5. Büttner, S., Funk, M., Sand, O., Röcker, C.: Using head-mounted displays and in-situ projection for assistive systems: a comparison. In: Proceedings of the 9th ACM International Conference on Pervasive Technologies Related to Assistive Environments, pp. 1–8 (2016)
6. Cook, J.: PTC technology accelerates Watson-Marlow's digital transformation plans. https://www.ptc.com/en/blogs/corporate/ptc-technology-accelerates-watson-marlow-digital-transformation
7. De Pace, F., Manuri, F., Sanna, A.: Augmented reality in industry 4.0. Am. J. Comput. Sci. Inf. Technol. **6**(1), 17 (2018)
8. Fraga-Lamas, P., Fernández-Caramés, T.M., Blanco-Novoa, Ó., Vilar-Montesinos, M.A.: A review on industrial augmented reality systems for the industry 4.0 shipyard. IEEE Access **6**, 13358–13375 (2018)
9. Ismail, I., Gamio, J., Bukhari, S.A., Yang, W.: Tomography for multi-phase flow measurement in the oil industry. Flow Meas. Instrum. **16**(2–3), 145–155 (2005)
10. Lavingia, K., Tanwar, S.: Augmented reality and industry 4.0. In: Nayyar, A., Kumar, A. (eds.) A Roadmap to Industry 4.0: Smart Production, Sharp Business and Sustainable Development. ASTI, pp. 143–155. Springer, Cham (2020). https://doi.org/10.1007/978-3-030-14544-6_8
11. Lorenz, M., Knopp, S., Klimant, P.: Industrial augmented reality: requirements for an augmented reality maintenance worker support system. In: 2018 IEEE International Symposium on Mixed and Augmented Reality Adjunct (ISMAR-Adjunct), pp. 151–153. IEEE (2018)
12. Ma, D., Gausemeier, J., Fan, X., Grafe, M.: Virtual Reality & Augmented Reality in Industry. Springer, Cham (2011). https://doi.org/10.1007/978-3-642-17376-9

13. Mann, R., Stanley, S., Vlaev, D., Wabo, E., Primrose, K.: Augmented-reality visualization of fluid mixing in stirred chemical reactors using electrical resistance tomography. J. Electron. Imaging **10**(3), 620–630 (2001)
14. Marner, M.R., Smith, R.T., Walsh, J.A., Thomas, B.H.: Spatial user interfaces for large-scale projector-based augmented reality. IEEE Comput. Graph. Appl. **34**(6), 74–82 (2014)
15. Mourtzis, D., Siatras, V., Zogopoulos, V.: Augmented reality visualization of production scheduling and monitoring. Procedia CIRP **88**, 151–156 (2020)
16. Noghabaei, M., Heydarian, A., Balali, V., Han, K.: A survey study to understand industry vision for virtual and augmented reality applications in design and construction. arXiv preprint arXiv:2005.02795 (2020)
17. Nolet, G.: Seismic Tomography: With Applications in Global Seismology and Exploration Geophysics, vol. 5. Springer, Heidelberg (2012). https://doi.org/10.1007/978-94-009-3899-1
18. Nowak, A., Woźniak, M., Rowińska, Z., Grudzień, K., Romanowski, A.: Towards in-situ process tomography data processing using augmented reality technology. In: Adjunct Proceedings of the 2019 ACM International Joint Conference on Pervasive and Ubiquitous Computing and Proceedings of the 2019 ACM International Symposium on Wearable Computers, pp. 168–171 (2019)
19. Nowak, A., Zhang, Y., Romanowski, A., Fjeld, M.: Augmented reality with industrial process tomography: to support complex data analysis in 3D space. In: Adjunct Proceedings of the 2021 ACM International Joint Conference on Pervasive and Ubiquitous Computing and Proceedings of the 2021 ACM International Symposium on Wearable Computers (2021)
20. Plaskowski, A., Beck, M., Thorn, R., Dyakowski, T.: Imaging Industrial Flows: Applications of Electrical Process Tomography. CRC Press (1995)
21. Primrose, K.: Application of process tomography in nuclear waste processing. In: Industrial Tomography, pp. 713–725. Elsevier (2015)
22. Rao, G., Aghajanian, S., Zhang, Y., Jackowska-Strumiłło, L., Koiranen, T., Fjeld, M.: Monitoring and visualization of crystallization processes using electrical resistance tomography: CaCO3 and sucrose crystallization case studies. Sensors **22**(12), 4431 (2022)
23. Romanowski, A.: Big data-driven contextual processing methods for electrical capacitance tomography. IEEE Trans. Ind. Inf. **15**, 1609–1618 (2019). https://doi.org/10.1109/TII.2018.2855200
24. Romanowski, A., et al.: Interactive timeline approach for contextual spatiotemporal ECT data investigation. Sensors **20**(17) (2020). https://doi.org/10.3390/s20174793. https://www.mdpi.com/1424-8220/20/17/4793
25. Satkowski, M., Dachselt, R.: Investigating the impact of real-world environments on the perception of 2D visualizations in augmented reality. In: Proceedings of the 2021 CHI Conference on Human Factors in Computing Systems, pp. 1–15 (2021)
26. Sobiech, F., et al.: Exploratory analysis of users' interactions with AR data visualisation in industrial and neutral environments (2022)
27. de Souza Cardoso, L.F., Mariano, F.C.M.Q., Zorzal, E.R.: A survey of industrial augmented reality. Comput. Ind. Eng. **139**, 106159 (2020)
28. Stanley, S., Mann, R., Primrose, K.: Interrogation of a precipitation reaction by electrical resistance tomography (ERT). AIChE J. **51**(2), 607–614 (2005)
29. Tapp, H., Peyton, A., Kemsley, E., Wilson, R.: Chemical engineering applications of electrical process tomography. Sens. Actuators B Chem. **92**(1–2), 17–24 (2003)
30. Wang, M.: Industrial Tomography: Systems and Applications. Elsevier (2015)

31. Zasornova, I., Zakharkevich, O., Zasornov, A., Kuleshova, S., Koshevko, J., Sharan, T.: Usage of augmented reality technologies in the light industry. Vlakna a textil (Fibres and Textiles) (28), 3 (2021)
32. Zhang, Y., Ma, Y., Omrani, A., et al.: Automated microwave tomography (MWT) image segmentation: state-of-the-art implementation and evaluation. J. WSCG **2020**, 126–136 (2020)
33. Zhang, Y., Fjeld, M.: Condition monitoring for confined industrial process based on infrared images by using deep neural network and variants. In: Proceedings of the 2020 2nd International Conference on Image, Video and Signal Processing, pp. 99–106 (2020)
34. Zhang, Y., Fjeld, M.: "I am told to be happy": an exploration of deep learning in affective colormaps in industrial tomography. In: 2021 2nd International Conference on Artificial Intelligence and Information Systems, pp. 1–5 (2021)
35. Zhang, Y., Fjeld, M., Fratarcangeli, M., Said, A., Zhao, S.: Affective colormap design for accurate visual comprehension in industrial tomography. Sensors **21**(14), 4766 (2021)
36. Zhang, Y., Fjeld, M., Said, A., Fratarcangeli, M.: Task-based colormap design supporting visual comprehension in process tomography. In: Kerren, A., Garth, C., Marai, G.E. (eds.) EuroVis 2020 - Short Papers. The Eurographics Association (2020). https://doi.org/10.2312/evs.20201049
37. Zhang, Y., Nowak, A., Romanowski, A., Fjeld, M.: An initial exploration of visual cues in head-mounted display augmented reality for book searching. In: Proceedings of the 21st International Conference on Mobile and Ubiquitous Multimedia, pp. 273–275 (2022)
38. Zhang, Y., Omrani, A., Yadav, R., Fjeld, M.: Supporting visualization analysis in industrial process tomography by using augmented reality—a case study of an industrial microwave drying system. Sensors **21**(19), 6515 (2021)
39. Zhang, Y., Yadav, R., Omrani, A., Fjeld, M.: A novel augmented reality system to support volumetric visualization in industrial process tomography. In: Proceedings of the 2021 Conference on Interfaces and Human Computer Interaction, pp. 3–9 (2021)
40. Zubizarreta, J., Aguinaga, I., Amundarain, A.: A framework for augmented reality guidance in industry. Int. J. Adv. Manuf. Technol. **102**, 4095–4108 (2019)
41. Zulfabli, H., Ismalina, H., Amarul, T., Ahmad, S.: Product development of mechanical practice: augmented reality (AR) approach. In: AIP Conference Proceedings, vol. 2129, p. 020055. AIP Publishing LLC (2019)

VAMR in Aviation

RETRACTED CHAPTER: Methods of Visualizing Landing Performance in Low-Visibility ILS Approaches (Preliminary Findings)

Theodore C. Mofle[1] , Inchul Choi[1] , Daniela Kratchounova[2(✉)] ,
Jeremy Hesselroth[3], and Scott Stevenson[3]

[1] Cherokee Nation 3S, Oklahoma City, OK, USA
{Theodore.C-CTR.Mofle,Inchul.CTR.Choi}@faa.gov
[2] Federal Aviation Administration Civil Aerospace Medical Institute, Oklahoma City, OK, USA
Daniela.Kratchounova@faa.gov
[3] Federal Aviation Administration Flight Technologies and Procedures Division,
Oklahoma City, OK, USA
{Jeremy.J.Hesselroth,Scott.Stevenson}@faa.gov

Abstract. The article discusses four different methods for visualizing touchdown point dispersion. By comparing and contrasting scatter plot, two-dimensional box plot, heat map, and contour graphs, we were able to produce multiple methods that are well suited for visualizing touchdown data. Of these, contour graphs showed the highest potential as the best method for conveying an intuitive touchdown visualization. The ability to calculate probability of an outcome provided a meaningful insight to the effects of different guidance types and runway visual range on touchdown dispersion. Results of applied aviation research are not only a concern to the scientific community but for all aviation stakeholders (e.g., pilots, policy makers, and researchers). Therefore, it is important to convey information in the most intuitive way without solely relying on statistical inferences to present study results. Furthermore, future research using contour graphs to display the probability of landing in a particular area of the runway may produce further evidence for identifying low-visibility ILS approaches safety margins.

Keywords: Graphing Methodology · Two-dimensional Box Plot · Heat Map · Contour Graph · Head-up Display (HUD) · Instrument Landing System (ILS) · Low-visibility Operations

1 Introduction

Aviation research has often relied on pilot performance data to evaluate the safety and applicability of novel flight deck technologies. The objective of this paper is to describe the process we used to arrive at a method that is best suited for visualizing touchdown performance data during low-visibility, precision instrument approaches.

The original version of this chapter was retracted: A retraction note to this chapter can be found at https://doi.org/10.1007/978-3-031-35634-6_51

J. Y. C. Chen and G. Fragomeni (Eds.): HCII 2023, LNCS 14027, pp. 539–548, 2023.
https://doi.org/10.1007/978-3-031-35634-6_39

2 Background

Each graphing method we explored is associated with distinct advantages and disadvantages for extrapolating information and identifying data trends (Table 1). Figure 1 shows the four methods we considered, in a side-by-side comparison. The graphs present touchdown data for all guidance type and runway visual range (RVR) conditions used for this research. It is important to note that while touchdown point dispersion is a single construct, it is bivariate in nature (i.e., a value on the x-axis and y-axis).

First, scatter plots allow identification of potentially extreme outliers in addition to trends and possible variable relationships (e.g., linear or curvilinear, positive or negative). Simultaneously, scatter plots do not have the ability to mathematically identify outliers with whisker lines representing upper and lower limits, or provide information about descriptive statistics such as median and quantiles. Furthermore, it is more difficult to identify the distribution properties of bivariate measures. In data sets with many points of overlapping values, scatter plots may not be very informative due to the inability to distinguish between similarly valued data points.

Second, traditional box plots provide a solution to graphing the upper and lower data limits (i.e., upper and lower fences). The disadvantage is single dimension box plots only display the distribution of a single variable. Two-dimensional box plots are a method to overcome the shortcomings of both scatter plots and single dimension box plots by displaying the median, interquartile range, and upper and lower limits (with whisker lines) based on the distribution of two variables independently [1, 2]. Using this method allows a more accurate identification of outliers and examining the distribution with reference to both dimensions of the variable. In contrary, the inability to depict important visual information, such as how many landings occurred in a specific area of the runway, is a serious limiting factor in using either scatter plots or any form of box plots to present the touchdown data from this research in an effective presentation. For example, with only a box plot, it is impossible to determine if the distribution within the interquartile range (between first and third quartiles) is bimodal or normally distributed.

Third, we considered heat maps as a viable alternative to the previous two methods. Heat map is a technique that uses color-coding to represent frequency of bivariate data. Commonly used in vision science, for this research, a heat map provides a method of plotting the data regarding the frequency of touchdown points on the runway and with respect to two variables (i.e., deviation from the runway aiming point and centerline). More specifically, plotted with dark green hexagons represent areas of the runway with more landings and lighter green hexagons represent areas with fewer landings (Fig. 6 and Fig. 7). Nevertheless, heat maps do not allow for visualizing proportion of landings on the runway.

Contour graphs are a method of plotting three-dimensional information on a 2-dimensional space, such as displaying terrain information latitude, longitude, and altitude. When applied to touchdown point dispersion, a contour graph presents the proportion of touchdown points clustered in an area. The area within each contour line represents the same value of probability density[1].

---

[1] Probability density is a statistical term used to infer the likelihood of an outcome given the stated parameters.

Table 1. Presented below are the advantages and disadvantages of each plotting method (e.g., scatter plot, heat map, and contour graph).

Graph type	Advantages	Disadvantages
Scatter plot	Easy to visually inspect data trends (e.g., relationship between x and y)	Cannot distinguish between overlapped values or similar values (i.e., if multiple landing occur in the same location, a single data point indicates all the occurrences)
Two-dimensional box plot	Provide easy identification of outliers. Provided the distribution information in respect to a bivariate measure on a single graph	Cannot provide detailed distributional information within a box and no distributional information is available out of the box
Heat map	Presents graphical representation of having more/less values (i.e., number of landings)	Visualization of data relies on size of the area of interest. Cannot provide probability of an outcome
Contour graph	Can present areas having similar values (i.e., landing probability)	Interpolation can be exaggerated with sparse data

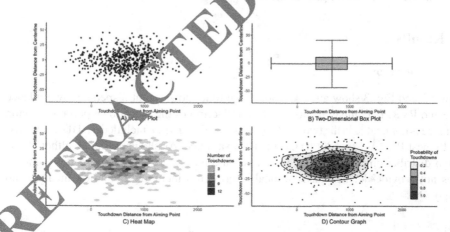

Fig. 1. Touchdown zone point dispersion for all conditions comparing different graphing methods for data visualization.

Using contour graphs to predict the probability of an area for a successful touchdown is conceivably a novel approach within the aviation research community. However, the Jet Propulsion Laboratory and Langley Research Center of the National Aeronautics and Space Administration (NASA) used similar techniques for the Mars Exploration Rover mission landings to quantify risk associated with different landings sites for the different missions [3]. Outside of the application to the Mars Rover missions [3], no additional literature reported using contour graphs to quantify the probability of landing within a specific area.

3 Method

The Civil Aerospace Medical Institute's (CAMI) Institutional Review Board (IRB) reviewed all study material and procedures to ensure compliance with ethical standards involving human research participants. All pilots recruited for the study received a briefing, signed an informed consent, and filled out a demographics questionnaire before participation. Data collection for this research effort took place in the Federal Aviation Administration's (FAA) B737-800 Level D simulator in Oklahoma City, OK and included 12 airline pilot crews. The participant pilots flew all scenarios manually, with the autopilot and auto-throttle "OFF", in daylight conditions only.

The study examined four guidance types: (a) raw data[2], (b) flight director (FD) on head-down display (HDD), (c) FD on HDD and head-up display (HUD), and (d) FD on HDD and HUD (AIII mode). The RVR values include a baseline condition set at the current lowest allowable CAT I minimums at 1800ft RVR with a 200ft decision altitude (DA). Additional examination of experimental visibility included 1400ft and 1200ft RVR with a 150ft DA, and a 1000ft RVR with a 100ft DA. To calculate and plot a single point of touchdown for each aircraft landing, we used the calculated center point between the main landing gear of the aircraft.

4 Results

4.1 Scatter Plot

Figure 2 and Fig. 3 show a scatter plot of the touchdown point dispersion by guidance type and RVR. In comparison to raw data, reduction of the touchdown point dispersion variance is noticeable in the two guidance type conditions that included a HUD. Similarly, the highest RVR value (1800ft) has the least variance. As shown in Fig. 3, although the rough distribution can be visualized based on the arrangement of the scatter points, it does not provide detailed distributional information including quantiles, median, and proportion.

---

[2] Data presented to the pilot in terms of separate indicators of localizer and glide slope deviation with no assistance from flight director.

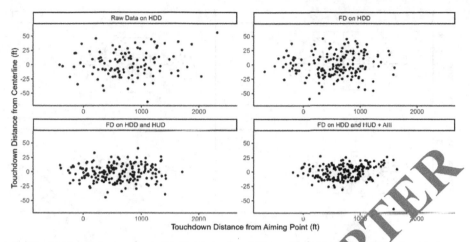

Fig. 2. Touchdown zone point dispersion by guidance types graphed with scatter plot.

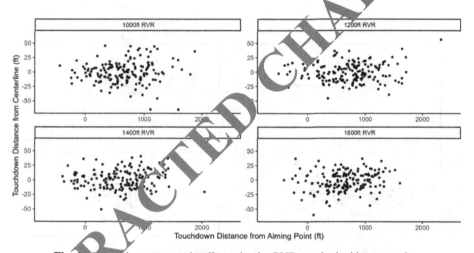

Fig. 3. Touchdown zone point dispersion by RVR graphed with scatter plot.

4.2 Two-Dimensional Box Plots with Scatter Plots

Figure 4 and Fig. 5 display a two-dimensional box plot of the data. Using a two-dimensional box plot offers an additional level of graphing capability to extrapolate outliers and overall trends when considering the distribution for distance from aiming point and runway centerline. However, estimating an unknown data value, such as the number of touchdowns each point on the graph represents as well as the ability to distinguish between closely related plotted values is not possible with this method [4].

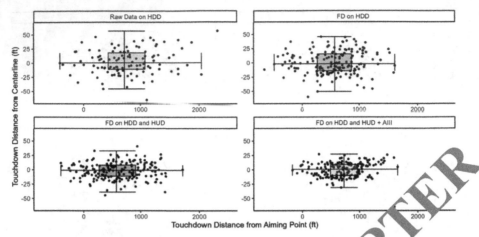

Fig. 4. Touchdown zone point dispersion by guidance type graphed with two-dimensional box plot.

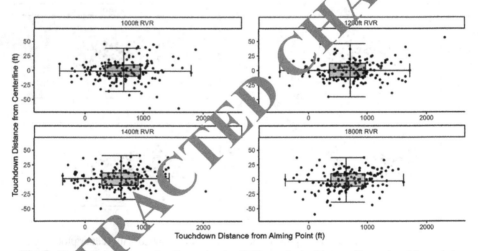

Fig. 5. Touchdown zone point dispersion by RVR graphed with two-dimensional box plot.

4.3 Heat Maps

Figure 6 and Fig. 7 shows the third method considered for visualizing touchdown point dispersion - heat maps. The changes in variance between the raw data and the FD on HDD and HUD (AIII Mode) conditions are still noticeable. But with using the heat map, it becomes clear how many landings occurred at the same point on the runway (e.g., in the two conditions using a HUD versus raw data). While heat maps are indeed an intuitive way to present data, assigning percentages associated with a particular outcome is not possible.

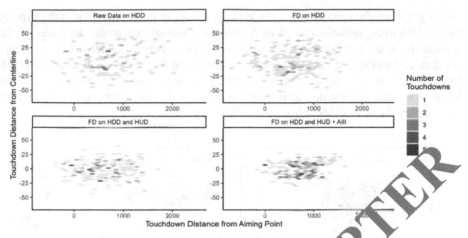

Fig. 6. Touchdown zone point dispersion by guidance type graphed with Heat map.

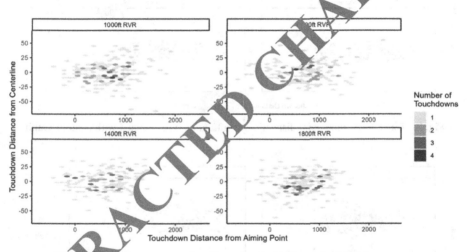

Fig. 7. Touchdown zone point dispersion by RVR graphed with heat map.

4.4 Contour Graphs

A contour graph was the final method we evaluated. Notionally, plotting the probability of landings that occurred in a given area of the runway would be possible if the different colors in heat maps were different levels of data density. For example, the outer most contour line in Fig. 8 and Fig. 9 accounts for 95% of the landings that occurred in the specific condition. Subsequent contour lines represent 80% of landings with each additional inner line decreasing the percentage by 20% (i.e., 60%, 40%, and 20%). The area outside of the outer most contour line is the area of touchdown points for the remaining 5% of landings. Another way to interpret contour graphs is to view the data as clusters with the same color saturation. For example, the darkest blue represents the highest density of data (Fig. 8 and Fig. 9).

In graphing the contour lines, the data presented in the scatter plot is the driving factor. However, unlike scatter plots or two-dimensional box plots, the bases of the contour lines are not dependent on measurements of central tendencies (e.g., mean, median, and mode); but rather, based on the density of the data (i.e., areas on the graph with the most tightly cluster data) to calculate the contour lines. As the color becomes lighter, the data are less dense. In addition, outliers do not affect the presentation of contour graphs as would be when using a box plot.

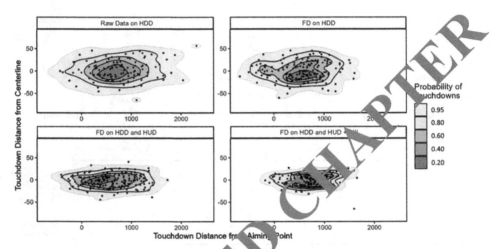

Fig. 8. Touchdown zone point dispersion by guidance type graphed with contour graph.

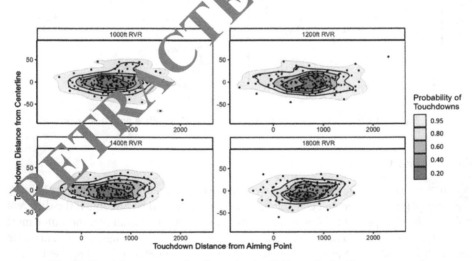

Fig. 9. Touchdown zone point dispersion by RVR graphed with contour graph.

5 Discussion

All of the touchdowns depicted in Fig. 2 through Fig. 9, regardless of their individual relative distances from the center point of the touch down zone, represent landings that were concluded safely. However, it is prudent to reflect on the graphs as valuable tools that aid in articulating important narratives that are of interest to the aviation community at large. First, it would be important to leverage the information contained within these different types of graphs to envision how a myriad of possible external factors effect landings. Second, it would be as important to know how different external factors can negatively impact safety margins, even when not yielding overtly or inherently unsafe conditions.

With respect to the first narrative, the graphing methods allow for early visualization of how external factors affect behavior in the aggregate without having gain that knowledge first-hand by flying the dozens of approaches themselves in conditions not commonly encountered in routine flight operations. Pilots colloquially refer to this mental exercise as "chair flying." By virtue of the consolidated data that the graphs offer, pilots can see how their colleagues tend to behave under certain conditions, mentally place themselves in similar situations, and think through how they themselves would respond. For example, lower RVRs might tend to lead to landings that are past the nominal touchdown zone.

To extend this example further, the fact that pilots are landing long in low RVR scenarios may be due to a shallowing out of the descent rate when the number of visual cues that a pilot would normally see is limited due to the low RVR. Subsequently, a pilot, who is now aware of this general tendency, can proactively mitigate against it by mentally reviewing the situation in advance of actually encountering it. Furthermore, this knowledge is not only useful to the pilot flying the aircraft. It is also of use to the pilot monitoring, who can verbalize any flight path deviations that lower RVRs potentially produce (e.g., shallowing out the descent rate over the runway threshold and landing further down the runway).

The second important point is that of a reduced safety margin, even when the landing itself could be considered safe. This information would be particularly useful to policy writers who must judge whether an approach, for example, has an adequate margin of safety to be conducted under certain combinations of weather conditions and runway infrastructure (e.g., approach lighting systems). Policy writers can utilize the types of graphs represented here to understand and communicate risk to approving officials. In this way, the graphs serve to illustrate pilot tendencies under certain conditions and can be used to build a shared mental model among teams who are charged with writing and approving policy.

6 Conclusions

In previous work, we examined the construct of safety margins and how they relate to crew workload during low visibility takeoffs [5]. Building on the same premise, the use of contour graphs may be a way to visualize and further examine touchdown point dispersion and its impact on safety margins. For example, landings would have a relatively larger safety margin if the touchdown point occurs in the highest color saturation region (i.e., innermost contour; [Fig. 8 and Fig. 9]). However, if the touchdown occurs in the outer regions, landings would have a relatively lower safety margin. Consequently, the effects of a new condition (e.g., the application of new technology) could be better interpreted in the context of specific flight operations without solely relying on results of statistical analyses. This approach would be similar to how NASA used contour graphing to predict risk associated with each landing site during the Mars Rover explorations [3]. Potential future research in this area may examine the relationship between crew workload profiles and touchdown point dispersion, as well.

References

1. Tongkumchum, P.: Two-dimensional box plot. Songklanakarin J. Sci. Technol. **27**, 59–866 (2005)
2. Wickham, H., Stryjewski, L.: 40 Years of Boxplots. Had.Co.Nz. 1–17 (20..)
3. Knocke, P.C., et al.: Mars exploration rovers landing dispersion analy.. In: Collection of Technical Papers - AIAA/AAS Astrodynamics Specialist Conference, vo. 2, pp. 805–821 (2004). https://doi.org/10.2514/6.2004-5093
4. Potter, K.: Methods for presenting statistical information: the box plot. Vis. Large Unstructured Data Sets **4**, 97–106 (2006)
5. Kratchounova, D., et al.: No one is superman: 3-D safety margin profiles when using head-up display (HUD) for takeoff in low visibility and high crosswind conditions. In: Chen, J.Y.C., Fragomeni, G. (eds.) HCII 2021. LNCS, vol. 12770, pp. 336–352. Springer, Cham (2021). https://doi.org/10.1007/978-3-030-77599-5_24

HUD Training and Extended Reality Solutions

Kyle Morrison[✉], Aaron Perkins, and Adrian Hanson

Collins Aerospace, Wilsonville, OR 97070, USA
kyle.morrison@collins.com

Abstract. Extended reality (XR) training offers pilots unlimited access to familiarize themselves with aircraft systems, instrument procedures, Head-Up Display (HUD) symbology, and Enhanced Flight Vision System (EFVS) features before entering full flight simulator (FFS) training. Historically, HUD training has been accomplished through computer-based training (CBT), paper-based training (PBT), and lower-level flight training devices, but the future of HUD and EFVS training will be through highly immersive XR training. This is an outline for current use cases, software and hardware best practices, and training outlines that are elevated through the use of XR. Collins has set a precedent in the aviation industry by proposing XR training to be approved for ground and flight training in the FAA's Boeing 737 FSB Report. This inclusion of XR in the report is a formal way for the FAA to acknowledge XR as an acceptable way to train pilots, paving the way for the wider adoption of XR solutions in pilot training programs.

Keywords: Extended Reality (XR) · Heads-Up Display (HUD) · Full Flight Simulator (FFS)

1 Introduction

1.1 Pilot Training Overview

Pilot training is a crucial aspect of ensuring aviation safety. It is imperative that pilots are well trained in all aspects of flight and are able to handle any situation that may arise during a flight. Ground training has traditionally been done through PBT and CBT methods. However, these methods of training are limited in their effectiveness, especially in the area of HUD training and EFVS training.

In the past, basic HUD training has been done through CBTs and low-level flight training devices (FTDs). Similarly, this method of training has been found to be less effective when compared to full FFS training. According to a study by the Federal Aviation Administration (FAA), FFS training provides a more immersive and realistic experience for pilots, allowing them to gain a better understanding of the various systems and procedures involved in flying an aircraft.

CBT and PBT have also been found to be lacking in providing pilots with unlimited access and time to familiarize themselves with HUD symbology, system behavior, eye scan pattern requirements, and operational techniques for instrument procedures. This

J. Y. C. Chen and G. Fragomeni (Eds.): HCII 2023, LNCS 14027, pp. 549–559, 2023.
https://doi.org/10.1007/978-3-031-35634-6_40

is particularly important for pilots who are new to using HUD in their aircraft, as it can take time to become fully familiar with the system.

XR-based flight deck (FD) training offers a highly immersive and realistic experience for pilots, allowing them to practice and gain proficiency in using the HUD. The HUD VR Trainer software is produced by Collins Aerospace and built to aid in the training of individuals in the use of a HUD. Our trainer uses XR technology to simulate the Head-Up Guidance System used in a variety of air transport, business jet, and military aircraft. Originally developed as a sales and marketing tool by the Collins Aerospace Head Up Guidance Systems (HGS) business unit, the trainer offers various training scenarios that can be loaded and utilized within the game engine-based software.

When working with XR and HUD training it can provide both instructor led training (ILT) and self-guided training (SGT). Not only that, a game engine-based XR solution allows for instantly interchangeable FDs, rehosts, and training scenarios. XR allows flexibility, coupled with its continuous updates and improvements to meet the ever-changing needs of the industry, which propels the growing adoption of this method of training. Training built with an XR framework, utilizing OpenXR (explained below), further enhances the training experience by providing a more immersive and interactive environment that can adapt and evolve with technological advancement (Fig. 1).

Fig. 1. Image of HUD VR Trainer Unity Architecture

Furthermore, the use of new XR advancements, such as haptics and hand-tracking, allows for more intuitive and natural interactions with the virtual environment. This can lead to a more efficient and effective training experience that feels familiar to pilots.

Overall, by utilizing and developing an XR training environment, new use cases have been discovered that offer new solutions to traditional training methods. These advancements have the potential to greatly enhance training and prepare individuals for not just the use of a HUD but all aspects of the FD. By integrating advanced FFS software with XR technology and state-of-the-art game engines, complemented by comprehensive training software, XR HUD training can be adapted into a proficient alternative to FFS training that caters to the growing requirements, many times in a shorter time period, with instructors and pilots.

2 Traditional Flight Deck Software

The software architecture that is traditionally suitable for FFS combines avionic rehosts, an out-the-window image generator (IG), and a simulation software base.

Integration of a next-generation IG, with the increased graphics fidelity and real-time rendering capabilities of modern game engines like Unreal Engine or Unity, has the potential to revolutionize FFS.

2.1 Avionic Rehosts

Systems like the HUD are powered by proprietary hardware and software when installed in a FD. Avionic Rehosting is a software package that transfers the avionics system of a physical FD to a simulated environment. We use avionic rehosting for testing, development, training, and verification of avionics systems without the need for flight testing. Rehosting is a safer and cost-effective way to validate new systems, and upgrade software and hardware configurations before deployment. Furthermore, avionic rehosts allow pilots to train and receive credit on simulated FDs.

2.2 Simulation Software

Simulation architecture provides a comprehensive and realistic aircraft simulation. The architecture is a detailed simulation of various aerodynamic and structural elements of the aircraft, including wing and body shapes, engine performance, and control surfaces. Our system is designed to provide basic autopilot functions such as altitude hold, heading hold, speed control, etc. It can be used for free flight or to provide a base-level of automation for more advanced training scenarios. Our simulation software is CORESIM. It is designed as a modified aero model for large commercial aircraft. A UDP connection is made between a game engine and CORESIM to control the IG, simulation software, and game engine interactions and visuals.

2.3 Image Generators

IGs are responsible for generating high-resolution images that simulate the view from the FD. IGs are typically divided into two main components: the image generation unit and the projection hardware. The IG software compiles 3D models and textures from a terrain database of real-world terrain, cities, and airports. The projection hardware projects visual components of the IG onto a display viewable in the FFS. Typically, this unit uses a combination of lenses and mirrors to project the images in a way that simulates a pilot's perspective on a FD.

2.4   Future of Image Generators and XR Integration

An IG built with a modern-day game engine like Unreal Engine or Unity has the potential to revolutionize aviation training. With the advanced graphics and real-time rendering capabilities of game engines, a game engine-driven IG will unlock a range of new features and capabilities that were previously unavailable with traditional IGs.

One of the key benefits of using game engines is the engine's ability to provide increased graphics fidelity. For example, CAE has shifted its focus to the Unreal Engine as its software platform for its next generation of visual solutions. The shift is a result of the advancements in visual systems technology and the advantages of Unreal Engine's ecosystem of content and community. CAE's Vice President of Technology and Innovation, Marc St-Hilaire, notes that the simulation industry was previously facing many challenges in creating an immersive and effective training solution, but these have now been solved due to advancements in game engine technology, GPU power, and other elements that make up a simulation solution. Coupling the power of Unreal Engine, satellite imagery, and digital terrain data sources rapidly develops large-scale gaming areas [1].

Beyond that, modern game engines also have built-in support for XR devices, enabling the possibility to create a next-gen IG that has XR support from the start. Beyond that, it removes the need for a projection system as the entire world becomes projected within the XR device. This support also comes in the form of compatibility with current and future GPUs. Furthermore, they have built-in support architecture to easily create and manage large-scale multiplayer games, and provide a powerful platform for building an IG that can support multiple users at once providing a more collaborative and interactive training experience.

3   Technology

Certain technology and hardware are more suitable for XR training. Rigorous trial and error has led to the development of a solution that is intuitive and useful for pilots. A significant challenge was posed by the inherent complexity of emerging XR technology, as each new headset, controller, and software update added more for pilots to learn and adapt to, taking away from the focus of actual flight training. Specific XR devices and SDKs eliminate these challenges providing easier access to high-fidelity training that surpasses CBT and PBT.

3.1   Hand Tracking

Hand tracking technology is produced by a depth-sensing camera that is mounted or built into the front of an XR headset. It is a newly viable user input system that has many benefits over existing physical controllers and has proven to be a better solution in regard to more natural interactions with the FD environment. Interacting with joysticks such as a yoke and throttle is a challenging task with hand controllers. With hand tracking, it becomes instantly easier and more intuitive. When using XR hand controllers you need to place them down to be able to interact with a physical yoke, joystick, or throttle. Beyond that developing hand tracking with OpenXR enables the system to be configured with most modern hand-tracking devices allowing easy upgrades and industry standardization (Fig. 2).

Fig. 2. HUD VR Trainer Hand Tracking | Extended Reality Lab | Collins Aerospace | Portland, OR

Not only does hand-tracking eliminate the need for users to learn how to use a controller, but it has been found to lead to more accurate and natural interactions with better retention in training. An IEEE study found that hand tracking led to better accuracy in the cognitive load task and participants used both hands more equally in hand-tracking mode than in controller conditions. Hand tracking reduces cognitive load and although it is still slower than controller tracking, the use of haptic cues can enhance accuracy for manual tasks. The study showed improved speed in completing the task with haptics and other forms of feedback. For example, the sound of a button press with a corresponding button motion can make up for the lack of haptics [7].

3.2 Haptics

The use of haptic devices with hand tracking has become increasingly popular in aviation training. Interacting with the simulation of a FD is more realistic and immersive with the combination of haptic devices and hand tracking than with hand controllers alone (Fig. 3).

This increased level of immersion can result in a more effective training experience for pilots. A study published in the Affective Computing and Human-Computer Interactions collection investigated the effects of haptic gloves on the retention of training in a virtual environment and its transfer to real tasks. The results showed that the

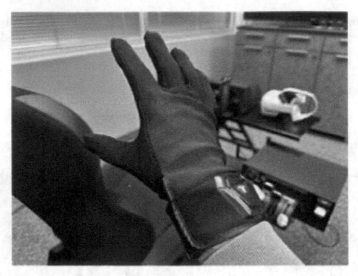

Fig. 3. Bhaptics TactGlove | Extended Reality Lab | Collins Aerospace | Portland, OR

use of augmented, multisensory cues such as haptic vibrations from gloves, improved both performance and user experience in the virtual environment and also transferred to improved performance in the real task. The use of haptic gloves was proposed as an effective and efficient way to represent cues such as torque and weight that are difficult to simulate in VR environments. Haptic gloves can enhance the transfer of training from virtual to real scenarios with higher knowledge retention [2].

3.3 XR Headsets and SDKs

At aviation trade shows and conferences you will see XR present at nearly every booth. XR devices have the potential to revolutionize aviation training by providing a more immersive and interactive experience for students, which leads to higher retention rates. For varying use cases, it is best to deploy different XR hardware based on the needs of the user. However, there are a wide variety of SDKs that tend to be platform-specific, closing the software off from different devices and use cases.

For a trainer that needs to be portable and will be used in various locations, headsets that offer standalone capabilities, like the Meta Quest platform and certain Vive headsets, allow students and instructors to transport and set up the device package easily. For higher fidelity, stationary, and mixed reality setups, the Varjo XR platform is emerging somewhat as an unofficial industry standard. Offering high-fidelity graphics and a high-fidelity passthrough camera, the Varjo platform allows for more complex setups that can even incorporate real-world avionic hardware.

There are several XR SDKs available, primarily OpenVR, Oculus VR, and OpenXR. OpenVR is a platform developed by Valve Corporation that is commonly used in gaming. Oculus VR is a platform developed by Meta and is commonly used in the gaming and entertainment industries. Then there is OpenXR, which is an industry-standard platform for XR devices, developed by the Khronos Group, that aims to provide compatibility between different XR devices and applications.

OpenXR allows for cross-platform compatibility, meaning that nearly any XR device can be used with software developed using OpenXR, regardless of the device's brand or model [9]. This feature greatly expands the potential user base for XR aviation training programs, as training facilities and pilots can use the XR device of their choice. It offers a comprehensive set of features and APIs (Application Programming Interfaces) that developers can use to create high-quality XR experiences. This includes hand tracking, eye tracking, and 6 degrees of freedom tracking, which allow for more realistic and intuitive interactions in XR environments. OpenXR also provides support for multiple rendering engines, including Unreal Engine and Unity, enabling developers to choose the engine that best fits their needs [9].

3.4 Game Engines

A game engine is software that provides a set of tools and functionality to game developers, enabling them to construct their games with professional and efficient methods (Unity, 2023). They provide a large library of assets and plugins that can be used to enhance the synthetic environment, such as weather effects, particle systems, and AI characters as well as marketplaces with user created content. Game engines also provide support for XR devices and require much less development time to integrate. Leveraging these provides an environment to which a synthetic FD can be crafted for training. Avionic rehosts and IGs can be integrated into the game engine directly off a pixel buffer and integrated with simulation software to populate a fully synthetic XR FD (Fig. 4).

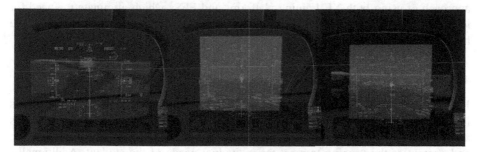

Fig. 4. HUD VR Trainer realistic representative HUDs in Unity

One of the main challenges with developing with a game engine for aviation training is the cost and complexity of developing and maintaining this kind of synthetic environment, as it can require significant programming expertise and specialized knowledge. It is important to note, building a synthetic XR FD environment requires not only systems and simulation engineers, but also engineers with knowledge of game engines, XR technology and development, and artists with knowledge of 3D software. Engineers and artists will need to have knowledge of modeling software (Blender), gaming engines (Unity and Unreal Engine), and editing software (Photoshop), as well as a knowledge of C#, C++, and networking standards for simulation control and multiplayer setup.

4 Training

Training demands in the aviation industry are currently at an all-time high, and limited resources for both instructors and FFSs are proving to be a challenge. According to Scott Kirby, the CEO of United Airlines, the shortage of pilots in the industry is a significant issue, and many airlines will be unable to reach their planned capacities in the next 5 years or more. He mentioned this during a quarterly earnings call in April [8]. In response, XR technology can significantly fill the gap. One of the primary advantages of XR technology is that it provides an immersive, interactive experience for pilots in training. With XR, pilots can interact with the virtual environment in a way that simulates the experience of being in the FD of a real aircraft. This allows them to practice and perfect the skills required for successful instrument flight procedures.

Another benefit of XR-based FD training is that it provides pilots with unlimited access to the training environment. Unlike traditional flight simulators, which are often in high demand and have limited availability, XR technology provides pilots with access to the training environment whenever they need it. Training can be done anytime, anywhere, for a fraction of the cost.

Furthermore, XR-based FD training allows pilots to familiarize themselves with the unique HUD symbology and system behavior of a particular aircraft. This helps to reduce the learning curve and time required that is associated with FFS training, allowing pilots to hit the ground running when they begin training on the FFS.

XR-based FD HUD training will enable the industry to train for both baseline HUD usage as well as provide for EFVS training requirements. HUD and EFVS training in the past have historically been accomplished through: 1) ILT, 2) SGT with CBT modules, 3) FTDs, and 4) Level D FFS. The future of HUD and EFVS training will be an integrated approach of using both XR training platforms and FFSs which eliminate the need for less effective solutions like CBTs and expensive FTDs. Training providers that utilize highly immersive XR training before FFSs will produce proficient pilots in less time.

4.1 Instructor Led Training

ILT has long been the dominant approach to training in the aviation industry, with students learning from an experienced instructor who provides direct guidance and feedback. This approach allows for the personalization of training, as the instructor can adjust the pace and content of the training to meet the individual needs of the student. Additionally, ILT provides a structured environment in which students can practice procedures and techniques in real-time with the instructor.

4.2 Self-guided Instruction

However, ILT can also be limited by the availability of qualified instructors and the cost of training, as well as the constraints of scheduling and location. In contrast, self-guided training provides a more flexible and cost-effective solution, allowing students to access training materials and resources at their own pace and convenience. This approach is particularly beneficial for reinforcing learning and improving skills, as students can revisit training materials as many times as needed.

The integration of a portable XR training platform that provides both types of training options has the potential to greatly benefit pilot training. A platform that combines the personalized guidance and feedback of ILT with the flexibility and cost-effectiveness of SGT can provide students with a comprehensive training experience that meets their individual needs. Furthermore, XR technology provides a number of benefits to the industry in terms of FD training, including unlimited access to the training environment and the ability to familiarize students with HUD symbology, system behavior, eye scan pattern requirements, and operational techniques for instrument procedures.

4.3 Flight Training Devices

As defined by FAA Part 60, FSTDs include FTD at levels 4–7, all of which are non-motion based. FTDs, depending on the level, are a clone of aircraft controls, equipment, instrumentation, and aerodynamic modeling. The FTD includes the hardware and software necessary to represent the aircraft operation in ground and flight conditions. FTD Level 4 is the lowest level approved for flight training credit and is a basic cockpit procedural trainer which often incorporates touchscreen displays. A FTD Level 5 requires generic aerodynamic modeling but must have physical representative controls for primary and secondary flight controls. All other controls may incorporate touch screen displays. A Level 6 FTD must have an aircraft specific aerodynamic model and all switches, controls, and knobs must physically replicate the aircraft. A Level 7 FTD is currently for helicopters only and must include a replica of all controls & systems with a type specific aerodynamic model, vibration system, and a visual system [5].

FTDs are being used by air carriers and flight training providers today to allow pilots to learn cockpit flows, system integration, and standard operating procedures. All of these training facets can be trained in an XR platform; and, because the FAA does not require FTD training for HUD or EFVS operations, XR training is poised to replace the use of expensive and resource-limited FTDs.

4.4 Full Flight Simulator Training

Level D FFSs provide full-motion immersive training which serves as the gold standard for preparing pilots to fly a specific aircraft [4]. The FAA does not require by rule that pilots use a Level D FFS for HUD training; however, the FAA FSB Reports do contain HUD specific maneuvers to be flown in a simulator prior to aircraft operation. For example, the Boeing 737 FSB Report requires a variety of maneuvers for HUD qualification such as straight and level flight, stall prevention and recovery, and unusual attitudes. Additionally, a number of instrument approach procedures are recommended such as CAT I, CAT II, and CAT III approaches with various environmental requirements relating to visibility, ceilings, and winds [6].

While XR FD training platforms won't replace FFS flight training for HUD, XR can be used to supplement and reduce the time required in a FFS. The benchmark that signals 'end-of-training' for the HUD is that a pilot must demonstrate satisfactory knowledge and flight proficiency during a check with an examiner. Proficiency is the requirement, not a set number of Level D FFS hours, which allows XR training solutions to provide the needed training for a pilot to become proficient before FFS training commences.

Collins has taken the next step in solidifying XR training by formally proposing training credit to the FAA for both ground and flight training for Boeing 737 Head-Up Guidance Training. Appendix 5 of the Boeing 737 FSB Report contains the existing requirements for HUD training; and, XR methods are expected to be adopted as a means of training for ground training as well as certain tasks required for flight training in the next revision of the document.

4.5 EFVS Training

EFVS flight training does differ from baseline HUD training in that the FAA has both a dedicated rule (61.66) and Advisory Circular (90-106B). The FAA specifies that EFVS flight training may be accomplished in an aircraft or in a FFS; but if a FFS is used, it must be in a Level C or higher FFS, and be equipped with an EFVS [3]. Just like baseline HUD training though, the FAA does not specify a minimum number of hours in a Level C FFS, instead, training is centered on certain tasks and maneuvers. CFR 61.66 requires flight training on tasks such as pre-flight and inflight preparation, EFVS use of display, controls, and modes. The rule also requires pilot techniques for taxi, takeoff, climb, cruise, descent, landing, and rollout conducted during both day and night conditions.

The tasks outlined above can be trained with an XR FD platform and mastered before spending any time in a FFS. Of greatest value perhaps comes with the XR training for learning how to use EFVS sensor imagery and gaining exposure to normal and abnormal EFVS system behavior. Trainees can use the XR training platform to look at EFVS artifacts like blooming and halo, as well as programing the training device to experience non-normal image presentations such as flipped, frozen or inverted images. A typical training program may only show these image abnormalities during ground training with videos because the FFS is not programmed for these failures or there's insufficient time to cover corner case failures; but, with XR training platforms pilots will be able to experience these enhanced vision anomalies 'real time' while flying an instrument approach and learn to apply corrective actions.

Just like baseline HUD training, XR FD training cannot replace the use of a FFS but training providers can make full use of XR and train all tasks and maneuvers until the pilot trainee is proficient and has mastered the system. By doing so, each training provider will deliver highly competent HUD and EFVS pilots into the FFS stage of flight training.

5 Conclusion

In conclusion, XR technology offers numerous benefits for aviation training, specifically in terms of preparing pilots for the use of HUD systems and EFVS. By incorporating haptic devices, hand tracking, IGs, avionic rehosting, and game engines, XR technology creates an immersive and interactive environment that can significantly improve the training experience for pilots. The use of hand tracking and haptic devices provides elevated realism and intuitive control, while IGs built with game engines like Unreal Engine provide a more dynamic and immersive synthetic environment with XR capabilities built in. The integration of OpenXR offers a comprehensive and flexible platform for XR device integration, offering users more choices in regard to hardware. XR technology's ability to allow pilots unlimited access to the training environment and to familiarize themselves with the HUD system at their own pace is another key benefit. XR technology addresses the challenges posed by limited resources for both instructors and flight simulators. Keeping pace with XR technology as it grows and evolves has the potential to revolutionize the training experience for pilots and prepare them for the use of HUDs in aviation.

References

1. Unreal Engine. CAE Pivots to Unreal Engine for Next-Gen Flight Simulators (2022). www.unrealengine.com/en-US/spotlights/cae-pivots-to-unreal-engine-for-next-gen-flight-simulators
2. Cooper, N., et al.: Transfer of training-virtual reality training with augmented multisensory cues improves user experience during training and task performance in the real world. PLOS ONE. Public Library of Science (2021). https://journals.plos.org/plosone/article?id=10.1371%2Fjournal.pone.0248225
3. Federal Aviation Administration, Advisory Circular 90–106B, Enhanced Flight Vision System Operations (2017)
4. Federal Aviation Administration. Flight Simulator Qualification Test Guide (2019)
5. Federal Aviation Administration. Code of Federal Regulations, Part 60 (2023)
6. Federal Aviation Administration, Boeing 737 Flight Standardization Board Report (2021)
7. Jamalian, N., Gillies, M., Leymarie, F.F., Pan, X.: The effects of hand tracking on user performance: an experimental study of an object selection based memory game. In: 2022 IEEE International Symposium on Mixed and Augmented Reality (ISMAR), pp. 768–776. Singapore, (2022). https://doi.org/10.1109/ISMAR55827.2022.00095
8. Josephs, L.: A severe pilot shortage in the U.S. leaves airlines scrambling for solutions, CNBC, CNBC (2022). https://www.cnbc.com/2022/05/15/us-pilot-shortage-forces-airlines-to-cut-flights-scramble-for-solutions.html. Accessed 20 Dec 20 2022
9. Khronos Group. OpenXR. (2020). https://www.khronos.org/openxr/

Impacts of Dual Head-Up Display Use on Workload in the Civil Aviation Flight Deck: Implications for Crew Coordination

David C. Newton[1]([⌧]) [iD], Jeremy Hesselroth[1], and Rebecca DiDomenica[2] [iD]

[1] Federal Aviation Administration, Oklahoma City, OK 73169, USA
David.C.Newton@faa.gov
[2] Cherokee Nation, 3-S, Oklahoma City, OK 73169, USA

Abstract. In a two-person flight crew, the ability of each crewmember to maintain a shared mental model during flight is foundational to flight safety. The addition of a head-up display (HUD) for the pilot flying (PF) represents a departure from traditional flight deck design where each pilot is able to view the same primary flight display. With a single HUD, the PF is able to use a display that is not available to the PM. As such, operating an aircraft with a single HUD may alter the shared mental model compared to operating an aircraft with dual HUDs. In the case of single HUD use during approach and landing, the PM does not see the primary flight information that the HUD superimposes onto earth-based reference points. The PM also is unable to maintain visual contact with out-the-window visual information while simultaneously monitoring flight information. As such, the PM may experience different workload levels when monitoring without a HUD compared to monitoring with a HUD. The present study attempts to uncover the contribution of dual HUD use to the optimization of crew workload by measuring pilots' workload during a series of simulated, low-visibility approach and landing scenarios in a flight simulator. After each scenario, pilot workload was measured using the NASA Task Load Index (NASA-TLX). Crew workload was evaluated as a function of dual HUD vs. single HUD use and runway visual range (RVR). The findings regarding crew workload, crew coordination, and HUD use are discussed.

Keywords: Head-up Display · Mental Workload · Civil Aviation

1 Introduction

1.1 Crew Coordination in Transport-Category Aircraft

In the civil aviation flight deck, the ability of each crew member to coordinate with one another during flight is a foundational component of flight safety. This is particularly the case in the traditional two-person transport-category flight deck, where responsibilities are divided based on the pilot flying the aircraft (PF) and the pilot monitoring the aircraft (PM) [1]. Crew coordination is the practical application of a shared mental model to a set of circumstances. This includes clear and concise communication, both verbal and

© The Author(s), under exclusive license to Springer Nature Switzerland AG 2023
J. Y. C. Chen and G. Fragomeni (Eds.): HCII 2023, LNCS 14027, pp. 560–571, 2023.
https://doi.org/10.1007/978-3-031-35634-6_41

non-verbal, to arrive at a shared understanding of the current status of the aircraft and the environment in which it is operating. Crew coordination involves the use of standardized language and phrases, in addition to Standard Operating Procedures, which direct the use of common communication-enhancing behaviors. An example of this is the 'call and response' model inherent in checklist usage and the verbalization and verification of changes made to levels of automation [2].

Crew coordination is further enhanced by a clear delineation of flight deck responsibilities. The PF is primarily responsible for flight path and aircraft energy management. The PM verifies the PF flight path and energy management, makes Flight Management System entries, runs checklists, manipulates flaps and gear, and is responsible for internal and external communications. Flight deck operations during a standard instrument approach to a full-stop landing are a useful example to describe how the PF/PM workload division contributes to the safe operation of transport category aircraft. The fact that workload responsibilities are divided in a known, reliable, and repeatable way allows the PF to concentrate on primary flight information (e.g., airspeed, altitude, glide slope, and localizer deviation) and manipulate the flight controls without having to allocate their cognitive resources to monitoring duties, which might compromise flying performance [3].

This division of responsibilities is especially beneficial during abnormal events (e.g., rapidly-changing weather, flight plan changes, and aircraft emergencies). For example, if cloud ceiling height and prevailing visibility are at the minimum levels required for the approach, the PF may find that the mental demands of flying a stabilized approach and acquiring the airfield visually consume substantially more cognitive resources, and that having to perform a PM task, such as answering a radio call, may result in a deviation from the intended flight path or aircraft energy state [4].

This same principle applies to other previously mentioned external factors, like aircraft system malfunctions and emergencies. When an aircraft malfunction presents itself, the pilot who recognizes it first makes a clear, declarative statement as to the nature of the malfunction. The PF will then call for the appropriate checklist, which the PM facilitates. These checklists often contain critical steps that require the PF to visually confirm before they are executed (e.g., shutting down an engine that is on fire). Some events take priority over the checklist; however, depending on the nature of the emergency and the position of the aircraft, the flight crew may elect to execute a missed approach and climb to a higher altitude before completing the checklist, thereby reducing the cognitive demand on the PF [5].

Taken together, crew coordination is a multidimensional, dynamic component of civil aviation flight that is characterized by continuous scanning and interaction with visual information located throughout the flight deck, shared awareness of critical flight information, and a common mental model of the current situation on the part of both crew members. Throughout this process, significant fluctuations in workload may occur that can affect the crew's ability to coordinate successfully with one another. As flight deck technology has advanced, it may be possible for new display technologies to facilitate shared awareness and successful crew coordination.

1.2 Head-Up Displays for Civil Aviation

The head-up display (HUD) is one advancement in flight deck technology designed to improve flight-crew performance and situation awareness, particularly during high-workload phases of flight, such as takeoff, approach, and landing. The HUD is a transparent display fixed in front of the PF that superimposes critical aircraft information (i.e., near field) on top of natural, out-the-window (i.e., far field) information [6].

HUD use during flight reduces the amount of effort and workload required to maintain awareness of critical flight information both inside and outside of the aircraft. The HUD allows the pilot to maintain visual contact with the far-field, out-the-window visual information, such as runway markings, airfield lighting systems, and other air traffic. In addition to reduced pilot workload, these benefits manifest as improved flight path tracking performance, and improved ability to detect expected changes in near- and far-field visual information [7].

The benefits and drawbacks described previously are with regard to HUD use by the PF. There is comparatively little scientific knowledge on how HUD use might impact the PM, who may use the HUD to monitor the aircraft's state. Based on what is known about the benefits and drawbacks of the HUD from a PF perspective, it is likely that many of these factors, including reductions in pilot workload, may transfer to the PM.

1.3 The Present Study

Given what is known about the impact of HUD use on pilot performance and workload for the PF, it is important to understand how HUD use by the PM might impact workload, particularly during the high-workload phases of flight (i.e., approach and landing). While the PF uses the HUD to manually control the aircraft and guide it toward the runway touchdown zone during an approach and landing, the PM uses the HUD to monitor primary flight information to ensure there are no anomalies in aircraft and pilot performance. As such, the relative workload profile between single and dual HUD use may be different for the PM, and it is important to understand this relationship. Therefore, the purpose of the present study is to explore whether the addition of a HUD for the PM produces any changes in workload compared to when the PM does not use a HUD.

2 Method

2.1 Participants

Twenty-four Airline Transport Pilot Captains from major airlines in the United States volunteered to participate in this research. The participants were paired into two-person flight crews for the study session, resulting in 12 crews. Crew members received monetary compensation in exchange for their participation. Each participant (a) held an Airline Transport Pilot (ATP) certificate; (b) was qualified and current as pilot-in-command in a Boeing 737; (c) had at least 100 h of flight time with a HUD; and (d) had flown with a HUD within 30 days of study participation.

2.2 Simulator and Study Materials

Simulated flights were conducted in a CAE Boeing 737–800 Level D, Full Flight Simulator, located at the Federal Aviation Administration (FAA) Mike Monroney Aeronautical Center in Oklahoma City, Oklahoma. In addition to replicating the flight deck and flight dynamics of a Boeing 737–800, the simulator includes a six-axis pneumatic motion system, night/dusk/day out-the-window visual model with a collimated out-the-window visual system, comprehensive weather and wind modeling system, and dynamic loading of flight controls. The simulator is equipped with dual Collins Aerospace HGS-6700 HUDs. In this study, the HUDs were set with AIII mode activated, providing automatic flight path guidance to touchdown and lateral guidance during rollout.

To measure crew workload, each participant was given a booklet containing 48 copies of the NASA Task Load Index (NASA-TLX) rating scale—one scale for each simulated flight scenario. The NASA-TLX evaluates crew workload across six subscales (i.e., Mental Demand, Physical Demand, Temporal Demand, Performance, Mental Effort, and Frustration) and is supplemented with a composite (Total) score by weighting tallies. NASA-TLX subscale scores can range from 0–20 and the total weighted score can range from 0–100, with larger scores indicating greater overall workload [8–10].

Along with the NASA-TLX, each participant also received a booklet containing approach procedure charts for each of the 48 simulated flight scenarios in the study. These approach procedure charts provided pilots with the information necessary to conduct an Instrument Landing System (ILS) approach into the runway in use for each scenario.

2.3 Simulated Flights

Each simulated flight scenario involved an ILS approach and landing beginning six miles from the runway threshold. At the beginning of each scenario, the aircraft was aligned with the final approach fix, traveling at the target airspeed, and configured for landing before control was transferred to the crew.

All of the experimental flight scenarios occurred during the daytime and involved overcast conditions. Winds were present in each scenario and were of a constant baseline velocity of 14 knots, with gusts up to 26 knots present from the start of the scenario down to the cloud ceiling, at which point the gusts died out and a constant wind of 14 knots was present. The wind direction was offset either 60 degrees left or 60 degrees right from the runway heading, resulting in a crosswind component of 11 knots.

2.4   Research Design and Variables

This study used a fully within-subjects design, with each two-person flight crew completing a total of 48 simulated approach and landing scenarios. There were two independent variables evaluated in this study: Display Type (Dual HUD vs. Single HUD) and Runway Visual Range (RVR; 1200 ft vs. 1000 ft vs. 600 ft vs 300 ft).

The primary independent variable in this study is Display Type—that is, whether both HUDs were deployed during the approach and landing (Dual HUD) or only the PF HUD was deployed (Single HUD). Scenarios where only the PF HUD was deployed are the baseline condition, representing the current state of HUD operations at the time of this publication. Scenarios where both the PF and PM HUDs are deployed are the experimental condition of interest, representing future flight deck operations where the PF and PM both have superimposed primary flight information available to them.

The second independent variable in this study is RVR, which is defined as the horizontal distance a pilot can expect to see down the runway, based on sighting either the High-Intensity Runway Lights (HIRL) or the visual contrast of other targets, whichever yields the greater visual range [11]. Four levels of RVR were implemented in this study: 1200 ft, 1000 ft, 600 ft, and 300 ft. The RVR levels in this study were selected based on the authorized minimum visibility levels for four major categories of ILS approaches: Special Authorization Category II (1200 ft RVR), Standard Category II (1000 ft RVR), Fail Passive Category III (600 ft RVR), and Fail Operational Category III (300 ft RVR) [12]. The purpose of this variable was to progressively reduce the saliency of out-the-window visual information, necessitating greater reliance on HUD symbology.

2.5   Procedure

The FAA Civil Aerospace Medical Institute Institutional Review Board approved all study procedures. Upon arrival, participants provided their consent to participate in the research and were provided an overview of the study's purpose and procedures. Participants then received a detailed briefing to help them become familiar with the flight scenarios they would be performing during the study session. This briefing also contained a description of the NASA-TLX, including an explanation of the six subscales and when to complete them. Participants then viewed a training video describing the HUD symbology specific to approach and landing. Following the briefing, participants received a flight deck walk-through and familiarization session led by a Boeing 737-type rated pilot.

Following the familiarization session, pilots completed the main study session, which consisted of a series of 48 ILS approach and landing scenarios into runways. To maximize participant engagement, unique runways were used for each of the approach and landing scenarios. All scenarios were conducted with the autopilot and autothrottles disengaged, requiring the pilot to manually control the speed, altitude, and attitude of the aircraft. Before each approach and landing, the experimenter briefed the crew on the runway and approach procedure in use, visibility, winds, and whether the PM HUD was deployed (the PF HUD was deployed in all flight scenarios). The crew then carried out an approach checklist to verify aircraft configuration and approach procedure. When the pilots announced that the checklist was complete, the experimenter cleared the aircraft for landing and began the simulation. After each scenario, each pilot completed the rating scale portion of the NASA-TLX. This procedure was repeated for each of the 48 simulated flight scenarios.

Following the main study session, participants completed the debriefing session, during which the NASA-TLX paired comparison procedure was carried out. In this procedure, participants were shown 15 paired combinations of the NASA-TLX subscale names and were asked to identify one of the two paired subscales that contributed the most to their workload during the flight scenarios.

3 Results

Each of the six subscale scores of the NASA-TLX and the total weighted NASA-TLX score were averaged between PF and PM, and plotted by RVR condition (i.e., 1200 ft, 1000 ft, 600 ft, or 300 ft) and between display condition (i.e., Single or Dual HUD). Patterns among the means indicate that NASA-TLX scores, and hence workload, generally increased with decreasing RVR, but there were no statistically significant differences between display conditions (see Fig. 1, 2, 3, 4, 5, 6 and 7).

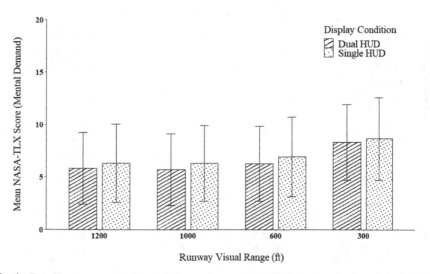

Fig. 1. Bar Chart presenting Mental Demand scores by RVR between single and dual HUD.

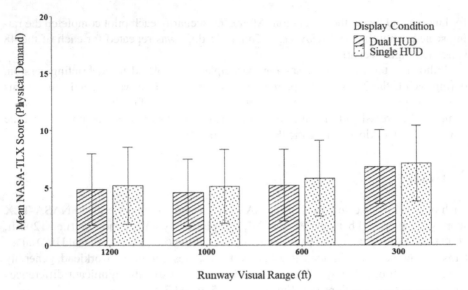

Fig. 2. Bar Chart for Physical Demand scores by RVR between Dual and Single HUD.

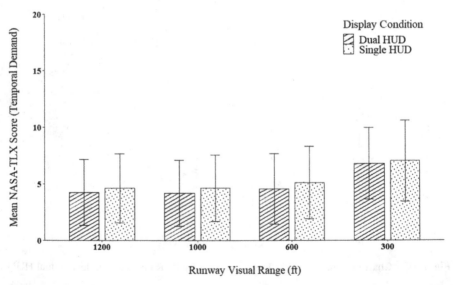

Fig. 3. Bar Chart for Temporal Demand scores by RVR between Dual and Single HUD.

Seven two-way Analysis of Variance (ANOVA) tests were conducted to assess the effect of visibility for RVR (with 4 levels, 1200 ft, 1000 ft, 600 ft, or 300 ft) and display type for HUD (with 2 levels, single or dual HUD) on NASA-TLX scores in normal scenarios. For analyses purposes, NASA-TLX scores for PM and PF in the same run were averaged for each of the six subscale and total weighted NASA-TLX scores. For example, a Mental Demand NASA-TLX subscale score for PM under the same scenario

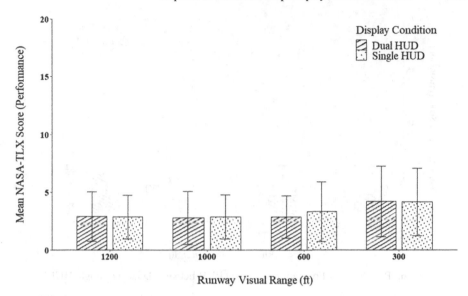

Fig. 4. Bar Chart for Performance scores by RVR between Dual and Single HUD.

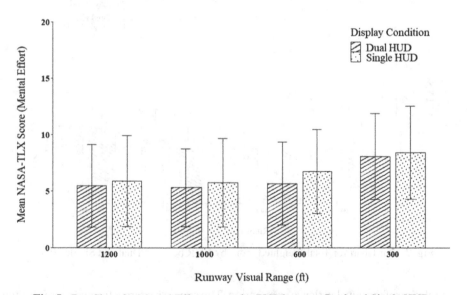

Fig. 5. Bar Chart for Mental Effort scores by RVR between Dual and Single HUD.

having a specific RVR and HUD condition (e.g., 1200 ft RVR and single HUD) was averaged with a Mental Demand NASA-TLX subscale score for PF.

The data were evaluated for normality and equality of variances. Performance and Frustration subscales violated the equality of variances assumption, and all subscales and total weighted NASA-TLX scores violated the normality assumption. A square root transformation was applied to Performance and Frustration subscale scores to address

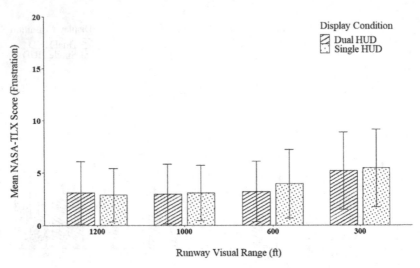

Fig. 6. Bar Chart for Frustration scores by RVR between Dual and Single HUD.

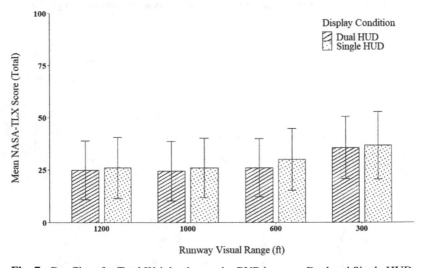

Fig. 7. Bar Chart for Total Weighted score by RVR between Dual and Single HUD.

the violation of the equal variance assumption. The square root transformed scores for the Performance subscale met the equal variance assumption, but the Frustration subscale still violated the assumption. Although normality remained violated for all NASA-TLX dimensions, ANOVAs are generally robust to violations of normality, and as such, this should not measurably affect results [13–15].

All ANOVA results including the six subscales and total weighted NASA-TLX scores are summarized in Table 1. For all ANOVA models, the interaction between HUD and RVR, as well as that of HUD were not significant, while the effect of RVR was significant. For example, there was no significant interaction between RVR and HUD with respect to the total weighted NASA-TLX scores; $F(3,376) = 0.20$, $p = .896$, $\eta^2 = 0.002$. There was no significant effect of HUD on the total weighted NASA-TLX scores; $F(1,376) = 1.70$, $p = .193$, $\eta^2 = 0.004$; however, there was a statistically significant effect of RVR on the total weighted NASA-TLX scores; $F(3,376) = 11.96$, $p < .001$, $\eta^2 = 0.087$. Tukey HSD pairwise comparisons were evaluated for RVR across all subscales and the total weighted NASA-TLX scores. NASA-TLX scores for 300 ft RVR were significantly higher than those of 600 ft, 1000 ft, and 1200 ft RVR in all subscales and the total weighted NASA-TLX scores, and no significant differences between 600 ft, 1000 ft, and 1200 ft RVR were observed.

Table 1. NASA-TLX Subscales and Total Weighted Score.

NASA-TLX Subscale	Display Condition			RVR		
	$F(1, 376)$	p-value	η^2	$F(3, 376)$	p-value	η^2
Mental Demand	2.07	0.151	0.005	9.73	<.001	0.072
Physical Demand	1.88	0.172	0.005	8.67	<.001	0.064
Temporal Demand	1.58	0.210	0.004	14.18	<.001	0.101
Performance*	0.15	0.695	0.000	5.29	=.001	0.040
Mental Effort	2.23	0.137	0.005	10.47	<.001	0.077
Frustration*	0.56	0.454	0.001	11.13	<.001	0.081
Total Weighted Score	1.70	0.193	0.004	11.96	<.001	0.087

Note. Performance and Frustration subscales were reported with respect to square root transformed values

4 Discussion

The purpose of this study was to evaluate whether the addition of a second HUD, used by the PM, produced changes in workload during approach and landing operations in a transport category aircraft compared to a baseline condition of single HUD use. The results indicate that a second HUD resulted in no measurable change in workload, both in terms of global workload as measured by the NASA-TLX weighted total score, as well as across the six dimensions of workload measured by the NASA-TLX subscales. Conversely, crew workload did increase significantly as RVR decreased, indicating that reduced saliency of out-the-window visual information is accompanied by increased cognitive demands on the crew. This suggests that HUD plays in crew coordination during low-visibility flight operations.

The absence of significant differences in NASA-TLX scores between the single HUD and dual HUD conditions indicates that crew workload is unaffected by the presence of a HUD for the PM. The takeaways from this finding are two-fold. First, this indicates that the HUD does not increase workload under conditions that were imposed in this experiment. The presence of the HUD for the PM has the potential to impose additional demands on workload because it increases the amount of information that the PM may be required to monitor during approach and landing operations. Second, this finding indicates that the presence of the HUD does not reduce crew workload, which could indicate that HUD use by the PM causes them to re-allocate their attentional resources during monitoring. It is important to note that the approach and landing operations conducted as part of the research presented herein involved strictly routine operations; that is, no non-routine failures or unexpected events occurred. Previous research suggests that non-routine events, such as engine failures, can elevate workload significantly beyond that which is experienced during routine operations [16].

There are a few limitations to note. The first limitation is related to the use of flight simulation, and the associated pitfalls of this method of evaluation compared to real flight tests. While a Level D flight simulator can reliably mimic many of the characteristics of real-world flight and are advantageous in terms of their consistency and data collection capability, they cannot replicate real-world flight. This is particularly the case in terms of the workload that pilots experience during flight. During simulated flight, workload levels often do not reach levels experienced during real flight, particularly during high-workload phases such as approach and landing [17]. A second limitation of this study concerns the magnitude of differences between RVR levels. The RVR levels in this study were selected based on the authorized minimum visibility levels for four major categories of ILS approaches: Special Authorization Category II (1200 ft RVR), Standard Category II (1000 ft RVR), Fail Passive Category III (600 ft RVR), and Fail Operational Category III (300 ft RVR) [11]. Evaluating use of dual HUD in the context of these approach procedures is important in determining the operational suitability of dual HUD use. However, the effect size afforded by the differences between these levels may be minimal from a workload standpoint. That is, it may be possible to detect greater changes across visibility levels if a wider range of RVR level is used.

Taken together, this research represents an initial investigation into whether the use of dual HUDs on a transport category aircraft flight deck changes the workload involved in approach and landing operations. Based on these findings, it is likely that crew workload is not significantly impacted by the addition of a second HUD used by the PM during routine low-visibility approach and landing operations. In the context of crew coordination, this may indicate that the baseline levels of workload and task engagement that facilitate optimal task management during the use of a single HUD are likely preserved when a second HUD is added. This could also indicate that cognitive resources are strategically re-allocated to maintain the same level of engagement or effort when a second HUD is added. Therefore, dual HUD use during approach and landing operations in transport category aircraft may be a promising method for optimizing pilots' awareness of primary flight information and facilitating crew coordination without significantly impacting workload.

References

1. Federal Aviation Administration: Roles and Responsibilities for Pilot Flying (PF) and Pilot Monitoring (PM) (SAFO No. 15011). Washington, D.C.: Federal Aviation Administration (2015)

2. Federal Aviation Administration: Crew Resource Management Training (Advisory Circular No. 120–5D). Washington, D.C.: Federal Aviation Administration (2001)

3. Faulhaber, A.K., Friedrich, M., Kapol, T.: Absence of pilot monitoring affects scanning behavior of pilot flying: implications for the design of single-pilot cockpits. Hum. Factors **64**(2), 278–290 (2022)

4. Dehning, P.: Crew coordination in aviation. In: Steiger, HJ., Uhl, E. (eds.) Risk Control and Quality Management in Neurosurgery. Acta Neurochirurgica Supplements, vol. 78, pp. 39–41. Springer, Vienna (2001) https://doi.org/10.1007/978-3-7091-6237-8_6

5. Jensen, R.S.: Pilot Judgment and Crew Resource Management. Routledge, Abingdon-on-Thames (2017)

6. Weintraub, D.J., Ensing, M.: Human Factors Issues in Head-Up Display Design: The Book of HUD. Dayton, OH: The Crew System Ergonomics Information Analysis Center (1992)

7. Martin-Emerson, R., Wickens, C.D.: Superimposition, symbology, visual attention, and the head-up display. Hum. Factors **39**, 581–601 (1997)

8. Grier, R.A.: How high is high? A meta-analysis of NASA-TLX global workload scores. Proc. Hum. Factors Ergon. Soc. **59**, 1727–1731 (2015)

9. Hart, S.G.: NASA Task Load load Index (TLX). Volume 1.0; Paper and pencil package. NASA Ames Research Center, Moffett Field, CA (1986)

10. Hart, S.G.: NASA-task load index (NASA-TLX): 20 years later. Proc. Hum. Factors Ergon. Soc. **50**, 904–908 (2006)

11. Federal Aviation Administration: Runway Visual Range (RVR) (Order No. 6560.10C). Washington, D.C.: Federal Aviation Administration (2011)

12. Federal Aviation Administration: Criteria for Approval/Authorization of All Weather Operations (AWO) for Takeoff, Landing, and Rollout (Advisory Circular No. 120–118). Washington, D.C.: Federal Aviation Administration (2018)

13. Lix, L.M., Keselman, J.C., Keselman, H.J.: Consequences of assumption violations revisited: a quantitative review of alternatives to the one-way analysis of variance F test. Rev. Educ. Res. **66**, 579–619 (1996)

14. Mena, B., José, M., Alarcón, R., Arnau Gras, J., Bono Cabré, R., Bendayan, R.: Non-normal data: Is ANOVA still a valid option? Psicothema 2017, **29**(4), 552–557 (2017)

15. Pearson, E.S.: The analysis of variance in cases of non-normal variation. Biometrika. **23**, 114–133 (1931)

16. Faulhaber, A.K.: From crewed to single-pilot operations: Pilot performance and workload management. In 20th International Symposium on Aviation Psychology, p. 283 (2019)

17. Dahlstrom, N., Nahlinder, S.: Mental workload in aircraft and simulator during basic civil aviation training. Int. J. Aviat. Psychol. **19**, 309–325 (2009)

Visual Attention in Extended Reality and Implications for Aviation Safety

Yves Valentin and HeeSun Choi[✉]

Department of Psychological Sciences, Texas Tech University, Lubbock, TX 7909, USA
heesun.choi@ttu.edu

Abstract. Visual attention is essential to select and process relevant visual information while filtering out irrelevant stimuli. Thus, the visual attentional function is critical for aviation workers to perform workplace tasks effectively and safely. Emerging extended reality technology, including virtual and augmented reality, is increasingly used in aviation. This technology may heavily impact the user's visual attentional processing due to its innovative methods of presenting visual information to the users, as well as its technical limitations. We reviewed various extended reality applications in aviation, which may involve differential demands and challenges for aviation workers' attentional performance. Then, we presented a multifaceted construct of attention involving distinct functions such as alerting, orienting, executive, and spatial attention. Prior research suggests that alerting, orienting, and executive attention may have unique impacts on how effectively users can process virtual cues presented via extended reality and resolve conflict in the combination of virtual and physical visual stimuli. Cluttering and decluttering in extended reality may significantly impact executive attentional performance. Furthermore, head-mounted display (HMD) extended reality may change the spatial distribution of visual attention due to its restricted field of view and use of a cluttered focal visual field. Future research is warranted to investigate whether this innovative extended reality technology could present significant, possibly permanent, changes to the user's various attentional functions.

Keywords: Visual Attention · Attention Networks · Spatial Attention

1 Background: Extended Reality Applications in Aviation

For improving aviation systems to ensure more reliable and safer air travel, innovative technologies to aid and train aviation workers have been developed and adopted in broad aviation workplaces. Among many emerging technologies, Extended Reality (XR) is one of the most prominent tools the aviation industry has increasingly adopted. Extended reality has the potential to provide effective cognitive aids to pilots and operators and to support other aviation fields, including engineering, navigation, and training and simulation (Safi et al., 2019). This section overviews extended reality use in aviation, focusing on their potential associations with visual attentional processing.

© The Author(s), under exclusive license to Springer Nature Switzerland AG 2023
J. Y. C. Chen and G. Fragomeni (Eds.): HCII 2023, LNCS 14027, pp. 572–584, 2023.
https://doi.org/10.1007/978-3-031-35634-6_42

1.1   Current and Future Extended Reality Applications in Aviation

Varying types of extended reality technology delivering immersive experiences are currently used in aviation, including Virtual Reality (VR) and Augmented Reality (AR). Virtual reality completely removes the user's real-world environment and replaces it with a virtual environment. Thus, VR fully immerses the individual into a virtual environment where they cannot view the real-world environment. Augmented reality uses a mechanism that displays real-world content combined with virtual content (Azuma, 1997). AR differs from VR, where in VR, the user could feel and behave in a computer-generated environment as they navigate a real-world environment (Hincapié et al., 2011). AR, on the other hand, allows an individual to see the real world with digital objects being superimposed onto the real-world scene (Hincapié et al., 2011). Although AR and VR are different, both may be considered types of the extended reality spectrum. Two main device types commonly used for varying extended reality experiences are Head-Mounted Displays (HMDs) and Head-Up Displays (HUDs).

Although not yet adopted in broader areas, there is also an emerging type of extended reality technology that is designed to conceal, eliminate, and see-through objects in a perceived environment, called Diminished Reality (DR) (Mori et al., 2017). DR differs from other common extended reality systems that are designed to create a fully immersive, visually rich and realistic experience or add additional virtual stimuli to the physical environment. The primary benefit of utilizing DR is to remove irrelevant information from the environment to help users to process relevant information more efficiently, which may come at the cost of losing situational awareness (McDonald et al., 2021). Although DR has only been introduced to limited domains, it has the potential to assist aviation workers' complex task performance.

Extended Reality for Navigation Tasks

Head-Up Display (HUD) extended reality has been frequently used in the aviation industry to assist aircraft operators with navigation tasks, such as approach and landing (Prinzell & Rissel 2004). The visual information found inside and outside the plane requires a pilot to divide their attention which stretches their capabilities to attend to multiple sources of valuable information (Wickens, 2021; Ververs & Wickens, 1998). For operating an aircraft effectively and safely, an aviator must maintain attention to the instruments that display in-flight information as well as landmarks and hazards outside of the cockpit (Fadden et al., 1998). Given the complexity of such tasks demanding greater visual attentional loads, HUD is useful for presenting information from both sources to be processed together. This placement eliminates the need to shift visual attention from the outside world to the inner domain of the cockpit to retrieve information, reducing the time spent to obtain display information (Fadden et al., 1998). HMD has also been considered for aviation applications, with the potential benefits of displaying near and far domain information without requiring to look down to receive various flight-related information from cockpit instruments. Extended reality-based navigation aid systems may lead to reduced visual travel, minimal eye accommodations, and an unlimited field (Newton, 2022). However, visual clutter may occur, leading to attentional tunneling, failed detection of critical events, and increased spatial disorientation (Prinzel & Risser, 2004).

Extended Reality for Air Traffic Control Tasks

As air traffic continues to increase, the workload of air traffic controllers and the complexities they face are expected to rise (Hofmann et al., 2012; Lee et al., 2020). Tower controllers are required to gaze out their windows to monitor the movement of airplanes, the weather, and lighting conditions while monitoring air traffic (Reisman & Brown, 2006; Hofmann et al., 2012). They also need to attend to computer displays to obtain information on runway and taxiway layouts, aircraft and vehicles position, and detection of actual/potential conflicts (Masotti et al., 2016). Switching back and forth from computer displays to outside the window can significantly decrease controllers' attention and situational awareness (Masotti et al., 2016). The aviation industry has developed augmented reality-based systems for air traffic controls to help increase air traffic controllers' performance by reducing heads-down time (Reisman & Brown, 2006). With augmented-reality systems, status information can be displayed in a user's line of sight, providing significant benefits for air traffic controllers' attention (Ellis et al., 2002; Safi et al., 2019; Reisman & Brown, 2006).

Extended Reality for Inspection and Maintenance Tasks

In the aviation industry, inspection and maintenance work can be characterized as a complex task with demanding attentional and cognitive loads, involving extensive manual work steps, a large amount of components to be handled, and a need to document in combination (Eschen et al., 2018). Prior research showed that extended reality applications could facilitate overall worker performance, allowing a task to be completed with lower effort and errors while increasing the quality of task performance (Tang et al., 2003; Herbet, 2019). Research also suggests that various XR applications can be used for communication where experts or instructors can view the camera feed from the operator headset and provide them with instructional guidance (Garcia et al., 2020). AR has been adopted in aviation workplaces to provide detailed information on complex inspection and maintenance tasks while allowing an operator to work simultaneously. For instance, using a head-worn device, AR can display virtual digital information overlaying the actual work scene during an assembly operation or present maintenance instructions to workers (Key et al., 2022; Wang et al., 2016). AR can be particularly useful in providing information that is not easily accessible and hard to retrieve, reducing the time and effort for workers to complete their tasks (Hincapié et al., 2011). Extended reality also supports design and optimization tasks by allowing engineers to visualize computer-aided design (Safi et al., 2019). For example, VR may be used in aero engine design, aircraft interior, and aero maintenance tasks (Stone et al., 2011).

Extended Reality for Training

Training using extended reality technology has a range of benefits, from reducing the cost of training, eliminating risk by putting individuals in simulation rather than a hazardous situation, and exposing people to situations they have not yet encountered in the real world (Kaplan et al., 2020). Prior research suggests that simulation-based training is beneficial for in-flight training and reduces the search time for relevant instructions in manufacturing tasks (Kaplan et al., 2021). In addition, learning with AR has been shown to be faster compared to paper-based training (Borgen et al., 2021). Training in simulations allows for immediate feedback, reducing attentional and cognitive loads, which in turn allows more efficient training (Kaplan et al., 2021; Garcia et al., 2020). Simulation-based training also provides more immersive and game-like experiences, allowing individuals to be more engaged in learning (Borgen et al., 2021). VR has been explored as a training tool for commercial and space pilots in various aviation industries, being investigated for its potential for various training, such as emergency, inflight disorientation and navigation problems, and spacecraft docking (Aoki et al., 2008; Loftin, 1994; Garcia et al., 2020; Olbrich et al., 2018; Piechowski et al., 2020).

2 Human Visual Attention

2.1 Visual Attention and Task Performance and Safety

The attentional function allows humans to select and process the most important information among vast competing stimuli and distractors in an environment (Carrasco, 2011). Attention helps us concentrate on a particular stream of information or process while ignoring irrelevant information or process, allowing us to perform everyday tasks successfully (Carrasco, 2011). Furthermore, impairments in attentional functions significantly increase injury risks due to increased failures in detecting and avoiding potential hazards (Ball et al., 1988). For example, older adults often experience age-related declines in attention, which contributes to their increased risks of involvement in fatal crashes (Ball et al., 1993; Owsley et al., 1995). Visual attention involves selective processing of relevant visual stimuli and filtering out irrelevant visual stimuli, which is particularly critical as the amount of visual information in any environment exceeds our processing capacity (Wickens, 2021). Aviation workplaces tend to involve highly visual task environments, where critical visual information, objects, and hazards must be selected and responded to. Visual attention would allow aviation workers, including pilots, air traffic controllers, and maintenance workers, to detect and process relevant visual stimuli to perform their job safely and effectively.

Attention is considered a complex and multifaceted rather than a unitary construct, consisting of multiple distinct aspects of attentional functions (Posner & Rothbart, 2007). Different aspects of attentional functions may have differential and unique impacts on our capabilities and performance. For instance, sustained attention is the ability to maintain a high level of focus over an extended time (Wickens, 2021). For example, air traffic controllers must continuously monitor the visual information and traffic status. Being inattentive at any given moment may result in missing critical events. Divided attention is the ability to attend to multiple processes concurrently (Wickens, 2021). Aircraft operators may need to divide their attention across multiple spatial locations (e.g., paying attention to the outside environment and the cockpit display), tasks (e.g., manipulating controls while talking to a co-pilot), or sensory stimuli (e.g., maintaining visual attention on the roadway while listening to instructions during taxiing). Prior research showed many aspects of attention are significantly associated with task performance and safety (Prinzel & Rizzer, 2004). As attention is multifaceted, examining the relationship between extended reality and specific attentional functions can help identify the precise impacts of extended reality technology use on a user's visual attention and address the potentials and concerns.

2.2 Attention Networks Model

A neurocognitive attention networks model lays out different neural networks associated with three distinct attentional functions: alerting, orienting, and executive attentional functions (Posner & Peterson, 1990; Raz & Buhle, 2006; Fan et al., 2002). Each function is unique yet essential in regulating an individual's task performance and behaviors. The alerting attention function involves achieving and maintaining a state of alertness in responding to incoming stimuli (Posner & Rothbart, 2007). There are two aspects of alerting attention: tonic and phasic alertness. Tonic alertness, or vigilance, refers to an ability to maintain a state of alertness over an extended period of time, and phasic alerting is considered the increased readiness to respond to stimuli after a cue. Alerting attention is necessary to effectively use warnings or signals preceding an event that may have critical consequences if missed. For example, air traffic controllers need to maintain a high level of sensitivity to respond to upcoming events that are potentially hazardous (Reisman & Brown, 2006; Ellis et al., 2002). The orienting attentional function involves switching attentional focus toward a particular stimulus (e.g., object or location) to select the most relevant information among many sensory inputs (Posner & Rothbart, 2007). Many aviation worker tasks involve processing dynamic and complex information often placed at various locations across a large physical space. Workers are often required to shift their focus in the environment to attend to the information that has the highest priority at the moment. For example, aircraft operators must be able to direct their attention to the most relevant area or objects inside the cockpit or the outside environment during operation (Fadden et al., 1998). Lastly, executive attention involves resolving conflicts among competing stimuli or processes of both internal and external (Posner & Rothbart, 2007). This function is critical for many aviation workers to complete their tasks; air traffic controllers need to make an accurate and prompt resolution when they detect conflicting or competing information in the display (Reisman & Brown, 2006). Extended reality technology may uniquely impact each of the alerting, orienting, and executive attentional functions, which could have differential implications for aviation workers' task performance and safety.

2.3 The Spatial Distribution of Visual Attention

Prior research suggests that the spatial coverage of visual attention is associated with various everyday task performance and safety outcomes (Carrasco, 2011; Feng & Spence, 2014). When attempting to process relevant information in both the focal and peripheral fields, an individual's capability to allocate visual attention is important. For instance, impairments in visuospatial attention can increase motor vehicle crash risks (Ball et al., 1993) and fall risks (Broman et al., 2004) due to an inability to detect and avoid potential hazards in peripheral visual fields. Visual stimuli in the peripheral region are typically processed with slower speed and lower accuracy than those in the central visual region (Carrasco & Chang, 1995; Carrasco & Frieder, 1997). Prior research suggests that the size of the attentional visual field may be impaired or declined, leading to increased safety concerns; for example, older drivers' increased crash risks are linked to declines in their inability to detect and process information in the visual periphery (Owsley et al., 1994).

The attentional visual field is the region where a person can sort out information without any head or eye movements (Hassan et al., 2008). A computerized task measuring the ability to localize a visual target in a wide area of one's focal and peripheral visual field can assess the attentional visual field. The Attentional Visual Field (AVF) (Feng et al., 2017; Mitchell & Choi, 2022; Mitchell et al., 2022) or the Useful Field of View (UFOV) task (Ball et al., 1988) uses a similar paradigm that displays a visual stimulus on a computer or extended reality display and asks locating the target among distractors while attending to a large visual field. Prior studies demonstrated that an individual's attentional visual field was associated with risk avoidance performances, as visuospatial attentional ability is critical to quickly noticing and responding to hazards (Ball et al., 1993). Decrements in the spatial distribution of visual attention may significantly impact worker task performance and safety in aviation work environments, where hazards may often be present and need to be responded to quickly.

3   Visual Attention Involving Extended Reality

3.1   Virtual Cues and Alerting, Orienting, and Executive Attention

Extended reality is widely used to display computer-generated visual cues and warnings in a virtual or augmented environment to aid the user's attention. For instance, extended reality provides visual warnings for air traffic controllers to direct their attention in the direction where critical situations may occur outside of their view (Bagassi, 2016). Similarly, XR-based aircraft operator guidance systems can display a directional cue to guide the operator's attention to proceed with a task. When the operator is looking in the correct direction, the system can then highlight a specific control or instrument that they need to use (Lallai et al., 2021).

Alerting and orienting attention is critical to effectively responding to virtual cues presented by extended reality. Alerting attention would determine the user's ability to maintain their readiness to select and process the most relevant information and make use of signals preceding a target or an event once an extended reality system presents a cue (Posner & Peterson, 1990; Posner & Rothbart, 2007). XR-based assistive systems presenting cues or warnings can help air traffic controllers or operators maintain alertness to detect and respond to targets or safety-critical events (Lallai et al., 2021). Similarly, orienting attention involves switching attention toward cues presented by XR systems (Posner & Petersen, 1990; Posner & Rothbart, 2007). Aviation operators and air traffic controllers are often required to orient and change their attention and eye fixations across multiple displays and controls (Hofmann et al., 2012; Newton, 2022). Through virtual cues, XR systems may assist users with orienting to direct their attention towards the most relevant area or objects during task performances.

Varying types of extended reality may have differential impacts on alerting, orienting, and executive attention due to the unique characteristics and mechanisms of how they present visual cues and warnings. For instance, augmented reality often displays virtual stimuli overlaying the physical environment or merging with real-world objects, which may create conflicts between virtual and physical visual stimuli (Gabbard et al., 2019; Wickens, 2021). Executive attention may be required to resolve these conflicts as conflicts in information from an XR display and the physical environment could disrupt the focus of attention. HMD AR headsets present multiple virtual and physical stimuli concurrently in a common visual field. Although this technology aims to integrate virtual information well into the physical world to provide a visually streamlined experience, some information may conflict due to its perceptual differences and varying visual depth (Gabbard et al., 2019). Executive attention would be particularly essential in processing virtual stimuli that are not aligned or congruent with real-world stimuli or the background physical context.

Furthermore, when a virtual cue is presented to direct the user's attention to specific visual information in the physical environment, the user may need to move their visual attention from the virtual to the physical environment (Gabbard et al., 2019). Also, when virtual information is presented on top of the physical visual field to be used to perform a task in the physical environment, the user may need to switch their attention between the two environments constantly, which may increase perceptual conflicts (Fadden et al., 2000). Individual differences in executive attention may determine the user's ability to resolve potential conflicts between virtual cues and the physical world and select and process relevant visual information while disregarding irrelevant information. Extended reality environments with significant perceptual incongruency are likely to overload executive attention, which could have detrimental impacts on the user's attentional performance.

3.2   Cluttering and Decluttering in Extended Reality and Executive Attention

Extended Reality-based cognitive aid systems and training present visually rich information by adding visual stimuli to the user's visual field (Safi et al., 2019). For instance, AR assistive systems can aid users in task performance by displaying additional visual information overlaying the physical environment. However, this may clutter the visual field and potentially negatively impacts visual attention (Ververs & Wickens, 1988; Wickens, 2021). In particular, extended reality systems with limited display sizes available to present visual information likely clutter a user's focal visual field substantially. Peripheral visual fields are not available for AR applications to display visual information could result in occlusions between virtual and real-world visual information cluttered in the focal visual field (Lallai et al., 2021). A cluttered visual field increases the user's overall visual attentional load, and it may be particularly detrimental to executive attention due to increased perceptual conflicts in the visual fovea (Alexander et al., 2012). Thus, if aviation XR technology users interact with an XR display with high visual intensity, conflicts in displayed information or between virtual and physical information would be more difficult to resolve. Furthermore, highly salient virtual information displayed on XR displays may severely impact visual attentional processing of the physical environment.

The aviation XR technology user's impaired or overloaded executive attention due to virtual information added to the natural visual field may significantly impact the user's performance and safety (Fadden et al., 2000; Ververs & Wickens, 1988). A cluttered XR display could deteriorate the ability of aviation operators and traffic controllers to resolve conflicts in safety-critical situations, where conflicting information in physical environments must be resolved quickly (Fadden et al., 2000; Prinzel & Risser, 2004). For instance, an operator might encounter a sudden warning activated while operating a plane. The warning may indicate a particular error in the plane's movement, while other visual cues may provide conflicting information. The operator's inability to resolve the conflicts in the information and quickly make a proper choice of action could result in severe consequences. Thus, the display intensity of aviation XR technology needs to be designed adequately with consideration of visual information loads of specific environments and tasks, as well as the intended user's executive attentional functions.

While many XR applications in aviation tend to add visual information to the visual field, other types of XR technology, such as diminished reality, may be used to reduce the amount of visual information in complex aviation work environments (Murph et al., 2021). Decluttering the visual field by de-emphasizing irrelevant visual information through XR can reduce potential conflicts in visual input. Thus, it may be beneficial for aviation workers' executive attentional performance, assisting in ignoring irrelevant visual information more effectively. However, contextual information may still be useful for resolving a conflict and selecting relevant information. Loss of such information due to the information being de-emphasized by extended reality could be detrimental to aviation workers' visual attentional performance.

3.3 Field of View (FoV) of Extended Reality and the Spatial Distribution of Attention

Head-Mounted Display (HMD) VR and AR devices use a display that presents computer-generated images to one or both eyes (Azuma et al., 1997; Hincapié et al., 2011). HMD XR headsets have a field of view (FoV) of restricted sizes and unnatural shapes that are different from the natural human FoV. For example, VR headsets in the current market have rectangular-shaped FoVs between 80 and 120° diagonally, with smaller vertical and horizontal FoVs, which is a significant reduction compared to a human FoV of approximately 180° (Mitchell & Choi, 2022). Microsoft HoloLens, a widely used AR headset, has a narrower field of view than most VR headsets, which is estimated to be 30° horizontally and 17° vertically (Lallai et al., 2021). The Hololens 2, which is a sequel to the Hololens, offers a maximum diagonal field of view (FoV) of 54°, thus improving on its predecessor. The restricted FoV size and shape of XR headsets may affect visual attentional processing with peripheral visual fields not available to display virtual objects; thus, users only see virtual objects in the center of the FoV (Lallai et al., 2021).

Furthermore, visual attentional demands increase in the focal visual field due to reduced or lost visual processing in the peripheral field in virtual or augmented environments. Mitchell and Choi (2022) examined the distribution of visual attention in a virtual environment when using an HMD VR headset with a limited FoV. The study revealed that visual attention could be distributed differently in a virtual environment. VR users tended to respond more accurately to visual stimuli presented in the horizontal and diagonal directions than those along the vertical meridian (Mitchell & Choi, 2022). The findings may suggest that the FoV constraints of an HMD VR device impact the spatial distribution of visual attention. Future research is warranted to investigate how the spatial distribution of visual attention differs in extended reality environments, where a peripheral visual field is not available (i.e., VR) or visual attention is enhanced over the focal visual field (i.e., AR), in comparison to a physical environment.

4 Potential Long-Term Effects of Extended Reality Use

With the expected increasing use among broader aviation workers, extended reality technology is likely to be used for longer hours and extended periods in the future. Despite the benefits of extended reality application for aviation, there could be unexpected, potentially adverse effects of long-term use of XR on users' cognitive functions. Prior research has shown that new technologies, such as video games, may present significant, permanent effects on the user's cognition (Green & Bavelier, 2006; Spence & Feng, 2010).

Long-term use of extended reality may have differential impacts on different aspects of attention. Extended reality may impact the spatial distribution of attention when exposed to a restricted visual field and increased visual clutter extensively. The potential impacts may vary and can be positive or negative, depending on the characteristics of different types of XR technology. For instance, augmented reality may result in enhanced attention in the focal visual field but not in the peripheral visual field, whereas virtual reality may deteriorate visual attention in the peripheral field (Fig. 1). Furthermore, long-term use of extended reality-based cognitive aids that present cues and warnings may lead to extensive training in exogenous attention (i.e., externally-controlled attention) rather than endogenous attention (i.e., internally-controlled attention). This may strengthen the XR users' attentional functions to be more responsive to external cues.

Prior research investigating the impacts of playing video games on attention may suggest that a positive training effect may occur as a result of extensive use of extended reality. Studies showed that playing video games may improve spatial attentional and cognitive functions (Green & Bavelier, 2006; Spence & Feng, 2010). Video game players showed superior performance in localizing targets compared to non-video game players in non-video game-related environments, suggesting that the effect of playing video games generalizes to untrained tasks and environments (Green & Bavelier, 2006; Spence & Feng, 2010). Choi and Lane (2013) further suggest that specific characteristics of a video game, such as in-game viewpoints (e.g., first-person perspective), may enhance spatial attentional functions after prolonged playing. Extended reality may have similar positive effects on visual attentional functions after long-term exposure, given its similarities with video games. Similar to action video games that could enhance visual attention, extended reality often requires multiple items to be processed simultaneously. Also, extended reality-based cognitive aids often demand skills to detect and respond to targets in a wide visual field while rejecting irrelevant distracting information in a visually challenging, immersive, and interactive environment. The potential positive effects of the long-term use of extended reality on visual attention may have implications for the development of attention training and intervention (Mitchell & Choi, 2022). Extended reality technology may be used as training and intervention tools for attentional performance for aviation workers as well as general populations.

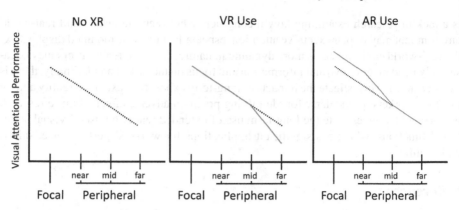

Fig. 1. Possible changes in visual attentional functions across the focal and peripheral visual field after prolonged use of extended reality.

5 Conclusion and Future Research Needs

The use of extended reality technology in aviation is expected to grow continuously, with its immense potential for improving aviation workers' task performance. Prior research has focused on expanding applications and investigating the benefits of extended reality for various tasks and workplaces in aviation. However, there is a limited understanding of the potential impacts of extended reality on the user's attentional and cognitive functions, which would have significant implications for aviation workers' safety and health.

Aviation work environments are often complex and involve dynamic task performance, requiring effective visual attentional performance. Prior research suggests that extended reality can assist aviation workers' alerting and orienting attentional functions with processing critical visual information occurring outside their visual focus. For instance, XR-based guidance systems can digitally highlight instruments and controls to facilitate aviation workers' task performance. A newer, diminished reality technology can be used to reduce conflicts among visual information in the physical environment. Thus, it has the potential to be used to help air traffic controllers and aviation operators select and process the most relevant visual information efficiently. However, due to the physical characteristics and restrictions of extended reality, such as the limited field of view of head-mounted display headsets and increased visual information, visual clutter can occur in the focal visual field. The user's visual attention may be overloaded as extensive virtual and real-world information is shown in the focal visual field. Also, users may need to resolve conflicting information coming from the virtual and physical environment. If the virtual and physical worlds are not aligned, it may hinder the users' ability to transfer their attention from virtual cues to real-world situations.

Future research can investigate how aviation workers' alerting and orienting attentional functions can be enhanced by virtual cues and warnings when using XR applications and how those enhancements may affect their primary task performance and safety. Empirical research is further needed to investigate the differential impacts of the varying sizes and shapes of FoV of HMD XR headsets on the user's ability to detect and respond to visual information in their central and peripheral visions. In addition, there is a lack of research examining how incongruency between the virtual and real-world environment may impair executive attention, especially with head-mounted displays. As the real-world environment is more dynamic in nature, extended reality users may occasionally need to ignore virtual information and focus on the task at hand. Finally, there is a critical need to investigate the impacts of long-term exposure to extended reality among aviation workers, particularly for identifying potential adverse effects. Future research is warranted to investigate the long-term use of extended reality on users' visual attentional functions, which has significant implications for workers' performance, safety, and health.

References

Alexander, A.L., Kaber, D.B., Kim, S.-H., Stelzer, E.M., Kaufmann, K., Prinzel, L.J.: Measurement and modeling of display clutter in advanced flight deck technologies. Int. J. Aviat. Psychol. 22(4), 299–318 (2012)

Aoki, H., Oman, C.M., Buckland, D.A., Natapoff, A.: Desktop-VR system for preflight 3D navigation training. Acta Astronautic 63(7–10), 841–847 (2008)

Azuma, R.T.: A survey of Augmented Reality. Presence Teleoper. Virtual Environ. 6(4), 355–385 (1997)

Ball, K., Owsley, C., Sloane, M.E., Roenker, D.L., Bruni, J.R.: Visual attention problems as a predictor of vehicle crashes in older drivers. Invest. Ophthalmol. Vis. Sci. 34(11), 3110–3123 (1993)

Ball, K.K., Beard, B.L., Roenker, D.L., Miller, R.L., Griggs, D.S.: Age and visual search: expanding the useful field of view. J. Opt. Soc. Am. A 5(12), 2210 (1988)

Bagassi, S., De Crescenzio, F., Lucchi, F., Masotti, N.: Augmented and virtual reality in the airport control tower. In: 30th Congress of the International Council of the Aeronautical Sciences (2016)

Broman, A.T., West, S.K., Muñoz, B., Bandeen-Roche, K., Rubin, G.S., Turano, K.A.: Divided visual attention as a predictor of bumping while walking: the salisbury eye evaluation. Investig. Ophthalmol. Vis. Sci. 45(9), 2955–2960 (2004)

Borgen, K.B., Ropp, T.D., Weldon, W.T.: Assessment of augmented reality technology's impact on speed of learning and task performance in aeronautical engineering technology education. Int. J. Aerosp. Psychol. 31(3), 219–229 (2021)

Carrasco, M.: Visual attention: the past 25 years. Vision. Res. 51(13), 1484–1525 (2011)

Carrasco, M., Chang, I.: The interaction of objective and subjective organizations in a localization search task. Percept. Psychophys. 57(8), 1134–1150 (1995)

Carrasco, M., Frieder, K.S.: Cortical magnification neutralizes the eccentricity effect in visual search. Vision Res. 37(1), 63–82 (1997)

Choi, H., Lane, S.A.: Impact of visuospatial characteristics of video games on improvements in cognitive abilities. In: Proceedings of the Human Factors and Ergonomics Society Annual Meeting, vol. 57, no. 1, pp. 1735–1739 (2013)

Ellis, S.R., et al.: Augmented reality in a simulated tower environment: effect of field of view on aircraft detection. NASA TM-2002-211853 (2002)

Eschen, H., Kötter, T., Rodeck, R., Harnisch, M., Schüppstuhl, T.: Augmented and virtual reality for inspection and maintenance processes in the aviation industry. Procedia Manuf. 19, 156–163 (2018)

Fadden, S., Ververs, P. M., Wickens, C. D.: Costs and benefits of head-up display use: a meta-analytic approach. In: Proceedings of the Human Factors and Ergonomics Society Annual Meeting, vol. 42, no. 1, pp. 16–20 (1998)

Fadden, S., Wickens, C., Ververs, P.: Costs and benefits of head up displays - an attention perspective and a meta-analysis. SAE Trans. **109**, 1112–1117 (2000)

Fan, J., McCandliss, B.D., Sommer, T., Raz, A., Posner, M.I.: Testing the efficiency and independence of attentional networks. J. Cogn. Neurosci. **14**(3), 340–347 (2002)

Feng, J., Craik, F.I.M., Levine, B., Moreno, S., Naglie, G., Choi, H.: Differential age-related changes in localizing a target among distractors across an extended visual field. Eur. J. Ageing **14**(2), 167–177 (2017). https://doi.org/10.1007/s10433-016-0399-7

Feng, J., Spence, I.: Upper visual field advantage in localizing a target among distractors. i-Perception **5**(2), 97–100 (2014). https://doi.org/10.1068/i0625rep

Gabbard, J.L., Mehra, D.G., Swan, J.E.: Effects of AR display context switching and focal distance switching on human performance. IEEE Trans. Visual Comput. Graphics **25**(6), 2228–2241 (2019)

Garcia, A. D., Schlueter, J., Paddock, E.: Training astronauts using hardware-in-the-loop simulations and virtual reality. In: AIAA Scitech 2020 Forum, p. 0167 (2020)

Green, C.S., Bavelier, D.: Effect of action video games on the spatial distribution of visuospatial attention. J. Exp. Psychol. Hum. Percept. Perform. **32**(6), 1465 (2006)

Hassan, S.E., Turano, K.A., Muñoz, B., Munro, C., Roche, K.B., West, S.K.: Cognitive and vision loss affects the topography of the attentional visual field. Investig. Ophthalmol. Vis. Sci. **49**(10), 4672–4678 (2008)

Hebert Jr., T.: The impacts of using augmented reality to support aircraft maintenance. Air Force Institute of Technology Wright-Patterson AFB OH Wright-Patterson AFB United States (2019)

Hincapie, M., Caponio, A., Rios, H., Gonzalez Mendivil, E.: An introduction to augmented reality with applications in aeronautical maintenance. In: 13th International Conference on Transparent Optical Networks, pp. 1–4 (2011)

Hofmann, T., König, C., Bruder, R., Bergner, J.: How to reduce workload – augmented reality to ease the work of air traffic controllers. Work **41**, 1168–1173 (2012)

Kaplan, A.D., Cruit, J., Endsley, M., Beers, S.M., Sawyer, B.D., Hancock, P.A.: The effects of virtual reality, augmented reality, and mixed reality as training enhancement methods: a meta-analysis. Hum. Factors: J. Hum. Factors Ergon. Soc. **63**(4), 706–726 (2021)

Key, K., et al.: Preliminary findings: Application of maintenance instructions displayed in augmented reality. In: Chen, J.Y.C., Fragomeni, G. (eds.) HCII 2022. LNCS, vol. 13318, pp. 221–232. Springer, Cham (2022). https://doi.org/10.1007/978-3-031-06015-1_16

Lallai, G., Loi Zedda, G., Martinie, C., Palanque, P., Pisano, M., Spano, L.D.: Engineering task-based augmented reality guidance: application to the training of aircraft flight procedures. Interact. Comput. **33**(1), 17–39 (2021)

Lee, Y., Marks, S., Connor, A.M.: An evaluation of the effectiveness of virtual reality in Air Traffic Control. In: Proceedings of the 2020 4th International Conference on Virtual and Augmented Reality Simulations, pp. 7–17. Association for Computing Machinery, Sydney (2020)

Loftin, R.B.: Virtual Environments for aerospace training. In: Proceedings of WESCON 1994, pp. 384–387. IEEE (1994)

Masotti, N., De Crescenzio, F., Bagassi, S.: Augmented reality in the control tower: a rendering pipeline for multiple head-tracked head-up displays. In: De Paolis, L.T., Mongelli, A. (eds.) AVR 2016. LNCS, vol. 9768, pp. 321–338. Springer, Cham (2016). https://doi.org/10.1007/978-3-319-40621-3_23

Milgram, P., Kishino, F.: A taxonomy of mixed reality visual displays. IEICE Trans. Inf. Syst. **E77-D**, 1321–1329 (1994)

Mitchell, D., Choi, H.: Assessing the spatial distribution of visual attention in a virtual environment: development and validation of a novel VR-based attentional visual field (AVF) task. In: CHI Conference on Human Factors in Computing Systems Extended Abstracts, pp. 1–7 (2022)

Mitchell, D.T., Leibman, D., Choi, H.S.: Development and validation of extended reality attentional visual field tasks. In: Proceedings of the Human Factors and Ergonomics Society Annual Meeting, vol. 66, no. 1, pp. 1992–1996 (2022)

Mori, S., Ikeda, S., Saito, H.: A survey of diminished reality: techniques for visually concealing, eliminating, and seeing through real objects. IPSJ Trans. Comput. Vision Appl. **9**(1), 1–14 (2017). https://doi.org/10.1186/s41074-017-0028-1

Murph, I., et al.: Diminishing reality: potential benefits and risks. In: Proceedings of the Human Factors and Ergonomics Society Annual Meeting, vol. 65, no. 1, pp. 164–168 (2021)

Newton, D.C.: Human factors considerations for head-worn displays in civil aviation. In: Chen, J.Y.C., Fragomeni, G. (eds.) HCII 2022. Lecture Notes in Computer Science, vol. 13318, pp. 233–250. Springer, Cham (2022). https://doi.org/10.1007/978-3-031-06015-1_17

Olbrich, M., Graf, H., Keil, J., Gad, R., Bamfaste, S., Nicolini, F.: Virtual reality based space operations – a study of ESA's potential for VR based training and simulation. In: Chen, J., Fragomeni, G. (eds.) VAMR 2018. LNCS, vol. 10909, pp. 438–451. Springer, Cham (2018). https://doi.org/10.1007/978-3-319-91581-4_33

Owsley, C., Ball, K., Keeton, D.M.: Relationship between visual sensitivity and target localization in older adults. Vision. Res. **35**(4), 579–587 (1995)

Piechowski, S., et al.: Virtual reality as training aid for Manual spacecraft docking. Acta Astronaut. **177**, 731–736 (2020)

Posner, M.I., Rothbart, M.K.: Research on attention networks as a model for the integration of psychological science. Annu. Rev. Psychol. **58**(1), 1–23 (2007)

Posner, M.I., Peterson, S.E.: The attention system of the human brain. Attent. Soc. World **13**, 25–42 (1990)

Prinzel, L.J, Risser, M.: Head up displays and attention capture. Tech. Memo. No. NASA TM-2004-21300, NASA Langley Research Center, Langley, VA (2004)

Raz, A., Buhle, J.: Typologies of attentional networks. Nat. Rev. Neurosci. **7**, 367–379 (2006)

Reisman, R., Brown, D.: Design of augmented reality tools for air traffic control towers. In: 6th AIAA Aviation Technology, Integration and Operations Conference (ATIO) (2006)

Safi, M., Chung, J., Pradhan, P.: Review of augmented reality in aerospace industry. Aircr. Eng. Aerosp. Technol. **91**(9), 1194–1197 (2019)

Spence, I., Feng, J.: Video games and spatial cognition. Rev. Gen. Psychol. **14**(2), 92–104 (2010)

Stone, R.J., Panfilov, P.B., Shukshunov, V.E.: Evolution of aerospace simulation: from immersive virtual reality to serious games. In: Proceedings of 5th International Conference on Recent Advances in Space Technologies, pp. 655–662. IEEE (2011)

Tang, A., Owen, C., Biocca, F., Mou, W.: Comparative effectiveness of Augmented Reality in Object Assembly. In: Proceedings of the SIGCHI Conference on Human Factors in Computing Systems, pp. 73–80 (2003)

Ververs, P.M., Wickens, C.D.: Head-up displays: effect of clutter, display intensity, and display location on pilot performance. Int. J. Aviat. Psychol. **8**(4), 377–403 (1998)

Wang, X., Ong, S.K., Nee, A.Y.C.: Multi-modal augmented-reality assembly guidance based on bare-hand interface. Adv. Eng. Inform. **30**(3), 406–421 (2016)

Wickens, C.: Attention: Theory, principles, models and applications. Int. J. Hum.-Comput. Interact. **37**(5), 403–417 (2021)

User Experience in VAMR

What Makes First Steps Users Rave About Virtual Reality? An Explorative Qualitative Study of Consumers' First VR Experience

Julie Abdinoor and Yingjie Chen

Purdue University, West Lafayette, IN 47907, USA
{jabdino,victorchen}@purdue.edu

Abstract. First experiences can make or break a new product. If consumers love it, they rave about the product and encourage others to try it. If they don't, they move on and discourage others from trying. Considering the slow consumer adoption of VR, we explored user attitudes, expectations, and behaviors during their first VR experience using qualitative methods. At first, we interviewed ten participants and studied their feelings about VR before, during, and after the Oculus First Steps tutorial. Despite initial concerns, participants formed a positive attitude toward VR. Six participants reacted enthusiastically to First Step's robot, which prompted us to conduct an online investigation of consumer discussions. Thematic analysis of users' posts and responses to the First Step's robot on Facebook, Reddit, and YouTube revealed strong positive emotions, which impacted users' attitudes and increased their likelihood of recommending VR to others. Implications for content developers and future studies is discussed.

Keywords: Virtual reality · First Steps robot · Qualitative VR research · Consumer behavior

1 Introduction

Why is the consumer adoption of immersive VR technology so slow? The diffusion of innovation isn't an exact science; possibly, the sale of VR headsets might follow the same trend as mobile phones. Maybe the "face computers" [41] of today are equivalent to the bricks we called "car phones" in the'80s. Perhaps when this wearable technology isn't so large and clunky [24], it will appeal to more buyers. VR could also follow the internet adoption rate, which academia and the military used for twenty years before the proliferation of AOL discs spiked consumer adoption in the '90s [32].

The sluggish adoption rate might be related to content and positioning. The focus on gamers has created a perception that VR is a tool for gaming [21]. However, COVID-19 did see a small spike in VR interest thanks to travel-related content and restless consumers stuck at home [16]. The Global Times reported in March 2021 that travel was a new growth category for consumers [2]. Yet broad consumer interest in VR just isn't there. In a Statista survey conducted in November 2021, only 9% of respondents said they were

© The Author(s), under exclusive license to Springer Nature Switzerland AG 2023
J. Y. C. Chen and G. Fragomeni (Eds.): HCII 2023, LNCS 14027, pp. 587–603, 2023.
https://doi.org/10.1007/978-3-031-35634-6_43

very interested in VR, while 46% said they were not at all interested [3]. Age doesn't appear to be a significant factor. In the same study, only 27% of 18–34-year-olds said they were very interested in VR [3]. It wasn't surprising to hear the Meta $3.3 billion loss in the fourth quarter last year or that they shifted VR employees to other company areas [8, 41].

The slow adoption had us wondering why. This study explored consumers' feelings during their first experience and the potential positive impact on consumer adoption. Consumers who are highly involved with a product and experience something unique and enjoyable are often compelled to share their feelings with others [1, 13]. As social media is a megaphone for product recommendations, the main aim of this study was to explore how consumers feel about their first VR experience and how their reactions prompted subsequent behavior. Our study included the following questions to understand how new users feel about VR:

- How do participants feel about VR before their experience?

  - What expectations and concerns do they have about VR?

- How do they feel during the First Steps experience?

  - What did they like and dislike? What surprised them?

- How does the experience change their attitudes and behavior toward VR?

2   Literature Review

Measuring consumer interest in VR using quantitative methods is challenging for researchers since most people haven't tried it. As of June 2022, only 23% of US adults have tried VR [5]. Asking people to answer survey questions about an unknown experience creates reliability issues. For example, Manis and Choi [28] developed the VR Hardware Acceptance Model (VR-HAM) to understand the adoption rate of VR. The survey was conducted on LinkedIn and asked participants to rate their perception of VR's usefulness. Without understanding the experience personally, consumers would have to guess based on preconceived notions.

A social media analytics study in 2018 revealed consumers were concerned about the performance of the headsets, the price point, and the amount of interesting content [26]. However, this analytics study was conducted a year before Oculus released the wireless headset, which might have made a difference in their findings.

Researchers recognize there are emotional components to the VR experience, such as perceived playfulness and enjoyment and the impact on the perceived usefulness [43, 44]. Studies suggest that hedonic variables determine whether consumers will accept a new technology [14, 35]. However, studies tend to focus on the consumer perception of VR, which leans toward gaming. A recent mixed methods study involving workshops, interviews, and several surveys suggests that consumers felt VR only had value in gaming [21]. This gaming perception could explain the broader market miss. Although 63% of US adults say they play video games in an average week, only 30% consider themselves gamers [45]. Since the gamer identity tends to be male and 58% of video game players in the US are 34 years old and younger [9, 10], VR research could be focused on understanding a younger male market and potentially missing an older segment.

2.1 Emotion Influence and the Pursuit of Happiness

Research suggests consumers in good moods select products consistent with both the valence of their affective state and their level of arousal [15]. Shoppers are more likely to buy in good moods, and intense affective reactions can last longer [40]. When people feel positive emotions such as happiness, excitement, and love, they will search for more information online, discuss the experience with friends and family, share in an online community, purchase products, and plan other experiences [40].

Frederickson [17] suggests what makes people happy is essential for people's well-being and mental health [17]. However, happiness doesn't necessarily mean the same to everyone. Mogilner et al. [30] found a temporal focus on the present or future impacted happiness, which can change as we age. For example, future-oriented people associated happiness with excitement, whereas present-focused consumers felt happiest with calm.

Despite an elusive definition, people seek happiness [42]. When Professor Santos offered a class in happiness at Yale in 2018, it was the most popular course in the university's history [37]. It was so popular that Santos filmed the content and made it free on Coursera. Over 130,000 people have enrolled in the course since it launched in the middle of 2018 [42]. Humans simply want to feel happy.

Consumers feel happier with experiences rather than simply purchasing products. Van Boven and Gilovich (2003) found participants were happier with experiences than with material purchases, even when matched in price [46]. The authors suggest people are happier because the experience is open to positive reinterpretations, adds a meaningful addition to personal identity, and helps contribute to social relationships [46].

How do these positive emotions work in virtual reality? Van Kleef (2017) explains positive emotions can be contagious to others simply by observing others' reactions, as expressions often signal an inferential process in the observers [47]. VR research suggests that humans react to virtual characters' expressions as they would watching a human and behave in the same way [12, 36]. Slater et al. (2009; 2010) explained lifelike characters in a VR setting may increase the sense of being there, called "presence" [38, 39]. When participants feel a high level of presence, they respond to characters in a realistic way [12, 36]. In essence, if created to do so, virtual characters can help humans feel happy.

3 Theoretical Frameworks

This study considered two theoretical frameworks: the Experiential Hierarchy of Effects attitude formation [27, 40] and Frederickson's [17, 18] Broaden and Build Theory of Positive Emotions which emphasizes the importance of positive emotional arousal for mental health and well-being.

3.1 Experiential Hierarchy of Effects

Lavidge and Steiner [27] created the Hierarchy-of-Effects model to describe how consumers reach a purchase decision by following specific steps during attitude formation. The consumer's level of involvement with the attitude object determines how the sequence of steps unfolds [27, 40]. A high-involvement purchase, for example, requires cognitive information processing versus a low-involvement purchase, where a consumer thinks about the need for a product, buys it, and then forms an opinion about their purchase after using the product [40]. In the Experiential Hierarchy of Effects, the consumer forms an attitude based on hedonic consumption [40]. In other words, consumers' emotional reactions to experiences drive their attitudes and actions [27]. Although the purchase of a VR headset falls into the high-involvement category, the purchase of the headset itself isn't the only purchase. The real purchase is the experience a consumer has while wearing the headset. In other words, it's the content. Attitudes towards VR shape when the consumer is wearing the headset and experiencing something extraordinary. Something memorable. Something exciting.

3.2 Broaden and Build Theory of Positive Emotions

Positive emotions broaden people's minds and contribute to good health and functioning [7]. Frijda [19] suggests positive emotions trigger a state of "free activation," where the participant's mind is open and receptive to trying new opportunities. Frederickson [17, 18] developed the Broaden and Build Theory of Positive Emotions to explain why experiencing positive emotions is not only a temporary lift but that it opens minds to explore new activities later. These positive emotions build over time and act as a reservoir when positive energy is needed [7]. VR content that stimulates positive emotional arousal could become an arsenal of positive energy for consumers to draw on later when they need it. Post-purchase satisfaction could expand when owning a VR headset becomes known as a tool for creating positive emotions rather than simply a toy to play games.

4 Methodology

Since the VR experience is unknown to so many consumers, participants needed to experience VR before they could understand and accurately reflect their feelings on VR. Therefore, a qualitative research approach is more suited to this study as people make meaning from the experience versus quantitative studies, where people already know and just need to be asked [29]. We not only wanted to explore how people made sense of their virtual reality experience, but we also wanted to understand how the experience itself changed their attitudes and opinions.

As VR is a unique experience with many options, we selected the consumer-friendly stand-alone Oculus Quest (1st Generation; Oculus, 2019) headset for a fully immersive experience and an introductory program to teach the basics. Although there are more expensive headsets on the market, the Oculus Quest is specifically priced to appeal to consumers for personal use ($399-$499)[1].

---

[1] Oculus Quest. (n.d). Wikipedia. https://en.wikipedia.org/wiki/Oculus_Quest. This model was discontinued September 2020 when Meta (formerly Facebook) introduced the Meta Quest 2.

The Oculus Quest First Steps tutorial (Version 1.0; Meta Quest, 2019) [31] is an ideal program for testing consumer reactions to a first VR experience. It's provided to Oculus Quest purchasers and is often used to set up their headsets. Although it's merely an introduction to what is possible to do in VR with an Oculus Quest headset and two hand controllers, first-time users are often surprised to learn they can touch, hold, throw objects, and grasp hands in the virtual space. The tutorial guides the user on operating the hand controllers and provides several practice objects, including blocks, paper airplanes, balls, and small rockets. First Steps is a straightforward guide to teaching someone how they use their "hands" in VR. Once they've mastered the hand controllers using the objects, the guide prompts the user to try two additional activities by inserting a cartridge into a virtual unit. One exercise involves shooting at flying boxes to score points. The other activity includes dancing in a virtual dance club with a robot partner. The friendly robot character extends his hands in greeting, and the participant can shake or hold his hands. As with a normal dance partner, the participant can spin the robot and dance or simply stand next to him if they wish. Either way, the robot is there to dance with rather than just standing and dancing alone.

5 Interviews

5.1 Data Collection

Following IRB approval, we conducted ten semi-structured interviews with individuals in a large midwestern university starting in the Spring of 2022. We met with eight participants in private offices on campus, one in an author's home, and another at her office in town. We met at scheduled times convenient for the participants. We obtained signature approvals from each participant. We recorded each interview using the Voice Memos (Version 2.2; Apple Inc., 2020) application. After each interview, we wrote memos recapping key learning points and further directions. We used REV.com for transcription services and NVivo (Mac Release 1.6.2; QSR International, 2021) for coding and data analysis.

5.2 Participants

We used criterion sampling [33] for this study as the tutorial had to be a new experience for participants, and they had to be curious about experiencing VR. Due to personal conversations, we also used snowball sampling [29]. Participants volunteered without pressure or financial incentives because they were curious to try VR and felt comfortable trying new technologies. The ten participants included six females and four males ranging in age from 19 to 61 ($M = 40.3$; SD $= 14.93$). Because our focus was on understanding the attitudes and opinions of first-time VR users, none of the participants considered themselves "gamers". Although their names are fictional, their ages and general professions are as follows:

- Sara, 19, Female, Undergraduate Student in Organizational Leadership
- Meg, 21, Female, Undergraduate Student in Technology Education
- Jen, 27, Female, Ph.D. Student in Learning Design & Technology

- Rusty, 32, Male, Ph.D. Student in Organizational Leadership
- Abby, 38, Female, Organizational Leadership Instructor
- Anne, 49, Female, Community Center Activities
- Anthony, 50, Male, Professor in Computer Design
- Sean, 51, Male, Professor in Computer Technology
- Dave, 55, Male, Medical Professional
- Susan, 61, Female, Staff Administration

Interviews ranged from 50 to 90 min. Discussion questions addressed their broader feelings towards technology and VR, their expectations towards the tutorial, their feelings during the tutorial, and their feelings after the tutorial.

After learning their age and occupation, we discussed their background and comfort level with technology and social media usage. We discussed their attitudes towards VR, if they knew anyone who used it, and any concerns and expectations about the experience.

After the initial discussion, we helped the participant put on the headset, which prompted the program to start. The volume on the headset was loud enough that the recording could pick up the guide's instructions throughout, which helped us understand the participant's progress. Although some participants wore face masks, which made it difficult to see facial expressions, we asked them to provide verbal comments to reflect their feelings. We noted their emotional reactions and asked them to describe what they were experiencing.

After completing the tutorial, which took about 20 min, they removed the headset, and we discussed their reactions. Participants explained what surprised them, what met or didn't meet expectations, and any changes in attitudes or opinions towards VR. We also discussed potential applications and how they could use it at home, school, and work.

We followed up with participants at various times post-trial to see if their attitudes and behavior towards VR had changed since the experience. We discussed what they did after the experience, such as discussions with friends and family and anything new they might have learned about the technology since the trial.

5.3 Data Analysis

We identified over 70 codes in the first analysis. All codes fell within three main categories: feelings they had towards VR before the tutorial, feelings during the experience, and feelings after the experience. Within each category, three main themes emerged: concerns for the technology, surprise with the quality, and enjoyment with the experience.

Feelings Before the Tutorial. All but two participants were curious and excited to try VR but also nervous. Sara and Meg were apprehensive about the technology overall since they had watched the film *Ready Player One* and an episode of *Black Mirror*. These programs portrayed VR as a necessary escape from a frightening dystopian reality. We later learned Sara had concerns about motion sickness, which she usually experiences while riding in a car, but it wasn't an issue in the tutorial. Anthony had concerns overall about making people more anti-social. "...*people are already isolated. I wonder if VR will make people more isolated*". Rusty raised an interesting point about adding yet another identity to maintain and was concerned that people would choose a digital life over a real one. *"So more push on this avatar life. For example, if I start enjoying this, would I want to spend more time with this"*. Meg discussed the trade-offs to technology changes that not everyone likes. *"I think it's kind of natural for technology to continue to evolve and for those things to happen... I don't know. There's a trade-off to both good and bad things that can come from it...The good? I'd be able to socialize with friends in a way that I've not ever been able to"*.

Sean and Anthony were less enthusiastic for different reasons and only participated out of professional courtesy. Neither participant felt particularly hopeful about the technology. Sean viewed technology from a practical standpoint and didn't see a useful reason for VR personally or professionally. However, he grudgingly accepted it had niche industry applications. Anthony had purchased two headsets for his children, ages nine and thirteen, and was disappointed in their limited interest. *"They only played with it the first week, and then it sat on the shelf"*. Anthony had not considered participating with his children in VR, and he couldn't foresee doing something in virtual reality would ever be better than real life.

Feelings During the Tutorial.   Sara, Meg, Jen, Dave, Susan, and Anne loved the experience overall and expressed their enthusiasm with lots of laughter and expressions of "cools" and "wows". They particularly enjoyed the dancing robot segment. Sara said, *"Oh, this is...Oh my gosh. This is so weird! I don't know what I'm doing.* (high-pitched squeal) *I'm dancing! Am I supposed to be dancing right now? Oh Yeah. I can dance with him. That's so fun. Can I make him spin?"* Meg felt the same. *"He waved at me! Sure. I'm gonna dance. That's fun. I'm in. I like this one"*. Susan and Anne were enchanted by the robot and liked holding his hands. Susan laughed a lot at the *"tiny little man with eyes"* who waved at her. *"We're getting down!"* She said, laughing. *"We're dancing!"* She elected to repeat the dance segment. *"He's kinda cute! Oh, I need this to exercise"*. Anne liked that he was *"right there"* with her and that she could *"reach out and touch him"*.

Five female participants preferred the dancing robot to the shooting segment and didn't spend much time shooting the guns. Meg explained the gun shooting was a traditional game experience, so not that exciting. *"It's like some old-style game, you know, just shooting them, and I will get points, and it's like easy for me to get bored of that game"*. She compared that to the dancing robot segment. *"There's a character and very cute, and like inviting me to dance, so I think it's really like relaxed and, I feel like I'm engaged with the environment more with that game instead of the shooting one"*. Anne felt the same way about the immersive environment and that she was moving, but wasn't stressed out. She thought of it as *"relaxing exercise"*.

Rusty, Sean, and Anthony preferred the shooting segment and were very uncomfortable with the dancing robot. *"I'm not a dancer,"* Rusty explained. He also wondered if he should fight him. *"He's saying hi. Do I need to fight with him?"* Although Anthony didn't explain his discomfort, he didn't spend much time with the robot. Sean tried his best not to show any dancing movements, but we observed his legs moving just a little to the music. He was also tempted to get down to the floor when the robot instructed him to *"get down!"* Sean also pretended to shoot objects at the interviewer, which seemed to make him happy.

In contrast, Dave, who loves to dance in real life, felt the *"little dude"* was a lot of fun. *"What?! Now there's a little dude in front of me. Wave to the little dude. Shaking his hand. Little dude's dancing!"*.

Dave also tried to blow up objects with the rocket. *"If I could accidentally hit the blimp with the rocket and try and blow it up. Yeah. Oh, it's coming right at me! Oh, man. It almost hit me, but I knocked it away with my hand"*. Rusty also enjoyed the rockets. *"I like this paper plane thing. So like, they really respond well. I like this rocket. More rockets"*. Jen enjoyed playing with the different objects and said "cute" a lot. The hot air balloon *"Oh, it sounds so cute... Okay. Fly. Oh, that's so cute"*.

The participants were impressed with the quality of the tutorial. Anthony felt it was a top-tier program and stressed he didn't believe there were programs with similar quality. Dave felt dancing was more fun than shooting, but he enjoyed other parts of the tutorial. *"I was super happy when I got to shoot stuff. I thought that was cool"*. He was surprised by the immersive 3D environment. *"That was way more fun to do than I thought it would be...Like, you're literally watching the rocket zoom around was pretty cool. That was pretty fun! And again, the rocket went where you expect the rocket would go at the speed you'd expect"*. Jen was surprised at how advanced VR had progressed. *"It's kind of exciting here...Yeah, it's fantastic. I just can't believe the VR technology has so advanced"*.

Feelings After the Tutorial. Sara especially liked the robot and laughed. *"It was cool. I would hang out with him again. I'd dance with him again"*. Dave was surprised at how much he liked the dancing robot. *"The dancing around was actually super, super fun. Like, I mean, I found myself wanting to just, you know, dance with this weird VR dance partner"*. He could also imagine having fun with others in the virtual space. *"I can imagine if you really turned it into an actual dance partner, you know, like I could see learning to dance, like learning swing moves in that environment"*. Meg thought it was *"freaky fun"* to dance with the robot. Susan loved the robot, wanted to name him and wanted to take him home with her. *"He was cute, and it was just fun compared to normal exercising"*. She liked the fact that he was right there with her rather than just watching people on TV. *"They aren't doing it with you"*. Anne felt the same way despite being married since her husband didn't dance. She loved the experience and could see picking out a character as a dancing partner. Exercise was important to Anne, who works with senior citizens every day. Not only was the tutorial great for movement, but she felt a *"great escape"* as well.

Concerns about the dark side of technology didn't go away after the tutorial. Sara mentioned it could be *"a slippery slope"* for people *"who don't have many friends"*. She explained, *"I feel like it could be really easy for someone who doesn't have many friends...just turn to this instead of actually interacting with other people. I think that could be a slippery slope"*.

Dave mentioned he would only meet with people he knew online, considering users only see an avatar and not the real person. *"If I know you're my buddy, it's different. It's different hanging out than if you're dancing with someone, and it might be Chuck, who's a 300-pound guy living in Detroit in his, you know, grandmother's basement"*.

We found the highly aroused participants promoted the experience to others. Sara was so excited by her experience that she told Meg, who then volunteered to participate in the study. Two additional women overheard Sara's enthusiasm in the hallway and also wanted to try it.

Purchase and use intention varied. Dave, who enjoyed the dancing, discussed the experience with his friends and family and planned to purchase headsets for himself and his teenage kids. Jen talked to her husband about her experience, and they went to Sam's Club to look at headsets. Sara spoke to her friends about borrowing a headset from the campus library and playing it together.

Anthony, who works in the computer graphics area, was impressed with the program's quality. He also discussed the need to focus technology solutions on adult women rather than college-aged students. He felt older women had been neglected as a segment and that they deserved further research.

Rusty wasn't interested in the personal use of VR but was very excited about the professional applications, particularly in remote meetings and usage in the classroom. In our follow-up discussion, he mentioned he was looking at VR companies for internship opportunities.

Abby's favorite part was playing tetherball. She wasn't interested in dancing with the robot; however, she thought it would be cool if he could teach her how to do something fun, like play tennis.

Sean was probably the least interested in VR, yet the next week commented that he watched a TV program featuring people who used VR to look at the bottom of the ocean. He reiterated that its usefulness lies in niche applications, but his voice was noticeably less harsh than it was during the tutorial, almost as if he was mulling over the possibilities.

Anne was going to talk to her two teenage kids about VR. She felt her 17-year-old son would be particularly interested in the travel applications. Anne could also see the potential for grocery shopping and the assistance of a personal shopper. She felt having a *"dietician on the side"* could help a lot of people on special diets.

5.4 Interview Findings

As suggested by the Experiential Hierarchy of Effects [40, 27], participants' attitudes towards VR formed from the emotions they felt during the experience. Despite their initial concerns with the technology, they felt positive emotions during the interaction. The participants' reactions also support Frederickson's Broaden and Build Theory of Positive Emotions [17, 18]. The positive emotion they felt from their VR experience sparked their interest and subsequent actions. Although their area of interest in the technology varied, they spoke with friends and family about their experiences. Most participants planned additional usage for personal or professional activities, or they planned to keep looking into it. Although each participant contributed to our understanding, the strong reactions to the robot prompted a broader study of what consumers were saying on social media.

6 Social Media Analysis

A Google search for "Oculus First Steps robot" returned nearly one million results. We felt online data would supplement the interview findings and offer a wider breadth of consumers' feelings towards the tutorial experience. We followed Kozinets' [25] netnography approach, which provides a structured process of collecting and analyzing online data. According to Kozinets [25], netnography is best used for understanding online cultures where the researcher is the instrument and data is collected from social media sites.

Online ethnography is an ideal method for understanding consumer feelings for several reasons. The internet is an open space for people to profess their feelings, opinions, and attitudes on various topics, particularly products, and services. Consumers like to share their experiences online with other consumers – or warn people to stay away [20]. Customer comments are unsolicited and voluntary, and there are limited regulations that prohibit researchers from reading what consumers feel. It's a popular resource for marketers to "listen" to what consumers like and dislike about a product or service. Rich details provided by texts, photos, videos, and memes can be significant and often reveal consumer trends and human connections, and emotions [25]. Online data can offer a deep cultural understanding of human experiences [23].

6.1 Data Collection

We followed Kozinets' [25] investigative data operation method and collected data from social media sites that are open to the public and do not require a login or password. Data is indexed by search engines and accessible via search results. We did not interact with participants or post content.

We chose Facebook, Reddit, and YouTube because conversations happen between posters and commenters, similar to natural communities [25]. These sites also offer a diversity of viewpoints and types of posts, including pictures, graphics, videos, and texts. Posts revealed many human emotions, including fear, happiness, excitement, and love. Kozinets [25] suggests originally posted content enables researchers to have a deeper understanding of their experience from an ethnographic view. Therefore, we retained comments in their original form.

We copied and pasted original posts and comments from these three sites onto word documents and uploaded them into NVivo (Mac Release 1.6.2; QSR International, 2021) for coding and analysis. The following is an overview of each site.

Facebook. The Facebook community "Oculus Quest 2- Beginner Friendly" (https://www.facebook.com/groups/983675928824765) had approximately 33.1K members at the time of our study. Consumers engage with other beginning VR enthusiasts in this community. They ask and answer questions, provide feedback, post comments and photos, and discuss their experiences. This is a public community where anyone can join. All posts and comments are visible to anyone, and data is indexed by search engines. Readers can click the like button (Thumbs up) to show support for the post. We included a March 20, 2022, post titled "Totally recommend Oculus first contact and First steps for oculus if you are brand new to Vr, so helpful!" and 18 comments. This particular post had 35 likes.

Reddit. The discussion site Reddit offers a subreddit forum R/OculusQuest (https://www.reddit.com/r/OculusQuest/). This community is open to anyone who wants to share and discuss the Oculus Quest and Quest 2. It was created on September 26, 2018, and had approximately 352K members at the time of this study. Members post pictures and videos and share their feelings with other members. Members can comment and show their support or approval of a post by "upvoting". Within this subreddit, we searched for comments using these search terms: "first steps", "1st steps", and "first steps robot". We selected only posts (and corresponding comments) that reflected their experience using the tutorial. For example, one of the posts, "My mom dances in First Steps", featured a video and had 44 comments. We collected a total of 10 posts and 208 comments. Table 1 shows the post title, the type of content, the date posted, the number of comments, and the percentage that upvoted the post.

Table 1. r/OculusQuest First Steps Posts and Number of Comments on Reddit

	Title	Content	Date Posted	Comments	Upvoted
1	My mom dances in First Steps	Video	1 year ago	44	98%
2	Forgot I recorded this right after launch. Caught her dancing with the first steps robot. 😄	Video	1 year ago	33	94%
3	Oculus Quest 1st steps is one of the best games on the quest.		1 year ago	21	69%
4	Blowing Minds		3 years ago	7	96%
5	Had some friends and family over for the weekend! First Steps Robot Dance gets em every time! 😄 😈 🎮 🐾	Video	3 years ago	13	94%
6	My son is absolutely obsessed with the dancing robot mini game in First Steps	Video	3 years ago	33	94%
7	Dad tries First Steps, sees the robot, and what's the first thing he does?		3 years ago	29	90%
8	Lead singer of Imagine Dragons (Dan Reynolds) also loved that dancing robot in First Steps	Video	3 years ago	13	94%
9	Can you save in first steps? I just want to robot 🤖 with the dance		2 years ago	3	91%
10	Some more love for that little robot in First Steps		3 years ago	12	90%

YouTube. YouTube is a public website for people to share and watch videos. Searching for "oculus first steps robot" returned a video tutorial by a gamer named AndyThePlayer titled "The Robot In First Steps is So Adorable (First Steps Oculus Quest Gameplay)" (https://youtu.be/J9MPY-bTsS4). This tutorial was posted on June 19, 2019, and had over 3,300 views, 67 likes, and 22 comments at the time of our research.

6.2 Data Analysis

We used thematic analysis to analyze the data since this study was a broad investigation of consumers' emotional reactions to their experiences using the First Steps tutorial. According to Braun and Clarke [6], thematic analysis is a method for identifying and analyzing patterns or themes within data and can often help decipher various directions of the research topic. As an exploratory study, we looked for key themes that involved reaching "across" the data for understanding [6]. We paid particular attention to data that shed light on answering the main research question: "how did they feel about their First Steps experience, and how did it change their attitudes and opinions about VR?".

After reviewing the data, we generated initial codes. This step revealed several possible themes, including feelings about the robot, converting people to try VR, dancing, first experience, men's and women's reactions, launching the rocket, and requests for similar content. After the second and third review of codes, four main themes emerged from the analysis: (1) consumers felt strong positive emotions toward the robot, (2) they felt it was a fantastic introduction to VR, (3) they asked for additional robot-like content, and (4) they enjoyed it so much they showed it to others to try.

Positive Emotional Reactions. Consumers described feeling love and excitement, and even overwhelming emotions towards the robot with words and emojis. *"I danced with this guy on my oculus for HOURS and I fell in love 😊"*. One poster was particularly moved. *"I nearly cried dancing with this cute little guy!"*.

Videos of people dancing with the robot prompted others to post their support and admiration and surprise at the robot's attention. *"That robot has gotten so many dates. He's the George Clooney of robot tutorials"*. Another poster commented on the ongoing robot discussions. *"I feel like "moms dancing with that robot in First Steps" is becoming a genre in and of itself"*.

One conversation string on Reddit titled *"Some more love that little robot in First Steps"* expressed naming the robot. One commented, *"I call him "Tommy" He is Tommy"*. Another person responded that they contacted Oculus to ask what they named him. *"I asked Oculus support what his name was -they didn't have one. So Tommy it is!"* Another poster replied, *"I just read today that the devs called him 'Monty.' It was on this sub"*.

Great First VR Experience. Consumers felt their first experience was fun and amazing, and they wanted to share their thoughts with others and recommended others share them as well. *"It's impossible not to have fun with that robot. First steps is a really amazing introduction to VR for non-gamers"*. One poster described her wow moment. *"That dancing robot was my first wow moment in VR"*. And they used the tutorial to show others. *"Had some friends and family over for the weekend! First Steps Robot Dance gets em every time!"*. Another poster agreed. *"Yeah, the robot dancing is great! I've done the First Steps demo probably 5 times by now and I always repeat the dancing and really get down with that little guy 😊 🤖 🦾 💃"*. Another poster added their thoughts. *"First Steps in general is IMO, the best thing to show new people and I make sure they leave the dancing for last"*.

Consumers Want Additional Robot-Like Content. The robot portion of the tutorial is just one part of the program, and users must get through the initial tutorial first.

Consumers expressed frustration at having to go through the entire tutorial just to get to the robot section. *"I really wish there was a way to skip ahead in First Steps"*. *"Any way to jump straight to the dancing robot without having to sit through the tutorial?"* *"It keeps forcing me to do the annoyingly long intro: (I just want to dance with the robot* 👹*"*. Some people talked about how fun they had and wished for additional content like it. They also addressed the lack of similar content on the market. *"I decided to go through First Steps again (because it's honestly a fun demo) and I was surprised that I was enjoying that little dancing part even more. No more figuring out how to grab his hands, etc. I just let myself go completely (no worries, my balcony door shades were down). So much fun! I wish there would be a whole game like this"*. Another poster agreed. *"Other developers need to follow this formula"*. Other people chimed in. *"They need to make some of the parts of first steps into bigger fleshed out separate games. Was trying to find a dancing game similar to that and couldn't find anything. Imagine they would make bank by getting you to buy first steps sub games separately"*.

Consumers Wanted to Share it with Others and Enjoyed Watching Other People Have Fun. Consumers were not only happy with their experience, but they also actively shared their experience with friends and family and encouraged them to try it. They expressed happiness when others enjoyed the experience. *"I almost get more enjoyment from just watching people experience VR for the first time! Sharing this amazing tech with others is a great feeling!* 🧑*"*. One poster described his experience, which led neighbors to search for a headset. *"Took the quest up to the local tap. My 65 year-old neighbor played it for 5 min and proclaimed they couldn't go a week without it in their life. They called around this morning until they found one at the Walmart in the next town"*. Some consumers felt frustration when others refused to try it. *"Sister and brother-in-law - both refused to try. Sister was convinced she would get sick and BIL had no interest, even though he is a flat gamer"*.

6.3 Findings

The online data suggests that experiencing the First Steps program is a positive emotional experience that prompts a positive evaluation of VR. The data supports the Experiential Hierarchy of Effects theory [27, 40] that VR can be an emotionally driven hedonic experience. The emotional connection to the robot in the dance experience prompted this positive reaction which mirrored our interview findings. Consumers who posted their feelings had a strong emotional response to dancing with the robot rather than shooting at blocks and scoring points.

There were many references to "girlfriend, mother/mom, aunt, grandmother" in the online discussions, but it is difficult to determine gender and age in online profiles. As this is an ongoing study, we plan to broaden our online data to other sites and media. Further study of online data could help build user personas, which in turn, could guide us in selecting additional participants to interview and observe. This research will assist in building segmentation strategies that could help the adoption rate. Based on the interview reactions in addition to the online data, the highly aroused segment may be older females, possibly mothers, but we need to interview more participants in this segment.

7 Discussion

The data suggest a new positioning strategy could help the sluggish adoption rate. Meta launched Oculus Quest 2 on National Fitness Day with the headline, "Cardio that Doesn't Suck is Ready" [11]. Perhaps a more effective positioning would be that VR provides a fun and happy escape with a cute robot. Additional content like the robot activity needs to be developed first, however. Purchasing the headset is only the first Step.

A potential limitation of the interview portion of the study concerned comfort levels. Watching people while they experienced the tutorial, particularly dancing, made some participants uncomfortable. Possibly observing participants through a two-way mirror might make them more comfortable. As one online person commented on dancing in front of others, *"I just let myself go completely (no worries, my balcony door shades were down)"*.

Future research could study which element of the robot experience is arousing. Several variables in the segment could stimulate emotions, including music, facial expressions, holding hands, and dancing. For example, Howard and Gengler [22] suggest receiver attitudes can be swayed if they see happy, smiling senders of those messages, but they need to see the facial expressions for it to work. The robot's facial expressions include friendly wide-eyed smiles and winks, which could explain why so many users felt positive arousal toward the robot. Testing individual variables would be insightful.

8 Conclusion

The data suggest the dancing robot content is an emotionally driven hedonic experience for first-time VR users. As the Experiential Hierarchy of Effects states, attitudes toward VR were formed during the experience itself [27, 40], confirming the importance of a positive first experience. Users who experience intense positive emotional arousal during their first experience may act as consumer advocates, driving adoption via word of mouth and social sharing.

The data suggest there is a potential to shift away from gaming and move towards positive experiences to appeal to women. The consumers that experienced positive emotional arousal are actively seeking additional robot-like content. Understanding who these customers are can offer insights to developers. Furthermore, content that is positively arousing, such as robot dancing, can be used as a tool for consumers' health and well-being. In addition to exercise and relieving isolation, as Frederickson [18] explained, building a repertoire of positive emotions can help consumers during trying times in life.

If the most emotionally engaged segment is indeed female and potentially older, the tech market will need more than a new content strategy. Most game developers are still predominantly male [9] and therefore create content that appeals to men. Adult women would be an entirely new segment to consider for content development. This new strategy could not only potentially speed up VR adoption, but it could help diversify the industry overall.

References

1. Aaker, D.: Secrets of social media revealed 50 years ago. Harv. Bus. Rev. (2011). https://hbr.org/2011/06/secrets-of-social-media-reveal
2. AFP: Pandemic fuels travel boom in virtual reality. Global Times (2021). https://www.globaltimes.cn/page/202103/1219713.shtml
3. Alsop, T.: Interest in virtual reality (VR) in the United States as of July 2020, by age. Statista (2021). https://www.statista.com/statistics/456810/virtual-reality-interest-in-the-united-states/
4. Apple Inc.: Voice Memos (Version 2.2) [Computer App] (2020). https://support.apple.com/guide/voice-memos/welcome/ARc
5. AR Insider: How Many Consumers Have Tried VR? AR Insider (2022). https://arinsider.co/2022/06/08/how-many-consumers-have-tried-vr-2/
6. Braun, V., Clarke, V.: Using thematic analysis in psychology. Qualit. Res. Psychol. 3(2), 77–101 (2006). https://doi.org/10.1191/1478088706qp063oa
7. Celestine, N.: Broaden-and-build theory of positive emotions. PositivePsychology.com (2022). https://positivepsychology.com/broaden-build-theory/
8. Clark, M.: Meta reportedly breaks up the 300-person team that was building a hybrid VR/AR OS. Meta isn't combining its AR and VR operating systems, for now. The Verge (2022). https://www.theverge.com/2022/2/25/22950710/meta-vr-ar-os-team-xros-breakup-hyper-tuned-focus
9. Clement, J.: Game developer distribution worldwide 2014–2021, by gender. Statista (2021). https://www.statista.com/statistics/453634/game-developer-gender-distribution-worldwide/
10. Clement, J.: Average age of U.S. video game players in 2019. Statista (2021). https://www.statista.com/statistics/189582/age-of-us-video-game-players/
11. Cohen, D.: Oculus Quest 2 An integrated campaign kicked off to mark National Fitness Day. Adweek (2021). https://www.adweek.com/social-marketing/facebook-reality-labs-wants-people-to-sweat-with-oculus-quest-2/
12. deBorst, A.W., deGelder, B.: Is it the real deal? Perception of virtual characters versus humans: an affective cognitive neuroscience perspective. Front. Psychol. 6, 576 (2015). https://doi.org/10.3389/fpsyg.2015.00576
13. Dichter, E.: How word-of-mouth advertising works. Harv. Bus. Rev. 147–166 (1966)
14. Diefenbach, S., Kolb, N., Hassenzahl, M.: The 'Hedonic' in human-computer interaction – history, contributions, and future research directions. In: Proceedings of the Conference on Designing Interactive Systems, pp. 305–314 (2014). https://doi.org/10.1145/2598510.2598549
15. Di Muro, F., Murray, K.B.: An arousal regulation explanation of mood effects on consumer choice. J. Consum. Res. 39(3), 574–584 (2012). https://doi.org/10.1086/664040
16. Fitzmaurice, R.: From sofa to Safari: the rise of virtual travel. Evening Standard (2021). https://www.standard.co.uk/escapist/travel/vr-travel-oculus-quest-2-virtual-tours-b901159.html
17. Fredrickson, B.L.: What good are positive emotions? Rev. Gen. Psychol. 2(3), 300–319 (1998)
18. Fredrickson, B.L.: The broaden-and-build theory of positive emotions. Philos. Trans. R. Soc. B: Biol. Sci. 359(1449), 1367–1378 (2004). https://doi.org/10.1098/rstb.2004.1512
19. Frijda, N.H.: The Emotions. Cambridge University Press, Cambridge (1986)
20. Ghelber, A.: Customer experience is key as consumers share more online reviews. Forbes Communication Council Post (2021). https://www.forbes.com/sites/forbescommunicationscouncil/2021/08/03/customer-experience-is-key-as-consumers-share-more-online-reviews/?sh=1e57fba45362
21. Hall, L., et al.: When will immersive virtual reality have its day? Challenges to IVR adoption in the home as exposed in studies with teenagers, parents, and experts. PRESENCE Virtual Augmented Reality 1–33 (2022). https://doi.org/10.1162/pres_a_00347

22. Howard, D.J., Gengler, C.: Emotional contagion effects on product attitudes: figure 1. J. Consum. Res. **28**(2), 189–201 (2001). https://doi.org/10.1086/322897
23. HYVE: Robert Kozinets: Netnography: The Essential Guide to Qualitative Social Media Research [Video]. YouTube (2020). https://youtu.be/CUnLAvyuQB8
24. Jenkins, A.: The fall and RiseVRf VR: the struggle to make virtual reality get real. Fortune (2019). https://fortune.com/longform/virtual-reality-struggle-hope-vr/
25. Kozinets, R.V.: Netnography the Essential Guide to Qualitative Social Media Research. 3rd edn. Sage Publishing (2020)
26. Laurell, C., Sandstrom, C., Berthold, A., Larsson, D.: Exploring barriers to adoption of virtual reality through social media analytics and machine learning – an assessment of technology, network, price and trialability. J. Bus. Res. **101**, 1–916 (2019). https://www.sciencedirect.com/journal/journal-of-business-research/vol/101/suppl/C
27. Lavidge, R.J., Steiner, G.A.: A model for predictive measurements of advertising effectiveness. J. Mark. **25**(6), 59 (1961). https://doi.org/10.2307/1248516
28. Manis, K.T., Choi, D.: The virtual reality hardware acceptance model (VR-ham): extending and individuating the technology acceptance model (TAM) for virtual reality hardware. J. Bus. Res. (2018. https://www.sciencedirect.com/science/article/pii/S0148296318304946?via%3Dihub
29. Merriam, S.B., Tisdell, E.J.: Qualitative Research: A Guide to Design and Implementation, 4th edn. Jossey-Bass, San Francisco (2016)
30. Mogilner, C., Aaker, J., Kamvar, S.D.: How happiness affects choice. J. Consum. Res. **39**(2), 429–443 (2012). https://doi.org/10.1086/663774
31. Oculus: First Steps (Version 1VR) [VR app] Meta Quest (2019). https://www.oculus.com/experiences/quest/1863547050392688/
32. Pardes, A.: Inside the Intense, Insular World of AOL Disc Collecting. Vice (2015). https://www.vice.com/en/article/kwxngw/inside-the-weird-world-of-aol-disc-collecting-511
33. Patton, M.Q.: Qualitative Research and Evaluation Methods, 3rd edn. Sage, Thousand Oaks (2001). [Chs. 1, 6, 9]
34. QSR International: NVivo Qualitative Data Analysis Software. [Computer App] (Mac Release 1.6.2) QSR International (2021). https://support.qsrinternational.com/nvivo/s/
35. Sagnier, C., Loup-Escande, E., Lourdeaux, D.: User acceptance of virtual reality: an extended technology acceptance model. Int. J. Hum.-Comput. Interact. (2020). https://www.researchgate.net/publication/338424401_User_Acceptance_of_Virtual_Reality_An_Extended_Technology_Acceptance_Model
36. Sanchez-Vives, M.V., Slater, M.: From presence to consciousness through virtual reality. Nat. Rev. Neurosci. **6**, 332–339 (2005). https://doi.org/10.1038/nrn1651
37. Shimer, D.: Yale's most popular class ever: happiness. New York Times (2018). https://www.nytimes.com/2018/01/26/nyregion/at-yale-class-on-happiness-draws-huge-crowd-laurie-santos.html
38. Slater, M., Lotto, B., Arnold, M.M., Sanchez-Vives, M.V.: How we experience immersive virtual environments: the concept of presence and its measurements. Annuario Psicolog. **40**, 193–210 (2009)
39. Slater, M., Spanlang, B., Corominas, D.: Simulating virtual environments within virtual environments as the basis for a psychophysics of presence. ACM Trans. Graph. **29**, 92 (2010). https://doi.org/10.1145/1778765.1778829
40. Solomon, M.R.: Consumer Behavior: Buying, Having, Being. 13th edn. Pearson (2019)
41. Stern, J.: Make your quest a better portal to the metaverse. Wall Street J. (2022). https://www.wsj.com/articles/meta-quest-2-review-metaverse-11645571617
42. Sugay, C.: How to measure happiness with tests and surveys (+ quizzes). PositivePsychology.com (2022). https://positivepsychology.com/measure-happiness-tests-surveys/

43. Sun, H.M., Cheng, W.L.: The input-interface of Webcam applied in 3D virtual reality systems. Comput. Educ. **53**(4), 1231–1240 (2009). https://doi.org/10.1016/j.compedu.2009.06.006
44. Tokel, S.T., İsler, V.: Acceptance of virtual worlds as learning space. Innov. Educ. Teach. Int. **52**(3), 254–264 (2013). https://doi.org/10.1080/14703297.2013.820139
45. Tran, K.: Why gamers are more valuable than companies think. Morning Consult (2023). https://morningconsult.com/2023/02/07/why-gamers-are-more-valuable-than-companies-think/
46. Van Boven, L., Gilovich, T.: To do or to have? That is the question. J. Pers. Soc. Psychol. **85**(6), 1193–1202 (2003). https://doi.org/10.1037/0022-3514.85.6.1193
47. Van Kleef, G.A.: Emotions as agents of social influence: insights from Emotions as Social Information (EASI) theory. In: Harkins, S.G., Williams, K.D., Burger, J.M. (eds.) The Oxford Handbook of Social Influence, pp. 237–255. Oxford Library of Psychology, Oxford University Press (2017). https://doi.org/10.1093/oxfordhb/9780199859870.013.19

Multi-user VR Experience for Creating and Trading Non-fungible Tokens

Lizhou Cao[✉][iD], Jackson Shuminski[iD], Huadong Zhang[iD],
Pruthviraj Solanki[iD], David Long[iD], David Schwartz[iD], Ihab Mardini[iD],
and Chao Peng[iD]

Rochester Institute of Technology, 1 Lomb Memorial Dr, Rochester, NY 14623, USA
{lc1248,jvs8230,hz2208,ps4100,dllppr,disvks,ixmfaa,cxpigm}@rit.edu

Abstract. Non-fungible tokens (NFTs) have shown a great potential in creating, identifying, and trading digital ownership, and can be used to build the economics in the future metaverse. It is important for the users to understand the basic concepts of NFTs before they engage in a virtual society or application that uses NFTs to represent digital assets. Traditional learning methods like reading articles are inefficient to support active learning of a new concept. In this work, we designed and developed a multi-user VR-based learning method that provides a learner-oriented experience for users to create their own digital assets, witness the process of minting the assets into NFTs, and trade the NFTs. We conduct a study with participants to understand the learning efficiency of the VR-based method in comparing to the traditional reading-based method. The evaluation result shows that the multi-user experience was more engaging than a solo reading-based experience, and the participants became more motivated to learn about NFT topics in the VR experience.

Keywords: Multi-user VR environment · informal learning · non-fungible tokens · metaverse

1 Introduction

Virtual reality (VR) technology enables immersive experiences. It has been praised for its capability to realize the concept of the metaverse, bringing a virtual society into existence [13,32]. The concepts like digital ownership, cryptocurrency, and trading among users are fundamental knowledge in the metaverse, in which non-fungible tokens (NFTs) play important roles [2,17]. NFTs are unique digital identifiers that have been commonly used to represent and protect photos, videos, audio, digital artworks, and many other digital collectibles [4,33]. Building a virtual society based on NFT technology has been explored [15,27]. As an example, Decentraland [11] presented a virtual society with NFTs. Pertinent elements of the Decentraland ecosystem include finite digital real estate, digital property design limitations, and blockchain-based construction and exchange. The key aspect of their work involved learning about what the general user base

J. Y. C. Chen and G. Fragomeni (Eds.): HCII 2023, LNCS 14027, pp. 604–618, 2023.
https://doi.org/10.1007/978-3-031-35634-6_44

might know about NFTs and their possible connections to VR navigation of the Decentraland metaverse. As the foundation for economic participation in Decentraland, the demystification of these virtual digital systems is key for full environment immersion and consumption.

When people enter a virtual society for the first time, many of them may not even have a basic understanding of the concept of NFTs. We did a pre-study interview and found that most of the users lack the relevant knowledge, and this may further impact the trust and confidence naive users have in taking full advantage of a natively digital ecosystem and its fundamental economic exchange mechanisms. However, the traditional materials do not have the features to engage people to focus on the learning process, which is not suitable for the users of metaverse.

To address the basic concept introductions of NFTs efficiently, we designed and developed a multi-user experience in VR. We created a virtual environment that simulates the metaverse virtual society, allowing multiple users to join simultaneously and learn the concept of the NFTs and its applications to the user-generated content and digital asset ownership [24], through a hands-on playful experience. In the multi-user VR experience, individual users are able to create original digital art, mint and transact NFTs for trading with each other. The motivation for creating this VR experience is to convey the concept of NFTs like decentralization and collaboration and prepare users for future consumption and exchange experiences in the metaverse. With the simulated experiences with NFTs in a VR environment, users will have more intuitive feel for the concept. We conducted a user study by analyzing the learning experience and outcome. The results showed that our multi-user experience significantly improved the user experience and increased the interest in learning about NFTs.

The contribution of this work is two fold:

- The design and development of a multi-user VR experience that maps the learning outcomes to the play actions of creating and trading NFTs.
- A comprehensive evaluation of the user experience and learning outcome through the comparison between the multi-user VR experience and the solo reading-based learning experience.

2 Related Work

2.1 Non-fungible Tokens

NFTs have received a lot of attention in recent years and are used to create the ownership of digital assets and a safe way for transaction [10,33]. Chohan [9] explained how the blockchain technology was used with NFTs and pointed out that the capability to secure the data while maintaining the transparency of the transaction has made the use of NFTs possible to protect digital assets. Wang et al. [33] discussed the opportunities and challenges of NFTs. They mentioned that current NFT solutions are at an early age and the usability of NFTs is a critical challenge. Choi et al. [10] developed a blockchain-based educational program for elementary students. Their program enhanced the user engagement. Wu et al. [34] reviewed the educational applications that use NFTs to reward students. They found that NFTs as rewards can be useful for confirming the course completion and can potentially enhance enthusiasm for learning.

Kugler et al. [20] and Trautman et al. [30] described that NFTs can be used in the creation of artworks in the future and protect them when trading. As more and more artworks are published digitally, seeking an effective way to protect copyrights is challenging. Different from physical artworks, people who have access to a digital pool of artworks could easily make copies of others' works. Bstech et al. [5] demonstrated a way to transform a traditional artwork into a digital one with NFT protection. They studied the market of traditional global artworks and digital artworks and were confident that NFTs could revolutionize the way the art market works. Valeonti et al. [31] discussed the possibility of creating crypto collectibles and digital museums and argued that the financial potential of the collectibles with NFTs is substantial.

NFTs are promising tools for building the economic system of a virtual society like Metaverse [22]. Joy and Zhu [17] demonstrated the relationship among Metaverse, digital fashion, and non-fungible tokens. Gadekallu et al. [14] reviewed the use of blockchain technology in different applications in Metaverse. They argued that the indivision and uniqueness of NFTs make them suitable for the identity representation.

2.2 Learning Approach

When people enter the virtual society, it is important for them to understand the concepts of NFTs and transactions. However, most of the learning materials about these subjects use traditional media, such as texts, images, and videos [25], which are inefficient in explaining the concept of NFTs, especially to new users who do not have prior knowledge. To promote active and hands-on learning experience, Dettling et al. [12] created a system that presents the blockchain technology with a simple simulation of the minting and transaction process. Au et al. [1] explored the method of using the simulation to convey knowledge of trading digital assets. The method resulted in a clear description of the transaction process but was also found to lack the engagement. In this work, we were guided by the idea of learning-by-doing – promoting users to create and use NFTs in a social scenario, as opposed to memorizing definitions, rules, and policies that are often emphasized in the traditional learning materials. Thus, we looked into the possibility to design and develop an immersive VR environment to situate users into the context and make them free to interact with each other during a trading event.

VR technology has been a great success in entertainment, training, and education [6,8,35]. It enhances the feeling of presence when the users access a digital environment or event. Yilmaz et al. [36] developed a virtual environment for NFT-based virtual auctions. Their findings suggested that the immersive virtual environment helps improve learning efficiency. Cao et al. [7] applied VR technology to enhance the learning experience of historical events of the Apollo projects. By driving the lunar rover and exploring the lunar surface in VR, users were more engaged in the learning process. Adding a multi-user mode could help further improve the learning efficiency when the learning objectives are composed of corporations and interactions [16,29]. Ibanez et al. [16] presented a multi-user language learning application found that the multi-user mode was able to promote collaborative activities. Barret et al. [3] developed a VR-based multi-user learning environment for language education. The results indicated an agreeable attitude towards applying VR and multi-user. Lerner et al. [23] used a multi-user VR platform for emergency medicine education. Their system increased the feeling of presence because the VR and multi-user mode simulated a reality scenario. They found the feeling of presence affected the training effectiveness significantly.

In this work, we implemented a multi-user VR experience that allows users to create and trade NFTs in a virtual society. Our goal is to explore and evaluate the effectiveness of this experience in learning the concept of NFTs and the potential to motivate the users to learn more about NFTs afterwards.

3   Game Design and Development

Our multi-user VR platform provides users with a game-like experience through two activities: artwork creation and trading. Figure 1 is an overview of the design and shows the mapping between the learning goals and the VR-based play components based on the instructional design theories [19,28]. In the artwork creation activity, each user creates an art piece using a spatial drawing tool and witnesses that the art pieces are minted into the blocks of NFTs. In the trading activity, the users are brought to a virtual trading plaza that simulates the transaction of the NFTs. Each user is able to bid on others' digital artworks and learn about the process of digital trading.

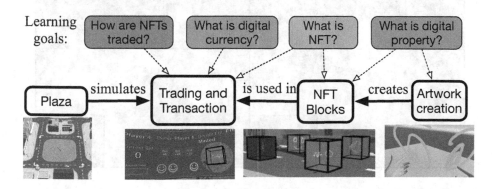

Fig. 1. The overview of the VR experience design. The dotted arrow lines indicates the mapping of the learning goals onto the play components.

Our platform allows four users to play together. We created a multi-user VR framework that connects the headsets to the same server and brings the users into the same virtual environment. The server synchronizes the visuals and interactions on the headsets, so that the users can view each other's avatars and artworks and communicate with gestures such as head-nodding and hand-waving. The artwork creation activity is implemented in the private space of the individual users. a user's hand movements and drawing actions can be seen by others, but the creation of the artwork can not be intervened by others. The trading plaza is implemented as a public space, where the bidding and transaction take place among all users.

3.1 Artwork Creation in Virtual Space

The main motivation of the artwork creation activity is to help the users understand the NFTs by creating art and then minting it themselves. This activity mimics a real world process of converting an art piece into an NFT and getting it ready for trading.

After all the users have entered the virtual environment, they start creating an art piece. The users can move around but are in the confines of a little area around them. They can draw new lines in the 3D space around them or erase the lines they have drawn using their hands, as shown in Fig. 2. At the same time, they listen to the narrator who speaks about NFTs and the minting process, in order to convey the foundational concepts of the NFT and boost the progress towards the learning goals.

Fig. 2. The images show four users creating their own art pieces.

The users are given unlimited time to make their art pieces. Once every user presses a button to finalize their art pieces, an animated minting process begins, where the art piece shrinks down and goes into the block of the same color as the user's identification color. These blocks that encapsulate the art pieces represent the NFTs, and they will be used in the later trading activity.

Users are free to draw any art they want. This simulates the fact that nearly any original artwork can be made into an NFT and traded on the marketplace. The 3D space for drawing provides further spatial freedom as to not limit the user's creativity in two dimensions. Also being able to move in a constricted zone would make it easier for the users to look at their own art pieces from different angles and help the creation as they can draw from different angles.

3.2 Trading

Once each user has created an art piece and minted it into an NFT, the users are brought to the trading plaza, where they trade the NFTs they created. The main motivation of the trading activity is to create an experience of NFT trading and convey the idea of smart contracts. The play achieves these two goals in two separate rounds of trading (Fig. 3).

Fig. 3. Screenshots from the trading activity. The left image shows the users can see and communicate to each other through gestures during the trading. The right image is the market place large screen displaying the bidding-related information.

The first round is a simple trading round where each user puts their NFT up for auction and the other three users bid on it using the bidding buttons. The users start with 100 in-game currency. They get familiar with the trading interface and gain a hands-on experience of trading NFTs via auctions. When the timer runs out the user with the highest bid takes the ownership of the NFT that was put for auction. During the auction, users can see the ownership of the NFTs and the name of the creator. They can also see how much other users are bidding on a particular auction item. Users can bid on the NFTs that are up for auction and they are not the owner of. The auction process shows the users the way ownership works as they were told in the artwork creation activity.

After all the NFTs are traded once, the second round demonstrates the smart contract functionality. In the second round, All the NFTs are put up for auction again one by one, and users bid on them once again to take the ownership.

But this time when a trade is made, 20% of the trade value is added to the creator's account, which is a commission no matter if the creator is involved in the transaction or not.

There is a large screen in front of the trading plaza that includes two interface modules for users to interact with: inventory and marketplace. In the inventory module, the user can see the NFTs they own and the available amount of the currency they can spend to bid. In the marketplace module, all the users see the trading deals that are on the marketplace and they are able to bid on those deals through this module.

In terms of the play mechanism, the trading activity gives the users choices to set their goal of either trying to own the NFTs as many as possible or gathering the in-game currency as large as possible. Based on the users' goals of play, it could turn into a competitive marketplace where the users scheme to gain advantageous trades or a cooperative marketplace where some users work together to get profit.

4   User Study

First of all, we conducted a pre-study survey to recruit random participants and ask them questions about metaverse, VR, and NFTs, in order to obtain a general understanding of what they know about the subject and how they would interpret these terms if they were not really sure of the meanings. 19 participants were recruited to answer the pre-study survey. 13 participants were not familiar with metaverse. 17 participants were not familiar with NFTs. We found that 16 participants had concerns about the protection of digital assets, but only 5 participants knew a method to protect digital assets. The responses from the pre-study indicate that most people do not know much about how to protect digital properties. 18 participants suggested that they need more knowledge prior to being ready to engage with a multi-user virtual society.

We implemented the multi-user VR system using Unity. The implementation was done on a Windows 10 workstation composed of Intel(R) Xeon(R) W-2145 CPU processor and NVIDIA GeForce GTX 1080 graphics card. The system runs through a Photon server to synchronize the VR contents among the four users' workstations. Then, the contents are ported to a Meta Quest 2 HMD through the Meta Quest Link.

The user study was conducted with a between-subject design: one experiment is the VR-based experience and the other experiment is the reading-based experience. For the VR-based experience, we recruited 28 participants, including 21 male, 3 female, and 4 non-binary. Their ages range from 18 to 28 (Mean = 20.9 and SD = 2.9). Every four participants were a group to create their own artworks and trade with each other. The VR experimental trials were video recorded for the post-analysis of the group interactions and activities.

For the reading-based experience, we recruited 15 participants, including 11 male, 3 female, 1 non-binary. Their ages range from 18 to 34 (Mean = 20.7, SD = 4.2). Individuals were presented with the reading materials about the metaverse,

NFTs, and digital properties and ownership, which were gathered from online resources and aimed at the same learning objectives as the VR-based experience. All participants read and listened to English without barriers.

Upon arrival, the participants signed the consent form and answered the questions in a demographic survey. For both VR-based and reading-based experiments, we found that 4 participants are very familiar with metaverse, 5 participants are very familiar with digital ownership, and 8 participants are very familiar with NFTs. For the VR-based experiment, 25 participants answered that they had experience with VR. The investigators informed the participants of the VR-based experiment that they would be in a shared virtual environment and trade digital artworks with each other, helped them wear the HMDs, and taught them how to use the handheld controllers. They were given enough time to practice the use of the controllers prior to starting the VR experiment. After completing the experiment, all participants of both experiments were asked to fill out the user experience questionnaire [21] and a post-study questionnaire (Table 1). In addition to these two questionnaires, the participants of the VR-based experiment filled out the Virtual Reality Sickness Questionnaire [18].

Table 1. Post-study questions were used in both VR-based and reading-based experiments to evaluate the learning outcomes of the participants about the NFTs. Q1 to Q5 are the questions related to the factual knowledge of NFTs. Q6 and Q7 are about potential impacts on the users after learning NFTs related knowledge.

Q1: What is a Non-Fungible Token (NFT)?
Q2: Who can create NFTs? How to create NFTs?
Q3: What kind of things do NFTs typically contain?
Q4: What are the three significant stages in the life of an NFT? What is the purpose of the second stage?
Q5: How can the smart contract let NFTs benefit digital creators?
Q6: Would you feel comfortable to turn your work into NFTs? Why and why not?
Q7: Would you like to learn more about digital ownership and NFTs? Please explain your answer

5   Evaluation and Discussion

We analyzed the participants' responses in the post-study questionnaire, UEQ, and VRSQ. We used the Wilcoxon rank-sum test to analyze Q1 to Q5 of the post-study questions and the Likert scale ranks (discrete data) for UEQ. All statistical results were based on the significant value of $\alpha = .05$. We also analyzed and discussed the feedback and observations on the VR-based groups.

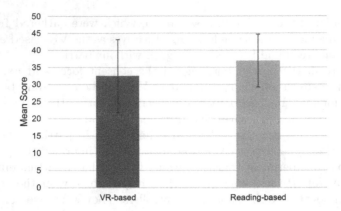

Fig. 4. The mean scores of VR-based and reading-based groups in Q1 to Q5 of the post-study questions. The error bar in the figure represents the standard deviation.

5.1 Learning Experience and Outcome Analysis

We analyzed the post-study questions to evaluate the learning outcomes. For Q1 to Q5, we invited the experts in NFTs to rate the participants' answers based on the learning scope of the given materials. Each question is worth 10 points, so the maximum score is 50. As shown in Fig. 4, the mean score of the VR-based group is 32.5 (SD = 10.66) and the mean score of the reading-based group is 36.93 (SD = 7.7). The p-value is 0.168, which indicates the results of the post-study questionnaire do not show any significant difference between the two groups in terms of the learning outcomes.

The reading group memorized the knowledge from the learning materials better than the VR-based group, but the difference is not significant. We observed that the VR environment itself and the interaction with other participants in VR can be factors of distraction for some participants and make them less focused on learning. This is likely the reason causing the lower mean score than the reading-based group. For instance, one participant in the VR-based group mentioned after the experiment that *"I heard things being said, but I was too busy looking around and trying to figure out how things work."*

For Q6 and Q7 in the post-study questions, we categorized the participants' answers into "Yes", "No", and "Maybe", which reflect the level of their willingness. As the results shown in Fig. 5, we found that 46.43% of participants in the VR-based group and 33.33% of participants in the reading-based group feel comfortable turning their work into NFTs, and 67.86% of participants in the VR-based group and 40% of participants in the reading-based group are willing to learn more about digital ownership and NFTs.

We used UEQ to evaluate the learning experience. We categorized the 26 items of UEQ into six scales [26]. The mean ratings of the VR-based and reading-based user groups in the six categories of scales are listed in Fig. 6. The attractiveness ($p < 0.001$), stimulation ($p = 0.005$), and novelty ($p < 0.001$) ratings of the VR-based group are significantly higher than the reading-based group.

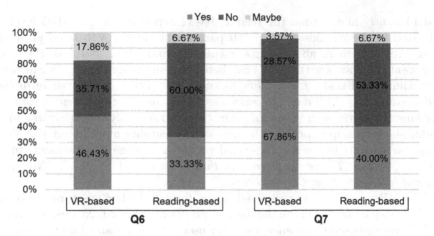

Fig. 5. The answer distribution of VR-based and reading-based groups in Q6 and Q7 of the post-study questions.

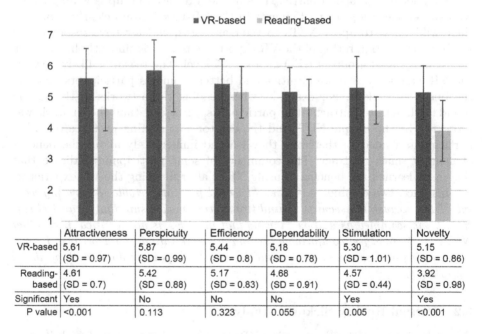

	Attractiveness	Perspicuity	Efficiency	Dependability	Stimulation	Novelty
VR-based	5.61 (SD = 0.97)	5.87 (SD = 0.99)	5.44 (SD = 0.8)	5.18 (SD = 0.78)	5.30 (SD = 1.01)	5.15 (SD = 0.86)
Reading-based	4.61 (SD = 0.7)	5.42 (SD = 0.88)	5.17 (SD = 0.83)	4.68 (SD = 0.91)	4.57 (SD = 0.44)	3.92 (SD = 0.98)
Significant	Yes	No	No	No	Yes	Yes
P value	<0.001	0.113	0.323	0.055	0.005	<0.001

Fig. 6. The UEQ data analyzed using Wilcoxon rank-sum test. The values are the mean ratings from VR-based and reading-based groups in terms of the six scales. SD is the standard deviation of the corresponding value. The error bar in the figure represents the standard deviation.

We observed that the VR experience is entertaining for the participants, and likely this is a reason to motivate them to engage with the experience. Correspondingly, in the UEQ data, the attractiveness rating of the VR experience is significantly higher than the reading-based experience at $p < 0.05$ level. As indicated in the responses of Q7, 19 participants in the VR-based group are willing to learn more about digital ownership and NFTs. Some of them said they want to know how the NTFs can benefit them in more detail. For instance, they commented that *"I would like to know more about exactly where to trade and auction them.";* *"I'd like to learn about how companies are kept accountable and how this works with copyright."* On the contrary, only 6 participants in the reading-based group expressed the demand in learning more about the NFTs. Some participants in the reading-based group wrote negative comments in Q7, like *"No, because I have no interest in them as a digital creator.";* *"Not really, I'm not interested in getting into them."*

The VR experience has received a significantly higher mean rating on the novelty category of UEQ than the reading experience at $p < 0.05$ level. Compared to the reading-based experience, the inter-user interaction and gamified contents in VR enhanced the novelty of the experience, as the participants can be free to explore the scene, move objects, and interact with other participants.

A higher percentage of participants in the VR-based group is willing to use NFTs after the study. 13 participants in the VR-based group clearly expressed their willingness to apply NFTs to their artworks, as they have responded in Q6. The stimulation rating of the VR experience is also significantly higher than the reading-based group in UEQ at $p < 0.05$ level. The reason is likely because the VR experience is more intuitive and better promotes participants' trust in the benefits of NFTs. For example, when trading the artworks in the second round with smart contracts, the participants witnessed that the artwork was protected by the unique NFT, and the creator was gaining profits after other participants traded it; therefore, they learned immediately about the benefits of using a smart contract. The comments of some participants indicate that they have learned the benefits of using NFTs after finishing the VR experience. For instance, two comments read as *"I would feel comfortable to turn my work into NFT because the security behind transaction makes sure that I can feel safe from being scammed as well as knowing that my NFT is not identical from other NFTs.";* *"I would feel comfortable turning my work into an NFT because I really like drawing and painting, so it would be nice to be paid to do something that I really enjoy."*

5.2   Virtual Reality Sickness Analysis

We evaluated the VR sickness using VRSQ. The ranking range of each item in VRSQ is from 1 to 4. As shown in Fig. 7, all the mean ratings are between 1 (Not at all) to 2 (Slightly), which does not indicate any serious sickness symptom, nor in our observation. This is partially because the experience is short (about 10 min of play). Another possible reason is because of the play mode we designed for the VR experience. The participants sat on the chairs during the play, and they were moving arms and hands to interact with only static objects or avatars of other participants. This made the participants feel that the environment was mostly stationary.

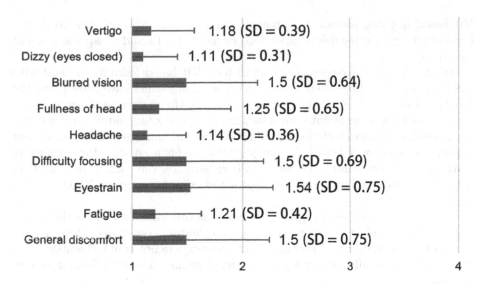

Fig. 7. The mean ratings of the VR-based group in VRSQ in terms of nine items. SD is the standard deviation of the corresponding value. The error bar in the figure represents the standard deviation.

5.3 Multi-user Environment

We collected feedback about the VR participants' preference for playing in the multi-user or single-user environment. Only 1 out of 28 participants preferred to play alone. Other participants gave very positive comments on the experience in the multi-user environment: *"I believe that it is very fun to play with others in the VR environment because it makes experiencing an all-new world all the more enjoyable and prevents it from ever becoming boring.";* *"It's more fun in multiplayer because things become more interactive and immersive.";* *"Yes, playing with other users allows for more innovation and creativity within yourself."* The multi-user environment is an important factor that improves the user experience in this study. The ability to discuss with each other and share the artworks in the multi-user environment is able to help users to engage with the learning experience. In addition, the ownership and trading of NFTs must be based on multi-user activities. The multi-user VR system is able to simulate an NFT use scenario very close to the cases in social reality, which would otherwise be difficult to simulate in a single-user environment.

6 Conclusion and Future Work

In conclusion, NFTs play an essential role in the economy system of the metaverse. The multi-user VR system presented in this work provides an immersive experience for the users to learn what the NFTs are and how to create and trade them, as they would do in the future virtual society. We found that such

VR-based learning method is important for the users who are new to digital currency to gain a hands-on experience of using NFTs and grasp the concept effectively.

In the study, we compared the multi-user VR-based learning method with the traditional reading-based learning method. The results have shown that the VR-based method is more effective in simulating the metaverse space and conveying the knowledge about digital ownership and digital trading. By enabling the game-like features including spatial drawing and multi-user interaction, user experience is enhanced, and the participants are engaged with the interactive learning activities. After finishing the VR experience, the participants are willing to learn more about the related topics and consider applying NFTs to their work.

For the future study, we plan to explore more insights into how the multi-user modes can affect the user experience and learning outcomes. More specific impact factors on the multi-user and single-user experiences will be identified and discussed to hopefully suggest a guideline for designing future NFT-incorporated VR experiences.

Acknowledgements. We thank Foundry Digital, LLC, for their financial support of this exploratory project and the RIT MAGIC Center for hosting this work. We also thank the anonymous participants to participate in the user study.

References

1. Au, C.H., Au, T.F., Fung, W.: Blockchain-simgame: how can simulation be used for facilitating corporate learning of blockchain technology? In: European Conference on Games Based Learning, pp. 847-XIII. Academic Conferences International Limited (2018)
2. Bao, H., Roubaud, D.: Non-fungible token: a systematic review and research agenda. J. Risk Financ. Manag. **15**(5), 215 (2022)
3. Barrett, A., Pack, A., Guo, Y., Wang, N.: Technology acceptance model and multi-user virtual reality learning environments for Chinese language education. Interact. Learn. Environ. **31**, 1665–1682 (2020)
4. Borri, N., Liu, Y., Tsyvinski, A.: The economics of non-fungible tokens. Available at SSRN (2022)
5. Bsteh, S., Vermeylen, F.: From painting to pixel: understanding NFT artworks (2021). Accessed 15 June 2021
6. Cao, L., Peng, C., Dong, Y.: Ellic's exercise class: promoting physical activities during exergaming with immersive virtual reality. Virtual Reality **25**, 597–612 (2021)
7. Cao, L., Peng, C., Hansberger, J.T.: Usability and engagement study for a serious virtual reality game of lunar exploration missions. In: Informatics, vol. 6, p. 44. MDPI (2019)
8. Cao, L., Zhang, H., Peng, C., Hansberger, J.T.: Real-time multimodal interaction in virtual reality-a case study with a large virtual interface. Multimed. Tools Appl. 1–22 (2023)
9. Chohan, U.W.: Non-fungible tokens: blockchains, scarcity, and value. Critical Blockchain Research Initiative (CBRI) Working Papers (2021)

10. Choi, E., Choi, Y., Park, N.: Development of blockchain learning game-themed education program targeting elementary students based on assure model. Sustainability **14**(7), 3771 (2022)
11. Decentraland: Decentraland, a virtual world on open standards (2023). https:// decentraland.org/
12. Dettling, W., Schneider, B.: Bloxxgame – a simulation game for teaching blockchain. In: Marfisi-Schottman, I., Bellotti, F., Hamon, L., Klemke, R. (eds.) GALA 2020. LNCS, vol. 12517, pp. 169–178. Springer, Cham (2020). https://doi. org/10.1007/978-3-030-63464-3_16
13. Dionisio, J.D.N., Burns, W.G., III., Gilbert, R.: 3D virtual worlds and the metaverse: current status and future possibilities. ACM Comput. Surv. (CSUR) **45**(3), 1–38 (2013)
14. Gadekallu, T.R., et al.: Blockchain for the metaverse: a review. arXiv preprint arXiv:2203.09738 (2022)
15. García, R., Cediel, A., Teixidó, M., Gil, R.: Semantics and non-fungible tokens for copyright management on the metaverse and beyond. arXiv preprint arXiv:2208.14174 (2022)
16. Ibáñez, M.B., García, J.J., Galán, S., Maroto, D., Morillo, D., Kloos, C.D.: Design and implementation of a 3D multi-user virtual world for language learning. J. Educ. Technol. Soc. **14**(4), 2–10 (2011)
17. Joy, A., Zhu, Y., Peña, C., Brouard, M.: Digital future of luxury brands: metaverse, digital fashion, and non-fungible tokens. Strateg. Chang. **31**(3), 337–343 (2022)
18. Kim, H.K., Park, J., Choi, Y., Choe, M.: Virtual reality sickness questionnaire (VRSQ): motion sickness measurement index in a virtual reality environment. Appl. Ergon. **69**, 66–73 (2018)
19. Kruse, K.: Gagne's nine events of instruction: an introduction. Retrieved the 10 (2009)
20. Kugler, L.: Non-fungible tokens and the future of art. Commun. ACM **64**(9), 19–20 (2021)
21. Laugwitz, B., Held, T., Schrepp, M.: Construction and evaluation of a user experience questionnaire. In: Holzinger, A. (ed.) USAB 2008. LNCS, vol. 5298, pp. 63–76. Springer, Heidelberg (2008). https://doi.org/10.1007/978-3-540-89350-9_6
22. Lee, L.H., et al.: All one needs to know about metaverse: a complete survey on technological singularity, virtual ecosystem, and research agenda. arXiv preprint arXiv:2110.05352 (2021)
23. Lerner, D., Mohr, S., Schild, J., Göring, M., Luiz, T., et al.: An immersive multi-user virtual reality for emergency simulation training: usability study. JMIR Serious Games **8**(3), e18822 (2020)
24. Min, T., Wang, H., Guo, Y., Cai, W.: Blockchain games: a survey. In: 2019 IEEE conference on games (CoG), pp. 1–8. IEEE (2019)
25. Nofer, M., Gomber, P., Hinz, O., Schiereck, D.: Blockchain. Bus. Inf. Syst. Eng. **59**, 183–187 (2017)
26. Schrepp, M., Hinderks, A., Thomaschewski, J.: Construction of a benchmark for the user experience questionnaire (UEQ). Int. J. Interact. Multim. Artif. Intell. **4**(4), 40–44 (2017)
27. Skalidis, I., Muller, O., Fournier, S.: The metaverse in cardiovascular medicine: applications, challenges, and the role of non-fungible tokens. Can. J. Cardiol. **38**(9), 1467–1468 (2022)
28. Smith, P.L., Ragan, T.J.: Instructional Design. Wiley, Hoboken (2004)
29. Thomas, J., Bashyal, R., Goldstein, S., Suma, E.: MUVR: a multi-user virtual reality platform. In: 2014 IEEE Virtual Reality (VR), pp. 115–116. IEEE (2014)

30. Trautman, L.J.: Virtual art and non-fungible tokens. Hofstra L. Rev. **50**, 361 (2021)
31. Valeonti, F., Bikakis, A., Terras, M., Speed, C., Hudson-Smith, A., Chalkias, K.: Crypto collectibles, museum funding and OpenGLAM: challenges, opportunities and the potential of non-fungible tokens (NFTs). Appl. Sci. **11**(21), 9931 (2021)
32. Wang, F.Y., Qin, R., Wang, X., Hu, B.: Metasocieties in metaverse: metaeconomics and metamanagement for metaenterprises and metacities. IEEE Trans. Comput. Soc. Syst. **0**(1), 2–7 (2022)
33. Wang, Q., Li, R., Wang, Q., Chen, S.: Non-fungible token (NFT): overview, evaluation, opportunities and challenges. arXiv preprint arXiv:2105.07447 (2021)
34. Wu, C.H., Liu, C.Y.: Educational applications of non-fungible token (NFT). Sustainability **15**(1), 7 (2023)
35. Xie, B., et al.: A review on virtual reality skill training applications. Front. Virtual Reality **2**, 645153 (2021)
36. Yilmaz, M., Hacaloğlu, T., Clarke, P.: Examining the use of non-fungible tokens (NFTs) as a trading mechanism for the metaverse. In: Yilmaz, M., Clarke, P., Messnarz, R., Wöran, B. (eds.) EuroSPI 2022. CCIS, vol. 1646, pp. 18–28. Springer, Cham (2022). https://doi.org/10.1007/978-3-031-15559-8_2

Investigating the Role of Vection, Presence, and Stress on Visually Induced Motion Sickness

Behrang Keshavarz[1,2](✉) (iD), Narmada Umatheva[1,2] (iD), and Katlyn Peck[1] (iD)

[1] KITE-Toronto Rehabilitation Institute, University Health Network, Toronto, ON M5G 2A2, Canada
behrang.keshavarz@uhn.ca
[2] Toronto Metropolitan University, Toronto, ON M5B 2K3, Canada

Abstract. Visually induced motion sickness (VIMS) is a common side-effect when using visual displays such as Virtual Reality applications. The goal of the present study was to further investigate how VIMS is related to the sensations of vection (i.e., illusory self-motion) and presence (i.e., feeling of "being there"). In addition, we explored how acute stress, anxiety, and discomfort may affect the severity of VIMS. A total of 53 participants were exposed to a 15-min-long VIMS-inducing visual stimulus while their level of VIMS was recorded before, during, and after stimulus exposure. Results showed significant, positive correlations between VIMS severity and vection frequency (i.e., the total amount of vection experienced), vection intensity, and presence. Only weak to moderately strong correlations were found for VIMS and stress. Interestingly, regression analysis revealed that vection frequency and the level of discomfort experienced prior to the experiment were the two best predictors of VIMS severity. The results of this study help to better understand how VIMS, vection, and presence are linked to each other and how individual and situational factors add to the experience of VIMS.

Keywords: Motion Sickness · Virtual Reality · Vection · Presence · Stress

1 Background

1.1 Visually Induced Motion Sickness

The use of visual devices such as smartphones, tablets, or Virtual Reality is an essential part of our daily lives. Today, visual devices can be considered mainstream, and they are becoming increasingly relevant in various domains, including entertainment, research, education, work, training, and/or art. However, with the growing popularity of visual devices comes an increased risk of experiencing potential side-effects, such as visually induced motion sickness (VIMS). VIMS is characterized by nausea, headache, disorientation, or oculomotor issues, and is a common sensation when using VR or other visual devices [1, 2]. For instance, a recent online survey with more than 330 participants showed that VIMS is common across different visual displays, with eyestrain being the most prominent symptom [3]. In addition, approximately 25% of participants reported

© The Author(s), under exclusive license to Springer Nature Switzerland AG 2023
J. Y. C. Chen and G. Fragomeni (Eds.): HCII 2023, LNCS 14027, pp. 619–633, 2023.
https://doi.org/10.1007/978-3-031-35634-6_45

that they sometimes or often experience nausea when using VR applications or simulators, suggesting that VIMS is a serious concern that may impact the usefulness and general acceptance of these novel technologies if not properly addressed.

The underlying causes of VIMS are not fully understood. A sensory conflict between the visual, vestibular, and proprioceptive systems are often considered to be at the root of VIMS, specifically when this sensory conflict is novel and the user has not yet habituated or adapted to it [4, 5]. For instance, VIMS may be triggered when the visual system conveys the sensation of self-motion, whereas the vestibular and/or proprioceptive sense suggests stasis. Alternative theories have highlighted the involvement of postural instability (i.e., the inability to maintain control over one's balance) [6, 7] and eye movements [8]. Although supporting evidence for all three theories can be found in the literature, the exact mechanisms involved in the genesis of VIMS remain unknown [9, 10].

1.2 Vection, Presence, and VIMS

Two concepts that are closely linked to the occurrence of VIMS are *vection* and *presence*. Vection describes the illusion of self-motion in the absence of actual physical self-motion [11, 12]. A common real-life situation leading to vection is when a passenger is sitting in a stationary train while looking at another stationary, neighboring train. Once the neighboring train initiates movement, the passenger often misperceives this motion as motion of their own train. In general, vection can be easily elicited by providing optic flow associated with self-motion to a large portion of the visual field, for instance in optokinetic drums, VR headsets, or large-screen simulators. Note that non-visual sensory cues (auditory, tactile) also contribute to vection, although to a lesser extent than visual cues [13–15].

For many modern visual applications, vection is often a desired sensation, as it increases the immersive experience of these applications [16]. For instance, a driving simulation experience feels much more realistic when the driver feels as if they are moving through the real world. At the same time, vection is also of functional relevance for VR applications, as it improves VR performance such as spatial navigation [17]. Thus, maximizing vection seems a desirable goal for many visual devices. At the same time, vection has historically also been considered one of the potential causes of VIMS [18], questioning the benefit of vection per se. However, the relationship between vection and VIMS is quite complicated [19]; on one hand, there is strong evidence that vection alone is not sufficient to cause VIMS, as many studies demonstrated that users can indeed perceive strong and compelling vection without experiencing any or only minimal VIMS. On the other hand, it has been argued that vection might be a prerequisite for experiencing VIMS, but this view has been challenged by studies showing that VIMS-like symptoms may occur in the absence of vection (for a summary and critical discussion see [10]). Thus, further delivering insights into the relationship between vection and VIMS and how they interact with other factors is highly relevant.

Presence is often described as a state of physically "being there" in a virtual environment [20, 21]. Like vection, presence is very much a desired phenomenon in VR applications, as it improves the overall VR experience and is positively associated with performance and enjoyment [22, 23]. Note that presence is different from immersion, with the former considered a psychological state and the latter describing how much a certain VR system blocks out features of the real world rather than a psychological state for the user. That is, an immersive system does not necessarily have to induce presence [24], and it is possible to feel a sense of presence when using low-immersive technologies such as books [25]. Unlike vection, the sensation of presence has been negatively linked to VIMS as concluded by a thorough review of the literature [26]. In their review, the authors compared studies that explored the relationship between presence and VIMS in VR systems and found that the majority of studies reported a negative correlation between VIMS and presence (11 out of 20 papers). At the same time, 6 studies found a positive correlation, and 4 did not find any correlation at all, suggesting a strong heterogeneity in the findings. Thus, it is obvious that the link between presence and VIMS is less clear than one might expect and requires further investigation.

1.3 Depression, Stress, Anxiety, and VIMS

To date, a coherent pattern of physiological changes associated with the experience of motion sickness and VIMS has yet to be identified. However, changes in various signals such as heart rate [27, 28], electrodermal activity [29, 30], or facial skin temperature [31] have been reported, likely driven by an increased activity of the sympathetic branch of the autonomic nervous system [32, 33]. These physiological responses are similar to an acute stress response [34] and result in an increased release of neurotransmitters and hormones such as acetylcholine or epinephrine respectively, when experiencing motion sickness [35, 36]. Although it seems obvious that VIMS leads to perceived stress, it is less clear whether the perception of stress itself increases the likelihood of experiencing VIMS. For instance, Golding [37] reported that the susceptibility to motion sickness was positively (but weakly) correlated with stress-related nausea, but other controlled studies investigating stress as a predicting factor for VIMS are rare.

There is also evidence suggesting that personality traits might be associated with VIMS, although this relationship is considered to be rather weak. For instance, Collin and Lentz [38] found that subjects who were highly susceptible to VIMS reported higher neuroticism and higher trait anxiety scores compared to those who were less susceptible to VIMS (see also [39]).

1.4 The Present Study

The goals of the present study were to further investigate the relationship between VIMS, vection, presence, and stress. To achieve this, participants were exposed to a VIMS-inducing visual stimulus while their level of VIMS, vection, presence, and stress were measured using subjective rating scales. Due to the heterogeneity of previous findings, we did not have directed hypotheses with regards to the relationship of VIMS with presence and vection; both negative and positive correlations seem possible. With regards to stress, we assumed that an increased level of stress prior to stimulus presentation is linked to increased levels of VIMS.

2 Methods

2.1 Participants

A total of 57 healthy adults were recruited to participate in this study. Of those, four participants were removed post-hoc due to increased sickness levels prior to the beginning of the experiment (SSQ-N score of > 50, n − 4) As a result, the final sample consisted of $N = 53$ participants, including 31 women ($M_{age} = 26.8$ years, range = 19–40 years) and 22 men ($M_{age} = 27.4$ years, range = 18–39 years). All participants self-reported to have no recent history of stroke, active vestibular disorders, disabling musculoskeletal disorder, acute psychiatric disorder, uncorrected visual impairments, diagnosed cardiovascular disease, diagnosed gastroinstestinal disorders, and/or a diagnosis of mild cognitive impairment or dementia. The study was designed following the principles of the Declaration of Helsinki and was approved by the University Health Network's research ethics board. All participants provided written consent prior to the study and were informed that they were free to withdraw from participating at any time without negative consequences. Participants were reimbursed with a $20 gift card for their time commitment to the study.

2.2 Stimuli and Apparatus

All participants were exposed to a visual stimulus that has been successfully used in previous studies to induce VIMS in most observers [40, 41]. The stimulus consisted of a 15-min-long video of a bicycle ride recorded from a first-person perspective, captured with a hand-held camera that was rigidly mounted on the handle-bars of a bicycle. The video contained segments of flat and bumpy terrain (see Fig. 1).

Fig. 1. A screenshot of the VIMS-inducing visual stimulus.

Participants were seated in a height-adjustable chair positioned 200 cm in front of a 2.90 m wide x 2.30 m high projection screen resulting in a visible field-of-view of 71° horizontally and 60° vertically. The laboratory room was dark (walls painted black, no windows) and temperature-controlled. The resolution of the video was 600 x 480 pixels with a refresh rate of 60 Hz. The seat height was individually adjusted to ensure that eye height was set to the center of the screen. Note that the current data presented here are a subset from a larger study that also investigated a variety of physiological measures (i.e., heart rate variability, skin conductance) with regards to VIMS. These physiological data are not reported here; for further details please see [31].

2.3 VIMS Measures

Fast Motion Sickness Questionnaire (FMS). VIMS was measured during stimulus presentation using the Fast Motion Sickness (FMS; [42]) scale. The FMS was administered at each minute while watching the stimulus video by having participants rate their level of VIMS (focus on symptoms of nausea and discomfort) on a scale from 0 (*no sickness at all*) to 20 (*severe sickness*). The FMS reliably measures the specific symptoms nausea and discomfort of VIMS and allows for continuous nausea and discomfort ratings. The peak FMS score (i.e., highest score participants reported during stimulus presentation) has been shown to strongly correlate with the Simulator Sickness Questionnaire in previous studies (e.g., [40]).

Simulator Sickness Questionnaire (SSQ). The Simulator Sickness Questionnaire (SSQ; [43]) was verbally administered once prior (SSQ-pre) and once after the video (SSQ-post). The 16-item standardized SSQ was used to assess various VIMS symptoms with responses recorded with a 4-point rating scale ranging from "*not at all*" to "*severe*" at that moment in time. Scores on the SSQ subscales aim to target the specific symptom clusters nausea (SSQ-N), oculomotor (SSQ-O), and disorientation (SSQ-D). In addition, a total score (SSQ-TS) can be derived. In order to control for potential group differences, the SSQ was administered prior to stimulus exposure to ensure that participants did not feel sick before watching the video.

2.4 Other Dependent Measures

Vection and Presence Ratings. Following stimulus exposure, all participants were asked to fill out a post-study questionnaire with questions assessing the frequency and intensity of vection experienced while watching the stimulus video. In order to familiarize participants with the phenomena of vection, the train illusion analogy was used, whereby passengers on a stationary train may feel self-motion when an adjacent train starts moving. Participants were asked to rate the frequency of vection after stimulus exposure via response to the question "*how often did you experience self-motion during the video, that is, how often did you feel that you were actually moving*" on a scale ranging from 0–100 percent of the time. Vection intensity was assessed by asking participants "*how strong was the feeling of self-motion*", using an 11-point rating scale ranging from 0 (*non-existent*) to 10 (*very strong*). The degree of presence was assessed by asking participants "*how strong was the feeling of being present in the virtual scenery*" on an 11-point rating scale ranging from 0 (*non-existent*) to 10 (*very strong*).

Depression, Anxiety and Stress Scale (DASS-21). To obtain a general assessment of mood, participants were asked to complete the DASS-21, a validated self-report 21-item questionnaire designed to measure three related, yet distinct symptoms of depression, anxiety, and stress over the last week [44]. The DASS-21 is particularly unique because it was constructed to further the process of defining, understanding, measuring, and potentially discriminating between dimensional emotional states usually described as depression, anxiety, and stress. The rating scale ranges from 0 (*did not apply to me at all*) to 3 (*applied to me very much, or most of the time*). Responses can be calculated to obtain three subscale scores (depression, anxiety, or stress) and a total score.

Stress and Discomfort Items. Visual analog scales were used to assess self-reported acute feelings of stress and discomfort prior to, and immediately after stimulus exposure. Thus, participants were asked *"how much stress are you feeling?"* and *"how much discomfort do you feel?"* using 11-point rating scales ranging from 0 (*no stress/discomfort*) to 10 (*worst possible stress/discomfort*). Participants were informed to base their responses on how they felt at that specific moment.

2.5 Procedure

Eligible participants completed the informed consent process upon arrival to the lab, and any questions were fielded by the experimenter. First, participants filled out the SSQ (SSQ-pre) and the experimenter attached the physiological equipment (as mentioned above, the physiological data is reported in [31], and is separate from the scope of this paper). Participants remained seated for a 10-min baseline period to acclimate to the lab environment. Following this period, participants were exposed to the visual stimulus. During stimulus presentation, participants verbally rated their level of VIMS using the FMS scale once every minute.

Following stimulus presentation, participants filled out the SSQ for the second time (SSQ-post) and were asked to fill out a post-study questionnaire. Stimulus exposure was terminated whenever participants reported moderate-severe sickness using the FMS scale as a barometer (e.g., score of 10 or higher out of 20) or when participants asked to stop. Participants were free to abort the experiment at any time without reasons and without negative consequences. In the case of reported sickness, participants remained in the lab under the supervision of the experimenter until all symptoms of VIMS had subsided and the participant felt comfortable leaving the lab. Before leaving the lab, participants were thoroughly debriefed and indicated that they were comfortable to leave the lab and that sickness (if any reported) had subsided appropriately. Each experimental session lasted for approximately 90 min.

3   Results

Of the 53 participants, 17 stopped the stimulus presentation prematurely due to increased levels of VIMS (11 women, 6 men). However, they still filled out the SSQ and provided FMS ratings; thus, their data were retained for statistical analysis and were not removed. The mean and standard deviation for all VIMS (SSQ, peak FMS score), vection, and presence measures are presented in Table 1. Non-parametric Welch t tests were conducted to compare the mean differences between female and male participants on all variables. No significant effects were found for any of the variables (p's > .20). These results suggest no sex-related differences in the reported scores.

Table 1. Mean (SD) for VIMS, vection, and presence measures separated by sex

Variable	Women (n = 31)	Men (n = 22)	Total (n = 53)
SSQ Nausea	71.4 (35.8)	63.3 (39.7)	68 (37.3)
SSQ Oculomotor	59.4 (34.2)	54.8 (34.8)	57.5 (34.2)
SSQ Disorientation	94.7 (63)	92.4 (70.5)	93.8 (65.6)
SSQ Total Score	82.8 (42.8)	76.7 (46.9)	80.2 (44.2)
Peak FMS Score	7.6 (4.8)	7.5 (4.6)	7.6 (4.7)
Vection frequency	39.7 (27.8)	50.7 (33.3)	44.3 (30.4)
Vection intensity	4.4 (2.8)	5.3 (2.9)	4.8 (2.9)
Presence	5 (2.8)	5.6 (2.5)	5.3 (2.7)

The mean and standard deviation for the DASS-21, stress, and discomfort measures are presented in Table 2. Again, non-parametric Welch t tests showed no differences between female and male participants for any of these variables (p's > .30).

Table 2. Mean (SD) for DASS-21, stress, and discomfort measures.

Variable	Women (n = 31)	Men (n = 22)	Total (n = 53)
DASS 21- Depression	2.2 (2.5)	3 (3.1)	2.5 (2.7)
DASS 21 – Anxiety	2.2 (2.4)	2.1 (2.3)	2.2 (2.3)
DASS – Stress	4.1 (2.8)	3.7 (3.1)	3.9 (2.9)
Stress item	1.1 (1.3)	1.4 (1.8)	1.2 (1.5)
Discomfort item	0.8 (1)	0.7 (0.9)	0.7 (1)

The relationships between VIMS, vection, and presence are illustrated in Fig. 2 through the representation of scatterplot correlations among the variables SSQ total score, vection intensity, vection frequency, and presence. With regards to the SSQ total scores, strong positive correlations were found with vection intensity ($r = .50, p < .01$), vection frequency ($r = .56, p < .01$), and presence ($r = .44, p < .01$). Additionally, strong positive correlation was found between presence and vection, ($r = .63, p < .01$) as well as presence and vection intensity ($r = .53, p < .01$).

Spearman correlations were conducted to further examine the relationship between vection frequency, vection intensity, presence, and all measures of VIMS (SSQ and peak FMS score). The correlation coefficients are depicted in Fig. 3. Overall, significant positive correlations (moderate to strong) were observed between most of the VIMS measures and vection frequency, vection intensity, and presence. These results suggest that more severe VIMS is associated with more intense and longer lasting vection and a more intense sensation of presence. The strongest correlation was observed between vection frequency and the SSQ subscale disorientation ($r = .61, p < .01$), followed by

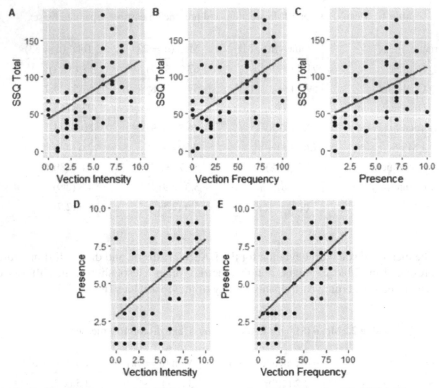

Fig. 2. Scatterplots between (A) SSQ total scores and vection intensity, (B) SSQ total score and vection frequency, (C) SSQ total score and presence, (D) presence and vection intensity, and (E) presence and vection frequency. SSQ = Simulator Sickness Questionnaire. The blue line represents the regression line.

vection frequency and the SSQ total score ($r = .56, p < .01$). However, the relationship between presence and the SSQ subscale nausea ($r = .27, p = .53$) and the peak FMS score ($r = .22, p = .12$) was weak and non-significant.

Spearman correlations were also conducted to determine the association between the VIMS measures and the DASS-21, pre-stress, and pre-discomfort measures. The results of the correlation coefficients are illustrated in Fig. 4. Results showed positive, significant correlations (moderately strong) between the SSQ subscale oculomotor and the scores of the three DASS-21 dimensions (depression, anxiety, and stress), suggesting that individuals who reported higher oculomotor issues tend to report higher emotional states of depression ($r = .29, p = .04$), anxiety ($r = .33, p = .02$), and stress ($r = .29, p = .04$). Additionally, the level of discomfort reported prior to stimulus exposure significantly correlated with all VIMS measures (positive, moderately strong). The level of stress reported prior to stimulus exposure was positively correlated only with the SSQ subscale oculomotor ($r = .33, p = .02$).

A stepwise regression was conducted to determine the best combination of predictors that would explain the most amount of variance in SSQ total scores. The best model was selected based on the Akaike's information criterion (AIC). As seen in Table 3, the

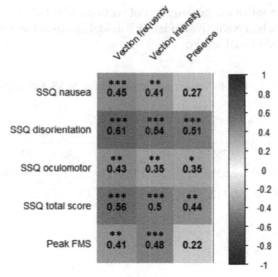

Fig. 3. Correlation plot of Spearman correlation coefficient matrix between variables of vection frequency, vection intensity, presence, and VIMS measures (peak FMS and SSQ scores). FMS = Fast Motion Sickness; SSQ = Simulator Sickness Questionnaire. ***$p < .001$, **$p < .01$, *$p < .05$.

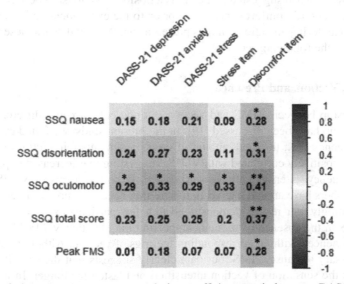

Fig. 4. Correlation plot of Spearman correlation coefficient matrix between DASS-21 (depression, anxiety, and stress) and VIMS measures (peak FMS and SSQ scores). DASS = Depression Anxitey Stress Scale; FMS = Fast Motion Sickness; SSQ = Simulator Sickness Questionnaire. **$p < .01$, *$p < .05$.

combination of two variables, the frequency of vection and initial feelings of discomfort, was identified as the best predictive model. This model accounted for approximately 37% of the variance in SSQ total scores.

Table 3. Summary of the best-fit linear regression model for the SSQ total score as the dependent variable

Variable	b	95% CI	sr^2	AIC	Adj. R^2
Vection frequency	0.76***	[0.43, 1.09]	.30	536.81	0.31
Discomfort (1 item)	12.62*	[2.32, 22.91]	.11	549.89	0.37

Note. $R^2 = .39$, adj $R^2 = .37$, $F(2, 50) = 16.095$. ***$p < .001$, *$p < .05$.

4   Discussion

The aim of the present study was to further investigate the relationship between VIMS, vection, and presence. In addition, we were also interested in exploring how mood (depression, anxiety, stress) may be linked to the severity of VIMS. Overall, we found supporting evidence for the notion that VIMS is positively linked to both vection and presence. Our data also suggested that there is a positive relationship between the levels of acute stress and discomfort experienced prior to the experiment and the severity of VIMS reported during and after stimulus presentation. We will discuss these findings in more detail in the following sections.

4.1   VIMS, Vection, and Presence

The relationship between VIMS and vection is quite complex and different facets of this relationship have been discussed [19]. In the present study, we found evidence that vection frequency (i.e., the total amount of time participants felt vection) and vection intensity are positively correlated with VIMS, suggesting that increased experiences of vection (frequency, intensity) are associated with increased levels of VIMS [18, 45]. Some researchers have argued that vection is neither necessary nor sufficient for VIMS [10]. Interestingly, our results demonstrated that few participants ($n = 4$) did indeed report VIMS in the absence of vection, supporting the idea that VIMS-like symptoms may be experienced without corresponding feelings of vection. Although vection may not be necessary to cause VIMS, our data clearly suggests that the severity of VIMS increased as the sensation of vection intensified and lasted for longer. In fact, vection frequency was the most important predictor for VIMS severity in our regression analysis, explaining a total of 30 percent of the variance in the VIMS data alone.

   Like vection, the relationship between VIMS and presence is not well understood. Based on the results of a systematic review provided by [26], it has been suggested that the two phenomena might be negatively correlated, with increased presence being associated with less VIMS. However, the present study contradicts this assumption, as we found strong positive correlations between presence and VIMS (see also [46, 47]). There are several possible explanations for this finding. First, a positive relationship between presence and VIMS seems plausible from a theoretical point of view. That is, similar to an increased sensation of vection, an increased sense of presence may amplify a perceived sensory conflict, with the visual system suggesting ego-motion that contradicts the veridical motion and position of the stationary user. Along this line of argumentation, we also found strong positive correlations between vection and presence, suggesting that both may impact VIMS in similar fashion.

Secondly, it is important to note that the studies included in [26] used immersive VR technologies that involved active engagement from their participants (e.g., actively navigating through the virtual scene). In contrast, participants in our study were passively exposed to a moving visual scene presented on a flat, non-stereoscopic projection screen. It is possible that increased levels of presence may only reduce VIMS when participants are actively engaged in a task and are experiencing a high degree of immersion within the virtual scene. Conversely, presence might be detrimental to VIMS in circumstances that limit the user's control of the virtual scene. Lastly, it is important to note that the impact of presence on the different aspects of VIMS varied in strength. For instance, the correlations between presence and the nausea aspect of VIMS, as measured by the SSQ subscales nausea and the peak FMS score, were weak and non-significant. Instead, presence showed the strongest correlation with the disorientation aspects of VIMS, suggesting that higher levels of disorientation were associated with increased presence. Given the multi-faceted nature of VIMS, it seems important that the different aspects of VIMS need to be considered when evaluating the precise relationship between presence and VIMS.

4.2   Depression, Stress, Anxiety, Discomfort and VIMS

Our study revealed some interesting insights into how anxiety, depression, and acute stress may contribute to VIMS. Overall, we found weak to moderately strong correlations between the above-mentioned measures, specifically with regards to the SSQ subscale oculomotor. Our findings suggest that stress experienced *prior* to a VIMS-inducing stimulus may affect the severity of VIMS to some degree. These results seem plausible given that VIMS is comparable to a stress response with accompanying physiological outcomes (e.g., [31]). It seems plausible that those who are already stressed prior to the experiment experienced enhanced levels of stress during stimulus presentation and, ultimately, increased levels of VIMS.

Interestingly, the level of discomfort experienced prior to the study was a good predictor of VIMS severity as one of the two predictors for the best-fit regression model. The correlation analyses mirrored this result, with significant, moderate-to-strong correlations between discomfort and all of the VIMS measures. This finding is potentially relevant in light of assessing an individual's susceptibility to VIMS. Recently, promising results were reported for estimating one's susceptibility to VIMS based on past experiences [48]. However, based on the present results, an accurate assessment of an individual's current state of well-being (*state*) in addition to their general susceptibility to VIMS (*trait*) could be beneficial for accurately estimating one's risk to experience

VIMS in certain situations. Hence, these factors should be taken into consideration for future research aiming at further optimizing the ability to predict VIMS susceptibility.

4.3 Limitations and Future Outlook

One of the main limitations of the current study is that presence was measured with a customized, single-item question. Although this approach provides a simple and effective method for gauging the level of presence, this single-item question does not account for the multifaceted nature of presence (e.g., social presence, physiological presence). Thus, our study is unable to accurately determine which aspect of presence is associated with VIMS. For future studies, a more thorough measure of presence–for instance via the well-established Presence Questionnaire [49] or other well-established presence scales–seems favorable. Another limitation of the present study is that participants did not actively engage with the visual scene but were instead passively exposed to it. As a result, our stimulus elicited only moderate levels of presence on average. Introducing active control of some elements of the VR scene may further increase the level of presence and allow us to better understand how strong levels of presence may affect VIMS. Lastly, our study was exploratory in nature, and we used correlation and regression analyses to gain insights into the relationship between vection, presence, and VIMS. Correlations do not allow for an assessment of causality; thus, future studies could aim to systematically manipulate the level of presence and/or vection as independent factors to investigate whether changes in presence affect VIMS ratings accordingly.

5 Conclusion

The results of the present study suggested that VIMS was positively correlated with vection and presence, resulting in increased VIMS severity as presence and vection intensified. In contrast, the relationship between VIMS and stress and anxiety was rather weak. However, the level of discomfort experienced prior to the stimulus presentation was also positively associated with VIMS and was one of the Top 2 predictors of VIMS severity together with vection frequency, explaining 37% of variance in VIMS as measured by the SSQ. The latter finding is particularly interesting for the development of methods trying to predict an individual's susceptibility to a VIMS-inducing situation.

Acknowledgements. This work was supported by Forvia. We thank Robert Shewaga, Bruce Haycock, and Susan Gorski for technological assistance. We also thank Sophia (Yue) Li for administrative support and coordination of project-related activities.

References

1. Keshavarz, B., Golding, J.F.: Motion sickness: current concepts and management. Curr. Opin. Neurol. **35**, 107–112 (2022). https://doi.org/10.1097/WCO.0000000000001018
2. Kennedy, R.S., Drexler, J., Kennedy, R.C.: Research in visually induced motion sickness. Appl. Ergon. **41**, 494–503 (2010). https://doi.org/10.1016/j.apergo.2009.11.006

3. Keshavarz, B., Murovec, B., Mohanathas, N., Golding, J.F.: The visually induced motion sickness susceptibility questionnaire (vimssq): estimating individual susceptibility to motion sickness-like symptoms when using visual devices. Hum. Factors **65**(1), 107–124 (2021). https://doi.org/10.1177/00187208211008687

4. Reason, J.T.: Motion sickness adaptation: a neural mismatch model. J. R. Soc. Med. **71**, 819–829 (1978)

5. Oman, C.M.: Motion sickness: a synthesis and evaluation of the sensory conflict theory. Can. J. Physiol. Pharmacol. **68**, 294–303 (1990)

6. Riccio, G.E., Stoffregen, T.A.: An ecological theory of motion sickness and postural instability. Ecol. Psychol. **3**, 195–240 (1991). https://doi.org/10.1207/s15326969eco0303_2

7. Smart, L.J., Jr., Stoffregen, T.A., Bardy, B.G.: Visually induced motion sickness predicted by postural instability. Hum. Factors **44**, 451–465 (2002)

8. Ebenholtz, S.M., Cohen, M.M., Linder, B.J.: The possible role of nystagmus in motion sickness: a hypothesis. Aviat. Space Environ. Med. **65**, 1032–1035 (1994)

9. Keshavarz, B., Hecht, H., Lawson, B.D.: Visually induced motion sickness: characteristics, causes, and countermeasures. In: Hale, K.S., Stanney, K.M. (eds.) Handbook of Virtual Environments: Design, Implementation, and Applications, pp. 648–697. CRC Press, Boca Raton, FL (2014)

10. Lawson, B.D.: Motion sickness symptomatology and origins. In: Hale, K.S., Stanney, K.M. (eds.) Handbook of Virtual Environments: Design, Implementation, and Applications, pp. 531–599. CRC Press (2014)

11. Palmisano, S., Allison, R.S., Schira, M.M., Barry, R.J.: Future challenges for vection research: definitions, functional significance, measures, and neural bases. Front. Psychol. **6**, 193 (2015)

12. Berti, S., Keshavarz, B.: Neuropsychological approaches to visually-induced vection: an overview and evaluation of neuroimaging and neurophysiological studies. Multisens. Res. **34**, 153–186 (2020). https://doi.org/10.1163/22134808-bja10035

13. Kooijman, L., Asadi, H., Mohamed, S., Nahavandi, S.: A Systematic Review and Meta-Analysis on The Use of Tactile Stimulation in Vection Research (2021). https://psyarxiv.com/pgj3m/

14. Väljamäe, A.: Auditorily-induced illusory self-motion: a review. Brain Res. Rev. **61**, 240–255 (2009). https://doi.org/10.1016/j.brainresrev.2009.07.001

15. Murovec, B., Spaniol, J., Campos, J.L., Keshavarz, B.: The role of visual, auditory, and tactile cues in the perception of illusory self-motion (vection). In: 3rd Interdisciplinary Navigation Symposium, Virtual Conference (2020)

16. Hettinger, L.J., Schmidt, T., Jones, D.L., Keshavarz, B.: Illusory self-motion in virtual environments. In: Hale, K.S., Stanney, K.M. (eds.) Handbook of Virtual Environments: Design, Implementation, and Applications, pp. 435–466. CRC Press (2014)

17. Riecke, B.E., Feuereissen, D., Rieser, J.J., McNamara, T.P.: More than a cool illusion? Functional significance of self-motion illusion (circular vection) for perspective switches. Front. Psychol. **6**, 1174 (2015). https://doi.org/10.3389/fpsyg.2015.01174

18. Hettinger, L.J., Berbaum, K.S., Kennedy, R.S., Dunlap, W.P., Nolan, M.D.: Vection and simulator sickness. Mil. Psychol. **2**, 171–181 (1990). https://doi.org/10.1207/s15327876mp0203_4

19. Keshavarz, B., Riecke, B.E., Hettinger, L.J., Campos, J.L.: Vection and visually induced motion sickness: how are they related? Front. Psychol. **6**, 472 (2015). https://doi.org/10.3389/fpsyg.2015.00472

20. Heeter, C.: Being there: the subjective experience of presence. Presence: Teleoper. Virtual Environ. **1**, 262–271 (1992)

21. Slater, M., Usoh, M., Steed, A.: Depth of presence in virtual environments. Presence: Teleoper. Virtual Environ. **3**(2), 130–144 (1994)

22. Cooper, N., Milella, F., Pinto, C., Cant, I., White, M., Meyer, G.: The effects of substitute multisensory feedback on task performance and the sense of presence in a virtual reality environment. PLoS ONE **13**, e0191846 (2018). https://doi.org/10.1371/journal.pone.0191846

23. Stanney, K.M., Kingdon, K.S., Graeber, D., Kennedy, R.S.: Human performance in immersive virtual environments: effects of exposure duration, user control, and scene complexity. Hum. Perform. **15**, 339–366 (2002). https://doi.org/10.1207/S15327043HUP1504_03

24. Nichols, S., Haldane, C., Wilson, J.R.: Measurement of presence and its consequences in virtual environments. Int. J. Hum. Comput. Stud. **52**, 471–491 (2000). https://doi.org/10.1006/ijhc.1999.0343

25. Baños, R.M., Botella, C., Guerrero, B., Liaño, V., Alcañiz, M., Rey, B.: The third pole of the sense of presence: comparing virtual and imagery spaces. PsychNology J. **3**, 90–100 (2005)

26. Weech, S., Kenny, S., Barnett-Cowan, M.: Presence and cybersickness in virtual reality are negatively related: a review. Front. Psychol. **10**, 158 (2019). https://doi.org/10.3389/fpsyg.2019.00158

27. Cowings, P.S., Suter, S., Toscano, W.B., Kamiya, J., Naifeh, K.: General autonomic components of motion sickness. Psychophysiology **23**, 542–551 (1986). https://doi.org/10.1111/j.1469-8986.1986.tb00671.x

28. Hu, S., Grant, W.F., Stern, R.M., Koch, K.L.: Motion sickness severity and physiological correlates during repeated exposures to a rotating optokinetic drum. Aviat. Space Environ. Med. **62**, 308–314 (1991)

29. Golding, J.F.: Phasic skin conductance activity and motion sickness. Aviat. Space Environ. Med. **63**, 165–171 (1992)

30. Warwick-Evans, L.A., Church, R.E., Hancock, C., Jochim, D., Morris, P.H., Ward, F.: Electrodermal activity as an index of motion sickness. Aviat. Space Environ. Med. **58**, 417–423 (1987)

31. Keshavarz, B., Peck, K., Rezaei, S., Taati, B.: Detecting and predicting visually induced motion sickness with physiological measures in combination with machine learning techniques. Int. J. Psychophysiol. **176**, 14–26 (2022). https://doi.org/10.1016/j.ijpsycho.2022.03.006

32. Muth, E.R.: Motion and space sickness: intestinal and autonomic correlates. Auton. Neurosci. **129**, 58–66 (2006). https://doi.org/10.1016/j.autneu.2006.07.020

33. Gianaros, P.J., Quigley, K.S., Muth, E.R., Levine, M.E., Vasko Jr, R.C., Stern, R.M.: Relationship between temporal changes in cardiac parasympathetic activity and motion sickness severity. Psychophysiology **40**, 39–44 (2003)

34. Harm, D.L.: Motion Sickness Neurophysiology, Physiological Correlates, and Treatment. CRC Press, Boca Raton (2002)

35. Choukèr, A., et al.: Motion sickness, stress and the endocannabinoid system. PLoS ONE **5**, e10752 (2010). https://doi.org/10.1371/journal.pone.0010752

36. Kohl, R.L.: Endocrine correlates of susceptibility to motion sickness. Aviat. Space Environ Med. **56**, 1158–1165 (1985)

37. Golding, J.F.: Predicting individual differences in motion sickness susceptibility by questionnaire. Pers. Individ. Differ. **41**, 237–248 (2006). https://doi.org/10.1016/j.paid.2006.01.012

38. Lentz, J.M., Collins, W.E.: Motion sickness susceptibility and related behavioral characteristics in men and women. Aviat. Space Environ. Med. **48**, 316–322 (1977)

39. Paillard, A.C., et al.: Motion sickness susceptibility in healthy subjects and vestibular patients: effects of gender, age and trait-anxiety. J. Vestib. Res. **23**, 203–209 (2013). https://doi.org/10.3233/VES-130501

40. D'Amour, S., Bos, J.E., Keshavarz, B.: The efficacy of airflow and seat vibration on reducing visually induced motion sickness. Exp. Brain Res. **235**(9), 2811–2820 (2017). https://doi.org/10.1007/s00221-017-5009-1

41. Peck, K., Russo, F., Campos, J.L., Keshavarz, B.: Examining potential effects of arousal, valence, and likability of music on visually induced motion sickness. Exp. Brain Res. **238**(10), 2347–2358 (2020). https://doi.org/10.1007/s00221-020-05871-2
42. Keshavarz, B., Hecht, H.: Validating an efficient method to quantify motion sickness. Hum. Factors: J. Hum. Factors Ergon. Soc. **53**, 415–426 (2011). https://doi.org/10.1177/001872081 1403736
43. Kennedy, R.S., Lane, N.E., Berbaum, K.S., Lilienthal, M.G.: Simulator sickness questionnaire: an enhanced method for quantifying simulator sickness. Int. J. Aviat. Psychol. **3**, 203–220 (1993). https://doi.org/10.1207/s15327108ijap0303_3
44. Henry, J.D., Crawford, J.R.: The short-form version of the depression anxiety stress scales (DASS-21): construct validity and normative data in a large non-clinical sample. Br. J. Clin. Psychol. **44**, 227–239 (2005). https://doi.org/10.1348/014466505X29657
45. Nooij, S.A.E., Pretto, P., Oberfeld, D., Hecht, H., Bülthoff, H.H.: Vection is the main contributor to motion sickness induced by visual yaw rotation: implications for conflict and eye movement theories. PLoS ONE **12**, e0175305 (2017). https://doi.org/10.1371/journal.pone. 0175305
46. Liu, C.-L., Uang, S.-T.: Effects of presence on causing cybersickness in the elderly within a 3D virtual store. In: Jacko, J.A. (ed.) HCI 2011. LNCS, vol. 6764, pp. 490–499. Springer, Heidelberg (2011). https://doi.org/10.1007/978-3-642-21619-0_61
47. Ling, Y., Nefs, H.T., Brinkman, W.-P., Qu, C., Heynderickx, I.: The relationship between individual characteristics and experienced presence. Comput. Hum. Behav. **29**, 1519–1530 (2013). https://doi.org/10.1016/j.chb.2012.12.010
48. Golding, J.F., Rafiq, A., Keshavarz, B.: Predicting individual susceptibility to visually induced motion sickness by questionnaire. Front. Virtual Reality **2**, 3 (2021). https://doi.org/10.3389/frvir.2021.576871
49. Witmer, B.G., Singer, M.J.: Measuring presence in virtual environments: a presence questionnaire. Presence: Teleoper. Virtual Environ. **7**, 225–240 (1998). https://doi.org/10.1162/105474698565686

Recovery Effect of Different Virtual Natural Environments on Stress in Short-Term Isolation Tasks

Yuqing Liu[1], Ao Jiang[2,3(✉)], and Junbo Dong[1]

[1] Xiangtan University, Xiangtan 411100, Hunan, China
[2] Imperial College London, London, UK
aojohn928@gmail.com
[3] Springer Heidelberg, Tiergartenstr. 17, 69121 Heidelberg, Germany

Abstract. On deep space missions, astronauts must endure isolated, confined and extreme (ICE) environments with no access to normal earthly comforts, which can cause severe physical and emotional stress. The use of virtual reality to relieve astronaut stress is an area of research with great potential. Further research on methods of recovery from psychological stress is needed. The aim of this study was to investigate the effects of using virtual reality to simulate the natural earth environment in different seasons on stress recovery for people in short-term isolation tasks. Through the evaluation (N = 24), we found that the natural scenes provided by the VR headset had a significant stress-reducing effect for people in isolated and enclosed environments. In addition, seasonal differences had varying stress relieving effect, and the spring group had the best subjective psychological effect on stress reduction. This paper contributes to the methodology of psychological support for people in isolated, enclosed environments and to future space exploration.

Keywords: Virtual reality · Decompression · Isolated environments

1 Introduction

The natural environment has a strong positive bearing on the regulation of people's emotions and the relieve of their psychological stress. The contact with nature can improve people's cognitive control [1], reduce their stress, help them recover from mental fatigue [2, 3], and reduce negative emotions [3]. Several studies have shown that regular participation in pleasant and stress-free natural environments is associated with psychophysiological benefits since the participants can gain restorative experiences in natural environments [5].

However, on deep space missions, astronauts will live in an isolated, confined and extreme (ICE) environment without interact with nature [7] and are exposed to great pressure due to their special working environment: During long-term space missions, environmental peculiarities, isolation and interpersonal relationships in particular, can all be sources of stress leading to psychological/psychosocial problems and even psychopathological symptoms or disorders [6]. It is in this sense that their stress can be relieved if they are accessible to the natural environment. Several studies have shown that exposure to such an environment can negatively affect crewmembers' sleep, which in turn leads to additional stress reactions and mental health challenges, and thus stymies the task performance [4, 8]. The psychological well-being of astronauts is of the utmost importance to the successful completion of space missions [10]. Therefore it is urgent to find effective measures to alleviate astronauts' psychological stress. In past space missions, the United States and Russia relieved astronauts' psychological stress in a variety of ways, including surprise gifts and food from the transport module, increased on-board music and lighting, real-time contact with people on Earth [35], and close cooperation with flight surgeons [12]. Future space missions will explore still more isolated environments [10], and for expeditionary missions, the long distances involved may encumber some of these supporting activities [12]. The astronauts may face isolated and enclosed environment for reasons such as signal delays. Therefore, finding ways to effectively relieve stress in an isolated, enclosed environment is an important means of safeguarding deep space exploration and especially long-term missions.

In human-computer interaction (HCI) research, well-being and mental health support are often the aim of investigation, and many well-being promoting technologies are popular [20, 21]. Among these, virtual reality (VR) technology has contributed to various mental health-related fields such as stress research [14], psychotherapy [36], and emotion management [37]. However, only nascent progress has been made in the field of using virtual reality in the space flight environment to relieve the psychological stress of astronauts. Few studies have been devoted to its use in maintaining psychosocial well-being during lengthy space missions [10]. Although there are already products that use VR to reduce the psychological stress of astronauts, such as the Network of Social Interactions for Bilateral Life Enhancement (ANSIBLE), which helps astronauts keep in touch with their families on earth [25], and the Motigravity treadmill [38] equipped with VR software. These stress relief methods often require a large space and good communication conditions, which are often difficult to achieve on deep space missions. Therefore, there is a demand to develop a more convenient and space-saving solution to relieve stress based on VR - using virtual reality to simulate the earth environment in order to relieve astronaut stress is a viable option.

With the applications (APP) in the VR allowing for deep immersion in the virtual environment (VE), we can use VR-driven simulated natural environment to help the astronauts relax. In this way, the above-mentioned deficiencies of other methods can be avoided, and the astronauts can enjoy the benefits of the natural environment to relieve their stress even in the outer space. It has been shown that VR headsets provide reductive natural scenes with relaxing and stress-reducing effects and simulated natural environments have similar efficacy to that of the real natural environments in terms of improving human's mental health [14]. One study found that six minutes of natural exposure in a mobile VR headset produced similar effects to six minutes of natural outdoor exposure [15]. Both situations are better than sitting indoors without exposure to nature [15]. This method of using simulated earth environments to achieve stress relief has been proven to be quite effective. And to further refine this method of stress relief, a series of studies have explored the factors that influence its stress-recovery effects from different perspectives, including the way in which virtual nature is visualized [23], the components of the virtual nature environment [16] and the immersion level of VR [14].

There are currently no studies dedicated to the effects of virtual reality simulated natural environment on people's stress recovery in different seasons. In real life, the effects of urban blue-green space in the natural environment on mental recovery vary with the seasons [18]. Also, videos of different seasonal landscapes shown on a monitor had an impact on the stress-relieving effect [39]. So we further explored the influence of the natural environment on astronauts' stress recovery in various seasons. Based on past researchers' exploration of the effects that the real and virtual environments exert on psychological stress reduction, we make the following hypotheses:(1) The use of simulated natural environments via VR have a stress-recovery effect on people in short-term isolation tasks; (2) The simulated natural environments in different seasons have different degrees of stress-recovery effects on people in short-term isolation tasks. In this paper, we will use virtual reality to simulate different natural environments and explore their impacts on stress reduction for people in short-term isolation tasks. The research aims to simulate a closed, isolated scenario on the space station and compare participants from different seasonal groups in an isolated, closed environment to test whether the use of virtual reality to simulate the natural environment in different seasons has different stress recovery effects on astronauts on space missions.

2   Methods

2.1   Subjects

This study recruited 24 healthy subjects, 12 of each sex, through a social networking site at Xiangtan University (Hunan, China), all of whom passed a medical examination. All subjects have normal vision or normal corrected vision which is better than 0.6 (1/min view) [56, 13], free from mental illness, in good health and none of the women pregnant or breastfeeding. Additionally, to avoid potential interference with the experimental results caused by subjects not being comfortable with the VR equipment, all subjects had experienced VR before. This study was approved by the Ethics Review Committee of Xiangtan Central Hospital, China. All subjects signed an informed consent form and obtained a participation fee in prior to participation in the trial.

2.2   Measurement Tools

This experiment measures the effect of pressure recovery in five areas: psubjective recovery, heart rate (HR), systolic blood pressure (SBP) and diastolic blood pressure (DBP). The Perceptual Recovery Scale (PRS) were used for the subjective questionnaire. The Perceptual Recovery Scale (PRS) can be used to categorize the effectiveness of subjects' emotional recovery in their environment [19]. Precedents can be found to have used the PRS scale for measuring subjective recovery and stress perception [14].

Blood Pressure and Heart Rate

The measurement of systolic and diastolic blood pressure has been widely used in research on emotions and stress [1]. Also, heart rate has previously been used to reflect psychological stress [14].

Perceptual Recovery Scale PRS

The Perceptual Restoration Scale (PRS) can be used for restorative evaluation in all types of environments, including natural environments [51]. Wang Xinxin et al. revised the Chinese version of the PRS scale in 2015, which has high-score reliability and validity [37]. At the same time, the Chinese version of the PRS scale has a high degree of representativeness and appropriateness of the entries, and is largely consistent with the framework of attention recovery theory [14, 51], and there are significant differences in the recoverability of different environments obtained by using the scale. Therefore, the scale was employed in this experiment, which has 22 graded entries, with higher scores indicating better recovery.

2.3 Experimental Equipment

The all-in-one Pico Neo3 VR machine was chosen for this experiment, featuring a Qualcomm Snapdragon XR2 processor with 8 cores and 64 bits, up to 2.84 GHz; 6 GB RAM; binocular resolution of 3664*1920; refresh rate: 120 Hz, 256 GB storage; TUV low blue light certification and eye protection mode enabled within the settings.

360° videos available for free download on Baidu (the Chinese equivalent to Google) were used for the VR environment, thus saving costs, and all the videos last around 6 min.

In this experiment, heart rate (HR), systolic blood pressure (SBP) and diastolic blood pressure (DBP) were measured using an arm blood pressure meter (YE690 series, Yuyue, China), which complies with the standards of the American Society for Medical Device Testing, the British Society of Hypertension and the European Society of Hypertension.

2.4 Materials

Given the diverse effects different seasons of environment exerted on people's stress recovery, we chose the natural environments that are as relaxing and stress-relieving as possible. Previous studies shows that people prefer places that are densely wooded and that people like places with open views [11]. Places with water sources (ponds, streams, lakes) or indirect sources (such as the sound of water and frogs) are also favored [43]. Wuhan is a subtropical monsoonal humid climate zone with four distinct seasons, and the dynamic link between blue-green space and psychological recovery in different seasons has been explored in probed into based on the Wuhan East Lake landscape [16]. Therefore, this experiment chose the Wuhan East Lake scenic area as the object of simulation, and four different natural scenes were simulated via VR, respectively selected from the spring, summer, autumn and winter Wuhan East Lake. (Spring: March - May, Summer: June - August, Autumn: September - November, Winter: December - January) (Fig. 1).

Fig. 1. Screen shots of the four sets of experiments

2.5 Study Design

This was a longitudinal study lasting for five days, and consent forms were signed by the subjects prior to the experiment. The experimental group for this VR experiment had four different experimental setups, and the only difference between them was the season in the natural environment simulated by VR. Figure 2 shows the experimental flow chart.

Each subject was isolated in a separate room of a ward at Xiangtan Central Hospital, which were single rooms of $14 \, m^2$ with the same facilities and layout including a separate toilet and bathroom compartment and basic furniture (table, chair, bed, bedside table and air conditioning).The windows were sealed to cut access to the natural environment, thereby ensuring that the subjects had no access to any objects that are connected to the outside world, e.g. mobile phones, television, etc., except for books in the rooms as the only source of entertainment. They woke up at 7.30 a.m. and went to bed at 11 p.m. to ensure a good night's sleep. The hospital served standardized food to the subjects at 8 a.m., 11.30 a.m. and 5.30 p.m.

Physiological data (heart rate, systolic blood pressure, diastolic blood pressure) was collected from 2:40–3:15 pm on Day 1, Day 3 and Day 5 from the four groups of subjects. A 360° video of the virtual reality simulation corresponding to different earth environments lasting 6 min was then provided to the different groups of subjects from 3:15–4:00 p.m. (time selected based on previous studies [50]). Finally, the stress test was administered to the subjects again on day 5 from 4:00–4:30 pm: a physiological test was administered before the subjects removed the VR glasses (time controlled within one minute), and then the subjects removed the VR glasses and filled out a questionnaire (PRS). Each stress test lasted approximately 10–15 min, and the results were recorded for subsequent analysis.

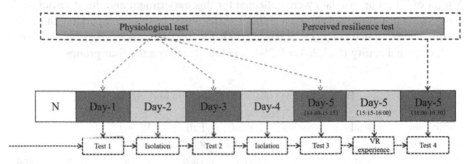

Fig. 2. Experimental flow char

2.6 Experimental Data Processing

In this experiment, we collected various pressure indicators from four groups of subjects on days 1 and 3 of isolation and these before and after relaxation with VR on day 5. Since the data of heart rate and blood pressure are only representative of a period of time,subjects were asked not to take off the VR glasses when measuring heart rate and blood pressure after VR relaxation to eliminate the potential external influence of other scenery. Heart rate and blood pressure tests before and after VR relaxation, as well as the PRS perceived recovery values measured after relaxation using VR, can be used to derive the degree of recovery for a given natural environment. Experimental data include: systolic blood pressure data and differences (SBP1, SBP2, SBP1-SBP2); diastolic blood pressure data and differences before and after the experiment (DBP1, DBP2, DBP1-DBP2); and perceived recovery values of PRS. The decompression indicators are: differential high pressure (SBP1-SBP2) values, differential low pressure (DBP1-DBP2) values and PRS perception recovery values are all positive.

One-way ANOVA was used to test the variables. Paired-samples t-tests were applied separately to each of the stress indicators measured during the isolation period to measure the effect of isolation emotions on stress. Paired samples t-tests were used on three pairs of data (heart rate, systolic and diastolic blood pressure) measured before and after the use of VR to detect differences in pressure before and after relaxation with VR.Thus, it can be concluded whether the VR simulation of the natural environment has a restoration effect.In addition, a one-way ANOVA was applied to the data from the four groups to detect differences in pressure-lowering indicators between the different seasonal groups, so as to derive the effect of season on the effect of pressure recovery. If there was a notable difference, the season with the best pressure recovery was then explored by comparing the mean of PRS values among the groups. All data analyses were carried out in SPSS (version 25.0).

3 Result

3.1 Statistic Results of Four Groups of Subjects Exposed to Four Simulated Seasons

A total of 24 groups of data were collected for this experiment and the statistics of the subjects in each group are shown in Table 1. After a two by-two comparison, there is no significant difference in age (F (3,20) = 0.327, p = 0.806), gender (F (3,20) < 0.001, p = 1), or visual acuity (F (3,20) = 0.294, p = 0.829) among the four groups.

Table 1. Subject characteristics of the four groups.

Participant characteristics	Total	Spring group	Summer group	Fall group	Winter group	F	p
Age	19.625	19.5	19.67	19.5	19.83	0.327	0.806
Gender (n, %)							
Male	12 (50%)	3 (50%)	3 (50%)	3 (50%)	3 (50%)	<0.001	1
Female	12(50%)	3 (50%)	3 (50%)	3 (50%)	3 (50%)	<0.001	1
Vision degree: mean (standard deviation)	5.04 (0.070)	5.05 (0.084)	5.05 (0.084)	5.017 (0.040)	5.05 (0.084)	0.294	0.829

3.2 Psychological Stress During Isolation Test for the Four Groups

A paired samples t-test was performed between the results obtained from each stress test during isolation.The first day of isolation yielded significant increases in subject heart rate (t = 4.701, cohens'd = 0.529, p = 0.021), systolic blood pressure (t = 12.356, cohens'd = 0.874, p = 0.003), and diastolic blood pressure (t = 11.281, cohens'd = 0.768, p = 0.007) compared to the pre-isolation experiment. On the third day of isolation, subjects had a significant increase in heart rate (t = 6.262, cohens'd = 0.572, p = 0.012), systolic blood pressure (t = 11.543, cohens'd = 0.743, p = 0.004) and diastolic blood pressure (t = 10.236, cohens'd = 0.692, p = 0.004) compared to the first day. In contrast, there was no significant difference in heart rate (t = 0.017, p = 0.516), systolic blood pressure (t = 0.092, p = 0.426) or diastolic blood pressure (t = 0.021, p = 0.462) between day 3 and day 5 of isolation. Figure 3, Fig. 4 and Fig. 5 show changes in the average value of each pressure indicator for each group.

3.3 Stress Relief Effects in the Four Groups

We performed a paired samples t-test on the data collected. As shown in Table 2, there are 3 pairs of measurements before and after relaxation with VR, with significant differences in 2 pairs of pressure indicators: systolic blood pressure (t = 10.865, p = 0.014), and

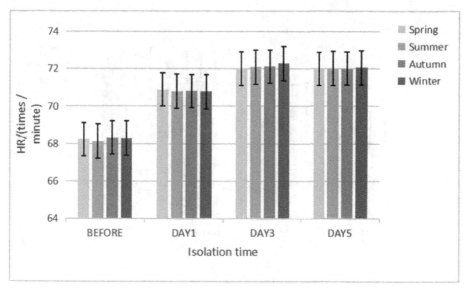

Fig. 3. Histogram of changes in HR

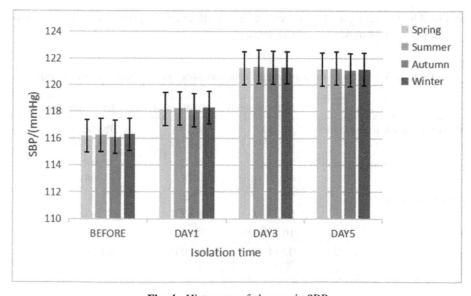

Fig. 4. Histogram of changes in SBP

diastolic blood pressure (t = 25.701, p < 0.001). The value of PRS is positive (PRS = 12.361 ± 8.356). It can be concluded that the subjects experienced a decrease in systolic and diastolic blood pressure i.e. a decrease in blood pressure after relaxing using the VR simulated natural environment. The data from the subjective questionnaires of the subjects as well as the physiological objective data show that the natural environment

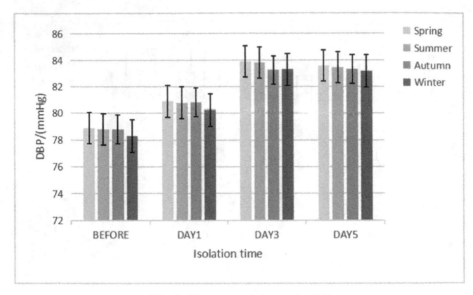

Fig. 5. Histogram of changes in SBP

provided by virtual reality has a stress-relieving effect on people in short-term isolation assignments. Thus hypothesis H1 is confirmed.

Table 2. T-test results for paired dependent variables (means (standard deviations))

	SBP (mmHG)	DBP (mmHG)	HR (times /minute)
Before using VR for relaxation	120.590 (12.213)	80.134 (0.975)	78.293 (10.354)
After using VR for relaxation	117.843 (12.354)	78.335 (1.781)	77.497 (7.368)
Mean difference	2.747 (11.783)	1.799 (0.893)	0.796 (6.342)
t	10.865	25.701	0.999
p	0.014	<0.001	0.125

3.4 Different Stress-Relieving Effects of the Four Groups

There are all together 4 stress indicators in this study, which are influenced by the VR-simulated seasons (spring, summer, autumn and winter) R. One-way ANOVAs were done for each of the 4 stress indicators in the four groups. As shown in Table 3, PRS ($F_{(3,20)} = 3.206$, $p = 0.045$) produce significant differences as the seasons changed, indicating a remarkable difference in the effect of VR simulated pressure recovery based on the natural environment in different seasons. The PRS values rank the highest in the spring group (M = 13.978, SD = 8.191) and lowest in the winter group (M = 9.195, SD = 8.791). The mean of this data set is highest in spring, followed by autumn, summer and winter, indicating that the stress recovery effect of the virtual reality simulation in the natural environment differs with seasons and is most significant in the spring group, which confirms hypothesis H2.

Table 3. Data for variables grouped by season (means (standard deviations))

	SBP1-SBP2	DBP1-SDPB2	HR1-HR2	PRS
Spring group	1.691	2.371	1.379	13.978
	(8.862)	(6.301)	(6.397)	(8.191)
Summer group	2.498	1.562	1.129	9.237
	(7.983)	(6.392)	(7.798)	(8.571)
Fall group	1.739	2.198	1.293	13.298
	(9.102)	(6.291)	(6.453)	(8.317)
Winter group	2.598	1.231	1.078	9.195
	(7.642)	(6.289)	(8.219)	(8.791)
F	0.917	0.816	0.714	3.206
p	0.451	0.500	0.817	0.045

4   Discussion

This was a longitudinal study that investigated the impact of seasonal factors in virtual earth environments on the use of VR simulations of natural environments for relaxation in isolated, enclosed environments. The results showed that the spring group showed the greatest reduction in stress compared to the other groups, meaning that using VR to simulate the natural landscape of spring provided the greatest relief from the psychological stress of isolation and enclosure.

Similar to previous studies [4, 47], on the first day of isolation, the subjects experienced a substantial increase in stress. This may have been caused by irritation from the loss of contact with the outside world resulting from the loss of electronic devices. Numerous studies have shown that astronauts living in isolated, enclosed environments are deprived of resources related to social interaction [24, 27] and are not able to communicate with family and friends by email or other means of communication. On the 5th day of isolation, the subjects' stress decreased slightly compared to the 3rd day. In numerous studies, crews became substantially more content towards the end of the experiment and stress eased steadily over time [22, 24, 42]. However, their stress levels were still significantly higher than before isolation.

This study simulated the closed environment on a space mission through a 5-day isolation experiment. After processing the data, it can be safely concluded that the natural environment simulated by VR has a restorative effect on stress, which is consistent with the results of several studies [44–46]. In addition, this experiment confirmed that there exists a significant difference in the recovery effect on stress of VR-simulated natural environment (in spring, summer, autumn and winter), among which the spring group exerted the most significant recovery effect on stress. In the measurements obtained after experiencing VR, the dependent variables systolic and diastolic blood pressure are markedly various, and only heart rate does not change much. This may result from of the limited five-day simulated space missions, especially in terms of obtaining reliable results for depression or anxiety [49] and have not yet affected heart rate. It is also likely that the time spent being immersed in the natural environment of the VR simulation is too short to reach a level of emotional intensity that could display significant changes in the heart rate.

4.1 Significance of the Study

This study provides a convenient and effective way for astronauts to get in touch with nature by providing them with a VR simulation of the natural environment, thus relieving them of the stress caused by the isolated and enclosed environment. VR is an advantageous stress reliever in the ICE environment [26] and is now used to rehearse aviation missions in advance and to treat various mental illnesses such as post-traumatic stress disorder [10]. Nevertheless, there is little research on the use of VR to reduce stress and prevent mental illness for astronauts on expeditionary missions. This study demonstrates the stress-relieving effects of VR-simulated natural environments on the isolated and enclosed environment. Furthermore, because people in those environments are often unable to see the natural environment for long periods of time, VR simulations of the natural environment may have an even greater stress-recovery effect on the astronauts than on the ordinary population. At the same time, this study illustrates that VR simulations of natural environments are similar to real ones in that their restorative effect on the mental changes with the seasons [18]. Seasonal differences may cause differences in the amount of vegetation and the colour and brightness of the virtual natural environment, which may affect the stress recovery effect of the natural environment. This study found that the best season for stress relief is spring, which could further promote the application of VR-simulated natural environments for stress recovery and contribute to the maintenance of astronauts; mental health during deep space missions. The study also inspired us to consider not only the components of the environment such as lakes and woods, but also the lighting, dominant colours and number of vegetation when choosing a natural environment for the VR simulation. This provides a new direction for optimizing the way VR-driven natural environments relieve stress.

4.2 Limitations and Future Work

In this study, the subjects have been isolated in a closed environment for 5 days and their stress state showed changes, while providing them with a VR simulated natural environment relieved the subjects' stress caused by isolation. However, the isolation period could be longer. Many studies have conducted the solitary confinement for 15 days or more. The short duration of confinement is not conducive to exploring the effects of long-term space missions on psychological stress [48] and should be extended to at least 15 days in subsequent studies. On top of that, this study can only recreate the survival conditions of astronauts in space flight under limited conditions, and cannot reproduce all the sources of stress that astronauts experience during a mission, such as those caused by microgravity conditions. The effect of seasons on the pressure-reduction in VR-simulated natural environments may be related to the intensity of light and the saturation of colors [34, 40, 41]. Therefore, the impacts of the hue [32, 33], color temperature [29–31], saturation and brightness of VR-simulated natural environment images should be explored in the future.

5 Conclusion

Twenty-four subjects were isolated for 5 days in Xiangtan Central Hospital, Hunan, China, and all subjects had registered significantly higher-pressure values on the fifth day. After a period of relaxation in the environment provided by the VR, their stress was considerably alleviated. This experiment verified that the reductive natural environment provided by VR could reduce the stress for people in a short-term isolation task; it also found significant differences in the stress-relieving effects based on different seasons with their positive effects in the order of spring, autumn, summer and winter. In addition, experiments have shown that the reductive natural environment provided by VR is more effective in subjective stress recovery than objective physiological recovery.

References

1. Berman, M.G., Jonides, J., Kaplan, S.: The cognitive benefits of interacting with nature. J. Psychol. Sci. **19**(12), 1207–1212 (2008). https://doi.org/10.1111/j.1467-9280.2008.02225.x
2. Depledge, M.H., Stone, R.J., Bird, W.J.: Can natural and virtual environments be used to promote improved human health and wellbeing?. J. Environ. Sci. Technol. **45**(11), 4660–4665 (2011). https://doi.org/10.1021/es103907m
3. Berto, R.: The role of nature in coping with psycho-physiological stress: a literature review on restorativeness. J. Behav. Sci. **4**(4), 394–409 (2014). https://doi.org/10.3390/bs4040394
4. Pagel, J.I., Choukèr, A.: Effects of isolation and confinement on humans-implications for manned space explorations. J. Appl. Physiol. 1449–1457 (2016). https://doi.org/10.1152/jap plphysiol.00928.2015
5. Jones, M.V., Gidlow, C.J., Hurst, G., et al.: Psycho-physiological responses of repeated exposure to natural and urban environments. J. Landscape Urban Plan. **209**, 104061 (2021). https://doi.org/10.1016/j.landurbplan.2021.104061
6. Marazziti, D., Arone, A., Ivaldi, T., et al.: Space missions: psychological and psychopathological issues. J. CNS Spectr. **27**, 536–540 (2021). https://doi.org/10.1017/S10928529210 00535
7. Dinatolo, M.F., Cohen, L.Y.: Monitoring the impact of spaceflight on the human brain. J. Life **12**(7), 1060 (2022). https://doi.org/10.3390/life12071060
8. Zivi, P., De Gennaro, L., Ferlazzo, F.: Sleep in isolated, confined, and extreme (ICE): a review on the different factors affecting human sleep in ICE. J. Front. Neurosci. **14**, 851 (2020). https://doi.org/10.3389/fnins.2020.00851

9. Zeng, C., Lin, W., Li, N., et al.: Electroencephalography (EEG)-based neural emotional response to the vegetation density and integrated sound environment in a green space. J. Forests **12**(10), 1380 (2021). https://doi.org/10.3390/f12101380
10. Salamon, N., Grimm, J.M., Horack, J.M., et al.: Application of virtual reality for crew mental health in extended-duration space missions. J. Acta Astronautica **146**, 117–122 (2018). https://doi.org/10.1016/j.actaastro.2018.02.034
11. Parsons, R., Daniel, T.C.: Good looking: in defense of scenic landscape aesthetics. J. Landscape Urban Plan. **60**(1), 43–56 (2002). https://doi.org/10.1016/S0169-2046(02)000 51-8
12. Goncalves Freitas, A.R., Schülke, A., Glaser, S., et al.: Conversational user interfaces to support astronauts in extraterrestrial habitats. In: 20th International Conference on Mobile and Ubiquitous Multimedia, pp. 169–178 (2021). https://doi.org/10.1145/3490632.3490673
13. Allen, M.J., Austen, D.P., Jones, A.E., Levene, J.R., Miller, S.: The Visual Standards for the Selection and Retention of Astronauts; NASA: Houston. TX, USA (1970)
14. Ding, X., Chen, Y.: The stress recovery effect of virtual reality natural scene with different immersion on knowledge talents. In: Proceedings of the 5th International Conference on Big Data and Education, pp. 399–406 (2022).https://doi.org/10.1145/3524383.3524409
15. Browning, M.H.E.M., Mimnaugh, K.J., Van Riper, C.J., et al.: Can simulated nature support mental health? Comparing short, single-doses of 360-degree nature videos in virtual reality with the outdoors. J. Front. Psychol. **10**, 2667 (2020). https://doi.org/10.3389/fpsyg.2019. 02667
16. Gao, T., Zhang, T., Zhu, L., et al.: Exploring psychophysiological restoration and individual preference in the different environments based on virtual reality. J. Int. J. Environ. Res. Public Health **16**(17), 3102 (2019). https://doi.org/10.3390/ijerph16173102
17. White, M., Smith, A., Humphryes, K., et al.: Blue space: the importance of water for preference, affect, and restorativeness ratings of natural and built scenes. J. Environ. Psychol. **30**(4), 482–493 (2010). https://doi.org/10.1016/j.jenvp.2010.04.004
18. Zhou, Y., Yang, L., Yu, J., et al.: Do seasons matter? Exploring the dynamic link between blue-green space and mental restoration. J. Urban Forestry Urban Green. 127612 (2022). https://doi.org/10.1016/j.ufug.2022.127612
19. Jiang, A.O.: Effects of colour environment on spaceflight cognitive abilities during short-term simulations of three gravity states (Doctoral dissertation, University of Leeds) (2022)
20. Sas, C., Höök, K., Doherty, G., et al.: Mental wellbeing: future agenda drawing from design, HCI and big data. In: Companion Publication of the 2020 ACM Designing Interactive Systems Conference, pp. 425–428 (2020)
21. Baghaei, N., Stemmet, L., Hlasnik, A., et al.: Time to get personal: individualised virtual reality for mental health. In: Extended Abstracts of the 2020 CHI Conference on Human Factors in Computing Systems, pp. 1–9 (2020)
22. Musilova, M., Foing, B., Beniest, A., Rogers, H.: EuroMoonMars IMA at HI-SEAS campaigns in 2019: an overview of the analog missions, upgrades to the mission operations and protocols. In: 51st Lunar and Planetary Science Conference, Harvard Press (2020)
23. Yeo, N.L., White, M.P., Alcock, I., et al.: What is the best way of delivering virtual nature for improving mood? An experimental comparison of high definition TV, 360 video, and computer generated virtual reality. J. Environ. Psychol. **72**, 101500 (2020). https://doi.org/ 10.1016/j.jenvp.2020.101500
24. Fucci, R.L., Gardner, J., Hanifin, J.P., et al.: Toward optimizing lighting as a countermeasure to sleep and circadian disruptionin space flight. Acta Astronaut. **56**(9–12), 1017–1024 (2005)
25. Wu, P., Morie, J., Wall, P., et al.: Maintaining psycho-social health on the way to Mars and back. In: Proceedings of the 2015 Virtual Reality International Conference, pp. 1–7 (2015)
26. Anderson, A.P., Mayer, M.D., Fellows, A.M., et al.: Relaxation with immersive natural scenes presented using virtual reality. J. Aerosp. Med. Hum. Perform. **88**(6), 520–526 (2017)

27. Kanas, N., Salnitskiy, V., Weiss, D.S., et al.: Human interactions during shuttle/Mir space missions. Aviat. Space Environ. Med. **48**(5–12), 777–784 (2001)
28. Anderson, A., Stankovic, A., Cowan, D., et al.: Natural scene virtual reality as a behavioral health countermeasure in isolated, confined, and extreme environments: three isolated, confined, extreme analog case studies. J. Human Factors 00187208221100693 (2022)
29. Jiang, A., Zhu, Y., Yao, X., Foing, B.H., Westland, S., Hemingray, C.: The effect of three body positions on colour preference: an exploration of microgravity and lunar gravity simulations. Acta Astronaut. **204**, 1–10 (2023)
30. Jiang, A., et al.: Short-term virtual reality simulation of the effects of space station colour and microgravity and lunar gravity on cognitive task performance and emotion. Build. Environ. **227**, 109789 (2023)
31. Jiang, A., Yao, X., Westland, S., Hemingray, C., Foing, B., Lin, J.: The effect of correlated colour temperature on physiological, emotional and subjective satisfaction in the hygiene area of a space station. Int. J. Environ. Res. Public Health **19**(15), 9090 (2022)
32. Yu, K., Jiang, A., Zeng, X., Wang, J., Yao, X., Chen, Y.: Colour design method of ship centralized control cabin. In: Stanton, N. (ed.) AHFE 2021. LNNS, vol. 270, pp. 495–502. Springer, Cham (2021). https://doi.org/10.1007/978-3-030-80012-3_57
33. Yu, K., Jiang, A., Wang, J., Zeng, X., Yao, X., Chen, Y.: Construction of crew visual behaviour mechanism in ship centralized control cabin. In: Stanton, N. (ed.) AHFE 2021. LNNS, vol. 270, pp. 503–510. Springer, Cham (2021). https://doi.org/10.1007/978-3-030-80012-3_58
34. Lu, S., et al.: Effects and challenges of operational lighting illuminance in spacecraft on human visual acuity. In: Stanton, N. (ed.) AHFE 2021. LNNS, vol. 270, pp. 582–588. Springer, Cham (2021). https://doi.org/10.1007/978-3-030-80012-3_67
35. Manzey, D.: Human missions to Mars: new psychological challenges and research issues. J. Acta Astronautica **55**(3–9), 781–790 (2004). https://doi.org/10.1016/j.actaastro.2004.05.013
36. Riva, G.: Virtual reality in psychotherapy. Cyberpsychol. Behav. **8**(3), 220–230 (2005)
37. Montana, J.I., Matamala-Gomez, M., Maisto, M., et al.: The benefits of emotion regulation interventions in virtual reality for the improvement of wellbeing in adults and older adults: a systematic review. J. Clin. Med. **9**(2), 500 (2020)
38. Del Mastro, A., Schlacht, I.L., Benyoucef, Y., Groemer, G., Nazir, S.: Motigravity: a new VR system to increase performance and safety in space operations simulation and rehabilitation medicine. In: Arezes, P. (ed.) AHFE 2017. AISC, vol. 604, pp. 207–217. Springer, Cham (2018). https://doi.org/10.1007/978-3-319-60525-8_22
39. Wang, Y., Xu, M.: Electroencephalogram application for the analysis of stress relief in the seasonal landscape. Int. J. Environ. Res. Public Health **18**(16), 8522 (2021)
40. Jiang, A., Foing, B.H., Schlacht, I.L., Yao, X., Cheung, V., Rhodes, P.A.: Colour schemes to reduce stress response in the hygiene area of a space station: a Delphi study. Appl. Ergon. **98**, 103573 (2022)
41. Jiang, A., Yao, X., Hemingray, C., Westland, S.: Young people's colour preference and the arousal level of small apartments. Color. Res. Appl. **47**(3), 783–795 (2022)
42. Nunes, A., Musilova, M., Cox, A., Agelini, J., Foing, B.: EMMIHS-2, the second euromoon-mars IMA HiSeas 2019 campaign: simulated moonbase outlook and outcomes-an engineering perspective. In: Lunar and Planetary Science Conference, p. 2405, no. 2326. Harvard Press (2020)
43. Völker, S., Kistemann, T.: Developing the urban blue: comparative health responses to blue and green urban open spaces in Germany. J. Health & place **35**, 196–205 (2015). https://doi.org/10.1016/j.healthplace.2014.10.015
44. Lee, J., Park, B.J., Tsunetsugu, Y., et al.: Effect of forest bathing on physiological and psychological responses in young Japanese male subjects. J. Public Health **125**(2), 93–100 (2011). https://doi.org/10.1016/j.puhe.2010.09.005

45. Song, C., Ikei, H., Kobayashi, M., et al.: Effects of viewing forest landscape on middle-aged hypertensive men. J. Urban Forestry Urban Green. **21**, 247–252 (2017)
46. Ulrich, R.S.: Natural versus urban scenes: some psychophysiological effects. J. Environ. Behav. **13**(5), 523–556 (1981)
47. Jiang, A., Schlacht, I.L., Yao, X., et al.: Space habitat astronautics: multicolour lighting psychology in a 7-day simulated habitat. J. Space: Sci. Technol. (2022).https://doi.org/10. 34133/2022/9782706
48. Bressane, A., Negri, R.G., de Brito, J.I., et al.: Association between contact with nature and anxiety, stress and depression symptoms: a primary survey in Brazil. J. Sustain. **14**(17), 10506 (2022). https://doi.org/10.3390/su141710506
49. Jiang, A., Yao, X., Schlacht, I.L., Musso, G., Tang, T., Westland, S.: Habitability study on space station colour design. In: Stanton, N. (ed.) AHFE 2020. AISC, vol. 1212, pp. 507–514. Springer, Cham (2020). https://doi.org/10.1007/978-3-030-50943-9_64
50. Li, C., Sun, C., Sun, M., et al.: Effects of brightness levels on stress recovery when viewing a virtual reality forest with simulated natural light. Urban Forestry Urban Green **56**, 126865 (2020)
51. Walvekar, S.S., Ambekar, J.G., Devaranavadagi, B.B.: Study on serum cortisol and perceived stress scale in the police constables. J. Clin. Diagn. Res.: JCDR, **9**(2), BC10 (2015). https://doi.org/10.7860/JCDR/2015/12015.5576

An Approach to Investigate an Influence of Visual Angle Size on Emotional Activation During a Decision-Making Task

Sebastian Oberdörfer[1]($\boxtimes$) (ID), Sandra Birnstiel[2] (ID), Sophia C. Steinhaeusser[1] (ID), and Marc Erich Latoschik[1] (ID)

[1] Human-Computer Interaction, University of Würzburg, Würzburg, Germany
sebastian.oberdoerfer@uni-wuerzburg.de
[2] Gamification Research Group, Friedrich-Alexander-Universität Erlangen-Nürnberg, Nürnberg, Germany

Abstract. Decision-making is an important ability in our daily lives. Decision-making can be influenced by emotions. A virtual environment and objects in it might follow an emotional design, thus potentially influencing the mood of a user. A higher visual angle on a particular stimulus can lead to a higher emotional response to it. The use of immersive virtual reality (VR) surrounds a user visually with a virtual environment, as opposed to the partial immersion of using a normal computer screen. This higher immersion may result in a greater visual angle on a particular stimulus and thus a stronger emotional response to it. In a between-subjects user study, we compare the results of a decision-making task in VR presented in three different visual angles. We used the Iowa Gambling Task (IGT) as task and to detect potential differences in decision-making. The IGT was displayed in one of three dimensions, thus yielding visual angles of 20°, 35°, and 50°. Our results indicate no difference between the three conditions with respect to decision-making. Thus, our results possibly imply that a higher visual angle has no influence on a task that is influenced by emotions but is otherwise cognitive.

Keywords: Virtual Reality · Decision-Making · Emotions · Iowa Gambling Task

1 Introduction

Decision-making is an important ability in our daily lives. While most daily decisions rarely have strong impacts, some decisions can cause severe consequences in the long run, such as financial ruin and life-threatening events. In these situations, people often must deal with uncertainties with regards to reward and punishment [6]. A good decision-making ability generally keeps people from consciously making disadvantageous decision. However, when the decision-making

© The Author(s), under exclusive license to Springer Nature Switzerland AG 2023
J. Y. C. Chen and G. Fragomeni (Eds.): HCII 2023, LNCS 14027, pp. 649–664, 2023.
https://doi.org/10.1007/978-3-031-35634-6_47

Fig. 1. Our virtual IGT is presented on the deck of a forest cabin.

ability is impaired, disadvantageous decisions might seem beneficial. A strong impairing influence can be emotions [2].

Decision-making situations can also take place when using immersive media, such as during training [22] as well as gaming [30] in immersive Virtual Reality (VR), and Augmented-Reality-based collaborative work [27]. With an increase in immersion, the visual angle on a particular stimulus can also be increased. Immersion is *"the extent to which the computer displays are capable of delivering an inclusive, extensive, surrounding, and vivid illusion of reality to the senses of a human participant"* [41]. The visual angle defines the total amount of available visual information. A higher visual angle can lead to a higher emotional response to audiovisual stimuli [12]. While this can lead to a stronger emotional response to emotionally designed Virtual Environments (VEs) [19,42] in general, it could also cause a stronger emotional activation in a decision-making situation.

As VR is not only used for entertainment [1] but also for learning [35], therapy [24], and scientific analyses [21], it is important to investigate whether a higher immersion and respective VR-factors impair a user's decision-making abilities. This research direction receives even a higher importance considering the fact that gambling games can be played in VR [13]. Research shows higher risk potential when playing a slot machine in VR instead of on a regular computer screen [14]. The required research should evaluate whether different visual angles influence a user's performance in a decision-making task.

Contribution

In this paper, we measure the influence of three different visual angles on a decision-making task in VR. We use the Iowa Gambling Task (IGT) as decision-making task [3] and present it in visual angles of 20°, 35°, and 50°. The design of the surrounding VE intends to evoke positive emotions in users. In particular, we designed a sunny forest environment allowing users to enjoy lush greenery from the deck of a wooden cabin as displayed in Fig. 1. In a between-subjects study, we measured IGT decision-making as well as positive and negative affect. Our results did not show a statistical difference between the three conditions with respect to affect and decision-making. While not ruling out an emotional influence of a higher visual angle on a stimulus, our results may suggest that visual angle sizes have no effect on a repetitive decision task that may be influenced by emotion but is otherwise cognitive.

2   Theoretical Background

Our research visualizes the IGT in three different visual dimensions in VR to investigate whether a higher visual angle causes a higher emotional activation and hence an influence on IGT decision-making. Research demonstrates that IGT decision-making potentially is impaired when completing the task in VR instead of on a regular computer screen [29]. However, research found no differences when the IGT was presented in the same visual angle size in a real laboratory environment using a computer screen and in a virtual replicate of the laboratory as well as in a virtual forest using a Head-Mounted Display (HMD) [28].

2.1   Iowa Gambling Task

The IGT has been used for more than 20 years in research to measure decision-making [6] and emotion-based learning [8]. The task simulates real-life decision-making and features uncertainties in regards to assumptions and outcomes. The task requires participants to win as much money as possible by drawing 100 cards from four card decks. Each card deck contains 40 cards. Following a fixed win and loss schedule, each card can result in an overall win or loss of money as shown in Table 1. The schedule results in two card decks making a profit and two card decks making a loss in the long run as shown in Table 2. Throughout the task, healthy participants cognitively develop an understanding for the underlying structure of the win and loss schedule [2]. The total number of advantageous minus disadvantageous selections determines a participant's IGT decision-making. A higher number of advantageous cards drawn indicates a better IGT decision-making. Splitting the results in blocks of 20 draws each allows for a more detailed analysis of the selection patterns [4]. The IGT proved robust to certain changes in its parameters, such as use in the original manual version with 40 cards [3], the computerized version with 60 cards [5], and the computerized version with a higher contrast value [23].

Researchers used the IGT to investigate the often underestimated effect of emotions on decision-making [2]. For example, induced arousal showed an influence on measurements [26,33]. Researchers also used the IGT to investigate the influence of emotion and mood induced by movie sequences on decision-making

Table 1. Overview of the win and loss schedule. Values are in $.

	1	2	3	4	5	6	7	8	9	10
Card Deck A										
Win:	+100	+100	+100	+100	+100	+100	+100	+100	+100	+100
Loss:	0	0	−150	0	−300	0	−200	0	−250	−350
Card Deck B										
Win:	+100	+100	+100	+100	+100	+100	+100	+100	+100	+100
Loss:	0	0	0	0	0	0	0	0	−1250	0
Card Deck C										
Win:	+50	+50	+50	+50	+50	+50	+50	+50	+50	+50
Loss:	0	0	−50	0	−50	0	−50	0	−50	−50
Card Deck D										
Win:	+50	+50	+50	+50	+50	+50	+50	+50	+50	+50
Loss:	0	0	0	0	0	0	0	0	0	−250
	11	**12**	**13**	**14**	**15**	**16**	**17**	**18**	**19**	**20**
Card Deck A										
Win:	+100	+100	+100	+100	+100	+100	+100	+100	+100	+100
Loss:	0	−350	0	−250	−200	0	−300	−150	0	0
Card Deck B										
Win:	+100	+100	+100	+100	+100	+100	+100	+100	+100	+100
Loss:	0	0	0	−1250	0	0	0	0	0	0
Card Deck C										
Win:	+50	+50	+50	+50	+50	+50	+50	+50	+50	+50
Loss:	0	−25	−75	0	0	0	−25	−75	0	−50
Card Deck D										
Win:	+50	+50	+50	+50	+50	+50	+50	+50	+50	+50
Loss:	0	0	0	0	0	0	0	0	0	−250
	21	**22**	**23**	**24**	**25**	**26**	**27**	**28**	**29**	**30**
Card Deck A										
Win:	+100	+100	+100	+100	+100	+100	+100	+100	+100	+100
Loss:	0	−300	0	−350	0	−200	−250	−150	0	0
Card Deck B										
Win:	+100	+100	+100	+100	+100	+100	+100	+100	+100	+100
Loss:	−1250	0	0	0	0	0	0	0	0	0
Card Deck C										
Win:	+50	+50	+50	+50	+50	+50	+50	+50	+50	+50
Loss:	0	0	0	−50	−25	−50	0	0	−75	−50
Card Deck D										
Win:	+50	+50	+50	+50	+50	+50	+50	+50	+50	+50
Loss:	0	0	0	0	0	0	0	0	−250	0
	31	**32**	**33**	**34**	**35**	**36**	**37**	**38**	**39**	**40**
Card Deck A										
Win:	+100	+100	+100	+100	+100	+100	+100	+100	+100	+100
Loss:	−350	−200	−250	0	0	0	−150	−300	0	0
Card Deck B										
Win:	+100	+100	+100	+100	+100	+100	+100	+100	+100	+100
Loss:	−1250	0	0	0	0	0	0	0	0	0
Card Deck C										
Win:	+50	+50	+50	+50	+50	+50	+50	+50	+50	+50
Loss:	0	0	0	−25	−25	0	−75	0	−50	−75
Card Deck D										
Win:	+50	+50	+50	+50	+50	+50	+50	+50	+50	+50
Loss:	0	0	0	0	−250	0	0	0	0	0

Table 2. Overall win and loss for each IGT card deck. Values are in $.

	Card Deck A	Card Deck B	Card Deck C	Card Deck D
Win	4000	4000	2000	2000
Loss	−5000	−5000	−1000	−1000
Combined	−1000	−1000	1000	1000

[9,17]. It was shown that a positive mood can lead to better IGT decision-making in the second block of the task lasting from game round 21 to 40 [9]. Moreover, subjects who were in an emotional state associated with certainty performed better than those who were in an emotional state associated with uncertainty [17]. Although not fully applicable, research showed an impact on IGT decision-making of subjects suffering from anxiety when anxiety-relevant stimuli were displayed on either the favorable or the unfavorable card deck [32].

In contrast to examining the effects of emotions on decision-making, several studies have also shown that the IGT can be completed with the development of, as well as access to, explicit knowledge and thus cognitive processes [10,25]. Typically, a participant goes through four phases: pre-punishment phase, pre-hunch phase, hunch phase, and conceptual phase [2]. During the *pre-punishment phase*, which lasts until about the 10th card, subjects have no knowledge about the distribution of the card decks. Until around the 50th card is drawn, subjects are in the *pre-hunch* phase and begin to develop a first hunch about the existence of good and bad card decks. Subsequently, in the *hunch* phase, which lasts until about the 80th card, they begin to show initial knowledge of the distribution of the card decks. Finally, for the remainder of the task, subjects develop a more detailed knowledge of the underlying principles in the *conceptual* phase. This is consistent with the observation that decision time decreases strongly during the first two blocks [8]. However, besides a cognitive development of knowledge, research has further shown that healthy participants with higher risk attitudes intentionally draw cards from riskier card decks [37].

Taken together, this results in a dichotomy of cognition and emotion in IGT decision-making [20,36]. While emotions have been shown to constantly influence IGT decision-making [15], they are not the only factor contributing to a person's behavior in the task [10].

2.2 Immersion and Emotion

Immersion evokes and directly affects presence [40,45]. *Presence* describes the subjective illusion of being in a real place even though one is physically in a different place [39]. Thus, presence refers to the perceived realness of a virtual experience [38]. Maintaining presence requires support from sensorimotor contingencies [39] and a continuous stream of stimuli and experiences [48]. The experience of presence is the precondition for emotional influence through the design of a VE [34]. Vice versa, higher emotional intensity of a predominant emotion in a VE can increase presence [19].

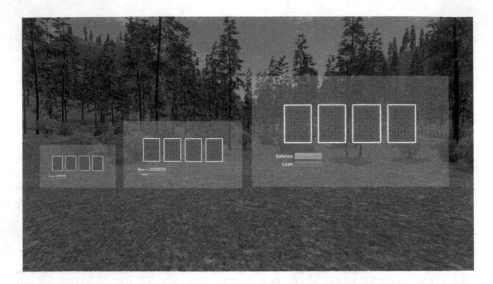

Fig. 2. Comparison of the three conditions: Visual angle of 20°, 35°, and 50°.

Research suggests that VR may serve as an ideal expressive medium for emotional challenge [31]. A recent publication discusses the influence of VE design on the emotional perception of VEs and provides design recommendations for joyful and fearful VEs [42]. Emotional positive VEs are characterized primarily by natural aspects such as lush vegetation, access to water, sunshine, and overall wide, colorful, and open spaces. In contrast, emotional negative VEs are designed to enclose the user in dark places with unbalanced light, harsh and dirty elements, and even signs of past violence.

2.3 Summary

The dichotomy of cognition and emotion makes the IGT ideal for our research. The sensitivity to emotions of this otherwise cognitive task allows for an investigation whether potential changes in emotional activation caused by different visual angles influence IGT decision-making. The results of this investigation provide first insights into the effects of visual angle size on emotional activation and decision-making in a cognitive task.

3   System Design

We embedded the IGT in a VE following recommendations for an emotional positive design [42]. The VE consists of a sunny forest environment featuring lush greenery and colorful flowers. The VE further features a wooden and cozy cabin as depicted in Fig. 1. Facing away from the cabin and towards the trees, we displayed the IGT on a semi-transparent white background as displayed in

Fig. 3. Visualization of our IGT interaction techniques.

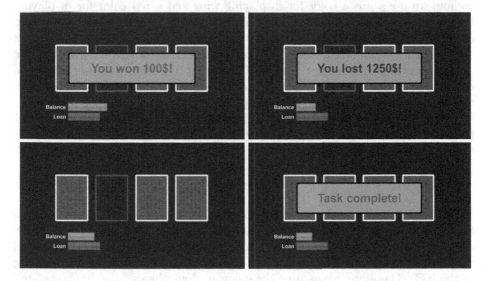

Fig. 4. The user interface of our virtual IGT uses emotional color-coding of wins and losses.

Fig. 2. The participants were positioned at the same distance to the IGT and the IGT was displayed in one of three dimensions thus yielding visual angles of 20°, 35°, and 50°.

3.1 Virtual IGT

Our implementation of the virtual IGT is based on the fixed schedule of win and loss of the original IGT version [3]. The VR application displays the four card decks with cards lying face down. Our virtual IGT provides two interactions: (1) *selection* of a card deck and (2) *drawing* a card from the selected card deck. We selected the HTC Vive Pro [16] as output device and hence mapped the interactions to the HTC Vive game controller as depicted in Fig. 3. The virtual IGT displays the position of a controller using its 3D model. We defined four zones on the touchpad each representing a card deck to allow for a selection of one of the four card decks. A user selects a card deck by merely touching a specific zone or moving the finger over the touchpad. The currently selected card deck is marked by a black frame. A user can draw a card from the selected card deck by pressing the touchpad. Subsequently, the virtual IGT first adds the respective card deck's payout to the player's balance before subtracting the drawn card's loss value. The VR application displays the player's current balance and initial loan with two labeled bars. While a green bar changes its length according to the win and loss of a game round to indicate a player's balance, an orange bar shows the initial loan. The virtual IGT displays respective wins and losses of each card directly over the four card decks for two seconds. Following emotional color coding, we use a green color for displaying wins and a red color for displaying losses. We made this decision to increase the emotional reaction to each decision as displayed in Fig. 4. A user cannot draw a new card while the win and loss information are displayed. After drawing 40 cards from a single card deck, the respective card deck becomes inactive. The virtual IGT informs a user about the completion of the task after the 100th card is drawn. The VR application logs the decision for each turn, thus allowing for an analysis of a user's performance.

We developed the virtual IGT with Unity 2019.3.10f1 [43] using the SteamVR plugin version 1.2.3 [44]. The virtual IGT is a prefab allowing for a free positioning inside of VEs.

4   Method

Based on the theoretical considerations in Sect. 2 and our design choices in Sect. 3, we assume that a higher visual angle on the IGT leads to a stronger emotional reaction to the results of a participant's card draws. As a consequence, the assumed change in mood in turn influences the participant's decision-making in the IGT. Therefore, we assume the following hypotheses.

- H1: A higher visual angle on the IGT causes a stronger affect.
- H2: IGT decision-making differs between the three visual angles.
- H3: IGT decision-making differs between the three visual angles in block 2.

We conducted a between-subjects design user study to investigate the effects of different visual angels on the IGT and to test our hypotheses. Our conditions only differed with respect to the visual angle on the IGT: $IGT20°$, $IGT35°$, and $IGT50°$. The participants were randomly assigned to either one of these conditions. Our study was approved by the Human-Computer-Media institutional ethics review board of the University of Würzburg.

4.1   Measures

We used the following measures in our user study.

Demographics. We assessed a participant's *age* (in years), *gender, video game experience*, and *VR experience* as demographic data. As an additional control variable, the demography questionnaire included the *Immersive Tendency Questionnaire (ITQ)* [48] to assess a participant's immersive tendency, their current alertness as well as fitness, and their ability to focus. Cronbach's alpha for ITQ was .62.

Decision-Making. We used our virtual IGT to measure decision-making. As described in Subsect. 2.1, the IGT requires participants to draw 100 cards from four card decks which are either advantageous or disadvantageous. The total number of advantageous *minus* disadvantageous selections determines a participant's IGT decision-making [3]. We analyzed the total score as well as the score per 20-card block. A higher number of advantageous cards drawn indicates a better IGT decision-making.

Positive Affect and Negative Affect. We use the *Positive and Negative Affect Schedule (PANAS)* [46] to measure a participant's affect. The PANAS consists of two 10-item 5-point Likert scales (5 = very much). Each scale measures one of the two primary dimensions of mood, i.e., positive (PA) and negative affect (NA). As we wanted to determine the overall effect of differences in the visual angle, we only administered the PANAS after the completion of the IGT. Cronbach's alpha was .86 for PA and .75 for NA.

Presence. Since presence is closely connected to the experience of emotions [19, 34], the study included the *presence questionnaire - version 3.0 (PQ)* consisting of the 19 core items [47] as a control variable. The PQ consists of 7-point Likert scales (7 = high perceived presence). We only report the total average score. Cronbach's alpha was .84.

4.2 Procedure

The study took place during the Covid 19 pandemic. To ensure protection and hygiene, we took the following precautions. (1) Each participant was required to disinfect their hands before and after the study, wear a mask at all times, and report if they were in a risk area or showed signs of illness. (2) The experimenter was required to disinfect their hands, wear a mask at all times, and report daily if they showed signs of illness. (3) The experimenter and participant were required to maintain a minimum distance of 1.5 m. (4) All surfaces touched and equipment used, such as HMD, controller, keyboard, had to be cleaned with a disinfectant after each experiment. (5) The laboratory had to be ventilated for at least 15 min after each experiment.

The experimental setup consisted of a desk, a chair, a computer (CPU: i7–9700K, RAM: 16 GB, GPU: RTX 2070), one 28 inches computer screen (resolution: 3840 × 2160 px), an HTC Vive Pro HMD (1440x1600 px resolution per eye, 110° field of view), a single HTC Vive controller, a mouse, and a keyboard.

After being welcomed, the experimenter told the participant to sit down at the desk, to read the study information, and to sign an informed consent form. Each participant had to fill in the Problem Gambling Severity Index (PGSI) [7]. We conducted the PGSI as a safety measure to protect them from gambling-related harm. This 9-item questionnaire measures the severity of a gambling addiction by considering a person's gambling behavior over the past year [11].

Table 3. Descriptive statistics per group.

Variable	IGT20°		IGT35°		IGT50°	
	M	SD	M	SD	M	SD
IGT score[a]	−8.08	22.97	−7.36	23.82	−4.54	25.49
PA[b]	2.69	0.57	2.35	0.59	2.65	0.82
NA[b]	1.36	0.37	1.51	0.50	1.59	0.44
ITQ[c]	4.43	0.63	4.39	0.57	4.36	0.45
Presence[c]	4.35	0.76	4.15	0.66	4.19	0.82

[a] Calculated means from −80 to 80.
[b] Calculated means from 1 to 5.
[c] Calculated means from 1 to 7.

We only allowed participants that scored 0 on the PGSI to participate. Afterwards, participants filled in the demography questionnaire. Upon completion of the questionnaire, the participants received written and illustrated instructions about the possible interactions with our virtual IGT. Here, we also used Fig. 3 to explain the card selection interaction technique. We also informed them about the functionality of the HMD and potential symptoms of cybersickness. The participants completed the IGT in their randomly assigned condition. After completing the IGT, the participants filled in the post-questionnaire consisting of PANAS and PQ. Finally, we explained the goal of the experiment as well as the IGT's fixed schedule of win and loss, showed a short educational video about problem gambling, reminded them of the effects of cybersickness, and thanked them for participating.

4.3 Participants

We recruited participants from the students enrolled in the bachelor programs Media Communication and Human-Computer Interaction at the University of Würzburg. Participants were rewarded with credits mandatory for obtaining their program of study's degrees. Overall, 76 individuals with a mean age of 21.75 ($SD = 2.70$) took part in the study. Twenty-nine participants self-indicated as male (age: $M = 21.69$, $SD = 2.73$), whereas the majority of 47 self-indicated as female (age: $M = 21.79$, $SD = 2.68$). None of the participants reported being diverse gender. Concerning video game experience, 9 participants had never played a video game before, whereas most of them played at a daily ($n = 11$), weekly ($n = 13$), monthly ($n = 19$), or at least yearly ($n = 20$) basis (one missing value). Four participants had only played video games in past studies. Regarding VR usage, the majority of 42 participants had only experienced VR in past studies and 17 persons had never experienced VR before. Only four participants used VR on a weekly basis, eight persons used VR once a month, and, last, five participants stated to use VR once in a year (one missing value).

Being randomly assigned to one of the three conditions, 26 participants completed IGT20° (9 male, 16 female; age: $M = 21.84$, $SD = 2.85$), while 25 persons

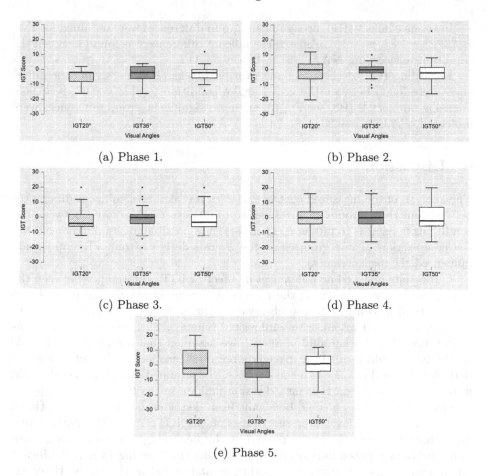

(a) Phase 1.

(b) Phase 2.

(c) Phase 3.

(d) Phase 4.

(e) Phase 5.

Fig. 5. IGT values per phase. Error bars display standard errors.

completed IGT35° (9 male, 16 female; age: $M = 21.92$, $SD = 2.53$). Last, 26
participants completed IGT50° (11 male, 15 female; age: $M = 21.50$, $SD = 2.73$).

5   Results

All analyses were conducted using *JASP* version 0.16.0.0 [18] and an alpha-
level of .05. Descriptive data is presented in Table 3. Calculated Levene's tests
indicated homogeneity of variances for all scales, $ps > .05$, whereas Shapiro-Wilk
tests revealed violation of the normality assumption for the overall IGT score
and NA.

First, we analyzed the control variables. No significant group differences were
spotted for **ITQ** values, $F(73, 2) = 0.10$, $p = .901$. Similarly, **presence** did not
significantly differ between the three conditions, $F(73, 2) = 0.53$, $p = .593$.

In terms of affect (H1), no significant group differences were obtained for **PA**, $F(73, 2) = 1.88$, $p = .161$. Alike, no significant difference was found between the conditions concerning **NA**, $\chi^2(2) = 4.38$, $p = .112$.

Regarding **IGT** decision-making over all blocks (H2), no significant differences were found between the visual angles conditions, $\chi^2(2) = 0.07$, $p = .965$. Focusing on block 2 (H3, see Fig. 5), again no significant group differences were indicated, $F(73, 2) = 0.30$, $p = .741$.

6   Discussion

The analysis of the measured control variables revealed no significant differences between our three groups with respect to immersive tendency and between the conditions in regards to presence. Therefore, it is possible to assume that neither the composition of our groups nor the overall design of our VR application influenced the measurements.

Our results revealed no differences in affect or IGT performance between the three groups after completing the respective version of the virtual IGT. These results stand in contrast to the observation that a larger visual angle leads to a higher emotional response to audiovisual stimuli [12]. Based on the analysis of the theoretical background in Sect. 2, we assumed that a higher visual angle on the IGT would result in a stronger emotional reaction to the outcomes of a participant's card draws. As a consequence, the assumed change in mood would in turn influence the participant's decision-making in the IGT.

One potential reason could be a shift from decision-making on an emotional level to a cognitive level over the course of the IGT. While the participants might have been emotionally activated at the beginning of the task, this emotional activation potentially declined over time, thus leading to non-significant differences in mood between the conditions at the end of the study. However, the insignificant IGT decision-making differences in the second block suggest that there was no emotional activation at the beginning of the task. The second block of IGT can be strongly influenced by a participant's mood [9]. Another potential explanation could be an execution of the IGT with primarily cognitive processes [10,25]. Instead of reacting in an emotional way to the outcomes of drawing cards, the participants might have cognitively analyzed the results to develop explicit knowledge about the task's underlying principles. Based on this assumption, it is possible to infer that visual angle size does not evoke or moderate emotional response to purely cognitive stimuli. Finally and in alignment with the previous explanation, the mood of the participants might not have been influenced by their performance in the IGT but by the surrounding emotional positive VE. This is supported by the rather low NA values and mid-range PA values indicating a predominantly positive state across all conditions. As IGT decision-making can be influenced by a participant's mood [9,17], the induction of a similar mood across all conditions using the same VE could account for the insignificant differences between the conditions with respect to IGT decision-making.

As a result of this, a higher visual angle on the IGT did not cause a stronger affect, thus leading to the rejection of **H1**. IGT decision-making also did not differ among the three conditions, either for overall performance or for decisions made in the second block. This leads to the rejection of **H2** and **H3**.

Taken together, our results suggest that a higher visual angle does not affect a task that is influenced by emotion but is generally cognitive. Combining these results with findings from Oberdörfer et al. [28], although emotional influences from a higher visual angle cannot be ruled out, this could mean that when transferring cognitive decision tasks from normal computer screens to VR, and thus potentially higher visual dimensions, there is no risk of influencing the outcome of the task through a higher level of emotion. This is an important insight as even scientific analyses can be carried out in VR [21].

7 Conclusion

As an approach to investigate the influence of visual angle size on emotional activation during a decision-making task, we measured IGT decision-making in VR. We embedded the IGT in an emotional positive VE and presented it in either one of three visual dimension to our participants.

Our results showed no statistical difference between the three visual angle conditions in terms of affect and decision-making. Although we cannot rule out an emotional influence of a higher visual angle on a stimulus, our results potentially suggest that the size of the visual angle has no influence on a repetitive decision task that may be influenced by emotions but is mainly cognitive.

Future work should investigate whether different sizes of visual angle lead to differences in decision-making in a purely emotional decision task. Another research direction is to investigate whether other VR factors such as embodiment or social presence influence IGT decision-making.

References

1. Beacco, A., Oliva, R., Cabreira, C., Gallego, J., Slater, M.: Disturbance and plausibility in a virtual rock concert: a pilot study. In: 2021 IEEE Virtual Reality and 3D User Interfaces (VR 2021), pp. 538–545 (2021). https://doi.org/10.1109/VR50410.2021.00078
2. Bechara, A., Damasio, A.R.: The somatic marker hypothesis: a neural theory of economic decision. Games Econ. Behav. **52**(2), 336–372 (2005)
3. Bechara, A., Damasio, A.R., Damasio, H., Anderson, S.W.: Insensitivity to future consequences following damage to human prefrontal cortex. Cognition **50**(1–3), 7–15 (1994)
4. Bechara, A., Dolan, S., Hindes, A.: Decision-making and addiction (part ii): myopia for the future or hypersensitivity to reward? Neuropsychologia **40**(10), 1690–1705 (2002). https://doi.org/10.1016/S0028-3932(02)00016-7
5. Bechara, A., Tranel, D., Damasio, H.: Characterization of the decision-making deficit of patients with ventromedial prefrontal cortex lesions. Brain **123**(11), 2189–2202 (2000). https://doi.org/10.1093/brain/123.11.2189

6. Brevers, D., Bechara, A., Cleeremans, A., Noël, X.: Iowa gambling task (IGT): twenty years after-gambling disorder and IGT. Front. Psychol. **4**, 665 (2013)

7. Caler, K., Garcia, J.R.V., Nower, L.: Assessing problem gambling: a review of classic and specialized measures. Curr. Addict. Rep. **3**(4), 437–444 (2016)

8. Cella, M., Dymond, S., Cooper, A., Turnbull, O.: Effects of decision-phase time constraints on emotion-based learning in the Iowa gambling task. Brain Cogn. **64**(2), 164–169 (2007). https://doi.org/10.1016/j.bandc.2007.02.003

9. de Vries, M., Holland, R.W., Witteman, C.L.M.: In the winning mood: affect in the Iowa gambling task. Judgment Decis. Making **3**(1), 42–50 (2008)

10. Dunn, B.D., Dalgleish, T., Lawrence, A.D.: The somatic marker hypothesis: a critical evaluation. Neurosci. Biobehav. Rev. **30**(2), 239–271 (2006). https://doi.org/10.1016/j.neubiorev.2005.07.001

11. Ferris, J.A., Wynne, H.J.: The Canadian Problem Gambling Index. Canadian Centre on Substance Abuse Ottawa, ON (2001)

12. Gall, D., Latoschik, M.E.: Visual angle modulates affective responses to audiovisual stimuli. Comput. Hum. Behav. **109**, 106346 (2020)

13. Griffiths, M.: The psychosocial impact of gambling in virtual reality. Casino Gaming Int. **29**, 51–54 (2017)

14. Heidrich, D., Oberdörfer, S., Latoschik, M.E.: The effects of immersion on harm-inducing factors in virtual slot machines. In: Proceedings of the 26th IEEE Virtual Reality Conference (VR 2019). IEEE, Osaka, Japan (2019)

15. Heilman, R.M., Crişan, L.G., Houser, D., Miclea, M., Miu, A.C.: Emotion regulation and decision making under risk and uncertainty. Emotion **10**(2), 257–265 (2010). https://doi.org/10.1037/a0018489

16. HTC Corporation: Htc vive (2011–2017). http://www.vive.com

17. İyilikci, E.A., Amado, S.: The uncertainty appraisal enhances the prominent deck b effect in the Iowa gambling task. Motiv. Emot. **42**(1), 1–16 (2018). https://doi.org/10.1007/s11031-017-9643-5

18. JASP Team: Jasp (2021). http://jasp-stats.org/

19. Jicol, C., et al.: Effects of emotion and agency on presence in virtual reality. In: Proceedings of the 2021 CHI Conference on Human Factors in Computing Systems (CHI 2021). Association for Computing Machinery, New York (2021). https://doi.org/10.1145/3411764.3445588

20. Kahneman, D., Frederick, S.: Frames and brains: elicitation and control of response tendencies. Trends Cogn. Sci. **11**(2), 45–46 (2007). https://doi.org/10.1016/j.tics.2006.11.007

21. Knote, A., von Mammen, S., Gao, Y., Thorn, A.: Immersive analysis of crystallographic diffraction data. In: 26th ACM Symposium on Virtual Reality Software and Technology. Association for Computing Machinery, New York (2020). https://doi.org/10.1145/3385956.3422097

22. Leder, J., Horlitz, T., Puschmann, P., Wittstock, V., Schütz, A.: Comparing immersive virtual reality and powerpoint as methods for delivering safety training: impacts on risk perception, learning, and decision making. Saf. Sci. **111**, 271–286 (2019). https://doi.org/10.1016/j.ssci.2018.07.021

23. Lee, W.K., Su, Y.A., Song, T.J., Chiu, Y.C., Lin, C.H.: Are normal decision-makers sensitive to changes in value contrast under uncertainty? evidence from the Iowa gambling task. PLoS ONE **9**(7), 1–10 (2014). https://doi.org/10.1371/journal.pone.0101878

24. Liszio, S., Graf, L., Masuch, M.: The relaxing effect of virtual nature - immersive technology provides relief in acute stress situations. In: Wiederhold, B.K., Riva, G.,

Bouchard, S. (eds.) Annual Review of Cybertherapy and Telemedicine (ARCTT), pp. 87–93. Interactive Media Institute, San Diego, CA, USA (2018)

25. Maia, T.V., McClelland, J.L.: The somatic marker hypothesis: still many questions but no answers. Proc. Natl. Acad. Sci. **101**(45), 16075–16080 (2004). https://doi.org/10.1073/pnas.0406666101

26. Miu, A.C., Heilman, R.M., Houser, D.: Anxiety impairs decision-making: psychophysiological evidence from an Iowa gambling task. Biol. Psychol. **77**(3), 353–358 (2008)

27. Mourtzis, D., Siatras, V., Angelopoulos, J.: Real-time remote maintenance support based on augmented reality (AR). Appl. Sci. **10**(5), 1855 (2020). https://doi.org/10.3390/app10051855

28. Oberdörfer, S., Heidrich, D., Birnstiel, S., Latoschik, M.E.: Enchanted by your surrounding? measuring the effects of immersion and design of virtual environments on decision-making. Front. Virtual Reality **2**, 101 (2021). https://doi.org/10.3389/frvir.2021.679277

29. Oberdörfer, S., Heidrich, D., Latoschik, M.E.: Think twice: the influence of immersion on decision making during gambling in virtual reality. In: Proceedings of the 27th IEEE Virtual Reality conference (VR 2020), pp. 483–492. IEEE, Atlanta (2020). https://doi.org/10.1109/VR46266.2020.00069

30. Oberdörfer, S., Latoschik, M.E.: Knowledge encoding in game mechanics: transfer-oriented knowledge learning in desktop-3d and vr. Int. J. Comput. Games Technol. 2019 (2019). https://doi.org/10.1155/2019/7626349

31. Peng, X., Huang, J., Denisova, A., Chen, H., Tian, F., Wang, H.: A palette of deepened emotions: exploring emotional challenge in virtual reality games. In: Proceedings of the 2020 CHI Conference on Human Factors in Computing Systems (CHI 2020). Association for Computing Machinery, New York (2020). https://doi.org/10.1145/3313831.3376221

32. Pittig, A., Brand, M., Pawlikowski, M., Alpers, G.W.: The cost of fear: avoidant decision making in a spider gambling task. J. Anxiety Disord. **28**(3), 326–334 (2014). https://doi.org/10.1016/j.janxdis.2014.03.001

33. Preston, S., Buchanan, T., Stansfield, R., Bechara, A.: Effects of anticipatory stress on decision making in a gambling task. Behav. Neurosci. **121**(2), 257 (2007)

34. Riva, G., et al.: Affective interactions using virtual reality: the link between presence and emotions. CyberPsychology Behav. **10**(1), 45–56 (2007). https://doi.org/10.1089/cpb.2006.9993

35. Seufert, C., Oberdörfer, S., Roth, A., Grafe, S., Lugrin, J.L., Latoschik, M.E.: Classroom management competency enhancement for student teachers using a fully immersive virtual classroom. Comput. Educ. **179**, 104410 (2022). https://doi.org/10.1016/j.compedu.2021.104410

36. Singh, V.: Dual conception of risk in the Iowa gambling task: effects of sleep deprivation and test-retest gap. Front. Psychol. **4**, 628 (2013). https://doi.org/10.3389/fpsyg.2013.00628

37. Singh, V., Khan, A.: Heterogeneity in choices on Iowa gambling task: preference for infrequent-high magnitude punishment. Mind Soc. **8**(43), 43–57 (2008). https://doi.org/10.1007/s11299-008-0050-1

38. Skarbez, R., Brooks, F.P., Jr., Whitton, M.C.: A survey of presence and related concepts. ACM Comput. Surv. **50**(6), 1–39 (2017). https://doi.org/10.1145/3134301

39. Slater, M.: Place illusion and plausibility can lead to realistic behaviour in immersive virtual environments. Philos. Trans. R. Soc. B **364**, 3549–3557 (2009). https://doi.org/10.1098/rstb.2009.0138

40. Slater, M., Linakis, V., Usoh, M., Kooper, R.: Immersion, presence, and performance in virtual environments: an experiment with tri-dimensional chess. In: Proceedings of the ACM Symposium on Virtual Reality Software and Technology (VRST 1996), pp. 163–172. ACM, Hong Kong (1996). https://doi.org/10.1145/3304181.3304216

41. Slater, M., Wilbur, S.: A framework for immersive virtual environments (five): speculations on the role of presence in virtual environments. Presence 6(6), 603–616 (1997). https://doi.org/10.1162/pres.1997.6.6.603

42. Steinhaeusser, S.C., Oberdörfer, S., von Mammen, S., Latoschik, M.E., Lugrin, B.: Joyful adventures and frightening places - designing emotion-inducing virtual environments. Front. Virtual Reality (2022). https://doi.org/10.3389/frvir.2022.919163

43. Unity: unity 2019.3.10f1 (2021). http://unity3d.com/get-unity/download/archive

44. Valve Coorperation: Steamvr plugin (2015–2022). http://assetstore.unity.com/packages/tools/integration/steamvr-plugin-32647

45. Waltemate, T., Gall, D., Roth, D., Botsch, M., Latoschik, M.E.: The impact of avatar personalization and immersion on virtual body ownership, presence, and emotional response. IEEE Trans. Vis. Comput. Graph. 24(4), 1643–1652 (2018). https://doi.org/10.1109/TVCG.2018.2794629

46. Watson, D., Clark, L.A.: Development and validation of brief measures of positive and negative affect: the Panas scales. J. Pers. Soc. Psychol. 54(6), 1063–1070 (1988)

47. Witmer, B.G., Jerome, C.J., Singer, M.J.: The factor structure of the presence questionnaire. Presence 14(3), 298–314 (2005). https://doi.org/10.1162/105474605323384654

48. Witmer, B.G., Singer, M.J.: Measuring presence in virtual environments: a presence questionnaire. Presence 7(3), 225–240 (1998). https://doi.org/10.1162/105474698565686

AR-Based Visitor Support System for Enhancing the Liveliness of Sightseeing Spots Using CG Humanoid Models

Kouyou Otsu[✉], Takuya Ueno, and Tomoko Izumi

Ritsumeikan University, 1-1-1, Noji-Higashi, Kusatsu, Shiga, Japan
k-otsu@fc.ritsumei.ac.jp

Abstract. When visiting an unfamiliar sightseeing spot, the absence of other individuals can make a visitor feel lonely and hesitant about visiting. In this paper, we propose an AR application that aims to eliminate this psychological reluctance to enter a spot when visiting for the first time. This application enables the user to know information about visitors (numbers of people and their attributes) who have visited a spot recently through a visualization mechanism in which CG human-shaped objects are overlapped on the spot image acquired by the camera on the visitor's own tablet PC. To examine the effectiveness of the proposed application in a controlled settings, we developed an experimental environment in which users can experience the proposed application in a VR space by operating a virtual tablet. The experimental results suggested that this visualization approach based on CG humanoid objects with motion and attributes contributes to the psychological ease of visiting spots and enhances the desire to visit.

Keywords: Tourist support system · VR/AR · Social presence

1 Introduction

In a tourism activity, a stroll around a town is an important way for visitors to learn about an unfamiliar but attractive place. In this paper, we discuss how technology can support encounters with new, attractive spots as visitors walk around a sightseeing area.

During a stroll around a town, we sometimes come across interesting spots (e.g. restaurants and stores we have not visited before), but if no other visitors are around, we may feel anxious and hesitant to visit. In this way, visiting a spot in the strolling context often creates psychological hesitation. Previous studies on tourist behaviors have indicated that some risks associated with services offered negatively affect a destination's image [1,3]. Additionally, research on factors influencing store visits has demonstrated that the social presence of other customers encourages customer visits [2,6]. Recently, review sites for restaurants and tourist attractions have become popular. This implies that access to other people's experiences reflects a desire to form a psychological sense of trust about a visit. In other words, confirming the presence of others who had experiences

© The Author(s), under exclusive license to Springer Nature Switzerland AG 2023
J. Y. C. Chen and G. Fragomeni (Eds.): HCII 2023, LNCS 14027, pp. 665–677, 2023.
https://doi.org/10.1007/978-3-031-35634-6_48

similar to those of a tourists might be considered a factor in encouraging that tourist to visit. Many tourism support systems have been proposed to assist visitors in strolling situations [4,5], but previous works have not focused on the reduction of psychological hesitation for visiting a spot.

Thus, this study aims at providing technical support to tourists who hesitate to visit spots due to the scarcity of other visitors around them, with a view to enhancing the desire to visit new spots. In this paper, we propose an AR application that conveys past visitors' information (number of people and their attributes) at a spot by overlaying CG human-shaped objects onto a video captured by a visitor using a mobile device (Fig. 1). When a visitor uses this application in front of a spot, CG human-shaped objects representing previous visitors overlap onto a video captured by built-in camera on a tablet PC along with movements to simulate the other visitors' entering the spot. Thus, the proposed method is expected to reduce hesitation to visit tourist attractions because it shows users the presence of tourists who have already visited those spots. However, it is not clear whether such a presentation method can encourage users to enter a spot, or what information about past visitors would be beneficial to present to them.

In this paper, we focus on whether presenting past visitors and/or their attributes (e.g. age or gender) as CG human-shaped objects effectively motivates users to visit a spot. We will also focus on the difference in effectiveness between CG and actual humans in motivating users to enter a spot, and discuss the possibilities and limitations of information presented by humanoid CG playing the same roles in helping recipients change their behavior as actual humans. Our contribution in this paper to the domain of AR applications for tourism support are as follows:

- We clarified that the visualization of past visitor attributes in human-like format is useful for enhancing interest and improving the ease of entering a spot, especially in situations where no one is around the user.
- We quantitatively demonstrated the difference in the effect of humanoid CG objects and actual humans attracting people to a spot in a controlled environment.

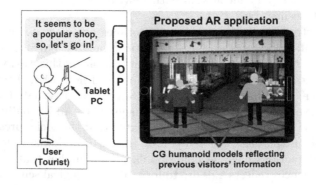

Fig. 1. Overview of the proposed method.

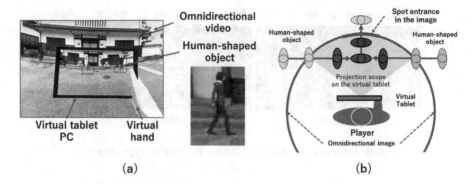

Fig. 2. Configuration of the VR experimental environment. (a) An example of the user's view while using the system and, (b) a schematic representation of VR space and human-shaped objects' behavior.

2   Experimental Environment

The purpose of this study is to clarify whether presenting information about other visitors through CG human-shaped objects is useful in improving the psychological ease of visiting tourist attractions. One typical approach to clarify this issue is to conduct a survey targeting real visitors to actual spots in the real field. However, in real-world experiment, environmental factors such as weather and the behavior of other visitors may affect one's impression of a tourist attraction. Therefore, it is desirable to conduct experiments in a controlled environment to verify the effect of presenting other people's behavior via the proposed method. For this reason, we developed an experimental system that allows users to experience the proposed method by operating a virtual tablet terminal in a VR space. The following section describes the details of the experimental system (Fig. 2).

2.1   Implementation of the Experimental System

The system enables users to experience visiting sightseeing spots in a VR space by projecting an omni-directional video image of the sightseeing spots via a head mounted display(Meta Quest 2, Meta Inc.). Figure 2 (a) shows an example of the user's view while using the system. In VR space, an omni-directional video image is always projected around the user. In addition, a virtual hand is displayed that corresponds to the right hand controller in the real world, and the user is always holding a virtual tablet by using it. By moving their own hand, users can hold the tablet up to the spot in their field of view. On the screen of the virtual tablet, images captured by a virtual camera mounted on the virtual tablet are constantly projected. When the user holds up the terminal so that the spot appears on the screen, CG human-shaped objects are also displayed on the screen of the virtual tablet. Therefore, the user can obtain past information about visitors to the spot.

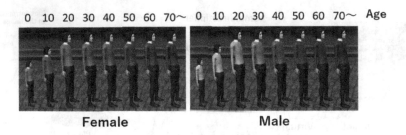

Fig. 3. Representation of attributes by human-type objects.

Figure 2(b) shows a schematic representation of the VR space and human-shaped object's behavior. In this system, the CG human-shaped objects start from the outside of the omni-directional image and moves toward the entrance of the spot by going around the inside of the image. In this case, the CG human-shaped objects are implemented so that they are only displayed through the screen of the virtual tablet when it is inside the omni-directional image. Therefore, the CG humanoid objects are seen by the user as if they were appearing from outside the virtual tablet screen and entering a spot on the screen.

2.2 Representation of Attributes by Human-Type Objects

In this system, the characteristics of past visitors to a tourist spot are represented by the size of the human-shaped object and the color of the clothing. These provide the user with visual information about the spot's visitors. This study deals with gender and age as visitor attributes. Specifically, the size of the human-shaped object and the color of the clothing are set to vary according to the age and gender of past visitors. Figure 3 shows the relationship between age, gender, and the appearance of the objects. As shown in Fig. 3, differently colored humanoid objects are used to represent gender differences. In addition, the brightness and saturation of the objects are changed for each age group. Finally, to explicitly present the number of child visitors, only the human-shaped objects corresponding to visitors in their 0 s to 10 s are set to display their height in a smaller size.

3 Experiment

3.1 Experimental Purpose and Hypothesis

In this experiment, we investigated the effects of differences in the presentation of human-shaped objects on the willingness to visit a spot. For this purpose, we evaluate the following hypotheses, H1 and H2, in this experiment:

H1 The interest in the spot is enhanced by the presentation of human-shaped objects with attribute information.

H2 The psychological cost of entering a spot is reduced by the presentation of human-shaped objects with attribute information.

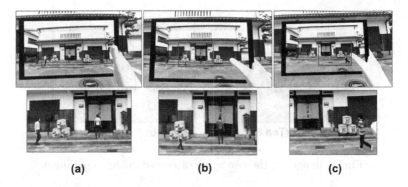

Fig. 4. The contents presented in each condition of the experiment. The group of images in the lower row are enlarged images of the upper row (the enlarged position is indicated by the red-framed rectangle). (Color figure online)

3.2   Experimental Settings

As participants, 20 university students (17 males and, 3 females) were recruited. They were asked to wear head mounted display (HMD) and view the omni-directional video of a sightseeing spot in the experimental environment described above. For this purpose, we set the following comparison conditions:

Condition I. Without the system: Scenario without the virtual tablet.

Condition II. With humanoid CG: Scenario with the virtual tablet and with humanoid CG objects presented but without reflecting attribute information (Fig. 4 (a)).

Condition III. With Humanoid CG and visitors' attributes: Scenario with virtual tablet and with humanoid CG objects reflecting previous visitors' attribute information (Fig. 4 (b)).

In Condition I, the participant can only view an omni-directional video of the spot, and they cannot experience the proposed system. In contrast, Condition II and III allow the use of a virtual tablet during the experience. Conditions II (Fig. 4(a)) and III (Fig. 4 (b)) differ in whether the attributes are reflected on the human-shaped objects in the virtual tablet. In Condition II, all humanoid objects that appear are wearing white clothing and their size is equal. On the other hand, in Condition III, information on the age and gender of past visitors is represented on humanoid objects by color and size.

In the experiment, the videos of the spot were recorded in advance using an omni-directional camera (THETA SC2, RICOH Inc, resolution: 3840×1920, 29.97 frames per second). These videos contain views of a sightseeing spot where Japanese traditional architecture is present, and the different spots are used as the objects for experiment. The degree of interest in the spots may vary depending on each participant's preferences. Therefore, to enable the experiment to proceed for spots in which participants are interested, we prepared videos of two different spots, α and, β, shown in Fig. 5. Then, we asked participants to select one spot of interest prior to the experiment and used the selected video in

Spot α (Tea Shop)   **Spot β (Brewery)**

Fig. 5. Images of the two spots discussed in the experiment

the experiment. Therefore, the visibility experienced in this experiment differed according to the interests of the participants.

In addition to the factors related to the information presentation method, we also set up two-level comparison conditions based on the presence or absence of an actual visitor, since the impression of a spot is considered to change depending on whether actual visitor is shown in the video. We examined the influence of the presence of an actual visitor to α and β in the omni-directional video of each spot by noting where an actual visitor appeared and where no one appeared. Figure 4 (c) shows an example of a view of the experimental system in the case where the actual visitor is shown in the omni-directional video. Thus, this experiment is designed with a two-factor intra-participant design with a two-level factor for the presence or absence of actual visitor in the video and a three-level factor for the information presentation pattern. Participants were asked to perform a total of six trials combining three patterns (I. without the system/II. with humanoid CG/III. with humanoid CG + attribute) and two types of videos(A: "no actual visitor"/B: "with actual visitor") to be compared. For the sake of a counterbalance, the order of the experiences was switched for each participant based on the four experimental patterns shown in Table. 1.

The attribute information of the human-shaped object presented in Condition III was set as a controlled fictitious context that was not based on actual visit information. To be precise, we specified that there would be six men and women in their 0 s to 30 s in Video A (no actual visitor condition) and six men and women in their 40 s to 70 s in Video B (with the actual visitor condition). In Conditions II and III, an animation of six human-shaped objects walking toward the spot in sequence was overlapped on the video. The length of each video and the duration of each experiment was set to 30 s.

3.3   Evaluation Metrics

After each trial, the participants were asked to respond to a questionnaire that asked about their impressions of the spot and their desire to visit it. After experiencing the system in each condition, the participants were asked to answer the 10 questions shown in Tables 2 and 3. In addition, after experiencing Condition III, participants were asked to answer the questions shown in Table 3 to investigate the characteristics of the presentation of attribute information. Q1–8, 9,

Table 1. The order (pattern) of the system experience of the participants in this experiment. "A:(II)" indicates that the visitor experiences the information presentation method with humanoid CG (Condition II) in Video A ("no actual visitor" condition).

Pattern	Trial 1	Trial 2	Trial 3	Trial 4	Trial 5	Trial 6
i	A:(I)	A:(II)	A:(III)	B:(I)	B:(II)	B:(III)
ii	B:(I)	B:(II)	B:(III)	A:(I)	A:(II)	A:(III)
iii	A:(I)	A:(III)	A:(II)	B:(I)	B:(III)	B:(II)
iv	B:(I)	B:(III)	B:(II)	A:(I)	A:(III)	A:(II)

Table 2. Question items Q1–Q8 for the questionnaire. These questions are based on the 7-point Semantic Differential (SD) scale.

No	Question
1	Lonely – Lively
2	Anxious – Secure
3	Cluttered – Orderly
4	Dark – Light
5	Boring – Fun
6	Disappointing – Intriguing
7	Empty – Full
8	Unattractive – Attractive

and 10 in Tables 2 and 3 are common questions asked after all experiments, they and asked about the impression, interest, and ease of visiting the spots using the 7-point semantic differential (SD) and Likert scale (1: not applicable at all to 7: very applicable), respectively. After the experience with Condition III, we asked Q11–13 in Table 4 about the degree of understanding of the presentation of attribute information and its relationship to the ease of entering the spot. Q11 asked about the degree of understanding of the customer base on a 6-point Likert scale (i.e., a 7-point Likert scale, excluding "neither"). Q12 asked the respondents who answered "4" or more in the affirmative (i.e., those who correctly identified the clientele) about the age of the humanoid model presented to them. This question had the following three options: "Most of the respondents were in their 40 s or older," "Most of the respondents were in their 30 s or younger," or "Not sure."

Table 3. Question items Q9–Q10 for the questionnaire. These questions are based on the 7-point Likert scale.

No	Question
9	Did you like to enter the spot?
10	Did you feel this spot easy to enter?

Table 4. Question items Q11–Q13 for the questionnaire. These questions are only asked after the experience of Condition III.

No	Question	How to answer
11	Have you identified the visitor's attribution of this spot?	6-point scale
12	Please select one item that applies to the displayed CG humanoid models	3-choice question
13	Did knowing the visitor's attribution affect the ease of entering the spot?	7-point scale

3.4 Procedure

At the beginning of the experiment, the participants granted informed consent after being made aware of health considerations about the VR experience. We obtained their agreement to participate in the experiment. After the participants were instructed to put on the HMD, they were asked to confirm the system operation for 30 s in the VR space for practice, which displayed an omni directional image containing scenes unrelated to the spot presented in the experiment and a static CG human-shaped object. In this case, the participants were asked to confirm that the controller corresponded to the virtual tablet in the VR space and that the CG human-shaped object was visible through it. We then presented images of the two spots shown in Fig. 5 and asked the participants to select the spot they were interested in. Thereafter, we started the first trial using the images of the selected spots. The trial was conducted six times in total, with the participants repeatedly experiencing the system and answering a questionnaire while changing the conditions in the order shown in Table 1.

4 Results

4.1 Evaluation of Impressions of the Spot

The average score for each question was calculated for each factor based on the presence or absence of an actual visitor and the presentation method of the humanoid model. A one-way Friedman test based on the presentation method was then performed to verify the difference in mean score based on differences in the method. In addition, a multiple comparison test based on the Steele-Douwas method was also performed for the questions for which a main effect was found. Figure 6 shows the average scores for each method of experiencing the system for Q1–8, by condition, with and without an actual visitor. Table 5 shows the results of the Friedman and multiple comparison test. In addition, box plot diagrams showing the trend of scores for Q9 and 10 are shown in Fig. 7. In the following, we will discuss the results of the experiment with and without actual visitor.

Results with No Actual Visitor. In the trial without actual visitor in the video, the mean scores of the SD-based questions Q1–8 were (1) < (2) < (3) for all items except for Q3, "Cluttered – Orderly". Thus, it is suggested that the impression evaluation of the spot tends to become more positive by adding the

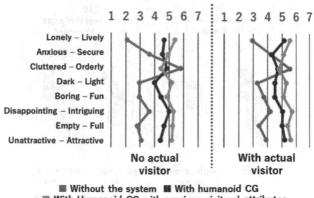

Fig. 6. Results of responses to Q1–8 in the questionnaire listed in Table 3.

Table 5. Results of Friedman and multiple comparison tests for the answers to questions 1–8 (** : $p<.01$, * : $p<.05$, n.s. : no significant difference).

Question	No actual visitor			With actual visitor		
	$(1)\times(2)$	$(1)\times(3)$	$(2)\times(3)$	$(1)\times(2)$	$(1)\times(3)$	$(2)\times(3)$
Lonely – Lively	**	**	n.s.	**	**	n.s.
Anxious – Secure	n.s.	*	n.s.	n.s.	n.s.	n.s.
Cluttered – Orderly	*	**	n.s.	n.s.	n.s.	n.s.
Dark – Light	n.s.	**	*	**	**	n.s.
Boring – Fun	*	**	n.s.	n.s.	**	n.s.
Disappointing – Intriguing	*	**	n.s.	n.s.	**	n.s.
Empty – Full	**	**	n.s.	**	**	n.s.
Unattractive – Attractive	*	**	n.s.	**	**	n.s.

humanoid model and its attributes. However, the mean score of Q3, "Cluttered – Orderly" was $(3) < (2) < (1)$, which was the opposite of the other items. This may be due to the increased amount of information on the screen that results from layering humanoid CG models and adding attributes such as color and size.

Between Conditions I and II, significant differences were found except on, Q2, "Anxious – Secure" and Q4, "Dark – Light". These results indicate that even a simple human-type presentation had some effect on the improvement of the impression evaluation of the spot. Furthermore, between Conditions I and III, there was a significant difference in all adjective pairs. Thus, it was found that adding attribute information to the human models improved the impression of the spot, including items related to "anxiety" and "brightness," which were not improved by only presenting the models. In particular, a significant difference was observed between Condition II and III for Q4, "Dark – Light". This suggests that the presentation of the humanoid CG model with colors gives a better impression of the spot as well as attribute information.

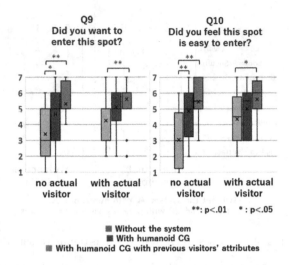

Fig. 7. Results of responses to Q9–10 in the questionnaire (** : p<.01, * : p<.05).

In the results for both questions Q9 and Q10, the difference in scores was significant between Conditions I – II, and I – III, respectively. These results indicate that the presentation of human-shaped objects is useful in arousing interest in entering and the perception of ease of entry, and the effect is further enhanced by the addition of attribute information. Therefore, the results support Hypotheses H1 and H2 under the condition of there being no actual visitor in this experiment.

Results with Actual Visitor. Similarly, in the condition with actual visitor, the mean scores were (1) < (2) < (3) for all items except for Q3, "Cluttered – Orderly". This indicates that even when the presence of actual visitor is felt, the impression evaluation becomes more positive by presenting visitor's information via the human-shaped model with attributes. In Q3, "Cluttered – Orderly", Condition II produced the greatest "clutter" impression, unlike the no actual visitor condition. However, there was no significant difference among conditions in terms of information presentation.

In the condition with actual visitor, unlike the condition "no actual visitor", the mean score for Condition I increased in Q2 "Anxious – Secure". However, it was not significantly different from the scores for Conditions II and III with actual visitor. Moreover, the difference between Condition I and II was not observed in Q6, "Disappointing – Intriguing" in the "with actual visitor" condition.

In the results for both questions Q9 and Q10, significant differences were found only between Condition I and III. In the Q9, where there was no actual visitor, there was a significant difference between Condition I and II, but not in the condition "with actual visitor". These results indicate that the feeling of the presence of real humans who are trying to enter a spot just like users has

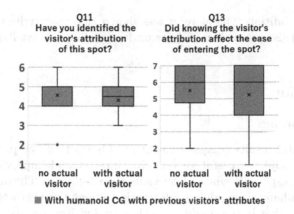

Fig. 8. Results of responses to questions 11 and 13 specific to Condition III.

a strong effect on the perception of safety and interest in the spot. From the results, it is also observed that the presence of visitors affected the presentation performance of the proposed method and the effect on the willingness to enter the spot is reduced. However, this result does not indicate that the effect of the proposed method disappears due to the presence of real visitors. For example, the difference between Condition I and III is significant for the Q6, "Disappointing – Intriguing" result and questions Q9 and Q10. Since the differences between Condition I and III are significant for questions Q9 and Q10, the results indicate that the provision of attribute information by a single current visitor and a group of past visitors with different characteristics works to arouse interest and increase "ease of entry". Thus, although the effect of the information is weaker in the "with actual visitor" condition than in the "no actual visitor" condition, the results support Hypotheses H1 and H2.

4.2 Evaluation of Information Provided by the System

Figure 8 shows the trend in scores for questions 11 and 13 for Condition III. For question 11, "Have you identified the visitor's attribution of this spot?", 18 out of 20 participants in the "no actual visitor" condition and 17 in the "with actual visitor" condition responded affirmatively with a score of 4 or higher. Theses results indicate that most participants understood the representation of the attributes based on the color and height of the humanoid CG model. To verify the correctness of their understanding, question 12 asked about the age of the displayed CG human-shaped models. As a result, In the "no actual visitor" condition, 15 out of 18 respondents answered correctly, two answered incorrectly, and one answered "Not sure" (correct response rate: 83.3%). In the condition "with actual visitor", 12 out of 17 respondents answered correctly, four answered incorrectly, and one answered "Not sure" (correct response rate: 70.6%). Thus, more than 70% of the participants were able to guess the visitor's attributes even in the experimental setting in which they paid attention to their surroundings, as in the visitor condition. Therefore, it was shown that the attribute presentation method using this system is useful for understanding the attributes of visitors in a spot.

5   Discussion

5.1   Our Findings

The experimental results suggest two things. One is that the presentation of a human-shaped object is useful for arousing interest and improving the ease of entering a spot, especially when a user visits the spot alone. The other is that the effect can be enhanced by adding information about the visitor's attributes. It should be noted that in the condition with actual visitor, the score in Condition I increased overall, and the score in Condition II was almost the same as in Condition I. This suggests that the mere addition of a CG representation of other visitors in the presence of other visitors is not sufficient to arouse interest and dispel the apprehension about entering the spot. On the other hand, the presentation in Condition II improved the ease of entering the spot regardless of the presence or absence of visitors. In other words, these results indicate that the presentation of past visitor's attributes can be a factor in providing an atmosphere of other visitors that cannot be provided only by presenting the social presence of others. Therefore, this presentation approach based on attributes is effective for improving the ease of entering the spot even in situations where there is a strong sense of the presence of others in the real world.

The experimental results also suggest that the presence of real-world visitor has a strong effect on improving impressions of a spot. Specially, for many of the scores in the "with actual visitor" condition, the difference between the scores in the "no actual visitor" condition and the "with actual visitor" condition was smaller than in the "no actual visitor" condition. This result suggests that the presence of actual humans attenuated the presentation effect of the system. This indicates that there is still a gap in the strength of the "attraction" to a spot between the CG humanoid model and the real visitor. Therefore, our findings may contribute to providing quantitative data on the difference in attraction ability between CG and realistic humans. As mentioned earlier, the experiment was conducted in a VR environment. However, the difference between CG models and actual humans may be more pronounced in the real world situation, where social presence is felt more acutely. Therefore, the results in this paper are not sure to support the same conclusions as those in the real world. However, the results in this paper show the potential of such CG humanoid models to support solitary users as a means of stimulating interest and motivation to visit in destinations where there are no visitors around.

5.2   Limitations

One of the limitations of the discussion in this paper is that this experiment was conducted in a VR environment, and the effects of the experiment in a real-world environment have not been studied. In addition, the present study was conducted by using fictitious visitor's attribution information. Thus, further research is needed to clarify whether it is effective by using actual customer information. On the other hand, from our experimental result, it is shown that this information presentation method may be useful in a solitary environment without the presence of others, and in electronic guidance using video images to enhance interest and visitation.

6   Conclusion

In this paper, we proposed an AR application that aims to eliminate the psychological reluctance to enter a place when visiting for the first time. This application allows the user to know the information about visitors (number of people and attribute) who have visited a spot in the past through a visualization mechanism in which a CG human-shaped object is overlapped on the image of a spot captured by the camera on the visitor's personal terminal. To test the effectiveness of the proposed application in a controlled environment, we developed an experimental system in which users could experience the application by operating a virtual tablet in a VR space. The experimental results showed that superimposing CG human-shaped objects with motion and attribute information overlapping on the spot images contributes to the psychological ease of visiting spots and increases the desire to visit. In the future, we plan to conduct experiments at real spots to verify the effectiveness of the system.

References

1. Chahal, H., Devi, A.: Destination attributes and destination image relationship in volatile tourist destination: role of perceived risk. Metamorphosis 14(2), 1–19 (2015). https://doi.org/10.1177/0972622520150203
2. Harrell, G.D., Hutt, M.D., Anderson, J.C.: Path analysis of buyer behavior under conditions of crowding. J. Mark. Res. 17(1), 45–51 (1980). https://doi.org/10.1177/002224378001700105
3. Hui, S.K., Bradlow, E.T., Fader, P.S.: Testing behavioral hypotheses using an integrated model of grocery store shopping path and purchase behavior. J. Consum. Res. 36(3), 478–493 (2009). https://doi.org/10.1086/599046
4. Kinoshita, Y., Tsukanaka, S., Go, K.: Strolling with street atmosphere visualization: development of a tourist support system. In: CHI 2013 Extended Abstracts on Human Factors in Computing Systems, CHI EA 2013, pp. 553–558. Association for Computing Machinery, New York (2013). https://doi.org/10.1145/2468356.2468454
5. Traunmueller, M., Fatah gen. Schieck, A., Schöning, J., Brumby, D.: The path is the reward: Considering social networks to contribute to the pleasure of urban strolling. In: CHI 2013 Extended Abstracts on Human Factors in Computing Systems, CHI EA 2013, pp. 919–924. Association for Computing Machinery, New York (2013). https://doi.org/10.1145/2468356.2468520
6. Wong, J.Y., Yeh, C.: Tourist hesitation in destination decision making. Ann. Tour. Res. 36(1), 6–23 (2009). https://doi.org/10.1016/j.annals.2008.09.005

Virtual Construction Simulation: Evaluating Impact of Immersion and Interactivity on Novice Designers

Stella Quinto Lima[1]([envelope]) [iD], Bimal Balakrishnan[2] [iD], and Jong Bum Kim[1] [iD]

[1] University of Missouri, Columbia, MO 65211, USA
{sqkqr,kimjongb}@umsystem.edu
[2] Mississippi State University, Starkville, MS 39762, USA
bbalakrishnan@caad.msstate.edu

Abstract. Typical curricula in architecture include history and theory, design studios, structures, and building construction courses. While studio classes mainly use active forms of learning, building construction courses often rely on passive techniques . Active forms of teaching with greater student interaction with learning content have shown better learning outcomes and more inclusive toward those on a different learning spectrum. Thus, creating meaningful hands-on experiences for students to learn building construction is crucial. Drawing on theories related to media psychology, human-computer interaction, and architectural education, this study aims to understand the impact of immersion and interactivity on the learning experience and knowledge gained by building construction students. The study was designed as a full-factorial, 2 (high vs. low immersion) × 2 (high vs. low interactivity) experiment. Participants were randomly assigned to one of four groups and learned how to assemble a bus shelter in virtual reality. The learning experience was measured through questionnaires that assessed their spatial presence, attention, engagement, and knowledge gain to increase accuracy. Their knowledge gain was measured through a questionnaire that included cued and free recall tasks, labeling of building components, identifying correct connections between components, and a detailed drawing task. The study's results provide insights into the relative contributions of various technology affordances and how they impact learning experiences and outcomes. The authors believe that understanding these nuances will allow for the customization of technology affordances to achieve desired learning outcomes, thus making virtual reality a more effective tool for teaching building construction.

Keywords: Virtual Reality · Building Systems · Interactive Simulation

1 Introduction

Educating architecture students about building construction techniques and processes is an integral part of their education, but it is a challenging endeavor for multiple reasons. These include, but are not limited to, the challenge of visiting active site constructions with projects relevant to the class, accessibility, and safety issues [1]. As a

© The Author(s), under exclusive license to Springer Nature Switzerland AG 2023
J. Y. C. Chen and G. Fragomeni (Eds.): HCII 2023, LNCS 14027, pp. 678–690, 2023.
https://doi.org/10.1007/978-3-031-35634-6_49

result, newly graduated architects often fail to meet employers' expectations regarding their knowledge of construction [2]. Current educational approaches mainly rely on 2D images that students often cannot fully comprehend [3, 4]. In recent studies, immersive virtual reality (VR) has shown promise [1, 5], but the relative contributions of its technology affordances, such as immersion or interactivity, on learning outcomes are still unclear. Therefore, this study aims to understand which aspects of VR media contribute to students' better understanding of construction subjects. Through a controlled experiment, we sought to answer the following question, "How do the level of immersion and interactivity impact the experience and knowledge gained by building construction students?"

Virtual reality can create two types of immersion: physical and psychological [6]. The first one is easier since the headset already manipulates vision, audio, and the haptic feeling with the controller. However, when changing perceived surrounding cues (such as noise, the field of view (FOV), and embodied navigation (EN)), the VR user will feel more immersed in the environment [6]. Immersive experiences, according to Winn et al. [7], increase participant engagement. Perceptual immersion appeals to the users' senses, inviting them to explore the new reality they are immersed in.

Furthermore, some people find it difficult to feel absorbed without sensory stimulation. As a result, the VR headset will operate as a shield against real-world distractions, allowing the user to concentrate on the task at hand. Interactivity is associated with the amount of interaction between people or people and content. In VR technologies, interactivity is usually considered from a recreational or enjoyment perspective, but it also has significant applications for learning [8]. Lee et al. [9] and Khoshnevisasl et al. [10] observed that more interactive applications increased engagement, attention, and positive learning outcomes. This paper also expands on earlier work by drawing on theoretical foundations from psychology, human factors, and usability research.

We developed a VR simulation prototype to teach building systems and construction techniques that can accommodate different learning spectrums. The simulation provides a first-person, immersive, and interactive experience for learning building systems and construction detailing that gives the students several ways to prototype and receive information. Students can study the assemblage of an existing bus shelter with a unique design in virtual reality.

2 Literature Review

2.1 Students' Learning Traits

Architecture requires professionals to be proficient in different fields of study to meet the challenges faced when designing and constructing buildings [11]. The coursework is divided between design studios, theoretical, and technical courses to impart multidisciplinary skills. During their undergraduate years, they develop skills such as spatial visualization, building construction, and time management that are not always in class. One important factor influencing a student's skill development is their learning traits. Felder & Silverman's [12] theory of learning styles and D'souza's [11] adaptation of Gardner's [13] multiple intelligences theory within the context of architecture suggest that students learn through different modalities and different processes.

Felder & Silverman [12] divide learning styles into four dimensions, each subdivided into two categories. A student can be placed in one category for each of the four dimensions. They are sensing and intuitive; visual and verbal; active and reflective; and sequential and global learners [12, p. 678]. Sensing learners collect data through their senses by observing and touching, while intuitive learners collect information by their perception and speculation [12, p. 676], [14, p. 22]. Visual students learn from graphics, images, and demonstrations, while verbal learners learn mainly through verbal communication, textbooks, and auditory lectures [14]. Active learners need to experience the information in the real world to understand it, and reflective learners must observe applications and have time to contemplate the information. Sequential learners acquire knowledge at a steady pace in an orderly manner, while global learners do not learn in a specific order [12, p. 679; 14, p. 25]. Gardner [13] suggests that intelligence should be considered a multidimensional set of cognitive abilities. D'souza [11] builds on Gardner's idea to suggest that architectural education should take advantage of these different dimensions, such as bodily-kinesthetic intelligence, to enhance learning. Taken together, these learning theories suggest great potential for emerging technologies such as VR to have a significant impact on learning.

2.2 Teaching Methodologies

The most common approach to teaching is lecture-based, which prioritizes an instructor-centered system that first passively provides all the learning material and later tests students with various forms of assessment such as assignments or tests. Instructors that use this technique assume that their students do not need to be active to understand the topic in the study [15]. Therefore, this is a passive teaching method. In contrast, we have seen the emergence of many active teaching methods, such as problem-based, inquiry-based, and experiential-based learning. These methodologies have the common characteristic of helping the student's learning process by encouraging them to be active. Problem-based learning usually prioritizes smaller classes. The instructor introduces a problem that the students independently research and tackle or collaborate with their peers to learn the topic at hand [16, p. 328]. The professor's task here is to guide and narrow the focus area to prevent information overload [16, 17].

There is an emerging consensus that active teaching methods are better than passive ones. For example, when Khoshnevisasl et al. [10] compared two groups of students, one receiving instructions through lecture-based learning and the other using problem-based learning, the latter group performed better [10]. Yoon and D'Souza [18] and Felder and Silverman [12] also support using a problem-based approach to teaching. Felder and Silverman [12] emphasize that some students who are different from others on the learning spectrum have issues comprehending information with passive teaching methodologies. For instance, active or reflective learners struggle with lecture-based learning as it does not allow the students to be active or have moments to reflect on the information they are receiving [12, p. 678]. Visual, global, and sensing students also struggle to learn with traditional teaching approaches [11, p. 678]. Thus, Felder and Silverman [12] and D'souza [11] affirm that the current educational system privileges one set of students over others, and active teaching methodologies might be the solution for a more inclusive classroom.

2.3 Building Systems Education

Architectural education is known for the studio-based pedagogy that can be seen as a particular type of problem-based learning and simulate the design process in a professional architectural firm. Another set of courses crucial for architectural education is the building construction courses that essentially introduce how various building components are assembled [19]. Ideally, the curriculum for such courses should include taking students on in-person site visits to analyze real structures and learn how they are constructed. Hands-on interactions are essential to improving knowledge of construction methods and help in the development of spatial visualization skills [20]. However, giving that opportunity may not be possible in most situations. The most common challenges are weather, safety issues on construction sites, classes with many students, or lack of valuable building examples [1, 20]. To fill the gap, instructors rely on slideshows and handbooks composed of 2D images and verbal information [3, 4]. On the other hand, the students still need to develop the necessary visualization skills to understand the underlying details of various building components and their connections. Also, when such courses rely heavily on lecture-based content, they disadvantage students with different learning styles. This creates a problem since most architecture students tend to be active learners [21]. As a result, many new architecture graduates fail to meet employers' expectations regarding construction process knowledge and accurate representation in construction documents [2].

2.4 Inclusive Teaching Media

A teaching methodology considering multiple intelligences and learning styles is fundamental to ensuring positive learning outcomes. Instructors can apply some pedagogical techniques to the lectures to enhance learning, such as: connecting the current subjects to what was studied before; providing factual and theoretical content in equal proportions; providing time for reflection and hands-on activities; using graphic aids in text and lectures; show the desired outcome of the topic and give the sequential explanation about it [12, 14]. Yoon and D'souza [18] suggested adapting problem-based learning to the student's needs by considering students' cognitive styles.

In those cases, virtual reality (VR) applications might be the ideal medium for building construction education since it eliminates obstacles and give students valuable hands-on experience, even though it is simulated. For example, schedule, weather, and safety hazards on building sites would not be a problem because the class would not need to leave the school. The number of students would also not be an issue because the professor can manage usage time and the number of headsets necessary for the course. This approach gives students valuable material in a medium that aligns with architectural students' learning styles. Therefore, the next section will analyze how instructors can use VR in architecture and construction education and the main characteristics that make it a valuable tool to aid student knowledge.

2.5 Virtual Reality Aid to Building Systems Education

Due to safety issues, class sizes, schedule problems, or lack of construction sites related to their studies [1], fewer and fewer programs can take students to construction sites to learn about building systems. Latta and Oberg [22] suggest that VR provides the opportunity to have a significant experience in a realistic virtual environment that people hardly have access to in the real world. The crucial aspect is that VR must provide an authentic experience, though many fail [22]. VR technologies have great potential to be used as educational tools, especially for architectural education. Researchers are already assessing the benefits of VR in different aspects of architectural education. An example is VRConDet [1], which aims to substitute on-site visits with guided tours of construction sites filmed in real-time. This method could solve the challenges of exposing real-world construction techniques and bringing real-life quality information to the students. Studies about the use of VR applied to education often state positive results. However, the relative contributions of its technology affordances on learning outcomes are still unclear. When teaching, the goal is to catch the student's attention, engage them in the content and maintain their focus. It is theorized that the immersion and interactivity of VR technologies are linked with better attention, engagement, spatial visualization, and knowledge gain levels. Therefore, it is crucial to understand the theory and past research on these two affordances.

Immersion. Immersion is a crucial affordance of virtual reality technology, and it accomplishes it through two channels: perceptual and psychological [6]. Bowman and McMahan's [23] research mentions that different human senses, such as auditory, proprioceptive, and visual senses, are linked to the feeling of immersion. The VR headsets influence the senses significantly since the display usually covers the user's eyes and visual field, headphones limit outside noise, and a haptic sensation from the controllers provides tactile feedback. However, the VR user will feel more immersed in the virtual environment when manipulating perceived surrounding cues (noise, the field of view, and navigation, for example). This study will focus on the visual and proprioceptive senses, concentrating on perceptual immersion.

The visual sense is characterized by the field of view (FoV), and the proprioceptive sense will be the navigation style (static/dynamic). The FoV is the area people can see in their direct and peripheral vision. A human usually has an FoV of 200 ° horizontally and 135 vertically [24]. Thus, the closer a VR headset can reach the human FoV, the better the immersion. There are many studies about the implications of FoV on immersion. They point out that VR headsets with wider FoV enhance immersion and while it is weaker in headsets with narrow FoV [25–27]. FoV also plays a part in achieving a sense of spatial presence. Wider FoV provides more environmental cues and suppresses outside stimuli [6]. In an early VR study [28], participants had a better memory of virtual environments when they were more immersed.

Proprioception is characterized by the self-perception of position, movement, and balance [29, p. 667]. Vision can trigger proprioceptive information when providing a virtual body and ambient cues. The brain can calculate the body's position relative to its surrounding environment [29]. An alternative is to provide environmental information, such as room corners or other details, so people can locate themselves to move around the environment [30]. Embodiment is essential to understand the world around us, and embodied navigation (EN) is closely related to memory, as was pointed out in studies by Buzsáki and Moser [31] and Leutgeb et al. [32].

Also, EN plays a part in the perceived actions that the user can have in a virtual environment which affects another dimension of this study: spatial presence [33, 34]. However, to internalize the possible actions of the simulation, the user needs to have minimal influence from the real world [35]. The subjects need to focus on what the virtual environment provides to assimilate the virtual body as their own. The more at ease the user feels with its motions and self-location, the more engaged the user becomes with the simulation. Therefore, with active EN and a wider FoV, we can predict that the spatial presence of the user will increase. Consequently, this will enhance engagement and attention toward the simulation, aiding the students' knowledge gain. Therefore, we can hypothesize that greater levels of immersion will increase spatial presence and knowledge gain.

Interactivity. Steuer [36] defined it as the freedom of the user to modify the form and content in a virtual environment. In VR technologies, interactivity is usually advertised for recreational purposes, but it also has significant applications for learning [8]. As discussed earlier, students are more successful when taught through active forms of learning [10], and many schools adapt their subjects to promote interaction with learning content. Recent studies have explored the gamification of education and how interactivity promotes engagement, attention, and learning [9, 37–39]. Sherman and Craig's [40] work suggests that engagement is key to virtual environment's success. Thus, if interactivity options in the simulation attract the user, it will be engaging. Barata et al. [41] described how the gamification of the class content led to greater student engagement. Steuer [36] also mentions that the user will achieve telepresence in a virtual environment if they have more freedom to move and interact with the environment around them. The presence will intensify if they have a task to complete in the simulation. Based on the information above, we can assume that interactivity will affect students' engagement and attention, leading to increased spatial presence and knowledge gain. Thus, the second hypothesis of this study is that greater levels of interactivity will positively affect spatial presence and knowledge gain.

3 Methodology

3.1 Research Design and Research Question

This research aims to assess the impact and relative contribution of immersion and interactivity of VR applications on students' learning about building construction. The study is designed as a 2 (high vs. low immersion) × 2 (high vs. low interactivity), full-factorial, controlled experiment. Their impact on engagement, attention, and knowledge gain is systematically measured. The primary research question in this study is: How do the level of immersion and interactivity impact the student's experience and knowledge gain?

3.2 Methods

Voluntary participants (N = 54) aged between 19 and 37 (M = 20.77, SD = 2.73) were recruited from an undergraduate design program at a large public university in the midwestern United States. All students were either enrolled in or had previously completed

the Building Systems course. Most of the participants were female (75%). Each participant experienced the virtual reality simulation individually and was randomly assigned
to one of the four experimental conditions. The participant was then briefed about the
study protocol and obtained informed consent. Each participant experienced the virtual
reality simulation corresponding to the experimental condition for an adequate time.
Then, they completed questionnaires and assessment tasks that measured their knowledge of what they learned through the simulation. After the study, the participant was
debriefed and thanked. Their responses were entered into a dataset, and paper-based
questionnaires were stored securely.

3.3 Experimental Stimuli

The Immersive Building System simulation (IBS) was created for this study. The IBS
is meant to be used by students as a construction guide to help them understand simple
building construction principles. Students could examine the assembly of a bus stop in a
virtual construction shop. The same structure was built physically by different students
in a previous semester. The simulation has four distinct scenarios corresponding to the
differing levels of Immersion and Interactivity. Participants were randomly allocated
to one of four groups to undergo the simulation (High Immersion and High Interactivity; High Immersion and Low Interactivity; Low Immersion and High Interactivity;
Low Immersion, Low Interactivity). Following the IBS simulation, individuals completed a questionnaire that measured their spatial presence, attention, engagement, and
knowledge gain.

3.4 Operationalization of Independent Variables

This experiment design had two independent variables based on the literature review
conducted for this study: immersion and interactivity. For this study, immersion was
manipulated through the visual and proprioceptive senses. The first uses different FOVs,
and the second uses different EN styles (static/dynamic). Field of View (FOV) and
Embodied Navigation (EN) were used to alter the first variable. The HTC Vive Pro
head-mounted display and controllers were used to implement the simulation. In the
high immersion condition, the horizontal FOV is 82.3°, the vertical FOV is 81.9°, and
the EN is dynamic because of the body motion tracking. In the low immersion condition,
the horizontal FOV is 72.9°, the vertical FOV is 71.7°, and the EN is passive, and
movement was achieved by teleportation using a button in the controller. The low-
interaction condition included seven pop-ups with information regarding the bus stop
building process and four animations showing the step-by-step procedure (See Fig. 1).
The "Do it Yourself" button is added to the high interactivity condition, allowing students
to build the bus stop from the ground up in the virtual environment (See Fig. 2).

3.5 Dependent Variables

Spatial Presence. The goal of the simulation was to locate the user in a construction
site and enable them to engage in the experience of assembling building components to

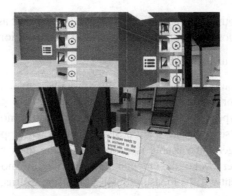

Fig. 1. Low Interactivity Condition

Fig. 2. High Interactivity Condition

form a structure. The VR technology shielded the student from the immediate physical environment and provided an experience similar to being at a construction site. Spatial presence was thus an essential aspect of the learning experience. Spatial presence was measured using MEC Spatial Presence Questionnaire [42].

Knowledge Gain. It is assumed that when the participants are engaged and attentive to the task, they will gain more knowledge. A questionnaire structured in a way similar to an in-class multiple-choice quiz was used to assess knowledge gain. It included information presented in the simulation. Another question asked the students to correctly identify all the tools used to construct the bus shelter. The next set of multiple choice asked students to identify the correct 3-dimensional rendering of the bus shelter from multiple perspectives and identify the accurate 2-dimensional section drawings. The last open-ended question asked the participants to draw exact details of the bus shelter by hand.

The scoring rubric for the open-ended question considered four aspects: drawing scale, line weight, usage of correct symbols, and material differentiation with hatches.

Additional Variables of Interest.

Engagement. The prototype aimed to aid the students' understanding of structures. However, the instructor must make it engaging for students to pay attention to a new subject. A VR prototype was developed because VR is still a novelty that catches the students' attention. Also, the gamification of the subject was appealing to the younger generation. The engagement variable is connected to the immersion and interactivity variables. So, the higher level of the independent variables, the more engaging the application. The engagement will be measured using O'Brien, Cairns, and Hall's [43] User engagement scale (UES).

Attention. With engagement, the students focused on the information being shown in the prototype. Thus, they pay attention to what they interact with in the simulation. The students' self-report attention to the application was used to define attention. It was measured using three 9-point scale statements from MEC Spatial Presence Questionnaire [42] adapted for this experiment.

Demographic Variables. Besides the measures used for attention, engagement, spatial presence, and knowledge gain, we also gathered self-report data on demographic variables. The information collected included gender, age, academic standing, undergraduate year, the overall experience in using simulations, and experience with various 3D software. In addition, they answered about their previous knowledge (or work) in architecture or similar areas.

Procedure. With approval from the Institutional Research Board (IRB), participants were recruited from a design department's undergraduate program in the midwestern United States. Upon the participant's arrival on the scheduled day, they were briefed about the study procedure and signed the informed consent form. Participants were randomly assigned to one of the four experimental conditions. First, they completed the demographic portion of the questionnaire. Before the simulation, they received instructions about using the HTC Vive controllers. Once comfortable with the VR headset and controllers, participants were given ten minutes to use the IBS. After exploring the simulation, they completed the second part of the questionnaire that measured their sense of presence and questions on knowledge gain.

4 Data Analysis

4.1 Index Construction and Preparation for Data Analysis

Individual items on the respective scales were averaged to construct indices for various dependent and control variables. These indices for also evaluated for their reliability. The self-location (Four items; Cronbach's $\alpha = 0.91$) and possibility for actions (Four items; Cronbach's $\alpha = 0.88$) showed good reliability. Similarly, engagement items measured using the User Engagement scale were organized into four indices corresponding to the four factors; (Reward factor, three items; Cronbach's $\alpha = 0.85$; Focused Attention, three items, Cronbach's $\alpha = 0.66$; Aesthetic appeal, three items, Cronbach's $\alpha = 0.70$; Perceived usability, three items, Cronbach's $\alpha = 0.68$) and attention (Three items; Cronbach's $\alpha = 0.94$) also showed good reliability. Higher Cognitive Involvement was measured using two items which were averaged to create the score. The four experimental conditions had more or less equal numbers of participants. All assumptions were checked to ensure satisfaction before undertaking statistical tests discussed in the next section. One outlier was removed based on the Mahalanobis plot. The normality of the dependent variables was evaluated using skewness and kurtosis and was ensured to be within an acceptable range ($\pm/-2$). The homogeneity of variance was tested using Levene's test.

4.2 Summary of Results

Multiple factorial analysis of covariance (ANCOVA) tests were conducted to evaluate the impact of two independent variables, immersiveness, and interactivity, on various dimensions of spatial presence. On the *possibilities for action* dimension, there was a significant main effect for *interactivity*, $F (1, 46) = 4.40$, $p < .05$, partial $\text{eta}^2 = 0.09$. Participants in the high interactivity condition felt they had a greater possibility for action (adj. $M = 7.30$, $SE = 0.28$) compared to those in the low interactivity condition (adj. $M = 6.46$, $SE = 0.27$). For other dimensions of spatial presence, the ANCOVA models were not significant. For the *reward factor* dimension of O'Brien's user engagement scale, there was again a significant main effect for interactivity, $F (1, 49) = 7.53$, $p < .01$, partial $\text{eta}^2 = 0.13$. The participants in the high interactivity conditions perceived a greater reward (adj. $M = 4.64$, $SE = 0.14$) than those in the low interactivity condition (adj. $M = 4.12$, $SE = 0.13$). The most relevant measure of knowledge gain was the drawing task which the authors were still scoring and analyzing at the time of this publication. There were no significant results for the multiple-choice responses that captured participants' cued recall.

5   Discussion

5.1   Theoretical and Practical Implications

The significant results indicate that greater interactivity resulted in an enhanced perception of possibilities for action (one dimension of spatial presence) and a greater perception of reward by the student participants. These results suggest that greater interaction in an immersive learning platform such as virtual reality has the potential for an engaging learning experience in building construction. While the immersion variable did not yield significant results, it could be the case that even with a reduced FoV, VR head-mounted displays limited distracting stimuli from the immediate physical environment. Preliminary results from this study validate the potential for using VR for building construction education. VR opens up more opportunities for an innovative educational approach allowing virtual site visits to construction sites. It also shows the potential of VR as an engaging platform where future students could experiment and interactively learn about components and their connections in the context of construction. We believe VR can enhance learning outcomes for students across various learning styles. When interactivity is added to the simulation, it can lead to engaged learning and positive learning outcomes.

5.2 Limitations and Future Directions

This paper reports preliminary results from a controlled experiment. From a methodological perspective, two aspects of this study could be further refined or improved. First, a more nuanced operationalization and implementation of immersiveness could provide more insight into the impact of immersiveness on the sense of presence and knowledge gain. Second, knowledge gain could benefit from a more rigorous theoretical and operational definition and the development of measures. Future studies could extend this effort by examining the impact of immersion and interactivity on more complex construction scenarios.

References

1. ElGewely, M., Nadim, W.: Immersive virtual reality environment for construction detailing education using building information modeling (BIM). In: Panuwatwanich, K., Ko, C.-H. (eds.) The 10th International Conference on Engineering, Project, and Production Management. LNME, pp. 101–112. Springer, Singapore (2020). https://doi.org/10.1007/978-981-15-1910-9_9
2. Celadyn, W.: Architectural education to improve technical detailing in professional practice. Glob. J. Eng. Educ. **22**(1), 57–63 (2020)
3. Arslan, A.R., Dazkir, S.: Technical drafting and mental visualization in interior architecture education. Int. J. Scholarsh. Teach. Learn. **11**(2), n2 (2017)
4. Chen, C.-T., Chang, T.-W.: 1:1 spatially augmented reality design environment. In: Leeuwen, J.P., Timmermans, H.J.P. eds. Innovations in Design & Decision Support Systems in Architecture and Urban Planning, pp. 487–499. Springer, Dordrecht (2006). https://doi.org/10.1007/978-1-4020-5060-2_31
5. Rahimian, F.P., Ibrahim, R.: Impacts of VR 3D sketching on novice designers' spatial cognition in collaborative conceptual architectural design. Des. Stud. **32**(3), 255–291 (2011). https://doi.org/10.1016/j.destud.2010.10.003
6. Oprean, D.: Understanding the immersive experience: examining the influence of visual immersiveness and interactivity on spatial experiences and understanding. University of Missouri-Columbia (2015)
7. Winn, W., Windschitl, M., Fruland, R., Lee, Y.: When does immersion in a virtual environment help students construct understanding.In: Proceedings of the International Conference of the Learning Sciences, ICLS, vol. 206, pp. 497–503 (2002)
8. Roussou, M.: Learning by doing and learning through play: an exploration of interactivity in virtual environments for children. Comput. Entertain. CIE **2**(1), 10 (2004)
9. Lee, E.A.-L., Wong, K.W., Fung, C.C.: How does desktop virtual reality enhance learning outcomes? A structural equation modeling approach. Comput. Educ. **55**(4), 1424–1442 (2010)
10. Khoshnevisasl, P., Sadeghzadeh, M., Mazloomzadeh, S., Hashemi Feshareki, R., Ahmadiafshar, A.: Comparison of problem-based learning with lecture-based learning. Iran. Red Crescent Med. J. **16**(5), e5186 (2014). https://doi.org/10.5812/ircmj.5186

11. D'souza, N.: Revisiting a Vitruvian preface: the value of multiple skills in contemporary architectural pedagogy. Archit. Res. Q. **13**(2), 173–182 (2009). https://doi.org/10.1017/S13 59135509990261
12. Felder, R.M., Silverman, L.K.: Learning and teaching styles in engineering education. Eng. Educ. **78**(7), 674–681 (1988)
13. Gardner, H.E.: Frames of Mind: The Theory of Multiple Intelligences. Basic Books (2011)
14. Felder, R.M., Henriques, E.R.: Learning and teaching styles in foreign and second language education. Foreign Lang. Ann. **28**(1), 21–31 (1995). https://doi.org/10.1111/j.1944-9720. 1995.tb00767.x
15. Struyven, K., Dochy, F., Janssens, S.: 'Teach as you preach': the effects of student-centered versus lecture-based teaching on student teachers' approaches to teaching. Eur. J. Teach. Educ. **33**(1), 43–64 (2010). https://doi.org/10.1080/02619760903457818
16. Wood, D.F.: ABC of learning and teaching in medicine: problem based learning. BMJ **326**(7384), 328–330 (2003). https://doi.org/10.1136/bmj.326.7384.328
17. Schmidt, H.G., Rotgans, J.I., Yew, E.H.: The process of problem-based learning: what works and why: What works and why in problem-based learning. Med. Educ. **45**(8), 792–806 (2011). https://doi.org/10.1111/j.1365-2923.2011.04035.x
18. Yoon, S.-Y., Souza, N.D': Different visual cognitive styles, different problem-solving styles? In: Proceedings of the International Association of Societies of Design Research 2009 Conference (2009)
19. Meijs, M., Knaack, U.: Components and Connections: Principles of Construction. Walter de Gruyter (2012)
20. Eiris, R., Wen, J., Gheisari, M.: iVisit: digital interactive construction site visits using 360-degree panoramas and virtual humans.In: Construction Research Congress 2020, pp. 1106–1116. Tempe, (2020). https://doi.org/10.1061/9780784482865.117
21. Mostafa, M., Mostafa, H.: How do architects think? Learning styles and architectural education. Archnet-IJAR **4**, 310–317 (2010). https://doi.org/10.26687/archnet-ijar.v4i2/3.139
22. Latta, J.N., Oberg, D.J.: A conceptual virtual reality model. IEEE Comput. Graph. Appl. **14**(1), 23–29 (1994). https://doi.org/10.1109/38.250915
23. Bowman, D.A., McMahan, R.P.: Virtual reality: how much immersion is enough? Computer **40**(7), 36–43 (2007)
24. Arthur, K.W.: Effects of Field of View on Performance with Head-Mounted Displays. The University of North Carolina, Chapel Hill (2000)
25. Lin, J.W., Duh, H.B.L., Parker, D.E., Abi-Rached, H., Furness, T.A.: Effects of field of view on presence, enjoyment, memory, and simulator sickness in a virtual environment. In: Proceedings IEEE Virtual Reality 2002, pp. 164–171 (2002) https://doi.org/10.1109/VR. 2002.996519
26. Stanney, et al.: Aftereffects and sense of presence in virtual environments: formulation of a research and development agenda. Int. J. Hum.-Comput. Interact. **10**, 135–187 (1998)
27. Prothero, J.D.: Widening the field-of-view increases the sense of presence in immersive virtual environments. Human. Interface Technology Laboratory Technical report (1995)
28. Usoh, M., Catena, E., Arman, S., Slater, M.: Using presence questionnaires in reality. Presence **9**(5), 497–503 (2000)
29. Stillman, B.C.: Making sense of proprioception: the meaning of proprioception, kin-aesthesia and related terms. Physiotherapy **88**(11), 667–676 (2002)
30. Wang, P., Wu, P., Wang, J., Chi, H.-L., Wang, X.: A critical review of the use of virtual reality in construction engineering education and training. Int. J. Environ. Res. Public. Health **15**(6), 1204 (2018). https://doi.org/10.3390/ijerph15061204
31. Buzsáki, G., Moser, E.I.: Memory, navigation and theta rhythm in the hippocampal-entorhinal system. Nat. Neurosci. **16**(2), 130–138 (2013)

32. Leutgeb, S., Leutgeb, J.K., Moser, M.-B., Moser, E.I.: Place cells, spatial maps and the population code for memory. Curr. Opin. Neurobiol. **15**(6), 738–746 (2005)
33. Wirth, W., et al.: A process model of the formation of spatial presence experiences. Media Psychol. **9**(3), 493–525 (2007). https://doi.org/10.1080/15213260701283079
34. Lee, K.M.: Presence, explicated. Commun. Theory **14**(1), 27–50 (2004). https://doi.org/10.1111/j.1468-2885.2004.tb00302.x
35. Schubert, T., Friedmann, F., Regenbrecht, H.: Embodied presence in virtual environments. In: Paton, R., Neilson, I. (eds.) Visual Representations and Interpretations, pp. 269–278. Springer, London (1999). https://doi.org/10.1007/978-1-4471-0563-3_30
36. Steuer, J.: Defining virtual reality: dimensions determining telepresence. J. Com-mun. **42**(4), 73–93 (1992). https://doi.org/10.1111/j.1460-2466.1992.tb00812.x
37. Hallifax, S., Serna, A., Marty, J.-C., Lavoué, É.: Adaptive gamification in education: a literature review of current trends and developments. In: Scheffel, M., Broisin, J., Pammer-Schindler, V., Ioannou, A., Schneider, J. (eds.) EC-TEL 2019. LNCS, vol. 11722, pp. 294–307. Springer, Cham (2019). https://doi.org/10.1007/978-3-030-29736-7_22
38. Hwang, G.-J., Sung, H.-Y., Hung, C.-M., Huang, I., Tsai, C.-C.: Development of a personalized educational computer game based on students' learning styles. Educ. Technol. Res. Dev. **60**(4), 623–638 (2012)
39. Tai, T.Y., Chen, H.H.J., Todd, G.: The impact of a virtual reality app on adolescent EFL learners' vocabulary learning. Comput. Assist. Lang. Learn. **35**, 1–26 (2022)
40. Sherman, W.R., Craig, A.B.: Understanding Virtual Reality: Interface, Application, and Design. Morgan Kaufmann, Burlington (2018)
41. Barata, G., Gama, S., Jorge, J., Gonçalves, D.: Engaging engineering students with gamification. In: 2013 5th International Conference on Games and Virtual Worlds for Serious Applications (VS-GAMES), pp. 1–8 (2013)
42. Vorderer, P., et al.: MEC spatial presence questionnaire, vol. 14, no. 2004, p. 2015 (2004). Accessed Sept
43. O'Brien, H.L., Cairns, P., Hall, M.: A practical approach to measuring user engagement with the refined user engagement scale (UES) and new UES short form. Int. J. Hum.-Comput. Stud. **112**, 28–39 (2018). https://doi.org/10.1016/j.ijhcs.2018.01.004

Gender Effects on Physical Contact in Social VR

Kanami Tsuda, Junko Ichino$^{(\boxtimes)}$ (iD), and Kouki Shimizu

Tokyo City University, Yokohama, Japan
{g1872063,ichino,g1872048}@tcu.ac.jp

Abstract. Despite increasing research on user perception, action, and behavior via avatars in virtual spaces, few studies exist on user behavior on social virtual reality (VR) platforms. We focus on physical contact, the most fundamental mode of human communication, and investigate the effects of gender factors on physical contact among social VR users in a virtual space. Using VRChat, a social VR platform, as a field, we collected data for 168 general users by observing their responses when a confederate approached them. We analyzed three factors: the apparent gender of the avatar of the interaction partner (2 levels: male and female), the actual gender of the interaction partner (2 levels: male and female), and whether their natural voice is used (2 levels: with and without voice). The results showed that when the actual gender of a user's interaction partner was female, the user had more frequent and intimate physical contact, such as hugging and patting the head. In contrast, the apparent gender of the avatar of the user's partner did not affect the frequency of physical contact. Furthermore, users had more frequent physical contact when not speaking than when speaking with their natural voice. These results suggest that the actual gender of a partner affects user behavior more than the apparent gender of the partner's avatar.

Keywords: Social VR · Avatar Appearance · Physical Contact · Gender · Field Study · VRChat

1 Introduction

Physical contact is a basic need and an essential form of human communication [1]. In clinical settings, for example, nurses make contact patients to form relationships with them and ease their pain.

What kind of physical contact occurs in the increasingly popular social-networking service metaverse (social VR) platforms? It is unclear how physical contact between avatars will be affected by their embodiment in the 3D virtual world, even if this is supposed to boost the reality of communication. Avatar appearance affects the perception, actions, and behaviors of users regarding communication, such as their liking [2], acceptable personal space [3], and gender bias toward avatars [4]. However, various avatar factors and their effects on physical contact have not been sufficiently studied. Furthermore, there have been few field studies on this question.

Therefore, we investigate how factors related to avatars affect physical contact through a field study of social VR platforms.

© The Author(s), under exclusive license to Springer Nature Switzerland AG 2023
J. Y. C. Chen and G. Fragomeni (Eds.): HCII 2023, LNCS 14027, pp. 691–705, 2023.
https://doi.org/10.1007/978-3-031-35634-6_50

2 Preliminary Observation and Research Questions

We conducted preliminary observations prior to conducting the field study. We used VRChat [5] (Fig. 1) for a total of 15 h to observe user behaviors. Because avatars of various appearances were present in VRChat, we focused our observations on the relationship between the avatar's appearance and physical contact. We observed that the degree and details of physical contact varied depending on the apparent gender of the avatar and the actual gender of the user.

We also observed that users often did not use the voice chat function (which enables conversations in the natural voice of the user and can be freely set; see Fig. 2) in VRChat, and the physical contact between users differed depending on whether they used this function. If users do not use the voice chat function, i.e., do not speak with their natural voices, their actual gender is hidden from other users. However, if they use the voice chat function, their gender is revealed to other users. Consequently, we anticipated a correlation between the actual gender of users and the use of this voice chat function.

Based on the aforementioned observations and considerations, we set the following research questions: **RQ1**: *Does the apparent gender of the avatar of the interaction partner affect physical contact in virtual spaces?* **RQ2**: *Does the actual gender of the interaction partner affect physical contact in virtual spaces?* **RQ3**: *Does speaking in one's natural voice affect physical contact in virtual spaces?*

Fig. 1. Tutorial World of VRChat, the social VR platform selected as the field for the study.

User nametag when voice
chat function is active

User nametag when voice
chat function is inactive

Fig. 2. User nametag showing the status of the voice chat function in VRChat. When a user activates the function, their nametag is surrounded by a blue line.

3 Related Work

3.1 User Perception, Action, and Behavior Regarding Appearance of Self-avatar

The literature on the extent to which self-avatar appearance affects users' perception, action, and behavior is extensive. The avatar's appearance is crucial, particularly in social situations [6]. Recent studies have shown that self-avatar appearance (for example, face [3, 7, 8], hands [9–12], and full body [12–14]) affects user perception, action, and behavior. For example, even with avatars having diverse appearances, users can feel embodied within that avatar to the extent that they identify with it and have some degree of ownership [15, 16].

Several studies have found that user perceptions, actions, and behavior regarding their self-avatar appearance also vary depending on the apparent gender of the self-avatar [2, 4, 17–19] and the actual gender of the user [2, 19]. For example, Schwind et al. [2] compared users' perceptions of self-avatars with six types of hands, including male, female, and androgynous, using hand-operated tasks such as typing and drawing. The results showed that female users had lower acceptance and perception of presence when their self-avatar had a male hand, whereas male users had a higher acceptance and perception of presence regardless of whether their self-avatar's hand was male or female. Beltran et al. [4] compared male and female self-avatars for the task of working in a virtual office from the first-person perspective. They found that users' implicit gender bias decreased when their self-avatar was female.

3.2 User Perception, Action, and Behavior Regarding Appearances of Other Avatars

Several reports exist on the effects of the appearance of other avatars on user perception, action, and behavior, although they are fewer than those on the appearance of self-avatars, which were described in the previous section. For instance, Bönsch et al. [3]

showed that the facial expression of approaching avatars can influence the level of personal space a user can tolerate. Smith et al. [20] and Abdullah et al. [21] found that communication between avatars in virtual environments involves rich nonverbal behaviors such as eye contact and gestures, which are similar to human communication in face-to-face situations.

A few studies exist on users' perceptions, actions, and behaviors regarding the apparent gender of other avatars. Lopez et al. [18] showed that gender bias is higher when the apparent gender of the other avatar is female than when it is male.

Thus, as shown in Sects. 3.1 and 3.2, studies on the relationship between avatar appearance in virtual space and user perception, action, and behavior have progressed in recent years. However, the question of how the apparent gender of the avatar and the actual gender of the user manipulating the avatar affect physical contact in virtual space has not yet been fully investigated. Furthermore, less research has been conducted in the field than in laboratories.

4   Field Study

Using an existing commercial social VR platform, we observed the behavior of public users when confederates approached and spoke to them. To obtain ecologically valid data, we did not divulge to the users that we were conducting a study. The study was conducted for a total of 50 h over two months, from October to December 2021.

4.1   Study Design

To answer the research questions described in Sect. 2, three factors were varied: the apparent gender of the avatar of the interaction partner (i.e., the apparent gender of the avatar of the confederate, two levels: male and female), actual gender of the interaction partner (i.e., actual gender of the confederate, two levels: male and female), and whether the users speak with their natural voices (two levels: with and without natural voice).

4.2   Study Environment

Existing commercial social VR platforms include VRChat, Facebook Spaces, Rec Room, and High Fidelity. From these, we selected VRChat as our field of study because it is the most common platform. Among the many worlds in VRChat, we conducted the study using the Tutorial World (Fig. 1), which is the first place that Japanese novices visit to learn how to use VRChat. Tutorial World has various types of users, not only novices but also experts who are willing to assist novices. VRChat users can identify if an avatar is using the voice chat function (i.e., whether the avatar speaks with their natural voice) described in Sect. 2 by the difference in the design of the user nametag displayed above the avatar's head (Fig. 2).

4.3 Participants

The study was conducted to ensure that the number of VRChat users for each level of each factor was approximately equal. Data were collected for a total of 168 users (Table 1).

Two confederates, C_1 and C_2, were paired to conduct the study. The same confederates were assigned to a person throughout the study. One confederate (C_1) was an interaction partner, while the other confederate (C_2) was a passerby and observed the interaction between confederate C_1 and the user. The actual gender of the two confederates was one male and one female, and C_1 and C_2 were switched according to the level of each factor (Sect. 4.1).

Table 1. Number of users for each level of each factor.

Apparent gender of partner's avatar	Actual gender of partner	With or without natural voice	Number of users
Male	Male	With	19
Male	Male	Without	23
Male	Female	With	22
Male	Female	Without	20
Female	Male	With	22
Female	Male	Without	23
Female	Female	With	21
Female	Female	Without	18
		Total	168

4.4 Procedure

A session was defined as the period from the time confederate C_1 approached a user up to 60 s had elapsed. The flowchart of a session is shown in Fig. 3. To ensure that the user recognized the actual gender of confederate C_1 (i.e., the user's interaction partner), the confederate C_1 greeted the user using their natural voice.

Confederate C_2 observed the interaction between the user and confederate C_1 from a short distance, noting details while avoiding being noticed by the user. The notes included the frequency of the user's contact with confederate C_1 and the body parts (head, hands, arms/shoulders, torso, legs, and upper body (hug)) with which the user made contact with the confederate C_1 during the session.

4.5 Design of Appearance of the Avatar of the Interaction Partner

Since the apparent gender of the avatar of the interaction partner (confederate) is a factor in this study (Sect. 4.1), we designed the appearance of the confederates' avatar to meet the following criteria: the gender of the avatar is apparent to anyone who sees it, while the degree of skin exposure is minimum (to avoid arousing mere sexual feelings), and the avatar design is conventional (to observe user responses in general, rather than those based on curiosity upon encountering an avatar with an unusual appearance). Avatars were created using Vroid [22] (Fig. 4). The size of the avatar was based on the standard size [23] of each body part of a Japanese person in their 20s.

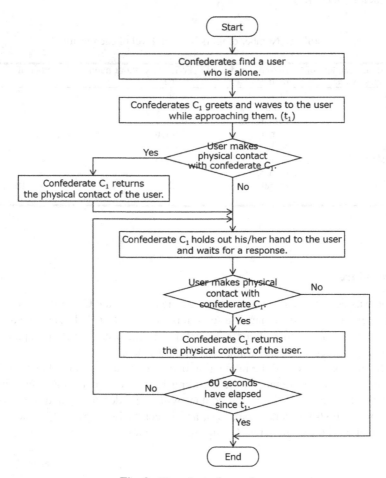

Fig. 3. Flowchart of a session.

Fig. 4. Appearance of confederate avatars (left: male, right: female).

5 Results

5.1 Effects of Three Study Factors

To examine whether the three study factors mentioned in Sect. 4.1 affected the contact frequency, 2 (apparent gender of avatar of the interaction partner) × 2 (actual gender of the interaction partner) × 2 (with or without natural voice) ANOVA was first performed on the frequency of the user's contact with the confederate C_1 during a session. If the main effect was significant, multiple comparison tests were performed using the Tukey–Kramer method as a post-hoc analysis. Table 2 shows the results of the analyses for the total contact frequency of all body parts in contact ([total] in Table 2) and for the contact frequency by body part in contact ([head] to [upper body] in Table 2). Figures 5, 6, and 7 show the total contact frequency of all body parts in contact for each factor. The error bars in the graphs in each figure represent the standard errors of the mean. The asterisks in each figure and table represent the significance levels (*: $p < 0.05$, **: $p < 0.01$, ***: $p < 0.001$).

For the total contact frequency, the ANOVA showed that the two main effects of the actual gender of the interaction partner and with or without a natural voice were significant. Post-hoc tests showed that the frequency was significantly higher when the actual gender of the interaction partner was female than when it was male (Fig. 6) and without the use of a natural voice than with it (Fig. 7).

5.2 Effect of the Body Part in Contact

To examine whether there is a difference in contact frequency for various body parts, the χ^2 test was performed to compare the total contact frequency of all users among the six groups: head, hands, arms/shoulders, torso, legs, and upper body (hug). If a significant difference was found, multiple comparison test was performed using the Ryan method as a post-hoc analysis.

The result of the χ^2 test was significant ($\chi^2(5) = 293.37$, $p < 0.001$). The post-hoc test showed that hands had a significantly higher contact frequency than all other body parts. The arms/shoulders had a significantly higher contact frequency than the torso, legs, and upper body (hug) (Fig. 8).

Table 2. Analysis results of contact frequency by each factor.

	Apparent gender of the avatar of the interaction partner		Actual gender of the interaction partner		With or without the use of natural voice		Interaction effects
	F (df1, df2)	p	F (df1, df2)	p	F (df1, df2)	p	
Total	2.46 (1,160)	0.119	18.17 (1,160)	<0.001*** M<F	10.98 (1,160)	<0.01** W<W/O	none
Head	0.38 (1,160)	0.536	9.33 (1,160)	<0.01** M<F	4.82 (1,160)	<0.05* W<W/O	none
Hands	4.31 (1,160)	<0.05* M<F	2.82 (1,160)	0.095	3.30 (1,160)	0.071	none
Arms/shoulders	0.12 (1,160)	0.731	7.07 (1,160)	<0.01** M<F	3.32 (1,160)	0.070	none
Torso	0.41 (1,160)	0.522	4.83 (1,160)	<0.05* M<F	0.01 (1,160)	0.932	none
Legs	0.04 (1,160)	0.840	0.74 (1,160)	0.391	4.04 (1,160)	<0.05* W<W/O	none
Upper body (hug)	0.07 (1,160)	0.793	6.77 (1,160)	<0.05* M<F	4.06 (1,160)	<0.05* W<W/O	none

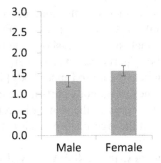

Fig. 5. Contact frequency by apparent gender of the avatar of the interaction partner. (left)

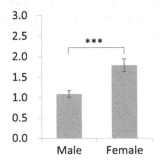

Fig. 6. Contact frequency by actual gender of the interaction partner. (center)

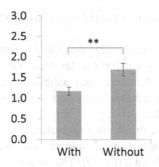

Fig. 7. Contact frequency with or without the use of natural voice. (right)

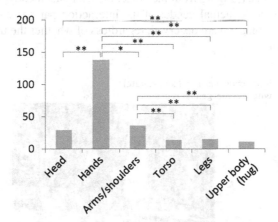

Fig. 8. Total contact frequency of all users by body part in contact.

6 Discussion

6.1 Effect of Apparent Gender of the Avatar of the Interaction Partner (RQ1)

The apparent gender of the avatar of the interaction partner did not affect physical contact in virtual spaces (Fig. 5). Given the previous study showing that the appearance of other avatars affect user perception, action, and behavior (Sect. 3.2), our result that the apparent gender of the interacting avatar (i.e., the other avatar) did not affect physical contact was unexpected.

6.2 Effect of Actual Gender of the Interaction Partner (RQ2)

The actual gender of the interaction partner affected physical contact in virtual spaces, and users made contact with their partner (confederate) significantly more when the actual gender of their interaction partner was female than when it was male (Fig. 6). It is interesting that the actual gender of the person manipulating the avatar of the interaction partner in the real world, rather than the apparent gender of the avatar of the interaction partner (i.e., other avatar for the user) in the virtual world (Sect. 6.1), affected the users' physical contact.

We will now discuss the reason why the contact frequency was higher when the actual gender of the interaction partner was female. In this field study, we did not ask the users their actual gender; however, their natural voices suggested that most users were male. Therefore, the contact frequency was higher when the actual gender of the interaction partner was female.

When the actual gender of the interaction partner was male, users often left before 60 s had elapsed from the start of the session and entered into a conversation from a distance after the initial handshake (Fig. 9). This was particularly noticeable when the actual gender of the user's interaction partner (confederate) was male and the user spoke with their natural voice (judging from the voice, the user was mostly male).

In contrast, when the actual gender of the interaction partner was female, longer periods of physical contact were observed, regardless of whether the user spoke in their natural voice or not.

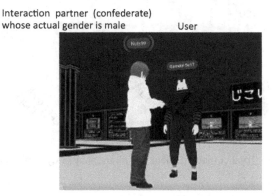

Fig. 9. Typical interaction when the partner's (confederate's) actual gender is male. After an initial light handshake, the user continued the conversation without physical contact from a distance.

6.3   Effects of Natural Voice (RQ3)

Speaking in one's natural voice affected physical contact in virtual spaces, and the users made contact with their partner (confederate) significantly more when the natural voice was not used (Fig. 10).

When the user did not use their natural voice, a higher contact frequency was observed, along with tendencies for longer contact durations and more intimate contact. These observations can be interpreted as users' attempts to express their interest in others using physical contact as an interaction method in situations where they cannot use their voices. The confederates, unable to hear the user's voice, could only guess what they aimed to say, for instance, "Your avatar looks funny," "Your avatar's clothes are cute," or "Your avatar's ears are cute," when they made contact the area of interest.

When the user used their natural voice, the conversation took precedence, and physical contact did not occur in most cases. This may be because hearing the partner's natural voice diminishes the sense of being in a virtual world and increases that of being in reality, which may have prevented physical contact in accordance with social norms in the real world.

Fig. 10. Typical interaction in which the user spoke with their natural voice. After an initial wave of the hands (left), they exchanged a light greeting and then transitioned to a more conversational interaction. In this example, the confederate held out their hand to the user; however, the user did not respond (right).

6.4 Conditions for Higher Contact Frequency: [Actual Gender of Partner is Female] × [Without Use of Natural Voice]

Sections 6.1–6.3 indicate that a user's physical contact is more frequent when the actual gender of the interaction partner was female and when the user did not speak with their natural voice. In addition, not only was the quantity of contact greater, but the quality of contact was also more substantial, and the following were observed: longer duration of contact, continued physical contact after the initial handshake, and more intimate contact such as hugging, patting the head, and touching the feet (Fig. 11).

Interaction partner (confederate)   User who did not speak
whose actual gender is female   with their natural voice

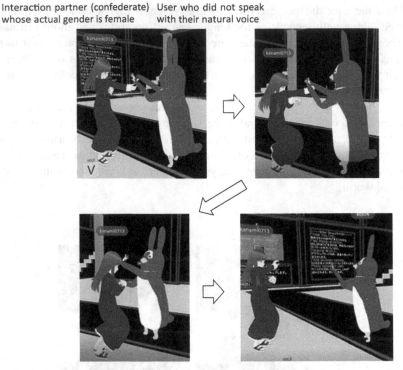

Fig. 11. Typical interaction in which the actual gender of the interaction partner (confederate) was female and the user did not speak with their natural voice. After shaking hands for the first time (upper left), the user made contact with the partner's arm (upper right) and then made contact with various points, including the head (lower left), to interact intimately. Finally, they parted with a wave (bottom right).

6.5 Effects of the Body Part in Contact

The body part with which contact was made affected the contact frequency. The order of contact frequency was hand, arm/shoulder, head, leg, torso, and upper body (hug). This order reflects the implicit social norms by which people interact in the real world.

We will discuss the reasons why the contact frequency via hands was high. In this field study, the confederates repeatedly held out their hands to (but did not make contact with) the users (Fig. 3). Most users responded by holding out their hands, and a handshake often followed (Fig. 12). A high hand-contact frequency probably resulted from this study procedure. While no statistically significant difference in the total frequency via all body parts existed ([total] in Table 2), only in the case of hands, the contact frequency was significantly higher when the apparent gender of the avatar of the interaction partner was female than when it was male. ([hands] in Table 2).

We will next discuss the bottom three contact frequencies: upper body (hug), legs, and head. In all three cases, the contact frequency was significantly higher without the use of a natural voice (Table 2). When a user does not speak with their natural voice, anonymity is high and the risk of identification is low. It is not surprising that users in such a situation made contact with the upper body (hug), legs, and head, which in the real world would only come into contact with each other in the case of extremely close relationships. In addition, when a user does not speak with their voice, the only means of interaction is nonverbal behavior. Therefore, the user might be attempting to add variety to the interaction by making contact with various body parts.

Fig. 12. Hand-to-hand contact (handshake) with the highest contact frequency.

7 Conclusion

We observed the physical-contact behaviors of 168 general users in VRChat, a social VR platform. We analyzed the user contact frequency based on the apparent gender of the avatar of the interaction partner, the actual gender of the interaction partner, and whether users spoke with their natural voices. We found that the contact frequency was higher when the actual gender of the user's interaction partner was female and when the user used their natural voice. Contrary to expectations, the apparent gender of the avatar of a user's interaction partner did not affect the contact frequency. These results suggest that the actual gender of the partner affected user behavior more than the apparent gender of the partner's avatar. These results also suggest that not only the representation of the avatar's appearance, which has been extensively explored, but also the representation of the avatar's voice will be important topics for future studies. We also found that users in the virtual world made contact body parts not typically made contact in the real world.

This study used the Tutorial World of VRChat, which has a wide range of Japanese users, as the target of observation. In the future, we must investigate whether similar trends can be observed on other social VR platforms. Because physical contact varies significantly by culture, users from cultures other than Japan must also be investigated. Physical contact is less common in Asian countries, including Japan, than in Western countries. This is particularly true in Japan, where people rarely engage in physical contact in public places. Using this field study, we confirmed that even Japanese people actively engage in physical contact in virtual spaces. In cultures where physical contact is a habit, this result may be more prominent.

Acknowledgments. We wish to express our gratitude to the VRChat users who cooperated with us as users of our field study.

References

1. Barnlund, D.C.: Communicative Styles of Japanese and Americans. Wadsworth Publishing Co Inc., Belmont (1988)
2. Schwind, V., Knierim, P., Tasci, C., Franczak, P., Haas, N., Henze, N.: These are not my hands!": effect of gender on the perception of avatar hands in virtual reality. In: Proceedings of the ACM CHI 2017, pp. 1577–1582 (2017). https://doi.org/10.1145/3025453.3025602
3. Bönsch, A., et al.: Social VR: how personal space is affected by virtual agents emotions. In: Proceedings of the IEEE VR 2018, pp. 199–206 (2018). https://doi.org/10.1109/VR.2018.8446480
4. Beltran, K., Rowland, C., Hashemi, N., Nguyen, A., Harrison, L., Engle, S., Yuksel, B.: Reducing implicit gender bias using a virtual workplace environment. In: Extended Abstracts of ACM CHI 2021, pp. 1–7 (2021). https://doi.org/10.1145/3411763.3451739
5. https://hello.vrchat.com/
6. Gonzalez-Franco, M., Steed, A., Hoogendyk, S., Ofek, E.: Using facial animation to increase the enfacement illusion and avatar self-identification. IEEE Trans. Visual Comput. Graphics **26**(5), 2023–2029 (2020). https://doi.org/10.1109/TVCG.2020.2973075
7. Seyama, J., Nagayama, R.S.: The uncanny valley: effect of realism on the impression of artificial human faces. Presence: Teleoperators Virtual Environ. **16**(4), 337–351 (2007). https://doi.org/10.1162/pres.16.4.337
8. Oh, S.Y., Bailenson, J., Krämer, N., Li, B.: Let the avatar brighten your smile: effects of enhancing facial expressions in virtual environments. PLoS ONE **11**(9), e0161794 (2016). https://doi.org/10.1371/journal.pone.0161794
9. Argelaguet, F., Hoyet, L., Trico, M., Lécuyer, A.: The role of interaction in virtual embodiment: effects of the virtual hand representation. In: Proceedings of the IEEE VR 2016, pp. 3–10 (2016). https://doi.org/10.1109/VR.2016.7504682
10. Lin, L., Jörg, S.: Need a hand? How appearance affects the virtual hand illusion. In: Proceedings of the ACM SAP 2016, pp. 69–76 (2016). https://doi.org/10.1145/2931002.2931006
11. Maister, L., Slater, M., Sanchez-Vives, M.V., Tsakiris, M.: Changing bodies changes minds: owning another body affects social cognition. Trends Cogn. Sci. **19**(1), 6–12 (2015). https://doi.org/10.1016/j.tics.2014.11.001
12. Ogawa, N., Narumi, T., Kuzuoka, H., Hirose, M.: Do you feel like passing through walls?: Effect of self-avatar appearance on facilitating realistic behavior in virtual environments. In: Proceedings of the ACM CHI 2020, pp. 1–14 (2020). https://doi.org/10.1145/3313831.3376562
13. Koulouris, J., Jeffery, Z., Best, J., O'Neill, E., Lutteroth, C.: Me vs. Super (wo) man: effects of customization and Identification in a VR Exergame. In: Proceedings of the ACM CHI 2020, pp. 1–17 (2020). https://doi.org/10.1145/3313831.3376661
14. Latoschik, M.E., Roth, D., Gall, D., Achenbach, J., Waltemate, T., Botsch, M.: The effect of avatar realism in immersive social virtual realities. In: Proceedings of the ACM VRST 2017, pp. 39:1–39:10 (2017). https://doi.org/10.1145/3139131.3139156
15. Gonzalez-Franco, M., Lanier, J.: Model of illusions and virtual reality. Front. Psychol. **8**, 1125 (2017). https://doi.org/10.3389/fpsyg.2017.01125

16. Kilteni, K., Groten, R., Slater, M.: The sense of embodiment in virtual reality. Presence: Teleoperators Virtual Environ. **21**(4), 373–387 (2012). https://doi.org/10.1162/PRES_a_00124
17. Shang, X., Kallmann, M., Arif, A.S.: Effects of virtual agent gender on user performance and preference in a VR training program. In: Arai, K., Bhatia, R. (eds.) FICC 2019. LNNS, vol. 69, pp. 482–495. Springer, Cham (2020). https://doi.org/10.1007/978-3-030-12388-8_34
18. Lopez, S., et al.: Investigating implicit gender bias and embodiment of white males in virtual reality with full body visuomotor synchrony. In: Proceedings of the ACM CHI 2019, pp. 1–12 (2019). https://doi.org/10.1145/3290605.3300787
19. Schwind, V., Henze, N.: Gender- and age-related differences in designing the characteristics of stereotypical virtual faces. In: Proceedings of the ACM CHI PLAY 2018, pp. 463–475 (2018). https://doi.org/10.1145/3242671.3242692
20. Smith, H.J., Neff, M.: Communication behavior in embodied virtual reality. In: Proceedings of the ACM CHI 2018, pp. 1–12 (2018). https://doi.org/10.1145/3173574.3173863
21. Abdullah, A., Kolkmeier, J., Lo, V., Neff, M.: Videoconference and embodied VR: communication patterns across task and medium. In: Proceedings of the ACM CSCW2, vol. 453, pp. 1–29 (2021). https://doi.org/10.1145/3479597
22. https://vroid.com/studio
23. Research Institute of Human Engineering for Quality Life.: Japanese Human Body Dimensions Database 2004–2006 (2007). https://www.hql.jp/database/cat/size/size2004

Retraction Note to: Methods of Visualizing Landing Performance in Low-Visibility ILS Approaches (Preliminary Findings)

Theodore C. Mofle⬤, Inchul Choi⬤, Daniela Kratchounova⬤,
Jeremy Hesselroth, and Scott Stevenson

Retraction Note to:
Chapter 39 in: J. Y. C. Chen and G. Fragomeni (Eds.):
Virtual, Augmented and Mixed Reality, **LNCS 14027,**
https://doi.org/10.1007/978-3-031-35634-6_39

The authors have retracted this conference paper because there was an erroneous assumption associated with the placement of the XYZ coordinate system zero point. This affected all calculations and the respective visualization of landing performance by skewing the touchdown points either before or after the actual touchdown points on a subset of the runways used for this research.

All authors agree with this retraction.

The retracted version of this chapter can be found at
https://doi.org/10.1007/978-3-031-35634-6_39

© The Author(s), under exclusive license to Springer Nature Switzerland AG 2024
J. Y. C. Chen and G. Fragomeni (Eds.): HCII 2023, LNCS 14027, p. C1, 2024.
https://doi.org/10.1007/978-3-031-35634-6_51

Author Index

J. Y. C. Chen and G. Fragomeni (Eds.): HCII 2023, LNCS 14027, pp. 707–709, 2023.
https://doi.org/10.1007/978-3-031-35634-6

Printed in the United States
by Baker & Taylor Publisher Services